CANNABIS
GROWER'S
HANDBOOK

QUICK
AMERICAN
PUBLISHING

CANNABIS GROWER'S HANDBOOK
The Complete Guide to Marijuana and Hemp Cultivation
Copyright © 2021 Ed Rosenthal
Published by Quick American Publishing
A division of Quick Trading Company
Piedmont, California, USA

Printed in Canada
Second Printing

ISBN 9781936807543
eISBN 9781936807550

Project Director: Jane Klein
Project Manager and Chief Editor: Angela Bacca
Copy Editor: Paula Dragosh
Editorial Review: Joey Ereñeta, Ellen Holland, Jeff Jones
Art Director/Cover Design: Christian Petke
Cover Photo: Phil Sullivan, HRS Agriculture/Team Terpene
Back Cover Photos: Ed Rosenthal by Tonya Perme Photography and
Trichome Macro by Kandid Kush
Interior Design: Scott Idleman, Blink
Production Editor: Christy Quinto
Photographs as noted.

Names: Rosenthal, Ed, author. | Flannery, Robert, 1978- author. | Bacca,
    Angela, 1986- author.
Title: Cannabis grower's handbook : the complete guide to marijuana and
    hemp cultivation / Ed Rosenthal, Dr. Robert Flannery, Angela Bacca.
Description: Piedmont, California : Quick American Publishing, 2021. |
    Includes bibliographical references.
Identifiers: LCCN 2021021606 (print) | LCCN 2021021607 (ebook) | ISBN
    9781936807543 (trade paperback) | ISBN 9781936807550 (epub)
Subjects: LCSH: Cannabis. | Marijuana. | Marijuana industry.
Classification: LCC SB295.C35 R6583 2021 (print) | LCC SB295.C35 (ebook)
    | DDC 633.5/3--dc23
LC record available at https://lccn.loc.gov/2021021606
LC ebook record available at https://lccn.loc.gov/2021021607

CANNABIS
GROWER'S
HANDBOOK

Ed Rosenthal
Dr. Robert Flannery and Angela Bacca

DEDICATION

This series continues to be dedicated to Pete Seeger (1919–2014).

God bless the grass that grows through the crack.
—Malvina Reynolds, "God Bless the Grass"

This edition of the *Cannabis Grower's Handbook* is dedicated to Dennis Peron (1945–2018).

All use of marijuana is medical. —Dennis Peron

William Tell has stretched his bow til it won't stretch no furthermore
And/or may it require a change that hasn't come before.
—"St. Stephen," Robert Hunter, The Grateful Dead

WARNING: Although marijuana may not be habit forming, growing it is.
—Ed Rosenthal

ACKNOWLEDGMENTS

Dabsel Adams, AEssenseGrows, Kristen Angelo, Justin Arriola, Jeremy Babbit, Barney's Farm, George Bianchini, Thomas Blank, PhD, Kristine Borghino, Lily Borghino, The Brand Family, Bruce Bugbee, PhD, Frenchy Cannoli, Sunshine Cereceda, Central Coast Agriculture, Julie Chiarello, Tommy Chong, Laura and Marty Clein, Remo and Sandra Colsanti, Chris Conrad, Jose Luis Cordovez, Lizzy Cozzi, Dank Duchess, Steve DeAngelo, Kymron DeCesare, Doobie Duck, David Downs, Daniel "Old E" and Brian "Bleezy" Eatmon of Mendo Dope, ECO Cannabis in Oakland, Mahmoud ElSohly, PhD, Phil Emerson, Joey Ereñeta, Nico Escondido, Bill Faulconer, Will Ferguson, Mike Finley, Tera Flannery, Mel Frank, Laura Galli, Emery Garcia, Reginald Gaudino, PhD, Gregory Gerdeman, PhD, Dan Grace, Bill Graham, Mark Gray, Mark Grayshock, GreenSourceGardens, Grow Magazine, GrowWeedEasy.com, Ellen Holland, Jake Holley, Humboldt Seeds, Dale Hunt, PhD, Dale Sky Jones, Jeff Jones, Kandid Kush, Autumn Karcey, Brandy Keen, Caleb King, Ted Kinsman, Jay Kitchen, Wendy Kornberg, John Kozlowski, La Osa, Donald P. Land, PhD, Troy Larkin, Gopi Lennon, Heiner Lieth, PhD, Helios Lima, James Loud, Mattie Mead, Jeff Lowenfels, Brian Lundeen, Brian Malin, Neil Mattson, PhD, Max Montrose, Miranda Moore, Kristin Nevedal, Amber O'Neill, Christian Petke, Phytonyx, Professor P, Christy Quinto, Rosa Raudales, PhD, Jesse Robertson, Felisa Rogers, Mary Shapiro, Autumn Shelton, SKUNK Magazine, Brian Spivey, Clayton Stewart, StickyFields, Stinkbud, Lucas Strazzeri, Phil Sullivan aka Team Terpene, Picture Fotografie, Seth Swanson, Dr. Robert Thornton, Chris Trump, Andy Unruh, Dan Vinkovetsky (formerly known as Danny Danko), Alexander Wild, Kale Worden, Giacobazzi Yanez, Zoom_Gardens

A special thanks to our sponsors:

AC Infinity, Advanced Nutrients, AgGas, Air Sniper, Apogee Instruments, ARBICO Organics, Bionova, Cannabis Training University, Cannatrol, Cryo Cure, DriFlower, Dyna-Gro, Dynasty Genetics, Earth Witch Seeds, Ecological Laboratories Inc., EYE Hortilux, Fresh Headies, Garden City Fungi, Genesys Global, GreenBroz Inc., Green Goddess Supply, Green House Seed Co., Greenshock Farms, Grobo, Grodan, Groundwork BioAg, Grow Glide, Growlink, Gutenberg's Dank Pressing Co., Hanna Instruments, Happy Tree Microbes, Harvest More, HiBred Seed, Horticulture Lighting Group, Lost Coast Plant Therapy, Humboldt Seed Company, Humidicorp, iHort, microBIOMETER, Microclone Tissue Culture, Miicrobial Mass, Mondi Products, Munch Machine, Neptune's Organics, North Atlantic Seed Co., Oaksterdam University, Paradise Seeds, Pinch and Pull, Plant Success Organics, Power Grown, Pulse Grow, Pure Pressure, Purple Caper Seeds, Reiziger Holland, Rocket Seeds, Royal Queen Seeds, Sasquatch Soil Company, Scynce LED, Sensational Solutions, Sensi Seeds, Smart Bee Controllers, Smart Pots, Spray-N-Grow, STM Canna, Suite Leaf, Surna, Taoshops S.R.O., The Seed Cellar, TNB Naturals, Tom's Tumble Trimmer, True Liberty Bags, Ultra Trimmer, Vital Garden Supply, Weed Guardians Family Tree

TABLE OF CONTENTS

PREFACE
by Steve DeAngelo

Ed Rosenthal and I emerged from the same underground cauldron of culture and politics known as the Youth International Party, more commonly referred to as "the Yippies" or sometimes even just "Yippie!" (The exclamation point was very important to us.) Although the Yippies were often written off as the court jesters of the New Left movement of

Steve DeAngelo speaking at the kickoff of the Hemp Tour at Penn State's Earth Day, circa 1987. Courtesy of Steve DeAngelo

the '60s and '70s, the Yippie! movement gave birth (or at least shelter) to a cadre of remarkably effective and absolutely determined cannabis activists who would go on to play crucial roles in the formation of the modern cannabis movement and industry.

Like old CIA officers, old Yippies never really retire. Ed and I are both fortunate to have now reached elder status, but in the early 1970s I was just about the youngest Yippie and Ed had been around the scene a lot longer; he was this impressive, distant figure I heard about long before we met. I think I first met him at the 1975 White House Smoke-In, though it could have been the 1977 White House Smoke-In, or possibly while smoking or even selling weed in a smoky commune somewhere.

Marijuana Grower's Guide, the original edition of this book, seems to have always been present in my life, and I recall my reaction upon first seeing it; it was one of the most powerfully subversive books ever written. Here was an extremely specific, detailed, impeccably researched and written guide to producing the best cannabis in the world. The only other instructions for growing cannabis that I had seen had been mimeographed handouts passed from hippie to hippie, or the rudimentary drawings sometimes published in underground newspapers. I could tell right away that this book was going to change our world.

At the time, almost all the cannabis consumed in the United States was imported from countries like Mexico, Jamaica, and Lebanon. Ed had produced a tool that would allow any reasonably dedicated cannabis consumer to liberate themselves from this very long, expensive supply chain and, with a steady application of effort, might also enable them to grow enough for their friends and family.

Marijuana Grower's Guide taught the earliest domestic growers how to produce higher-quality cannabis than what was coming from other countries. Appreciation for imported cannabis began to wane. More people began to consume it as higher quality became more available, and the earliest cannabis breeders built on the foundation Ed had laid. In a stroke of good fortune (or divine intervention), this high-quality cannabis was abundant in California during the AIDS crisis, where it played a key role in preserving and enhancing the quality of life of AIDS patients. This real-life demonstration of the therapeutic properties of cannabis convinced the voters of California, and eventually other states and nations, to pass cannabis initiatives.

Today the millions of people who have been introduced to cannabis since the first publication of *Marijuana Grower's Guide* have coalesced into a powerful movement that will ensure that everybody who needs cannabis has safe and affordable access to it and that one day the prison doors are thrown open and every single cannabis prisoner on Planet Earth comes home to their family—with the resources they need to rebuild the lives that were stolen from them.

Thank you, Ed, for all you have done to teach and guide us on our common mission. Always Onward, Forever Free!

Steve DeAngelo in Canada, 2019. Photo: Giacobazzi Yanez

FOREWORD
by Tommy Chong

Photo: Kerry Reynolds

Well, here we go again. Ed has written another book. Just as before, all my close friends are still potheads, and Ed is still not only a pothead, he is the pot-growing expert who holds the distinction of turning more people on to pot than Cheech and Chong.

What has changed since the last foreword I wrote is that he is not worrying so much about the DEA chasing down the hundreds of thousands of growers currently tending gardens all over America because, hey man, it's getting legal everywhere!

I admire and respect Ed because he is a great revolutionary and "anti establishment" hippie who likes to wear weird clothes while he outs corrupt federal officials who can no longer freely enforce America's sadly outdated drug laws. In 2003, Ed faced 20 years in federal prison for doing pretty much what he had been doing for the past 30 or so years—growing pot and teaching others to grow their own. The feds insisted Ed broke the law, and Ed would agree with them and then explain, "It's a terrible law!"

Another reason why I admire and respect this man is that writing is hard, comedy is easy. Ed's books have been every grower's go-to textbooks when it comes to growing good pot and combating disease, thieves, and other pests that could waste an entire growing cycle. He hasn't just taught people to grow, he is one of many advocates who fought to bring about the dearly needed changes in the law so that pot growers are treated much like any other farmer in America.

My memory is good, my brain is so good, and it is thanks to weed. It is all about weed. Our bodies are like computers. If you know what button or what app to hit, you can learn everything there is to know. And, if you know how to get the energy source, you know how to recharge the batteries.

Ed has the whole field covered. Ask Ed. I do on occasion still ask Ed. Ed is probably one of the most intelligent men I know, and he does have the answer to quite a few problems facing Americans today. So, if you have the time and the inclination, read what he has to say. Things are changing for the better, and even the United States government has backed off when it comes to arguing with Ed. I have to say that as the pot laws are changing and, one by one, begin to disappear, we can take a moment before we light up that now legal joint and say a silent, "Thanks, Ed Rosenthal," because he stood in front of the government tank and faced it down . . . and he was totally zonked out of his mind when he did it.

Thank you, Ed. —Tommy Chong

THE CANNABIS USER'S BILL OF RIGHTS

Photo: La Osa

- Adults shall not be prohibited from using or possessing cannabis.
- All adults, medical patients, and caregivers of medical patients shall have the right to grow their own cannabis for noncommercial use.
- Laws regulating commercial cannabis markets should be fair, open, regulated for health and consumer protection, and allow easy access for buyers and sellers.
- A "medical use" designation shall be determined by patients in consultation with their doctor without interference from the government.
- Cannabis users shall not be discriminated against by employers and landlords.
- Cannabis use shall not be considered when determining child custody.
- There shall be no taxes or fees on personal use cultivation.

THE TOMATO MODEL

The model for what cannabis legalization should look like is already out there. It's tomatoes. More tomatoes are grown in America by home gardeners than are produced commercially, yet there is a robust commercial market for tomatoes and tomato products of all types: canned, vine

ripened, organic, sauces, soups, ketchup, and so on. At the same time, small-scale specialty cultivators do well selling their produce at farmers' markets, and home gardeners with extra tomatoes share the bounty with neighbors as gifts, in trade, or through informal sales. Cannabis should be handled in the same way. Commercial growers can thrive side by side with home and specialty cultivators.

INTRODUCTION
by Angela Bacca

"After legalization, elementary botany classes could use this guide as a casebook for learning about a common plant."
—Raymond A. Sokolov, *New York Times* book review of *Marijuana Grower's Guide*, by Mel Frank and Ed Rosenthal, April 16, 1978

The earliest iterations of this book were a call to action: "Overgrow the Government."

In 1971, President Richard Nixon formally declared the War on Drugs, and in 1973 he created the Drug Enforcement Administration (DEA), one of several agencies that would receive ever-increasing federal funding for the purpose of eradicating illegal drugs and the illegal drug trade. Of the many weapons used in the war against marijuana production and use, the US government sprayed both domestic and Mexican-grown crops with Paraquat, a deadly pesticide.

In 1978, the *Washington Post* summed up the policy in a column titled "Marijuana Outrage." "The irony is simply this: the government that failed over many decades to convince the public that marijuana was dangerous finally has helped make it dangerous."

When *Marijuana Grower's Guide* by Ed Rosenthal and Mel Frank was published in 1974, it was the first-of-its-kind gardening guide about the cannabis plant since federal prohibition began with the Marihuana Tax Act of 1937. It was more than a DIY gardening book; it was a guide to active protest.

In turn, the American grow-your-own movement flourished in the late 1970s and early 1980s. As the preface to the 1984 edition of *Marijuana Grower's Handbook* by Ed Rosenthal put it, "The more the government stepped up its eradication attempts aimed at imports, the more mini-gardens and mini-farms began to develop in the U.S. In simple-to-understand language, Marijuana Grower's Guide made experts out of hardening hobbyists."

Generations of growers around the world would learn to grow cannabis by reading and sharing Ed's early books, articles, and "Ask Ed" columns, which originated with the founding of *High Times Magazine* in 1974 to answer readers' cannabis questions. Nearly 50 years later, new and experienced cultivators around the world are still reading his columns in their local cannabis publications and sending Ed their questions, photos, and observations from their unique home gardens.

Cannabis grower-researchers inspired by these early writings fueled the global innovation and study of indoor agriculture. Through artificial lighting, climate controls, and hydroponics, not only did indoor gardeners evade law enforcement, but they provided the controls necessary to experiment, breed, and innovate.

In the late 1980s and early 1990s, Ed was a prominent advocate in the creation of the nation's first medical cannabis laws, first with the passage of Proposition P in the City of San Francisco in 1991 and next as a part of a broader coalition to support the passage of California's Proposition 215 in 1996, the first state-level medical cannabis law in the United States. Both measures were championed by the late Dennis Peron, to whom we have dedicated this edition of the *Grower's Handbook*.

This early regulation-free legislation in California led to the proliferation of cannabis gardens, varieties, innovations in cultivation practices, by-products, and methods of ingestion. It also solidified California as the epicenter of the burgeoning global industry. *The Marijuana Grower's Handbook* was updated in 1998 to include new technologies, as more and more growers found their way to the cannabis plant and indoor cultivation.

In the early 2000s, the first city-sanctioned dispensaries and grow operations appeared in the San Francisco Bay Area, and Ed was deputized by the City of Oakland to oversee the large-scale production of starter plants (clones) to supply state legal growers through these storefronts.

In 2002, the DEA carried out several predawn raids on San Francisco dispensaries and Ed's Oakland home publishing office, where he was arrested and put on trial as the "kingpin" of a major illegal drug operation. The judge barred Ed's defense from testifying that he had been deputized by the city or that the operation was in compliance with local ordinances and state law.

Many of the original members of the Youth International Party, aka The Yippies, went on to become pivotal figures in the cannabis legalization movement and industry, including Ed Rosenthal, Steve DeAngelo, and Dana Beal. The Yippies were memorialized in the 2020 Netflix movie *The Trial of the Chicago 7*.

Using the Yippie tactic of drawing attention to injustice through spectacle, Ed attended his federal trial in a "Wizard of Weed" costume. The international media attention this garnered helped swell the crowds of protestors outside the federal courthouse.

"They had to lie in order to win, so who was actually on trial?" Ed asked. "By the time it got to *The New York Times*, the law was on trial."

The jury was forced to convict Ed on the evidence presented, but many jurors publicly denounced their verdict when they learned the government had barred them from hearing the truth. The public backlash from the political prosecution and public statements from jurors largely factored into Ed's June 2003 sentencing to one day in federal prison with credit for time served in a local jail the day of the arrest.

"This is day one in the crusade to bring down the marijuana laws. The federal government makes no distinction between medical and recreational marijuana. They're right, all marijuana should be legal," Ed said in a press conference after the sentencing, vowing to fight his conviction despite the lenient sentencing. The appeals would continue unsuccessfully until 2007.

I started working for Ed in the summer of 2008 at the end of the George W. Bush era, which was characterized by the sort of political prosecutions against state-legal cannabis that Ed endured. My first project was a revised edition of *Marijuana Grower's Handbook*. Early on in the production of the book the newly inaugurated Obama administration signaled a sea change in federal priorities regarding cannabis. The so-called Ogden Memo stated the new administration's look-the-other-way policy on state medical cannabis laws.

A flood of growers and aspiring cannabis entrepreneurs made their way to Oakland to attend classes at Oaksterdam University and learn from Bay Area pioneers in the business, including Ed and Dennis Peron. Oaksterdam's founder, Richard Lee, put up over $1 million of his own money to place a legalization initiative (Proposition 19) on the California ballot in 2010. While we went to print that year truly believing cannabis would be legal within months, the narrow defeat of Proposition 19 paved the way for the successful passage two years later of the first adult-use legalization laws in Colorado and Washington state.

While the previous edition of this book ushered in the Green Rush, this edition comes at a time when marijuana, now exclusively referred to as "cannabis," has mainstreamed. Real and meaningful research is being conducted on cannabis cultivation, genomics, medicine, processing, and use. Most people who will pick up this book can grow legally, either for personal or for medical use or as a licensed commercial grower. More and more schools offer courses on cannabis cultivation.

This book is for everyone: the home grower, those looking to get into the commercial industry, and especially for seasoned educated growers who wish to continue to learn and expand their techniques and knowledge. It's designed to be a useful educational tool that breaks down general concepts and explains and applies them for both home and commercial gardens. While some may choose to read it cover to cover, others will use it as a staple reference in the garden, for the answers to any and all of their questions lie within these pages.

Last time we knew the contributions and reviews from a handful of credentialed scholars, academics, and researchers added to the legitimacy and respect of the book. Still, most contributed their writing under pseudonyms or (as requested) reviewed content without recognition. This time, we are particularly proud of the accomplished contributors who have made this edition the new groundbreaking standard for all cannabis grow books to come and who can finally claim their bylines.

This edition adds two coauthors: Dr. Robert Flannery of Dr. Robb Farms, and the author of this introduction, Angela Bacca.

Dr. Robert Flannery is the first PhD in the United States with technical training and expertise in commercial cannabis cultivation. He has a PhD in plant biology with an emphasis in environmental horticulture and a specific expertise in hydroponic crop optimization for cut-flower production from the University of California at Davis. Dr. Flannery has managed commercial horticultural cultivation since 1999. While working on his doctorate, he began advising cultivators throughout Northern California on modern horticulture practices.

I have been editing and writing cannabis-specific content ever since I was a student journalist at San Francisco State University in 2006. I edited and managed the 2010 edition of *Grower's Handbook* while working on an MBA at Mills College and (with Ed) supporting the Proposition 19 campaign in any way I could. Since that time I have edited several books and magazines in the field and specialized in long-form journalistic coverage of the economic and political rollout of commercial cannabis markets in different states from a business, horticulture, economics, and ethics perspective.

In addition to contributions from Dr. Robb and me, what makes this edition so special are all the outside contributors and editors who have ensured that *Cannabis Grower's Handbook* is the most thorough and comprehensive cannabis cultivation guide available.

Part I: The Cannabis Plant describes how cannabis produces its range of effects in humans, outlines the plant's taxonomy and history, and breaks down cannabis varieties and basic breeding.

In the previous edition of the book, one of the nation's leading cannabis researchers, under the pseudonym G. Lee PhD, wrote about how cannabis works with human physiology. In this edition, Dr. Gregory Gerdeman is able to formally claim his byline and update the content to reflect the advances of scientific understanding over the last decade. Dr. Gerdeman is a neuroscientist and educator who has the distinction of studying the endocannabinoid system (ECS) for nearly three decades. His graduate research included some of the world's first discoveries that endocannabinoids act as "retrograde messengers" that regulate synaptic plasticity in the brain, findings that have become a foundation to modern understanding of the ECS and the neuroprotective actions of cannabinoids.

Corrections to common misconceptions about female cannabis flower anatomy were provided by Mel Frank, the co-author of the original *Marijuana Grower's Guide* (1974).

In the review of cannabis varieties, we have included an expanded feature on autoflowering plants by Jeff Lowenfels, a "reformed lawyer" and author of *Teaming with Microbes* and the whole *Teaming With* book series. These quick-harvesting varieties have emerged as the most intriguing new cultivars in many commercial markets and home gardens, and cannabis breeders are producing more and more of them.

Our terpene section has been expanded to include new research and newly identified cannabis terpenes. This content was revised by the team at Royal Queen Seeds and Ellen Holland, a longtime cannabis journalist and editor who contributed greatly to the production of this book.

This edition also includes a chapter on basic breeding by Professor P of Dynasty Genetics and Will Ferguson. Supplemental information about genomic testing, breeding, and cannabis intellectual property was provided by Dale Hunt, JD, PhD, of Plant & Planet Law Firm and Breeder's Best. Content about producing diploid and triploid seeds was provided by Emery Garcia of Oregon CBD.

Part II: The Limiting Factors explains the key inputs that drive the process of photosynthesis and therefore plant growth: light, carbon dioxide, water, oxygen, nutrients and fertilizers, and air temperature, humidity and qualities. Each chapter breaks down basic concepts, techniques, products, and how to apply this information to the garden.

The Light chapter was revised and expanded by Jake Holley, who at the time of first printing is earning his PhD in horticultural biology with a specialty in plant lighting at Cornell University, where he conducts research. This chapter received further technical review by Bruce Bugbee, PhD, professor at Utah State University and founder of Apogee Instruments. The Water chapter was revised and edited by Rosa Raudales, PhD, a professor at the University of Connecticut. The Nutrients & Fertilizers chapter was revised and edited by Neil Mattson, PhD, professor at Cornell University. The Air Temperature, Humidity & Qualities chapter was revised by the authors with contributions from Oaksterdam University horticulture professor Joey Ereñeta, Autumn Karcey and Mike Finley of Cultivo, Inc., and Brandy Keen

Part III: Setting Up the Garden covers choosing a plant growth medium and/or nutrient-delivery system as well as the basic elements of indoor and outdoor garden design for personal and commercial operations. Because there is no one right way to grow, we included a showcase of garden profiles that cover a range of styles, from fully organic regenerative outdoor gardening techniques to high-efficiency indoor gardens.

The Soil chapter was revised by Brian Malin of Vital Garden Supply, with supplemental information about regenerative farming, living soils, and permaculture provided by Jeff Lowenfels. The Hydroponics chapter has been revised and expanded by Neil Mattson, PhD, professor at Cornell University.

Basic small- and large-scale indoor garden setups were written by Bill Faulconer, author of *Design & Build a Room to Grow: Money Can Grow on Trees*, with scaling considerations provided by Justin Arriola of Automated Growth Solutions. Extra considerations for indoor design optimization and electrical safety were provided by Joey Ereñeta of Oaksterdam University.

In the last part of this section we have included a showcase of alternative gardens, growing styles, and strategies from growers we admire: the late Dennis Peron, Dan Vinkovetsky (formerly Danny Danko of High Times), Daniel "Old E" and Brian "Bleezy" Eatmon of Mendo Dope and Mark Grayshock of Greenshock Farms, Remo aka @UrbanRemo, Sunshine Cereceda of Sunboldt Grown, Tyler LeBlanc of Apollo Green, Kristin Nevedal of the International Cannabis Farmers Association, Autumn Shelton and the Brand Family of Autumn Brands, Jeremy Babbitt of 918 Oklahoma Grown and Andy Unruh of Sticky Flower Farm, Trent Hancock of Creswell Oreganics, Marty and Laura Clein of Martyjuana, Wendy Kornberg of Sunnabis, and Chris Trump. These profiles were written by the authors unless otherwise noted.

Finally, for the first time we have included an overview of concepts of sustainability, for all types of gardens. This content was provided by Dale Sky Jones, chancellor of Oaksterdam University, and other Oaksterdam faculty, with supplemental content by the authors.

Part IV: The Plant Life Cycle focuses on each stage of the plant's life cycle: propagation, vegetative growth, and flowering. These chapters were written by the authors and edited by Jay Kitchen of Uptown Growlab. Jay is the author of Uptown Growlab's *The Kitchen* and the *2021 Cannabis Annual*. After a career as an administrative law judge in New York City, Jay came out of the cannabis closet and relocated to the Pacific Northwest, where he hosts the popular Uptown Growlab live show on YouTube.

Finishing and flushing products and processes are covered by the authors.

Part V: Harvesting & Processing details the harvesting process, how to choose a harvesting date, and all the different ways the crop is processed after it has been cut down.

The process of ripening is covered by the authors, with original study on the evolution of the chemical profile found in the trichomes throughout the flowering process by Caleb King, Thomas Blank, PhD, and Reggie Gaudino, PhD, of Front Range Biosciences, and Kymron DeCesare and Donald P. Land, Ph.D, consultants to Front Range Biosciences.

Picking, trimming, drying, curing, and storing were written by the authors with editorial review by Clayton Stewart, an environmental technologist, post-harvest specialist, and consultant who has worked with large-scale commercial facilities in Canada. Clayton also wrote the Automation chapter and originated a study on drying and curing to expand this section.

To close out this section, the authors cover solventless extraction and concentration methods.

The appendices cover propagation methods: cloning, tissue culture, producing seeds, and regeneration, as well as a pest and disease guide designed for problem-solving in the garden.

The Pest & Disease appendix was revised by integrated pest management expert Saul Alba. The Cloning appendix was revised by Ellen Holland. The Producing Seeds appendix was written by the team at Humboldt Seeds.

The guide to tissue culture was written by Bill Graham of Microclone Tissue Culture. Bill is a founding member of the Cannabis Group of the Society of In Vitro Biology.

Finally, we have included a list of incredible garden consultants who contributed to the production of this book, a thorough glossary, and extensive bibliography and resources section.

While the laws, tools, and techniques will continue to evolve rapidly after the publication of this edition of Ed's best-selling cultivation guide, now the *Cannabis Grower's Handbook*, the fundamentals will never change. We hope that new and experienced growers who pick up this book will continue the legacy of innovation and social change that inspired the readers of the first and subsequent editions.

In the introduction to the 2010 edition Ed warned, "Using marijuana isn't addictive but growing it is." Over the last 50 years cannabis has become the gateway to gardening for many people in many more places. Although cannabis will not be truly legal until everyone has the right to grow their own, we hope the publication of this new edition leads to further research, understanding, and freedom of this world-changing plant.

Foreword to *Marijuana Grower's Guide*, 1974

Over the past 10 years there have been revolutionary changes in the values of young people. The empty materialism of the fifties and liberal idealism of the sixties have been washed away by a pragmatic re-evaluation of lifestyle and political structure.

To a great extent this is the result of the widespread use of the psychoactive herbs and drugs which burst upon the scene in 1967. These substances seem to break down the ego and defense mechanisms and allow individuals to re-evaluate the sets and set perceptions based upon behavior patterns no longer relevant.

Marijuana, the most popular of the psychoactive herbs, has helped millions of people to a broader understanding of themselves. It is for precisely this reason that governments all over the world view it as a dangerous drug. How can they control their people if they see through the hypocrisy and self-serving purpose of the leaders' actions?

The use of marijuana has become so widespread that the government's repressive efforts, such as Operation Intercept, have resulted in almost total failure, and contempt for the inept efforts by the rulers of a system which hears its death-knell but does not understand the sounds.

However, the economic system which makes marijuana seem like just another commodity, rather than the sacrament that it should be, must be replaced. This book will help you make marijuana free.

FREE GRASS   FREE YOURSELF   FREE THE WORLD

PART I:

THE CANNABIS PLANT

Photo: Jesse Robertson / Sticky Fields

UNDERSTANDING THE EFFECTS OF CANNABIS

by Gregory Gerdeman, PhD

Cannabis and the Endocannabinoid System

For thousands of years, cannabis followed humans, carried from one civilization to the next as a cherished plant companion.

The human-cannabis relationship is a powerful example of what biologists call mutualism, when two species mutually benefit the survival of the other. By selecting for the traits that breeders most valued, humans shaped cannabis evolution and continue to do so. In turn, this companion plant has contributed greatly to human societies through its use for food, clothing, shelter, medicine, manufacturing, religion, recreation, and other aspects of commerce and culture (Clarke and Merlin 2013).

It has been hypothesized that modern humans coevolved with cannabis. The implication is that cannabis has helped shape not only our cultural history but also our genetic code, the underlying biology of who we are (McPartland and Guy 2004). This is an extraordinary idea, that during the natural history of human cannabis use the relationship changed humans in a heritable way and thus affected the evolutionary trajectory of our species.

What is known for sure is that the reasons we have cultivated cannabis as a beneficial companion are inherent in our biology and helped create our evolutionary success. In a manner of speaking, we were predisposed to the relationship well before we became ecologically entwined. It is inherent in the biochemistry of how our bodies function and how cannabis touches us at the cellular level.

It is quite evident from history, as well as the present-day resurgence of cannabis as medicine, that cannabis enhances human survival and helps protect from injury and disease. Cannabis is a medicine that improves quality of life. The biologically active metabolites of cannabis support human health at molecular and cellular levels by acting at a physiological mechanism called the **endocannabinoid system**, which evolved as a key component of animal, and thus human, biology (Pellerin 2020).

Cannabis, The Medicine Flower

Some of the earliest discovered examples of written language describe cannabis as a medicine, as do medical texts from prominent cultures that flourished in the intervening millennia. Cannabis use since antiquity was widespread, and it was not just low-THC hemp. Archaeological evidence, supported by modern lab tests, shows that in parts of the ancient world that were quite distant from one another, ritual-medicinal uses of THC-rich cannabis not only existed but were revered and sacred (Russo 2007).

Before the invention of writing, cannabis was recognized as a vital crop unlike any other because of its multitude of uses for survival. But it's the truly extraordinary flower, distinctive among all others in nature, that is the reason there is such interest in the plant.

The many uses of cannabinoids found on these flowers range from lifting the mood to relaxing spastic muscles and even brain seizures. Cannabis eases aches and pains and can safely amplify the analgesic effects of other, more dangerous painkillers. It can distract thoughts from the passage of time, helping us forget, while often enhancing the emotional joys of exercise, sex, and eating.

In the decade since the previous edition of this book, there has been an explosion of scientific discovery about how cannabis provides such a broad range of therapeutic and enjoyable effects. To understand it, consider what each side of this relationship brings to the table. What is in cannabis that affects us so? What is it in humans that cannabis interacts with?

Cannabinoids

Cannabis produces well over 100 structurally related chemical compounds called cannabinoids. The production of these cannabinoids occurs primarily in and around the tightly clustered flowers that are the pride and joy of sinsemilla growers. The so-called bud is actually a leafy inflorescence, and it is covered with nearly microscopic, bubble-like trichome glands filled with a sticky, cannabinoid-rich resin. These glandular trichomes of cannabis are more than simply photogenic; they are marvels of chemical synthesis, creating a host of metabolites that supports the survival of the plant.

The most abundant of the cannabinoids are Δ^9 tetrahydrocannabinol (THC) and cannabidiol (CBD). These are the superstars that drive the psychotropic and medical uses of cannabis. THC and CBD are truly sister molecules, derived from the very same parent compound, the "mother cannabinoid" cannabigerol (CBG). More accurately, the true parent precursor is the "raw" or acid form, cannabigerolic acid (CBGa), which is converted to THCa or CBDa (or to a lesser extent CBCa) in a genetically controlled process (de Meijer 2016).

Like fraternal twins, THC and CBD share some characteristics but are definitely not identical and do not behave the same. THC is profoundly psychotropic and is the driver of the cannabis "high." This, of course, is very well known, and for decades following the elucidation of THC's chemical structure in the early 1960s, most of the world assumed that Δ^9 THC was the entire story behind why people enjoy using cannabis. This was validated by the observation that pure THC oil replicates the hashish high using no other components (Mechoulam and Ben-Shabat 1999).

THC is the dominant psychotropic player in cannabis, but can pure THC faithfully replicate a full cannabis experience? No. This is a simplification. Behavioral measures don't need to be very sophisticated to show that a shot of straight THC can get a human highly stoned or render a lab rat unable to move. The isolated focus on THC does not take into account "the entourage effect," where other cannabinoids or terpenes affect the experience too and lead to a spectrum of varying effects on people, not all of them psychotropic (Russo 2011).

UNDERSTANDING MEDICAL CANNABIS
Cannabinoids and Their Relationships

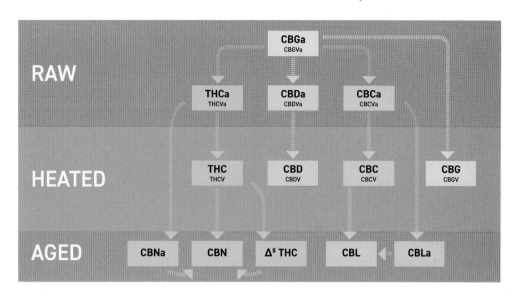

In the glandular trichomes of cannabis, the "mother cannabinoid" CBG is converted either to THC, CBD, or CBC in different amounts based on competing enzyme activities. The different cannabinoid ratios found in cannabis are mostly due to genetic variation in these cannabinoid synthase enzymes. Selective breeding has led to cannabis varieties that make neither THC or CBD, accumulating high levels of CBG instead. CBC is a lesser-known daughter of CBG. Although CBC is a minor component of contemporary cannabis, it is part of the therapeutic cannabinoid ensemble, and breeding efforts will generate more CBC-rich varieties. SOURCE: Steep Hill Lab and Elemental Wellness.

What is a cannabinoid?

There is inconsistency out there about when to use the term. Originally a moniker for secondary metabolites unique to cannabis, today it tends to define function more than origin, referring to those molecules that are active at cannabinoid receptors. In addition to endocannabinoids described in this chapter, there are synthetic cannabinoids constructed by chemistry labs for research and pharmaceutical drug development. Some have turned into illicit products sold as Spice, K2, and other names. On the other hand, the natural terpene **β-caryophyllene** has been called a cannabinoid because, like THC, it stimulates CB2 cannabinoid receptors (but not CB1), thereby representing a clear example of the herbal "entourage effect" inherent to cannabis (Gertsch et al. 2008). It is not a classic cannabinoid in structure, and is common not only in cannabis but in the essential oils of other dietary herbs such as black pepper, cloves, and copaiba. Some prefer to call caryophyllene a **cannabimimetic**, a name used for non-cannabinoid molecules that are known to act on the human ECS, such as compounds found in frankincense, liverwort, and echinacea (McPartland et al. 2014).

The therapeutic properties of the other twin, CBD, alleviate inflammation and consequent pain states, relieve anxiety and psychosis, decrease seizure frequency, and alleviate muscle spasms. Bold as these claims are, they are supported by many high-quality preclinical scientific studies, as well as numerous patient surveys and clinical anecdotes (Crippa et al. 2018). There is evidence, however, that CBD works more effectively in the presence of THC and/or other components present in full-spectrum cannabis extracts (Gallily et al. 2015; Sulak et al. 2017).

"Minor" Cannabinoids

Of the over 100 unique cannabinoids, very little about the pharmacology of most of them is known, but some of the more prominent "minors" are of great interest and may well be important players in commercially available cannabis. One key example is CBG, the "mother cannabinoid," which in 2021 is being grown in abundance thanks to successful breeding to develop high-CBG flowers. Both CBG and **cannabichromene** (CBC) influence the cannabis high and have therapeutic properties ranging from inhibiting tumors to bacterial infections (Russo and Marcu 2017).

Also present in cannabis is **cannabinol** (CBN), which is merely an oxidative breakdown product of THC, but is now produced in labs more than it occurs in nature. Similarly, Δ^8-THC is a natural isomer of THC that only minimally occurs in the flower but has recently garnered interest because it can be easily lab-manufactured through a chemical conversion of CBD. Both Δ^8-THC and CBN act relatively weakly at some of the same cellular receptors described later in this chapter (Pertwee and Grazia Cascio 2014) and are sometimes called "THC light." These molecules are surging in popularity, but it is important to realize that the chemistry that creates Δ^8-THC, Δ^{10}-THC, or even CBN also generates other by-products, depending on the precise conditions of the chemical reaction. Quality control is critical if these products are to be trusted for long-term use.

Breeding programs have also brought out increasing concentrations of the "varin" cannabinoids: **THCV** and **CBDV** (Lewis et al. 2018). These are also called "propyl cannabinoids" based on the 3-carbon tail in their molecular structures. They have numerous influences on the psycho-therapeutic properties of any flower that contains them. As refined drugs, both are in clinical studies.

Last but not least, the raw acid forms such as THCa and CBDa, which are what actually occur in the fresh, unheated plant material, have a variety of biological activities that make them compelling players in the ways that cannabis can support human health and well-being (Russo and Marcu 2017). Calling the cannabinoid acids "minor" is a bit funny, since they are what the plant actually makes, but in most all of the ways that cannabis is processed or heated during consumption, the acids are efficiently decarboxylated ("decarbed") into the better-known forms.

The Terpene Entourage

The range of fragrances that cannabis produces is well known. They are produced in the same place as cannabinoids, in the glandular trichomes. The diverse palate of scents to be found in cannabis is not due to cannabinoids, which have no odor, but to aromatic terpenes.

Unlike cannabinoids, terpenes are not unique to cannabis at all but are also abundant in most other plants. Most flower odors and other fragrant resins are composed of terpenes. The therapeutic properties of medicinal herbs, and their essential oils that are used for perfumes, flavorings, and aromatherapy, are often due to the terpenes they contain.

An important concept is that this natural ensemble of botanical metabolites, the entourage of cannabinoids and terpenes found in whole cannabis, work together to support health in ways that are superior to single molecules acting alone as isolated drugs.

It has long been appreciated by cannabis enthusiasts that the smell of the flower can, to some degree, predict the nature of the high it will elicit. The aroma is therefore linked to variation in biological effect. Other evidence comes from clinical studies that found that whole-plant extracts may produce superior outcomes than isolated ingredients (Gallily et al. 2015; Blasco-Benito. et al, 2018).

In addition to shaping the taste and smell that may distinguish one variety of cannabis from another, the bouquet of terpenes creates the "entourage effect" that determines, together with the cannabinoids and other bioactive molecules, the "shape and feel" of the cerebral experience, or the specific medicinal value.

Anthocyanins and other flavonoids bring out deep purples, fall colors and health-promoting properties in cannabis. Photo: Dr. Greg Gerdeman

Flavonoids

While the floral, skunky, and "fuel" smells of cannabis are famous, people who do not cultivate the plant are often surprised to learn that it can also be quite colorful. Like many plants, when shorter light cycles begin to diminish **chlorophyll** levels, the dominant green progressively gives way to underlying hues of yellow, red, and purple. The pistil hairs and even tiny trichome heads take on an orange coloration. In some varieties, the flower itself naturally matures into a striking purple, which is often reflected in the cultivar name. In addition, most any cannabis plant will turn purplish if it is shocked by cold temperatures.

All these colorations are the product of pigment molecules called **flavonoids**. Aside from aesthetics, flavonoids are an important part of the health benefits of fruits, berries, vegetables, and cannabis. Often called polyphenols, which is a reference to their molecular structure, they are not known to be psychotropic or to affect the cannabis "high" in any way.

Flavonoids are strong antioxidants, which all by itself could contribute to an entourage effect of enhancing well-being. Research has indicated that low dietary intake of flavonoids is associated with increased risk of cardiovascular disease and cancers, suggesting that a diet rich in flavonoids may be protective. Other experiments have found that flavonoid consumption enhances healthy blood flow to the brain (Rees et al. 2018). Most of the flavonoids in cannabis are common in other plants, such as the **anthocyanins** that are responsible for those purple colors. Cannabis also has at least two unique flavonoids called **cannflavin A and B**, which have been shown to have potent anti-inflammatory properties (Russo and Marcu 2017).

How does the entourage of cannabinoids, terpenes, and flavonoids team up? It is known that from one chemotype (chemical profile) to the next, the subjective experience of a "high" can be very different. What about cannabis as medicine? Are there distinct metabolite profiles in certain varieties that make them more effective than others for treating particular symptoms or diseases? The internet abounds with such claims, but the evidence behind it is mostly very poor, confounded by inaccurate product labeling, inconsistent dosing, and the inability to set up clinical trials to control the many variables of an entourage study, including placebo effects. The truth is still unknown. To date, there is not enough science to clearly prove such a wishful logic, but there are plenty of reasons to hope that a full exploration of the bioactive ensembles in cannabis could lead to this kind of understanding.

Having given this introduction to the complexity that cannabis brings to the relationship, attention must now be paid to the biochemistry and physiology of humans, and the ways in which humans have evolved to respond to cannabis. Here again, the story is much richer than imagined until recent years.

The Endocannabinoid System (ECS)

The key to it all — how cannabis alters physical and mental states and eases symptoms of so many injuries and illnesses — is a complex, integrative mechanism in human bodies called the **endocannabinoid system** (ECS). The ECS regulates vital cellular activity of animal bodies. It works to protect against toxic stresses, to promote homeostasis (which means a normal physiological balance), and to support general health and well-being. Undetected until the very end of the last century, the biology of the ECS provides a scientific rationale to explain humanity's innate therapeutic use of cannabis.

The ECS consists of:
- Various **cannabinoid receptors** used by cells to communicate, maintain balance, and sense the outside (and internal) world. They are activated by cannabinoids in cannabis.
- The **endocannabinoids** (eCBs), signaling molecules produced within the body that

act on those receptors, as a way that cells communicate with one another to maintain homeostasis.

- The **ECS enzymes** that either create or break apart the endocannabinoids. Changing the function of these enzymes dictates how many endocannabinoids are present and available in any given place and time within the brain and body.

> "Signaling molecule" is a general term for chemicals used by cells to communicate within the body. For example, neurotransmitters are signaling molecules used by brain cells (neurons) to communicate. Endocannabinoids are used not only by neurons but by nearly every type of cell in the body.

The endocannabinoid system is referred to as a "master regulator" of human physiology. The first big breakthrough came in 1988 and following years, when scientists discovered that there are receptors on the surface of brain cells that grab onto THC as though they evolved just to do so (Devane et al. 1988). These molecular locks, unlatched and activated by THC, quite naturally earned the name "cannabinoid receptors" because they were found through a deliberate search to decipher the secrets of cannabis's psychotropic effects.

Two subtypes were later recognized, encoded by different (but similar) genes, and expressed in different preferred areas of the body. These receptor proteins were called CB1 and CB2 (Herkenham et al. 1990; Munro et al. 1993).

The CB1 Receptor: A Choreographer of the Brain

Endocannabinoids in the Nervous System

The ECS is a master choreographer of nervous system activity. Neurons release endocannabinoids (eCBs) from their cellular membranes, which act at CB1 receptors in order to dampen down or fine-tune synaptic connections between brain areas. Brain circuits related to pain, emotional regulation, appetite, and higher thinking are all highly regulated in this way. This partly explains many of the most recognized actions of THC, which boosts ECS function as an outside CB1 activator. Some neurons of the cerebral cortex even use eCBs to self-regulate their own electrical activity, which is believed to play an important role in generating certain brain rhythms. Even target cells in the body use eCBs to give feedback to inputs from the nervous system, thereby shaping autonomic responses to stress, for example.

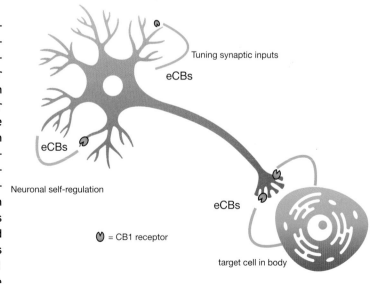

Tuning synaptic inputs

eCBs

eCBs

Neuronal self-regulation

eCBs

◒ = CB1 receptor

target cell in body

Graphic: Dr. Greg Gerdeman

THC affects mood, senses, and clarity of memory. Under the influence of cannabis, one might perceive the passage of time differently. Anxious thoughts can be replaced by sensory attention to something funny in the here and now, whether it is something mundane or something profound. Appetite may increase, while motor coordination may fall off. All of these are effects of THC working at CB1 receptors in different areas of the central nervous system, which includes the brain and spinal cord.

The human brain contains hundreds of different kinds of receptors that respond to dozens of neurotransmitters and hormones. It is part of the cellular biochemistry that makes this gray blob behind the forehead the most complex structure in the known universe. Of all those receptors, none are more prominent than the CB1 cannabinoid receptor.

The brain is literally teeming with CB1 receptors it uses to choreograph the rhythm of the circuits and keep feedback loops functioning in a healthy way that integrates brain with body, experience, and intention.

Of course, no cannabis is required for this to be so special and so important for biology. Animal bodies make their own endocannabinoids (eCBs), a shortened term for "endogenous (internal) cannabinoids." The name itself reflects that the endocannabinoids are very similar to THC, the phytocannabinoid (from the plant) that showed their existence. The first endocannabinoid discovered was named **anandamide** by its discoverer, from the Sanskrit word ananda, meaning "internal bliss," a wonderful homage to the beneficial properties of cannabis (Devane et al. 1992). A second endocannabinoid that is actually more abundant is **2-AG**. Anandamide and 2-AG are the actual playmakers used by cells throughout the brain and body to promote homeostasis by acting at cannabinoid receptors CB1 and CB2.

How is it that the ECS acts as a master regulator, or conductor of the neural symphony? Neurons in the brain release endocannabinoids to regulate and fine-tune their own inputs (Gerdeman 2007).

Consider what happens when a brain suffers a seizure, as in the case of someone with epilepsy or acute brain injury. Neurons are electrically active cells, and they are arranged in circuits in the brain. In a seizure, those circuits go haywire, barraging neural receptors with excessive electrical activity, one cell jolting the next with waves of excitatory neurotransmitters that push the cycle forward. The seizure ripples in waves across the brain, causing muscle spasms, blackouts, and the various outward symptoms of losing control over one's body.

CB1 receptors normally help prevent this from happening. When a cell starts receiving a surge of excitatory stimulus, for whatever normal reason, it responds by quickly generating endocannabinoids and releasing them to the signal producer. This is called retrograde signaling. They bind to the original sender neuron's CB1 receptors that are mostly found on the end-tips of the neurons, where the release of neurotransmitters occurs.

In this way, when a cell is receiving excessive inputs that are pushing it to be more electrically active than it should normally be, the release of endocannabinoids provides a negative feedback loop that says, "Slow down," and returns the system to balance (Katona and Freund 2008).

With epilepsy, stroke, and other brain injuries, the therapeutic implications for cannabis are really quite clear. The endocannabinoid system is protective, part of the brain's frontline defense against excitotoxicity damage. By directly stimulating CB1 receptor activity, cannabis is a supplement for the ECS, a boost for the endocannabinoids that need help to control the situation.

Cannabinoids and terpenes interact within the brain to influence the neural circuits of sensation and mood, including for the treatment of injury and disease.

CB1 is found virtually everywhere, regulating neural activity to keep it in balance. When pain-transmitting nerves carry their signals to the brain, healthy CB1 receptors help to keep the signal in check so that pain is appropriate, not pathological.

When the brain perceives a threat, the ECS acts through CB1 receptors to keep an initial fear response, and the momentary stress that motivates a proper fight-or-flight response, from turning into debilitating and chronic stress. Even the ability to forget or move past a traumatic experience, called "fear extinction," involves a well-studied mechanism of endocannabinoids acting at CB1 receptors in the so-called fear center of the brain, the amygdala (Morena et al. 2016).

The CB2 Receptor: A Thermostat of the Immune System

Whereas CB1 is most densely but not exclusively found throughout the nervous system, the CB2 receptor is found on the surface of cells that make up the immune system. Crawling and circulating throughout the body, the immune system is also enormously complex, with moving parts. Communication is key, and here again, the ECS plays a master role to regulate immune system communication and activity. Endocannabinoids act primarily at CB2 receptors to turn down excessive inflammation and to prevent tissue-damaging outcomes that can occur when an amped-up immune system starts to turn on its own body (Maccarrone et al. 2015).

Just as neurons release neurotransmitters to communicate, and how endocrine glands release hormones to send signals throughout the body via the bloodstream, immune cells communicate through the release of signaling molecules called cytokines. Many of these cytokines are pro-inflammatory, meaning that they stimulate a ramped-up immune response that recruits more and more first responders to the scene of an injury or infection. This leads to swelling, fever, and feelings of malaise that help to keep a person off their feet to allow for recovery. Just as CB1 receptors dial down the release of neurotransmitters in the brain, CB2 receptors respond to cannabinoids by inhibiting the release of pro-inflammatory cytokines.

The ECS: A Cellular Mechanism of Integrative Physiology

What is called an "endocannabinoid system" is more accurately a fundamental cellular *mechanism*. It isn't that some cells make up the ECS and others don't. Nor is it just in the brain and the immune system. Rather, cells of every tissue type utilize this mechanism. Some cells release endocannabinoids, others respond to them, often doing both. This ECS is integrative because it assists in the proper function of all physiological systems, helping to promote balance and integrate systems into the healthy balancing act that makes up a whole human being.

The ECS is an Entourage Too!

CB1 and CB2 receptors are important players in maintaining human health, and their discovery opened the door to reintroducing cannabis as an accepted part of medicine, yet they are not the whole story to the extended ECS and how the entourage of cannabis exerts its effects. It turns out that there are numerous other ways eCBs work, involving other receptor targets, which also promote pathways of maintaining homeostasis.

First are the TRP channel receptors. This important class of cell surface ion channels allows cells to monitor and respond to their sensory environment (Kaneko and Szallasi 2014). Depending on the subtype, TRP channels are activated by a number of physical stimuli such as temperature, acidic pH, osmotic swelling, or other mechanical stretching. They are also activated by a variety of essential oils from culinary and therapeutic herbs. The TRPV1 channel, for example, is activated by capsaicin from hot chili peppers. It is literally responsible for why humans feel pain from heat. Ever wonder why hot cream rubs are used for topical pain relief? It is because after the capsaicin creates a hot sensation, it stays stuck to the TRPV1 channel and causes it to desensitize. It is the same reason one can adjust to hot spicy food after the first few bites. When researchers searched for an endogenous activator for this hot pepper receptor, they were surprised to learn that it is none other than anandamide and 2-AG. Unlike capsaicin, the eCBs — and also CBD (but not THC) — simply desensitize the receptor rather than allowing it to open. CBD topicals do not feel hot, but their mechanism of pain relief is directly related to hot rubs. Recent research found that β-myrcene also inhibits TRPV1 activity (Jansen et al. 2019). This is only one example out of at least six different TRP channels that are known to be modulated by other phytocannabinoids and terpenes *in vitro* (experiments using cells in a petri dish; Muller et al. 2019).

Second, a pair of proteins called PPARs have long been studied as regulators of metabolism, and they too are regulated by both eCBs and phytocannabinoids (O'Sullivan 2016). In particular, PPARγ (gamma) is a so-called nuclear receptor because when it is activated, it moves into the nucleus of the cell and turns on genes associated with improving metabolism. PPARγ is activated by a class of drugs called glitazones, which are FDA-approved for the control of type 2 diabetes. Animal research has found both CBD and THCa, and likely others, can similarly activate PPARγ. This may help to explain repeated epidemiological findings that cannabis users tend to have a lower body mass index compared to non-users (Alshaarawy and Anthony 2019).

The ECS Discovery is Truly Revolutionary

The scale of influence the ECS exerts as a regulator of homeostasis at levels all over the body is a uniquely impressive aspect of human biochemistry. What we call an endocannabinoid "system" is more accurately a fundamental and distributed cellular *mechanism*. It isn't that some cells make up the ECS and others don't. It isn't just in the brain and the immune system. Rather, cells of every tissue type utilize this mechanism, with some cells releasing eCBs, others responding to them, and often doing both. The ECS is integrative because it assists in the proper function of all physiological systems, helping to promote balance and integrate systems into the healthy balancing act that makes up a whole human being.

The ensemble of cannabinoids, terpenes, and flavonoids in cannabis is so extraordinary because of the many ways they collaborate to influence the homeostatic functions of the ECS. All the various ECS receptors and enzymes evolved to be key players in health and are regulated not only by the cellular release of endocannabinoids in our bodies but also by the medicinal metabolites of cannabis.

Consider, for example, some known actions of CBD:

- Enhancing anandamide activity by inhibiting its breakdown by the FAAH enzyme.
- Tempering neurological effects of THC by tweaking its signaling at the CB1 receptor
- Regulating TRPV1 channel activity to influence pain and inflammation.
- Regulating serotonin in the brain to improve mood.
- Influencing metabolic health through PPAR activation. Remarkably, all these actions seem to tip toward anti-inflammatory, mood-regulating benefits that echo the innate functions of the ECS.

Science is revealing more about how the minor cannabinoids and terpenes also touch all these players of the ECS and the combination of ensembles that can occur when humans meet plants. This is how complex the entourage effect is and why it seems so compelling that humans are an ideal evolutionary match.

So while the ECS was discovered out of a quest to understand marijuana as a "drug of abuse," to be avoided and treated as a toxin, it has actually revealed profound lessons about human health and what it means to be well. The ECS is the biological rationale behind using this most ancestral of teacher plants.

Bob Marley famously said, "When you smoke the herb, it reveals you to yourself." Getting to the root of how cannabis interacts with the human body opens the promise of understanding its benefits, best uses, and potential for negative outcomes. The science of this pursuit has added dizzying details not only about the plant but about human biology. It somehow all fits within the ganja-inspired insights of Marley: when humanity studies the herb, it reveals humans to themselves.

Ayahuasca Purple Photo: Barney's Farm

THE CANNABIS PLANT

Cannabis evolved from plants native to the high altitudes of the Tibetan plateau and the Himalayan foothills. Its origins are clouded by the plant's early symbiotic relationship with humans, a relationship at least 6,000 years old. The use of cannabis and its products migrated with humans throughout the world, and the plant is now cultivated in climatic zones from the Arctic to the equator. Cannabis evolved on its own prior to its discovery by our human ancestors, but since then, it has been bred intensively to optimize particular characteristics.

Cannabis is cultivated for one or more of three useful products:
- the nutritious seeds
- the fibrous stalks
- the resinous flowers

Cannabis seeds are rich in oil and protein and are used as a food and as animal feed, as well as a source of oil for fuel and skincare products. The seeds have almost as much protein as soybeans, and they provide all nine of the essential amino acids that humans cannot create on their own and must obtain through diet. The lipid profile of the seeds is high in polyunsaturated fatty acids, especially omega-3 fatty acids. The seeds are also substantial sources of dietary fiber.

Researchers from the University of Manitoba showed that adding hemp seed and hemp seed oil to chicken feed greatly increased the ratio of omega-3 to omega-6 fatty acids in the resulting egg yolks and showed a 12-fold increase in alpha-linoleic acid (an essential omega-3 fatty acid) in the lipid profile of the eggs.

Cannabis fiber, produced from the stalks of the plant, is used to make tough cloth, paper, and rope. Though all cannabis plants are of the same species, the varieties typically cultivated for their seeds or fiber are known as hemp.

Phytocannabinoids Aren't Just In Cannabis

Cannabinoids get their name from the genus of plants (*Cannabis*) where they are primarily found in nature; however, other plants produce phytocannabinoids as well. A few species in the daisy plant family (*Asteraceae*) and a species of liverwort from New Zealand (*Radula marginata*) also produce compounds that bind to the cannabinoid receptors in the human body. In addition to other plant species, black truffles produce an endocannabinoid called anandamide. Anandamide is named for the Sanskrit word *ananda*, meaning "joy, bliss, delight," and interacts with the human body similarly to THC. Frankincense and cocoa may also contain compounds that bind to some of the same receptors that cannabinoids from cannabis bind to. (*See Understanding the Effects of Cannabis*).

The third product, the flowers and the resin that coats them, is used therapeutically and recreationally. Cannabis resin contains the group of substances collectively known as cannabinoids, of which Δ^9 **Tetrahydrocannabinol (THC)** is the chief psychoactive component. THC and at least 143 other cannabinoids are unique to cannabis. Plants grown for their THC content are commonly called cannabis, whereas cultivated varieties of cannabis that are primarily grown for their fiber and seed products are commonly referred to as hemp.

What's the difference between cannabis and hemp?

The term "cannabis" refers to all varieties of the cannabis plant. Hemp, on the other hand, has two definitions: botanical and legal. Traditionally the term "hemp" has referred to a collective group of varieties of cannabis that are grown for their seed and fiber content, while plants that are grown for the resinous female flowers have, until recently, been referred to as "marijuana." Both US and international laws have arbitrarily defined hemp by its content of THC, meaning any cannabis plant with under 0.3% THC content is considered "hemp," including resinous flowers high in other compounds such as CBD and CBG. The word "marijuana" is no longer the preferred term and is generally replaced in popular use by the word "cannabis." This book is a guide to producing cannabis and "hemp" plants grown for their resinous flowers, rather than traditional "hemp" grown for seed and fiber.

The many uses of this multifaceted plant have historically made it a valuable crop, and today there are collectively more breeding programs for cannabis than any other crop. The historical illegality of cannabis has unintentionally resulted in a robust breeding program that is pushing the genetic limits of what cannabis can produce as far as cannabinoid and terpene content, yield, and more. The escalation of the US government's War on Drugs forced innovative cultivators and breeders to work underground to provide a sufficient supply of seedstock to serve their own needs. The War on Drugs restricted transport of cannabis from Mexico, so American cultivators had to get creative in sourcing. Because of seed scarcity in the commercial market and the fact that cannabis is one of the few plants that casual farmers and breeders can easily grow from self-produced seed, many gardeners have become self-reliant and created their own seed stock.

Gardeners who take this path join an international breeding program as soon as they transfer some of their genetics (i.e., seeds) to someone else. In the 50 years of this modern cannabis breeding program, growers have developed diverse varieties and cultivation methods that are quite efficient at producing the desired product: large, dense buds of sinsemilla—that is, a profusion of unpollinated female flowers.

Cannabis varieties differ in many ways, including growth characteristics such as:

- height
- width
- branching traits
- leaf size and shape
- flowering time
- yield

- potency
- taste
- physical and mental effects
- aroma
- cannabinoid and terpene profile

The final harvest of a plant is a result of its "nature" and "nurture." The potential for high-potency cannabis is determined by genetics, or nature. However, environmental conditions, or nurture, affect the plant's growth and yield. Some plants have the genetic potential to produce high-quality cannabis and others do not. The goal of the cultivator is to provide the optimal environment to nurture the plants so they reach their full genetic potential.

Cannabis is a fast-growing annual plant, although some varieties in warm areas can overwinter by going dormant as the days shorten, then grow and flower again the next summer. The plant evolved on the Tibetan plateau, where the altitude averages 10,000 feet (3,000 m). Cannabis has evolved to grow, flower, and seed before the autumn snow in order for the population to survive to grow the following season.

Cannabis does best in a well-drained, nutrient-rich growing medium and requires long periods of bright, unobstructed light daily. Cannabis is usually dioecious, meaning plants are either male or female. Annual dioecious plants are rather unique in the plant kingdom.

Occasionally monoecious plants, or hermaphrodites, appear and produce both male and female flowers; however, this is often a function of a plant being stressed to induce hermaphroditism. Hermaphroditic plants are most common among some varieties native to south Asia, but can also result from inadequate light, poor nutrition, or switching from long uninterrupted nights to short or interrupted dark periods and back again. Because monoecious plants produce male flowers that can pollinate females, they are undesirable and should be removed from the garden as soon as they appear to avoid a pollination event.

Cannabis grown in the wild or with traditional methods outdoors has an annual cycle that begins with seed germination in the early spring. The plant grows vigorously in a vegetative state for several months as the days get longer and they begin to flower as the lengthening darkness reaches a critical period in late summer or early fall.

Vegetative growth means that the plant is developing new leaves, buds, stems, and roots; however, there is no production of its sexual organs (flowers).

The flowering time of landrace varieties depends on the variety's native latitude, but occurs in late summer as the night length increases. Most indicas are varieties from high latitudes and need less darkness to flower than most sativas, which are varieties from lower latitudes and equatorial regions. Most varieties set seed in the fall because they are genetically programmed to start flowering when the dark period reaches a critical length of time on consecutive nights of uninterrupted darkness. As winter approaches, the seeds drop and are ready for the next season as the plant dies.

Controlled environment agriculture, as seen in indoor or greenhouse production, allows the cultivator to control when the plants receive the critical length of uninterrrupted dark period. This gives the grower the ability to determine when the plants will be forced to flower, and when they will be ready to harvest.

Botanical Description: *Cannabis sativa* L.

The word "cannabis" is an ancient one, dating back past Roman and Greek to Thracian or Scythian times. Scholars have even identified biblical references to a plant known as "kaneh-bos" as early as the 15th century BCE.

As the contemporary name of a type of plant, *Cannabis sativa* L. was formally conferred in 1753 by Carolus Linnaeaus in his famous taxonomy. Linnaeaus, who devised the modern system for classifying and naming species through binomial nomenclature, concluded that the genus Cannabis had but one species, which bears the same botanical name. The genus is currently classified as belonging to the Cannabaceae family, which also includes hops (*Humulus* sp.). Recent phylogenetic studies and gene sequencing suggested that *Cannabis sativa* L. is closely related to members of the Celtidaceae family, which also includes the many species of Hackberry tree (genus Celtis); however, plant taxonomists have recently moved the members of the Celtidaceae family under an expanded Cannabaceae family. This was not the first time that *Cannabis sativa* L. has been reclassified, as it was formerly categorized as part of the Nettle (Urticaceae) or Mulberry (Moraceae) family.

Binomial nomenclature refers to the two-name system to classify species. The first name is the generic name, which is commonly referred to as the genus. The second name is the specific epithet, or species. The genus name is capitalized, whereas the species name is not. These names are derived from Latin and are always italicized. Cannabis is also the common name for Cannabis sativa, so when it is used as the common name, it does not need to be italicized or capitalized.

Hops provide a lot of the aroma and flavor characteristics for beer. In fact, opening a particularly "hoppy" beer like a Double IPA can give an aroma reminiscent of cannabis. Cannabis and hops are in the same plant family, and they share some similar qualities. For example, they produce similar terpenes. One of the many terpenes found in cannabis as well as hops is called humulene, which gets its name from the genus name of hops, *Humulus*.

There has been a similar evolution of thinking on how many species of *Cannabis sativa* L. should be recognized. In 1785, soon after Linnaeus identified it as a single species, the influential biologist Jean-Baptiste Lamarck claimed that the plant he found in India should be classified as a separate species, which he named *Cannabis indica*. This name would be included in various pharmacopoeias to designate cannabis plants that are suitable for the manufacture of medicinal preparations.

In the 19th century, some botanists proposed separate species classifications for cannabis plants indigenous to China and Vietnam. But by the 20th century, difficulty with definitively distinguishing between any of them due to intense breeding and hybridization had led most botanists to conclude, as Linnaeus did, that all cannabis plants belong to a single species.

What was once known as Cannabis indica would now be classified as a subspecies of *Cannabis sativa* (*Cannabis sativa* subsp. *indica*). Certainly, all cannabis plants satisfy one of the chief criteria of a species: they can interbreed. There are different ways to define a species. Wide disparities in cannabis plants' geographic location and primary characteristics have led many to argue that three species should be recognized, based on whether they are cultivated for fiber (sativa) or drugs (indica), or grow wild (ruderalis); however, defining a species by its ability to interbreed or hybridize has led taxonomists to conclude that sativas and indicas fall under one species.

Although it has been speculated that ruderalis is the progenitor wild variety, the fact that most of its alleles are recessive is an indication that it is a mutation. Although ruderalis can be hybridized with sativas and indicas, it grows in a fundamentally different manner and looks very different from the other members of the genus. For instance, flowering in ruderalis begins soon after germination and is not dependent on the length of daylight. Breeding cannabis varieties with ruderalis can create new varieties that will automatically start flowering ("autoflowering") regardless of the length of uninterrupted darkness. With careful breeding the hybrids will retain their highly resinous nature, as ruderalis is not typically as resinous as sativas or indicas.

The genetic makeup of cannabis varieties, also known as the **genotype**, is what drives the cannabinoid and terpene profile of the plant. The physical expression of the genotype is referred to as the **phenotype**. The plant's phenotype includes physical traits like plant height, yield, leaf size, terpene profile, cannabinoid ratios, flavonoid content, and time to harvest. The **chemotype** is the plant's phenotype, but specifically in reference to the chemical makeup of the plant. In other words, the chemotype of a cannabis variety is the genetic expression of its chemical makeup: cannabinoid potency, ratios, and content, terpene profiles, and flavonoid content.

Taxonomy of Cannabis

Kingdom: Plantae – Plants
Subkingdom: Tracheobionta – Vascular Plants
Superdivision: Spermatophyta – Seed Plants
Division: Magnoliophyta – Flowering Plants
Class: Magnoliopsida – Dicotyledons
Subclass: Hamamelididae
Order: Rosales
Family: Cannabaceae – Hemp Family
Genus: *Cannabis* L. – Hemp

Formal Botanical Description

Cannabis is an annual, dioecious, flowering herb. The leaves have serrated leaflets. The first pair of leaves usually have a single leaflet, the number gradually increasing to a maximum of about 13 leaflets per leaf (usually seven or nine), depending on variety and growing conditions. At the top of a flowering plant, this number again diminishes to a single leaflet per leaf. The lower leaf pairs usually occur in an opposite leaf arrangement and the upper leaf pairs in an alternate arrangement on the main stem of a mature plant.

Cannabis normally has imperfect flowers, with staminate male and pistillate female flowers occurring on separate plants. Occasionally, individual plants bear both male and female flowers and are referred to as hermaphrodites. Although monoecious plants are often referred to as hermaphrodites, true hermaphrodites (which are less common) bear staminate and pistillate structures on individual flowers, whereas monoecious plants bear male and female flowers at different locations on the same plant.

Cannabis is wind-pollinated and produces seeds that are technically fruits called achenes. Most varieties of cannabis are short day/long night plants, with the possible exception of *C. ruderalis* and some equatorial *C. sativa* varieties that are commonly described as auto-flowering and may be day-neutral. Cannabis is diploid, having a chromosome complement of 2n=20. Polyploid individuals have been artificially produced. (See *Basic Breeding*.) Cannabis plants produce a group of chemicals called cannabinoids, which are secreted by glandular trichomes that occur most abundantly on the bracts of female plants.

Since plants are not mobile, they can't outrun predators or pick up and relocate when competing plants move into the neighborhood. As a result, they have amassed other defenses against predators and competitors. One of their main strategies is chemical warfare. They produce oils and other chemicals designed to repel enemies. Others kill, sicken, delay maturation, or affect their metabolism. Plants use other aromatics to attract either pollinators for reproduction or predators that attack the plants' enemies. THC and the terpenes were developed as part of this arsenal.

The diversity of the cannabis plant's geography and morphology is considerable; cannabis grows in very different ways and places. The stems reach a height between three and 15 feet (~1 and 4.5 m) or more, and the plants range from thin and reedy to thick and bushy. While the plant is native to the Hindu Kush valley and the Himalayan foothills of the Tibetan Plateau, it has migrated with humans throughout the world and can now be found growing feral on every continent but Antarctica. Since there are no laws prohibiting it in Antarctica, where researchers from many countries work, it is safe to assume that cannabis has spread its roots there, too.

Cannabis sativa L. is one of only a few dioecious annual plants (including spinach)—that is, each plant is distinctively either male or female—though hermaphrodite plants do occur. Also unusual is the fact that cannabis is an annual, yet its closest botanical relative, hops, is a perennial. That, combined with the cannabis plant's ability in Nepal and similar climates to overwinter or regenerate in spring suggests that the plant's evolutionary path from being a perennial to an annual may have been relatively recent.

Even the plant's iconic leaves, instantly recognizable even to those who have never seen a cannabis plant growing, come in very different sizes and subtly different shapes. The palmate leaves can range from a spread of a few inches (about 5 cm) to more than a foot (30.5 cm), while the one to 13 (or more) sharply serrated leaflets vary from long and thin to broad and stubby. The cannabis plant's combination of extreme genetic variability and ease of interbreeding is part of what makes it so exciting to grow. The range of characteristics that selective breeding can produce is astonishing.

Anatomy of the Female Flower: Correcting the Record
By Mel Frank

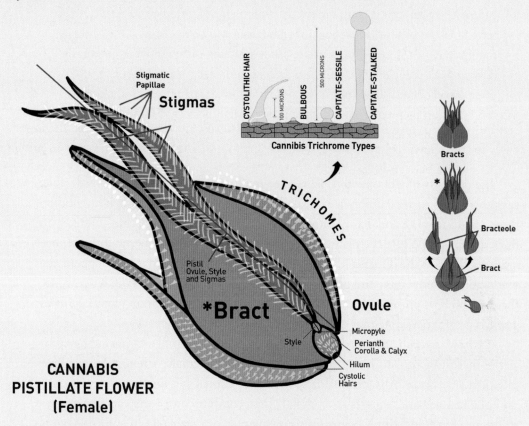

CANNABIS PISTILLATE FLOWER (Female)

Stigmatic Papillae — Stigmas

Pistil Ovule, Style and Sigmas

*Bract

Style — Ovule

Micropyle

Perianth Corolla & Calyx

Hilum

Cystolic Hairs

CYSTOLITHIC HAIR — BULBOUS — CAPITATE-SESSILE — CAPITATE-STALKED

100 MICRONS — 500 MICRONS

Cannibis Trichrome Types

TRICHOMES

Bracts

*

Bracteole

Bract

SOURCE: UrbanBotaniCanna™

In the cannabis industry, the general terms—bud, cola, nug—are easy enough and universally accepted, but when discussing specific plant parts with botanical terms, confusion reigns. Foremost are the incorrect uses of **calyx** and **pistil**. Growers read or hear about swollen calyxes being a sign of maturity and an indication of readiness for harvesting. What are incorrectly called calyxes or false calyxes are correctly identified as **bracts**.

Cannabis female flowers do have calyx cells, but not a defined calyx. The female calyx cells and corolla cells make up the perianth, a nearly transparent, delicate tissue that partially encloses the ovule (prospective seed). Each female flower has a single ovule, which is encapsulated by a bract. Bracts are small modified leaves adapted to enclose and protect the ovule (and the seed a fertilized ovule becomes) in what some growers refer to as the seed pod. Bracts have the densest covering of capitate-stalked resin glands of any plant part, and it is within the heads of these resin glands that the plant synthesizes and holds the highest concentrations of cannabinoids and terpenes of any plant part. Bracts make up most of the substance and weight of high-quality flowers (buds).

Each female flower has two stigmas that protrude from a single ovule; they are "fuzzy" (hirsute), about ¼ to ½ inch long, usually white, but sometimes yellowish, or pink to red and, rarely, lavender to purple. Stigmas are the pollen catchers. Some writers identify stigmas as pistils, and this too is incorrect. The pistil is all of the reproductive female flower parts. The pistil consists of two stigmas and an ovule (prospective seed). The term is misused in many books and seed catalogs that describe a single flower as having two pistils.

By definition, a perianth consists of a corolla and a calyx. In more familiar showy flowers, the corolla often is the brightly colored petals generally appreciated by looking at flowers, and the calyx often is the smaller green cup (sepals) holding the petals at the flower's base. Bright showy colors, large flower sizes, and enticing fragrances evolved to attract insects such as bees and flies, or animals such as birds and bats to collect and transfer pollen (unintentionally) to other flowers. Cannabis flowers are not brightly colored, large, or enticingly fragrant (at least to most nonhumans); they are wind-pollinated with no need to attract insects or animals to carry the males' pollen, and hence cannabis flowering parts never evolved into significant, attractive, or showy parts.

If a flower is pollinated, the ovule becomes a single fruit, an achene, essentially a single seed. The perianth tightly clasps the seed and usually contains tannins, which give mature seeds their markings or spotted coats. Between a thumb and finger the perianth can be rubbed off a seed. A well-pollinated typical bud develops from 50 to 150 seeds, a cola easily holds many hundreds, and even a small but thoroughly pollinated female can bear thousands of seeds.

Female flower X25 with mature seed. Here the perianth covers about 60% of the seed. Dark splotches are likely made up of corolla cells. Photo: Mel Frank

Terpenes

Revised by Ellen Holland, with additional content provided by Royal Queen Seeds

Terpenes are major components of cannabis resin, just as they make up the largest percentage of aromatic essential oils contained in most plants. The scent of most flowers, herbs, and spices are composed of these oils. When therapists use plant oils in aromatherapy, or when they are used in natural incense, perfume, or other scents to set the mood, the aromas they create are from various combinations of terpenes. They have the power to energize, relax, focus, and ease anxiety.

The presence of terpenes is apparent when buds are pinched or rubbed between the fingers to volatilize (evaporate) them and release their scent. The signature odors of cultivars like Grapefruit, Silver Haze, Blueberry, and Real Skunk brings a recognition of the type of mental and physical effects that the sample is known to produce.

Plants produce terpenes for one of three reasons:

- to attract pollinators
- to repel or kill herbivores
- to attract predators of herbivores

These odor molecules, which are costly for the plant to produce, increase as the plant's investment in reproduction increases. Before flowering, the odors are faint. As flowering progresses and the plant is more invested in protecting itself, the odor grows. As the bud ripens, whether seeded or sinsemilla (unpollinated), the odor increases substantially. Cannabis is wind-pollinated, so it doesn't need to attract pollinators, and outdoors it is resistant to insect predation, as the odors are a signal to experienced mammals to stay away. This indicates that the odors deter animals that would eat the plant, including larger grazers. In other plants terpenes and essential oils are insect repellents, such as those derived from citronella, clove, and wintergreen, which makes them the base for many natural pest removal garden sprays.

By temporarily altering brain function, terpenes affect mood, sensitivity, and perceptions, including balance and pain.

Chemically speaking, terpenes are composed of repeating units of isoprene, which is a 5-carbon unit chain or ring with eight hydrogen atoms attached (C_5H_8). Terpenes use the simple isoprene units as blocks to build molecules with 10, 15, 20, 30, and 40 carbon units; they also twist and turn the molecular structure to form simple chains or three-dimensional (polycyclic) structures. Most significant for the cannabis plant, terpene pathways are key enzymatic steps in the plant's production of THC. In addition, terpenes can form bonds with other molecules, which affects how animals and plants react to them. Depending on how terpenes stack against each other, they create different aromas.

Most of the aromas associated with plants are the result of terpenes and flavonoids, a group of natural substances found in many other plants including fruits, vegetables, tea, and wine that add to the color and flavor of the plant. Both flavonoids and terpenes are **hydro-carbons**, with either long carbon chains or carbon rings. Flavonoids are similar to terpenes and also play a role in the flavor and medicinal properties of cultivars by contributing anti-oxidative and anti-inflammatory properties. The health effects associated with cannabis are due to the synergistic effects of its components working together, a phenomenon known as the entourage effect.

Humans can smell and taste these compounds, but that is not the only way they are affected by them. Aromatherapy uses the inhalation of essential oils to regulate mood, sleep patterns, acuity, and healing processes. For example, lavender oil (rich in linalool) is a soothing agent and smooth muscle relaxant; rosemary is used to focus attention and provide a sense of satisfaction. These effects are a result of the combination of terpenes and other chemicals found in the oils of these plants.

While terpenes affect the brain in their own way, they also modify the effect of THC within the brain, adding subtleties to the high. Some terpenes may affect the high because they lock into receptor sites in the brain and modify its chemical output. A few, such as thujone, one of the main terpenes in wormwood (which is used to make absinthe), bind weakly to the CB1 receptor. Others alter the permeability of cell membranes or the blood brain barrier, allowing in either more or less THC. Others affect serotonin and dopamine chemistry by shutting off their production, affecting their movement, binding to their receptor sites, or slowing their natural destruction. **Dopamine** and serotonin, two of the main regulators of mood and attitude, are affected by some terpenes, as well as THC.

> Myrcene has been rumored to increase the permeability of the blood-brain barrier to the cannabinoids; however, hard evidence for this claim is yet to be found. The terpene borneol, on the other hand, has been shown to increase the rate of cannabinoid delivery across the blood-brain barrier by increasing its permeability.

By temporarily altering brain function, terpenes can affect mood, sensitivity, and perceptions, including balance and pain. When terpenes are mixed, as they are in natural plant oils, they each play a role in affecting brain function. Some combinations may work synergistically and others antagonistically, but each "recipe" of terpenes affects moods and feelings in its own way.

Over 100 terpenes have been identified in cannabis, but there likely are more that have yet to be identified, especially considering the multiple variations of each terpene. For instance, the characteristic citrus odor found in orange and lemon rinds differs by type and even variety. Their terpenes, called limonenes, are mirror versions of each other. This is due to slight differences in the amounts of limonene, as well as other compounds that contribute to the variation in citrus scent profiles.

Now companies are creating cannabis extracts that use terpenes derived from cannabis as well as other botanical sources such as lavender and clove. These lab-created products can then be reverse engineered to recreate the chemical makeup of cultivars. While using terpenes extracted from something like mint instead of cannabis or hemp is more cost effective for the producer, the potential negative health effects of vaporizing botanical terpenes at high temperatures are still unknown.

Creating the flavoring for cannabis vape pens also includes the use of terpenes that originated in a lab, which are widely used in cologne and perfume. The safety of vaporizing lab-originated terpenes remains undetermined; however, they are chemically identical to terpenes produced in cannabis or other terpene-producing plants. These lab-created terpenes typically have more intense smells and flavors, which makes their effects additionally complex, since odor impressions may change based on terpene concentration.

About 10–30% of cannabis smoke resin is composed of assorted terpenes. Some terpenes appear only occasionally in cannabis, while others are found all the time. The percentage of particular terpenes and the ratios in which they are found vary by plant variety and are driven by the plant's genetics.

Hops and both groups of cannabis contain similar complements of terpenes. The oil of common black pepper (*Piper nigrum*) also has a group of terpenes similar to cannabis (β-caryophyllene being the primary terpene). Terpenes are produced in the trichomes, the same glands where THC is produced.

> The term "essential oil" is not in reference to the oil being essential to humans' health; rather, the term is derived from their extractions from their respective plants being the "essence" of the plant itself. For example, lavender oil is the "essence" of the lavender plant.

Age, maturation, and the time of day can affect the amount, and perhaps ratios, of terpenes. One reason is their high volatilization rates at temperatures as low as 75°F (24°C). As plants mature, their odor gets more intense and sometimes changes as they ripen. Plants are constantly producing terpenes, but they volatize when exposed to sunlight and warm temperature. That means plants have more terpenes at the end of the dark period than after a full day of light. This can be easily tested by a home grower by checking a plant's odor early in the morning and at the end of a sunny day. There will be more pungency earlier in the morning.

Climate and weather also affect terpene and flavonoid production. The same variety of cannabis can produce different quantities and perhaps even different types of oils, depending on the type of soil in which it is grown in or the fertilizers used. The terpenes described below are those generally most abundant in cannabis, though individual plants may differ widely both in total percentages of terpenes and in their ratios.

FLUCTUATION IN TERPENE VOLATILITY

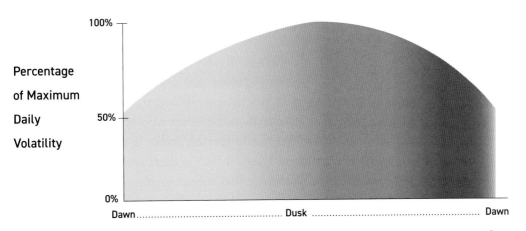

Percentage of Maximum Daily Volatility

Dawn .... Dusk .... Dawn

This chart represents fluctuation in terpene volatility over a 24-hour period. As the sun rises and/ or temperatures increase, the volatility of terpenes will also increase. Terpene retention is prioritized during harvest, which is why harvests should occur at dawn, when the terpene volatility is at its lowest.

Hops

Mango

β-Myrcene is the most prevalent terpene found in most varieties of cannabis, but little is found in hemp. It is also present in high amounts in hops, lemongrass, West Indian bay tree (used to make bay rum), verbena, and the plant from which it derives its name, *Myrcia*. Myrcene is often referred to as one of the most "earthy" smelling terpenes, with musky notes somewhat similar to cloves. Additionally, it has a slight odor of red grape and balsamic and a hint of mixed spice. Myrcene also appears in small amounts in the essential oils of many other plants and can be found abundantly in mangoes. Its odor is variously described as clove-like, earthy, nutty, green-vegetative, and citrus. The various odors are the result of slight differences in the essential oil's chemical makeup. All of these odors are commonly used to describe cannabis.

Myrcene is a potent analgesic, anti-inflammatory, and antibiotic. It blocks the actions of cytochrome, aflatoxin B, and other pro-mutagens that are implicated in carcinogenesis. It is also present in small amounts in many essential oils associated with antidepressant and uplifting effects.

Myrcene is a monoterpene that is an essential precursor to forming other secondary terpenes. The compound has been known to compose up to 50% of the total terpene content found in individual cultivars. Cultivars containing more than 0.5% myrcene are most likely to induce sedative effects classically attributed to indicas.

Lemon

Orange

Grapefruit

Limonene is found in citrus peels, mint, juniper, rosemary, pine, and cannabis. It is used in food, drugs, cosmetics, and biotechnology. Limonene is often the second, third, or fourth most prevalent terpene in cannabis resins. Citrus peel resins are a familiar source of limonene: the oil explodes into the air when a fruit is peeled. The exact odor is determined by the structure of the terpenes. Plants use limonene to repulse predators. For instance, flies have a group of receptors wired directly to the fly brain that are similar in function to the taste buds on human tongues. One of them detects noxious chemicals and responds to limonene as a toxin.

Limonene is one of the most commonly used terpenes. It appears as an ingredient in food, drugs, cosmetics, detergents, and cleansers, and it also finds applications in the biotechnology industry. After myrcene, limonene is the most abundant terpene in most cannabis cultivars.

Limonene has very low toxicity, and humans rarely encounter adverse effects from it. However, just like many terpenes and solvents, limonene may irritate skin and the respiratory system, causing symptoms such as watery eyes and vasodilation.

Limonene has antibacterial, antifungal, and anticancer effects. It inhibits the RAS cancer gene cascade, which promotes tumor growth. Since limonene is such a potent antifungal and anticancer agent, it is thought to protect against the *Aspergillus* fungi and carcinogens sometimes found in cannabis smoke streams.

Limonene synergistically promotes the absorption of other terpenes by penetrating cell membranes. In humans, limonene's design facilitates a direct response by quickly permeating the blood-brain barrier. The result is increased systolic blood pressure. In tests, participants reported an increase in alertness and restlessness. Various limonene analogs can cue the brain to sexuality, buoyancy, or focused attention. Limonene sprays are used to treat depression. This terpene interacts positively with cannabinoids THCa, CBDa, CBCa, CBC, and CBG, and with other terpenes such as caryophyllene and linalool. Further, the increased cell permeability caused by limonene facilitates the assimilation of other substances by the human body.

Limonene assists in modulating the body's immune system, resulting in an anticancer effect. It plays a role in healing damaged skin and regenerating cellular tissues. Limonene has potent anti-inflammatory properties, making this terpene a promising option in the treatment of certain forms of cancer.

β-Caryophyllene is a major terpene found abundantly in black pepper (15–25%), clove (10–20%), and cotton (15–25%). It is found in smaller percentages in several other herbs and spices. It has a sweet, woody, dry-clove odor and tastes pepper-spicy with camphor and astringent citrus backgrounds. It contributes to black pepper's spiciness and is used industrially to enhance tobacco flavor.

Black pepper

β-Caryophyllene, ingested in large amounts, blocks calcium and potassium ion channels. As a result, it impedes the pressure exerted by heart muscles. Applied topically, it is an analgesic and one of the active constituents of clove oil, a preferred treatment for toothache. It docks on the CB2 receptor site, the same site for which CBD has an affinity. Thus, it may help reduce inflammation. It may also contribute to giddy, goofy, and good feelings induced by cannabis use.

Cloves

Caryophyllene has also been found to play the role of a cannabinoid by targeting the CB2 receptor. Cannabinoids that target the CB2 receptor can potentially help treat disorders such as arthritis and multiple sclerosis, without the inconvenience of psychotropic effects. The CB2 receptor is involved in the regulation of emotional behavior and could be a potential therapeutic target when it comes to anxiety and depression. Caryophyllene may reduce inflammatory pain responses and also reduce spinal neuroinflammation.

Cotton

α- and β-Pinene provide the familiar odor associated with pine trees and their resins. α-Pinene is responsible for the distinct scents in pine needles and the herb rosemary, whereas β-pinene is the molecule responsible for the unmistakable smells of basil and dill. Pinene is likely to give the true skunk varieties, ones that stink like the animal, much of their odor.

Pine

Pinenes are the primary component in turpentine and are found in noticeable amounts in many other plant essential oils including rosemary, sage, and eucalyptus.

Pinene is one of the most researched terpenes. It is effective at protecting the lungs against certain types of viral infection. Pinene is used medically as an expectorant and topical antiseptic. It crosses the blood-brain barrier easily, where it

Rosemary

Basil

Dill

Sage

Wormwood

Thyme

acts as an acetylcholinesterase inhibitor, that is, it inhibits activity of a chemical that destroys an information-transfer molecule, resulting in better memory. Largely due to the presence of pinene, rosemary and sage are both considered "memory plants." Concoctions made from their leaves have been used for thousands of years in traditional medicine to retain and restore memory.

It is an anti-inflammatory as well as a bronchodilator, so each breath results in increased oxygen absorption. The invigorating experience of taking a deep breath while hiking through a pine forest may be a function of pinene's bronchodilator function.

It increases focus, self-satisfaction, and energy, and is known to increase alertness and to ease the potential short-term memory loss associated with consuming high amounts of THC. It can also help to combat negative sensations, such as paranoia.

Borneol smells much like the menthol aroma of camphor and is easily converted into it. It is found in small quantities in many essential oils. Commercially, it is derived from *Artemisia* plants such as wormwood and some species of cinnamon.

Borneol is one of several terpenes that insects and parasites hate. Humans, on the other hand, are usually quite attracted to these unique scents. The camphor-like overtones of many of the Haze cultivars are unmistakable. The high of these varieties has a calming effect, in addition to its psychedelic aspects, which is indicative of the relatively high concentrations of borneol present in these varieties. It is considered a "calming sedative" in Chinese medicine. Borneol is used to relieve certain kinds of pain, facilitate digestion, improve blood circulation, and even to help treat respiratory diseases. Its refreshing action is used for fever reduction and other cooling purposes. In Asia, this substance is also used as a preventative treatment for cardiovascular diseases.

Borneol naturally occurs in ginger, rosemary, sage, camphor, marjoram, thyme, mugwort, and other plants. Its oxidation generates the substance commonly known as camphor, which can itself be extracted from plants like camphor laurel and used as a source of borneol.

Borneol has anti-inflammatory, antioxidant, anticoagulant, and anesthetic properties. Research is beginning to reveal neuroprotective and antioxidant properties as well (Hur, Pak, Koo, and Jeon 2012).

Small amounts of borneol naturally contained in cannabis and other herbs are completely safe, while pure borneol can irritate the eyes, skin, and respiratory tract. Pure borneol is also harmful if swallowed.

Borneol increases the bioavailability of other active compounds and improves the transportation of substances toward brain cells.

Δ³-Carene has a sweet and hearty smell with notes of lemon, musk, and pine. It can be found in basil, pepper, cedar, pine, rosemary, and turpentine. This bicyclic monoterpene can be effectively extracted from several plants, and it's a component of many essential oils used in aromatherapy. It's also used in cosmetics, as a food flavoring, and as an insect repellent.

This terpene has some valuable properties still under investigation. Among its potential benefits for the body and brain are anti-inflammatory and antifungal effects. One of the most interesting therapeutic characteristics of carene is its role in supporting bone healing. Together with its anti-inflammatory action, carene speeds up bone repair and growth, especially in cases of malnutrition or injury.

Like other terpenes, carene is nontoxic, but it may cause irritation when inhaled. The cannabis flower often develops carene among its protective chemical compounds, though it is not one of the most abundant terpenes. Carene may contribute to the dry eye and dry mouth experienced by cannabis users. In aromatherapy, cypress oil, which is high in Δ³-carene, is used to dry excess fluids, tears, runny noses, excess menstrual flow, and perspiration.

Juniper essential oil is mainly composed of pinene and carene. Both are known to have powerful antifungal abilities and have been tested as treatments for candida, aspergillus, and dermatophytes fungi causing infections of the skin, hair, and nails.

Linalool has a floral scent reminiscent of spring flowers such as lily of the valley, but with spicy overtones. It is refined from lavender, neroli, and other plants. Humans can detect its odor in the air at rates as low as one part per billion.

Linalool acts on the human body in a number of beneficial ways. It has been used as a natural soporific, anti-inflammatory, anxiolytic, and topical skin application for millennia.

Lily of the Valley

Lavender

Catnip

Peppermint

Ginger

Ginseng

Insomniacs of the Renaissance and continuing to the present keep parcels of lavender under their pillows. It is still used to treat scars today.

Linalool is being tested for treating several types of cancers. It is a powerful anti-inflammatory and analgesic. It is also a component of several sedating essential oils, which makes sense, since it is shown to be a smooth muscle relaxer. In tests on humans who inhaled it, it caused severe sedation. In tests on rats, it reduced their activity by almost 75%.

Pulegone has a minty-camphor odor and flavor that is used in the candy industry. It is found in catnip, peppermint, and pennyroyal, among other plants. It is implicated in liver damage when used in very high dosages. It is found in tiny quantities in cannabis. Pulegone is an acetylcholinesterase inhibitor, that is, pulegone interferes with the action of the protein that destroys acetylcholine, the chemical the brain uses to store memory. Pulegone may counteract THC's effect of lowering acetylcholine levels, which may result in forgetting less if THC is accompanied with pulegone.

Humulene is also found in hops, basil, coriander, cloves, ginseng, and ginger. It has a woodsy, earthy flavor with spicy undertones. Humulene gets its name from the genus name for hops, which is *Humulus*. Hops is also found in a recognizable plant family: Cannabaceae. A very hoppy beer such as a Double IPA sometimes smells of cannabis because of humulene and other such terpenes.

Humulene is always part of the cannabis terpene profile. Therefore, this prolific oil plays a part in all the modified genotypes of different cultivars.

While this terpene may be known best for the aroma and flavors it provides to beer through hops, it's used for its anti-inflammatory properties and analgesic effects that block pain and relieve fear and stress.

Humulene is an isomer of β-caryophyllene, meaning that they have the same chemical formulation, but their bonds are arranged differently. In this way, both terpenes are known for the potential to suppress cancer tumors.

Humulene is an antibacterial agent and has anticancer and anti-inflammatory properties. It is frequently invoked as an appetite suppressant. This may lead to its more widespread use in the future.

Humulene is released when hops are steeped and can be used as an effective sedative. In the same vein, pepper and ginseng both contain humulene and are used as natural antibiotics.

Terpinolene is characterized as having herbaceous piney scents and tastes combined with hints of citrus and floral notes. It's found in other plants and herbs such as cardamom, conifers, cumin, lilac, marjoram, nutmeg, rosemary, sage, and tea tree. Also known as Δ-terpinene, terpinolene's woody aroma is often accompanied by citrusy and floral tones, which vary by isomer. Terpinolene's strong scent is used in fragrances for household products to provide pine and lemon fragrances in cleaners.

Termites excrete terpinolene as an alarm pheromone to signal a threat to the colony. Terpinolene is antibacterial and antifungal and has a sedative effect, so it can be used to reduce insomnia. Terpinolene is often found in sativa-dominant cultivars and is one of the primary components of the terpene profiles found in Jack Herer cultivars.

Terpineol has a pleasant odor that varies between apple blossom, citrus, lilac, and lime and is used in perfumes and soaps for fragrance.

Terpineol is a minor constituent of many plant essential oils and is derived commercially by processing other terpenes. It may account for the couch-lock effects of some cannabis, although terpineol's odor is not usually associated with body highs. That may be explained by the fact that terpineol is often found in cannabis with high pinene levels, as mentioned above. Its odor is masked by the pungent woodsy aromas of pinene. It is one of the terpenes that induces sleepiness but goes undetected, hidden by stronger odors.

Nerolidol is a sesquiterpene, which means it is less volatile and more aromatic than monoterpenes and other evaporative substances. Several plants contain nerolidol in their essential oils, including citrus peel, ginger, jasmine, lavender, lemongrass, tea tree, and many other plants. It has a floral woodsy odor with a hint of citrus. Plants produce it in response to insect attacks.

Nerolidol is used in many industrial products including candies, cleansers, cosmetics, and perfumes. It has antifungal, antibacterial, anxiolytic, and antioxidant properties. It is effec-

Tea tree

Marjoram

Cardamom

Jasmine

Lemongrass

tive against parasites, spider mites, head lice, and other pests. It is also known for potent antimalarial properties.

Humans can safely ingest and inhale nerolidol. It has been traditionally used for its relaxing, sedative, and sleep-assisting effect. It's also commonly used as a food-flavoring agent. Cultivars containing substantial amounts of it are antidepressant, ease social interactions, and seem to promote positive attitudes.

Nerolidol is nontoxic and enhances skin penetration of cannabis topicals. Formulators of balms, creams, and lotions might consider it for improving absorption of topicals when choosing ingredients.

Chamomile

α-Bisabolol is produced in moderate amounts only in chamomile flowers and a few other plants, such as the Candeia tree (*Vanillosmopsis erythropappa*), *Myoporum crassifolium*, and some cannabis cultivars.

It is a sedative and an antidepressant that works well for stress reduction.

Bisabolol is a monocyclic sesquiterpene alcohol. It has a warm floral aroma similar to honey, apples, and chamomile. Bisabolol has anti-inflammatory, anti-irritant, antioxidant, antimicrobial, antifungal, and analgesic properties. As with some other terpenes, it penetrates the skin easily and enhances the absorption of other molecules.

Bisabolol stimulates gastrointestinal tract receptors, so it has a calming effect on the stomach. It bonds with specific chemical messengers, including inflammatory proteins, reducing the production of inflammatory cytokines. Bisabolol has also shown to be effective against leishmaniasis, an infection caused by parasites (Corpas-López, Morillas-Márquez, et. al. 2015).

Parsley

Ocimene is a tropical terpene that has a sweet, fruity, woody odor that evokes flavors of citrus, guavas, mangos, papayas, and pine. It's found in fragrant herbs such as mint, parsley, and basil. It plays a key role in the social regulation of honeybee colonies, leading researchers to look into the idea of drug-sniffing bees.

Ocimene is believed to have a variety of medicinal benefits. It has anti-inflammatory and antifungal properties.

Eucalyptus

Mugwort

Eucalyptol/Cineole is the main ingredient in eucalyptus oil. It has a camphor-minty odor similar to pulegone. It is also found in other fragrant plants and in minor amounts in cannabis. It's responsible for the pleasurable and cooling scents found in eucalyptus, mint, rosemary, tea tree, mugwort, bay leaves, sweet basil, sage, and some varieties of cannabis.

Eucalyptus oil is considered centering, balancing, and stimulating. It's probably the stimulating and thought-provoking part of the cannabis smoke stream. It's used to increase circulation and pain relief, among other topical uses. Eucalyptol/cineole easily crosses the blood-brain barrier and triggers a fast olfactory reaction.

Eucalyptol/cineole is found in many mouthwashes and cough syrups. It helps to control the secretion of mucus, making it a good terpene to encourage optimal breathing. Like the name implies, it's also found in eucalyptus and contains minty, cool tones. This terpene is also known as cineol and is showing promise in treating memory loss associated with Alzheimer's disease.

Eucalyptol/Cineole has been studied intensely and has been shown to have numerous potential applications within the domain of medicine. Eucalyptol/cineole may contribute to improved cognition and have a positive effect on Alzheimer's due to its potential to enhance memory and learning. Cineole may also alleviate another element of Alzheimer's. It has been reported to decrease the inflammation caused by amyloid beta plaques. Additionally, it is antifungal, antibacterial, antioxidant, and has anticancer properties (Murata, Shiragami, Kosugi et. al. 2013).

Terpene Interaction

The way terpenes interact with one another and their resulting effect on brain activity provide fascinating territory for another level of exploration and creativity for seed breeders. By learning the odors of the terpenes, breeders can predict the mind-altering properties that each lends to a bud.

Photo: Jesse Robertson / Sticky Fields

INDICA, SATIVA, RUDERALIS & HYBRIDS

Most cannabis grown in the United States is derived from the hybridization of three distinct groups of cultivars: sativa, indica, and ruderalis. These groups were geographically separated and evolved along different paths to best survive in different environments.

The Etymology of Sativa, Indica, and Ruderalis

The term "sativa" refers to a plant that is widely cultivated as a domestic crop. It often is correlated with a plant that promotes good health as well. "Indica" came about when the famous French naturalist Jean-Baptiste Lamarck categorized a "new species" of cannabis in 1785. He named it *Cannabis indica* because the plant specimens were collected from India. Finally, "ruderalis" also gets its name from where it was found in nature. A ruderal plant is one that colonizes recently disturbed land. *C. ruderalis* was first identified along the Volga River in southern Siberia in 1924. It was growing along the rubble from the riverbed, hence the recently disturbed land.

Plant varieties originating in lower latitudes have less variation within their population. The reason is that the weather patterns, temperature, and rainfall in equatorial areas tend to vary less year to year. An equatorial population can home in on a more specific type of environment. As a result, the plants that thrive in a geographic location with little varying environmental factors will lead to a homogeneous genetic profile in the population.

All of these are sativas. They tend to grow tall so they can maintain their positions capturing light at the top of the canopy. They have long branches with thin leaves, since the light is so intense that the leaves don't have to grow wide to capture it. They have fewer chloroplasts because they don't need as many, when the light keeps the ones they have working at full speed. For this reason, equatorial leaves look paler than temperate plants' leaves. Since these plants are growing in areas where there isn't a threat of a freeze, they can take their time flowering and maturing. The landrace cannabis cultivars from equatorial regions show more homogeneous growing patterns as a result of evolving in more consistent environmental conditions.

What Is a Landrace?

Cannabis originated in Central Asia (the Tibetan Plateau), so any cannabis "native" to anywhere else on the planet was actually brought there through human migration. A variety that has been domesticated in a particular region and has been isolated from new genetics for many generations is called a landrace. Landrace varieties are the result of human input and natural conditions. A landrace variety, like Acapulco Gold, was introduced to Mexico by humans; however, it started growing ferally around what is now Acapulco. Its time as a feral plant allowed it to continue its evolution and then humans started selecting. The interplay of natural conditions and human guidance led to the landrace.

Landrace varieties have more "ancestral" genetics than most of the modern cannabis cultivars, which provides for breeding opportunities to reintroduce cannabinoid content from some of the lesser-known cannabinoids. For example, Durban Poison is a landrace from South Africa that has a particularly high concentration of tetrahydrocannabivarin (THCV). Breeding with Durban Poison has the potential of introducing genetics for higher THCV concentrations in modern varieties.

Terminology of Genetic Populations

Feral

Feral refers to a population of plants that were domesticated but that have returned to the wild and are living independently of humans. Examples are the hemp patches in the northern Midwestern United States. These populations escaped from cultivation and naturalized.

Landrace

Landraces are domesticated, locally adapted, traditional varieties of a plant that has developed over time, through adaptation to its natural and cultural environment of agriculture and pastoralism, and due to isolation from other populations of the species.

Naturalized

To "naturalize" means to adapt, grow, and spread as if the plant were a native. For example dandelions, native to Europe but not native to North America, have become established in many parts of the continent independent of human efforts.

Wild

Wild refers to a plant population that grows spontaneously (without human introduction) in self-maintaining populations in natural or semi-natural ecosystems and exists independent of direct human action. Examples are plants growing in a pristine uncultivated environment.

In temperate climates there is wider variability in weather—one year may be cold and rainy, the next hot and dry. In order to cope with this variability, temperate region cannabis populations evolved a more heterogeneous gene pool, so plants with one set of genes do better one season and another set does better under different conditions. That way, both the population and the genes are preserved. The landraces that have a more genetic variability evolved around the 35th parallel north. These include Southern Africans, Northern Mexicans, Moroccans, Lebanese, Nepalese, and Hindu Kush.

Plants within these groups look slightly different from each other and have different maturities, cannabinoid profiles, and potency. The variation in climate in midlatitude temperate zones explains their heterogeneity, the same as the higher latitudes' variation in climate affects the heterogeneity of cannabis found there.

Midlatitude varieties exhibit a wider selection of adaptations to cope with the variety of climatic challenges they face. This prepares them for unique weather conditions that may occur in an abnormal growing season.

Most cultivated varieties grown for commercial purposes are derived from hybrids of these types of cannabis. Starting in the 1970s, breeders crossed different varieties from the midlatitudes to combine the best characteristics from those populations to create some of the first domestic cannabis varieties, including Afghani-Kush, Big Bud, Haze, Hash Plant, Northern Lights, Skunk #1, and William's Wonder. These first domesticated varieties were derived from Afghani, Indian, Colombian, Mexican, Thai, and Vietnamese cannabis. A second generation of breeders included landraces from Brazil, South Africa, and Burma.

Within a few years, breeders started working with these domesticated varieties to hone the hybrids and find novel cannabis with desired characteristics, such as more sophisticated and complex highs, fast maturity, uniform flower development, bigger buds, larger yields, higher cannabinoid potency, pest resistance, more compact growing style, and so forth. Most of the varieties offered today are many hybridizations away from the original landraces from which they started. They have been totally domesticated to modern standards and tastes.

100% Indica Shiskaberry by Barney's Farm

Indica

As noted above, indica plants developed in central Asia between the 25th and 35th parallels north, where the weather is variable. Cannabis evolved in this region to reflect the variable weather patterns by developing a variety of different populations to cope. Thus, in any season, no matter what the weather, some plants will do better than others.

Indicas, including Kush varieties, tend to have broad general characteristics: they mature early, have compact short branches and wide, short leaves that capture much more light than thin leaves, which are dark green, an indication of the high number of chloroplasts in the leaves needed to most efficiently capture light energy. Their buds are usually tight, heavy, wide, and thick, rather than long. They smell "stinky," "skunky," or "pungent," and their smoke is thick—a small toke can induce coughing.

Indica plants were bred to develop varieties of cannabis for resin content, which was removed from the flowers to make hashish. It was only after these varieties found their way to the Americas were their buds widely consumed. The market for hashish to this day is still more popular in Europe, North Africa, and Central Asia. The best indicas have a relaxing "social high" and full-body calming effect, which allows the user to sense and feel the environment without analyzing the experience.

Kush varieties are indicas that were developed in the Hindu Kush valley, which stretches through northern Afghanistan, Pakistan, and India. They are a variant of indicas and have many of the same characteristics. Kush varieties tend to develop extra-wide leaf blades; however, the difference between Kush varieties and other indicas is one of nuance, rather than distinct difference.

Plant Characteristics: Indicas vs. Sativas vs. Ruderalis

	Indica	Sativa	Ruderalis
Height	2 to 6 feet (60 to 180 cm)	5 to 25 feet (1.5 to 7.5 m)	1 to 2 feet (30 to 60 cm)
Shape	Conical to bushy	Tall, Christmas-tree shape	Short, upright
Branching	Lots of side branching, usually wider than tall	Moderate branching, wide at base, single stem at top	Little to no branching with thin fibrous branches
Nodes	Short stem length between leaves	Long stem length between leaves	Short stem length between leaves
Leaves	Wide short leaves, short wide blades	Long leaves, thin long blades	Large, wide leaves with fewer blades
Color	Dark green to purple	Pale to medium green	Medium green
Flowers	Wide, dense, bulky	Long sausage-shaped flowers	Wide, dense, bulky
Odor	Pungent, fruity	Sweet to spicy	Pungent, earthy
High	Inertia, desensitizing	Psychedelic	Calming (low THC with high CBD content)
Flowering	6 to 9 weeks	8 to 15 weeks	5 to 7 weeks

Even in traditional cannabis-growing countries, the varieties found there are often the result of several crossed lines. For example, Jamaican ganja is probably the result of crosses between hemp, which the English cultivated for rope, and Indian ganja, which arrived with the Indian immigrants who came to the country.

The term for cannabis in Jamaica is "ganja," the same as in India. The traditional Jamaican term for the best weed is Kali, which is the name of the Hindu goddess of destruction. However, tourists in Jamaica today are likely to be solicited with terms such as "kush" or "purple"; it is very difficult to find the original landraces there.

100% Sativa Dr. Grinspoon by Barney's Farm

Sativa

Sativas are found throughout much of the world, but are most famous for the varieties found in the tropics/subtropics. Potent varieties such as Colombian, Panamanian, Mexican, Nigerian, Congolese, Indian, and Thai are found in equatorial and subequatorial zones. These plants usually require a long time to mature, due to their having been naturalized and evolved in climates with longer, more consistent growing seasons. They are famous for their THC potency and resulting high. The highs they produce are described in such terms as psychedelic, dreamy, spacey, energizing, and creative. The buds usually smell sweet, fruity, or tangy, and the smoke is smooth, sometimes deceptively so.

An Exception to the Rule

Although a sweet, tangy, and/or fruity aroma and flavor profile is usually associated with the sativas, there's always an exception to the rule. The cannabis variety "Mango" is classified as an indica. This variety gets its name from its aroma and sweet taste of mangoes.

Sativa plants grow in a conical, Christmas-tree form. The leaves have long, narrow serrated blades, wide spacing between branches, and vigorous growth. They often grow very tall outdoors and are difficult to control indoors. Sativas tend to grow more vertically, while indicas exhibit more horizontal growth.

Sativas have long, medium-thick buds when grown in high-light conditions found under full equatorial sun. Under lower light conditions, in temperate climates with lower light intensity and shorter days, or with indoor grows under inadequate artificial lighting, sativa stems are prone to elongating at a faster rate than indicas. This stem elongation causes "larfy" (wispy, fluffy, or airy) buds to form along the stems. The buds run, or are thinner and longer and don't fill out completely, since the plant has stretched between the bud sites. In areas with short growing seasons, the sativa buds may not fully mature before first frost.

Ruderalis

Ruderalis is a wild or feral variety of autoflowering cannabis native to the Caucasus mountains in Russia. Unlike indicas and sativas, ruderalis is not a photoperiodic plant. A few weeks after the seeds germinate, the plants begin to produce flowers while continuing to

Ruderalis Skywalker OG Auto by Barney's Farm

grow. They tend to be short, between one and three feet (30–90 cm), and varieties differ in flowering growth. Unfortunately, ruderalis is a less resinous plant than either indica or sativa, producing significantly less cannabinoid and terpene content.

Nevil Schoenmaker's The Seed Bank, which later merged into Sensi Seeds, tried using a Romanian variety that grew flowers along its new growth in an indeterminate pattern. In the early summer, the flowers were apparent, but they didn't develop into colas with significant density. In the fall, the plants continued to grow and formed small buds, but the flowers didn't produce heavy glandular development as they matured. Some varieties that are available commercially are more determinate. They produce flowers as the plants grow larger, and when a critical time period occurs, they quickly stop growing vegetatively and form a denser, more desirable bud.

Ruderalis is primarily seen as a way to introduce automatic flowering and genetics that lead to a more compact plant into indica and sativa varieties. Since ruderalis in nature is not as resinous and does not heavily produce flowers, most breeders do not see ruderalis as a valid source of genetics for crop yields or cannabinoid potency. However, developing a new variety with all the floral characteristics of a potent sativa that is shorter and matures sooner is highly desirable. Most cannabis varieties with ruderalis genetics in them are autoflowering versions of their sativa or indica cousins.

Hybrids

If indica and sativa varieties are considered opposite ends of a spectrum, most cannabis plants today fall somewhere in the middle. Because of cannabis's long symbiotic relationship with humans, whether for potent flowers or strong fibers, seeds have constantly been procured or traded across borders so that virtually all existing plant populations have been hybridized with foreign varieties at one time or another. Since the 1980s, seeds from the Dutch and other seed companies have been introduced in traditional cannabis-growing areas all over the world including Colombia, Mexico, Jamaica, and Thailand. For the most part, the only true landraces existing today are in the hands of collectors.

50% Sativa 50% Indica Hybrid Ed Rosenthal Super Bud by Sensi Seeds

After 50 years of dedicated prohibition breeding, the cannabis plant has been substantially changed. Breeders began with landraces and then widened the selection. Now thousands of varieties are available from countries all over the world. Hybrids, hybrids of hybrids, stabilized crosses, and remarkable "cuttings-only" varieties propagated only by cloning are all widely available (*See Appendix A: Cloning*).

Hybrid varieties are, simply put, hybridized versions of their indica and sativa ancestors. Indicas and sativas by themselves are described in their unique growing patterns and the types of high they induce. Hybrids tend to be defined more by their associated types of high. For example, the popular variety Blue Dream is a sativa-dominant hybrid. Blue Dream does not necessarily grow the way archetypal sativas do; however, it does induce the typical full-body calming effects from its Blueberry indica heritage in tandem with a more robust, invigorating cerebral effect from its Haze ancestry. Thus, Blue Dream is a sativa-leaning/dominant hybrid variety.

What About Hemp?

The biggest difference between "hemp" and "cannabis" is the name, although that is a gross oversimplification. The word is adapted from the proto-Germanic word "hanapiz," which was likely derived from the Greek word "kánnabis." The Old English version of "hanapiz" evolved into "henep," which later became "hemp."

Fiber hemp field, Heilongjiang, China, June 2019. Photo: Chris Conrad, TheLeafOnline.com

Hemp is a group of varieties of cannabis that were selected for their fibers and nutritious seeds rather than their medicinal flowers. Hemp fibers have been farmed in China for at least 6,000 years. The *Ch'i Min Yao Shu* is an agricultural encyclopedia written by Jia Sixie in the 6th century CE. The title translates to "Essential Ways for Living of the Common People." Jia Sixie was an agronomist and wrote this book to describe important crops in China. Hemp is the only plant mentioned for its fiber quality in the book.

Hemp cultivation in Europe may have started as early as 3,500 years ago and, once again, was primarily used for its fiber content. Researchers see ample evidence of its cultivation in places like Turkey, around 700 BCE. Hemp fabric was found in a Phrygian Kingdom gravesite, near modern-day Ankara.

Ancient breeders selected for cannabis plants with longer stalks to get longer fibers. Eventually those cannabis plants' morphologies became what is seen in hemp plants today: long, singular stalks.

Hemp seed consumption is also an important part of hemp's history with humans. Hemp plants provided nutrition to Paleolithic humans but was cultivated for food in China through the Han Dynasty. Hemp seeds are an easily digestible source of omega-3 and omega-6 fatty acids and essential proteins. The seeds can be pressed to create hemp oil, or they can be eaten raw straight from the plant. In some areas of present-day China, farmers will make a porridge of milled hemp seeds. Pressed hemp seeds were more than just a food source; the oil was also used as a fuel source for burning in lamps during ancient times.

There are many uses for hemp fibers and oils, which continue to expand in modern times. Just like indica, sativa, and all the hybridized cannabis varieties were and continue to be bred; however, they were bred for their effects more than anything else. Hemp varieties were and continue to be bred for their fiber and food properties. Modern hemp and cannabis varieties all started from ancient cannabis plants that early humans came across growing in the wild. Those prehistoric humans cultivated and bred the plants to reflect traits that people desired. Modern-day hemp is being used for raw materials such as fiber and food, but new end uses are being developed all the time.

Cannabis has a tremendous number of possible uses. From feeding the stomach to feeding the mind to feeding livestock to creating eco-friendly building materials and plastics that don't last in nature indefinitely, the future of cannabis is robust; however, that future was greatly influenced by cannabis' past interactions with humans as they migrated across the globe with hemp seeds in tow.

Above: hemp house constructed by Hempitecture.
Photo: Courtesy of Hempitecture
Inset: close-up of hempcrete brick by Hempitecture.
Photo: Sofia DeWolfe

AUTOFLOWERING VARIETIES

by Jeff Lowenfels

Cannabis ruderalis refers to autoflowering varieties of cannabis plants. While most cannabis varieties are triggered to flower by photoperiod (the ratio of light to uninterrupted darkness), ruderalis plants flower soon after germination and ripen according to their chronological age. They continue to grow vegetatively as they flower, devoting more energy to it as they near maturity.

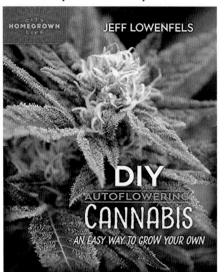

DIY Auto-flowering Cannabis by Jeff Lowenfels covers the history and benefits of autoflowering cannabis, the origins, chemistry, and growing habits, and includes step-by-step growing methods, tips, tricks, supplies, seed sourcing, and how to harvest, process, and breed new plants.

The advantage of these plants is that they grow very fast, going from germination to harvest in 60–90 days as opposed to 150 days or more for most other varieties. Because they flower regardless of light period, they can be grown any time of year that the weather is favorable.

When ruderalis was first discovered a century ago growing wild in the Volga River region of the Russian Ural Mountains, it produced little to no THC and was only a foot (30 cm) tall at maturity. Ruderalis varieties were subsequently found outside Russia in northern climates such as Canada, where the growing seasons are naturally short.

Breeders have crossed ruderalis plants with high-grade temperate zone sativas and indicas and have continued to improve upon the quality of the crosses while maintaining the autoflowering trait. The first stable, commercial variety, "Lowryder," circa 1971, was under a foot tall and often grown for its novelty and uniqueness. The THC level had improved, but it wasn't very high, and the yield wasn't large enough for either most commercial or hobby growers to take much more than a passing interest.

Still, the ability to have a cannabis plant grow from seed to harvest in seven to nine weeks and to do so regardless of photoperiod was enough to keep breeders' interest. More breeders started working with autoflowering ruderalis plants, and the cultivars kept improving. Ruderalis now takes its place alongside its larger cousins, with equal THC content.

Improved high-THC Lowryder varieties are still available for purchase, but breeders have developed far bigger plants. There are two basic types of autoflowering cannabis, small and "super autoflowers." The small plants are considered the standard for home gardeners. They grow to two to three feet (60–90 cm) high. Super autoflowers grow to four to five feet (1.2–1.5 m) high and up to four feet (1.2 m) wide.

Planted on two-foot (60 cm) centers, an acre (~2.5 hectares) of autoflowering plants can be high yielding. In one Oregon commercial garden, two-foot (60 cm) spacing of autoflowers resulted in 6,000 pounds (~2,725 kg) of production per acre versus 3,000–4,000

Big Auto Tao by Top Tao Seeds is an award-winning autoflowering variety bred out of a desire to blend the traits of a favored indica parent with the autoflowering trait. It was bred in 2009 from a Super Auto Tao mother and a Taomatic father, both from Bohemia (Czech Republic). Big Auto Tao is high in limonene, turpentine, and pinene, and smells and tastes like pine and citrus fruits. The effects are euphoric, happy, trippy,  and psychedelic, with a strong body high. It grows in temperate climates with four distinct seasons and is suitable for high altitudes. While this variety regularly tests between 15 and 20% THC, it also produces a significant amount of CBD, between 5 and 10%.

pounds (~1,360–1,815 kg) when using sativas and indicas.

There are several advantages of autoflowering plants to the grower. For outdoor cannabis growers in the northern hemisphere working with shorter growing seasons where cool weather and frosts hit before plants mature, autoflowers eliminate that problem because they almost always ripen within 80 days. They can be planted in the last half of June, grow through July and August and be ready to harvest at the end of the month or earlier.

Sometimes gardeners lack the space to grow larger plants. Both regular and super autoflowers grow well in 5–10 gallon (19–38 l) containers, suitable for a deck or a closet. A plant or two won't take over all the space of an outdoor in-the-ground garden, either.

Autoflowering cannabis plants are easy to grow at home. They have been compared to tomatoes when it comes to ease, that is, they grow themselves. They do well in the same soil and with the same fertilizers recommended for tomatoes. Just start them in their final container or location or transplant them from starter pots when they are 7–10 days old and let them do their thing. They grow and flower so fast that there isn't time for them to develop many problems.

Since autoflowers do not have to rely on day length to bloom, they can be grown under many light regimens, but they do best when grown under 18 to 24 hours of light. They do not need a dark period to rest. In areas with long growing seasons two crops are possible. Autoflowering plants still yield well when they receive short days of intense light, such as in a grow space.

Outdoors in lower latitudes, with long nights all year long, they lose their advantage because most higher-latitude plants initiate flowering quickly under long night conditions. The more intense the light, the higher the yield.

Autoflowering plants also have advantages for commercial growers because they are easier to care for than bigger cannabis plants. They don't have to be staked or tied, branches don't fall from weight, inspecting plants is easier, and harvesting is infinitely easier and safer because there is no need for ladders.

Ayahuasca Purple Photo: Barney's Farm

CHOOSING PLANTS TO GROW

There are more cannabis cultivars available now than ever before through seed banks and nurseries in Europe and North America.

Growing from seed has its advantages, but also some issues. Seeds are easier to transport and store than cuttings (clones) from a nursery. Cannabis grown from seed is not genetically identical. The degree of homogeneity varies from breeder to breeder. Although plants of the same variety will be closely related, only skilled breeders can create a uniform crop. Starting from seed results in decreased uniformity in the canopy, which is undesirable because it reduces yield in larger operations. Home growers and those with smaller farms may not mind the decreased uniformity in the crop.

Large-scale farmers are more likely to prefer uniformity, so choosing varieties from a nursery that takes cuttings from mother plants or from tissue culture will help provide those identical genetics that drive uniformity in the canopy.

Whether growing from seeds or from clones, choosing the right cultivar is paramount because they differ not only in their effects but also in how they grow.

Cultivar vs. Strain

The word "cultivar" is derived from "cultivated variety." Although in popular culture cannabis cultivars are referred to as "strains," the term "strain" is more appropriately used when referencing viruses, bacteria, or fungi. The use of "strains" in the cannabis industry is widely accepted and understood, however. This book uses "varieties" to refer to groups of related plants and the term "cultivar" to refer to specific varieties that are named landraces or the result of a dedicated breeding program.

Cultivars that do best in outdoor gardens tend to need more light than cultivars that grow better indoors. Some cultivars have very little branching, while others prefer to spread their branches and leaves horizontally. Some are heavy yielders with large colas that will need support as the flowers approach final maturity.

While some varieties may finish in 50 days, it can take as long as 12 weeks before the plant can be harvested. Choosing the variety of cannabis best suited to the grower's goals can be a daunting task; however, it almost always is a pleasurable one. The right variety is the variety of cannabis that meets those goals, whether they are the plants' medicinal properties, style of growing, taste, aroma, or any other trait desired by the breeder. There is no single perfect variety of cannabis other than the variety that works perfectly for the grower.

Choosing Cultivars

Choosing which cultivar to grow is one of the most important decisions to make when designing a garden. The two most important factors are the quality of the effects and suitability for the growing environment.

Find cultivars that produce desired flavors, aromas, highs, or medicinal qualities. Each cultivar has a genetic blueprint that determines how the plant will react to its environment, and therefore each cultivar will respond differently to different climates and garden setups.

New cultivars are the result of the intense competition among seed breeders hoping to find the next big thing. How cannabis has been bred and for which traits has changed over the years as well. In 1964, THC was isolated and its molecular structure was described. It was understood that THC was driving all of the plant's effects, which drove breeders to narrowly focus on THC content.

New cultivars were also bred for many other characteristics such as yield, flavor, aroma, medicinal effects, size, and maturation length, but no other aspect of the cannabis flower has been selected for more than THC potency. Popular varieties from the '60s and '70s usually had a THC potency that ranged between 6 and 12%, but ordinary Mexican tested in the range of 2 to 4%.

Breeders selected for a wide variety of desirable traits in new varieties. At first they concentrated on increasing potency, decreasing ripening time, and decreasing the growth-to-yield ratio. Later they developed more of an interest in terpenes, which provide the odor as well as "personality" of the high, as well as for cannabinoids other than THC, such as CBD and CBG. Outdoor environments have come into favor due to legalization, as well as a proliferation of autoflowering varieties, homogeneity, and a more scientific approach to obtaining intentional results and micro-adaptation to specific outdoor environments.

Cannabis is particularly easy to breed because it is dioecious, meaning unlike almost all other annual plants, plants are either male or female. This makes it easy to control pollination; separate all males from the females and only use pollen from selected males to pollinate females. Cannabis is wind-pollinated, so a male in proximity to a female plant will pollinate it. Flowers can also be hand pollinated. For this reason, it is relatively easy for a grower to experiment with breeding.

Compare cannabis breeding to tomatoes. Not only does each tomato plant carry both sexes, but tomatoes have "perfect" flowers, meaning each flower carries both sexes. To breed them, the stamen from the designated female must be removed before it matures, which requires tweezers and a sharp eye. Then pollen must be collected from the candidate male, which is painstaking.

As a result of the ease of breeding there are literally thousands of companies producing cannabis seed for commercial sales, so obtaining seeds has never been easier. They are available over the internet as well as in dispensaries. Many of these companies advertise in magazines that feature cultivation articles.

Clones are also available. Just as many people prefer to use tomato starts rather than germinate seed, clones provide a head start and save 10–15 days of cultivation. Another advantage of clones is that they have identical genetics and respond to the environment in a uniform way.

The "ideal" environment for one variety may not be optimal for another. Having cultivars that are genetically identical optimizes large-scale production, since all the plants will thrive under the conditions that the cultivator provides. Creating many microclimates to accommodate the different varieties is expensive and difficult to do if the commercial grower's goal is to increase yield without compromising quality.

Home gardeners' preferences tend to be more varied, and their cultivar selections reflect that diversity. Home gardeners have different goals in mind, which is why growing from seed or having many different varieties in the same garden is perfectly acceptable. Home gardeners may be less interested in crop yields than they are with crop quality. They tend to grow different varieties so they can harvest at different times and choose from a selection of cannabinoid potencies, qualities of the high, tastes, and aromas.

It is true that the heterogeneity of maturation times and types of cannabis grown in the same garden often result in smaller yields than from a homogeneous garden. Heterogeneous gardens require more individualized attention to the different cultivars, resulting in more individual care. Most home gardeners don't mind, especially when they see the fruits (or flowers) of their labor.

Plant Size

The height and spread of the canopy are two varietal characteristics to consider when choosing which cultivar works best in the garden. This is particularly important whether the garden is indoors or outdoors. Sativa-dominant cultivars tend to grow taller and stretch farther than indicas. An outdoor garden with abundant sun and plenty of room for plants to spread out works well with strong sativa varieties such as Sour Diesel, Lemon Skunk, Vanilla Frosting, Lemon Tree, Runtz, Orange Creamsicle, or Lemongrass. These tall cultivars thrive in outdoor gardens with no height restrictions, and the extra intensity of direct sunlight keeps the plants from stretching too much. If they are pruned early in vegetative growth, they will bush out more rather than grow tall. The higher light intensity promotes shorter branching and thus denser buds.

Indoor gardens typically have size restrictions. Tall varieties can potentially grow close to or into the lights, causing damage to the plants and undesirable flowers that are light and airy. Shorter varieties such as those associated with most indica-dominant and many hybrid varieties are ideal for smaller indoor grows. Cultivars such as Do-Si-Dos, Wedding Cake, Grease Monkey, Lava Cake, Northern Lights, or Super Skunk have indica characteristics and thrive in indoor climates. However, an indoor garden does not mean it has to be relegated to only growing indicas. There are plenty of sativas and hybrids such as Sour Diesel and OG Kush that thrive in even the smallest of indoor settings if they can be grown with either the SOG or ScrOG method. (*See Vegetative Growth*)

Maturation Speed

Cannabis varieties have different rates of maturation once they are set to flower. Typically, this ranges from seven to 11 weeks. The time it takes to reach maturity affects the choice of variety in a couple of significant ways. First and foremost, quicker-maturing varieties allow for more harvests per year. If a grower is looking to maximize yield, and streamline production, quicker plants are a big plus. The other significant reason is that late-season varieties are inappropriate to grow in areas with short growing seasons.

Outdoor growers consider maturation speed depending on the weather in autumn, which can be cold and moist, but varies regionally. Gardens in climates that remain warm through the fall may work best with varieties that have longer flowering times. Finishing the flowering cycle while temperatures are still hot outside can cause the flowers to be less dense and lose a lot of their terpenes (aroma and flavor). Flowering later when temperatures are cool will delay ripening (*See When & How to Harvest*). Conversely, outdoor growers in climates that experience early frosts should plant cultivars that are ready to harvest early in the fall. A lot of the autoflowering varieties flower quickly and still have a lot of the original qualities that make them so great.

Yield

Once the size and maturation speed of the varieties have been decided, maximizing yields is often the next decision that needs to be considered when choosing which cultivar works best for a garden. High-yielding crops provide more medicine after harvest. These varieties are vigorous growers and will usually have higher cannabinoid potencies as well.

Maturation speed has a negative correlation with crop yield. In other words, the faster the maturation time, the lower the yield tends to be, and vice versa. Slower maturing varieties have more time to develop flowers, and thus the yields tend to be larger. However, a quick maturation time and low yield are not mutually exclusive. If it is a necessity to have a quick maturation time, the resulting smaller plants can be more densely planted to fill out the given canopy with more buds.

Examples of heavy yielders are Blue Dream, Sour Diesel, Big Bud, Critical Kush, Super Silver Haze, and White Widow.

Flavor, Aroma & High

The quality of the flower is more important than the yield for many growers. The flavor and aroma of cannabis comes exclusively from the terpene profiles of the varieties. Some cultivars have very distinct noses. The decision to grow a specific variety based on flavor and aroma is a personal decision that is best decided by the end user.

Some people prefer fruity cultivars such as Strawberry Cough or Blackberry Kush. Others prefer a sweet flavor from varieties such as Durban Poison, GSC, or some of the "cake" varieties such as Wedding Cake or Ice Cream Cake. Sour Diesel, Chemdawg 4, and Hindu Kush all have gassy noses due to a relatively high concentration of limonene. Flavor and aroma preferences are personal, but they are also very closely related to the high that comes from smoking/vaping these varieties as well.

The high from cannabis comes from the interplay of the different cannabinoids and terpenes found in the plant. With hundreds of active ingredients, there are practically endless terpene and cannabinoid combinations. Finding the high that works best for different situations is part of the fun of exploring cannabis. Terpenes such as α-pinene and limonene are bronchodilators and tend to give an uplifting energetic high. β-caryophyllene and linalool are smooth muscle relaxers and are generally found in varieties that provide a relaxing, calming high. Cannabinol (CBN) is the only cannabinoid that is regularly mentioned in lab testing that is also a smooth muscle relaxer and can cause that calming high. Many consumers use cannabis to ease anxiety and will look to cultivars with higher than average cannabidiol (CBD) content, such as AC/DC, Cannatonic, Sour Tsunami, Harlequin, and Ringo's Gift.

Cannabinol (CBN)

CBN is the product of aged THC. Over time, THC naturally degrades into CBN, but that's not necessarily a bad thing. Because CBN is a smooth muscle relaxer, it's used as a sleep aid. Storing cannabis in consistent cool temperatures around 60°F (15.5°C) and preventing light penetration can produce finely aged flowers with a higher than usual CBN content: a smooth smoke that helps with relaxing and sleeping at night.

Mold Resistance

Cannabis is susceptible to gray mold (*Botrytis cinerea*) and powdery mildew, which is caused by a number of fungal species. Both of these fungal infections thrive in stagnant, high-humidity environments. Gardens with humidity controls or naturally low humidity and substantial air movement around the plants are less susceptible to mold and fungi. However, cannabis is grown all over the world, and there are a number of regions where high-quality cannabis is grown in high-humidity environments. Cultivars that are grown in high humidity gardens need to have some level of mold resistance.

Cultivars derived from varieties and hybrids from Thailand, Vietnam, and other countries in Southeast Asian where it is humid have a higher resistance to mold. Varieties such as Pineapple Thai, Super Lemon Haze, Voodoo, and Juicy Fruit have Thai ancestry and are less prone to fungal infection.

VARIETY SHOWCASE

Breeders are a breed apart. Breeding is not easy. It requires a keen eye, an acute sense of taste, and most important, an ability to discern a plant with outstanding qualities. Over the years, breeders have expanded their work, seeking out higher levels of cannabinoids other than THC, unique terpene profiles, and fast-harvesting, high-yielding, and beautifully colored new varieties. Any good harvest starts with great genetics, and the following pages showcase several classic and up-and-coming varieties from some of the best breeders in the world.

Kiwi by Dynasty Genetics

Heritage & Genetics
Mother: C99/White Widow (American Pacific Northwest)
Father: Blue Heron (Blue Magoo Bx1) (Oregon)
Type I: THC Dominant
Created: 2016
Sativa-dominant Hybrid

Grow Conditions
Climate: Temperate (four seasons)
Ripening time: approx. 9–10 weeks
Suitable for high altitudes
Resistance: pest and disease
Height: Grows between 4 and 6 feet (1.2–1.8 m)

Smells & Effects
Terpenes: terpinolene
Smells: berry, citrus, floral, haze, lavender, licorice, pine, sweet, tart, kiwi
Effects: active, alert, body high, cheerful, functional, happy, positive, social, talkative, uplifting

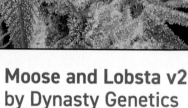

Moose and Lobsta v2 by Dynasty Genetics

Heritage & Genetics
Mother: Kali Snapple (Oregon)
Father: Oregon Huckleberry (Oregon)
Type I: THC Dominant
Created: 2014
Sativa-dominant Hybrid

Grow Conditions
Climate: Fog & Cloud Forests (cool, humid)
Ripening time: approx. 9–10 weeks
Height: Grows to 3 to 4 feet (90–120 cm) indoors and 6 to 8 feet (1.8–2.5 m) outdoors
Resistance: mold, fungus, pests, extreme temperatures

Smells & Effects
Terpenes: ocimene isomer II dominant
Smells: acrid, berry, caramel, floral, haze, musky, pineapple
Effects: relaxation, even head/body high, functional, happy, long-lasting, munchies, sensual

Marula
by Earth Witch Seeds

Heritage & Genetics
Mother: Farm Reserve Indica (Mendocino)
Father: Mozambican Indica (Mendocino & Mozambique)
Type I: THC Dominant (with significant quantities of THCV)
Created: 2015
Indica-dominant Hybrid

Grow Conditions
Climate: Mediterranean (mild, sunny, semi-arid)
Ripening time: approx. 7–8 weeks
Height: Up to 13 feet (4 m)
Resistance: powdery mildew, botrytis
This variety is well-suited for high altitude.

Smells & Effects
Terpenes: myrcene, limonene
Smells: candy, fruity, cherry, cotton candy
Effects: blissful, euphoric, heady

Witchy Wonder
by Earth Witch Seeds

Heritage & Genetics
Mother: Heirloom West Indies Sativa (West Indies)
Father: Af/Pak (Chitral Valley of Pakistan and Afghanistan)
Type I: THC Dominant (with significant quantities of THCV)
Created: 2002
Indica-dominant Hybrid

Grow Conditions
Climate: Fog & Cloud Forests (cool, humid)
Ripening time: approx. 8 weeks
Height: Grows up to 9–13 feet (3–4 m)
Resistance: high humidity, botrytis, bud rot

Smells & Effects
Terpenes: myrcene, limonene, α-santalol, β-santalol
Smells: floral, fruity, sandalwood, sour, kushy, tropical fruit
Effects: euphoric, narcotic, heavy

Garlic Haze by Earth Witch Seeds

Heritage & Genetics
Mother: Garlic Bud (California)
Father: Lake County Haze
(California)
Type I: THC Dominant (with
significant quantities of THCV)
Created: 2013
Sativa-dominant Hybrid

Grow Conditions
Climate: Mediterranean (mild, sunny,
semi-arid)
Ripening time: approx. 9–10 weeks
Height: Up to 16 feet (5 m)
Resistance: bud mold and rot

Smells & Effects
Terpenes: limonene, nerolidol, terpinolene
Smells: citrus, lemon, spicy, garlic
Effects: blissful, electric,
euphoric

Pumpkin Punch by Earth Witch Seeds

Heritage & Genetics
Mother: Pre-98 Bubba Kush (California)
Father: Heirloom Jamaican Sativa
(Jamaica)
Type I: THC Dominant (with significant
quantities of THCV)
Created: 2015
Sativa-dominant Hybrid

Grow Conditions
Climate: Fog & Cloud Forests (cool,
humid)
Ripening time: approx. 8–9 weeks
Height: Up to 9–13 feet (3–4 m)
Resistance: mold and disease, drought
tolerant
*This variety is well-suited for high
altitude.*

Smells & Effects
Terpenes: linalool, α-pinene, β-pinene
Smells: fruity, sweet, tropical, pumpkin
Effects: blissful, clear, euphoric

Cloud Walker by Green House Seeds

Heritage & Genetics

Mother: Punto Rojo (Colombia)
Father: Mendo Breath (Unknown)
Type I: THC Dominant
Created: 2018
Sativa-dominant Hybrid
Feminized seeds available

Grow Conditions

Climate: Mediterranean (mild, sunny, semi-arid)
Ripening time: approx. 9–10 weeks
Height: Grows very tall and will double or triple in size during flower, supports needed

Smells & Effects

Terpenes: high in myrcene and limonene, low caryophyllene
Smells: tropical pineapple, sweet vanilla, caramel, earthy undertones
Effects: uplifting, psychedelic, body high

Tropical Sleigh Ride by Greenshock Farms

Heritage & Genetics
Mother: Purple Candy Cane (California)
Father: Mean Gene's Pina/In the Pines (Mendocino)
Type I: THC Dominant
Created: 2016
Sativa-dominant Hybrid

Grow Conditions
Climate: Mediterranean (mild, sunny, semi-arid)
Ripening time: approx. 8 weeks
Height: Grows up to 8–12 feet (2.4–3.6 m)

Smells & Effects
Terpenes: ocimene, limonene, myrcene, linalool
Smells: candy, citrus, floral, fresh, fruity, grapefruit, lemon, mango, orange, pine, pineapple, sweet, sandalwood
Effects: active, blissful, relaxation, clear, electric, happy, munchies, social

Hawaiian Platinum Koffee by HiBred Seed

Heritage & Genetics
Mother: Platinum Huckleberry Cook-
ies/NL1 x Koffee Cake/Sky Cuddler
Kush F3 (Alaska)
Father: Hawaiian Dream (Colorado
& Georgia)
Type I: THC dominant
Created: 2020
Indica-dominant Hybrid

Grow Conditions
Climate: Mediterranean (mild, sunny,
semi-arid)
Ripening time: approx. 8–9 weeks
Resistance: some resistance to mold
and pests
Height: Indoors plants grow up to 6
feet (1.8 m), outdoors 10 feet (3 m)
or more
Suitable for high altitudes.

Smells & Effects
Smells: berry, candy, coffee, fruity,
sweet
Effects: blissful, body high, relaxation, cheerful, dreamy, long-lasting,
positive, sensual, trippy

Blueberry Muffin by Humboldt Seeds

Heritage & Genetics
Mother: Razzleberry (Oregon)
Father: FKA formerly known as PPD (Humboldt County, California)
Type I: THC dominant
Created: 2008
Indica
Feminized seeds available

Grow Conditions
Climate: Temperate (four seasons)
Ripening time: approx. 8–9 weeks
Height: Grows up to 12 feet (3.6 m)
Resistance: very resistant to extreme weather, pests, molds, and mildews
Suitable for high altitudes

Smells & Effects
Terpenes: myrcene, bisabolol, β-caryophyllene
Smells: berry, candy, creamy, fresh, fruity, hash, sweet, tart
Effects: active, alert, blissful, calm, cheerful, clear, energetic, euphoric, functional, happy, playful, talkative

L.A. Amnesia by Paradise Seeds

Heritage & Genetics
Mother: Original Amnesia
Father: Afghan Kush
(Afghanistan)
Type I: THC dominant
Created: 2017
Sativa-dominant Hybrid
Feminized seeds only

Grow Conditions
Climate: Mediterranean (mild, sunny, semi-arid)
Ripening time: approx. 8–9 weeks
Resistance: extreme temperatures, as low as 50°F (10°C) and as high as 104°F (40°C)
Indoor plants grow to 5 feet (1.5 m), outdoors to 10 feet (3 m)
Well suited for high altitude.

Smells & Effects
Terpenes: limonene, myrcene
Smells: citrus, haze, mango, spicy frankincense
Effects: active, relaxation, euphoric, intense, uplifting

Auto Wappa
by Paradise Seeds

Heritage & Genetics
Mother: Wappa
Father: Skunk x Ruderalis
Type I: THC dominant
Created: 2013
Indica-sativa Hybrid
Autoflowering
Feminized seeds only

Grow Conditions
Climate: Temperate (four seasons)
Ripening time: approx. 8–9 weeks (from germination)
Resistance: fungus
Height: Indoor plants grow to 3 feet (90 cm), outdoors to 3.6 feet (1.1 m)
Well suited for high altitude

Smells & Effects
Terpenes: myrcene, caryophyllene, linalool
Smells: fruity, sweet
Effects: blissful, relaxation, positive, uplifting

El Dorado OG by
Paradise Seeds

Heritage & Genetics
Mother: OG Kush
Father: Thin Mint GSC
Type I: THC dominant
Created: 2020
Indica-dominant Hybrid
Feminized seeds available

Grow Conditions
Climate: Mediterranean (mild, sunny, semi-arid)
Ripening time: approx. 7–8 weeks
Resistance: mold and disease, drought tolerant
Height: Indoor plants grow to over 3 feet (1 m), outdoors to 8 feet (2.5 m)
Well suited for high altitude.

Smells & Effects
Smells: fuel, lemon, pine, woodsy, earthy
Effects: relaxation, clear, even head/body high, functional

Mac Daddy by Purple Caper Seeds

Heritage & Genetics
Mother: MAC6 (Alien Cookies x (Columbian x Starfighter)) (Colombia)
Father: Grand Caper (California)
Type I: THC dominant
Created: 2018
Indica-dominant Hybrid
Feminized seeds available

Grow Conditions
Climate: Temperate (four seasons)
Ripening time: approx. 8–9 weeks
Height: Grows up to 10 feet (3 m)
Resistance: Very resistant to pest and disease, heat and drought tolerant

Smells & Effects
Terpenes: linalool, humulene, caryophyllene, limonene
Smells: acrid, berry, candy, fuel, ice cream
Effects: relaxation, even head/body high, intense, long-lasting, mind-numbing, narcotic, sedative, social

Luxor THCV by Purple Caper Seeds

Heritage & Genetics
Mother: DEVI (Humboldt County, California)
Father: Durban Kwazulu (Africa)
Type I: THC dominant, high in THCV
Created: 2020
Sativa

Grow Conditions
Climate: Temperate (four seasons)
Ripening time: approx. 9–12 weeks
Height: Can grow between 15 and 20 feet (4.5–6 m) outdoors
Resistance: Very resistant to pest and disease, heat and cold tolerant
Suitable for high altitudes

Smells & Effects
Smells: acrid, floral, fresh, fruity, herbal, licorice, musty, pepper, spicy, earthy
Effects: active, cheerful, clear, electric, energetic, functional, happy, positive

Cookies Gelato by Royal Queen Seeds

Heritage & Genetics
Mother: Wappa
Father: Skunk x Ruderalis
Type I: THC dominant
Created: 2013
Indica-sativa Hybrid
Autoflowering
Feminized seeds only

Grow Conditions
Climate: Temperate (four seasons)
Ripening time: approx. 8–9 weeks (from germination)
Resistance: fungus
Height: Indoor plants grow to 3 feet (90 cm), outdoors to 3.6 feet (1.1 m)
Well suited for high altitude

Smells & Effects
Terpenes: myrcene, caryophyllene, linalool
Smells: fruity, sweet
Effects: blissful, relaxation, positive, uplifting

Shogun by Royal Queen Seeds

Heritage & Genetics
Mother: Amnesia Haze (Netherlands)
Father: Royal Gorilla (USA)
Type I: THC dominant
Created: 2020
Sativa-dominant hybrid
Feminized seeds available

Grow Conditions
Climate: Mediterranean (mild, sunny, semi-arid)
Ripening time: approx. 9–11 weeks
Height: Plants grow up to 6.25 feet (1.9 m) outdoors and 4.5 feet (1.4 m) indoors

Smells & Effects
Terpenes: pinene, limonene, β-caryophyllene, humulene
Smells: pine, earthiness
Effects: alert, calm, functional

Glue Sniffer (GG#4 x GG#4 x The Whip! BX4) by The Seed Cellar

Heritage & Genetics
Mother: GG#4
Father: The Whip! (Afghanistan)
Type I: THC dominant
Created: 2019
Sativa-dominant Hybrid
Feminized seeds available

Grow Conditions
Climate: Temperate (four seasons)
Ripening time: approx. 6–7 weeks
Height: Grows up to 12 feet (3.6 m)
Resistance: Some resistance to cold, mold, and pests in northern latitudes.

Smells & Effects
Terpenes: limonene, myrcene, pinene, caryophyllene
Smells: fuel, lemon, pine, sour, woodsy
Effects: body high, relaxation, couch lock, eye droop, heady, munchies, narcotic, sedative

Silver Fire
by Sensi Seeds

Heritage & Genetics
Mother: Silver Haze
(Netherlands)
Father: Fire OG (USA)
Type I: THC dominant
Created: 2019
Sativa-dominant Hybrid
Feminized seeds available

Grow Conditions
Climate: Mediterranean (mild, sunny,
semi-arid)
Ripening time: approx. 9–10 weeks
Resistance: bud mold and rot

Smells & Effects
Terpenes: high in myrcene and limonene, low
caryophyllene
Smells: citrus, fuel, lemon, spicy, earthy
Effects: blissful, relaxation, calm, euphoric,
happy, contented

Black Domina
by Sensi Seeds

Heritage & Genetics
Mother: Northern Lights x Ortega
(Netherlands)
Father: Hash Plant x Afghani SA
(Afghanistan)
Type I: THC dominant
Created: 1996
Indica

Grow Conditions
Climate: Mediterranean (mild, sunny,
semi-arid)
Ripening time: approx. 7 weeks
Resistance: mold and disease, drought
tolerant
Well suited for high altitudes

Smells & Effects
Terpenes: high in myrcene, moderate
amount of pinene and low caryophyllene
Smells: berry, hash, musky, pepper,
blackberry, charas
Effects: relaxation, couch lock, dreamy,
intense, long-lasting, narcotic, sedative

Flubber Funk by Weed Guardians Family Tree

Heritage & Genetics
Mother: Flubber (Colorado)
Father: Scott's OG x Tangerine Kush (Colorado)
Type I: THC dominant
Created: 2016
Indica-dominant Hybrid

Grow Conditions
Climate: Mediterranean (mild, sunny, semi-arid)
Ripening time: approx. 8–10 weeks
Height: Grows up to 6 feet (1.8 m) tall
Well suited for high altitudes

Smells & Effects
Smells: berry, candy, creamy, fuel, hash, melon, sour, strawberry, sweet, dough, pie, cake mix
Effects: body high, relaxation, cheerful, happy, narcotic, positive

Project X67 by Weed Guardians Family Tree

Heritage & Genetics
Mother: GMO Foster (Colorado)
Father: Bellagio Gelato (Las Vegas, Nevada)
Type I: THC dominant
Created: 2019
Indica-dominant Hybrid
Feminized seeds available

Grow Conditions
Climate: Mediterranean (mild, sunny, semi-arid)
Ripening time: approx. 9–10 weeks
Height: grows up to 6 feet (1.8 m) tall
Best grown indoors and suited for high altitudes

Smells & Effects
Smells: berry, caramel, creamy, mango, sweet, offensive, rotten, banana, pawpaw fruit
Effects: body high, relaxation, couch lock, eye droop, giggly, long-lasting, narcotic, sedative

Male buds will soon open to simple
five petal flowers, releasing pollen.
Photo: Picture Fotografie

BASIC BREEDING

By Professor P of Dynasty Genetics and Will Ferguson

The progenitor of cannabis and hops originated in the Himalayan foothills at a time when there were seasonal differences but the weather was warm enough throughout the year to sustain active vegetative growth. This plant was probably a short-lived perennial that lived and flowered annually but survived for several years. Because it had no need for it, this plant never developed a way to deal with freezing weather.

The plant adapted as the climate changed to be more temperate with more varied seasons. It had to deal with an annual cold period that included freezing temperatures. The progenitor plant developed two paths to cope with the new circumstances.

Hops remains a perennial plant. The above-earth canopy dies back each autumn but has a woody root system that can stretch deep into the soil, storing energy produced by the previous season's photosynthesis. In the spring it grows feeder shoots to harvest nutrients found in the shallower soil sections and regrow the canopy. Hops is propagated by seed and rhizomes that stretch from the plants and lay down roots in suitable areas.

Cannabis became an annual plant that germinates, grows, flowers, produces seed, and dies in a single season. Cannabis can also regenerate after flowering in warm climates, where the weather encourages plant growth throughout the year.

Researchers think that the early symbiotic relationship between plants and humans helped cannabis travel the world. One of its unique qualities is that unlike most cultivated plants it can become feral and invasive. The alternation of cultivation and feral growth and contact between these populations played a crucial part in the development of modern cultivars.

> Varieties of cannabis that have "gone feral" and grow in the wild after having been cultivated by humans are found throughout the world. Varieties that have been cultivated in an area in isolation for many generations, an interplay between humans and nature, are commonly called "landraces."

Plants growing in temperate areas experience a varied environment. One year it's rainy, the next year sunny, cool, or cloudy. Temperate cannabis adapted to these vagaries and maintained a heterogeneous gene pool. When a population has a wide array of alleles, a percentage of the plants will do well or less poorly than others no matter the weather.

Random vs. Intentional Breeding

Left: A male branch with flowering pollen sacs. Right: close-up of male flowers at the node. Photo: Phil Sullivan / Team Terpene

Random breeding is when the seed collector who mixes all the acquisitions grows them out and allows for uncontrolled pollination. The theory is that the seeds are from good cultivars, so it's possible that they will result in some outstanding crosses to select from.

Although this technique is exciting, the "hang it up and see what tomorrow brings" method of breeding has fallen out of style because there is no provenance, no crosses that can be verified. This makes it difficult to register the hybrid as intellectual property.

The other classical technique is to study the various characteristics of plants and then to choose which to cross based on characteristics such as resistance to disease or predation, ripening time, growth pattern, and profile of cannabinoids and terpenes.

Modern commercial breeding uses genetic profiling to help make selections. DNA is found in the chromosomes, which are always found in pairs in nature. For instance, by analyzing certain snippets of DNA, it can be determined if a plant is autoflowering or if it will produce THC or CBD. Some of the analysis can be quite specific. Anyone who has used a genetic service such as 23andMe or Ancestry.com is aware of just how "personal" it can be, and the same goes for each plant and its DNA.

Some of these techniques are already being used commercially and by hobbyists.

Cannabis is the most widely bred plant in the world. Between hobbyists, breeders, and all the small and large seed companies, it is an enormous research pool that no other crop enjoys. One reason for the proliferation of cannabis breeding is that it's far easier to breed than most other crops.

Unlike almost all other annual plants, cannabis is dioecious, that is, it has separate male and female plants. This is another clue that it began as a perennial, because a small percentage of perennial plant species are dioecious.

Monoecious plants have either separate male and female flowers or "perfect" flowers—defined as having both male and female reproductive organs. To breed a perfect flower one has to use a tweezer to pull out the male organ, the pistil, before it matures, gather the pollen from the pistil of a different plant and paint it on the stigma. This is a painstaking task.

Cannabis is easy to propagate because it is dioecious. There are several techniques, but the most commonly used are the following:

- Male and female plants are separated. All males are destroyed except for the ones to be used for breeding. The pollen is gathered from the selected male(s). This is easily done by laying the male plant down horizontally and placing tarps under and over the plant. It will shed pollen that can be collected. Then the pollen is painted onto female flowers with a watercolor brush.

- Males and females are separated. All males except for breeding candidates are destroyed. All females to be pollinated and the selected male are placed in a pollen-tight space. A fan keeps the pollen circulating in the air until it's captured by the stigmas and used to produce seed.

Chromosomes are composed of genes and are the blueprint for everything about the plant. A gene can have any one of many versions, but they are found in pairs, one in each chromosome. Some alleles (versions of the gene) are dominant, some are partially dominant, and some are recessive.

A dominant allele imposes its traits without regard to the other allele. An example of this is the known model for THC potency in cannabis (Campbell et al. 2020). THC potency is not just phenotypically represented by a single allele; it is a complex group of alleles that all show signs of dominance. This is likely why early cannabis breeders were able to relatively easily focus on THC concentrations in the offspring of bred varieties. The alleles were dominant and were more likely to be expressed.

A partially dominant allele pairs with the other allele to combine the trait. For instance, a tall and a short plant may produce one between the parents' two heights.

A recessive allele gets sublimated by a dominant allele. When crossed with a non autoflowering plant the resulting plant will be autoflowering.

There are many methods and terms used in breeding.

- **F1** is the first generation from a cross. If the lines are stable this generation will be uniform because all the plants are receiving similar alleles. One half of the pair comes from each parent.
- **F2** is a cross between two F1s. These plants receive one allele from each parent, but the parents have mixed pairs of alleles, so they sort out into many combinations.
- **Backcross** refers to a plant that has a desirable characteristic (A) that one wants to transfer to another plant (B). First the two plants are crossed, and then a product of the cross (C, which is 50% B) is crossed back to B. In the next generation (D, which is 75% B), only some of the plants will have the desirable characteristic. One of the Ds with the characteristic is crossed back to B to produce E, which is 87.5% B. This may continue for several more generations to generate a plant with similar genetics of B with an A characteristic or B with the desired characteristic from A.

What Is Seed Stability?

Stability in cannabis breeding refers to how uniform the offspring are.

If a male and female plant are bred together, this means that their genetics are being crossed through sexual reproduction. The offspring are genetic mixtures of the parents. If the offspring exhibit different traits (such as varying heights), they are said to be unstable. However, if the seeds produce plants that show uniform traits, they are said to be stable.

Breeding for uniformity and stability is important for growers who grow from seed as opposed to clones. Growing from stable sources of genetics allows for a greater uniformity in the final product, which is a goal for commercial growers. Hobbyists may find genetic stability less valuable, as they are more open to seeing what the randomness of sexual reproduction brings them.

Essentially, stable cannabis varieties have more homozygous dominant traits than an unstable variety, which would have more heterozygous alleles. Stable parents typically produce predictable offspring, which is desirable for large-scale growers who cultivate from seeds. To achieve this desired goal, breeders will cross varieties with themselves (called "selfing") or crossing with their siblings. Backcrossing is when the offspring is bred with a previous generation (mom/dad, grandma/grandpa, etc.). Inbreeding the genetics with siblings or previous generations will, over many generations, result in offspring that have more uniform, homozygous, predictable, and hopefully desirable phenotypes.

Overview of Genetic Testing in Cannabis: Tools and Uses
by Dale Hunt, PhD, JD

In recent years there have been great advances in genetic testing. It has become increasingly powerful and inexpensive and offers a number of tools that can aid breeders and growers to achieve a wide variety of goals. It is useful to classify genetic testing tools into the kinds of questions they can answer.

As with human genomic sequencing services like 23andMe or Ancestry.com, there are lab tests available to break down what can be known about cannabis DNA and help elucidate what can be learned in the future. Here are some of the common ways cannabis genetic testing is being used by breeders and growers.

Identity and Relatedness establishes the equivalent of a fingerprint or barcode for one plant cultivar that is unique to that cultivar and shows the degree to which two plants are related, as well as mapping the relatedness of groups of plants.

Forensics is a subset of Identity and Relatedness; it determines intellectual property (IP) infringement by showing whether one plant is genetically the same as or different from a second plant.

Traits correlates DNA information with specific traits and uses the information in plant breeding to achieve improvement or modification of the traits.

Functions allows for understanding of molecular and biochemical characteristics and processes in terms of the genes controlling them.

Conditions and Interactions detects and assesses non-cannabis DNA to identify the presence and amounts of different pathogens or symbiotic organisms.

Whole Genome analysis involves sequencing all of an organism's DNA to obtain the full complement of information it contains. Since the total genome carries so much information, it can be hard to use for specific purposes without powerful analytic tools. In many cases, even if a full genome sequence is feasible and affordable, it can amount to a form of information overload.

Marker analysis involves sampling several much shorter sequences from specific portions of the genome. If the whole genome is a complex layout of information like a very large map, markers define specific spots on the map, like buildings and intersections. Some locations in the genome have much higher sequence variability than other segments. By determining an individual plant's sequences only at these locations, it is possible to create a set of markers that can uniquely identify one plant in comparison to another plant. Since the most useful markers are selected because they are highly variable, two unrelated plants are more likely to have different sequences at a given marker location than to have the same sequence at that location.

Genotype: the genetic composition of an organism
Phenotype: the physical expression of the organism's genotype
Chemotype: the chemical expression of the organism's genotype

The environment plays a role in the expression of the genotype and can affect phenotype and chemotype.

For example, indica-dominant cultivars tend to be shorter than sativa-dominant cultivars. This is driven by genetics. However, indica-dominant cultivars can stretch and get taller if there is not enough light for them. The genotype and environment interact to express the phenotype, or physical trait. Even though an indica's genotype is for a shorter growing pattern, the phenotype takes the environment into account as well. A low-light situation can make even a short plant stretch tall for sunlight.

For example, the Phylos Bioscience "Galaxy," which is a visual representation of the relationships between cannabis varieties, is based on assessing about 2,000 markers. Since these markers are highly variable, it is statistically improbable that two plants would be the same for all 2,000 markers unless the plants are substantially the same. Thus, marker matches and mismatches between compared plants can clearly establish whether different samples are the same variety or are different, and they can also provide a numerical indication of how similar or different they are.

There are tens of thousands of markers that have been identified and that are used for genotyping plants, studying correlations between a set of markers and a plant trait (phenotype), and using this knowledge for marker-assisted breeding. Some markers indicate the presence of a Y chromosome, indicating a male, enabling early and rapid sex testing of seedlings long before the plant is manifesting any male morphology.

Transcriptome analysis involves identifying subsets of genes based upon which ones are actively being expressed (transcribed, hence the term "transcriptome") in a given part of a plant such as a flower, a leaf, or a root, and/or at a given stage such as germination, trichome development, seed formation, and so forth. This permits the identification and understanding of the detailed genetic and biochemical processes that characterize that structure or stage of development.

In more scientific terms, the mRNA molecules are transcribed from the DNA in the nucleus of the plant cell. The mRNA then leaves the nucleus to be translated into proteins in the cell's cytoplasm. The transcriptome is the collective mRNA at any given moment in the cell's developmental stage.

Pathogen Genomics tests the non-cannabis DNA present in a sample as a way to show which other organisms are present and in what amounts. These tests are rapid and sensitive ways to detect pathogens early, before they can do major harm to the plant, and can also aid in understanding the interactions between a plant and the beneficial organisms that interact with it.

Cannabis breeders have all of these tools at their disposal, subject to cost considerations, of course. Generally, though, these tools are becoming less expensive and more powerful. If breeders want to create varieties that combine traits of different landraces and traits of other plants that perform well agronomically, they can use genetic markers to pick which varieties to use in their breeding program because those markers can reveal information about relatedness and ancestry of the parent plants for the original cross. If certain markers are known to correlate with traits, breeders can do marker assisted breeding, enabling early selection of offspring from a cross that will eventually express the desired traits.

The greatest challenge to marker-assisted breeding is finding the correlations between the many thousands of known genotypes and phenotypes, whose inheritance and manifestation can be very complex. This requires analyzing large amounts of genetic and phenotypic information. Data sharing, such as through the Ethical Data Alliance, a project of Green Aid, a nonprofit corporation registered in California, will significantly aid in defining these correlations that, in turn, will make marker assisted breeding all the more powerful.

Feminizing Seed

Feminized seeds produce female plants. When they germinate, there will be few males among them if they are produced correctly. The threat of accidentally pollinating crops by misidentifying a male as a female is minimized.

The only ways to preserve the exact genetics of a plant are by cloning or regeneration. (*See Appendix D: Regeneration.*) One reason to use this technique is because a plant crossed with itself produces seeds that retain its parents' favorable characteristics. Another reason to use this technique is to create a hybrid of two female plants.

A female plant can be manipulated to produce male flowers, and thus pollen to pollinate female flowers even with no male plants around. Feminized seeds are produced by inducing a normal female, not a hermaphrodite, to grow male flowers with viable pollen.

Cannabis is similar to humans in that each plant has a specific gender, male or female, that is designated genetically by an X or a Y chromosome. Pollen produced from male flowers borne on a female plant will have only the X chromosome. The progeny will inherit an X from the male flower's pollen and an X from the egg. The resulting seeds can only inherit two X chromosomes, which means that virtually all the resulting seeds will be female.

Getting only female plants was the motivation for creating feminized seeds, but they offer other advantages. Feminized varieties are more uniform (homogeneous) than "regular" seeds. Plants from feminized seeds tend to look more like each other and produce a more uniform harvest.

Even when using feminized seeds, there is still a small chance that a few plants will be hermaphrodites (truly both male and female) or males. If feasible, plants should be monitored through the entire growth stage to check for these oddities. Maintaining stable growing conditions is the best way to prevent male or hermaphroditic plants. Environmental stresses such as light, disruption, or over pruning will encourage female plants to produce pollen. If a male or hermaphrodite is found, remove it.

Feminized seeds are not as mysterious or weird as they might seem. In mature human females, taking male hormones causes masculinizing changes such as breast shrinkage, muscle bulking, and a lowering in voice pitch. The primary sex organs have already been formed, but they shrink.

A similar thing happens when female plants are treated with masculinizing chemicals. The difference is that while a mature human has already formed sex organs, every time a plant produces a new flower, it is growing a new sex organ. Plants under chemical influence grow viable male flowers: even though the plant is still a female with two X chromosomes, the pollen has only female chromosomes.

There are several methods used to produce feminized seed. By far, the easiest method was developed by the noted breeder Soma. He noticed that when colas of many varieties reached late ripeness, a few viable male flowers (often called bananas) developed. This is also a sign that the buds are ripe. Harvest the pollen using a fresh watercolor brush and brush it directly on the flowers or store it in a small glass or metal container. Not all varieties produce male flowers at the end of ripeness, but many do, and they do it reliably. Very small amounts of pollen are produced using this method, but a little pollen applied properly goes a long way.

Some varieties flower normally outdoors but experience indoor growing conditions as stressful and produce male and female flowers as a result. The pollen from the male flowers can be used for breeding, provided that the resulting plants are going to be grown outdoors, where they won't exhibit the unwanted hermaphroditism. This method has inherent risks of hermaphroditism in the resulting plants.

Plant stresses such as irregular light cycles and heat sometimes induce hermaphroditism. However, stress techniques are not reliable. They only seem to work when unwanted; most environmental stress regimens are unreliable in invoking male flower production. Should this happen accidentally in a garden with a valuable variety, opportunistic growers often collect the pollen, even when there are no immediate plans to use it.

Laboratories and commercial seed producers use three chemicals to induce male flowers in female plants: gibberellic acid, silver nitrate, and silver thiosulfate. They each inhibit the plant's production of ethylene, a hormone that promotes female flowering. Without ethylene, female flower production is reduced or stopped. The actions of these chemicals are localized. If only one branch of a plant is sprayed, that branch will be the only one affected.

The rest of the plant will continue growing female flowers, not males.

Gibberellins are the plant hormones that are most famous for stem elongation.

Gibberellins are hormones that plants produce to regulate many phases of their growth. Several of the gibberellins, such as GA3, 4, 5, and 7, induce male flowers when they are sprayed on female plants before they begin flowering. GA3 is the most effective and the gibberellin most commonly available commercially. For best results, use a solution of 0.01% (0.1 gram GA3 in a liter of distilled water).

Gibberellin must be used carefully. Lower doses result in fewer male flowers. Higher amounts have an inhibitory effect. Lightly spray the tops of the plant for five consecutive days and then force the plants to flower by increasing the uninterrupted dark period to 12 hours a day. The sprayed area will stretch a bit, but within two weeks, the first signs of male flowers will appear. They will be ripe and ready to release pollen in another two weeks.

Silver thiosulfate is more effective than silver nitrate, that is, it induces more male flowers. Sometimes the two chemicals are used together. It is usually recommended to spray the plant until the liquid drips off the leaves. Then immediately change the light regimen from vegetative to flowering. It is usually suggested that the leaves will droop and stop growing for a few days, yellow a bit and then regain turgidity. Male flower growth will become apparent in a couple of weeks. The flowers will ripen a few weeks later. However, drenching until drip-off has experimentally resulted in extremely stressed plants that produce few flowers. Lightly spraying the leaves as the light deprivation regimen is begun and then again once a week for two weeks results in stalks that produce flowers with fertile pollen.

Silver thiosulfate is made by combining two water solutions, one containing silver nitrate and the other, sodium thiosulfate. Silver nitrate alone can also be used to induce male flowers. Spray a solution of 0.02–0.03% on the plant, and then turn the lights to a 12-hour flowering cycle. The leaves will droop for a day or so and then resume turgidity. Male flower growth will become apparent in a couple of weeks and ripen a few weeks later. To make a 0.02% solution, add 0.1 gram of silver nitrate in half a liter of distilled water.

Because of market demand, almost all the seed companies offer most of their popular varieties as feminized seed. They are the best choice for most gardeners. The exception is gardeners interested in breeding.

Stubbornly Seedless Cannabis
By Emery Garcia

There are few things more detrimental to a grower's success than discovering the crop has been unknowingly pollinated. Not only is seeded flower virtually worthless for anything but extraction, cannabinoid content and overall usable flower production numbers are also drastically decreased. Once a plant starts putting its energy into reproduction, all other duties are largely ignored.

The cannabis plant's desire to reproduce has played a huge role in suppressing its use for fiber, fuel, and food. Sinsemilla, or seedless cannabis, cannot be produced within miles of even a tiny population of male plants. Unless a farmer carefully culls every male in the field, pollination ensues. Even feminized plants sometimes can become hermaphrodites, pollinating all the plants around.

The problem is that cannabis is wind-pollinated, and its pollen travels. Microscopic grains are capable of flying hundreds of miles in the wind. In the US Midwest, hemp pollen

In both photos, diploid plants (stem cell 2x) are on the left and triploid plants (stem cell 3x) are on the right. Courtesy of Oregon CBD

is tracked and tagged as one the most prolific of all pollen irritants in the air, fueled almost entirely by feral populations. With the CBD-driven hemp industry booming and the drive to use hemp as a sustainable plastic replacement increasing, growing a seedless cannabis crop is becoming more difficult.

According to Oregon CBD, an industrial hemp breeding firm out of Independence, Oregon, there is a solution. Led by the plant research breeder Dr. Hsuan Chen, the company developed the first triploid varieties, incapable of producing seeded cannabis. Triploid plants don't produce viable pollen, nor will females produce seed.

Triploids are already common in other commercial agricultural crops producing seedless fruit such as grapes, bananas, citrus, and hops. Oregon CBD's triploids are a first for cannabis.

"We have run many trials including covering flowering triploid plants with pollen. Like other plants in nature with odd numbers of chromosome pairs, triploids are sterile and never produce more than a few tiny immature seeds," said Dr. Chen.

Triploids have plenty of other benefits. Because each cell has 50% more genetic material than a regular (diploid), the entire organism is more vigorous, grows faster, and produces bigger and better flowers without seed. According to Oregon CBD's preliminary studies, the triploid plants produce up to double the yield and increase terpene production by about 30%.

Triploids are produced by chemically altering the mitosis process, so when cells attempt to split, the DNA splits apart, making two pairs in the somatic cells instead of one. These tetraploid seeds are grown out and crossed with diploids, creating triploids, as stubbornly sterile as mules.

For fed-up cannabinoid farmers, this development offers a lifeline for two industries already suffering at the hands of rogue pollen—be it from feral populations, careless farmers who don't pull their males, or large-scale fiber producers who have no intention to do so. Medical and recreational growers can rejoice at the prospect of a future where potent sinsemilla will continue to grow freely outdoors. For cannabinoid-chasing hemp farmers it means thousands of hours saved walking rows searching for those sneaky males or hermaphrodites and a higher-quality seedless product.

The Science Behind Triploids

Cannabis in the wild is almost exclusively a diploid (2n) species. In diploids, every plant receives one set of chromosomes from each parent. Though rare, spontaneous mutations can occur that result in a doubling of the diploid genomes and lead to tetraploid (4n) individuals even in controlled breeding populations.

Dr. Chen and Brendan Rojas, research plant breeders at Oregon CBD, designed a series of experiments to treat diploid cannabis tissue with compounds known to inhibit cell division. According to Dr. Chen, the process approximates the tetraploid-inducing events that occur in nature at a very low rate but does so more consistently. Treated plants are screened using a flow cytometer, a device that can measure the physical size of a plant genome, and compared with their diploid counterparts to detect the desired doubling of genome size. Success results in tetraploids, or plants with four sets of homologous chromosomes (4n) and an identical doubled version of the mother. This screening process is repeated a number of times in subsequent generations of cuttings to prevent reversion to the diploid state.

"We have to clone the tetraploid plants we produce and retest them many times to make sure they stay tetraploids, sometimes parts of the plants grow diploid shoots," adds Dr. Chen. "If they do, we have to start over because we can't use them for breeding."

Tetraploid cannabis plants have been described by two other research groups (Mansouri and Bagheri 2017 and Parsons et al. 2019), and their findings mirror those said to have been found at Oregon CBD; distinct morphological changes and increased nutrient consumption are apparent, but chemical composition (ratios and total amounts produced) is relatively unchanged, albeit with a marked increase in aromatic compounds. So far, evidence suggests that tetraploids offer little if any performance increase over diploids, with the exception of louder olfactory notes.

The real magic begins when a tetraploid plant is crossed with a diploid plant. Two copies of the tetraploid parents' chromosomes are carried over and one set from the diploid parent. The resulting offspring are not only sterile, but come with a variety of gains seen in other commercial agriculture crops such as overall essential oil production.

Polyploidy (anything possessing more than two sets of chromosome pairs) is already understood to increase secondary metabolite production in other crops, particularly those compounds responsible for flavor or aroma. Cannabis, thankfully, is not an exception to this trend, and the breeders say aroma compounds such as terpenes, esters, and aldehydes in their triploid varieties are heightened significantly.

PART II:

THE LIMITING
FACTORS

Pineapple   Photo: Theo Oldfield

THE CANNABIS PLANT LIFE CYCLE

Understanding how plants live provides insight into how to optimize their growth and production.

Plants are **sessile organisms**, meaning they are immobile, so they evolved ways to survive in a world in which they cannot walk, swim, or fly away from danger.

The vast majority of plants use the sun's energy to make their food from carbon dioxide (CO_2) and water. Plants have less access to inputs than motile organisms, so they evolved compounds needed to survive or to give them an advantage over competitors. In cannabis these compounds include chlorophyll, lignin to strengthen cell walls, suberin to diminish water loss, and THC and the rest of the cannabinoids and terpenoids to protect against different stresses, including pests and UV light. Flavonoids protect against photooxidative stress.

The Beginning

A cannabis plant starts its life cycle as a seed, a packet containing a plant embryo that is in a state of suspended animation just waiting for an external signal to germinate.

Germination occurs when the plant embryo exits its state of suspended animation, starts growing, and emerges from within the seed coat. This happens when it comes in contact with water, which changes the ratio of internal hormones, spurring growth. Germination usually occurs two to five days after planting. However, old age and low temperature can cause a delay of a week or more. The radicle, which is the beginning of the tap root, grows down, orienting itself by sensing gravity.

As the root grows, the embryo inside the seed coat uses the enclosed energy package to grow its shoot, that is, the parts above ground, the stems and leaves. The first parts of the shoot that emerge from the seed are the cotyledons (embryonic leaves). Cannabis has two cotyledons and thus is classified as a type of plant called a dicot.

Once the cotyledons break through the soil or growing medium, the plant relies on light energy for growth. The cotyledons expand and orient themselves to maximize exposure to light. Auxin is used to orient stem growth toward the source of light energy.

Plants Make Their Own Food
Sometimes plant fertilizers are referred to as "plant food," but this is fundamentally incorrect. Plants make their own food through the process of photosynthesis. The photosynthetic equation is as follows:

$$6CO_2 + 6H_2O \xrightarrow[\text{Chlorophyll}]{\text{Light}} C_6H_{12}O_6 + O_2$$

Carbon dioxide + Water → Sugar + Oxygen

Light is the energy used to make the food in this equation. The products are glucose ($C_6H_{12}O_6$) and molecular oxygen (O_2) gas. Glucose is a simple sugar that cannabis uses to power metabolism, that is, life processes. Sugar is moved around the plant to support maintenance and growth. When nitrogen, phosphorus, and potassium join the mix, the plant produces amino acids, which are turned into tissue. Cannabinoids and terpenes are carbon heavy. For instance, THC is a 21-carbon molecule. The carbon used to create THC comes from the 6-carbon atoms in the glucose molecule.

Plant nutrients are analogous to vitamins that humans need to thrive. These nutrients help the plant to create the compounds needed to photosynthesize. For example, the middle of the chlorophyll molecule is a magnesium ion, which gets absorbed through the roots and moved to the leaves to create chlorophyll. A magnesium deficiency, among other things, hinders photosynthesis.

Vitamins are detrimental if taken in excess. Similarly, too much fertilizer can be detrimental, preventing the plant from absorbing water. Plants are more efficient in absorbing nutrients that are given in small amounts over a longer period of time. This also diminishes waste runoff, resulting in using less water and fertilizer, saving money, and more important, gardening more sustainably.

Roots and shoots support each other; the root absorbs water and nutrients, and the shoot absorbs light. Water and nutrients absorbed by the roots are transported up to the shoots, where water in the leaves is required for photosynthesis.

The sugars that the leaves produce is transported to all other plant tissues, including the roots. The roots use the sugar to grow as they explore the growing medium in pursuit of water and nutrients. The sugar from photosynthesis is also transported to the top of the stem in a specialized tissue called the **shoot apical meristem (SAM)**, where it is used to begin expansion and growth. The SAM was there in the embryonic stage of the plant, but now it emerges from between the cotyledons.

Meristematic tissue in plants is akin to stem cells in animals. The SAM is a group of undifferentiated cells that create stems, leaves, and everything else included in the shoots of the plant. As the plant continues to expand and grow, it develops the seedling's first node after the cotyledons.

Nodes are the part of the stem where a new leaf and axillary bud are borne. It is easy to identify where the node is, since it is where the **petiole** of the leaf attaches to the stem. The petiole is the part of the leaf that extends the leaflets, or leaf blades, away from the stem.

This allows for better airflow around the leaf, but more important, extends the leaf away from the stem and provides the leaflets a better chance to capture more light.

The **root apical meristem (RAM)** is the roots' counterpart for the SAM. The RAM differentiates into root tissue so that the cannabis plant can grow its roots into the growing medium.

The SAM and RAM produce different plant hormones that get transported away from the meristematic tissue. For the SAM, auxin is produced and transported down to the roots. The RAM produces cytokinin, which is transported up to the shoots. The ratio of these two plant hormones dictates many things.

As the SAM continues differentiating new shoot tissues, the stem continues growing taller, creating new leaves and axillary buds. **Axillary buds** are borne on the stem in the axil of where the petiole and stem meet. These buds start off as being dormant. They require hormonal stimulus to come out of dormancy. This occurs when the hormonal balance between auxin and cytokinin shifts toward a higher concentration of cytokinin as compared with auxin.

Plant Hormones Control When Buds Come Out of Dormancy

Plants, cannabis included, evolved a method to control when buds come out of dormancy and create a new main stem. The shoot apical meristem (SAM) produces new axillary buds that usually stay dormant until a disruptive external event occurs that shifts the ratio of the plant hormones auxin and cytokinin in the bud tissue.

SAM produces auxin and transports it toward the roots, while the root apical meristem (RAM) produces cytokinins that are transported to the shoots. If something drastic occurs to the SAM, such as an animal eating the top of the plant, wind breaking it off, or a grower cutting it off, the flow of auxin to the roots stops.

Since the RAMs are still producing and transporting cytokinins to the shoots, the ratio of auxin to cytokinin at the bud sites on the shoots is shifted in favor of a higher concentration of cytokinins from the roots as compared with relatively equivalent concentrations between the two hormones.

The axillary bud recognizes this as a signal to come out of dormancy and to produce new branches. Each of the axillary buds also have SAMs, and when they leave dormancy, they start to produce and transport auxin to the roots. Eventually the ratio of auxin to cytokinin returns to its normal state.

However, instead of one main stem, lateral branches have replaced the primary stem as sources of auxin. SAMs create all parts of the stem, including flowers. If a cultivator removes the primary stem and there are three or four dormant axillary buds below it, the plant replaces the primary stem with three or four separate top colas of cannabis flower instead of just one.

The developing buds eventually become side (lateral) branches of the main stem, which can develop side branches of their own. If the plant is never trimmed from the top (topped), plants will take on the characteristic look of a Christmas/fir tree, a wider bushy plant, or a single stem with minimal lateral branching.

During this early stage of the cannabis life cycle, the plant grows vegetatively; it develops new leaves, stems, and roots, building infrastructure so that it can support heavy flower growth.

A plant with heavy flowers can fail if the branches are not strong enough to support it. The vegetative stage focuses on building stems, leaves, and roots as well as creating a robust plant prepared to produce a bountiful crop of flowers.

Most cultivars continue to grow vegetatively until they receive the environmental cue to start flowering related to the length of uninterrupted darkness the plants receive daily. This phenomenon is called photoperiodism and is essential for triggering flowering.

Photoperiodism

Broken down into its components, the word "photoperiodism" indicates its definition; "photo" refers to light, and "periodism" indicates length of time. Cannabis flowers when the length of darkness increases to a critical level in late summer and fall. Plants with this characteristic, including chrysanthemums and poinsettias, are often referred to as short-day plants.

Cannabis emerged in the evolutionary tree about 28 million years ago in the Tibetan plateau at latitude 33° north. This was at a time when two tectonic plates were thrusting the Tibetan plateau up, changing the environment from mild to temperate. At that latitude there are seasonal differences in the ratio of day to night hours. Using the seasonal environmental stimulus, cannabis evolved from a perennial to an annual, but remained dioecious, flowering and seeding by the end of the season. Had cannabis evolved closer to the equator, without much seasonal variation in that ratio, it could not use photoperiodism to determine flowering time. Cannabis uses this aspect of nature to trigger flowering through a photoreceptor called **phytochrome**. Phyto is derived from "plant," and chrome is "color" in Greek. Phytochrome literally means "plant color."

Toward dusk the light spectrum reaching Earth's surface shifts. More red light is filtered out, so the ratio of red to far-red changes, favoring far-red light.

As long as there is a higher ratio of red to far-red light, the phytochrome stays in its active form, P_{fr}, inhibiting flowering. Without red light illumination, it shifts to its inactive form, P_r, over a two-hour period. The far-red light at the end of the day gives the phytochrome photoreceptors a head start in their nightly process of decaying into the ground state. In the presence of far-red light without red, the P_{fr} quickly shifts to P_r, giving the plant the equivalent of an extra hour of darkness. The critical time period of darkness needed to induce flowering varies by cultivar.

How to calculate a cultivar's critical dark period outdoors: Check the plants for flowers every day. Count back one week from when they first appear. The length of the dark period at that time, from dusk to dawn, is the length of darkness that is required for flowering to be forced. This method works with natural light; indoors, adjust the dark period gradually to find the critical dark period.

In early summer there is enough red light for a long-enough period so that the amount of darkness is not enough to induce flowering.

Far-red light catalyzes the switch back to P_r; however, phytochrome receptors usually rely on long nights (uninterrupted periods of dark) for the P_{fr} to P_r conversion. When the sun rises the following morning and sunlight reaches the plant, phytochrome quickly returns to the P_{fr} state.

Cannabis shifts from a vegetative growth pattern to its flowering stage when enough phytochrome receptors decay to the ground isoform on a consistent nightly basis.

An interruption of the dark period with even a short period of light resets the phytochromes to their active states. Cannabis can be maintained in its vegetative growing pattern by providing light all the time, which prevents phytochrome decay into the ground state. The vegetative state can also be maintained by breaking up the night with a short period of light to convert the P_r back to P_{fr} and not allowing P_r to build to that critical level to trigger flowering. After roughly five days of long uninterrupted darkness, the cannabis plant starts investing its resources into flowering.

Indoor cultivators emulate the natural environment by regulating the light cycle to trigger flowering. Growing under either continuous light or a minimum of 18 hours of light keeps the plants in a vegetative growth state. Adjusting the light cycle so that the plants receive 12–14 hours of light and 10–12 hours of darkness triggers the flowering response.

Watching a plant grow as it transitions from a vegetative growth pattern to flowering is truly a surreal experience. Indoor cannabis plants typically start their vegetative growth cycle with their leaves barely filling out the canopy. When the light cycle is adjusted to a minimum of 10 hours of darkness and 14 hours of light, the plants switch to flowering and the results become very apparent. In the second week of consistent long, uninterrupted dark periods, flowers become visible at the nodes. The third week of production sees an increase in the number of overall flowers.

A ripe Strawberry Bliss cola. Photo: Theo Oldfield

Buds and Colas Are Inflorescences, Not Individual Flowers

What most people see as a single flower in cannabis, which some call a "bud" or "cola," is actually many, many individual flowers grouped together in what is called an **inflorescence**. The term "cola" is the Spanish word for "tail." Large inflorescences of cannabis can resemble a cat's tail sticking straight up in the canopy.

The famous Eagles song "Hotel California" makes a reference to these colas: *"On a dark desert highway / Cool wind in my hair / Warm smell of colitas / Rising up through the air."*

Traditionally, most indoor growers set the flowering cycle at 12 hours on and 12 hours off, but by inducing flowering under a shorter dark period, the plant is given up to an extra 2 hours of light energy that it uses for growth. (*See Flowering.*)

Each cultivar ripens at a different pace. Over the years, breeders have developed new cultivars with unique qualities. Breeders focused on yield, potency, maturation time, and many other characteristics.

Ripening times range from 6 to 10 weeks. About 2 weeks before harvest, the flowers contain the highest percentage of THC. After that point, they add just a little weight and greatly increase their production of terpenes, while THC declines slightly (Potter 2014). The buds get thicker and denser and show an overall increase in biomass. The stigmas, which start off as a white color, transition to a brown or beige color.

What Are Stigmas?

Stigmas are the part of the female flower that capture and collect pollen. Since cannabis is a wind-pollinated plant, the female flowers produce these protrusions that look somewhat like little hairy roots. The "hairiness" enlarges the surface area of the stigmas so they can filter more air and increase the likelihood of capturing a pollen grain.

Many kinds of plants develop trichomes to protect themselves by repelling and catching insects and other herbivores and protecting leaf tissue from excessive light.

It is theorized that one reason cannabis produces trichomes is to protect leaves and flowers from excessive UV light. As the season progresses, the plant begins to grow flowers. As its investment in the flowers increases, the plant becomes more protective, increasing the production and density of trichomes. The plant's most important organs at this point are the female flower and specifically the seed. That is where trichomes are most concentrated.

Cannabis evolved on the Tibetan plateau, which ranges between 4,500 and 5,000 meters (14,800 and 16,400 feet) in altitude. For comparison, the "Mile High" city of Denver, Colorado, sits at 5,280 feet (1,609 meters) in altitude. UV light is much more intense at these altitudes than at sea level, so protecting the flowers' embryos in the developing seeds from excessive UV light is paramount. Many cannabinoids, including THC, absorb UV light.

Top left: Seedling Photo: Ed Rosenthal   **Top right: A rooted clone.** Photo: Dr. Robb Farms
Bottom left: Plant in early flowering. Photo: Ed Rosenthal   **Bottom right: Flowered plant ready to harvest.** Photo: Professor P

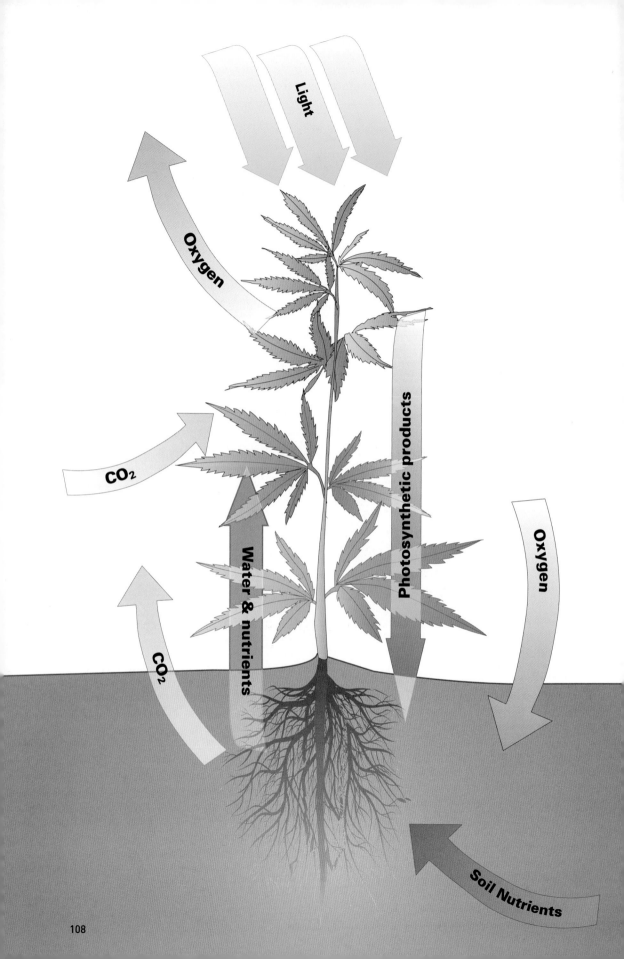

Light

Oxygen

CO₂

Water & nutrients

CO₂

Photosynthetic products

Oxygen

Soil Nutrients

PHOTOSYNTHESIS

Plants make their own food using a complex set of biochemical processes catalyzed by light from the sun or artificial lighting to convert two reactants (water and CO_2) into sugar (glucose) and oxygen, as described in the following equation:

$$6CO_2 + 6H_2O \xrightarrow[\text{Chlorophyll}]{\text{Light}} C_6H_{12}O_6 + O_2$$

Carbon dioxide + Water → Sugar + Oxygen

Glucose is the plant's basic building block. Carbon dioxide and water get converted into glucose and oxygen through the process of photosynthesis. Glucose ($C_6H_{12}O_6$) provides the energy to run the plant's metabolism; grow new tissue, including leaves, roots, and buds; actively absorb nutrients; and create cannabinoids and terpenes. THC is a 21-carbon molecule, and it is the carbon from glucose and thus from CO_2 that goes into building THC.

Leaves evolved to maximize the plant's surface area to collect light energy from the sun to drive photosynthesis. Carbon dioxide is collected from the air through pores on the bottom side of the leaves called **stomata**. These pores are also where the oxygen is released and where water transpires.

Photosynthesis evolved in cyanobacteria (blue-green algae) between 2.5 and 3.5 billion years ago. They evolved photoreceptors that capture light from the sun to use as an energy source. Water is split into its elements, hydrogen and oxygen, through the energy of light. The oxygen is eventually released as oxygen gas. The CO_2, in combination with the hydrogen from water, binds to an already existing sugar and, using a series of reactions, results in glucose. Atmospheric oxygen concentration started at roughly 1% and is now around 21%, the result of carbon mineralization and photosynthesis.

Plants Sweat Too

Plants transpire water from the roots, through the stems, into the leaves, and out the stomatal pores on the underside of the leaves. When the water evaporates (goes from liquid to vapor), it has the same effect as human sweat in cooling the body. This is why if plants do not have enough access to water in the root zone, they can overheat and suffer from heat stress.

In plants, photosynthesis occurs in an **organelle** called the **chloroplast**. Thousands of these organelles reside inside each leaf cell. It is widely accepted in the scientific community that chloroplasts evolved in free-living organisms similar to cyanobacteria. The ancestral "chloroplast" was consumed by its host, which likely was intending to digest it; instead, the two organisms formed a mutually beneficial relationship, where the chloroplast provides sugar to the host cell and the host cell provides protection and nutrients for the chloroplast. This theory is called endosymbiosis.

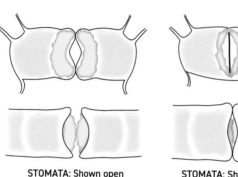

STOMATA: Shown open and cross-section (below)

STOMATA: Shown closed and cross-section (below)

An actual cannabis stoma under extreme magnification. Photo: Ted Kinsman, *Marijuana Under the Microscope* (2018)

Chloroplasts contain a number of photoreceptors. The most widely known is chlorophyll. Photoreceptors are pigments that each absorb different spectra of light and use the light's energy to power an electrical-chemical reaction that transfers energy from light into chemical energy in the form of glucose.

The pigments in plants associated with the chloroplast absorb mostly red and blue light and reflect some green light, which is why most plants have that characteristic green color. The chloroplasts arrange the pigments in large symmetrical protein structures collecting sunlight, analogous to antennas collecting radio signals. These antennas channel the light-excited electrons to a chlorophyll molecule, where the light reactions of photosynthesis occur. Other plant pigments such as carotenoids funnel energy from the light they absorb from other spectrums to drive photosynthesis. (*See Light.*)

Photosynthesis Examined

In 2009, Drs. Suman Chandra, Hemant Lata, Ikhlas Khan, and Mahmoud El-Sohly, research scientists at the University of Mississippi, published a landmark paper in cannabis physiology, "Photosynthetic Response of *Cannabis sativa* L. to Variations in Photosynthetic Photon Flux Densities, Temperature and CO_2 Conditions" (Chandra et al. 2009).

This study laid the groundwork for a better understanding of the whole plant physiology of cannabis. Like the title of the journal article implies, these researchers explored the effects of different light intensities, temperatures, and CO_2 concentrations on the rate of photosynthesis of cannabis.

The scientists grew cannabis under different environmental conditions and measured the photosynthetic rate and stomatal conductance of the plant. Stomatal conductance is the inverse of the resistance of water movement out of the plant's leaves. A high stomatal conductance means that a relatively high amount of water is leaving the plant. Low stomatal conductance means that a low amount of water is leaving the plant.

They discovered that the photosynthetic rate maxed out under very high light conditions (1,500 $\mu mol \cdot m^{-2} \cdot sec^{-1}$) and temperatures between 25 and 30°C (77 and 86°F). Higher light intensities and temperatures had adverse effects on the rate of photosynthesis and water use efficiency (WUE). Once it was determined what light levels and what temperature ranges were optimal for photosynthesis, the scientists explored the effects that different CO_2 concentrations have on the rate of photosynthesis, WUE, and rate of transpiration.

The rate of photosynthesis and WUE decreased by 50% and 53%, respectively, when the ambient CO_2 concentration was decreased to 250 ppm from the ambient level (at the time of publication) of 350 ppm. Increasing the CO_2 levels to 750 ppm resulted in a significant boost in photosynthesis and WUE: 50% and 111%, respectively. The rate of transpiration decreased by 29% at that level of CO_2 when compared with the ambient level. The researchers did not test CO_2 at the higher rate of 1,250 ppm.

This research reveals that cannabis is capable of taking advantage of very high light levels. Ambient CO_2 concentrations become the limiting factor when light intensity continues to increase. Injecting CO_2 into the plant canopy has a beneficial effect on photosynthesis, WUE, and overall plant performance. Cannabis plants close their stomata sooner in response to increased ambient CO_2 concentrations, decreasing the amount of water they need to perform at an optimal level.

Photosynthesis Plus is a complete ecosystem of micro-life in a bottle that promotes plant vigor, reduces the cost of inputs, and increases yield. Photosynthesis Plus enhances plant functions at the foliar level and the root zone in both soil and soilless substrates. It aids in photosynthesis and biological function by allowing plants to capture and utilize radiant energy more efficiently, thus speeding uptake and distribution of essential macro- and micronutrients required for all plant metabolic functions and growth. *Also sold as Photosynthesis Plus C (CA), Plus O (OR), Plus OK (OK), Plus IL (IL)*

The Limiting Factors

Cannabis plants are dependent on their environment for energy and nutrients. There are six essential factors that affect cannabis growth and productivity: light, carbon dioxide, water, oxygen, nutrients, air.

Each of these inputs is required in adequate amounts for photosynthesis and growth. Additionally, the six factors must be available at adequate levels so that the plant's productivity is not limited. If all these factors are adequately available, the crop will live up to its potential. For example, as the intensity of light increases, the plant's ability to utilize it depends on the availability of the other five factors. For this reason, the six factors are called "limiting factors."

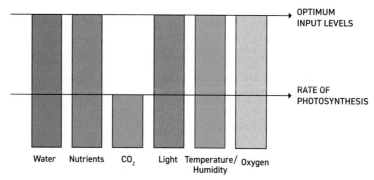

SIX LIMITING FACTORS: NECESSARY COMPONENTS IN PLANT GROWTH

A deficiency of any single factor limits growth to the level that factor supplies. No matter how well other factors are supplied they cannot be utilized. For example, insufficient amounts of CO_2 limit the use of light, water, nutrients and temperature/humidity.

The limiting factor, that is, the factor that is not sufficiently available, determines the rate of growth. Insufficient supplies of any one factor slow or stop growth.

It is unlikely that either water or nutrients are limiting factors for most indoor grows, since they are easily supplied; however, pH of the nutrient solution can affect the plant's ability to absorb nutrients. For example, when the pH of the nutrient solution becomes too alkaline, iron falls out of solution, making it unavailable to the plant's roots.

The metabolic rate of cannabis, or the speed of the cumulative rate of burning sugar to grow and maintain plant tissues, is heavily dependent on the ambient temperature. Animals such as humans are endothermic, "warm-blooded," and are capable of maintaining a steady metabolic rate by controlling their temperature internally. Organisms that do not internally control their temperature are exothermic and rely on environmental temperature to regulate metabolic rate.

Plants are exothermic, meaning they operate like cold-blooded animals. They rely on the external temperature to regulate their metabolic rates. In cooler weather, exothermic organisms such as cannabis function slower and thus grow slower.

CO_2 concentration is most often seen as a limiting factor in indoor cannabis cultivation, especially in indoor cultivation facilities without proper ventilation. Ambient CO_2 concentrations are around 420 ppm (in 2021). As concentrations fall, the photosynthetic rate slows. When it descends to 200 ppm, the plant has difficulty mining it from the air, leading to the cessation of photosynthesis. This is why supplementing the plant's environment with CO_2 is necessary.

Breathing around the plants is effective at increasing the CO_2 concentration; however, it is better to supplement with tanks or generators, which burn natural gas or propane. Filtered air from an enclosed animal shelter or a barn can be an inexpensive source of CO_2. Another source is natural gas-powered appliances such as water heaters, gas stoves, and clothes dryers.

Why Some Cannabis Flowers Are Purple

Purple flowers are a favorite among cannabis aficionados, with a growing list of cultivars available commercially such as Ken's GDP, Purple Haze, Purple Urkle, Sour Grape, Purple Space Cookies, Purple Cheese, Purple Kush, Lavender Jones, Purple Trainwreck, and so many more.

What makes these cultivars turn purple? The answer involves a genetic predisposition. Those cultivars of cannabis are genetically programmed to create a specific group of flavonoids called anthocyanins, which concentrate primarily in the top flowers and leaves.

Some cultivars turn purple from top to bottom, but most purple cultivars focus this "purpling" in the topmost parts of the plant, and there's a very good reason why.

Anthocyanins are pigments found throughout the plant kingdom, and they can range in color from deep purples to blues and reds. The compounds are strong antioxidants. The purpling of cannabis in some cultivars is for protection from too much light. The flowers on top turn the deepest shade of purple, while some shaded flowers remain deep green. The top flowers produce anthocyanins, which absorb some of the light, protecting the photosynthetic apparatuses from damage.

Some cannabis cultivars are just genetically predisposed to produce more anthocyanin than others, so they turn purple no matter what the grower does. Other cultivars turn purple when given the appropriate environmental factors. This is analogous to melanin in the skin of humans. Some people produce more melanin in their skin as regulated by their genetics, and some people will tan after exposure to sunlight. For both humans and cannabis, the production of melanin and anthocyanins is to protect from excessive light exposure.

Some cultivars produce purple flowers given the right environmental conditions. The purpling occurs because photosynthesis slows down under cool conditions, which pushes the plant to produce more anthocyanin.

Maintaining high light intensity while decreasing the temperature is one way cannabis growers can manipulate some cultivars to produce more anthocyanins. Purple cultivars are known to have lower cannabinoid potency. This makes sense because the plant is allocating carbon to produce anthocyanins instead of cannabinoids.

Photo: Dabsel Adams

LIGHT

Revised by Jake Holley, with additional content on design optimization by Joey Ereñeta

Proper lighting is the foundation for productive and healthy plants. Light is important for providing plants with the energy needed for growth while also signaling the way they grow. Many different light sources exist, and properly choosing a source and using light to the best potential is a process that is evolving rapidly. This chapter covers all aspects of light: why it is important and how to make educated and calculated decisions and recommendations about how to purchase and use it.

Properties of Light

Plants use light for different purposes, including growth pattern (photomorphogenesis), growth direction (phototropism), response to day length (photoperiodism), and photosynthesis. Each of these processes significantly affects the growth and productivity of plants.

- **Photomorphogenesis** is a plant's growth patterns in response to light, including leaf size, thickness, distance between leaves (internode length), and branching patterns.
- **Phototropism** describes the preference of a plant to grow and align leaves and chloroplasts to best use light.
- **Photoperiodism** is the response of plants to day length, including control of flowering (Gupta 2017).

The most amazing thing plants do with light is photosynthesis, the process that provides the foundation for most of life on Earth. Plants use photosynthesis to power the process of making sugar ($C_6H_{12}O_6$) from water (H_2O) and carbon dioxide (CO_2). Plants also use photosynthesis to convert the sugars they make into starches and then into complex molecules such as cellulose. Add some nitrogen atoms, and the result is nucleic acids and amino acids, the building blocks of all proteins.

Light Attributes

The three attributes of light are quantity, duration, and quality. Light is both a particle and a wave, and will be referred to in both ways in this chapter.

- Quantity of light is measured in particles and is another way to describe intensity or brightness of light. Providing plants with bright light is critical for healthy plant growth.

- Duration of light is the length of time plants experience light. Light duration is important for allowing the plant to both adequately photosynthesize and signal the plant to flower or stay vegetative.
- Quality, described as a wave, refers to the color of light and can be described by its spectrum. The spectrum of light given to a plant makes a large difference and is an important consideration when purchasing grow lights.

Light Quantity

There are two important ways to measure the quantity of light: instantaneous, which measures how much light is coming in at any given second, and cumulative, or the total amount over the course of a day.

There are several methods to measure instantaneous light, each designed to best describe a different aspect of light. Candela, lumens, lux, and foot-candles all describe how humans perceive the brightness of light. Watts per meter squared ($watts \cdot m^{-2}$) measures the total energy of light.

The most accurate way to describe light for plants is the number, or quanta, of photons. The unit of measurement for this is micromoles per meter squared per second ($\mu mol \cdot m^{-2} \cdot s^{-1}$). An important aspect to note is that these units cannot be easily converted between one another, especially with different spectra of light. For example, red and blue LEDs will have very low values in lux or foot-candles, since they do not contain green light, but they are much higher in $\mu mol \cdot m^{-2} \cdot s^{-1}$ and can be effective for plant growth.

Candela, Lumens, Foot Candle & Lux

The candela (or candle, or candle-power) is the most basic international unit for measuring emitted light and is defined as the illumination created by a common candle. Candela is calibrated for the perception of the human eye, being most sensitive in green and less so in red and blue.

Lumens are derived from this, as a single candela light source that radiates equally in all directions produces exactly 4π (12.6) lumens.

Foot-candles and lux describe the number of lumens per unit area, with foot-candles measuring in lumens per square foot and lux being the metric equivalent, lumens per square meter. These units of measurement are accurate in describing how bright a room or lit street will appear, but do not correlate well with how plants photosynthesize and grow.

Watts per Square Meter (watts/m²)

Watts/m² describes the total amount of light energy and is often used for weather and by the solar energy industry. Shorter wavelengths, like blue, contain higher energies per photon of light in comparison with longer wavelengths like red, and watts/m² accounts for this. Watts/m² is useful to determine how much the ground will heat up for weather prediction or how much power a solar panel will produce. However, since plants use red photons more efficiently in photosynthesis, this measurement is not as accurate for estimating plant growth as micromoles ($\mu mol \cdot m^{-2} \cdot s^{-1}$).

Micromoles ($\mu mol \cdot m^{-2} \cdot s^{-1}$)

The most accurate measurement of light in relation to its usefulness to plants is micromoles per meter squared per second ($\mu mol \cdot m^{-2} \cdot s^{-1}$), often simply referred to as "micromoles" of **photosynthetically active radiation (PAR)**. PAR includes the wavelengths of light from 400–700 nm. Some researchers have proposed that since far-red light affects photosynthesis, PAR should also include wavelengths from 701–750.

Sunlight at noon on a clear early summer day produces about 2,000 $\mu mol \cdot m^{-2} \cdot s^{-1}$ (10,000 fc or about 110,000 lux) at latitude 39° north in Maryland, which lies in a middle latitude of the US. At higher latitudes, the light is weaker; at lower latitudes, it is stronger.

Photosynthetic photon flux (PPF) is the total number of photons ($\mu mol \cdot s^{-1}$) produced by the lighting source. **Photosynthetic photon flux density (PPFD)** measures the density of the photons ($\mu mol \cdot m^{-2} \cdot s^{-1}$) from the light source falling on the canopy over a given time. This measurement most accurately describes light received by plants, since it weighs all photons of light in the PAR spectrum equally, unlike lux. As mentioned earlier, this will be important in later sections because LED lights emit in many wavelengths and cannot be accurately compared with other lighting sources using lux or foot-candle measurements. Since PAR is usually expressed in moles, which measure light quanta (photons), PAR is also called quantum light. Measuring quantum light is the only way to be certain that plants are getting all the usable light they need.

In addition to measurements of instantaneous light, the cumulative total amount of light is important, especially in outdoor or greenhouse settings, where the brightness of sunlight changes throughout the day and seasonally. For indoor setups where the light output is constant, knowing a lamp's intensity at the canopy works well enough because the total for the lit period is easily calculated. But for outside or in greenhouses, an integrated light measurement that measures instantaneous light and adds it up throughout the day is more meaningful, and daily light integral ($DLI/mol \cdot m^{-2} \cdot day^{-1}$) is a common way to express this.

Daily Light Integral (DLI) $mol \cdot m^{-2} \cdot day^{-1}$

Daily light integral (DLI) is quantified in moles per square meter per day ($moles \cdot m^{-2} day^{-1}$), or moles for short, and is a summation of how much light a space receives in a day. To convert $\mu mol \cdot m^{-2} \cdot s^{-1}$ to daily light integrals in $mol \cdot m^{-2} \cdot day^{-1}$, multiply by the number of seconds per hour (3,600) and number of hours of light, and divide by one million. For outdoor measurements, use the average light intensity over the entire day.

$$DLI \ (moles \cdot m^{-2} \cdot day^{-1})$$
$$= \frac{Light \ Intensity \ (\mu mol \cdot m^{-2} \cdot s^{-1}) * 3600 \left(\frac{seconds}{Hour}\right) * \frac{Hours \ of \ Light}{Day}}{1{,}000{,}000 \ \left(\frac{\mu mol}{mole}\right)}$$

For example, if plants are growing indoors with a light that produces 1,000 $\mu mol \cdot m^{-2} \cdot s^{-1}$ for 20 hours per day, that would be 1,000 x 3,600 (seconds in an hour) x 20 hours for 72 $mol \cdot m^{-2} \cdot day^{-1}$.

$$72 \, moles \cdot m^{-2} \cdot day^{-1}$$
$$= \frac{1000 \, \mu mol \cdot m^{-2} \cdot s^{-1} * 3600 \, \frac{seconds}{Hour} * \frac{20 \, Hours}{Day}}{1,000,000 \, \frac{\mu mol}{mole}}$$

For a 12-hour photoperiod, this would be 43.2 $mol \cdot m^{-2} \cdot day^{-1}$.

$$43.2 \, moles \cdot m^{-2} \cdot day^{-1}$$
$$= \frac{1000 \, \mu mol \cdot m^{-2} \cdot s^{-1} * 3600 \, \frac{seconds}{Hour} * \frac{12 \, Hours}{Day}}{1,000,000 \, \frac{\mu mol}{mole}}$$

The DLI for outdoor gardens varies considerably depending on latitude, season, and weather. For example, in the middle latitudes of the US a sunny summer day produces a DLI of roughly 26 moles per day. If it's cloudy, the DLI drops to about 12 moles per day. In midwinter, a sunny day yields a DLI of approximately 9 moles per day, and cloudy conditions reduce that to a mere 3 moles.

Faust DLI maps

DLI changes by season. Fortunately, the changes in DLI by area have been quantified, and there is a great interactive map online to see how much light can be expected outside during any month at any location in the United States (endowment.org/dlimaps/) (Korczynski 2002; Faust and Logan 2018).

The DLI chart shows how much the moles per day change from August through October. In August, the DLI ranges from 35–40 $mol \cdot m^{-2} \cdot day^{-1}$ in the eastern US to 50–55 in the west. In October the patterns change between north and south. The southwest receives 35–40 $mol \cdot m^{-2} \cdot day^{-1}$, but the rest of the country, except for the far north, receives only 20–30 moles per day. In addition to the low light levels, the sun delivers very little UVB light by mid autumn.

Light Duration

The term for the total duration of light a plant experiences in a day is "photoperiod," usually measured in hours. Photoperiod is important, as it both affects how much photosynthesis can be done by the plant and signals to the plant whether to flower.

DLI and Photoperiod

Duration is important to photosynthesis, as plants grow more with a longer photoperiod

Daily Light Integral (mol·m^{-2}·d^{-1})

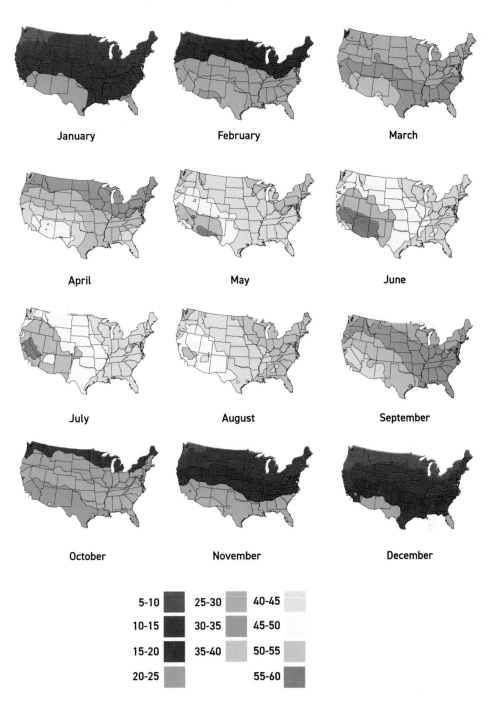

January

February

March

April

May

June

July

August

September

October

November

December

5-10	25-30	40-45
10-15	30-35	45-50
15-20	35-40	50-55
20-25		55-60

This chart shows how much light plants receive daily over the course of a year in the continental United States. During the fall and winter, the amount of light is based mostly on latitude. Light levels drop dramatically in September, just as the plants are ripening. By October, light has dropped in half as compared with June. By December it is down by nearly two-thirds. During the summer light intensity varies more by longitude. For example, the western half of the US receives 50% more light than the eastern half.

if the DLI is consistent (Koontz and Prince 1986). With an equal DLI, lower light for longer times is better than bright light for a shorter time. During vegetative growth, most cultivators use between 16 and 24 hours of light. The plants must not experience a long uninterrupted dark period.

These are tomato plants grown at various photoperiods with the same DLI. Labeled on each pot are two numbers, the photoperiod, ranging from 12 to 24 hours, and the DLI, being 20 across all plants. Data consistently showed an increase in biomass and growth up to 21 hours, then either flattening off or decreasing depending on species. Leafy greens like lettuce were not different between 21 and 24 hours, but plants like tomatoes, cucumbers, and petunias were significantly smaller under 24 hours of light compared with 12 hours. Photo: Jake Holley

Photoperiodism

The cannabis flowering cycle is induced by short days, but the term "short-day" is something of a misnomer: what cannabis needs to flower is a sufficiently long dark period.

Flower Initiation

Most cannabis cultivars (except autoflowering) flower only if they have a daily regimen of dark period that varies tremendously depending on variety. Setting the lights to a 12-hour light and 12-hour dark cycle is most commonly used to induce a strong flowering response. This time period is based on tradition; however, a shorter critical period of darkness can be used. When this critical dark period occurs for five to seven consecutive days, the plant changes its growth from vegetative to flowering.

Photoperiod Interruption

Cannabis is a "short-day plant." It measures the number of hours of *uninterrupted* darkness to determine when to initiate flowering. It does this by constantly producing a group of light-sensitive proteins collectively called **phytochrome**. They are inactivated by red light, which the plants receive all day. When darkness occurs, they become active over about two hours or immediately in the presence of more far-red than red light, which occurs at sundown. When the level of phytochrome reaches a certain level, flowering is induced. Each cultivar has a critical period that is the minimum number of hours of *uninterrupted* darkness that it requires to flower.

Cannabis is sensitive to light during the dark period, and too much light exposure at any time during the flowering cycle negatively impacts, or even inhibits, flowering. Red light (660 nm) most effectively inhibits flowering.

A very low intensity of light, only two micromoles, is required for only a few seconds to interrupt the dark cycle. Think of a water spray that wets all the vegetation. That is the light "spray." The entire plant must be "sprayed" with light, because the flowering reaction is localized. Parts of the plant that are not sprayed will flower, while the sprayed part will be inhibited.

Using this information, gardeners can manipulate when the plants flower outdoors as well as indoors. Indoors, the gardener turns the lights off and blocks all light from the flowering room.

Outdoors, gardeners can use light sprays to prevent flowering.

Light deprivation, covering the plants with an opaque covering so no light reaches them, is used to induce and maintain flowering during periods of short nights such as late spring and summer. (*See Flowering*.)

Beware of using green light: it is not as "safe" as often believed (Baskin and Baskin 1978). Although green light is not as powerful at inhibiting flowering as red, too much green light for too long of a duration does inhibit flowering (Park and Jeong 2019).

If there is a need to do any work or view plants during the dark period, it is important to be brief and to use the least amount of light possible. An occasional green light will not stop the plants from flowering for two reasons:

- The interruption of the dark period preventing flowering must take place each evening (Borthwick and Cathey 1962). An occasional light foray won't stop the flowering process; however, it can reduce yield or slow down maturation time, producing fewer flowers and taking more time to ripen if it occurs frequently.
- Plants are much less sensitive to green than red light, so they won't be affected as much.

Plants are much more affected by light interruption during the first few weeks of flowering than in later stages. Turning on lights during the last weeks of flowering will have far less effect on the process than light pollution during early flowering.

Light Quality

The quality of light is its color, or spectrum. Light spectrum is useful for directing the plant's growth habits, as well as contributing to healthy photosynthesis. Comparing this to a car, if light intensity is the gas pedal to increase speed of photosynthesis, light quality would be the steering wheel. Using different colors of light allows growers to affect the plant in terms of yield, flavor, color, growth, flowering, and even the severity of pests and diseases (Davis and Burns 2016).

Light color, as described in this text, is part of the electromagnetic spectrum that lies between wavelengths of 280 and 800 nanometers (nm) and is influential for plant growth and development. In horticulture, the rainbow of colors is abbreviated to only a few: blue (400–499 nm), green (500–599 nm), and red (600–699 nm). White light is created by combining all wavelengths between 400 nm and 700 nm. Ultraviolet light is between 200 nm and 399 nm, with UVC (200 to 279 nm), UVB (280 to 315 nm), and UVA (315 to 399 nm). In addition, far-red light lies from 700 to 750 nm, although most far-red light sources emit at 730 nm (Both et al. 2017). The reality of defining light by color is far more complex, as wavelengths within a color (425 vs. 450 nm) can affect growth differently, and different wavelengths are also known to have synergistic effects with one another.

Photosynthetically Active Radiation (PAR)

Several defined regions of the spectrum and their associated acronyms are used to describe the wavelengths of light for plant growth, specifically photosynthetically active radiation. PAR defines light that plants can use to gain energy for photosynthesis, from 400 nm (blue) to 700 nm (red), although wavelengths of light up to 752 nm can still positively affect photosynthesis (Cathey 1980; Sager 1984; Hogewoning et al. 2012; Zhen et al. 2019). Light from 280–399 nm and 700–750 nm can elicit responses in plants, such as the production of terpenes and cannabinoids, or affect flowering, while not necessarily contributing to photosynthesis. These wavelengths are sometimes included in a wider spectral range than PAR, which is referred to as photo-biologically active radiation (PBAR) because the wavelengths can affect more than just photosynthesis. Understanding the differences in light spectra and the effect they have on plants can help the careful cultivator ensure that the plants are getting everything they need to thrive.

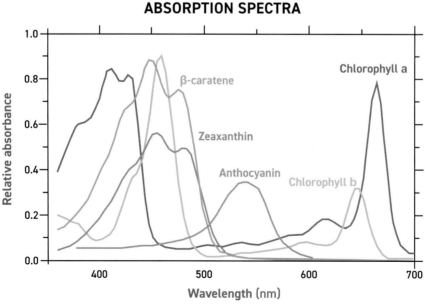

This chart represents relative absorbance of various plant pigments across the spectrum of photosynthetically active radiation. These pigments primarily absorb light in the blue and red spectra, however there is still absorbance in the green/yellow/orange spectra that also drives photosynthesis.

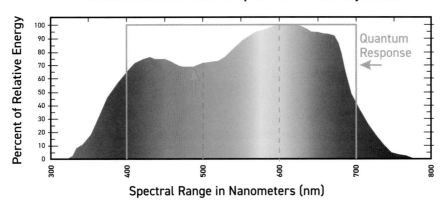

THE MCCREE CURVE - Active Spectrum of Photosynthesis

Y-axis: Percent of Relative Energy
X-axis: Spectral Range in Nanometers (nm)
Label: Quantum Response

The McCree Curve depicts the photosynthetic quantum efficiency across the spectrum of photosynthetically active radiation. It shows a plant's real world photosynthetic efficiencies. This curve provides insight when designing spectral output from artificial lighting. SOURCE: Smart Grow Technologies

Light Spectrum Effects

White (400–700 nm)
White light is a combination of all wavelengths of visible light, sometimes referred to as broad spectrum. The sun emits white light, and plants have evolved to use this light effectively. Since plants have evolved to use a broad spectrum of light, they require some variation in light color for healthy, optimal growth.

Red (600–699 nm)
Red light is the most effective light for promoting photosynthesis (McCree 1971). Plant lighting favoring high ratios of red light grows plants more effectively than other spectra of light; however, it is not an effective light to use by itself (Massa et al. 2008; Hernandez et al. 2016).

Far-Red (700–750 nm)
Far-red light has important implications for photosynthesis, photomorphogenesis, and flower induction in plants. Far-red light increases the photosynthetic rate of other light sources in a synergistic way that is more than the addition of these light sources independently, despite being outside the PAR range (Zhen and van Iersel 2017; Hogewoning et al. 2012). In addition, far-red light has also been shown to be beneficial for inducing flowering responses in short-day plants (Cathey and Borthwick 1957).

Red to Far-Red Ratio
One of the best-known spectral effects comes from the ratio of red to far-red light. A low ratio (i.e., high amounts of far-red light) causes plants to stretch and leaves to expand. Using incandescent bulbs for night interruption will cause plants to stretch for this reason. Having a high ratio of red to far-red light will help keep plants stout (Franklin 2008). Using

far-red at the start of the dark period in an attempt to promote flowering causes stretching and taller plants (Lund 2007).

Phytochrome

The main active photoreceptors for red light are phytochromes. Phytochromes come in two interchangeable forms: "red absorbing" P_r and "far-red absorbing" P_{fr}. If P_r absorbs light, it will shift to P_{fr} and vice versa. Although P_r absorbs most strongly at 660 nm and P_{fr} absorbs most strongly at 730 nm, both states absorb some light anywhere from 300 nm to at least 750 nm (Butler et al. 1964; Stutte 2009). Phytochromes can be induced to P_{fr} with green and yellow wavelengths (Shinomura et al.1996; Wang and Folta 2013). The balance of P_r to P_{fr} is known as the phytochrome photostationary state (PSS) and is altered anytime light is present. This is important for some of the differences in growth habits observed with different spectra. In addition to absorbing light, P_{fr} will naturally transition to P_r in darkness, and this forms the basis of dark periods being required for flowering (Borthwick and Cathey 1962).

Blue (400–499 nm)

Blue light has been shown to be critical for producing healthy plants, as chlorophyll development needs blue light and will not properly occur under only red light (Massa 2008). High ratios of blue light help keep plants stout (Hernandez 2016a, 2016b). In addition, blue light helps induce secondary metabolite production similar to having a higher light intensity (Hogewoning 2010). Although research has not been validated with cannabis, more blue light may increase THC and CBD production.

Cryptochromes, Phototropins & Light-Oxygen-Voltage Sensors

Blue light is effective for promoting photosynthesis while also activating a myriad of critical photoreceptors, including cryptochromes, phototropins, and light-oxygen-voltage sensors (LOV). These photoreceptors are important for chloroplast development, stomatal opening, circadian rhythm, and secondary metabolite production (Cashmore 1999; Ouzounis 2015; Pocock 2015; Kopsel et al. 2015).

Green (500–599 nm)

The perception and use of green light by plants is a commonly misunderstood topic. Photosynthesis driven by absorbing green light is almost as efficient as blue light and may in fact contribute more to full-plant photosynthesis, as it has greater leaf and canopy penetration than red and blue light (McCree 1972; Smith et al. 2017). There is even a green-light-specific photoreceptor theorized to exist (Pocock 2015; Mccoshum and Kiss 2011; Folta and Carvalho 2015; Zhang and Folta 2012). Green light is not wasted light, or invisible to plants, and plays an important role in both photosynthesis and signal transduction in plants.

Somewhere over the Rainbow: The Argument to Include Far-Red in PAR

The electromagnetic spectrum is the range of frequencies of electromagnetic radiation, from the high-energy, short-wavelength, ionizing radiation in gamma rays to low-energy, long-wavelength radio waves. There is a range in the spectrum where the wavelengths are between 400 and 700 nm that is especially important to plants. The radiation within this range is called photosynthetically active radiation (PAR). Radiation with a wavelength at 400 nm is blue light, whereas at 700 nm, it is red. Everything in between is part of the visible spectrum of light, seen when sunlight shines through mist or rain as a rainbow.

PAR is also the range of light that plants can absorb for photosynthesis; however, chlorophyll primarily absorbs red and blue light. Historically, chlorophyll's absorption spectrum was measured by extracting chlorophyll from a leaf using specific solvents and then passing visible light through a solution of the extracted pigment. This does not mean that accessory pigments are not absorbing other colors in the PAR spectrum. Plants reflect a lot of green light, which is why leaves appear to be green, but they also utilize green light to drive photosynthesis quite efficiently (Terashim et al. 2009).

In 2020, Drs. Shuyang Zhen and Bruce Bugbee published two papers that suggest PAR may need to be extended to include more than just light within the 400-700 nm range (Zhen & Bugbee 2020). Far-red light (700-750 nm) is just above the PAR spectrum.

Historically, plant scientists have described far-red light as integral to regulating photoperiodism in plants such as cannabis, but not as part of the spectrum that drives photosynthesis. This new research suggests that this may not be the case. Drs. Zhen and Bugbee designed experiments to measure photosynthetic rates in various crops when provided with PAR or PAR with far-red light. The treatment with the far-red light produced an increase in photosynthesis equivalent to providing extra light in the 400–700 nm spectrum. Far-red light alone increased photosynthesis, but only minimally. This suggests that far-red light, when paired with light in the 400–700 nm range, is just as effective at driving photosynthesis as PAR.

Far-red light increases the rate of photosynthesis, but does that translate into increased yields? Drs. Zhen and Bugbee tested that as well with lettuce. They treated lettuce with lights within historic PAR range and then others with PAR plus far-red. The PAR plus far-red had 15% more far-red added and 15% PAR removed, so the treatments had the same light intensity. Treatment with far-red light increased net photosynthesis and carbon capture, and increased yield by 29–31%.

UVA & UVB

UVA light is at the wavelength of the invisible portion of emissions from blacklights. It helps reverse damage done to plant DNA by UVB light.

UVB light affects the potency of high-quality plants. The amount of cannabinoids and terpenes that a plant produces increases as it receives more UVB light. This light can be provided to indoor plants with proper lighting. Outdoors, the amount of UVB light is highest at the beginning of summer and begins to decline in late summer, depending on the latitude. By early fall, the amount is a fraction of summer levels. (For more information on using UVB light to increase potency, *see Flowering*.) In humans, UVB causes tanning and sunburn.

UVR8

UV sensing by plants is governed by the UVR8 photoreceptor. This receptor has been linked to the reactions seen with UV light, including pigmentation, leaf expansion, and tolerance to UV-B light (Jenkins 2014). Activation of UVR8 stimulates the production of terpenes, anthocyanin, and other flavonoids (Folta and Carvalho 2015).

The weather app on iPhones provides UV level readings on a scale of 1-11+.

Other Light-Capturing Plant Pigments

Chlorophyll

For photosynthesis, light energy is captured by chlorophylls A and B, primarily from the red and blue portion of the spectrum. Light absorption by chlorophyll A peaks at 430 nm in the blue band and 663 nm in the red, and chlorophyll B peaks at 453 nm in the blue and 642 nm in the orange-red bands. Total chlorophyll absorbance peaks at 435 nm and 445 nm in the blue spectrum and 640 and 675 nm in the red wavelengths. Although chlorophyll is not the only plant pigment that absorbs light to drive photosynthesis, it is the pigment most closely related to the plant's photosystems. Thus, supplemental and indoor lighting designers have focused much of their energy on these specific wavelengths, which is why purple LEDs are abundant in the industry. This is not necessarily the best path, especially since there are other pigments that absorb light in different spectra and also drive photosynthesis.

Carotenoids

Chlorophyll is not the only light-sensitive part of the plant. Carotenoids are a group of orange pigments that capture light in the blue portion of the spectrum, at about 448 nm in the blue spectrum and 475 nm in the blue-green range. Carotenoids not only contribute to photosynthesis but also protect the chlorophyll from excess light that could have destructive effects.

When a photon is absorbed by a chlorophyll, carotenoid, or another light-harvesting molecule, its energy is transferred to an electron and it ceases to exist. Several things can happen to this excited electron. The energy absorbed can be lost either as heat, when the excited electron drops back to its ground state, or as light, causing fluorescence at longer wavelengths. Most important, it can be transferred to another molecule nearby, causing a chemical reaction that results in photosynthesis.

Other Pigments Related to Light

Anthocyanin and other flavonoid pigments absorb blue and UV light to protect chlorophyll from photo-destruction. Another pigment that appears to play a role in plant health is xanthophyll. This yellow pigment captures light in the range from 400–530 nm, violet (400–450 nm), blue (450–490 nm), and cyan (490–520 nm), but is usually hidden from human view by the green of chlorophyll. If a leaf loses its chlorophyll—because of a nitrogen deficiency, for instance—xanthophyll's bright yellow color becomes apparent.

Xanthophyll has several functions. First, it acts as a light and heat regulator. At dawn, it is in its low-energy form, violaxanthin, which has peak reactions to light at 480 and 648 nm. As the light increases to levels that might hurt the thylakoids and lead to photo-oxidation of the chlorophyll molecules, violaxanthin siphons off the photons, excess energy of using them to create its high-energy form, zeaxanthin. When light intensity decreases, the zeaxanthin returns to its low-energy state, violaxanthin, in a cycle that can take anywhere from a few minutes to several hours.

These chemical processes enable plants to cool themselves during lighted periods and stay warm during cool nights. Plants bank energy during the day and release it at night by shifting xanthophyll to its low-energy form, releasing heat. During the day, some of the light energy may also be transferred to chlorophyll by releasing an electron to be used for photosynthesis. Other plant pigments also gather energy from spectrums not used by chlorophyll. Neoxanthin, lutein, and zeaxanthin each transfer more than half the energy they gather to chlorophyll.

Light Meters

Most growers have not used a light meter because they have grown great gardens with excellent buds just by calculating the wattage input of the lights used. However, light meters are used to identify "hot spots" and dimmer areas of the garden, providing readings on how much light the plants are receiving and have received cumulatively. Light meters are well worth the investment because the information provided can be used to determine "hot" or dim spots so that the space is lit evenly, to control supplemental lighting, and to use energy most efficiently. Some models use phone apps. Rather than estimate the light reaching the garden, the meters provide an accurate reading.

A light "hot spot" is a localized area in the plant canopy that is getting significantly higher light intensity than surrounding areas. This is especially undesirable in large canopies, as it disrupts canopy uniformity.

Purchasing a Quantum Sensor

Many different tools can be used to measure light, but quantum sensors that accurately measure light can be difficult to find. Although quantum sensors can be more expensive than other lux and foot-candle meters, they are the most accurate and reliable tool to use to ensure that the plants are getting enough light and that it is evenly distributed. The main companies producing quantum sensors are LI-COR and Apogee. LI-COR is known for its accuracy and has an unrivaled history of producing quality plant-measuring tools, but it's more expensive and less user-friendly than Apogee. Apogee Full Spectrum quantum sensors are an excellent alternative that can interface with laptop computers easily via USB and free software, and can be used to log data without any additional equipment. In addition, they are easy to recalibrate using the Clear Sky Calculator website, ensuring years of quality use. For serious growers, these are a must-have for determining the life of fixtures and checking for dead spots. The record-keeping capability can ensure that the timers are functioning properly.

Apogee's MQ-500 is a full-spectrum Quantum PAR meter that accurately measures the photosynthetically active radiation of all grow lights, including LEDs, with a spectral range of 389 to 692 nm ± 5 nm.

Properly Lighting Plants

Cultivar Light Recommendations

Proper plant light is based on the variety being cultivated. Here are the general lighting requirements on different lines of cultivars.

Sativas require the most light because they evolved near the equator, between the 30th parallels, and are adapted to long periods of intense sun. They are followed by sativa-indica hybrids, indica-sativa hybrids, then indicas. Sativa-indica hybrids need less intense light than sativas, but still do best in more intense light. Indica-sativa hybrids are more light forgiving than sativa-based plants. They can function in the mid-to-low light range. Indicas need the least intense light of any of the varieties. They evolved at the 35th parallel in the Tibetan plateau and are the best bet for lower-light gardens.

Minimum Light Requirements for Indoor Cultivation

During the vegetative growth cycle, most varieties will do well with a minimum of 400–

Apogee's DLI-500 can spot-measure PAR levels and also log and display the daily light integral for the current day and last seven days. It also records and displays the photoperiod in hours of light that the area received each day.

500 $\mu mol \cdot m^{-2} \cdot s^{-1}$ (2,000–2,500 fc, 21,500–27,000 lux), although, with long-length photoperiods, the plants can efficiently use 1,000 $\mu mol \cdot m^{-2} \cdot s^{-1}$ (5,000fc, 54,000 lux) or more. The more total light (DLI) they receive during vegetative growth, the faster their growth and the sturdier their stems. When grown under low light, under a leafy canopy, or when shaded by trees or other tall plants, all varieties develop long internodes (spaces on the stem between the leaves) due to the enhanced far-red light. Plants with equatorial genetics are more affected by this.

During the flowering cycle, equatorial sativas need intense light and a minimum of 800–1,000 $\mu mol \cdot m^{-2} \cdot s^{-1}$. With less light, the buds will be loose and lanky. Sativa-dominant hybrids require bright light. They will produce luscious buds when illuminated with as little as 700–800 $\mu mol \cdot m^{-2} \cdot s^{-1}$. Indica-dominant hybrids require less light and can produce well using a minimum of about 600–700 $\mu mol \cdot m^{-2} \cdot s$-1. Indicas need the least amount of light to thrive. Some indicas produce well starting at about 550 $\mu mol \cdot m^{-2} \cdot s$-1, though others need higher levels to produce nice, tight buds. With more light (800 $\mu mol \cdot m^{-2} \cdot s^{-1}$), the indica and indica-dominant hybrid buds will be larger, tighter, and more potent.

Outdoor Growing

Why Use the Sun?

The best source of light is the sun. It requires no electricity or expense. During the summer, the sun is brighter during parts of the day than indoor lighting and is self-regulating. Outdoors, on a clear day at the beginning of summer, when sunlight hits Earth at the most direct angle, the light's intensity can reach upward of 2,000 $\mu mol \cdot m^{-2} \cdot s^{-1}$ (15,000 fc, or 161,000 lux) at noon, the brightest part of the day. Plants may not be able to process all the light at its peak, since cannabis plants are probably not able to use more than 1,500 $\mu mol \cdot m^{-2} \cdot s^{-1}$ (7,000–7,500 fc, or 75,000–80,000 lux). Only about 50% of sunlight is PAR (Boyle 2004). The rest of the light spectrum is not used by plants. The excess light is converted into heat and then dissipated through transpiration, reradiated as infrared heat, or dissipated using biochemical processes.

Cannabis plants do best under full light all day. Gardeners can use the sun as the primary source of light if they have a garden, greenhouse, terrace, patio, roof, skylights, or even a directly lit window. Bright spaces that are lit from unobstructed sunlight at least five hours a day usually need no supplemental light during the summer.

Autumn light can be more problematic. If the garden continues to receive direct sunlight, there is usually enough light for the buds to mature. However, if the direction of the light changes in the fall so that the plants get little direct sun, they will need artificial light to supplement the weak sunlight, overcast conditions, and oblique angles that create shadows. Without the additional light, buds do not develop properly. They grow loose and airy and are not particularly potent. Natural light can be supplemented using the same kinds of lights used for indoor production.

Checking Adequate Sunlight

To find out exactly how much light plants are getting, use a light meter. If the garden receives a minimum of 900 µmol·m^{-2}·s^{-1} (4,500 fc, or 48,375 lux) of light for five hours or more, the space is bright enough for a moderate harvest. Lower light levels result in less growth, slower ripening, and lower yield and quality. The converse is also true.

Cultivar Choice

In higher latitudes, plants must be harvested early in the fall to accommodate climatic conditions. This is due to the natural lengthening of darkness to the threshold to induce flowering. Unfortunately during autumn, when the plants are finishing flower growth and ripening, both the length and intensity of light diminishes, which reduces yield potential. There are three possible solutions: grow early-maturing or autoflowering plants, force the plants to flower early, or supplement the sunlight with electric lighting.

Supplementing Natural Light in Autumn

One rule of thumb is to supplement autumn's low light levels to a minimum of 900 µmol·m^{-2}·s^{-1} for at least five hours a day during daylight. White LEDs or CMH lamps can be used safely. Both light sources supply heat to the plants, which can be helpful in autumn.

Greenhouses

Greenhouses provide a middle ground between outdoor and indoor production. Many allow for year-round production in any climate, yet take advantage of natural sunlight. Others extend the growing season. This is extremely beneficial, as one of the largest single costs of indoor production is electricity to run lights. Greenhouses are still affected by season, and proper lighting controls should be used to both reduce electricity consumption and produce consistent, quality products.

Greenhouses benefit from three systems to control light: blackout curtains, shade cloth, and supplemental lighting.

Blackout curtains are opaque curtains used to block all light to allow for the necessary dark period for flowering during the long days of late spring to late summer. Blackout curtains can be pulled manually or using an automated, motorized system. They are closed and opened at the same time each day to block natural sunlight and lengthen the dark period.

Shade curtains are necessary with crops that can be scorched by sunlight. Although cannabis grows well under full sun, shade cloth can be used to acclimate young plants started indoors and to reduce temperature in summer.

With cannabis they are used only on the hottest days, when other systems are inadequate to handle the heat load. Supplemental light using LEDs or high intensity discharge (HID) lamps such as high pressure sodium (HPS) and ceramic metal halide (CMH) is necessary for consistent, year-round production in all climates. They can be used to supplement natural sunlight on cloudy days or seasonally. They can also be used to break up the dark period to delay flowering during long nights.

The most sophisticated greenhouses contain all three systems working together to produce the most consistent crops.

Light inside a Greenhouse

Despite being covered in glass or other clear glazing materials, greenhouses reduce the amount of sunlight reaching crops anywhere between 10 and 50%. Even if the outdoor sunlight provides a DLI of 60 $mol·m^{-2}·day^{-1}$, inside the greenhouse may only receive a DLI of 30 $mol·m^{-2}·day^{-1}$. During winter months, especially at higher latitudes, supplemental lighting will be necessary for healthy plant growth.

Proper Lighting Intensity

Supplemental lighting has been common in vegetable and floriculture greenhouses for several decades. Typical intensities of supplemental lighting in these greenhouses are between 100 and 200 $μmol·m^{-2}·s^{-1}$. In greenhouses growing cannabis, the most important time to provide supplemental light is during flowering, which is often limited to just a 12-hour photoperiod. This has pushed many growers to install lighting intensities of 300 to 400+ $μmol·m^{-2}·s^{-1}$, which provides an additional 13–17 $mol·m^{-2}·day^{-1}$ of light. This is especially important in higher latitudes, where natural lighting may provide only 5–10 $mol·m^{-2}·day^{-1}$ of light on the darkest days of winter. Since lights are one of the largest purchases a greenhouse owner will make, it is important to understand the climate, electrical costs, and expectations of production to make the best decision on light intensity.

Seasonal & Daily Differences

Perhaps the largest challenge to greenhouse lighting is the variable nature of sunlight. Seasonally, the amount of sunlight increases during summer, with longer days where the sun is higher in the sky, while the winter experiences short days, with the sun's zenith much lower. Seasonal impacts should not be underestimated. During the winter or on cloudy days, DLI values can be less than half, compared with a sunny summer day. This is especially true in higher latitudes such as Canada, Tasmania, and New Zealand.

In addition, weather affects light intensity on any given day, often more so than seasons. Days with complete cloud cover in the summer often have lower DLIs than bright sunny days in the winter. With the goal of consistent production, greenhouses need to be equipped with a light control system that measures and responds to light-intensity changes throughout each day.

Controlling Greenhouse Lighting

Greenhouses are best maintained through control systems to manage all aspects of the growing environment. Lighting control systems come in three forms: time clock, threshold control, and sophisticated computer-controlled systems.

Time clock systems run the same as in indoor production: circuits are wired to be powered on and off based on an internal clock. Lights turn on and off at the same time every day. These systems are good to have as a backup when plants are flowering, but they may not take into account season or weather and need to be adjusted based on the time of year and daily sunlight to properly light plants without wasting power. More sophisticated controllers use sensors to control lighting. If not automated, timers must be adjusted manually to prevent both overlighting and underlighting.

Threshold control offers a step up in control in comparison with time clock systems. Threshold incorporates timer control to set a photoperiod while monitoring the incidental sunlight to turn lights on and off. If sunlight is below a preset intensity decided by the grower, lights turn on; if sunlight is above that intensity, lights turn off. This is a step above time clock systems because lights automatically turn on and off based on the current weather. Better threshold systems track DLI through changing seasons and weather conditions.

There are many greenhouse control systems available that maintain a consistent DLI within set photoperiods. Some also control CO_2 and take electric rates into account to provide the cheapest and most consistent growing environment possible given seasonal variability and weather. Some computer-controlled systems have the goal of never needing to be adjusted, making them "set it and forget it" tools.

The level of lighting and control utilized depends on the location, size, and level of investment of the greenhouse. Small, backyard greenhouses can be run automatically with lights on a timer, an air conditioner or ventilation system, heater, humidifier, and dehumidifier, all set by thresholds, and watered using either automated irrigation or a passive system. Adding a blackout curtain and shade cloth increases the flexibility of the greenhouse.

Using Artificial Light in Windows & Terraces

During autumn, gardens in windows and on terraces may receive direct light, as the light comes from a more oblique angle. Sometimes window spaces that are shaded in the summer get direct light in the fall as the sun's angle changes seasonally. If the plants receive direct sunlight, they are probably getting enough light. If plants get only indirect light, even bright light, they require supplemental lighting. Using artificial lights to supply light to plants on a patio or terrace, or in a greenhouse or a window, need not cause suspicion. Use a ceramic metal halide (CMH) lamp or white LED, which both emit a clear light that blends in with natural light. High-powered LED security lights may be a solution for backyard gardens.

Indoors

Plants in indoor gardens require very bright light to grow well and yield a good crop. However, cultivars differ in the amount of light they require to support fast growth and high-performance flower development.

Gardeners have a wide selection of lights to choose from. These include LEDs, fluorescents, ceramic metal halide, and high-pressure sodium lamps. Growers rarely use incandescent or quartz halogen lights. These lamps are inefficient, converting only about 10 to 20% of the energy they use to light while wasting the rest by creating heat.

The recommendation table and next section help a grower decide how many lights are needed to grow an average hybrid indoors. Once the lights are set up and running on timers, no more thought may be needed for indoor gardens in terms of lighting.

	Intensity			Duration
	Fair	**Better**	**Ideal**	
Seedling + Vegetative	400 µmol·m^{-2}·s^{-1}	500 µmol·m^{-2}·s^{-1}	600 µmol·m^{-2}·s^{-1}	18–24 hours
Flowering	500 µmol·m^{-2}·s^{-1}	750 µmol·m^{-2}·s^{-1}	1,000 µmol·m^{-2}·s^{-1}	12–14 hours
Mother	400 µmol·m^{-2}·s^{-1}	500 µmol·m^{-2}·s^{-1}	600 µmol·m^{-2}·s^{-1}	18+ hours
Cuttings	100 µmol·m^{-2}·s^{-1}	150 µmol·m^{-2}·s^{-1}	200 µmol·m^{-2}·s^{-1}	24 hours

Cultivar-Specific DLI Requirements

Optimal PPFD and DLI requirements vary by cultivar and stage of development. Despite evolutionary adaptations to high- or low-light environments, most hybrid cultivars grown indoors under consistent light intensity optimize illumination around 1,000 PPFD (µmol m^{-2} s^{-1}).

Excessive light saturation can lead to photo-inhibition (reduced photosynthesis) and photo-oxidative stress, which causes damage to chloroplasts, plant pigments, lipids, proteins, and nucleic acids, and can lead to suboptimal CO_2 assimilation rates (Pintó-Marijuan and Munné-Bosch 2014).

Determining the optimal light levels for each cultivar may require some trials. Start with the genetic lineage of each variety and then examine its phenotypical and morphological expressions. Adjust light levels and monitor for growth response and any signs of stress, including chlorosis or leaf burn.

Most commercial cultivars are highly hybridized, so their "native" genetic lineage is less indicative of their light needs than morphological growth traits. Wide-leaf varieties tend to have darker green coloration due to a higher concentration of chlorophyll. These traits indicate a higher photosynthetic efficiency and lower PPFD and DLI requirements. Thin-leaf varieties tend to have a lighter green coloration, indicating lower chlorophyll density. This may lead to lower photosynthetic efficiency and higher PPFD and DLI requirements.

Optimal Indoor Light Conditions

Growth Stage	# of Weeks	PPFD	Photoperiod	Average DLI
Stem Cuttings	2	150–200	24	13–17
Transition	1	200–400	18	13–26
Seedlings & Vegetative	2–3	400–600	18	26–39
Early Flowering	1–2	600–800	12	26–35
Mid-Flowering	4–6	800–1,000	12	35–43
Late Flowering	1	600–800	12	26–35
Ripening	1	500–600	12	22–26

This is an example of how PPFD and DLI might be adjusted weekly throughout the life cycle of many hybrid cultivars. Other light formulas vary from these recommendations. These higher levels of illumination require all other conditions for growth to be optimized. (*See The Limiting Factors.*) These light intensities can be achieved by using dimmable LEDs. HID lights have deleterious spectrum changes when dimmed.

Lighting Design

To calculate lighting design, the light-intensity goal (PPFD) is determined based on the DLI and photoperiod requirements of the cultivar in each cultivation zone. The amount of canopy to be illuminated determines the number and strength of lights needed to achieve this goal based on the lamps' wattage and efficacy.

Each lamp's or fixture's horticultural light intensity is rated in photosynthetic photon flux (PPF), or the total number of PAR photons emitted by the fixture. When the concentration of PAR photons from the lights is measured in a certain area of the canopy, lighting can be optimized based on the PPFD goal.

By adjusting the height and spacing of the lights, the PPFD is adjusted, because the photons are spread apart or concentrated, decreasing or increasing the density of the finite number of photons received by the plant canopy. Once the light spacing and height is established, light controllers are used to dim or ramp up the light intensity for the particular cultivars in each zone.

The height of the lights has less impact in larger spaces. In a large space with good light reflectors, virtually all the light gets to the garden. Although the density from an individual light decreases over a given area, as the height increases, the cumulative density of all the lights remains the same because almost all the photons reach the canopy. The cross illumination achieved with higher mounting height also creates a more uniform light intensity across the canopy, minimizing illumination "peaks and valleys." This is why it is common for large grow rooms to utilize a high-bay lighting design. In smaller gardens more of the light strays outside the garden's perimeter.

Unless the light is directed back by reflective material, it is lost to the canopy.

Different lighting technologies have different efficiencies at converting electricity (electrons) into light (photons). Calculating the power draw of the fixture (wattage) versus the output of the lamp (PPF) is essential to choosing the right light. Using the PPF rating of the lights, the number of lamps required and their configuration can be determined.

The PPFD goal for each cultivation zone is dictated by the DLI requirements of the cultivars being grown, the stage of growth, and photoperiod provided.

Area is calculated by multiplying length and width of the space. For example, in a cultivation zone with dimensions of 12 by 8 feet (3.6 x 2.4 m), the total area of the canopy is 96 square feet (9 m^2).

12 x 8 feet (3.6 x 2.4 m) = 96 square feet (9 m^2) = total area

It will vary by application and cultivar, but the goal is to provide approximately 1,000 μmol m^{-2} s^{-1} PPFD of lighting in a flowering room. To determine the total lighting (PPF) requirements for the space, the total canopy square footage is converted to square meters and multiplied by the PPFD target.

9 m^2 x ~1,000 μmol m^{-2} s^{-1} = ~9,000 μmol s^{-1} = approximate lighting goal in PPF

Lighting fixtures are rated in PPF. After calculating the total PPF lighting needs for the canopy (~9,000 μmol s^{-1}), choose from available lighting options to create a configuration that will achieve or exceed the light-density goal of the cultivars in that zone, and then spread the lights evenly over that canopy area.

In this example, six 631-watt LED fixtures rated at a PPF of 1,550 μmol s^{-1} would provide ~9,300 μmol s^{-1}. Or, four double-ended HPS fixtures (1150 watts), each rated at a PPF of 2,400 μmol s^{-1}, provide ~9,600 μmol s^{-1}. This slightly exceeds the calculated PPF target. The LEDs can be adjusted down using a light control module. The HPS lamps' spectrum will change adversely when they are dimmed. Placing the six LED fixtures in two rows of three lights per row, or the HPS fixtures in two rows of two lights per row, will provide the best coverage across the 12 by 8 foot (2.6 x 2.4 m) canopy, slightly exceeding the 1,000 μmol m^{-2} s^{-1} PPFD target.

This approach can be used to measure and convert an area of any size of plant canopy into a lighting goal. Use the highest-desired PPFD, measure the canopy to be illuminated, and calculate the total PPF required for that space. Then, using the rated intensity output (PPF) of various lighting solutions, create a lighting design (lighting fixture type and how many rows/lights per row) that will properly and evenly illuminate the canopy. It doesn't always work out perfectly, so it is common to slightly oversize canopy illumination potential. With LEDs, use light controllers to adjust intensity based on the plants' needs. With HIDs, adjusting light is more complex. With high bays, it is best to shut off a percentage of lights instead of dimming. Another solution is to give the plants a little more light than originally planned.

Choosing a Light

All electrical work should be permitted and done only by licensed electricians. Input voltage (volts), current (amperage, or amps for short), and power consumption (wattage) are important factors for selecting a light source. Most household voltages operate around 120 volts; however, there are often outlets to 240 volts for appliances that require more power. Greenhouses and industrial warehouses may have access to 277 or higher voltage. The advantage of higher voltages is better electrical efficiency. When buying lights, ensure the voltage matches the available power service, as lights manufactured in Europe or Japan may not run using lower than 200 volts. (*See Electricity Basics.*)

The amperage of lights is an important factor to consider when determining how to set up multiple lights. For example, many home circuit breakers operate on a 20-amp limit on a 120-volt circuit. For safety consideration, the circuit should only be run continuously at 80% capacity, meaning only 16 amps of power should be run. This places the safe limit on a single circuit at 1,920 watts, which wouldn't even allow for two 1,000-watt fixtures. As mentioned before, if the lamps were to run at 240 volts, a 20-amp circuit would allow for double the wattage capacity of a 120-volt circuit.

The next factor to consider is the wattage, or overall power draw of the light. Higher wattages result in brighter lights. For instance, a 1,000-watt HPS produces more than double the light of a 400-watt HPS.

The last important factor to consider is the efficacy of the lighting source. For lights, the term "efficacy" is used instead of "efficiency," although they mean similar things. **Efficiency** is measured as a percentage, while efficacy is an independent value. For example, an LED may have an efficiency converting energy to light of 40%, and the efficacy may be 3.0 μmols/J. Despite these values being two ways to describe how much energy is needed to create light, efficacy allows for more direct calculations to estimate lighting.

The measure of lighting efficacy for plant use is μmols/J. This measures the lighting output (μmols of PAR photons, or PPF) and the power required to make the light (J, joules, or watt·second). Some lighting manufacturers will list this as μmols/watt; however, μmols/J is the most correct unit. A higher μmol/J rating produces more light with the same power.

Different lighting technologies (LED, fluorescent, HID) have various efficacies, and not all lighting within the same technology has equal efficacy (some LED fixtures are more efficacious than others). If the power of μmol/J and the footprint of a lighting fixture is known, an estimate (with some error due to light escaping or diminishing due to reflectance) of the light intensity of the grow area can be made.

Calculating Average Light Intensity (PPFD)

$Average\ light\ intensity\ (\mu mol \cdot m^{-2} \cdot s^{-1})$
$$= \frac{Number\ of\ lights \cdot fixture\ power\ draw\ (watts) \cdot efficacy\ (\mu mols/J)}{lighting\ footprint\ or\ area\ (m^2)}$$

If there is one light fixture that operates at 1,000 watts with an efficacy of 2.0 μmols/J, it will produce 2,000 μmols·s^{-1}. If this fixture lights four square meters (43 ft^2), it would light the space at an average intensity of 500 μmol·m^{-2}·s^{-1}. Again, this is only an estimate, as some light will be lost, so the actual intensity will be lower and the hang height of a fixture and optics will affect the lighting footprint. Reflectors help reduce light loss and make this calculation more accurate. Larger areas and more fixtures also improve accuracy.

$$\frac{1\ light \cdot 1,000\ watts \cdot 2.0\ (\mu mols/J)}{4\ (m^2)} = 500\ \mu mol \cdot m^{-2} \cdot s^{-1}$$

Calculating the Number of Lights Needed

This equation can be rearranged to determine how many lights are needed based on the area of the cultivation space and the target light intensity. At least 30 lights are needed to illuminate a 6 by 10 meter (20 x 32 foot) space, or 60 m^2, to 1,000 μmol·m^{-2}·s^{-1} using 1,000-watt lights with an efficacy of 2.0 μmols/J.

$Number\ of\ lights$
$$= \frac{Average\ light\ intensity\ (\mu mol \cdot m^{-2} \cdot s^{-1}) \cdot lighting\ footprint\ or\ area\ (m^2)}{fixture\ power\ draw\ (watts) \cdot efficacy\ (\mu mols/J)}$$

$$\frac{1,000\ (\mu mol \cdot m^{-2} \cdot s^{-1}) \cdot 60\ (m^2)}{1,000\ (watts) \cdot 2.0\ (\mu mols/J)} = 30\ lights$$

Again, this equation assumes 100% of the light reaches the target area. Factors like hang height, light footprint, reflectors, and even the color/reflectivity of walls affect this. Designers and manufacturers of large greenhouses or indoor grows use software, such as AGi 32, to most accurately quantify and implement light to ensure proper coverage at the right intensity.

Horticultural Lighting Labels

Choosing a light requires knowing as many details about its output, spectrum, and electrical requirements as possible. Unfortunately, a standard horticultural light label has not yet been agreed on. With lights for human use, several important measurements are included on package labels: lumen output, color rendering index (CRI), and correlated color temperature (CCT). These measurements are important to know the impact of the bulb on the brightness of a room, how well colors can be differentiated, and overall mood of the appearance of a room for people, but are not particularly useful for describing how effective lights are for growing plants.

As referenced in the light measurement section earlier in the chapter, the perception and use of light by plants does not correlate well with the human eye. Research is ongoing about ideal spectrums. However, horticultural lighting labels typically include power consumption parameters (volts, amps, wattage), spectral output of the lamp, and the μmols/J efficacy or PPF of the fixture.

Manufacturer	Model	Type	PPF (μmol·s⁻¹)	Radiation Percentage				Efficacy (J·s-1)	Wattage
				Blue	Green	Red	Far-Red		
Aelius	REDD 690w	LED	1,883	15%	26%	53%	6%	2.83	690
AGNETIX	A3 DD	LED	2,850	40%	40%	20%		2.45	1,200
California Lightworks	SolarSystem 1100	LED	1,864	20%	22%	58.%		2.35	800
Cultilux	CL PGZX	CMH	540	23%	28.%	49%		1.72	315
Cultilux	CL-LPC7	LED	1,750	24%	34%	40%		2.5	700
DormGrow G8LED	C2	LED	1,400	18%	34%	48%		2.6	1,150
Fluence	VYPR 3p; Dual R9B	LED	2,195	4%	0.1%	96%	0.3%	3.51	1,000
Green Rooster Lighting	630 CMH DE	CMH	1,116					1.77	630
Green Rooster Lighting	1000 HPS DE	HPS	2,100					2.1	1000
Heliospectra	Mitra Bellatrix	LED	1,820	24%	36%	40%		2.8	650
Horticulture Lighting Group®	HLG Scorpion Diablo	LED	1,920	16%	40%	44%		2.93	650
Mammoth Lighting	Mammoth Fold	LED	2,240	3%	75%	21%		2.8	600
P.L. Light Systems	HortiLED TOP 2.0	LED	1,084	7%	8%	84%	1%	3.17	342
Philips GreenPower	DRW_LB	LED	1,700	11%	5%	84%		3.3	325
SanLight	PQ6W gen2	LED	624	11%	29.%	52%	8%	2.7	245
Scynce	Raging Kush	LED	1,631	12%	33%	55.%		2.51	650
Scynce	Raging Kale	LED	583	36%	45%	36%		2.33	250
SolisTek	B9 LED	LED	1,825	17%	19%	45%		2.53	7,200

Most manufacturers of non-LED lights did not provide information requested for this chart. This sort of data comparison on lighting specifications explains why LEDs are quickly becoming the industry standard. Most companies provide data when asked; many more are found online.

Lighting Technologies

Many technologies exist today for providing light for plant growth. LEDs are the most-recommended light source for growing cannabis, but there are a variety of lamps that can also be used; high intensity discharge (HID), which include high-pressure sodium (HPS) and ceramic metal halides (CMH), and fluorescent bulbs. These light sources all differ in initial cost, efficacy, and spectrum.

The heat produced by a light (or any piece of electrical equipment) is directly related to the wattage the fixture consumes, regardless of the technology. A 1,000-watt LED produces as much heat as a 1,000-watt HPS. A 500-watt LED can be equivalent in light intensity to a 1,000-watt HPS, so there is less of a need for cooling fixtures. Heat from the fixtures is based on their wattage.

LED Lights

Price per light: High

Efficacy: Low to excellent (based on model), 0.9–3.2 µmols/J (Nelson and Bugbee 2014)

Spectrum: Customizable and can be excellent for either growth or secondary metabolite production. Some LEDs are adjustable and give growers the option to change spectral ratios or intensities.

HLG 650R commercial indoor horticulture LED LAMP is designed to replace a double-ended 1,000-watt HID lamp. This lamp uses full-spectrum, high-efficiency Quantum Boards® powered with Samsung's latest LM301H and Deep Red 660nm LED. This unit is dimmable, with wattage output from 60 to 630 watts.

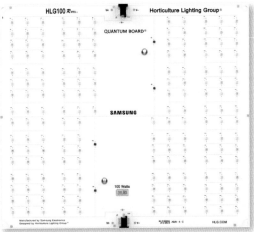

HLG 100 RPSEC® produces over 15,000 lumens with just 95 watts of power and is equivalent to a 200-watt T5 or a 300-watt fluorescent or metal halide. This fixture is ideal for vegging, supplementing, or powering a small garden.

HLG Scorpion is designed for commercial indoor gardens with low ceilings or vertical racks. HLG Scorpion uses six Quantum Boards® for an even light spread at just 12 inches (30.5 cm) from the canopy. This lamp uses Samsung's latest LM301H and Deep Red 660nm LED. This unit is dimmable, with wattage output from 60 to 630 watts.

Light-emitting diodes (LEDs) come in many configurations, including floodlights, panels, bars, circles, and rectangular fixtures. LEDs are highly efficient, using less electricity than HIDs and fluorescents. As a result, LEDs create less heat, and fixtures are only three or four inches (7–10 cm) deep, so they make great lamps for closet cultivation or vertical, tier-based production, where height is an issue.

LEDs are unique among lighting systems because they can be made with diodes that emit light in an unusually narrow spectrum. In addition, white LEDs can be made by phosphor-coating blue LEDs to provide a broad emission of wavelengths within the PAR range. LED fixtures are designed to provide plants with exactly the spectrum intended. These factors make LEDs an excellent source of plant lighting (Morrow 2008).

LEDs have a wide range of efficacies due to many different factors, including the generation of diode, spectrum, cooling strategy, adjustability, and additional features on the fixture. Diode manufacturers are continually improving on efficacy, following what is called Haitz's law (similar to Moore's law for computer chips): "The brightness of LEDs increases 20-fold per decade and decreases in price 10-fold per decade" (Steigerwald et al. 2002; Haitz and Tsao 2011). LEDs will eventually reach a theoretical maximum of 4.6–5.1 μmols/J in the coming years, depending on diode spectrum. Diode spectrum is important to determining efficacy, as red diodes are the most energy efficacious, currently followed by blue diodes. Other colors are not nearly as efficacious as red and blue, particularly monochromatic green, UV, and far-red. When LED fixtures are manufactured with these diodes, they have lower μmols/Js. "White" LED light is a combination of red, green, and blue, which is an effective way to get green light to the plant.

The cooling strategy of the fixture also affects efficacy. LEDs contain a large aluminum heat sink to cool the diodes. These can be actively cooled by fans or passively by ambient air. When a fixture uses fans to cool the heat sink, they must be powered, lowering fixture efficacy. LEDs have the ability to be adjusted for light intensity. Some fixtures have the option of adjusting specific channels of diodes, changing spectrum. Unfortunately, the circuitry that allows adjustability adds inefficiency to the fixture and lowers efficacy.

Currently, the most efficacious fixtures are passively cooled fixtures with fixed spectrums that are manufactured with the latest, most efficacious LEDs and use red, blue, or white LEDs. Still, the addition of other colors, including far-red, may be worth the minor loss of efficacy, as it may have a dramatic impact on plant growth and flowering.

Light from LEDs can be combined with HPS and CMH lamps, so there is no reason to scrap digital HID lamps. Adding LEDs to the other lights increases the amount of light delivered to the garden. For instance, a garden using a 400-watt HPS is increased to the

Using Scynce LED's "full power spectrum tuning," the grower has complete control over the spectrum delivered to the plants and can perfect cultivar-specific light recipes. Light intensity is not compromised as the spectrum is adjusted, so there is no need to swap out bulbs or fixtures. Secondary optics help focus this fine-tuned light energy over and deep below the canopy, eliminating the "pin-point" intensity that plagues most LEDs and some traditional lights.

EYE HORTILUX's LED 700-ES extends the standard LED growing spectrum by providing energy outside the PAR range to include ultraviolet (UV) and far-red, which promotes stronger plant growth with heavier flowers. Far-red light spectrum promotes increase in plant biomass, triggers flowering, enhances flower size, and improves the efficiency of the overall spectrum.

equivalent of 600 watts using 100 watts of LEDs. Adding 400 watts of LEDs can create the equivalent of a 1,000-watt HID system. An advantage of using a combination of HPS and LED lights is that the plants will receive all the spectrums needed to thrive.

LED fixtures cost more than HID lights, but save money in the long run.

LED lamps are capable of using significantly less electricity compared with HIDs per unit of PAR light produced. LEDs can save significant electrical costs per year when compared to the cost of running a 1,000-watt HID for 12 hours a day. To calculate the overall cost of purchasing and running a light for a period of time, add the cost of the fixture, any cost of maintenance over the running period (bulb replacements), and then multiply the cost of electricity by the hours run. This formula compares the cost of owning an LED fixture with an HPS lamp with similar light output for a year:

$$\left(\frac{Fixture\ Wattage\ (Watts)}{1000\left(\frac{watts}{kWatt}\right)} \cdot Cost\ of\ electricity\left(\frac{\$}{kWatt \cdot hr}\right)\right) \cdot Run\ Time\left(\frac{hours}{day}\right) \cdot 365\frac{days}{year})$$

Alternatively, this equation can be modified to include two fixtures to determine how long a fixture must be owned in years when comparing two fixtures:

$Return\ on\ Investment\ (years)$

$$= \frac{Difference\ in\ fixture\ cost\ (Fixture\ 1 - Fixture\ 2)}{Difference\ in\ maintenance\ and\ run\ cost\ per\ hour\ (Fixture\ 2\ run\ cost - Fixture\ 1\ run\ cost)}$$

$$\div\ Run\ Time(\frac{hours}{day}) \div 365\ (\frac{days}{year})$$

With

$$Difference\ in\ fixture\ cost = Fixture\ Price\ 1 - Fixture\ Price\ 2$$

$$Maintenance\ and\ run\ cost\ per\ hour\ of\ fixture = \frac{price\ of\ bulb}{lifetime\ of\ bulb} + (\frac{Fixture\ Wattage\ (Watts)}{1000\frac{watts}{kWatt}} \cdot$$

$$Cost\ of\ electricity(\frac{\$}{kWatt\cdot hr}))$$

$$Difference\ in\ maintenance\ and\ run\ cost\ per\ hour\ of\ fixture =$$

$$Maintenance\ and\ run\ cost\ per\ hour\ of\ fixture\ 2 - Maintenance\ and\ run\ cost\ per\ hour\ of\ fixture\ 1$$

Below are the parameters and fixture specifications compared within the equations. The two fixtures selected have similar light output and should be comparable to each other in terms of plant growth and yield.

Run time: 20 hours per day
Cost of electricity: $0.10 /kWatt·hr

LED Lamp

Price of LED: $1,500
Wattage of LED: 630 watts
Maintenance: $0

HPS Lamp

Price of lamp: $350
Wattage of lamp: 1000 watts
Maintenance: $55 for new bulb every 5,000 hours of run time

$$Difference\ in\ fixture\ cost = \$1,350 - \$350 = \$1,000$$

$$Maintenance\ and\ run\ cost\ per\ hour\ Fixture\ 1 = None^* + (\frac{630\ (Watts)}{1000\frac{watts}{kWatt}} \cdot 0.10(\frac{\$}{kWatt\cdot hr}))\underline{=}\$0.063$$

*LEDs do not need bulb replacement or maintenance

$$Maintenance\ and\ run\ cost\ per\ hour\ Fixture\ 2 = \left(\frac{\$100\ per\ bulb}{5000\ hours\ run}\right) + (\frac{1000\ (Watts)}{1000\frac{watts}{kWatt}} \cdot 0.10(\frac{\$}{kWatt\cdot hr}))\underline{=}\$0.12$$

The final equation is

$$Return\ on\ Investment\ (years) = \frac{\$1,000}{(\$0.12-\$0.063)} \div 18(\frac{hours}{day}) \div 365\ (\frac{days}{year}) = 2.67\ years$$

If the cost of electricity were $0.20 per kilowatt hour, the return on investment would be about one year.

Although the initial cost of the LED fixture is more than HPS, it pays for itself in a short period of time. There are more savings with the LED that are not included in this. For example, since there is less cooling equipment required for the LED fixture, this reduces the cost of equipment needed to run the lights and the operating cost of running cooling equipment. There are also efficiency rebates offered by many power companies for using LED lighting instead of conventional light technologies. As LEDs continue to drop in price and increase in efficacy, it will become even more advantageous to choose them over other lighting sources. LEDs have such a long life that they will not be replaced until more efficacious lamps are available. For these reasons, LEDs are often the best option.

High Intensity Discharge

High Intensity Discharge (HID) is a significant step forward in brightness and efficacy of light compared with fluorescent. These lights occupy less space and offer intensities bright enough for greenhouse supplemental lighting or as a sole source of light. HID fixtures come in two different bulb types that vary in efficacy and spectrum: HPS lamps, which are more popular, and CMH lamps.

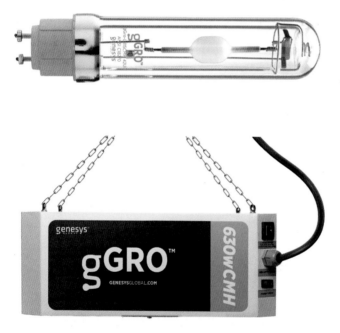

TOP: gGRO™ Ceramic Metal Halide (CMH) by Genesys Global lamps offer full-spectrum output with +14% more red and +104% more far-red spectrum, promoting growth and higher yield. The halides present are optimized to provide UV content for higher THC, broad spectrum for higher growth quality, and enhanced reds for more growth volume during flower stage.

BOTTOM: gGRO™ can be tailored to combine gLED™ and gHID™ to optimize around variables, including but not limited to business location, climate, and facility architecture, through every stage of plant growth.

Ceramic Metal Halide Lamps (CMH)

Price per light: Moderate
Efficacy: Moderately good, 1.5 µmols/J (Nelson and Bugbee 2014)
Spectrum: Good for growth, excellent for secondary metabolites and overall quality
Ceramic metal halide (CMH) lamps are the type of lamp used outdoors to illuminate sports events because they emit a white light. They were originally promoted as the best

light to use during the vegetative stage of plant growth, before the plants are forced to flower, but now it is generally recognized that plants also grow well vegetatively under HPS and LED lamps as under CMH. CMH lamps do have the advantage of minimizing internodal stretching during vegetative growth due to their high blue and low far-red light output.

CMH lamps, like fluorescents, come in many spectrums. This is very important for figuring how effective a lamp is. In general, 15% of the energy used by CMH lamps is emitted as PAR, as compared with 13% for HPS, but the crisp white light emitted by standard CMH lamps is low in the red spectrum. Since plants need red spectrum light for photosynthesis and flowering, its absence is felt. Nonetheless, under metal halides, plants grow quickly and flowering is profuse, with heavier budding than under fluorescents.

CMH lamps may be the solution to plant lighting problems indoors and out. During the fall, ceramic metal halide lamps can be used in backyard gardens to supply the extra energy boost needed to ripen. Run the lights during the day to supplement the ambient light. Although the light they emit is very bright, it is white, not the unusual amber color emitted by HPS lamps, so it is not as likely to look unusual.

CMH lamps can be used during the vegetative stage. They come in 315-, 630- and 1,000-watt sizes. The 315-watt lamps can easily illuminate a three by three (90 by 90 cm) to four by four foot (1.2 x 1.2 m) garden. The 630-watt lamp can illuminate a garden up to five by five feet (1.5 by 1.5 m). The 1,000-watt lamp can illuminate a garden up to six by six feet (1.8 by 1.8 m). This varies by cultivar. Additional light can be provided to increase intensity during flowering.

CMH lamps are convenient to use. The complete unit consists of a lamp (bulb), fixture (reflector), and ballast. The fixture and lamp are lightweight and easy to hang. A chain or rope is used to suspend the fixture, which takes up little space, making it easy to gain access to the garden.

Lights become dimmer as they age, but may need to be replaced after a year or less. A light meter is required to properly determine if the lights are still viable. Smartphone applications are available to perform light metering.

Ceramic Metal Halides & Ultraviolet Light (UV)

Ultraviolet (UV) light, as discussed earlier in the chapter, is composed of spectrums beyond blue that are invisible to humans but are visible to many animals. UV light is divided into three bands—UVA, UVB, and UVC. UVB is critical to the development of THC. The potency of cannabis is dependent on the amount of UVB light it receives. Ceramic metal halides emit UV light and can be used for this purpose.

Even if plants are being grown under HPS lamps, potency increases significantly if they are replaced with ceramic metal halides during the last two weeks of flowering. Some CMH fixtures are air-cooled and use a protective glass that absorbs UV light before it gets to the garden. The only way to benefit from the UV output is to remove the glass and take other steps for cooling. However, it is not recommended to remove the glass in an air-cooled hood, especially when there are so many newer options that do not require it. Modern CMH fixtures require less air-cooling, so they are no longer manufactured with the protective UV-light blocking glass.

 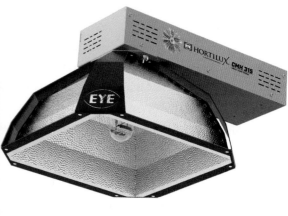

The EYE HORTILUX CMH 315 grow lamp was designed specifically for horticulture, rather than for use in retail spaces, like most ceramic metal halide lamps. These CMH lamps allow an effective amount of UV to pass through, more than 50% compared with other lamps, increasing cannabinoid content of cannabis flowers.

High-Pressure Sodium Lamps (HPS)

Price per light: Moderately low

Efficacy: Good, 1.7 µmols/J (Nelson and Bugbee 2014)

Spectrum: Excellent for growth, good for secondary metabolites and overall quality

High-pressure sodium (HPS) lamps emit an orange or amber-looking light. HPS lamps are commonly used as street lights. Their spectrum is heavily concentrated in yellow, orange, and red, with only a small amount of blue. HPS lights are usually used for flowering because they supply more orange and red light than CMH lamps, and are slightly more efficacious. The increased red and yellow light seems to promote more flower production.

Gardeners usually use HPS sizes of 400, 600, or 1,000+ watts, all of which are sold in indoor garden shops. The 600-watt HPS lamps are about 7% more efficient than the other sizes.

HPS lamps support fast growth during both vegetative and flowering stages. They need no supplemental lighting during any stage of growth, though they may produce more internodal stretching in vegetative plants than their CMH counterparts. HPS lamp brands and models differ in both the amount of light emitted per watt and in the spectrum that is emitted. Some HPS lamps emit enhanced levels of blue light, which encourages stout short stems and branches. Since light of each particular spectrum is processed differently by plants, some lamps produce more growth and flowering than others.

Fluorescent Lights

Price per light: Low

Efficacy: Fair, 0.8–0.9 μmols/J (uncited 1.1) (Nelson and Bugbee 2014) (Wallace and Both 2016)

Spectrum: Moderate for growth, excellent for secondary metabolites and overall quality

Growers have used fluorescent tubes to provide light since the early years of indoor cultivation in the 1960s. They are inexpensive, easy to set up, and moderately efficient. Plants grow and bud adequately under them. However, fluorescents do not create the intensity of light emitted by other technologies, so they usually don't produce the large, tight buds the more powerful lamps do.

Fluorescents can produce various spectral outputs, which are determined by the type of phosphor used to coat the surface of the tube. Each phosphor type emits a different set of light colors, rated in kelvin, and identified as "warm white," "cool white," and "daylight," or "natural white." These names signify the kind of light the tube produces, with daylight or natural white coming closest to approximating the sun's spectrum. Lamps of different spectrums can be used in the same fixtures.

Cool white fluorescents emit more blue light than warm white. They are useful during the vegetative stage because the blue light promotes stout, compact stem growth.

Warm whites emit more red light than cool whites and are often used during flowering because the red spectrum promotes flower growth.

Several brands of special "plant growth" lamps are also available. They concentrate their light emissions in the red and blue spectrums to provide plants with more energy, but they produce less total light.

T12s are the widest fluorescent lamps and consume less power, produce dimmer light, and emit lower heat. High output (HO) fluorescents are supercharged. They use almost 60% more power than standard T12 fluorescent lamps. They can illuminate a smaller garden very brightly and are an alternative light source, using a high-intensity discharge lamp. They are readily available in T-5 tube size.

T-5 Straight-Length Tubes

T-5 tubes are 5/8 inches (1.5 cm) wide and are available in a variety of lengths. Their more compact size means it is possible to fit four T-5 tubes in each foot (30 cm) of width. T-5 tubes are available in high output models, which are the ones usually sold in shops. A 4-foot (1.2 m) high output tube uses 54 watts and emits roughly 5,000 lumens, almost twice as much output as a conventional T-5. A bank of eight, four-foot (1.2 m) T-5 high output tubes emits 40,000 lumens and uses about 435 watts, as compared to a 400-watt HPS that actually uses 440 watts and produces about 50,000 lumens. T-5 HO fluorescents use about 60% more electricity than regular T-5s.

Compact Fluorescents (CFLs)

Compact fluorescents are often the most convenient lamps to use in small gardens. Unlike other fluorescent bulbs, they have ballasts built into the bulb assembly, so they can screw into standard incandescent sockets. They are available as floodlights, twisted tubes, and straight mini-tubes. Another advantage of CFLs is that they deliver a lot of light from a small point. Unlike tube fluorescents that deliver their light over a large area, often spanning several feet, the compact "point of light" emissions make it easier to increase light intensity by grouping them close to each other. Large-wattage CFL lamps are available in sizes of 25, 50, 100, 150, 200, and 250 watts. LEDs have largely supplanted the use of CFLs.

HID Ballasts

HID lamps have electrical systems that require conversion to higher voltage than is delivered through the electrical grid. The ballast converts incoming current to the appropriate voltage. Some ballasts are remote from the light, connected by a long electrical cord. The convenience of this is that the heavy ballasts do not hang from the ceiling or other supports, while the lighter and less cumbersome reflector and bulb are stationed above the plant canopy. In most large commercial indoor gardens and greenhouses, the ballast and lamps are configured together.

Old-style magnetic ballasts are dedicated to a particular type and wattage lamp and a single grid voltage, such as 110 or 220. They are very heavy and use almost 200 watts to power a 1,000-watt lamp.

Most digital ballasts can be used for both CMH and HPS lamps of the same wattage and with both 110 and 220 voltage. Some can power different wattage lamps.

Solid state digital ballasts are even more efficient and produce a steadier light that increases growth. They are used extensively by commercial growers.

Compared with magnetic ballasts, digital ballasts are more convenient. They are more electrically efficient, using only 50–100 watts, are lighter weight, and do not make any sound. They are also gentler on the bulb during start up and regulate current more precisely. Some are also capable of running both CMH and HPS bulbs. They are also safer than magnetic ballasts, as they incorporate safety features that ensure shutdown if problems occur.

Lighting Accessories & Light Reflectors

Light doesn't become weaker or disappear with distance. It appears to dim as the light beam widens over a larger area. As it spreads, its intensity dissipates. Just think of a flashlight. If the beam is tightly focused, it will have the same intensity at the focus point as it had at the point of emission. The larger an area of the garden that a lamp illuminates, the less intense the light that plants receive.

Reflectors are a way to keep the light focused where it is needed. The three other types of lamps other than LEDs discussed—fluorescents, CMH, and HPS—all emit light in all directions. Even a portion of LED light, although low in comparison with the other light sources, is emitted sideways, causing light to be lost. Only a portion of the light shines directly on the garden. Unless it is redirected, the light illuminates the wall and ceiling.

Any light emitted by the lamps that doesn't reach the plants is wasted and might as well not have been produced. There are many solutions, and all but a few involve the use of light reflectors.

Fluorescent Light Reflectors

The shape of a fluorescent reflector determines, to a great extent, how much light the plants receive. Use the best reflector available. Almost all fixtures with reflectors place the tubes too close to one another, so that only about 60% of the light is actually transmitted out of the unit. The rest is trapped between the tubes or bounces back and forth between the tubes and the reflector. This light may as well not be emitted, since it is not hitting the plants.

Like other fluorescents, CFL bulbs emit light in all directions. Inexpensive clamp-on fixtures with bowl reflectors help direct the light to the garden. Commercial reflectors are available for larger size CFLs. Good reflectors can double the light intensity the garden receives from CFLs.

The fluorescent tubes that fit inside shop lights can be fitted using LED tubes. They will produce more light cheaper. New fixtures with 4-foot (1.2 m) LED tubes are dimmable and come with remote controls.

CMH & HPS Reflectors

Both CMH and HPS bulbs emit most of the light along their length, so it comes out of the sides of the bulb. Many fixtures orient the bulb horizontally to take advantage of this. The reflector must direct the rest of the light downward.

There are many reflector models, but they can be classified into two general types depending on which position the bulb is held: horizontally or vertically. For most gardens, horizontally held lamps are preferred.

Horizontal Reflectors

Horizontal lamps deliver more light directly to the garden because of the position of the bulb and the direction that light is emitted. Manufacturers have created many designs, and each leaves its own illumination footprint. Some focus light in a small area; others are designed to distribute it over a large space. The best reflector for a particular garden depends on the garden's dimensions and design.

Small one-light or two-light gardens do better with focused reflectors. The light is directed downward, so most of it goes directly to the garden. Focused beam reflectors minimize the light that goes off to the sides. Larger gardens grow more vigorously when the reflectors in the center spread the light over a larger area. The plants receive light coming from different directions, minimizing shadows and giving a larger portion of the plant the opportunity to actively photosynthesize. Reflectors closer to the perimeter should still be close focused so that light remains in the garden.

Vertical (Parabolic) Reflectors

When a bulb is held vertically, almost all the light comes out the side and follows a horizontal path to the walls. This light must be directed down to the garden. None of the vertical reflectors are designed to keep the light in the area directly below the reflector, so lots of light leaks out of the garden if not directed back using additional reflectors. The light they redirect is broadcast over a very wide area. Some reflectors have adjustable bulb positioning, so the light is controlled somewhat, but most reflectors are too shallow and miss a large portion of light, and it is lost to the garden. Because of their poor design, vertical reflectors are very inefficient at directing light to the garden. They are considered old technology.

Air-Cooled Lights

Lights emit a lot of heat. Each 1,000 watts of light input creates about 3,412 Btus of heat, regardless of whether lights are fluorescent, HID, or LED. Just three 1,000-watt lamps release the same amount of heat as two standard electric space heaters. If all this heat is released into a room temperature garden, it has to be removed either through ventilation or air-cooling.

Air-cooled light reflectors solve part of the problem by removing the hot air before it gets into the room. The fixtures have a glass bottom, so the lamp is totally enclosed, trapping much of the heat. They come with four-, six- or eight-inch (10, 15, or 20 cm) flanges on either side of each reflector. An equally sized inline fan is attached to each row of air-cooled reflectors using flexible ducting. This inline fan draws cool air, typically from outside the room, and supplies it to each reflector in its row. Ducting attached to the other side of the reflectors exhausts much of the heat from the light out of the room. The cooling air travels through the sealed ducting and reflectors and never has contact with the air in the garden. It picks up the lamps' heat but absolutely no odor from the room. The air can be safely exhausted from the room or used to heat another interior space.

Depending on the quality of the air-cooled reflector, up to half of the lamp's heat is removed from the room, simplifying temperature management. The one problem with air-cooled CMH lights is that the bottom glass in the fixture absorbs UVB light and other spectrums, so the heat is eliminated at the cost of light, which is more expensive.

Another strategy is to use air-cooled lights with no enclosing glass. Air is drawn from the garden space through the tubing and then cooled and returned to the room or cleaned of odor using an inline carbon filter so that it can be exhausted outside or used for heating another interior space. Air above the canopy is pulled up into the reflector, drawing the heat with it. This keeps the canopy cool, and the CMH's UV light is directed to the garden.

Light Movers

No matter what kind of light reflector is used for HID lamps, they deliver light in an uneven pattern. Usually the center area, directly under the lamp, receives the most light. The intensity of the light tapers off as the distance from the center increases. Light movers help eliminate differences in light intensity by moving the center around so the angle of light changes. As the lamps move, each plant section comes directly under the light repeatedly. Instead of plants in the center receiving more light than those on the edge, the light is distributed more equally throughout the garden.

Shuttles move lights back and forth in a straight line along a track. The movers have a standard-issue 6-foot (1.8 m) movement area. However, some models have shorter lengths, and the distance they travel can be adjusted. Even if the light is only being moved a single foot (30 cm), the angle of light to the plant changes. Areas that were in constant shadow see the light and respond with increased growth. Using attachments, light movers can move several fixtures at the same time. They use little electricity, so they won't add much to the electrical budget.

These units increase the efficiency of the light and garden in several ways.

Moving lamps distributes light evenly. There are fewer hot spots, so plants grow more uniformly. Plants of a single cultivar grow to the same size and ripen at the same time.

In smaller gardens, lights can be placed closer to the plants, so they receive more intense light with less directed outside the plant canopy.

Total garden growth and yield increases. Getting light to the formerly light-deprived areas of the garden increases their growth. Expect a 10–20% increase in yield using light movers in small gardens. Even in larger spaces, moving the lights increases yield.

Reflective Materials

To maximize the light, it should be directed to the canopy, rather than illuminate spaces outside of it. White paint or reflective materials are used to ensure more light is directed to the plants. This is especially important with smaller garden spaces as compared with larger spaces, where there is a higher ratio of perimeter to plant canopy. Unless the light is reflected back from the perimeter, it is wasted.

Many self-contained units or tents have built-in reflective materials. Painting the walls, floor, and ceiling is the most common option in indoor spaces. Black or dark walls absorb light; white reflects it. Highly reflective white epoxy paint is an easy option to ensure light is reflected back onto the plants from the walls, floor, and ceiling, but other techniques are also used:

- Mylar is a commonly used wall liner, although it can become crinkly and is harder to clean.
- Panda (white and black) polyethylene plastic is highly reflective, easy to clean, and reusable.
- Aluminum foil can be used. It is inexpensive and recyclable.
- Aluminized bubble wrap doubles as insulation and is easy to clean, reusable, and can be recycled as packing material.

Photo: AgGas

CARBON DIOXIDE (CO_2)

Carbon dioxide (CO_2) and water are the two raw materials required for plant photosynthesis. CO_2 constitutes roughly around 0.042% or 420 parts per million (ppm), and rising, of the Earth's atmosphere at the time of writing.

Cannabis uses CO_2 only in the presence of light. CO_2 supplementation during the dark period has no benefit to the plant. Photosynthesis and CO_2 absorption occur immediately after the plant receives light, and the plant's stomatal pores open.

The plant mines CO_2 from the air by opening its stomata, tiny organs found primarily on the underside of the leaf. The stomata are responsible for the gas exchange of oxygen (O_2) and CO_2 into and out of the plant, and for transpiration, or regulating how much water evaporates from the leaf through the pores. While human skin pores sweat to regulate temperature and moisture, plants use their stomata to regulate how much water evaporates from the leaf to cool off the plant.

Once CO_2 is absorbed into the plant, it is directed to the chloroplasts—the plant organelles that contain light-absorbing pigments—where photosynthesis takes place.

Photosynthesis consists of a complex series of reactions in which light energy is used to convert CO_2 and water to sugar, releasing O_2 as a by-product.

The Process
Chlorophyll converts light energy into an electrical charge, a free electron that is used to cleave water into its constituent elements hydrogen (H) and oxygen (O). The O is released into the air and the H is combined with CO_2 to make sugar.

The amount of CO_2 in the air has a profound effect on the rate of photosynthesis and plant growth. As long as there is enough light to power the process, photosynthesis speeds up as the amount of CO_2 in the air increases. Conversely, as the CO_2 content of the air falls, photosynthesis slows to a crawl and virtually stops at a concentration of around 200 ppm, no matter the other conditions.

Plants that lack CO_2 continue respiration and growth for a short time, until their sugars are used up, before slowing down their metabolism to conserve energy. This occurs on evenings following brightly lit days. The plant creates excess sugar, some of which is used to continue plant growth and maintain cellular function during the dark period. Only when light and more CO_2 is available can the plant processes continue.

Cannabis Is a C3 Plant

Cannabis is a C3 plant: CO_2 is fixed to a 3-carbon sugar molecule during photosynthesis. The plant gathers carbon dioxide only when it is photosynthesizing. With adequate light and water, the plant absorbs more CO_2 when the concentration in the air increases. This increases the plant's photosynthetic efficiency, producing more sugars and resulting in faster growth.

Plants absorb CO_2 into their intracellular spaces through pores called stomata found on the underside of the leaf. Every time a stomatal pore opens up to allow CO_2 to diffuse inside, it transpires water.

Outdoors, breezes and the exchange of gasses in the air constantly replace CO_2 that plants consume. This provides enough atmospheric CO_2 for vigorous growth. Until recently outdoor growers rarely thought of the gas as a limiting factor. Now, some farmers are supplementing outdoor gardens and fields.

In fact, the 420 ppm of CO_2 found in the Earth's atmosphere is on the low end of the continuum of C3 plants' ability to use it as an ingredient for photosynthesis. Outdoor plants growing in the bright light of summer grow heavier and faster when supplemented with CO_2.

Raising the level of CO_2 up to 0.15% (1500 ppm), or a little less than four times the amount usually found in the atmosphere, increases plant growth rate significantly.

EFFECT OF CO$_2$ ON NET PHOTOSYNTHESIS

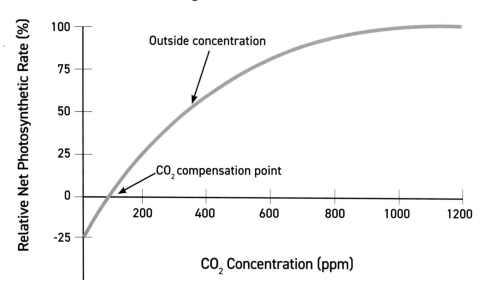

The orange line on this chart represents relative net photosynthetic rate at different CO_2 concentrations. The rate of photosynthesis continues to increase quickly and then flattens out as the continued addition of CO_2 no longer improves the photosynthetic rate.

Enhancing growth outdoors using increased CO_2 is discussed at the end of the chapter. When plants are growing in an enclosed area, there is a limited amount of CO_2 for them to use. Under bright lights, CO_2 is used up quickly. Enclosed gardens with no ventilation are also rapidly depleted to the point where the photosynthetic rate slows to a virtual stop at 200 ppm. Only when more CO_2 is added to the air does photosynthesis resume.

A closed closet or other small gardening space can be recharged with CO_2 simply by opening the door or curtain to let in fresh air. This increases the CO_2 content of the closet passively, as air naturally equalizes the concentrations of O_2 and CO_2 inside and outside the growing space, exchanging the higher O_2 levels from the plants with CO_2 from outside. Adding a small fan expedites the air exchange.

The rate of photosynthesis has the greatest increase as the CO_2 level climbs from 0–200 ppm. Under low-light conditions the rate of photosynthesis continues to increase as CO_2 rises to atmospheric levels. Increasing the CO_2 concentration beyond that without increasing light intensity does not result in a higher rate of photosynthesis. The plant cannot take advantage of higher CO_2 levels until the light intensity increases.

At high light intensity the photosynthetic rate increases as CO_2 concentrations increase to atmospheric levels. The rate of increase declines a bit after that, but the photosynthetic rate continues to increase as CO_2 levels reach 800 ppm. Increasing the light intensity encourages the plants to absorb even more CO_2, which increases growth and yield. Above 800 ppm of CO_2, photosynthesis continues to climb but at a slower rate, until it levels off at about 1,500 ppm.

> CO_2 is a nonflammable gas. It is nontoxic at the low levels growers employ. According to OSHA, CO_2 can pose health risks in extreme concentrations (above 5,000 ppm), but this level is more than three times the maximum plants find useful.

CO₂ Enrichment

Augmenting CO_2 in the garden increases photosynthesis, resulting in faster growth and bigger yields. Optimal levels range between 800 and 1,500 ppm. These concentrations are much higher than atmospheric carbon dioxide levels and can be achieved only through supplementation. Plants do not absorb CO_2 during the dark period, so CO_2 enrichment is only implemented when the lights are on. Achieving optimized results also requires increased lighting and temperature.

There are various ways to augment carbon dioxide in closed environment grow rooms. The most convenient way to do this is with a sensor, regulator, and tank kit. Other methods include using a sensor-regulated CO_2 generator that burns propane or natural gas. Metabolic and chemical processes such as fermentation also produce CO_2 and can be used to supplement a garden.

Common Myths about CO_2

The following assertions are completely false:
- Plants can overdose on CO_2
- All that is needed is good ventilation—extra CO_2 will not help
- Plants need fresh air, keeping them in a closed system is imprisonment
- The only time plants need CO_2 is when other conditions aren't right
- Plants grow immune to CO_2
- Plants need CO_2 supplemented both day and night

The use of CO_2 involves serious life-safety issues; CO_2 is regulated by OSHA as an asphyxiant. Any system used to apply it will need to include appropriate monitoring and alarm protocols, which are generally enforced by local authorities.

For both human and plant safety, food-grade bulk CO_2 delivered in liquefied form is the safest source, is certified as an organic practice by the USDA, and will not lead to any product contamination during testing. The use of propane burners to generate CO_2 gas is banned by some state and local fire codes. Note that incomplete combustion can produce deadly carbon monoxide, as well as ethylene, which is highly toxic to plants and can result in crop loss.

CO_2 Tanks

The easiest way to supply the gas is to use a CO_2 tank kit. The kit consists of a CO_2 meter, pressure regulator, flow meter, and a solenoid valve. For most gardeners, 20 or 50 pound (9–22 kg) tanks (the weight of the gas) are the most convenient. Tanks can be bought or rented. Steel tanks weigh twice as much as aluminum tanks, so a steel tank that holds 20 pounds (9 kg) of CO_2 has a gross weight of 50 pounds (22 kg), and an aluminum tank weighs about 40 pounds (18 kg) filled. The 50 pound (22 kg) tanks weigh, respectively, 170 and 110 pounds (77–50 kg) when filled.

Although CO_2 tanks are a bit cumbersome to lug around and are more expensive than burning propane or natural gas, they are still the best solution for most growers. They don't run the risk of degrading the garden environment, as compared with gas burners. Tanks release nothing but cool CO_2, while CO_2 generators release heat and water vapor, neither of which is helpful in most gardens.

Using burners to generate CO_2 runs the risk of producing a small amount of ethylene gas. Ethylene (C_2H_4) is also a plant hormone that is bioactive at concentrations as low as one part per billion. Ethylene can have many effects on the plant depending on the stage of growth the plant is in. It causes faster fruit ripening.

CO_2 tank systems use a regulator and emitter to control the amount of gas being released and, consequently, the concentration of CO_2 in the garden. These are the parts for a complete CO_2 supplementation system:

1. A regulator that standardizes the pressure.
2. An adjustable CO_2 flow meter that controls the amount of gas released over a given time period.
3. A solenoid valve that shuts the gas flow on or off.

These systems are usually sold as a single unit. Most systems include a CO_2 sensor that constantly measures the ppm of CO_2 in the air and turns the flow on or off to maintain the ppm the gardner sets. These systems keep an accurate gauge of the CO_2 in the air, eliminating guesswork and unwanted fluctuations.

CO_2 System Setup

In most tank systems CO_2 should be released just above the plants or circulation fans. The gas is heavier and cooler than the air, so it sinks. As it flows down, it reaches the top of the canopy first. This is where most of the light touches the leaves and where most of the plants' CO_2-consuming photosynthesis takes place. A good way to disperse the gas is by using inexpensive "soaker hoses" sold in plant nurseries and gardening stores. These soaker hoses have tiny holes along their length that disperse the gas.

Some systems circulate air through the plant canopy, drawing it up toward the ceiling. In this kind of system, the CO_2 should flow from the tube just below the canopy, so it is pulled up to the top. Another method of enriching a space with CO_2 is to add it to the air intake, so all new air is enriched. This is especially useful when a space has constant or frequent ventilation. Whichever setup is chosen, tanks should be placed in a space where they can easily be moved so that they can be refilled.

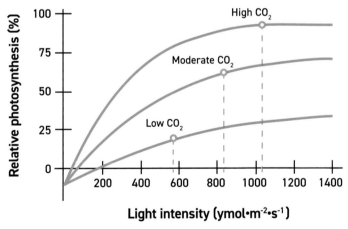

The three lines represent relative photosynthetic rates at various light intensities. The three curves represent the rates of photosynthesis when the ambient CO_2 concentrations are low, medium, and high. The increase of relative photosynthetic rate is largest when the CO_2 is highest and lowest when the CO_2 concentration becomes a limiting factor.
SOURCE: Erik Runkle, Michigan State University

Use of CO_2 in Commercial Gardens

In many jurisdictions the application of CO_2 to gardens is regulated for safety reasons. In some areas the use of portable 20 and 50 pound (9 and 23 kg) tanks are regulated, and safety precautions are in effect. They might include handling procedures as well as CO_2 detectors, which alarm when the levels exceed 2,500 ppm, which is considered a precautionary health hazard. Sometimes small tanks must

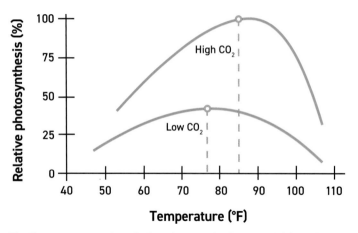

The lines represent the relative photosynthetic rate at high and low CO_2 concentrations across various temperatures. The optimal (highest) rates are represented by the peaks of the curves. At low/ambient CO_2 concentrations the optimal rate is closer to 78°F (26°C). At high CO_2 concentrations the optimal rate is closer to 85°F (30°C). SOURCE: Erik Runkle, Michigan State University

be held in a safety zone outside the structure. The gas is transported to the growing area via tubing.

Commercial cultivators often use micro-bulk CO_2 tanks with capacities of thousands of liters of compressed, liquid CO_2. These tanks are mounted on a pad on the exterior of the facility. The liquid carbon dioxide is converted to a gas and is either piped directly to sensor-controlled valves in each grow space or supplied via specialized HVAC systems that can simultaneously provide air conditioning, dehumidification, and supplemental carbon dioxide to each cultivation zone. These large-capacity tanks can last for many weeks, depending on the size and needs of the facility. Tanks can also be outfitted with a communications module that alerts the gas supplier when it is running low, so they can schedule on-demand, CO_2 deliveries to the site.

CO_2 Generators

Generators are much less expensive to operate than bottled CO_2 injection systems. They create carbon dioxide inexpensively by burning either natural gas or propane. They are safe to be around and burn cleanly and completely without leaving toxic residues or creating carbon monoxide, a colorless, odorless, poisonous gas.

Generators emit CO_2, water, and heat. Each pound of natural gas or propane burned produces about three pounds (1.36 kg) of CO_2, one pound (0.45 kg) of water, and about 21,800 British thermal units (Btu's) of heat. Other gasses and fuels produce different amounts of energy per unit burned.

One pound of CO_2 (~0.5 kg) = 8.7 feet^3 (0.246 m^3)

If the growing area is cool or cold, the heat from a CO_2 generator can be useful in keeping the space warm, as well as supplying CO_2 and humidity to the garden. In a warm space, the generator's heat must be dissipated to maintain the moderate temperature levels necessary for optimal growth. Some CO_2 generators use water-cooling to absorb the heat. The heated water is cooled outside the garden area, eliminating the temperature problem. However, the CO_2-enriched air still contains the moisture that was created.

Nursery supply houses sell large CO_2 generators especially designed for greenhouses. Indoor garden centers typically sell smaller generators more appropriate for indoor gardens.

Even a small generator unit can raise CO_2 levels very quickly. Commercial use of CO_2 generators in some areas has been banned, so check local and state regulations.

CO₂ CONCENTRATION IN CLOSED-LOOP GROW SPACE

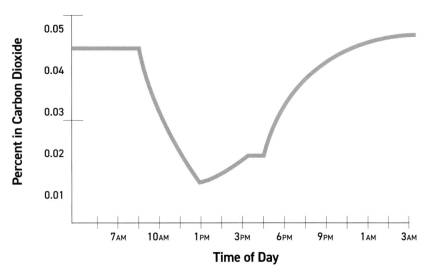

The orange line represents average CO_2 concentrations throughout a 24-hour period in a closed loop space with minimal ventilation. As lights turn on and photosynthesis starts, the CO_2 concentration dips as the plants absorb CO_2. Many plants close their stomata between 150 and 200 PPM CO_2. The curve bottoms out when the plants stop photosynthesizing. As photosynthesis slows, the CO_2 concentration increases. At night the plants are respiring and releasing CO_2, which is illustrated by the higher than ambient concentrations of 420 PPM CO_2 at night.

Alternative Methods to Enrich Air with CO_2

Other ways to bring CO_2 into the garden space include chemical reactions and biological processes such as composting, fermentation, and animal respiration.

Vinegar & Baking Soda

When vinegar and baking soda are combined, they make a salt and release CO_2.

In small gardens, a simple method for creating a controlled release of CO_2 is to drip vinegar into a solution made of baking soda and water. As the vinegar combines with the solution, CO_2 is released. Regulating the frequency of the drip controls the amount of CO_2 generated. This is not cost effective because baking soda and vinegar are expensive to purchase in the quantities needed to create significant amounts of CO_2.

To generate one cubic foot of CO_2, combine three quarts of 5% vinegar with 3.7 ounces of baking soda. Generating one cubic meter of CO_2 requires 106 liters of 5% vinegar and 3.7 kg of baking soda.

Fermentation

Fermentation is the process used to brew beer and make wine. All that is required to fer-

A single TNB Naturals CO_2 Enhancer can supplement 1,200 ppm of CO_2 in a 144 square-foot (13 m²) space for up to two weeks. The Enhancer is made from 100% organic ingredients and is activated by adding four cups (1 liter) of lukewarm water and shaking. Shake daily for optimal performance. Canisters should be placed or hung above the canopy, as the CO_2 will sink to the floor.

ment alcohol and make CO_2 is a jug or container, malt or another source of sugar, and yeast. Yeast are single-cell microorganisms that have been used in baking and fermenting alcoholic beverages for thousands of years. In fermentation, yeast digest sugar and release alcohol and CO_2. A gross simplification of this process is:

$$(\text{Sugar} => \text{Alcohol} + \text{Carbon Dioxide } (CO_2))$$
$$C_6H_{12}O_6 => 2(CH_3CH_2OH) + 2(CO_2)$$

As yeast feast on the sugars, they release about half the weight of the sugars' CO_2, so one pound (~0.5 kg) of sugar yields about half a pound (0.25 kg), or 4.35 cubic feet (0.12 m³), of gas. The yeast complete their meal in about four days. Then the solution must be replaced.

Beer-Making Kit

Yeast have a hard time processing sugar as the alcohol content climbs. Most beer yeast slow down as the liquid approaches about 5–8% alcohol. The maximum amount of sugar that yeast can process well is about one-tenth of the weight of the water. A gallon of water weighs 8 pounds (3.6 kg), so about 13 ounces of sugar is used. A liter of water weighs 1,000 grams, so use 80 grams of sugar.

Human Respiration

Each breath taken by humans releases CO_2. A 150-pound (68 kg) human produces an average of about 1 kilogram (2.2 lbs) CO_2 per day. In an hour a human releases 0.326 cubic feet of the gas (0.0092 m³).

Outdoor CO_2 Supplementation

Although carbon dioxide supplementation is a common practice when growing indoors, it is not as well known that outdoor supplementation is possible as well. Plants grown outdoors can benefit from CO_2 supplementation. They will grow sturdier and produce higher yields. Plants grown in tunnels or in greenhouses also benefit from CO_2 supplementation because they rapidly deplete the air of CO_2 as they photosynthesize, so air enrichment is very effective at increasing their growth.

Because CO_2 is expensive, it takes an automated prescriptive delivery system for it to be economical in ventilated environments. This requires "in-grow" sensors that measure light, temperature, humidity, and CO_2 levels, so that the gas is only applied when it is needed. It's also important to target the application of the CO_2 directly into the foliar canopy, which is where plants take it in through stomatal pores in their leaves.

If done right, CO_2 enrichment can generate yield improvements of 50% or more. This is because it does the following:

- Helps create larger root structures, healthier stems, and more leaves during the vegetative state
- Improves a plant's heat-tolerance by up to 10°F (~5°C), allowing photosynthesis to continue at high summer temperatures when plants would normally "shut down"
- Helps reduce plant transpiration and therefore foliar canopy humidity (think mold)
- Supplies added carbon during the flowering stage, leading to bigger and denser buds

Large Outdoor Spaces

CO_2 release is most efficient in large fields, where it is less likely to leave the cultivation site, even if it is moved by a breeze. Because CO_2 is heavier than air, it tends to move more horizontally rather than vertically. If it's released in a field, it will spread to other plants rather than be lost to the air.

Releasing CO_2 to rows of plants in a field during calm, sunny weather can increase yields by 50% or more. Coordinating CO_2 release to fields from CO_2-generating facilities will remove it from the atmosphere and may result in carbon credits.

ExHale by Garden City Fungi is a natural source of CO_2 that creates a steady sustainable supply that can meet the enrichment needs of enclosed gardens of all sizes, from small personal to large-scale commercial gardens. Inside each ExHale cultivator bag is a non-fruiting mycelial mass that is growing on organic matter. This mycelial mass cultivates CO_2, and the micro-porous breather patch releases it continually into the garden. No manure is used, so it is odorless.

Outdoor CO$_2$ Tanks

CO$_2$ from tanks can be applied to plants growing outdoors, in small and large gardens as well as in fields. To enrich the air around a plant outdoors, run a CO$_2$ line from a tank up the stem of the plant so that the gas disperses around the canopy. CO$_2$ is heavier than air and is cool coming out of the tank, so it will sink after it is released. It is best to set up the CO$_2$ line at the level of the canopy to be as close to where the leaves absorb CO$_2$.

There are several conditions that should be taken into consideration, particularly light, temperature, and wind velocity. CO$_2$ is most effective in warm conditions. It will help when the canopy leaf temperature is above 70°F (21°C) and becomes more effective as it climbs into the 80s. Ideal conditions for this method are sunny or very bright with low wind speed, especially in small gardens.

There are several commercial systems that regulate release based on three factors: light, temperature, and the amount of CO$_2$ in the space's atmosphere. Sensors and switches can be installed that are sensitive to weather conditions, so CO$_2$ is turned on only when there is bright light, little wind, and warm temperatures. Very often there is a period daily during summer and fall when the sun is shining and there is little wind. This most often occurs between 11 a.m. and 4 p.m., when the sun's rays are most intense.

These systems utilize appropriately sized CO$_2$ tanks that are refilled by gas companies in much the same way as propane is delivered.

In small gardens it works best when the emitters are placed around the top of the plant in a Christmas tree-like spiral draped down around the plant, or by placing the emitters along the central stem. Emitters can also be placed on the top of the canopy of rows of smaller plants.

Compost Piles

Compost piles produce considerable CO$_2$ and can be placed in the center of a densely planted outdoor garden. As the CO$_2$ is emitted by the pile, breezes will carry it through the plants. A small compost container can be placed under a large plant. Because compost piles generate heat, the emerging gas will be warmer than the surrounding air and will drift up through the plant's canopy. Moist organic mulches or thin layers of compost can also be placed over the soil. When they are provided with a bit of nitrogen, the microorganisms they hold become very active and release extra CO$_2$. Their activity is regulated by temperature, so they produce more CO$_2$ during the warmer daylight hours, rather than at night.

Compost can be used to increase the CO$_2$ content of both outdoor and greenhouse gardens. It is not necessarily smelly and yields a large amount of CO$_2$. Using compost or vermicompost (compost with worms) to generate CO$_2$ is environmentally friendly. When it's ripe, the compost can be used to enrich the soil or to make compost tea.

About a sixth to a quarter of a compost pile starting wet weight is converted to CO$_2$, so a 100 pound (45 kg) pile could contribute 33–50 pounds (15–22 kg) of carbon to the gas. Carbon makes up about 27% of the weight and volume of the gas, and oxygen makes up 73%, so that the total amount of CO$_2$ created is 61 to 93 pounds (27.6–42 kg), produced over a 60-day period, in warm conditions. That comes to two to three pounds (0.9–1.3 kg) or 16–25 cubic feet (0.45–0.7 m³) a day. The gas is supplied both day and night, so much of it is produced when the plants won't utilize it.

Adding a heavy layer of organic compost or mulch on top of the soil provides warmth and protection from the elements while increasing the CO_2 content around the plants as microorganisms feed on it, releasing the gas.

CO₂ & Roots

Roots have no use for CO_2 because they don't photosynthesize. In fact, CO_2 in the soil or water can pose a problem because it can drive out much-needed oxygen. (*See Oxygen.*)

Supplementing CO₂ Outdoors

Mendocino Grasslands ran a trial of outdoor CO_2 supplementation in its tunnel greenhouses. AG Gas systems were installed in three greenhouses. As a control, three additional greenhouses with no CO_2 supplementation were set to the same conditions with the same cultivars.

This technology was tested and validated at the Center of Irrigation Technology in conjunction with California State University at Fresno and the University of California at Davis. The technology was used to determine if CO_2 injection could improve yields for outdoor, field-grown tomatoes. The data from this experiment showed a 120% increase in the yield of tomatoes (Goorahoo, Cassel, and Carstensen 2003).

Mendocino Grasslands reported yield increases of 27 to 52%, with some seasonal variance in the greenhouses that were supplemented. The lowest increase was reported for a cooler season crop, while the highest yield increase was reported for a warm season crop.

Photo: AgGas

After two seasons it was decided they had used a control crop long enough and added CO_2 enrichment to all the greenhouses. Since then, the gas has been added to an open field.

The gas is delivered to the plants the same way in both the greenhouses and the open field. Pressure-compensating drip tubing with microholes facing down is held in place about 15 inches (38 cm) above the plants. The height of its support poles

The Carbogation "black box" control unit adjusts gas flow in real-time to deliver optimum results based on extant field conditions. The unique configuration allows for prescriptive delivery of CO_2 gas to the plants. Photo: AgGas

is adjustable, so it is raised as the plants grow.

CO_2 is used by plants only when there is enough light for photosynthesis. The system controls when the gas is released, and its flow rate from the tank is controlled by a software algorithm with sensors to measure light intensity, temperature, vapor pressure deficit, wind speed, and ppm of CO_2 in real time and to make adjustments continuously.

At first there were sensors in each greenhouse, but their reports were averaged so that all greenhouses received the same amount of gas. This was changed, so now each greenhouse gets individualized treatment.

Based on environmental conditions, the algorithm figures the correct CO_2 and ppm, and sensors measure and adjust it much like a thermostat. The algorithms controlling greenhouse and open field differ a bit in their calculations. The gas is used from the nursery stage until harvest, although CO_2 enrichment in the last 10 days is not that crucial, since plant growth has slowed.

At the farm it is stored in a rented 14-ton (13 metric tons) vacuum-jacketed tank, which keeps the gas cool without refrigeration. A tank this size provides enough gas for most of the summer. It is resupplied by the local gas company, which delivers it.

In general the best time for the plants to experience the gas release is during the brightest time of the day, under clear skies, between 10:30 a.m. and 4:30 p.m. This unit uses sensors to control the release of gas by time, light, vapor pressure deficit (VPD), temperature, humidity, wind, and desired ppm.

In spaces where swamp coolers are used, there is a ventilated flow of air, but CO_2 still makes sense because it increases yield so much.

In greenhouses ventilated using roof vents or reticulated roofs, the application of CO_2 will not be greatly affected for three reasons: CO_2 is being directed into a downward flow, toward the canopy; CO_2 is heavier than air so it naturally sinks; and CO_2 is being released from a tank where it is compressed. As it leaves the container, the CO_2 decompresses and cools. With horizontal air circulation in the greenhouse, the CO_2 will stay at plant level until it is used or vacated by fans.

Not all cultivars react the same way to CO_2 enrichment. Increased CO_2 does not affect quality.

Aside from the increased yield, Chance Franck, vice president at Mendocino Grasslands, made some interesting observations after using it for three years:

- The plants have less mold and fewer insect infestations.
- The plants seem to be healthier and less prone to stress.
- The buds are denser.

Notice the CO₂ tubing placed over the canopy. Photo: AgGas

WATER

Revised by Rosa Raudales, PhD

Not all water is created equal; the chemistry of water differs by source. Three key measures of water chemistry that affect plants are alkalinity, pH, and the concentration of dissolved minerals. Mineral content is reported as the concentration of individual elements such as calcium and sodium or total salts. The total concentration of salts is reported as electrical conductivity (EC, measured in millisiemens per centimeter, or mS/cm) or total dissolved salts (TDS, measured in ppm).

Alkalinity is the ability of the water to buffer acids. When water contains components that behave similar to limestone such as carbonates (H_2CO_3), or bicarbonates (HCO), then water pH is not affected as much by the addition of acidic substances such as a water-soluble fertilizer with high ammonium or urea. Water alkalinity reacts with acids to prevent dramatic changes in pH. Water with low or zero alkalinity will result in fast and dramatic drops of pH because there is nothing in the water to react with or buffer the acid in the solution.

Water with no dissolved minerals and no alkalinity is considered "pure water" or "soft water." The electrical conductivity and alkalinity of pure water are zero. The benefit of this water is that it is a clean slate to develop a nutrient program. The grower has full control;

OPTIMUM pH LEVELS FOR CANNABIS GROWING

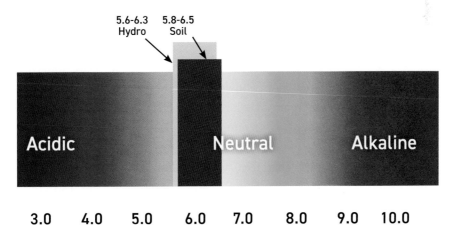

Optimum water pH in a hydroponic system is 5.6–6.3. In a soil system the pH should be between 5.8–6.5. Different nutrients can require a different pH, always check the package.

it is easy to add elements. The disadvantage is that with no alkalinity, there is no buffering ability, so the pH fluctuates.

Adding a small amount of an acidic substance has extreme effects on the pH of pure water; however, alkalinity can also be added in a measured and controlled way to pure water. An ideal water alkalinity is around 125 to 150 ppm of calcium carbonate equivalents because it represents some buffering capacity, but not so much that large amounts of acid have to be added to adjust the pH. Water alkalinity can be added by injecting soluble limestone that contains carbonates or oxides, which are typically associated with calcium or magnesium. Cal-Mag can be used to adjust the water.

Waters from different areas vary dramatically in quality. Even within a close distance, two water sources might differ. For example, well water near coastal areas tends to have high calcium content due to shells, surface water near agricultural fields might have a high concentration of phosphorus or nitrogen and a low pH caused by eutrophication (algae blooms, for instance), deep wells may have low oxygen and high iron and manganese, and some water sources in northern areas may have contamination from road salt.

Water with a high concentration of one element or total dissolved salts takes a large effort to adjust to nutrient programs, which is costly because it requires blending the water with a purer water source, or removal of these elements by treating water with reverse osmosis, deionization, or demineralization.

Water districts and companies continuously test the water they supply. The test results are public records and are available from the water district or company. Results may be posted on the internet. In addition to measures of alkalinity, dissolved solids, and pH, reports show some contaminants. While these tests are useful to track changes over time, they may be insufficient for agricultural purposes and not always timely to develop nutrient programs, prevent nutrient disorders, or chlorine toxicity. In some situations it is advisable to send water samples to a horticultural laboratory for testing two or three times a year or more frequently for closed-loop production systems.

Water Quality

Water is a chemical molecule composed of two atoms of hydrogen (H) and one of oxygen (O). H_2O has a relatively simple chemistry, but its role in the world cannot be underestimated: it is essential for life. Among many functions, water is a key element for plant growth; it is involved in photosynthesis, movement of solutes across cell membranes, nutrient uptake and redistribution, regulation of plant temperature, and flower and fruit development.

While the quality of the molecule itself does not change, water has the ability to dissolve and mix with many molecules. Therefore, water quality refers to chemical, microbial, and physical parameters that water carries and may affect its suitability for a specific use.

The quality of irrigation water strongly affects plant health and the efficacy of irrigation systems.

Water chemistry factors to consider when developing fertilizer programs are alkalinity, the concentration of dissolved ions or salts, and pH.

Alkalinity

Alkalinity refers to the buffering capacity of a solution, or its capacity to neutralize acids. Alkalinity is determined primarily by the total concentration of carbonates and bicarbonates in the water. These bi/carbonates associate with elements such as calcium (Ca), magnesium (Mg), and sodium (Na). Other compounds such as hydroxides, sulfides, phosphates, silicates, and borates may also contribute to alkalinity, but their concentration is usually low in irrigation water. Alkalinity determines how solutions respond to acid.

Water alkalinity should not be confused with alkaline pH (pH > 7.0). A simple way to understand alkalinity is that alkalinity behaves in the same way as dissolved limestone in the water. The following chart illustrates how alkalinity works and why decisions should be made based on the water analysis and not just following the recommendations from other operations.

Water alkalinity is typically reported as equivalents of calcium carbonate ($CaCO_3$) or calcium bicarbonate ($Ca(HCO_3)_2$) in water analysis. Water alkalinity greater than 150 ppm $CaCO_3$ is considered high and increases the pH of the substrate over time.

Alkalinity Units and Conversions

50 ppm calcium carbonate ($CaCO_3$) = 61 ppm calcium bicarbonate ($Ca(HCO_3)_2$)
= 1 mEq/L
1 ppm = 1 mg/L

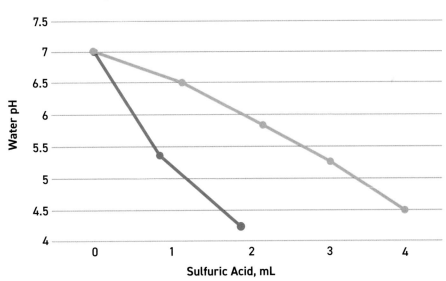

A solution with high alkalinity (blue line) has a relatively high amount of carbonates and/or bicarbonates in solution. The bi/carbonates react with acids, when an acid is added, buffering the solution from pH change. A solution with no bi/carbonates (orange line) will not buffer pH changes with the addition of acid. To exemplify how alkalinity buffers a solution, it took 4 mL of 0.5 M (Molar) sulfuric acid to bring a neutral, buffered solution's pH to 4.5 or less. A neutral, non-buffered solution of the same volume only required 2 mL of 0.5 M sulfuric acid to bring the pH to 4.5 or less, half as much as the buffered, high-alkalinity water.

Alkalinity can be managed by the type of fertilizer used. Alkalinity between 150 and 250 ppm can be managed by using fertilizers that result in an acid reaction in the substrate. Fertilizers result in acidic reactions when they have less than 20% or more of the total nitrogen in the form of ammonium (NH_4+) or urea. The higher the proportion of NH_4+ and urea in the fertilizer, the more acidic the reaction. These fertilizers must be used with caution, because in addition to being strongly acidic, high concentrations of ammonium can be toxic to crops.

In contrast, fertilizers with all the nitrogen in the form of nitrate have a mildly neutral reaction. Nitrate is not toxic to crops. Therefore, when the alkalinity is above 250 ppm, it is necessary to first inject acids to bring down the alkalinity to approximately 100 ppm $CaCO_3$ or 2 mEq/L and then use fertilizers with low ammonium/urea concentration. Never rely solely on fertilizers to manage extremely high alkalinity to prevent crop toxicity.

Use digital calculators available online to estimate the amount of acid to inject to lower alkalinity. An alkalinity between 60 and 150 ppm is an ideal range and should be matched with fertilizers with a more neutral reaction (20–30% NH_4+/urea of the total N). Water alkalinity under 60 ppm $CaCO_3$ is considered low and can be managed by using fertilizers with mostly nitrate (less than 10% of the total nitrogen from ammonium or urea). In addition, limestone can be incorporated in the substrate, or flowable limestone can be sporadically injected in the nutrient solution to increase the buffering capacity of substrates.

Water alkalinity is a standard measurement in the analysis of irrigation suitability in horticultural crops, especially in protected agriculture. Industrial or home water tests do not typically include water alkalinity. Instead they measure water hardness, which is also presented in $CaCO_3$ equivalents. However, water hardness and water alkalinity are not related and should not be confused despite the complicated use of the same units.

Water Hardness

Water hardness is the concentration of dissolved calcium, magnesium, and other cations in water. Water hardness can be carbonated (e.g., $CaCO_3$) or noncarbonated (e.g., $CaCl_2$). Water hardness is relevant to domestic and industrial use because high values reduce the solubility of soap and can result in scaling of water heaters. However, when it comes to irrigation water, the actual values of individual elements such as calcium, chloride, or carbonates are more informative to select nutrient programs and water treatments.

The concentration of calcium and magnesium is not a major concern for agriculture because these elements are essential for plant growth at high concentrations and are added in with fertilizers. Therefore, water hardness by itself is not a major concern in horticulture production.

Water alkalinity can be measured in-house by using kits that promote a reaction, measuring the pH after the reaction, and then matching the results to a conversion table. The alkalinity of water sources does not change frequently, so there is no need to measure it often or in-house. There isn't a direct meter that can perform the test; a pH kit must be used.

pH

Water pH refers to the concentration of hydrogen ions (H+) in relation to hydroxide ions (OH-) and is an indicator of the acidity of a solution. The pH scale ranges from 0 to 14—where less than 7 is acid, 7 is neutral, and greater than 7 is basic, also known as alkaline.

HYDRO-WATER SYSTEM

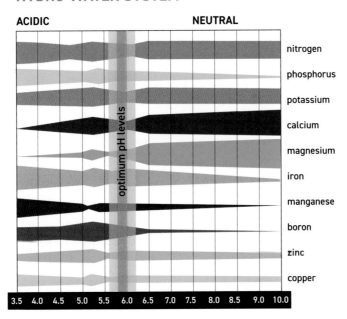

Acceptable pH range for hydro systems: 5.6–6.4. Optimum pH levels are 5.8–6.2.

SOIL

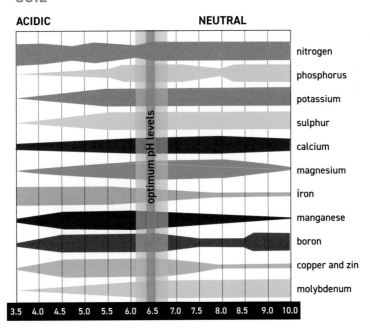

Acceptable pH range for soil gardens: 5.5–6.5. Optimum pH levels are 6.0–6.3.

The ideal starting pH for irrigation water is between 5 and 7, because it is close to the pH required by most crops (5.8–6.2).

Water pH affects the availability of iron, manganese, boron, zinc, and copper. As pH increases, the solubility of these elements decreases, and vice versa. The solubility of some agrochemicals such as fertilizers, fungicides, insecticides, and plant growth regulators is also affected by water pH.

For example, iron is very soluble and available for plants at low pH. While the total concentration of iron does not change when the pH increases, iron precipitates and becomes a solid, rust-colored precipitate that accumulates on surfaces and irrigation systems and is unavailable for plant uptake. The pH of the water can also affect the efficacy of agrochemicals. Growers should pay close attention to the directions on agricultural additive labels and adjust the pH to the recommended level to maximize the efficacy of products.

Growers using organic-based substrates in containers, such as peat or coconut coir, should focus on managing the pH of the substrate by selecting fertilizers that are compatible with water alkalinity and crop needs (*see Nutrients & Fertilizers*), instead of adjusting the water pH.

In contrast, growers using free-floating solutions, such as deep-water culture or nutrient film technique, or inorganic substrates such as rockwool or perlite, should focus on the pH of the solution, since this is where roots take up nutrients. If the pH is outside the recommended range, adjust the pH first and add the fertilizers afterward to prevent excessive nutrient fallout. With mineral fertilizers, two signs of nutrient fallout are cloudiness in the water or precipitate at the bottom of the tank. Check the pH again after fertilizers are added and adjust as needed. Remember the pH is being adjusted to increase nutrient availability.

The pH of water can be adjusted by adding acids or bases to the solution. Nitric, phosphoric, sulfuric, and citric acids are options to lower water pH. All these acids, except citric, are mineral acids that add elements (N, P, or S) to the solution. Citric acid is an organic acid that does not add additional elements to the solution and is considered a milder and "safer" acid compared with mineral acids. From a technical perspective, any acid will achieve pH reduction, for example, pH Down and pH Up contain acids such as citric acid, phosphoric acid, or nitric acid, or bases such as potassium hydroxide, as their active ingredients.

Select an acid based on (1) the elements (N, P, or S) that may be convenient to add to the solution, (2) organic versus mineral sources, (3) worker safety, of which citric is milder, nitric is the most hazardous to handle, and phosphoric and sulfuric are in the middle, and (4) cost.

To properly estimate how much acid to add to achieve a target pH, the water alkalinity must first be known. Online tools help calculate how much acid to use to reach a target pH. Many growers inject acids until they reach the target pH without using a calculator. While this may work, it can also lead to a lot of guessing that results in adding too many additional nutrients.

To increase the water pH, use flowable limestone or hydroxides. Flowable or soluble limestone dissolves well in water and often includes magnesium carbonate, and calcium or magnesium oxide. Depending on the composition of the product, the label will make recommendations of how much to add to increase a given pH by a specific amount. All acids and bases should be handled with caution and adequate personal protection equipment.

Advanced Nutrients' scientists developed pH Up with caustic potash and pH Down with phosphoric acid, enabling growers to easily calibrate their pH levels for optimal nutrient absorption. Each product features highly stable buffers, affording growers precise control of pH after dilution or adjustments between reservoir changes.

Be patient when adjusting the pH of the solution and test frequently. Mix the solution well and allow the acid or base to react before measuring the pH and adding more product. Water pH can be easily monitored and adjusted in-house with hand-held or inline meters. It is inexpensive to get an inline automatic injector system that adjusts the pH of solutions. However, these systems can only be as accurate as the maintenance they receive. Test and calibrate the meters frequently. The temperature of the water also affects pH. Meters are usually calibrated at 68°F (20°C). Temperature compensating meters are preferred.

The GroLine Waterproof Portable pH/EC/TDS Meter HI9814 from Hanna Instruments is designed to bring simplicity to nutrient testing. This single device will provide high-accuracy readings of the water-nutrient solution's pH, EC, TDS, and temperature with a single amplified probe, which is immune to interference from humidity and electrical noise.

The pH & Alkalinity Relationship

There is a connection between pH and alkalinity; however, pH does not equate to alkalinity because they are two different measurements. Water alkalinity refers to the concentration of carbonates and bicarbonates, while pH refers to the concentration of hydrogen ions.

Alkalinity in the water reacts with hydrogen ions to increase the pH (as in this equation: $H+ + HCO_3- \rightarrow H_2O + CO_2$). Typically, water with high alkalinity will have a high pH. However, water with high pH does not necessarily have high alkalinity. Water with a pH of 4.5 has zero alkalinity.

Water alkalinity is a stronger base than water pH; the pH of the substrate is affected by water alkalinity more than water pH. For example, water alkalinity of 50 ppm $CaCO_3$ (very low) would have the same effect in the growing media as water with a pH of 11 (very high). Water with a pH of 8.0 would have the same effect in the medium as alkalinity of 0.05 ppm $CaCO_3$.

Although the rhizosphere is temporarily affected while watering, the water pH has only a little effect on the substrate pH over time. Water alkalinity, which behaves like limestone, significantly increases the pH over time.

Dissolved Ions

Dissolved ions in a solution can be measured by estimating the concentration of total salts or individual elements. Both affect how water can be managed and used. Extremely high levels of dissolved elements affect the suitability of a water source.

Electrical conductivity (EC) is the ability of a solution to carry electrical current and an indicator of the total concentration of salts in a solution. Water EC indicates whether the salts, in general, are high or low, but it does not point to which specific elements are abundant. Adding fertilizer to water that already has a high EC (greater than 1mS/cm) can result in burnt roots and shoots. Therefore, water with low EC is desirable to give growers room to determine the amount of nutrients that can be used before harming the crop.

Electrical conductivity (EC) units:
1 mS/cm = 1 mmho/cm = 1dS/m = 1000uS/cm

EC can be easily measured, and the value can be used to track changes over time. Source water with an EC less than 0.5 mS/cm is ideal because it indicates there is a low concentration of dissolved salts. Water sources with levels above 0.5 mS/cm should be sent to an analytical laboratory for a complete nutrient analysis.

The goal of a complete nutrient analysis is to identify if any element is at a level that can be phytotoxic to crops or if any element that is essential for plant growth is high enough that fertilizer programs need adjustment. Water with an EC higher than 0.7 mS/cm can result in salt accumulation in substrates or nutrient solutions, hard and stunted growth, and lead to damage on the foliage in propagation.

High EC is problematic because it leaves little room to provide nutrients through fertilizers. Therefore, any water source with an EC greater than 1.0 should be treated by blending the water with a purer water source such as rainwater or reverse osmosis (RO) treated water.

The treatment choice will depend on a combination of factors specific to an operation, including cost and access to alternative water sources.

RO treatment can be expensive and time-consuming, and creates toxic wastewater, but in many circumstances it is the only option. Sometimes switching to a different water source might be the best option—from a technical and financial perspective.

Electrical Conductivity (EC) in Water Sources and Management Recommendations

EC (mS/cm)	Interpretation of result	Actions to prevent problems*
<0.5	Low concentration of dissolved ions and unlikely to be a problem for irrigation water in terms of total salt accumulation.	No action needed.
0.5–1.0	Moderate levels of dissolved ions are likely to lead to salt accumulation in the substrate or recirculating solution, affecting plant growth.	Treatment such as reverse osmosis or carbon filtering, blending with a purer water such as rainwater or RO-treated water, or leach during irrigation is recommended.
>1.0	High concentration of salts that will likely result in salt accumulation in the substrate or recirculating solution, affecting plant growth.	Treatment such as reverse osmosis or carbon filtering, blending with a purer water such as rainwater or RO-treated water, or leach during irrigation is required.

*Further testing is needed at all EC levels to determine which elements are present, including fertilizer nutrients, alkalinity, chloride, and sodium.

Water Testing

The chemical parameters of water sources do not change frequently. However, depending on the region and water source, differences might be observed seasonally. For example, the concentration of specific or total salts may be high in the summer when the water table is low, and vice versa in the winter. Contamination of surface or groundwater sometimes occurs from adjacent field or road salt applications.

Growers should send samples of the water for complete nutrient analysis at least twice per year. Growers who see nutrient disorder problems should test water quality, substrates, and nutrient solutions.

East Bay Municipal Utility District Annual Report 2020

Water Quality Parameters	Orinda
Alkalinity, total as $CaCO_3$	25–48 ppm
Calcium	4–9 ppm
Hardness as $CaCO_3$	16–36 ppm
Magnesium	1–2 ppb
pH	8.5–9.5
Potassium	<1–1
Silica	8–11
Sodium	5–11 ppm

The table above provides useful information for certain industrial and home applications. This report comes from the Orinda plant for East Bay MUD, which provides water for the eastern San Francisco Bay Area. Local water-quality reports are publicly available and can be checked for any region.

Specific Elements

Water often contains elements essential to plant growth as well as nonessential elements. Elements essential for plant growth are nitrogen (N), phosphorus (P), potassium (K), calcium (Ca), magnesium (Mg), sulfur (S), boron (B), chlorine (Cl), iron (Fe), manganese (Mn), zinc (Zn), copper (Cu), and molybdenum (Mo). Silicon (Si) is not considered essential but increases plant vigor and resistance to stress. Ca, Mg, S (in the form of sulfates, SO_4^-), B, Cl, Fe, Mn, Zn, Cu, carbonates, and sodium are often found in natural water sources.

Management of macronutrients (N, P, K, Ca, Mg, and S) in the water is relatively easy because they are needed in large amounts by plants and very rarely, with the exception of calcium, are they present in amounts larger than what the plants need.

Shallow wells in agricultural areas are often contaminated by agricultural runoff. Water from deep wells occasionally contains a high concentration of iron but is rarely contaminated by agricultural runoff.

The quality of surface water such as ponds, lakes, and rivers depends on the surrounding areas. The only way to know a water is to have it analyzed. It will prevent risks from unhealthy chemicals and help to determine how it needs to be treated for agricultural purposes.

N, P, and K in water indicates contamination from agricultural runoff because these elements are not found in high concentrations naturally. This may not be a significant issue from a nutrient management perspective, but there is a greater possibility of contamination with plant growth regulators, pathogens, pesticides, herbicides, and/or fungicides.

Any essential nutrient in the water that is below the level required for plant growth does not require removal (with reverse osmosis or blending with pure water sources). To properly use this water source, fertilizer levels can be decreased to accommodate the nu-

A healthy vegetative plant. Photo: Angela Bacca

trients already present. For example, if there are 20 mg/L of N in the water source and the plant requirement is 100 mg/L N, then the amount of N is reduced from fertilizers and only 80 mg/L is applied.

Micronutrients (B, Cl, Fe, Mn, Zn, Cu, and Mo) and nonessential elements (sodium and fluoride) in water sources are more difficult to manage because even small concentrations can cause plant phytotoxicity or affect the efficacy of irrigation systems.

The specific characteristics of water sources are difficult to predict. However, there are some common trends.

Rainwater and drinking water treated by cities are usually low in dissolved elements.

The type of dissolved elements and their quantity in groundwater is highly dependent on regional geological characteristics and the minerals that weathered into water sources. For example, high concentrations of sodium and calcium are common in coastal areas.

Reverse Osmosis (RO)

RO is a filtration system that uses a pressurized, ultrafine, semipermeable membrane to remove salts and other particles from water. Osmosis is a process in which a solution moves from a low concentration of solutes to a higher concentration. In reverse osmosis the pressure and the charge of the membrane forces the inverse process, moving the solution from high to low concentration and therefore removing impurities from the water.

Reverse osmosis can be used to remove excessive amounts of salts from irrigation water that contains excess sodium, chloride, or other micronutrients. Boron and some agricultural chemicals are difficult to remove with RO systems.

Water flow slows when RO systems are in line because the filter pore size is small. RO can easily be clogged by suspended solids such as sand, silt, organic matter, chemical precipitates (Fe, Mn, carbonates, pesticides), or bacteria and algae, so prefiltration of suspended solids is essential before membrane filtration to prevent clogging or damage.

Many argue that starting with RO-treated water is essential to develop nutrient programs. However, water with an EC of less than 0.5 mS/cm does not need treatment.

If the target element is a micronutrient that is above the toxicity threshold or a salt that cannot be managed with the nutrient program and no alternative water source is available to blend the water, RO treatment should be considered.

RO treatment is an effective technology and in many situations is the only option available to deal with high concentration of salts. However, its environmental footprint is a concern that must be considered. Brine is a solution with high concentration of salts and a by-product of RO treatment.

Brine discharge is regulated because the high concentration of salts may affect the ecosystem. There is ongoing research to identify applications for brine; until then, most of it is discharged back into water sources where it disrupts the balance of elements in water bodies and affects wildlife.

Secondary Nutrients & Micronutrients

Element	Ideal level (mg/L)	Interpretation	Management
Calcium (Ca)	40–100	High concentrations of calcium can result in scale buildup via $CaCO_3$ and other compounds precipitating out of solution (clogging irrigation lines and emitters). High levels of calcium can result in cation antagonism, causing a deficiency in phosphorus or magnesium.	Low calcium levels are managed by amending the irrigation water with calcium containing nutrients such as CalMag or calcium nitrate ($CaNO_3$). High calcium levels are managed through reverse osmosis or water softening (preferably with a potassium-based salt as opposed to a sodium-based salt).
Magnesium (Mg)	25–50	High concentrations of magnesium can result in scale buildup (clogging irrigation lines and emitters).	Low magnesium levels are managed by amending the irrigation water with magnesium containing nutrients such as CalMag or epsom salts ($MgSO_4$). High magnesium levels are managed through reverse osmosis or water softening (preferably with a potassium-based salt as opposed to a sodium-based salt).
Sulfur (S)	<10	High sulfur or sulfate levels in irrigation water may result in high hydrogen sulfide gas (H_2S) levels. Hydrogen sulfide smells of rotten eggs and is toxic in highly concentrated forms.	If high hydrogen sulfide levels are at or below 2 mg/L, aerating the water is ideal to convert the H_2S back to SO_4. Reverse osmosis or dilution with clean water should be used to remove/reduce excess ion concentrations including sulfate. The addition of calcium nitrate will decrease the rate of hydrogen sulfide formation.

Element	Ideal level (mg/L)	Interpretation	Management
Iron (Fe)	<0.3	Iron levels above 0.3 mg/L increase the risk of iron bacteria (slime that clogs emitters) and/or iron precipitation (rust particles), which cause discoloration of plant leaves in propagation or clogging of irrigation equipment.	Water treatments that oxidize the iron ions can remove them from the water. Treatments include aeration and settling in ponds, or chemical oxidation with chlorine, ozone, or potassium permanganate followed by sand filtration. The iron in the water sample is unlikely to be chelated unless it is from recycled water, so it is likely that additional chelated fertilizer iron will be needed for crops.
Manganese (Mn)	<0.3	Mn levels above 0.3 mg/L increase the risk of manganese bacteria (slime that clogs emitters) and precipitation in irrigation equipment (also causing clogging).	Water treatments that oxidize the manganese can remove these ions from the water. Treatments include aeration and settling in ponds, or chemical oxidation with chlorine, ozone, or potassium permanganate followed by sand filtration.
Zinc (Zn)	<0.5	Risk of zinc toxicity in plants. Symptoms may include chlorosis, reduction in leaf size, necrosis of tips, and distortion of foliage.	Fertilizer levels applied to crop plants are usually less than 0.75 mg/L. Do not apply additional zinc in fertilizer.
Boron (B)	<0.5	Boron at 1 mg/L or higher can cause toxicity characterized by leaf tip burn.	Boron is the only ion that cannot be effectively removed with reverse osmosis purification. Manage high boron levels in irrigation water (>1.0 ppm) by keeping the substrate pH above 6.0 and use calcium-based fertilizers, or blend with a more pure water source.
Molybdenum (Mo)	<0.1	Phytotoxicity is unlikely from Mo in water or soils.	Do not apply additional Mo in fertilizer.
Sodium (Na)	<70 mg/L	Sodium increases the electrical conductivity of the water—increasing the risk of salt burn of foliage and roots.	Remove with reverse osmosis or reduce by blending with rainwater. Restore nutrient balance and prevent salt buildup by leaching the substrate or replacing the recirculating nutrient solution periodically.
Chlorine (Cl)	<70 mg/L	Chloride levels above 70 mg/L increase the electrical conductivity of the water—increasing the risk of salt burn of foliage and roots.	Remove with reverse osmosis or reduce by blending with rainwater. Restore nutrient balance and prevent salt buildup by leaching the substrate or replacing the recirculating nutrient solution periodically.
Fluorine (F)	< 0.5 mg/L	Fluorine is added to drinking water to promote human health but can cause phytotoxicity symptoms.	Remove fluorine with activated carbon filters. Maintain the substrate pH above 6.0 and use calcium-based fertilizers.

Water Quality beyond Nutrient Programs

The quality of water affects plant production in other ways than just nutrient programs. Water can be a source or dispersal mechanism of plant pathogens or a carrier of elements and particles that clog the irrigation system or contain chemicals that are detrimental to crop quality.

Chemical Parameters

Chlorine

Drinking-water treatment facilities apply up to 4 ppm fluoride and chlorine (the sanitizer, not to be confused with the chloride ion) in the water. These levels are within the US Environmental Protection Agency standards for drinking water. It is rarely a problem for annual crops, and can be rinsed from the medium with flushing.

Chlorine is an essential micronutrient for plants, but plants' needs for chlorine are rather low. Most of the time water treatment facilities use a lower range, and chlorine dissipates as it moves in the water distribution systems, but the grower has little control or knowledge on when these changes might happen. Chlorine and fluoride can be easily removed by having an activated carbon filter. Chlorine can be monitored in-house by using colorimetric kits or having an inline meter.

Agrichemical Residues

Agricultural runoff can include agrichemicals such as herbicides, pesticides, fungicides, plant growth regulators, nutrients, and plant pathogens. Agricultural runoff can be present in surface water or groundwater where growers have very little control. Agricultural runoff increases in the water source when it is connected to the runoff or if nutrient solution is recirculated.

Think about water treatment as a risk management strategy, and implement an approach that has a continuous treatment point in place as a preventative mechanism. Carbon filtration is a good option. The goal is to have a proactive rather than reactive approach. Carbon filters also remove most agrichemicals. However, it is not known if they affect plant pathogen survival.

Chemical Precipitates

At high concentrations, greater than 4 mg/L, iron can precipitate, accumulating and clogging irrigation systems and staining surfaces of plant tissue or walls.

Iron is in solution in its dissolved form or when the pH is less than 6.0. As the pH increases, iron precipitates, forming into a solid form of rust. Precipitated iron accumulates in irrigation lines and can clog irrigation emitters and main pipes. Additionally, it stains the leaves with overhead irrigation.

Iron also precipitates when it goes from low to high oxygen levels, which happens when it is pulled from deep wells. Iron is typically a problem when using deep wells. Although not all wells have high iron concentration, problems with high iron are mostly observed in deep wells. Iron in water can be managed using a system that includes oxidation, which promotes precipitation, followed by filtration.

An effective method is injecting potassium permanganate (at 1:1 ratio) as an oxidizer, followed by filters with glauconite greensand. Aeration or other types of chemical oxidations (chlorine) can also be used. However, potassium permanganate is ideal because it injects K as a by-product, which is an essential macronutrient. Aeration can be slow, and chlorine can be phytotoxic.

Calcium in the water reacts with bicarbonates (HCO_3^-) or sulfates (SO_4^{-2}), and precipitates. This reaction happens when both elements are at high concentrations (Ca greater than 150 mg/L and bicarbonates greater than 180 mg/L, sulfates greater than 120 mg/L). This is why calcium is separated from other elements in stock solutions.

A quick fix to this problem is to inject acid to dissociate the bicarbonate ions. A more expensive solution is to use membrane filtration (e.g., reverse osmosis) to remove salts. Membrane filtration should only be used if the levels are extreme and cannot be managed with acid.

Dissolved Organics

Dissolved organics include agrochemicals and humic acids. Carbon filtration, reverse osmosis, and ozone remove a vast amount of agrochemicals from water.

Biological Parameters

Waterborne microbes that may affect crop production include plant pathogens, algae, and bacteria associated with clogging. Water sources vary in the risk that they pose by carrying detrimental microorganisms. Surface water tends to harbor microorganisms including plant pathogens and biofilm-forming bacteria at a larger concentration and diversity than any other water source.

Growers should be aware of the different risks they face when using different water sources. Deep wells, rainwater, and drinking water tend to have very low concentration of microorganisms. Iron and manganese oxidizing bacteria can be found in wells both deep and shallow. Any water source with agricultural runoff, including recirculated water within an operation, is likely to have plant pathogens.

Plant Pathogens

Irrigation water can be an inoculum or dispersal mechanism of plant pathogens. Water sourced from the ground, rain, or cities does not have plant pathogens. In rare cases groundwater can be contaminated from agricultural runoff.

Surface water bodies such as ponds and lakes and recirculated, but not precipitated, water can have a high concentration and diversity of plant pathogens. Subirrigation systems, regardless of the source, are at high risk of dispersing pathogens from container to container. This problem is exacerbated because the solution containing pathogens moves from one container or zone to another and also because organic debris such as plant matter or planting medium on floors or benches protects pathogens from desiccation or dehydration.

Waterborne plant pathogens include bacteria, oomycetes, and fungi. Oomycetes, also known as "water molds," include organisms that cause common diseases such as seedling blight, damping-off, and root and stem rot. They persist really well in water and produce swimming spores called *zoospores* that actively swim toward root exudates.

Two common oomycete pathogens found in water that affect cannabis are several species of *Pythium* and *Phytophthora*. Fungi such as *Fusarium* and *Rhizoctonia* are also present in the water. Recent research from the University of California has also found that sand filters can remove oomycetes from irrigation water (Lee and Oki 2013).

Unlike oomycetes, fungi do not swim freely; instead, they are carried in organic debris or overwintering structures. This is one reason, among others stated below, why removing organic debris is an important step in water sanitation.

Biofilms

Biofilms are a group of microorganisms, mostly bacteria, that form a polysaccharide coating that protects them from desiccation. Think of them as slime. In irrigation systems when water-soluble fertilizers are used, biofilms also harbor algae. Biofilms frequently accumulate in fine emitters, filters, or main irrigation pipes and clog the system. Biofilms are not well understood in irrigation. There is no one silver bullet to combat biofilms because they are diverse in composition. However, a general approach is recommended to prevent and remove them. First, follow the sanitation recommendations below. (*See Water Sanitation.*)

Flush the system with water at high pressure to remove the amount of organic and mineral residues that may be sitting on the system and physically (partially) destroy the biofilm. Use highly acidic water to dissolve some of the slime. After flushing the system, inject chemical sanitizers such as chlorine dioxide (ClO_2), hypochlorous acid (HOCl or HClO), peroxyacetic/peracetic acid ($C_2H_4O_3$), or hydrogen peroxide (H_2O_2) at high concentration—this is known as shocking the system.

The concentration used to shock the irrigation system is higher than the doses recommended for use during production and are toxic to crops. The system should be shocked only when the space is empty. If possible, the solution should be allowed to stay in the irrigation system overnight and be rinsed with abundant water at high pressure to push out the slime.

Algae

Algae are omnipresent. No matter how clean an operation, when there is light reaching a solution, it ends up accumulating algae. Prevent algae by stopping light from reaching the nutrient solution and clean up and dry out wet spots.

Water Sanitation

Water treatment options include sanitizers that kill organisms, chlorination, activated peroxygens, quaternary ammonium, ozone, UV light, heat treatment, chlorine dioxide, hypochlorous acid (HOCl or HClO), hydrogen peroxide (H_2O_2), peroxyacetic/peracetic acid ($C_2H_4O_3$), copper, biofungicides, and more. Little is known about the tolerance of cannabis to some of these sanitizers, so it is best to start with a low dose. Regardless of the target organism, here are some general rules to make sanitation effective:

1. **Select a sanitizer.** Sanitizers differ in their residual activity, or how much control they provide throughout the irrigation. Point treatments such as ultraviolet (UV) light and heat treatment can control organisms when the solutions are in direct contact with the treatment system, and they leave no residues in the solution.

   In contrast, injectable sanitizers continue to react throughout the irrigation. The residual activity of the injectable products varies by their inherent properties and the concentration applied. The benefit of residual activity is sustained control throughout the system; the disadvantage is the risk of phytotoxicity when the product is applied at high doses or if it accumulates in closed-loop irrigation systems.

   Sanitizers vary in their efficacy to control specific organisms. However, in irrigation sanitation the goal is not to sterilize the solution but to reduce the risk caused by microbes without causing plant phytotoxicity. Water sanitation is only one part of the whole integrated plant disease management.

2. **Filter first, sanitize later.** Sanitizers are nonspecific and react with any organic matter in the solution. To achieve a higher degree of sanitation, it is essential to remove non target organic matter or debris such as dead roots, leaves, and substrates from the solution via filtration and then apply the sanitation step.

3. **Extend contact time.** When possible, apply the sanitizer and allow it to have a prolonged contact time with the solution before irrigating crops. Storage tanks are an essential component of water management and sanitation because they provide the ability to slow water flow and reduce the size of the equipment or dose needed to treat water. The longer the water is in contact with a sanitizer product or treatment, the higher the microbial mortality.

4. **Filter multiple times.** Multiple-stage filtration is a must for any water distribution system. Install filters in series, from coarse to fine pores, to improve filtration efficiency and reduce the need of cleaning filters (use filters with automatic backwash). Filtration will help remove the organic debris discussed above. Having multiple stages will prevent the system from clogging too frequently.

5. **Monitor the efficacy of the system.** All water sanitation systems require constant monitoring to ensure proper sanitation and prevent phytotoxicity. A system will

only be effective if it is functioning properly. Include sampling valves to take samples or inline meters to measure active ingredients. In commercial operations, staff must be trained on how to monitor and adjust the system.

6. **Match the system to the culture of the operation.** While one technology might be "better" than others, at the end of the day the treatment option that will work best is the one that is well understood and maintained. Choose a technology that fits the operation's culture. Many operations like high-tech options, but many prefer simplicity. All options can work if there is someone who stands behind it and maintains it properly. Speak with other growers about how effective the systems are, the service the companies provide, and how easy the system is to manage.

7. **Think beyond water treatments.** Water sanitation is only one part of integrated plant disease management to prevent waterborne microbial problems. Use resistant cultivars when available.

The entry of pathogens from other sources include:
- Infected cuttings and liners
- Uncleaned tools
- Workers bringing in infections from outdoors
- Workers moving infections from one section to another
- Overwatering, which promotes bacteria and other root diseases

Physical Parameters

Physical parameters of water quality include any particles in suspension (not dissolved) that accumulate and clog the irrigation systems. They can be organic or inorganic.

Organic particles include debris such as plant parts, particles from media substrates, and even algae. Sand filters remove microbial loads and large organic particles. Screen and media filters are also effective in removing large organic debris and weeds. Media filters can easily clog if the debris is too coarse, so they must be monitored and cleaned.

Inorganic particles and debris include fine granular minerals such as sand, clay, and silt. These contaminants can be physically removed with "paper," sock, screen, or disc filters. Reverse osmosis or other membrane filtration should not be used to remove suspended inorganic particles and debris because they can physically damage the membranes.

Water treatment needs to be an integrated system that should be designed to target the combination of potential risks in an operation. Therefore, before installing a system, it is essential to understand the problem, match the treatment option to the problem, and develop a management plant to monitor proper functioning.

Water Treatment Options by Target Problem

Problem	Water Treatment Options	Objective
Microbial: Plant pathogens, biofilm, and algae	Sanitizers: chlorination, activated peroxygens, ozone, UV light, heat treatment, chlorine dioxide, hypochlorous acid, and copper.	Reduce inoculum. Remove established populations.
Chemical: High concentration of salts	Adjust nutrient program or pH. Reverse osmosis.	Manipulate chemistry to make it suitable for plants. Remove high concentration of ions.
Chemical: Agrochemicals	Carbon filtration or ozone.	Remove agrochemicals from water.
Physical: suspended particles	Filters: screen, disc, media, or membrane filters.	Remove debris.

Temperature, Oxygen & Carbon Dioxide

The temperature of the water affects plant growth, microbial activity, and the ability of water to hold oxygen. The optimum root zone temperature for oxygenated hydroponic solutions is 68°F (20°C). When the water temperature in the root zone is lower, plants are less efficient using energy, their metabolisms slow down, nutrient uptake reduces, and therefore yields are affected. When water is too warm, it holds less oxygen and can be cooled using water chillers or by blending with lower temperature water. When roots have access to enough oxygen, planting media temperature can be higher.

Water is an excellent conductor of temperature, and most greenhouses use hot water to increase root zone temperatures. Water at 100°F (38°C) is passed in pipe loops under the production benches or concrete floor to increase the root zone temperature during winter months, thus avoiding the need and cost of heating the whole facility.

Root respiration (intake of oxygen) is required for root growth and nutrient mobilization. Oxygen is available to the roots in air spaces in growing media or as dissolved oxygen (DO) in hydroponic solutions. DO is a measure of the amount of gaseous oxygen in water.

A DO of 6 ppm or more is ideal for hydroponic solutions. DO under 4 ppm has negative effects on plant growth, including stress and reduced growth and nutrient movement. Increasing the DO above 6 ppm has little to no effect on plant health, quality, or yields in hydroponically grown crops. Maintaining an optimum level can be achieved by promoting water movement or injecting air from the environment and avoiding stagnation in storage or production tanks. Here are some methods:

- Air pumps with bubblers
- Pumping a cascade or shower
- Injecting nano oxygen bubbles
- Adding H_2O_2
- Electrolysis

Water in deep wells may have low oxygen; however, as soon as the water reaches the ground-surface, enough oxygen dissolves into the water from the air.

Water in ponds or storage tanks with no aeration can accumulate anaerobic bacteria, which may smell bad or clog the system. A simple system (e.g., a pump) that promotes water movement is sufficient to prevent water stagnation. DO can be easily monitored with meters, very similar to a pH meter.

Temperature and DO have an inverse relationship. As water temperature rises, oxygen solubility goes down. For example, water at 50°F (10°C) can hold 11.3 ppm DO, whereas 77°F (25°C) can only hold 8.6 ppm DO. This relationship is especially important when producing in deep-water culture, where the roots are only exposed to the solution.

In container production the oxygen is stored in the pockets of air in the substrate. In other hydroponic systems the oxygen is obtained from the DO in the nutrient solution as it moves.

Carbon dioxide (CO_2) is very soluble in water. Most of the CO_2 in water comes as a by-product of algae, root, and microbial respiration (use oxygen and extrude CO_2). Ponds with a lot of algae (or plants) tend to have large pH fluctuations during the day.

Algae and plants use CO_2 and release oxygen when photosynthesizing during the sunny portions of the day. When light is not present (as is expected in the root zone for most plants), plant roots release CO_2 as they metabolize sugars. CO_2 reacts with water and forms carbonic acid, which lowers the pH of the water. This reaction is similar to what happens in hydroponic solutions, and that is why the pH of nutrient solutions tends to go down as plant biomass increases. Prevent algae accumulation by avoiding nutrient runoff into the pond and by having a good aeration system.

Electrolyzed Water

Electrolyzed oxidizing water (EOW), or electrolyzed water, is a potent disinfectant and has been shown to be effective in sanitizing food crops (Siddiqui 2018). The use of EOW for sanitation purposes is gaining traction in the cannabis industry as well. The disinfecting solution is nothing more than hypochlorous acid that can be created by using the process of electrolysis with a chloride-containing salt (NaCl or KCl) dissolved in water. Electrolysis is the process where water molecules are split into their atomic components through a direct electrical current:

$$2\,H_2O \rightarrow 2\,H_2 + O_2$$

During this process, hydrogen gas accumulates around the negative electrode (cathode), and oxygen gas forms around the positive electrode (anode). With dilute NaCl dissolved in the water, the electrolysis process results in two solutions: one with sodium hydroxide (NaOH) and one with hypochlorous acid (HOCl). Hypochlorous acid is a weak acid that has strong oxidizing powers that can neutralize colonies of *Escherichia coli*, *Salmonella typhimurium*, and *Listeria monocytogenes* (Park et al. 2009).

Similar to using ozonation for sanitation, electrolyzed water can be created on demand with few inputs. Ozonation requires an ozone generator; likewise, electrolyzed water requires an EOW generator. The EOW generator only requires water, salt, and access to electricity to create a sanitizing solution on demand. Electrolyzed water can also be purchased in a stabilized form as a disinfectant spray.

There is not much research identifying the benefits of using electrolyzed water on the growth of cannabis; however, it is known that when hypochlorous acid comes in contact with fertilizers in nutrient solution, especially nitrates, it quickly degrades into chloramines. Chloramines are a significantly weaker group of oxidizing agents and are not as effective as hypochlorous acid when it comes to antimicrobial activity.

EOW is an effective biofilm eliminator when it is used in pure water. Again, coming in contact with fertilizers, the acid quickly produces chloramines, which are not effective in treating biofilms in irrigation lines.

Direct application of electrolyzed water to the root zone of cannabis plants can run the risk of phytotoxicity. It is widely known that excessive use of hypochlorous acid in the root zone can harm the growth of plants. In low concentrations that are usually seen as safe for direct application to plant roots (<2.5mg/L), hypochlorous acid successfully inactivated a pathogen commonly found to cause root rot in cannabis, *Rhizoctonia solani* (Serge et al. 2019).

Electrolyzed water is a potent antimicrobial agent, so direct application to a living soil has a detrimental effect on the beneficial microorganisms that provide benefit to the plants' productivity. A healthy and diverse microbiome in the root zone provides protection from pathogens that may take advantage of a decimated microbial community.

Electrolyzed water's safest application is cleaning and disinfecting equipment, grow rooms, tables, pots, and irrigation systems. The effectiveness of EOW in combination with its ease of access from on-demand production makes it a very attractive product for sanitation purposes; however, the effects of direct use on plants is unknown.

Photo: Courtesy of AEssenseGrows

OXYGEN

All of the plant's living tissues require oxygen for aerobic respiration, from the bottom of the roots to the tops of the shoots. If oxygen becomes a limiting factor for any of those plant parts, the plant's rate of respiration will dip, and its ability to perform its normal activities will decrease. Theoretically, oxygen can be a limiting factor in the stems, leaves, and flowers; however, in practice, it is nearly impossible for that to happen. Oxygen stress is only a real possibility in the root zone, when oxygen uptake by the plant's roots outpaces oxygen's replacement there.

Oxygen Sources for Plants

Plants have three sources of oxygen:

- Oxygen released during photosynthesis but held in the plant structure
- Oxygen in the atmosphere
- Oxygen dissolved in water, which the roots absorb

Cannabis is terrestrial, meaning its roots explore the soil or whatever growing medium they are in. Underground roots do not see the light of day, and therefore do not have access to atmospheric oxygen.

Atmosphere

There is a lot of oxygen available in the atmosphere, which is about 21% oxygen. The roots' source of oxygen is through diffusion to the root zone.

Oxygen diffuses 10,000 times slower through water than it does through air. Roots growing in compacted soil or degraded growing medium with little air porosity can lose access to oxygen very quickly. It is imperative that the growing medium or soil has enough air porosity that oxygen can diffuse through the small air spaces between the soil particles. If the plant's roots are actively respiring, oxygen stress can occur within 20 to 30 minutes.

The primary way roots get oxygen is through diffusing through the air pores in the soil or growing medium or via water that is saturated with dissolved oxygen. When soil is watered from the top, the draining water creates a vacuum in its wake that pulls fresh air into the ground.

Dissolved in Water

Roots can also absorb oxygen that is dissolved in water or nutrient solution. As long as the water is saturated with oxygen, every time plants are irrigated or fertigated the roots get a fresh delivery. As temperatures rise, the rate of respiration in the roots increases.

Although oxygen in the atmosphere is at a concentration of about 21%, oxygen dissolves in water and maxes out at 8.3 ppm at 77°F (25°C). At 68°F (20°C), the dissolved oxygen concentration in water maxes out at 9.1 ppm.

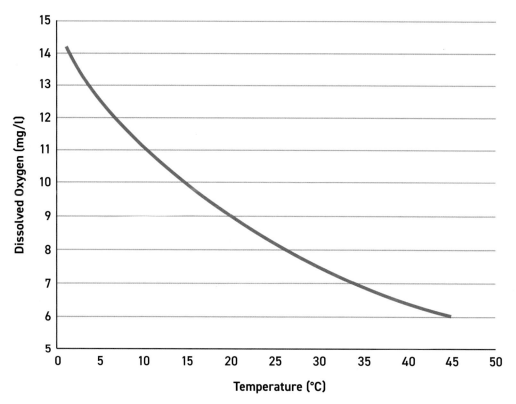

The orange line represents maximum saturation levels of dissolved oxygen at different temperatures. As water temperatures increase, the capacity to store dissolved oxygen decreases.

As water temperatures decrease, the saturation level increases. The question arises: Does it make sense to decrease the root zone temperature to increase oxygen availability to the roots? Unfortunately, a decrease in root zone temperature also drastically decreases the rate of root respiration, lowering the roots' metabolism and productivity. Even though more oxygen may be available in a cooler root zone, slower root respiration rates slow delivery of water and nutrients to the canopy. The ideal root zone and nutrient solution temperature should range between 68°F (20°C) and 72°F (22°C) in water culture and up to 75°F (24°C) in planting mix, where the water is interspersed with air. Planting media temperatures can run slightly warmer.

Dissolved oxygen (DO) is the primary source of oxygen for roots in aeroponic production. Growing in a physical growing medium requires frequent fertigations with oxygen-saturated nutrient solution.

Normal versus Low Oxygen Levels

Normoxic conditions mean that the level of oxygen is not a limiting factor for respiration in the root tissue. The roots are actively growing and absorbing nutrients and water sufficiently. Root respiration is heavily dependent on temperature and oxygen concentration. If the oxygen concentration declines with a constant root temperature, the rate of respiration will also slow down. As respiration rates drop, the amount of energy available to do work also decreases. This is the energy the roots need to grow, absorb nutrients, and maintain cellular integrity.

The root environment goes from normoxic to hypoxic when the concentration of oxygen in the root zone drops to a level so low that not enough energy is available from respiration for the roots to properly function. Hypoxic root conditions lead to several problems for the plant. The rate of nutrient absorption declines, and root growth decreases and dies. Plant roots signal to the leaves to close the stomata. Water absorption through the roots declines and then stops. This decreases the plant's ability to photosynthesize, since the stomata are closed and no longer allow CO_2 to enter the leaves. The combined effects of a hypoxic root zone range from a smaller yield to plant failure.

Wilting & Overwatering

Plants that are growing in poor, low air porosity soils or growing media may wilt not because they don't have enough water but because they have too much water. It is entirely possible to overwater a plant, especially if a growing medium does not have much air porosity. The media can be saturated or flooded with water that quickly becomes hypoxic.

Oxygen can diffuse relatively quickly through air but much slower through water. If a growing medium has very fine particles, it may have low porosity. If it is never allowed to dry out a bit so that air can diffuse into the root zone, the roots will suffer.

Hypoxic roots signal the leaves to close their stomata because the roots cannot keep up with the amount of water absorption needed to supply the shoots. When roots are continuously flooded, the plant wilts. A grower may see the wilting plant and think that it needs more water, when in fact more water would only make the problem worse. Although it may seem counterintuitive, the thing to do is actually let the root zone dry out enough to open up the pores inside the growing medium to let oxygen diffuse through.

As oxygen concentrations continue to decrease in a hypoxic root environment, the root zone eventually becomes anoxic, that is, it has virtually no oxygen. Root respiration stops completely and usually results in root die-off. Not only does this decrease the surface area for nutrient and water absorption, but the dying roots provide entry points for microbial pathogens such as *Phytophthora cinnamomi* (Jacobs et al. 1997).

An oxygen-enriched environment makes a big difference in plant vigor; more so for unrooted cuttings than rooted plants, but both benefit from sufficient oxygen concentrations. Root initiation requires more oxygen than regular root maintenance, which is why unrooted cuttings see a bigger benefit. Root growth and overall root mass accumulation are improved when oxygen is not a limiting factor. Root growth and development is best with oxygen-saturated media, which is why it is so important to have high oxygen levels when taking cuttings for vegetative propagation. Root initiation from shoot tissue requires adequate oxygen levels.

Increasing Oxygen in the Root Zone

Passive approaches capitalize on how roots get their oxygen. Oxygen naturally diffuses through the air spaces of a porous growing medium for soil. Using a growing medium with particles large enough to leave space for air once the soil drains is essential for allowing the passive movement of oxygen-containing air through the root zone.

Proper management of the irrigation schedule is crucial in optimizing oxygen availability for the roots. Growing plants in fine-grain or compacted soil or a growing medium that has low porosity leaves little breathing room for the roots.

Cannabis suffers from a waterlogged soil because it is more likely to be hypoxic, since the pores in the soil are filled with water.

Irrigating with low-oxygen water without allowing the soil to dry out between watering is the worst scenario, since oxygen never gets the chance to diffuse through the pores of the growing medium. The water being introduced into the root zone is not bringing oxygen with it. Allowing for the growing medium to dry out a bit between irrigations promotes oxygen availability in fine-textured soils.

Irrigating with oxygen-saturated water is another way to passively introduce oxygen to the roots. Waterlogged soil is not harmful to the plants as long as the root zone has plenty of oxygen. Plants can be irrigated continuously as long as the nutrient solution is saturated with oxygen.

The theory behind growing in aquaponic production is the roots are constantly being showered with nutrient solution that is always exposed to air. The high exposure to oxygen allows for constantly saturated water raining down on the roots.

Increasing oxygen concentrations in water is not difficult to do. There is so much oxygen available in the atmosphere that actively bubbling air through water in a storage tank with an aquarium pump attached to an air stone is sufficient.

A pump-over or cascade can also be used to oxygenate water in a storage tank. A pump creates a spray or jet that splashes back into the water and mixes with the air. This increases the DO saturation. The larger the surface area of air-to-water interaction that occurs, the quicker the water becomes saturated with oxygen.

Increasing the dissolved oxygen (DO) concentration in fertigation solutions can be done through several methods.

The simplest is a venturi system. Air is drawn into a flowing liquid so that when a hole is drilled into the pipe and tubing is attached, the water is automatically aerated as it flows. The Mazzei Airjection Irrigation system makes it easy to introduce oxygen-laden air into the water-nutrient solution. Just hook it up to the irrigation line, and it draws air into flowing water automatically. It requires no power and has no moving parts.

Bubbling air through the stock solutions and water storage tanks is one of the best ways to introduce oxygen into the system, as it is inexpensive and easy to maintain. Some air pumps can increase the temperature of the nutrient solution, which should be monitored.

Other than air, there are other products available that increase dissolved oxygen concentrations that also sanitize the water. Ozone (O_3) and hydrogen peroxide (H_2O_2) are strong oxidizing agents that neutralize microorganisms in the water. Both compounds naturally break down to produce oxygen:

Ozone breakdown
$$2O_3 \rightarrow 3O_2$$

Hydrogen peroxide breakdown
$$2H_2O_2 \rightarrow 2H_2O + O_2$$

Constantly running an air pump through stored water is a great way to get the dissolved oxygen concentration of the water to saturation level within a handful of minutes; however, the running of the air pump can start heating up the water. The pump motor's constant running eventually will warm up, and therefore warm air will be bubbled through the water. Be sure to monitor water temperatures.

Ozone has a half-life of about 20 minutes at room temperature. It is an extremely powerful oxidizer and has strong antimicrobial properties. Ozone can be produced on-site with an ozone generator. Ozone generators can be used to bubble ozone through water. Water should be ozonated at night in storage tanks and allowed sufficient time to break down before being applied to the plants. High-concentration ozone in the nutrient solution can oxidize nutrients and potentially damage roots.

Ozone is dangerous to breathe. It is such a strong oxidizer that it destroys the plasma membrane of pathogens, but it also can damage the lungs if breathed in. Ozone exposure can cause chest pain, coughing, shortness of breath, and sore throat. Ozone does have a distinct aroma, so if it is detected, leave the area immediately. Short exposures typically do not cause irreparable damage. **If ozone is bubbled through water storage tanks, it should be done at night when people are not around.**

Hydrogen peroxide also has oxidative properties, although nowhere near as strong as ozone. Hydrogen peroxide should be diluted down to a maximum of 1% of the water volume. (It comes in various percentages from 3% to about 30% solution.) It also breaks down quickly, so it does not stay oxidative for too long. Exposure to light breaks it down fast, so it should be stored in an opaque container in a dark location. Much like ozone, hydrogen peroxide has strong antimicrobial properties, which means that it, too, can damage root tissue if exposed at too high of a concentration. Neither ozone or hydrogen peroxide leaves a residue, and both break down into molecular oxygen that is available to the roots.

Ozone and hydrogen peroxide neutralize pathogenic bacteria and fungi; however, they also can eliminate beneficial microbes in the root zone. A robust and diverse microbial community in the root zone is beneficial to the health of the plant. When using ozone and hydrogen peroxide to oxygenate the water, it is best to wait before applying so that the ozone and hydrogen peroxide molecules have broken down.

How to Tell When the Root Zone Needs More Oxygen

In the absence of oxygen, roots die off. If hypoxia is suspected, use a soil moisture meter. If the plant can be popped out of its container, the roots can be inspected. Healthy roots are typically white in color and fuzzy with root hairs near their growing tips. In some water culture systems, no root hairs are present. Slimy, brown roots are unhealthy roots; however, some staining from soil, planting media, or nutrients and additives can be normal.

Anaerobic bacteria flourish when a root zone is low in oxygen. These microbes produce ammonia-smelling compounds. Musty or acrid smells are usually indicative of persistent low-oxygen in the root zone.

Anaerobic bacteria flourish when a root zone is low in oxygen. The roots "rot" or turn brown, slimy, and smell like ammonia. Photo: Courtesy of GrowWeedEasy.com

These roots were grown using a Current RDWC system from Current Culture H2O at High Latitude Farms in Hood River, Oregon. Photo: Courtesy of Current Culture

Indica Chocolate Photo: Stinkbud

NUTRIENTS & FERTILIZERS

Revised and expanded by Dr. Neil Mattson

The goal of nutrient supplementation is to provide the elements that plants require for metabolism and growth. The aim is to fertilize effectively and responsibly so that plants receive the nutrients they require for optimum performance, without applying excess. This saves fertilizer costs and prevents discharging excess nutrients to the environment.

There are many fertilizer choices available. They include prepared mixes with balanced and complete hydroponic fertilizers, liquid organic fertilizers, and slow-release solid organics. There is no one-size-fits-all fertilizer program. It will depend on the growing system, environmental conditions, and most important, the grower's preferences.

Plant demand for essential nutrients changes throughout the life cycle. Cannabis uses more nitrogen overall during the vegetative stage than in later stages. Flowering plants require more phosphorus to promote flower formation and potassium for bud development.

Overall, to account for the plant's changing needs for nutrients, one should adjust the nutrient supplementation program during these four life stages:

1. propagation of seeds / rooted cuttings
2. vegetative growth stage
3. flowering stage
4. ripening stage prior to harvest

Nutrient supplementation programs are adjusted for changes in environmental conditions such as light intensity, temperature, and humidity. Plant nutrient uptake is tied to transpiration, the evaporation of water from leaf stomata.

Plants transpire faster under bright light, warm temperatures, and low humidity. Because plants are using so much water, nutrients can concentrate in the canopy; therefore, nutrients (including nitrogen) should be diluted by 10–20%. When the flow rate is increased due to higher rates of transpiration and photosynthesis, nutrients build up when applied at a normal rate.

Conditions that slow down plant transpiration are low light, cool temperatures, and high humidity. Under low transpiration the nutrient solution concentration (including nitrogen) should be increased by 10–20% because plants will not absorb as much water, helping ensure sufficient nutrient supply to the plant.

N-P-K Ratios at Different Stages of Growth

Cannabis has different nutritional needs at different stages of growth.

Nitrogen (N), phosphorus (P), and potassium (K) are the nutrients needed most abundantly by plants. The amount of each nutrient varies as cannabis grows from seedling or cutting to a full-grown plant ready for harvest.

Nitrogen is necessary for creating new proteins and nucleic acids. Access to nitrogen early in the life cycle is important to develop new leaves, stems, and roots. As a result, the need to supply it to young plants is greater through the vegetative cycle, when new plant tissue growth is most substantial. The type of nitrogen (nitrate/NO_3^- vs. ammonium/NH_4^+) also plays a role. Nitrate has a near-neutral pH and keeps plants shorter, which is desirable.

Phosphorus is vital for plant growth, as it is also a component of DNA like nitrogen, but it has other roles in the plant. It is essential for photosynthesis, metabolism of sugars, cell division and elongation, and energy balance. When phosphorus is plentiful, plants grow taller and improve their flower quality. Shorter internodes typically result in higher-quality flowers, so limiting the amount of phosphorus during the vegetative and early flowering stages promotes better flower production.

Potassium has many functions in plants but is primarily responsible for regulating water movement and activating enzymes necessary throughout plant life cycles. Most nutritional guidelines suggest keeping potassium at medium to high levels from start to finish.

As plants transition from one stage in their life cycle to the next, their nutritional needs shift. They have two general stages of development, vegetative growth and flowering, but these can be broken down further:

- **Vegetative Growth**
  - Germination / stem cutting
  - Early growth / transition
  - Vegetative cycle
- **Flowering**
  - Early flowering
  - Mid-flowering / rapid flower growth
  - Late flowering / ripening

Nutritional guides differ, but the general rules to follow are high nitrogen / low phosphorus in vegetative growth and a shift to low-to-medium nitrogen and medium-to-high phosphorus in flowering. Potassium is maintained at medium-to-high levels the entire time. Some cultivators maintain lower concentrations of potassium during vegetative and transition to high in flowering. Each nutritional guideline is dependent on the individual cultivator's setup, preference, cultivar, and sometimes just plain trial and error for what works best for each specific system. Below are some examples of more specific N-P-K ratios that have been successful in other grow facilities.

Recommended N-P-K Ratios by Growth Stage

Growth Stage	Authors' Recommendations (N-P-K)	Authors' Recommendations (EC, dS/m)	Autoflower Seed Shop	General Hydroponics
Germination/ Clones	2-1-3	0.6–0.8	2-1-2	2-1-3
Early Growth	3-1-2	0.8–1.2	4-2-3	4-3-5
Vegetative Growth	3-1-2	1.2–1.6	10-5-7	10-5-12
Preflowering	3-1-2	1.6–2.0	1-1-1	9-5-12
First Flower- ing (Bud Set)	1-2-2	2.0–2.4	5-10-7	8-5-10
Rapid Flower Growth	1-3-4	2.4–3.0	6-15-10	8-5-10
Ripening & Flush	0-0-1	0.0–0.6	4-10-7	4-10-7

These are generalizations for hydroponic production. Adjust by growing conditions, media, and cultivar as needed. No matter what fertilizer instructions say, successful growers believe their eyes.

The "flush" stage is optional and is usually the last week before harvest. During a flush, some cultivators provide nothing more than clean water with no nutrients at the appropriate pH to the plants. Others will use the final ripening ratios for N-P-K, but at lower concentrations. It is all a personal choice, and there are schools of thought that support a complete flush versus a mild flush versus changing nothing during the final week of flower. (*See Finishing & Flushing.*)

Fertilizer Delivery Methods

The choice of fertilizers depends on the growing system and the grower's preferences.

For example, it is common to use prepared liquid or water-soluble conventional fertilizer mixes in hydroponic systems when plants are rooted in inert, soilless substrates such as light expanded clay aggregate (LECA) pebbles, perlite, rockwool, or vermiculite. Fertigation is common in hydroponic systems using these media. The term "fertigation" is a combination of fertilizer and irrigation and refers to the fact that plants receive water-soluble fertilizer every time they are irrigated.

Planting mixes that contain peat, bark, coconut coir, or compost have greater nutrient-holding capacity, so granular-controlled or slow-release fertilizers (including organic fertilizers) can be incorporated into the potting mix. Some nutrients, such as nitrogen, phosphorus, and potassium, may be used up quickly, so they are supplied through fertigation.

Nutrient Additives/Supplements

Be wary of supplement lines. Growers have been growing great buds for decades using pure water, hydroponics, and basic nutrients. Some supplements improve yield or quality, but others just supply phosphorus and potassium at inflated prices. Try the supplement with a few plants, but leave some of the same variety untreated (controlled). That is the only way to determine the effectiveness of the supplement.

Reading a Fertilizer Label

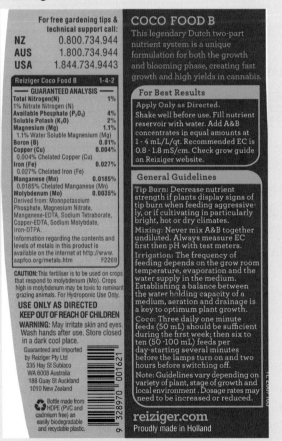

Every fertilizer label supplies the same types of information.

The most basic information found on all fertilizer labels is the three numbers separated by dashes, such as 2-1-6, which refers to the percentage by volume of the three macronutrients nitrogen (N), phosphorus (P), and potassium (K). Note that by convention in the US the percentage of phosphorus is given in the form of phosphate (P_2O_5) and potassium is given in the form of potash (K_2O).

Second, the label lists the guaranteed minimum analysis for macronutrients, calcium, sulfur, and magnesium (in percentage). There is no maximum analysis, so recipes may differ from the minimum guarantee.

Third, the label lists fertilizer salts the nutrients are derived from, for example, ammonium phosphate, magnesium carbonate, and so on. The derived-from information is particularly helpful if the grower wishes to get more in-depth at combining multiple fertilizer products. Some fertilizer salts are incompatible, thus referencing the derived-from information with fertilizer compatibility charts is useful. As a general rule, sticking to commercial products in the same series that are recommended for use together avoids compatibility issues.

Fourth, information on the application rate. Some labels chart application rates according to crop growth stage and how to use the fertilizer along with other products in the same series. It may list mixing instructions, and other instructions for use.

Fifth, storage instructions.

Water-Soluble Fertilizers

Water-soluble fertilizers are nutrients that are liquid or dry fertilizer that are readily dissolved in water and applied through a hydroponic or irrigation system. Water-soluble fertilizers can come from a single fertilizer salt (such as calcium nitrate or monopotassium phosphate), but more commonly they are commercially prepared by blending multiple fertilizer salts into a formulation that is semi complete or complete, and contains many or all the essential plant nutrients.

Great care must be taken when mixing fertilizer salts. Some fertilizer salts can interact with each other and cause precipitation, a chemical reaction in which the salts flocculate, or recombine into an insoluble form, usually a sludge that does not dissolve in water and can clog irrigation equipment.

A common precipitate issue occurs when combining calcium-based fertilizer salts (such as calcium nitrate) with fertilizer salts that contain phosphates or sulfates. Precipitation is mainly a problem when using concentrated fertilizer salts—this is why most hydroponic nutrients come as two- or three-part systems, since they can't be combined at high concentrations.

In general, it is safest to combine products only from within the same product line. Because of the precipitation issue, when preparing fertilizer solutions, always fill the reservoir with water first. Then completely dissolve one fertilizer before adding the next one.

When purchasing water-soluble fertilizers, many people prefer preformulated liquid fertilizer products because they are easy to measure (by volume), dissolve quickly in the nutrient reservoir, and usually have clear instructions for mixing with other products in the

Reiziger® Grow Booster is widely used by craft cannabis cultivators because it is formulated with a high concentration of powerful botanical ingredients that provide the plant the energy it needs to fortify its natural defense process and elevate terpenes, increase resin production, and elevate aroma and color.

same product line to provide a complete nutrient solution.

However, liquid fertilizers are very expensive compared with the quantity of dry fertilizer salts they contain. In addition, shipping these products is costly because of the weight of the water they contain. Dry powdered hydroponic water-soluble fertilizers contain the complete set of plant essential nutrients. They are much cheaper per unit of nutrient solution and more sustainable to ship. However, initially they require a bit more care to measure out and dissolve in the nutrient reservoir.

Home garden fertilizers can be used for cannabis, but care must be taken to make sure

Advanced Nutrients Big Bud® has a proven track record of helping plants pack on bud weight throughout the bloom phase. A team of scientists engineered this bloom booster with an optimal potassium and phosphorus ratio to amplify yields and maximize bud bulk while reducing the risk of heavy metal contamination.

These two-part base nutrient systems feature precise NPK ratios for vigorous vegetation and robust flowering. Advanced Nutrients' scientists engineered these revolutionary products with their proprietary pH Perfect Technology®, ensuring a balance-free pH that frees growers from tedious adjustments.

all plant essential nutrients are provided. For example, a common garden fertilizer is 10-10-10. This product provides N-P-K but may not provide the other essential nutrients. Other fertilizers are more complete and suitable for use without supplementation.

When larger gardens use fertigation, it is common to hold concentrated fertilizer in stock tanks. As compared with mixing nutrients at the dilute amounts the plants would receive in a larger reservoir, concentrated fertilizer stock tanks save space and the time spent frequently remixing the fertilizer.

Using a fertigation system, the concentrated fertilizer is introduced to the irrigation water using a proportioner to dilute the fertilizer to the final concentration the plants receive. This dilution can be done by a simple proportioner, which uses suction to draw up the concentrated fertilizer and mix it with the water source at the proper ratio.

A positive displacement injector is more likely to be used in commercial gardens. These injectors use a piston with a fill chamber to more accurately inject the proper ratio of nutrients into the irrigation water. These injectors typically have a higher ratio, for example, 1:64 to 1:200 1:100 is quite common and makes calculations easier (the fertilizer stock tank is prepared with 100x concentration). Remember that some fertilizers cannot be combined in a concentrated form. To account for precipitation, growers may have two to three or more fertilizer stock tanks with fertilizer injectors connected in series.

Controlled- & Slow-Release Fertilizers

Controlled- and slow-release fertilizers are dry fertilizers in a pellet or granular form. They are used not in solution-culture hydroponics but in soil or substrate grows. These fertilizers can be incorporated into the potting mix before transplanting or can be top-dressed onto the substrate surface.

Controlled-release fertilizers are typically formulated with all or most of the macro- and micronutrients required by the plant. They have a coating, often a polymer, which controls the release rate and pattern of the nutrients. Products are available with different release periods such as three to four month, five to six month, or eight to nine month.

The release rate is affected by substrate temperature; warmer temperatures lead to a quicker release rate. For example, a three-to-four-month product will release 90–95% of its nutrients during that time if substrate temperature averages 70°F (21°C), but will release more quickly with warmer conditions.

A benefit of controlled-release fertilizers is that they can provide the majority of the plant's fertilizer needs, thus reducing the need for water-soluble fertilizers. These slow-release nutrient forms reduce leaching of nutrients to the environment, making the feeding regimen more sustainable.

However, it can be difficult for a plant to achieve its full yield potential using only controlled-release fertilizers. Cannabis requires high amounts of fertilizers, and it can be difficult to meet all the plant's nutrient needs using controlled release alone. It is best used as the initial base fertilizer, and then liquid fertilizer can be added to supplement it.

Another issue with controlled-release is that once the fertilizer has been added, it cannot be removed, so it is important not to over apply it. During hot conditions, the fertilizer releases faster than the labeled rate, so salts can build up quickly. Monitor root zone salinity (as described below) and leach with clear water to remove excess soluble salts if there are readings in the danger zone.

Slow-release fertilizers do not have a polymer coating, and their rate of nutrient release is not as precise. They are not typically complete fertilizers but can be an inexpensive way to add specific elements. Examples of these include sulfur-coated fertilizers (such as sulfur-coated urea, a form of nitrogen), slowly soluble fertilizers such as gypsum (calcium sulfate), triple superphosphate (a source of phosphorus), and limestone. Standard limestone is a source of calcium and is also used to increase substrate pH. Dolomitic limestone is also used to raise substrate pH and is a source of both calcium and magnesium.

Soil test kits provide individual readings of nutrients. Meters provide only an overall reading.
Photo: Angela Bacca

Organic Fertilizers

Organic fertilizers come from animal or plant matter and naturally mined materials. Examples include compost, fish emulsion, guanos, limestone, manure, ground minerals, plant extracts, plant meals or rock phosphate, seaweed, and worm castings. Organic fertilizers may contain some immediately available nutrients; however, much of their nutrition is slow release and requires either weathering or microbes to break down complex organic molecules and make nutrients available. Meeting the plant's nutrient demands with organic fertilizer requires some experience, so it may be difficult to get the same yields initially with organic fertilizers as with conventional. Their use is especially nuanced when used in substrate or hydroponic systems.

Organic fertilizers often raise pH. The benefits of using organic fertilizers include reuse of waste streams (compost) as well as the potential for reduced leaching to the environment (if applied properly) because they are slow-release nutrient forms. Some connoisseurs consider organically grown buds to be the highest quality.

There are many organic fertilizer mixes on the market. Many are solid (granular, powdered, or pelleted) and are added directly to the soil or substrate prior to transplanting or to the topsoil while the crop is growing. Other organic products are readily available, soluble formulas added to the water. Many will include macronutrients as well as micronutrients; however, read the label carefully and ensure all essential nutrients are supplied either from one product or by combining materials.

Traditionally, single-source materials were used (such as plant or animal meals or manures). Most single-ingredient organic fertilizers are not complete; they are more often used as a supplement or combined with other ingredients. Many complete, balanced, organic fertilizers, containing several ingredients, are available.

Time is required for microbe-mediated nutrient availability; however, much of organic fertility is ultimately available after the first four to six weeks of application. For this reason, more available nutrients such as liquid organics may be required to spur initial growth. Then, as the microbes consume the organics in the planting mix, nutrients will gradually be released. The mix may be more "live" and fertile when it is used for a second crop. As long

Neptune's Harvest Fish & Seaweed Fertilizer (2-3-1) is an organic (OMRI listed) cold-processed fertilizer made from post-fillet ocean fish from Norwegian kelp in the North Atlantic that not only contains macro- and micronutrients, but also trace elements, vitamins, minerals, amino acids, enzymes, and omega fatty acids. Neptune's Harvest Fish & Seaweed Fertilizer repels deer, eliminates powdery mildew as a foliar feed, and is a great rescue product for plant stress.

Neptune's Harvest Crab & Lobster Shell (5-3-0) is a dry organic fertilizer made from organic matter that breaks down slowly while both aerating soil and helping it retain moisture. It is high in calcium (12–17%) and magnesium (1.3–1.7%) and controls root nematodes, grubs, ants, slugs and fungus.

as the mix retains its structure and is not subject to infection or disease, it can be reused.

Water-soluble organic fertilizers are delivered through the irrigation system. They work best when there is a substrate or soil where microbes are abundant, because they break down the complex nutrient compounds into soluble salts that the plants can absorb. They are not recommended for hydroponic systems because they ferment in reservoirs and lead to biofilm, which can coat roots, clog up systems, and deprive the plants of sufficient dissolved oxygen.

Compost

Compost is organic matter subjected to decomposition. It is a valuable soil or substrate amendment that increases organic matter content, nutrient-holding (or cation exchange) capacity, and is a source of beneficial microbes and slow-release nutrients.

Controlled compost piles are maintained at 130–160°F (54–71°C) for pasteurization for a minimum of three days. This kills harmful microbes and weed seeds.

Compost should represent only 10–20% of the substrate. Percentages depend on the quality of the soil that it is being added to and the level of dissolvable salts in the compost. Used as a large percentage of some mixes, it holds too much water and is too rich in nutrients. Only mature compost should be used. Immature compost can be high in ammonia and volatile organic compounds, which injure the plants.

Care should be taken to avoid transmitting human pathogens such as E. coli or Salmonella when animal manures are used. Manures should be fully composted or heat-treated before using as fertilizers, or if they are added to soil, they should be incorporated at least 90 days before harvesting a crop. Pet waste (dog and cat) can contain a number of pathogens and parasites harmful to humans and should never be used as a fertilizer or substrate amendment.

Compost teas are made by soaking organic matter or compost in water, which serves to transfer beneficial microbes, fine particulate organic matter, and some soluble nutrients to the water. The beneficial microbes can improve nutrient retention and availability to the roots as well as help the plant fight off diseases and insects. Commonly used ingredients for compost tea include vermicompost (worm-worked compost), well-composted manures, blood meal, coffee grounds, plant meals, minerals/ground rock, and oyster shells.

Similar to using manures, only materials known to not be a source of human pathogens should be used. Live (aerated) compost tea requires equipment to "brew" it with a lot of oxygen or airflow. Without proper aeration, compost tea will become infected by anaerobic bacteria, which causes plant diseases. Some hydroponic stores brew teas on-site.

Compost tea must be used within a few hours after brewing or kept aerated until use. Extracts or non aerated compost tea can also be used. With extracts, oxygen is not introduced during the steeping process, and the feedstock may be steeped in water for several days. An extract will not have the same large number of microbes as aerated compost tea; however, it is more shelf-stable and does not have to be used right away. The nutritional value of compost teas and extracts varies according to the ingredients and processor. These are rarely well described on their labels. It is important to find a processor that uses high-quality ingredients and follows a consistent process that provides reliable results.

Some compost tea recipes suggest using molasses as an ingredient of the brew. However, teas using it may become infected with pathogenic E. coli bacteria. For this reason, use honey, beet juice, malt, or sugar as a substitute.

SOME COMMON ORGANIC FERTILIZERS

Fertilizer	% N	% P	% K	Remarks
Bloodmeal	15.0	1.30	0.70	N readily available.
Bone meal	4.0	21.0	0.20	Releases nutrients slowly.
Cow manure	0.29	0.17	0.35	Fresh, 80% water. Excellent soil conditioner; apply in winter or composts for use in spring. Medium availability.
Coffee grounds	2.0	0.36	0.67	Highly acidic; best for use in alkaline soils.
Corn stalks	0.75	0.40	0.90	Breaks down slowly; chopped stalks make excellent conditioner for compact or dense soils.
Cottonseed meal	7.0	2.5	1.5	Highly acidic; nutrients become available over the course of the growing season.
Dried blood	13.0	3.0	-	More soluble than blood meal.
Fish scrap	7.75	13.0	3.80	Use in compost or turn under soil several months before planting; usually highly alkaline.
Greensand	-	1.5	5.0	Mined from old ocean deposits; used as soil conditioner; it holds water and is high in iron, magnesium, and silica.
Chicken manure	1.65	1.5	0.85	Dried; fast-acting fertilizer. Breaks down fastest of all manures.
Horse manure	1.65	1.5	0.85	Fresh, 60% water; medium breakdown time.

Monitoring Plant Fertility

The pH of the hydroponic reservoir or root zone substrate has a large impact on nutrient availability. The pH is a measurement of how acidic or basic (alkaline) a solution is and varies from 0 (most acidic) to 14 (most basic). (*See Water.*) The pH affects nutrient availability; at a higher pH, 6.3–6.7 in hydroponics and soilless substrates, micronutrients such as iron, manganese, zinc, and copper become increasingly unavailable.

At a lower pH, calcium and magnesium become increasingly unavailable, and some micronutrients become available at toxic levels for the plant. Nutrient disorders are often due to root zone pH, rather than a lack or excess of nutrients.

A pH meter is used to measure pH. There are many models available. Handheld meters are accurate and invaluable tools. Other models are placed in a tank or reservoir and constantly monitor the water. Automated devices automatically adjust the pH.

These meters can be used to measure the pH of the source water, fertilizer solution, or hydroponic nutrient reservoir. To test root zone pH, a solution sample must be prepared (described below). There are pH meters available with soil probes.

Periodically, the meter should be calibrated using at least two standards (pH 4 and pH 7). The pH sensor reading can drift over time, so it is important to calibrate frequently according to the manufacturer's instructions (typically every day to every week) to have accurate readings. If the meter can be calibrated with only one standard, it is only accurate close to that standard reading.

The sensor end of the pH meter, the electrode, should be kept in a pH storage solution between uses. It should not be stored in distilled water or allowed to dry out. It may need to be soaked in a storage solution for one to two hours if the sensor dries out. The pH electrode needs to be replaced when it does not calibrate or give reliable readings.

The pH of hydroponic reservoirs and in the root zone of soilless substrates can fluctuate quite rapidly depending on the alkalinity (a measure of the carbonates and bicarbonates in the water) and in response to plant uptake of nutrients. The larger the reservoir and the higher the alkalinity, the slower pH changes.

In particular, the form of nitrogen in the fertilizer has a large impact on pH. Ammonium-based fertilizer in the rhizosphere causes the pH to decrease, while nitrate-based fertilizer causes the pH to increase slightly.

In "true" hydroponics, where plants are growing directly in a nutrient solution, or in an inert substrate such as LECA or rockwool, it is recommended to test and adjust the pH daily to be around 5.5–6.0. In soilless substrates with organic components (coir, peat, or compost), pH does not fluctuate as rapidly, so it should be tested weekly and maintained at 5.8–6.2.

It's also important that the fertility level of the hydroponic reservoir or growing medium is checked so that the right amount of fertilizer is added to the water. The concentration of nutrients in the reservoir and substrate changes over time as the plants absorb nutrients and evaporate water. An accurate measurement is the only way to be sure that the plants are getting the optimal level of ingredients for maximal growth. At a minimum, growers should have parts per million (ppm), electrical conductivity (EC), or total dissolved solids (TDS) meters, which give a measure of overall fertility. However, they do not measure the levels of individual nutrients. Chemical test kits are available that are more detailed; they provide a measurement of each nutrient.

All three meters measure nutrient levels indirectly, based on the amount of electricity the nutrient solution conducts. The meters measure how efficiently electrons travel between probes through the solution. Pure, distilled water conducts virtually no electricity. The more nutrients and minerals in the solution, the more electricity is conducted. Electrical conductivity is the opposite of electrical resistance (measured in ohms), so the unit is the mho or, in metric units, the siemens. Since the current in even highly concentrated solutions is tiny, meters typically read in either 1/1,000th of an mho (a milli-mho per centimeter, abbreviated as mMhos/cm), or 1/1,000th of a siemens (a milli-siemens, abbreviated as mS/

cm). Tap water EC usually varies from 0.2 to 1.0 mMhos/cm (= mS/cm). A moderately strong fertilizer solution will have an EC of 1.5 to 2.5 mMhos/cm (= mS/cm). Thus, if tap water EC is 0.4 and fertilizer EC is 1.8, the resulting fertilizer solution would have an EC of 2.2 mMhos/cm (= mS/cm). Some EC meters are meant for more precise applications and use units of micromhos (1/1,000th of a mMhos); the units are µMhos/cm. Thus, 1,000 µMhos/cm = 1.0 mMhos/cm. Following the example above, the fertilizer solution EC of 2.2 mMhos/cm = 2,200 µMhos/cm.

Some meters provide readout in EC, and others read out as total dissolved solids or parts per million. Even those that read directly in TDS or ppm are measuring EC and then using a conversion to estimate the concentration of solids. A measurement of 1,000 ppm means that 1,000 units of nutrients are present for every million units of water.

The ppm/TDS readouts don't provide any more information than EC meters; they simply measure EC and then use a conversion factor to give a ppm readout. The conversion calculation is based on what manufacturers consider a typical hydroponic solution. The most common are based on measurements of two types of solutions—either 4-4-2 (40% sodium sulfate, 40% sodium bicarbonate, 20% sodium chloride) or sodium chloride (NaCl)—but they produce different results. The conversion factor for a 4-4-2 solution is approximately 700 x EC in mS/cm. The NaCl conversion is roughly 500 x EC. This means that the same solution, producing the same EC of 3.0 mS/cm, converts to either 2,100 ppm or 1,500 ppm, depending on the scale the manufacturer has chosen. These conversion differences reflect the disparity in conductivity between different nutrients.

Just like pH meters, EC/TDS meters need to be maintained through periodic recalibration as well as careful cleaning and storage. If the probe is contaminated or dirty, it affects the accuracy of the meter's reading. Rinse the probe in distilled water between readings and blot to dry with a lint-free wipe. Manufacturers include instructions for how to properly store the probe. EC electrode cleaning solution is also recommended for some models.

Nutrient types and calibration are not the only things that can affect an EC or TDS meter's readings. The EC of the solution also varies based on its temperature, since the speed of electron travel is measured. It increases as the solution gets warmer. Some EC/TDS meters measure temperature and automatically compensate for it (automatic temperature compensation, ATC).

If a meter does not have automatic compensation, measurements should be taken at close to the same temperature each time. This isn't an issue if the system is heated with an aquarium heater or other method of maintaining consistent solution temperature. If the gardening space (and nutrient solution) gets warmer after the lights have been running, nutrient readings should be taken at the same time of day or point in the light cycle.

Even a properly calibrated and maintained meter used under perfect conditions will not provide a precise reading of the nutrient concentration. Even expensive meters are only accurate in the range of approximately +/-5%.

EC/TDS meters are used to directly measure the overall fertilizer strength (total ions) in a hydroponic nutrient solution. EC/TDS changes over time as plants absorb water and nutrients.

Consider the situation when plants transpire 50% of the water in a reservoir. The solution's salt concentration (EC/TDS) can become dangerously high. Similarly, because plants take the nutrients they need from the solution and leave the rest, unused salts can build up because there is an imbalance between what the fertilizer provides and what the plant uses.

As the EC (ex: > 2.5) or TDS (ex. > 1,250–1,750, depending on the conversion factor) levels climb, roots have an increasingly difficult time extracting the water they need from the root zone because the osmotic pressure is strong and they must use more energy to extract water from the salt solution.

Because plant fertility needs change over time, a lower EC is used during the propagation and early vegetative stages and a higher EC for late-vegetative stage and flowering.

The general strategy to use for EC/TDS is to monitor and adjust over time. If EC goes up over time, the plants are being overfertilized. If EC goes down over time, the plants are being underfertilized, providing less fertilizer than the plant needs in proportion to its water usage.

In hydroponic gardens, the nutrient solution's EC should be checked every one to two days. This is especially important if the reservoir is small in relation to the garden. Add water to replenish the reservoir and decrease EC, and then add fertilizer if EC goes below target. In soilless substrates, the pH and EC should be checked and adjusted weekly. Because the probes cannot be placed directly into the substrate, a solution sample needs to be collected. This is usually done using either the PourThru method or the 1:2 dilution method.

The PourThru Method

This method does not require the collection of the medium, but it is less accurate. A small sample of distilled water is poured on top of the medium in the container and the leachate sample collected in a bowl. Measure using an EC meter. This method is most accurate when conducted on 5 to 10 pots using an average reading.

The 1:2 Dilution Method

Small samples of substrate are taken from 5 to 10 pots. This is mixed and combined with two parts of distilled water by volume. Because the two methods use different volumes of water, the recommended EC ranges are different depending on the method. Allow to soak for 60 minutes and measure using an EC meter.

Saturated Media Extraction (SME)

SME is more accurate than the PourThru method but is more time-consuming. The sample should be taken when the medium is moderately moist so that the root ball stays together. Samples are gently collected from the middle of the container of 5–10 pots and placed into another container. Distilled water is added to the point of saturation, with a little moisture visible on the surface. Allow to soak for 60 minutes and measure using an EC meter.

RECOMMENDED EC RANGES BY CROP STAGE

Development Stage	1:2 Dilution (mS/cm)	PourThru Top Irrigation (mS/cm)
Early Vegetative	0.3 to 0.45	1.0 to 1.5
Late Vegetative	0.45 to 0.59	1.5 to 2.0
Peak Flowering	0.59 to 0.77	2.0 to 2.5
Pre-Harvest	0.45 to 0.59	1.5 to 2.0

Source: "Nutrient Monitoring in Cannabis Cultivation: A Step-By-Step Guide". *Cannabis Business Times* (Cockson and Veazie 2020)

Steps for the PourThru method:
- The containers are fully watered with the fertilizer as usual. A few drops of water should drain from the bottom of the container.
- After the container drains for about an hour, it's at capacity, its maximum water-holding potential.
- A saucer is placed under the container.
- Distilled water is slowly poured over the top of the container medium. The amount to use depends on the container size. For a one gallon (3.75 l) container, use about 150 mL or 12 fluid ounces; for a three gallon (11.3 l) container, use 350 mL or about 12 fluid ounces.
- The leachate (runoff) sample is tested for pH and EC.

Steps for the 1:2 dilution method:
- A small amount of substrate is removed from the middle of the container where the roots are actively growing. Collecting a sample from the top or bottom of the container can cause inaccurate readings.
- The samples from 5 to 10 representative plants are pooled.
- One cup (240 mL) of the pooled substrate sample is mixed with two cups of distilled water.
- The sample steeps for 30 minutes.
- The pH/EC of the substrate solution is measured.

Note that fertilizer solution EC is different from root zone EC. Usually root zone EC is a bit higher than fertilizer solution EC because of accumulated salts. If root zone EC is substantially higher than the fertilizer solution (or higher than recommended PourThru or 1:2 dilution EC), then leaching with clear water to flush out excess salts is indicated. This should be done by irrigating the substrate with clear water until about 30% of the water leaches out of the pot each time.

Overall, careful monitoring of the hydroponic reservoir and substrate pH/EC/TDS reaps dividends in plant health and yield. Because EC and TDS only give a total measure of fertilizer strength (and total salts), they do not indicate specific deficiencies.

Periodic use of chemical test kits provides more detailed information than meters because they test the levels of specific elements. Commercial laboratories can test nutrient solution, substrate, and leaf tissue to determine specific mineral element levels.

Visual Symptoms of Nutrient Deficiencies and Corrective Actions

Beyond monitoring the nutrient solution and root zone pH, EC, and TDS, one can detect nutrient deficiencies by carefully observing plant leaves. Healthy leaves have a vibrant green to purple color. Leaves turning yellow (**chlorosis**) or brown (necrosis), or exhibiting other growth abnormalities such as curling, rolling, or misshapening, are important clues to the problem. Beyond the color of the symptoms, it is also important to note their pattern.

Depending on the deficiency, yellow or brown patterns can appear across the entire leaf, on its edges (margins), or between the veins (interveinal). Finally, the place on the plant where nutrient deficiencies first appear tells a lot about which nutrient is deficient. The location of the leaf on the plant (top or bottom of the individual shoots or branches) correlates to the age of the leaf. Young, immature leaves show different deficiencies from older, more mature leaves, which is very informative for determining specific nutrient problems in the plant.

Leaf age is an important diagnostic criteria because some nutrient deficiencies show up first on young leaves. That indicates that the deficient nutrient(s) are immobile; the plant cannot move them from older lower leaves to new leaves growing at the top of the canopy.

Immobile nutrients where deficiencies are apparent first on young leaves include iron, manganese, copper, zinc, boron, and calcium. Boron and calcium are the least mobile, and deficiencies show up on the youngest parts of the plant.

Nutrients that are mobile can be translocated from older leaves to provide nutrients to the new leaves. Mobile nutrients, including nitrogen, phosphorus, potassium, and magnesium, show deficiency symptoms first on old leaves.

When plants show visual symptoms of nutrient deficiency, their growth and yield may already be impaired. Therefore, beyond managing pH/EC, it is important to carefully and frequently observe plants and correct nutrient deficiencies as quickly as possible.

If the correct nutrient is added to cure a deficiency, the plant usually responds in apparent ways within three to five days, depending on the deficiency. Usually the first indication is that the symptom stops spreading and plant parts that were only slightly damaged begin to repair themselves, with the exception of a calcium deficiency, which causes permanent damage during cell growth. Calcium is one of the nonmobile nutrients.

Leaves and other parts that were slightly discolored may return to normal, although plant parts that were severely damaged, or suffered necrosis, will not recover. The most dramatic changes can be monitored through new growth: an observer can easily differentiate between plant parts that grew before and after the deficiencies were corrected.

Some nutrient deficiencies can look similar. The best way to differentiate between them is to note the part of the plant in which they are occurring. If in doubt, the only way to truly determine the issue is a laboratory tissue analysis.

Macronutrients

Photo: Ed Rosenthal

Nitrogen (N)

Nitrogen deficiency is the most commonly occurring nutrient deficiency of cannabis. N is the first number of the three numbers found on all fertilizer packages, which list N-P-K always in that order.

Role in plant nutrition

N is directly responsible for the production of chlorophyll and amino acids, and it is essential to photosynthesis. It is an essential element of tissue; without it, growth quickly stops.

Symptoms

N can travel anywhere on the plant. Usually deficiency starts on the lower portion of the plant because N travels to new growth. Lower leaves first appear pale green. Then the leaves yellow and die as the N travels to support new growth. The deficiency symptoms travel up the plant until only the new growth is green, leaving the lowest leaves to yellow and wither. Lower leaves die from the leaf tips inward. Other symptoms include smaller leaves, slow growth, and a sparse profile. The stems and petioles turn a red-purple tinge.

Too much N causes a lush dark green growth that is more susceptible to insects and disease. The stalks become brittle and break from lack of flexibility.

General discussion

Without high amounts of N, especially during the vegetative growth stage, the plant's yield is greatly reduced. Water uptake slows from vascular breakdown in the plants. N issues happen throughout the entire growth cycle. Plants should never experience an N deficiency during vegetative growth. However, overfertilizing with N causes problems too.

As the photoperiod changes, tapering off the use of N promotes flowering rather than vegetative growth. However, a small amount of N is always necessary in order for the plant to manufacture amino acids, which use N as an ingredient. This supports flower growth and utilization of P and K. Some "Bloom Boosters" have N-P-K ratios of "0-50-30." While high numbers sound impressive, using this fertilizer too early causes the flowers to be smaller than they could have been. If there is not enough N available, the plants are not getting the most out of the fertilizer.

In the middle to the end of the flowering stage, plants frequently show an N deficiency. They're using the nutrients that were stored in the leaves and dropping their oldest, bottom, fan leaves. To prevent the deficiency from getting extreme, switch over to bloom nutrients gradually unless the bloom fertilizer contains some N.

DEFICIENCIES OF NUTRIENT ELEMENTS IN CANNABIS

Suspected Element

Symptoms	N	P	K	Mg	Fe	Cu	Zn	B	Mo	Mn	Over-fertilization
Yellowing of:											
Younger leaves					x					x	
Middle leaves									x		
Older leaves	x		x	x			x				
Between veins				x						x	
Old leaves drop	x										
Leaf curl over				x							
Leaf curl under			x			x					x
Leaf tips burn:											
Younger leaves								x			
Older leaves	x						x				
Young leaves wrinkle & curl			x				x	x	x		
Necrosis			x	x	x		x			x	
Leaf growth stunted	x	x									
Dark green/purplish leaves and stems		x									
Pale green leaf color	x								x		
Mottling							x				
Spindly	x										
Soft stems	x		x								
Hard/brittle stems		x	x								
Growing tips die			x					x			
Stunted root growth		x									
Wilting						x					

Problem solving

Any water-soluble N (especially nitrates, NO_3) is quickly available to the roots. Insoluble N (such as urea) needs to be broken down by microbes in the soil before the roots can absorb it. After fertilization, N-deficient plants absorb N as soon as it is available and start to change from pale to a healthy-looking kelly green. Deficient plants usually recover within a week, but the most-affected leaves do not recover.

Any water-soluble fertilizer much higher in N than P and K can be used to solve N deficiencies very quickly. Most hydro "Vegetative Formulas" fall into this category.

Calcium nitrate $(Ca(NO_3)_2)$ is water-soluble and fast acting. It can be used as a foliar fertilizer and in the water-nutrient solution. It is often one of the two ingredients in CalMag. Magnesium sulfate, known as epsom salts $(MgSO_4)$, is the other.

Urine, fish emulsion (5-1-1), and high-nitrogen bat or seabird guano also act quickly. In soils, high-N fertilizers such as alfalfa and cottonseed meals, manure, feather meal, and fishmeal all supply N fairly quickly.

Photo: Kristen Angelo

Phosphorus (P)

Phosphorus deficiency occurs occasionally. P is the second number found on fertilizer packages. The numbers are always listed in the order N-P-K.

Role in plant nutrition

P aids in root and stem growth, influences the vigor of the plant, and helps seedlings germinate. P is extremely important in the reproductive stages and flowering. Plants use higher amounts of P during flowering. Without adequate or even abundant supplies, it results in lower yields.

Symptoms

Plants deficient in phosphorus grow slowly and are stunted with small leaves. P is mobile, so older leaves are affected first. They turn dark green and become weak, then develop dull blue or purple hues. The edges of the leaves turn tan/brown and curl downward as the deficiency works its way inward. The lower leaves turn yellow and die.

The stems and petioles turn purple or red. Some cultivars, however, normally possess red or purple stems and petioles, so these traits are not a surefire sign of P deficiency.

General discussion

Deficiency during flowering results in lower yields, but overfertilizing can result in a chemical and/or metallic taste or burn the plant. Cold weather (below 50°F/10°C) makes P absorption very troublesome. For this reason, highly available P, such as found in water-soluble bloom formulas, can add flower yield in cool weather.

Problem solving
Water-soluble fertilizers containing high P fix the deficiency. Bloom fertilizers are high-P formulas. High-P guano also provides readily available P. Rock phosphate and greensand are also high in P and gradually release it. The affected leaves do not show recovery, but no additional growth is affected and new growth appears healthy.

Photo: Kristen Angelo

Potassium (K)
Potassium is the third number found on fertilizer packages, always listed in the order N-P-K. K deficiency occurs occasionally in both planting media and outdoors in soil, but rarely in hydroponics.

Role in plant nutrition
K is found in the whole plant. It is necessary for all activities having to do with water transportation, as well as all stages of growth; it's especially important in the development of buds. K aids in creating sturdy and thick stems, disease resistance, water respiration, and photosynthesis.

Symptoms
Plants suffering from minor deficiencies look vigorous, even taller than the rest of the population, but the tips and edges of their bottom leaves die or turn tan/brown and develop necrotic spots. Mottled patches of red and yellow appear between the veins, which remain green, accompanied by red stems and petioles. These leaves eventually turn brown and die off. Deficiency results in slower growth, especially during the vegetative stage. Severe K shortages cause leaves to grow smaller than usual.

Excess K causes fan leaves to show a light to dark yellow or white color between the veins. K is mobile.

General discussion
Even in rich, well-fertilized soil, plants often suffer from mild K deficiencies, usually caused by improper fertilization. Many organic fertilizers such as guano, fish emulsion, alfalfa, cottonseed, blood meals, and many animal manures contain minor amounts of K relative to N and P.

Cold weather slows K absorption, as does too much calcium or ammonium (NH_4+). High levels of sodium displace K.

Problem solving

Although symptoms of minor K deficiency affect the cosmetic look of the plant, it does not seem to affect plant growth or yields.

Water-soluble fertilizers containing high K fix the deficiency. Bloom fertilizer usually contains high K levels. Highly alkaline K is used in the formulas mostly to balance the pH of highly acidic P.

Liquefied kelp, bloom fertilizers, and wood ash are commonly used and work quickly to correct K deficiencies, as does potassium bicarbonate ($KHCO_3$), potassium sulfate (K_2SO_4), and potassium dihydrogen phosphate (KH_2PO_4). Potassium silicate (K_2SiO_3) is used to supply silicon and has 3% K in it. Granite dust and greensand take more time to get to the plant and are not usually used to correct deficiencies, but to prevent them.

Damaged leaves never recover, but the plant shows recovery in four to five days with applications of fast-acting products.

Photo: Mel Frank

Calcium (Ca)

Calcium is a secondary nutrient generally listed as part of a label's guaranteed analysis. Ca deficiency is rare outdoors except in very acidic soils.

Role in plant nutrition

Ca strengthens plant cell walls and therefore stems, stalks, and branches, and it aids in root growth—mostly the newer root hairs. It plays a role in plant response to stimuli by regulating the permeability of stomata. It travels slowly and concentrates on roots and older growth. It plays a role in pistil development. Ca also enhances the uptake of K.

Symptoms

Ca deficiency stunts plant growth and makes the leaves turn dark green. Large necrotic (dead) blotches of tan, dried tissue appear mostly on new growth but also on other plant parts along leaf edges. Young shoots crinkle and get a yellow or purple color. In severe cases they twist before they die. Necrosis appears along the lateral leaf margins. Problems migrate to the older growth, which browns and dies. Stems and branches are weak, lack flexibility, and crack easily.

The root system does not develop properly, leading to bacterial problems that cause root disease and die-off. The roots discolor to a sickly brown. Ca is semi mobile.

General discussion

The deficiency is occasionally found in planting mixes and is more common in hydroponics.

Rhino Skin is a next-generation potassium silicate additive that increases stalk rigidity, bolstering plants with an optimal foundation for supporting heavy bud weight. With availability in mind, Advanced Nutrients' scientists carefully selected the most soluble forms of this naturally thick and solid element for cannabis plants.

However, Ca should be used when planting mixes are being constructed or when the pH of the mix is too low.

Distilled and reverse osmosis water lack dissolved Ca. This can lead to Ca deficiency unless the water is supplemented with it.

Some hydro fertilizers contain only small amounts of Ca, as the amount of Ca dissolved in the supply water varies. If the water contains more than 125 parts per million dissolved solids, it is probably providing the plants with enough Ca. If the water contains less, Ca has to be added to the water to bring it up to 125 ppm.

Problem solving

Outdoors, add Ca to acidic soils to bring them into the pH range of 5.8–6.3. Dolomitic lime, or garden lime, can be added to planting mixes before potting. It provides Ca and also helps stabilize pH over time.

Both planting media and hydro systems can be fertilized as directed using a commercial calcium-magnesium (Ca-Mg or "CalMag") formula; this provides instant availability to the plant. It can also be used in planting mixes. Growers often use Ca-Mg acetate.

Calcium nitrate $Ca(NO_3)_2$ is a water-soluble fertilizer that supplies both Ca and N. It provides a very soluble form of Ca to the roots and can also be used as a foliar spray. This formula gets Ca to the plant very quickly.

DIY CalMag

Dissolve 2.25 ounces of calcium nitrate $Ca(NO_3)_2$ and 6 ounces epsom salts $(MgSO_4)$ into one gallon of water. Use at same rate as commercial CalMag.

There are a number of brands of liquid Ca or liquid lime that are absorbed by the roots.

One teaspoon of hydrated lime per gallon of water provides relatively fast absorption. Dolomitic limestone, which contains Mg and Ca, takes longer to absorb. It is a good ingredient to amend into planting mixes to prevent deficiency.

Ground eggshells, fish bones, and seashells also break down over the season and add Ca to the soil. They can be softened and made more available by soaking in vinegar or lemon juice before use.

Gypsum, Ca sulfate $(CaSO_4)$, can be added to soils to increase Ca content without affecting the pH too much. It should not be added to soils with a pH below 5.5 because it interacts with aluminum (Al), making it soluble and poisonous to the plants.

Magnesium (Mg)

Role in plant nutrition
Magnesium helps support healthy veins and maintains leaf production and structure. It's required for chlorophyll production and enzyme breakdowns.

Symptoms
Mg is mobile, so deficiency symptoms start in the lower leaves. The veins remain green while the rest of the leaf turns pale yellow, exhibiting chlorosis. The leaves eventually curl up and die. The edges of affected leaves feel dry and crispy.

As the deficiency continues, it moves from lower leaves to the middle to upper half. Eventually the growing shoots change from a pale green to white color. The deficiency is quite apparent in the middle leaves. At the same time, the stems and petioles turn purple. Some cultivars, however, normally possess red or purple stems and petioles, so these traits are not a surefire sign of deficiency.

General discussion
Mg deficiency is common in all constructed soilless media and hydro. It is not commonly deficient outdoors. It occurs more frequently if using distilled, reverse osmosis water or tap water that has low ppm count. Usually water with 125 ppm dissolved solids contains adequate amounts of Mg.

Problem solving
Mg deficiency is one of the easiest nutrient deficiencies to diagnose and cure.

Water-soluble nutrients containing Mg fix the deficiency. Such nutrients are Mg sulfate ($MgSO_4$, epsom salts) and Ca-Mg for fast absorption, and dolomite lime or garden lime and worm castings for moderate absorption.

In hydro and planting mixes Mg deficiencies are easily fixed using 1 teaspoon (5.7 cc) of epsom salts per gallon (1.3cc per liter) of water in reservoirs. In planting mixes use 1 teaspoon per quart (5cc per liter) of soil in planting mixes. After the first treatment, use one-quarter dose with each watering or change of reservoir. Ca-Mg can also be used.

For fastest action, epsom salts can be used as a foliar treatment at the rate of 1 teaspoon per gallon (1.3cc per liter). Ca-Mg can be used foliarly as directed.

Dolomitic limestone contains large amounts of Mg. It can be used to raise the pH of soils and planting mixes and supply Mg at the same time.

Sulfur (S)

Sulphur deficiency is rare. Like iron (Fe), S moves slowly in the plant. Warmer temperatures make S harder for the plant to absorb. Unlike Fe, S is distributed evenly throughout the plant, mainly in the big fan leaves.

Role in plant nutrition

S is essential during vegetative growth and plays an important role in root growth, chlorophyll supply, and plant proteins.

Symptoms

The first signs of S deficiency are yellowing of young leaves. S deficiency starts at the back of the leaves and creeps toward the middle.

Leaf growth is slow; leaves become brittle and narrower than usual, and are small and mutated. Buds die off at the tops of flowering plants. Overall growth is stunted. Some S deficiencies show orange and red tints rather than yellowing. In severe cases the veins of the growing shoots turn yellow with dead areas at the base of the leaf where the blades join. The stems become hard and thin, and may be woody. They increase in length but not in diameter.

Too much S stunts the plant and leaf size, and the leaves look brown and dead at the tips. An excess of S looks like salt damage: restricted growth and dark color damage. This is rare.

Problem solving

Both organic soils and inorganic fertilizers contain high levels of available S, so plants are unlikely to suffer from a lack of the element. However, a deficiency is easily solved using epsom salts ($MgSO_4$). The plant is watered with epsom salts until the condition improves. One teaspoon per gallon (1.3–2.6cc per liter). It can be applied both foliarly and to the irrigation water.

One of the reasons why S deficiency is unlikely is that many commercial fertilizers contain nutrients as sulfates, so adding nutrients containing S fixes the deficiency. Mix at recommended strength to avoid nutrient burn. Any water-soluble fertilizer that uses S in the trace minerals also works. Other sources are elemental garden S, potassium sulfate (K_2SO_4), which is often used in commercial fertilizers.

Gypsum, composed of Ca and S, is sometimes used to improve problematic soils, since it contains two secondary nutrients and helps make the soil more friable. Do not use gypsum on acidic soil (pH less than 5.5); it affects the availability and absorption of soil aluminum, which is toxic to plant roots at relatively low levels.

Micronutrients

Boron (B)
Boron deficiency is not common. B is not mobile.

Role in plant nutrition
B is important in the processes of maturation, pollen germination, and seed production. It also aids in cell division, protein formation, healthy leaf color, and plant structure formation. Proper amounts keep stems, stalks, and branches strong and help plant cells maintain rigidity. It helps calcium maintain solubility.

Symptoms
The first sign of a B deficiency is the browning or graying of the growing tips followed by their death. Soon after, the lateral shoots start to grow, but then die. Shoots appear sunburned, twisted, and bright green. The leaves develop small brown necrotic dead spots that look like strawberry seeds and are surrounded by an area of dying tissue between leaf veins. B deficiency resembles a calcium deficiency, but can be differentiated by the small size of the necrotic areas.

Stems and petioles (leaf stems) are brittle and show signs of hollowness. B deficiency only affects newer growth.

Roots become stunted, and the smaller secondary roots become short and swollen as the root tips die. The roots are vulnerable to fungal and bacterial attacks that rot the root hairs and cause discoloration.

Excess B is more common in outdoor soil gardens. It is sometimes delivered in irrigation water and then becomes part of the soil matrix. Indoors and in containers it is rare and usually caused by overuse of fertilizers. B deficiency causes the yellowing of the leaf tips, which progresses inward. The leaves drop and the plant dies.

Problem solving
Even using reverse osmosis, B is difficult to remove. Treat a B deficiency foliarly or through the irrigation water, using one teaspoon (4.9cc) of boric acid (available in drug stores) per gallon of water (1.3cc per liter). Fast-acting solutions also include borax, compost, and compost teas.

Copper (Cu)
Copper deficiencies are rare. Cu has a low mobility.

Role in plant nutrition

Cu is essential to healthy plant production and reproduction and maturity, and assists in carbohydrate metabolism and oxygen reduction.

Symptoms

Cu deficiency first appears in young leaves, which exhibit necrosis and coppery, bluish or gray with metallic sheen at the tips and margins. The young leaves turn yellow between the veins.

Other symptoms include limp leaves that turn under at the edges and eventually die, and wilting the whole plant. New growth has difficulty opening. Flowers do not mature or open in males, and in females the stigmas don't grow properly.

Cu toxicity is rare but fatal. As the plant approaches death, its leaves turn yellow from its inability to use iron (Fe). The roots are abnormally sized and then start to decay.

General discussion

Cu deficiencies are often confused with overfertilization.

Problem solving

Foliar feeding with copper fungicides such as copper sulfate ($CuSO_4$) and chelated copper adjusts a deficiency. Any hydroponic micronutrient formula containing Cu helps as well. Compost, greensand, and kelp concentrates are good natural sources.

Soaking dimes or quarters in water and then using the water to irrigate the plants also supplies Cu, because these coins are 92% Cu and 8% zinc. (Pennies contain mostly zinc.) An acid solution such as pH Down, K fertilizer, lemon juice, or vinegar dissolves the Cu faster.

Iron (Fe)

Iron deficiency occasionally occurs outdoors and in planting media.

Role in plant nutrition

Fe is necessary for enzymes to function and acts as a catalyst for the synthesis of chlorophyll. Young actively growing tissues need Fe to thrive.

Symptoms

Fe deficiency starts in the new leaves, which lack chlorophyll but have no necrotic spots. This causes interveinal chlorosis, or the yellowing of the leaves except for the veins, which remain green. New leaves start to experience chlorotic molting, first near the base of the leaflets so that the middle of the leaf appears to have a brown mark. The veins remain dark green. Note that a Fe deficiency looks similar to a Mg deficiency except for its location. Fe deficiency affects the new growth but not the lower leaves, while Mg deficiency affects the middle and lower leaves first. Fe moves slowly in the plant.

Problem solving

An Fe deficiency may indicate a pH imbalance. Fe precipitates with even a moderately high pH. Fe may be present but not available to the plants. If it is present, it will dissolve if the pH is lowered to the preferred range (5.8–6.2).

Foliar feed with Fe chelated fertilizer containing Fe, Zn, and Mn, since these deficiencies are often found in combination. Other Fe-bearing supplements include compost, Fe chelates (often found in hydroponic micronutrient supplements), iron oxides (Fe_2O_3, FeO), and iron sulfate ($FeSO_4$) for fast absorption. Supplements should be added both foliarly and to the planting medium. Adding rusty water also works.

Manganese (Mn)

Manganese deficiency is rare and almost always associated with Fe-Zn deficiencies.

Role in plant nutrition

Mn helps enzymes break down for chlorophyll and photosynthesis production, and it aids in making nitrates available for protein production.

Symptoms

Mn deficiency is generally found in the young leaves. The leaf tissues turn yellow, and small areas of tan or brown dead tissue (necrotic areas) appear in the middle of the leaf. The leaf veins usually stay green. The leaf becomes outlined in a ring of dark green along its margins. Too much Mn in the soil causes an iron deficiency. In addition, the plant shows a lack of vigor. Mn is not mobile.

Problem solving

For fast relief, foliar feed with a water-soluble fertilizer high in Mn such as Fe-Zn-Mn fertilizer, hydro micros, or Mn chelate. Then add the fertilizers to the water-nutrient solution. Compost and greensand also contain Mn but are absorbed more slowly than the water-solubles.

Molybdenum (Mo)

Molybdenum deficiency is very rare but is more likely to occur in color-changing cultivars in cold temperature conditions. Mo is mobile.

Role in plant nutrition

Mo is contained in enzymes that help plants convert nitrates to ammonia, which is required for protein production.

Symptoms

The middle leaves turn yellow. As the deficiency progresses toward the shoots, the new leaves become distorted or twisted. A Mo deficiency causes leaves to have a pale, fringed, and scorched look, along with undersized or strange-looking leaf growth. Older chlorotic leaves experience rolled margins, stunted growth, and red tips that move inward toward the middle of the leaves.

Sometimes Mo deficiency is misdiagnosed as an N deficiency. However, N affects the bottom leaves first. Mo affects leaves in the middle of the plant first and then moves up to the newer growth.

Excessive Mo in cannabis looks like Fe or Cu deficiency.

General discussion

Generally a Mo deficiency most often occurs when S and P are deficient. Mo toxicity does not tend to wreak havoc on plants, but excess Mo causes severe problems in humans, so extra precautions should be taken when using it. Follow directions carefully.

Problem solving

Foliar spraying with water-soluble fertilizers aids in overcoming the deficiency. Because plants need Mo in such small amounts, a hydroponic micronutrient mix is often the most efficient way to supply it. These fertilizers can be used as foliar sprays or applied to the soil, as well as their customary use in hydroponic nutrient solutions.

Silicon (Si)

Silicon deficiency is very rare. Si is not mobile.

Role in plant nutrition

Si has not been proved necessary for plant growth. However, the presence of Si promotes the development of strong leaves, stems, and roots. It also increases resistance to fungal and bacterial diseases and insect infestation. When available to the plant, it is added to the structure of cell walls, strengthening them and making them more resistant to a number of environmental stresses, including drought, pests, and disease. It strengthens stem and branch structure, and as a result it promotes growth and development. The plant also exhibits an increase in photosynthetic activity and overall yield increases.

General discussion

Si is abundant in nature, but it is not included in hydroponic fertilizers, so it should be used as a supplement.

Problem solving

Diatomaceous earth can be added to the soil or planting mix. The Si is dissolved by acids in the medium into a soluble form that the roots absorb.

Liquid Si is found in Si supplements. It is immediately available to the plants.

Photo: Mel Frank

Zinc (Zn)

Zinc deficiency occurs occasionally. With low levels of Zn in the plants, the yields are dramatically reduced. Zn is not mobile, so symptoms occur mainly in the newer growth.

Role in Plant Nutrition

Zn aids in plant size and maturity, as well as in the production of leaves, stalks, stems, and branches. Zn is an essential component in many enzymes and in the growth hormone auxin. Low auxin levels cause stunted leaves and shoots. Zn is also important in the formation and activity of chlorophyll. Plants with high levels of Zn can tolerate longer droughts.

Symptoms

New growth has radically twisted leaf blades. Zn deficiencies are identifiable by spotting, chlorosis, and yellowing between the veins of older leaves. Interveinal yellowing is often accompanied by overall paleness. During the flowering stage, buds may contort, twist, and turn hard. When the deficiency first appears, the spotting can resemble that of an Fe or Mn deficiency, but it affects the new growth. Zn excess is very rare, but produces wilting and even death in extreme cases.

Problem solving

Use an Fe-Zn-Mn micro mix to solve the deficiency. Zinc sulfate ($ZnSO_4$), chelated zinc, or zinc oxide (ZnO) also adjust the deficiency.

Photo: Miranda Moore, HoneyDew Farms

AIR TEMPERATURE, HUMIDITY & QUALITIES

With contributions from Joey Ereñeta, Autumn Karcey, Mike Finley, and Brandy Keen

Cannabis and the air that surrounds it have an intimate relationship. The stem and leaves are bathed in it and are affected by its temperature and humidity. Air temperature plays a major role in determining leaf temperature, and relative humidity affects how easily plants can absorb CO_2, which is required for photosynthesis. The effects of climatic conditions on the plant are found in its relationship to vapor pressure.

Ideal temperature is tied to light and humidity conditions. The combination of temperature and humidity is used to calculate the vapor pressure deficit (VPD). As more light is available, the ideal temperature for normal plant growth increases.

Cannabis grows well in moderate temperatures, between 70 and 85°F (21–29°C). Both high and low temperatures slow the rate of metabolism and growth. Plants grow best when the temperature at the leaf surface during the lighted period is kept between 72 and 79°F (22–26°C). When CO_2 augmentation is used, plants function better when the temperature is a few degrees warmer, between 79 and 85°F (26–29°C). Individual cannabis varieties differ in their temperature preferences by a few degrees, so some experimentation is required to find the ideal temperature and humidity for the specific cultivar.

Plants growing under moderate intensity lighting should be kept on the low side of the recommended temperature range. Plants growing under higher-intensity lighting should be kept on the warmer end of the scale. Strong light and low temperatures slow growth and decrease stem elongation. Conversely, when plants are given high temperatures and only moderate light, the stems elongate.

During dark periods, the temperature can be kept as much as 10°F (5°C) cooler than the lit period without any negative effects. Wider temperature differences cause slower growth, stem elongation, and delayed flower ripening. Plants that experience a large diurnal shift, the differential between day and night temperatures, suffer from stretching and slowed growth rates.

Plants that are kept at a constant temperature day and night grow stouter, sturdier stems and have denser bud growth. It lowers the chances of botrytis and powdery mildew infections, which prefer cooler temperatures. Maintaining temperature also eliminates higher humidity created by falling temperature.

At temperatures below 60°F (15°C), photosynthesis and plant metabolism slow, stunting growth until conditions improve. As soon as the temperature rises, the plant resumes full functioning. When the temperature falls below 40°F (4°C), cannabis plants experience tissue damage and require about 24 hours of warmer conditions to resume growth. However, young plants are tolerant of low temperatures; when outdoors, seedlings may pierce snow cover without ill effect. Low temperatures during ripening, even just overnight, delay or prevent bud maturation. Some equatorial varieties stop growth after a few nights when the temperature dips below 40°F (4°C). Wind exacerbates these conditions.

Ideal Temperature Ranges by Growth Cycle

Germination: 70–78°F (21–25°C)   Flowering: 68–85°F (20–30°C)
Vegetative: 68–85°F (20–30°C)   Cloning: 75–85°F (24–30°C)

EFFECT OF TEMPERATURE ON PHOTOSYNTHESIS

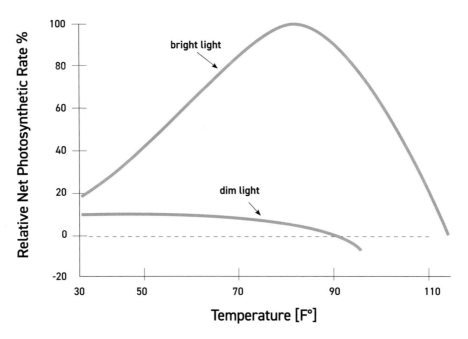

Plants photosynthesize more rapidly in high light and high CO_2 conditions when the temperature is around 85°F (30°C)

When using vapor pressure deficit (VPD) to guide the climate, "finite control" is essential. VPD parameters are incredibly tight. The difference of one degree Fahrenheit (half a degree Celsius) at the leaf, two degrees Fahrenheit (~one degree Celsius) of the air, or 5% relative humidity drastically changes a targeted VPD range.

Most high-end instruments have an accuracy range of +/- one degree Fahrenheit (half a degree Celsius) and 1.5% relative humidity. At temperate conditions, this can be challenging when calculating multiple differentials around a target

VPD. A good solution is to use a quality hygrometer such as a digital sling psychrometer to measure relative humidity. Walk around the garden, focusing first on room and canopy consistency, then compare with the other sensor's readings. Stationary hygrometers can be used; however, they must be calibrated to provide accurate results.

One way to control humidity is to use a fogger and dehumidifier both controlled by the same sensor to keep temperature and humidity within the dead band. If they are on separate sensors, they must be coordinated so that they don't fight each other.

Air Circulation

The steady movement of air in the garden provides many essential benefits for growing plants. Airflow homogenizes the temperature and humidity in the space, ensuring that all plants experience the same conditions. As heat builds up underneath cultivation lights, and moisture accumulates in the plant canopy, good airflow circulates cool, dry air from the air conditioner and dehumidifier. This air movement strengthens plant stems and vascular tissues. Plants that sway from optimal airflow respond by creating thicker stems and increased vascular pathways for the uptake and translocation of water and other valuable resources. This makes the plant more stress tolerant. Later, thicker-stemmed plants will be able to support the increased flower weight accumulated during the reproductive stage.

Airflow in the room eliminates "dead" zones where insects and fungus are more likely to create an infection. Airflow across the plant canopy also boosts vapor pressure deficit, providing additional protection from mold and fungus and driving transpiration.

Carbon dioxide is heavier than air and concentrates closer to the floor of the grow room. However, airflow keeps it moving through the plant canopy. Wall and ceiling-mounted fans can be used to move cooler, CO_2-rich air out from underneath tables and racks and back into the parts of the room where it can be used by the plants. Horizontally mounted fans circulate air through the canopy. As the CO_2 is used up by leaves and flowers, this air is blown away, replacing it with CO_2-enriched air.

Biosecurity

Climate control conditions affect the overall biosecurity of the garden in a number of ways:
- Humidity fluctuations invite fungal growth such as bud mold and powdery mildew.
- Plants expend energy responding to or recovering from poor climate conditions. This energy is diverted from growth-reducing yield and quality.
- Under poor environmental conditions, plants' natural defenses are compromised, leaving them more vulnerable to infestation or infection from fungus or pathogens.
- Unsanitary ventilation systems can be a source of pest infiltration and infection colonies.

- Filtration and air sterilization systems are often incorporated into the HVAC system.

Besides temperature and CO_2 content, other things to consider about the air in the garden include dust content, electrical charge, and humidity.

Dust

The dust content of the air affects the efficiency of the plant's ability to photosynthesize. Although floating dust blocks only a small amount of light, dust accumulated on leaves blocks large amounts of light.

"Dust" is actually composed of many different-sized solid and liquid particles that float in the gaseous soup of the atmosphere. The particles include organic fibers, hair, other animal and vegetable particles, bacteria, viruses, smoke, and such odoriferous liquid particles as essential oils and water-soluble condensates. Virtually all dust particles have a positive electrical charge because they are missing an electron, which causes them to float in gasses such as air.

They are captured in HEPA and carbon filters, both of which can be used in all garden spaces.

Negative ion generators charge oxygen molecules with an extra ion, which is unstable and easily jumps from the O_2 to a positively charged molecule floating in the air. The neutralized dust particle precipitates to a surface rather than continuing to float. One way negative ions are created is by crashing water such as fountains or waves at a beach. Negative ion generators produce them in copious amounts and use an extremely small amount of electricity. They are considered healthful and stress reducing for both plants and animals, including humans, and are sometimes used in schools and offices.

Ions can be used in rooms adjacent to rooms where ripening or mature buds are being grown or stored, but not inside them because the ions will interact with the terpenes. Ion generators can be used in spaces with plants in vegetative growth and during the first few weeks of flowering.

Ozone generators create ozone (O_3), which has a unique odor. As a gas, oxygen forms a molecule composed of two O atoms (O_2). Using an electrical charge, three O_2 molecules are combined into two O_3 molecules.

Ozone is unstable: the third atom jumps from the molecule to dust particles, spores, and bacteria. It is not safe to be around, either for plants or for humans, but degrades into O_2 over time. It can be used to clean uninhabited spaces but should not be used around living or cut plants or humans. Ozone generators are often used in air exhaust systems because of their effectiveness in eliminating odors.

If the leaves are dusty, wash them off using a mist or "shower" setting on sprayer nozzles. Be careful when using water sprays around hot lights because the lamps will shatter if even a little water hits the hot glass. Before spraying, make sure the lights are higher than the spray range or shut them off and let them cool down.

Temperature

Cannabis plants are hardy and survive outdoors in a wide range of temperatures. As the temperature rises from the high 70s into the 80s Fahrenheit (20–25°C), plants spend more energy staying cool and maintaining faster cell metabolism. Under high light conditions, photosynthesis increases as the temperature rises, resulting in a net gain in plant growth. Photosynthesis reaches its apex at about 85°F (30°C) and about 1,500 PPFD (Chandra et al. 2009).

As the temperature rises past 85°F (30°C), photosynthesis slows until it stops at between 90–95°F (32–35°C). At this point, plants go into preservation mode; photosynthesis stops as the plants spend energy acquiring water and transpiring it through the stomata in order to keep cool.

Outdoor plants facing long, hot spells should be encouraged to develop deep roots by providing deep penetration irrigation followed by moderate soil drying. Later in the season, when the roots are stressed to supply water, they will be able to draw on adequate supplies with less effort from the deeper level. As soil dries out, water tension increases, and the soil holds the remaining water tighter. Keeping the soil moist makes it easier for the plant to draw it from the medium.

Many or most cultivars withstand extremely hot weather, up to 120°F (49°C), for short periods, as long as they have adequate supplies of water and a large root system. When plants wilt in hot weather, either the medium is drying or the root system is not robust enough to supply the amount of water the plants are transpiring to keep cool. The plants can be cooled using cooling misters or a misting fan. If the temperature cannot be controlled directly, place a 20–30% shade cloth over the plants to reduce stress. Another solution is to spray a nontoxic antitranspirant, which will slow transpiration by blocking the stomatal openings somewhat and slow their release of water.

Excessive heat can be a problem indoors, too, though it is easier to control. Gardens using high wattage lamps generate a lot of heat; an unprotected 1,000-watt lamp emits about 3,412 Btus. During the winter, the heat produced may keep the garden space comfortable, but during the summer, the space may get too hot, particularly if there are several lights heating up the space.

The temperature of the uppermost foliage is the specific area of interest. The space in the aisles or the floor may be cool, but that doesn't matter to the plants. What is important is the temperature of the canopy under the lights where the plants are producing new growth. Even when the overall temperature of the room is in the optimal range, the areas directly under the bulbs can be very hot.

Different lighting technologies produce different amounts of radiant heat, which means the ambient temperature and the leaf temperature can be dramatically different between different lighting technologies.

Each type of lighting technology produces direct waste heat (the electricity that isn't converted to light) and radiant heat (the heat that is created when light strikes a surface and is converted from light energy to thermal energy). The result is that the leaf surface temperature beneath a high-intensity discharge (HID) light is higher than the leaf surface temperature beneath an LED, even in the same room with the same PPFD and air temperature.

Because of this, accurate air temperature measurements cannot be made in direct light when temperature readings are taken. Measurements taken in direct light are actually surface temperatures, not air temperatures. For best accuracy, temperature probes controlling the heating, ventilation, and air conditioning (HVAC) system should be out of direct light, and temperatures under direct light should also be taken periodically to understand the differential between the air temperature and the leaf temperature of the plants. An infrared thermometer provides the most accurate reading. Other sensors such as direct light or wet bulb thermometers are not as accurate.

An inexpensive way to get a temperature reading in direct light is to hang the temperature sensor at canopy level, but shaded. A white paper cup is very effective at providing that shade. Put a hole in the bottom of the cup so that the temperature sensor can be pushed through. Pull the wired temperature sensor through the hole until the sensor itself is almost to the rim of the cup. Now turn the cup upside down at the level of the plant canopy. This creates a shaded temperature sensor that can constantly take measurements even in direct light. It is important to use a white or other reflective color cup. A dark-colored cup will absorb more heat and give a false reading.

Although the air temperature affects leaf temperature, taking the measurement of air temperature is an indirect method of determining canopy conditions. A more accurate method, though not widely used, is to measure the leaf temperature at the top of the canopy, where most of the photosynthesis is taking place, using an infrared (surface temperature) thermometer, and regulating the air conditions based on this reading. The reasoning is that the general environmental conditions are not as relevant as the environment that the plant is experiencing. Under this regimen the air temperature is controlled based on leaf temperature measurements.

Relative Humidity (RH)

The ideal humidity for a cultivation space varies based on plant maturity level, temperature selection, and VPD goals. Maintaining proper humidity is a critical consideration, particularly during mid-to-late-stage flowering when the plant is especially vulnerable to mold.

In general, RH should be about 70% in the pre-rooted propagation stage. This is easily achieved using a humidity dome. The vegetative growth stage should be 55–65%. While this is a basic overview and general range, using VPD calculations is more precise. However, excessively low humidity creates an overly rapid transpiration of moisture, resulting in stunted growth and a poor-quality harvest.

Vapor Pressure Deficit (VPD)

The primary benefit of VPD is optimizing transpiration and gas exchange for photosynthesis and increasing nutrient uptake. Two other factors make VPD important to any indoor garden: producing high-quality cannabis without the use of harmful pesticides, and lowering production costs.

Plants require a flow of water in order to bring nutrients up from the roots and maintain temperature through transpiration, as well as for photosynthetic and metabolic processes. The rate that the water can evaporate from the leaves depends on the air's temperature, humidity, and the difference between how much water the air is holding and how much water it is capable of holding. This is called vapor pressure deficit. For example, at the same temperature, a given amount of water will evaporate more quickly when the air is drier than when it is more humid. If the air is fully saturated and no longer has the capacity for more moisture, the plant cannot transpire.

Temperature plays an important role as well. When the water is warmer, in this case in the plant, it is closer to its point of "phase change" from liquid to vapor. This relationship is represented in the evaporation point and boiling point of an element or compound. The connection is transversely represented in dew point and freezing point.

The leaves' surface area to air is also a factor in determining the exchange rate. The plant's evaporation rate is called transpiration; the climate is responsible for its transpiration speed. VPD becomes the plant's circulatory system in which photosynthesis is the driver. Vapor pressure is the measurement of the plant's water pressure to transpire.

Instead of measuring and calculating it repeatedly, a chart is much easier to follow, as some values remain relatively stable. For example, a properly transpiring plant's leaf temperature in a balanced, stable environment will remain stable.

Calculating Vapor Pressure Deficit (VPD)
By Pulse Grow

Air is made up of many gasses. It is about 78% nitrogen, 21% oxygen, and much smaller parts of other gases. Water vapor, the gaseous form of water, is one of those other gases. The amount of water vapor in the air (expressed as pressure) is called "vapor pressure."

Air can hold only a certain amount of water vapor at a given temperature before it starts condensing back to liquid water (in forms such as dew or rain). The maximum amount of water vapor that air can hold at a certain temperature is called "saturation vapor pressure," (SVP).

As the air gets hotter, the amount of water that the air can hold (its SVP) increases. As air cools down, the SVP decreases, meaning that the air can't hold as much water vapor. That is why there is dew all over everything after a cool morning.

The air just gets too full of water, and the water condenses out.

Similarly, the current actual amount of water vapor in the air is called the "actual vapor pressure," or AVP.

Some key points:

$$AVP / SVP \times 100 = RH\%$$

RH is just the proportion of water the air is currently holding versus its maximum capacity. That's why it's called "relative" humidity.

The maximum the AVP can be is the current SVP.

That means RH = 100%. If AVP reaches SVP, any additional moisture will precipitate out of the air as liquid water (dew, etc).

The full vapor pressure deficit (VPD) formula is saturation vapor (SVP) pressure minus actual vapor pressure (AVP), or:

$$VPD = SVP - AVP$$

Vapor Pressure Deficit Estimates

RH%

Temp (°F)	80	78	76	74	72	70	68	66	64	62	60	58	56	54	52	50	48	46	44	42	40	38	36	34	32	30	28	26	24	22
66	0.6	0.6	0.7	0.7	0.8	0.8	0.9	0.9	0.9	1.0	1.1	1.1	1.1	1.2	1.2	1.2	1.3	1.3	1.4	1.4	1.5	1.5	1.6	1.6	1.6	1.7	1.7	1.8	1.8	1.9
68	0.6	0.7	0.7	0.8	0.8	0.9	0.9	1.0	1.0	1.0	1.1	1.1	1.2	1.2	1.3	1.3	1.4	1.4	1.5	1.5	1.6	1.6	1.7	1.7	1.7	1.8	1.8	1.9	1.9	2.0
70	0.7	0.7	0.8	0.8	0.9	0.9	1.0	1.0	1.1	1.1	1.2	1.2	1.3	1.3	1.4	1.4	1.5	1.5	1.5	1.6	1.7	1.7	1.8	1.8	1.9	1.9	2.0	2.0	2.1	2.1
72	0.7	0.8	0.8	0.9	0.9	1.0	1.0	1.1	1.1	1.2	1.2	1.3	1.3	1.4	1.4	1.5	1.5	1.6	1.7	1.7	1.8	1.8	1.9	1.9	2.0	2.0	2.1	2.1	2.1	2.2
73	0.8	0.8	0.9	0.9	1.0	1.0	1.1	1.1	1.2	1.3	1.3	1.4	1.4	1.5	1.5	1.6	1.6	1.7	1.8	1.8	1.9	1.9	2.0	2.1	2.1	2.2	2.3	2.3	2.3	2.4
75	0.8	0.9	0.9	1.0	1.0	1.1	1.2	1.2	1.3	1.3	1.4	1.4	1.5	1.6	1.6	1.7	1.7	1.8	1.9	1.9	2.0	2.0	2.1	2.2	2.2	2.3	2.3	2.4	2.5	2.5
77	0.8	0.9	1.0	1.0	1.1	1.2	1.2	1.3	1.3	1.4	1.5	1.5	1.6	1.7	1.7	1.8	1.9	1.9	2.0	2.0	2.1	2.2	2.2	2.3	2.4	2.4	2.5	2.5	2.5	2.7
79	0.9	1.0	1.0	1.1	1.2	1.2	1.3	1.4	1.4	1.5	1.6	1.6	1.7	1.8	1.8	1.9	2.0	2.0	2.1	2.2	2.2	2.3	2.4	2.4	2.5	2.6	2.6	2.7	2.8	2.8
81	0.9	1.0	1.1	1.2	1.2	1.3	1.4	1.4	1.5	1.6	1.7	1.7	1.8	1.9	1.9	2.0	2.1	2.1	2.2	2.3	2.4	2.4	2.5	2.6	2.6	2.7	2.8	2.9	2.9	3.0
82	1.0	1.1	1.1	1.2	1.3	1.4	1.5	1.5	1.6	1.7	1.8	1.8	1.9	2.0	2.1	2.1	2.2	2.3	2.4	2.5	2.6	2.7	2.7	2.8	2.8	2.9	3.0	3.0	3.1	3.2
84	1.1	1.1	1.2	1.3	1.4	1.5	1.5	1.6	1.7	1.8	1.9	1.9	2.0	2.1	2.2	2.3	2.3	2.4	2.5	2.6	2.6	2.7	2.8	2.9	3.0	3.0	3.1	3.2	3.3	3.4
86	1.1	1.2	1.3	1.4	1.5	1.5	1.6	1.7	1.8	1.9	2.0	2.0	2.1	2.2	2.3	2.4	2.5	2.5	2.6	2.7	2.8	2.9	3.0	3.1	3.1	3.2	3.3	3.4	3.5	3.6
88	1.2	1.3	1.4	1.4	1.5	1.6	1.7	1.8	1.9	2.0	2.1	2.2	2.3	2.3	2.4	2.5	2.6	2.7	2.8	2.9	3.0	3.1	3.1	3.2	3.3	3.4	3.5	3.6	3.7	3.8
90	1.2	1.3	1.4	1.5	1.6	1.7	1.8	1.9	2.0	2.1	2.2	2.3	2.4	2.5	2.6	2.7	2.8	2.9	2.9	3.0	3.1	3.2	3.3	3.4	3.5	3.6	3.7	3.8	3.9	4.0
91	1.3	1.4	1.5	1.6	1.7	1.8	1.9	2.0	2.1	2.2	2.3	2.4	2.5	2.6	2.7	2.8	2.9	3.0	3.1	3.2	3.3	3.4	3.5	3.6	3.7	3.8	3.9	4.0	4.1	4.2
93	1.4	1.5	1.6	1.7	1.8	1.9	2.0	2.1	2.2	2.3	2.4	2.6	2.7	2.8	2.9	3.0	3.1	3.2	3.3	3.4	3.5	3.6	3.7	3.8	3.9	4.0	4.1	4.2	4.3	4.4
95	1.5	1.6	1.7	1.8	1.9	2.0	2.1	2.2	2.4	2.5	2.6	2.7	2.8	2.9	3.0	3.1	3.3	3.4	3.5	3.6	3.7	3.8	3.9	4.0	4.1	4.3	4.4	4.5	4.6	4.7
97	1.5	1.7	1.8	1.9	2.0	2.1	2.3	2.4	2.5	2.6	2.7	2.8	3.0	3.1	3.2	3.3	3.4	3.5	3.7	3.8	3.9	4.0	4.1	4.3	4.4	4.5	4.6	4.7	4.8	5.0
99	1.6	1.8	1.9	2.0	2.1	2.3	2.4	2.5	2.6	2.7	2.9	3.0	3.1	3.2	3.4	3.5	3.6	3.7	3.9	4.0	4.1	4.2	4.4	4.5	4.6	4.7	4.9	5.0	5.1	5.2
100	1.7	1.8	2.0	2.1	2.2	2.4	2.5	2.6	2.8	2.9	3.0	3.2	3.3	3.4	3.6	3.7	3.8	3.9	4.1	4.2	4.3	4.5	4.6	4.7	4.9	5.0	5.1	5.3	5.4	5.5

This chart is in Fahrenheit and designed for the vegetative growth stage. The band in blue/green is the ideal range. Visit PulseGrow.com to use the VPD calculator or make a custom chart.

To achieve a target vapor pressure deficit (VPD), "finite control" is essential. VPD parameters are incredibly tight. The difference of one degree Fahrenheit (half a degree Celsius) at the leaf, two degrees Fahrenheit (~one degree Celsius) of the air, or 5% relative humidity, drastically changes a targeted VPD range.

The "optimal" VPD has been the subject of much debate, but anecdotal evidence points to somewhere between 1.2 and 1.6 kilopascals (kPa) in flowering plants. As the same VPD can be established at various temperature and humidity selections, it's important to consider each variable independently and not just VPD as a target.

For instance, a VPD of approximately 1.33 kPa can be achieved at temperature-humidity pairings of 82°F (28°C) and 64% RH, and 70°F (21°C) and 47% RH. Even though each of these selections results in the same VPD, the higher temperature and humidity ranges result in faster growth and require less cooling than the lower temperature and humidity ranges.

It's also important to note that although VPD is a significant consideration, it's not the only consideration. Temperature and humidity must also be considered as independent metrics.

While understanding the simple principles of VPD is crucial, it is critical to observe the plants in their environment. Due to the variations between cultivars, the chart will get the grower close, but the plants will ultimately guide the way. Through combining useful data logging and consistent genetics, multiple cycles can be analyzed for beneficial trends and "best seasons" for repeatable optimal conditions in greenhouses and indoor environments.

While the fundamental laws of VPD are universal in principle to outdoor, indoor, and greenhouse cultivation, the control and manipulation humans have over VPD are vastly different between all three methodologies.

Climate Controls

Humidity Control

The moisture in the garden air affects the vapor pressure deficit and the rate at which plants transpire and perform gas exchange. If humidity is too high, plant transpiration is stifled and fungal pathogens can thrive. Humidity that is too low leads to excessive transpiration and stress responses such as wilting and stomatal closure. Optimal humidity and VPD allow the plants to transpire and uptake carbon dioxide at highly efficient rates, which can significantly increase photosynthesis and rates of growth.

The primary source of grow room humidity is plant transpiration, followed by evaporation of moisture from the planting medium and irrigation system. During periods of optimal growth, plants release almost as much moisture as the grower provides to them on a daily basis. To counteract this, dehumidifiers are regularly used to remove excess water from the air.

In other cases, humidification is used to elevate RH. This can occur when growing in

a particularly dry climate and is commonly used in propagation rooms for rooting cuttings. Both humidifiers and dehumidifiers are typically equipped with a hygrometer for measuring RH and a hydrostat for setting the desired humidity levels in each zone.

Sizing Dehumidifiers

Dehumidifiers are rated by the amount of moisture they can remove from the surrounding air on a daily basis. The dehumidification capacity required can be calculated based on the total wattage of lighting and the lighting type used. The power of the lights to drive photosynthesis determines the plants' rate of transpiration.

The Growlink Platform virtually connects all the technology in the cultivation space. Growlink captures massive amounts of valuable crop-level data using custom wireless mesh canopy sensors to drive yields, reduce losses, optimize irrigation, prevent disease, and reduce energy consumption. The system comes with the 24/7 support, on-site commissioning, and training.

The more powerful the lighting, the faster plants transpire. The more transpiration, the greater the dehumidification capacity needed. Lighting type plays a big factor in this calculation because different light technologies have different levels of efficacy. For example, LED lights have a different efficacy factor than high-intensity discharge (HID) lights, in that they produce more photons per watt of electricity consumed. A 600-watt LED produces more light and drives more photosynthesis and transpiration than a 600-watt HID light. Therefore, there are slightly different rules of thumb for sizing dehumidifiers depending on the light technology used.

On average, 0.02 pints (0.095 l) of dehumidification is needed per watt of HID light, or 0.03 pints (0.14 l) of dehumidification per watt of LED light.

To properly calculate the dehumidification capacity required, use the equation above and follow these steps:

1. Add up the total wattage of lighting in the garden.
2. Based on lighting type, multiply the total lighting wattage by 0.02 pints (0.095 l) for HID or by 0.03 pints (0.14 l) for LED.

For example, using 3,000 watts of HID light in the space: 3,000w x 0.02 pints (0.095 l) = 60 pints (28 l)

In this room, a dehumidifier that has a minimum rating of 60 pints (28.4 l) per day is required.

Using 3,000 watts of LED light in the space: 3,000w x 0.03 pints (0.14 l) = 90 pints (42.6 l)

In this room, a dehumidifier that has a minimum rating of 90 pints (42.6 l) per day is required.

Cooling Indoors

There are several ways to manage heat in indoor gardens:

- Don't create a hot environment. In small gardens using HIDs, air-cooled lights prevent heat from being trapped in the garden space.
- Keep heat-producing ballasts outside the growing area.
- Run lights at night. If the room is lit exclusively by lamps, the day/night cycle can be reversed so heat is generated at night, when it is cooler outside. It's also a financial savings because electricity is cheaper at night.
- Ventilate the garden area with filtered air. During the winter and in the evening, outdoor air may be cool enough to lower the temperature of the garden. Don't ventilate if the outside air is too hot or cold.
- Install an air conditioner. Air conditioners can be set up to exchange the heat in the room without venting telltale odors. Portable air conditioners work well. Window models can be installed in a window or an internal wall to vent the heat into a central area.
- Use an evaporative or "swamp" cooler. Warm dry spaces can be cooled using portable air coolers. These appliances cool the air using evaporation. Air is drawn through a wet filter; as the water evaporates, it cools the air. This works best in low-humidity situations.

Even without lights, an enclosed space such as a greenhouse can get hot rapidly when sunlight is illuminating it or when outdoor temperatures rise. Sunlight is converted to heat energy when it hits an opaque surface in the greenhouse. The heat is trapped, so the temperature increases throughout the day. Some greenhouses have roofs that open to let hot air escape and draw cooler air in.

For ventilated greenhouses, swamp coolers are very effective. Water runs through fibrous plastic mats as fans blow air, lowering the greenhouse temperature. Because swamp coolers work by evaporation, they are most effective in hot, dry areas.

Another evaporation technique uses five-micron spray nozzles, or cooling fans, to pulverize water into small particles less than five microns in diameter. The water pieces are so small that they immediately evaporate as they are sprayed into the hot air, lowering the ambient temperature. Spray coolers and water misters are available through nursery and patio supply houses.

Air Conditioning

For proper cooling, air conditioning (AC) is the most common and effective choice. Air conditioners pass air across coils filled with a refrigerant. Heat from the air is transferred to this fluid, and the air is blown back into the garden at a lower temperature. All air conditioners produce condensate—moisture collected by the coils in the air handler—that must drain from the unit. Many ACs have a condensate tube, which can be sent to a drain. Some cultivators capture the condensate from their ACs and dehumidifiers for recycling. (*See Sustainability.*) If so, this water must be regularly tested and filtered to ensure that it is safe for reuse in the garden.

For a small garden, a portable or window AC unit may be the easiest option to provide sufficient cooling. They are inexpensive to purchase; however, they are less energy efficient and more costly to operate than higher-efficiency commercial units. Because the air handler, coils, and condenser are all combined into one packaged unit, some portable and window air conditioners release unfiltered odor with the warm air they exhaust. ACs that exchange heat but not air are preferable.

Commercial facilities commonly use a split or ducted air conditioning system. Split ACs have separate air handlers and condenser units. The air handler sits inside the grow room, while the compressor sits outside the facility. Although split systems are more expensive to purchase than packaged window and portable ACs, they are more efficient at converting power into cooling capacity. Additionally, split ACs are better than some single-unit ACs at odor mitigation because all the air that is pulled into the air handler is cooled and blown right back into the grow room. The refrigerant used for heat transfer is the only thing that travels between the indoor and outdoor environments.

A ducted air conditioner utilizes commercial cooling and air handling equipment, which should be specifically sized for the application. If installing such a system, or retrofitting an existing one, it's best to seek out a professional who specializes in cannabis projects. It's easiest to use products from HVAC manufacturers that manufacture equipment designed for

Traditional HVAC systems designed for comfort cooling can lower yields, contaminate crops, damage plants, and increase energy consumption and costs. Surna offers integrated and stand-alone climate control systems. Integrated systems coordinate the cooling and dehumidification functions, usually with the same pieces of equipment and provide far greater precision and more energy-saving options.

the indoor horticulture industry. They offer units that provide cooling, heating, dehumidi-fication, and CO_2 supplementation.

Selecting and Sizing HVACs

The amount of heat produced by grow room equipment (heat load) and the cooling capac-ity of an air conditioner are generally rated in British thermal units (Btus). AC capacity is also often rated in units called "tons." One ton of air conditioning is equal to 12,000 Btus of cooling capacity. When the heat loads in the room are known, such as lights, fans, and other electronic equipment, calculations can be made to determine how many Btus (or tons) of cooling power are needed to maintain temperatures within the optimal range.

All electrical devices produce 3.412 Btus of heat per watt of energy consumed. Because grow lights are the greatest heat load in an indoor garden, air conditioning needs are esti-mated based on the amount of lighting in each space. The rule of thumb is between four and six Btus of AC for every watt of lighting. Since lights only produce 3.412 Btus per watt, this range factors in a buffer of additional cooling to account for all other potential heat loads in the grow room. Additional heat loads include dehumidifiers, CO_2 generators, pumps, fans, and other electrical devices, as well as people. Using this equation, the range of cooling required for any grow room can be calculated by simply adding up the total lighting wattage and multiplying by four to six Btus.

For example, a grow room with 3,000 watts of lighting will need:

3,000w x 4 Btus = 12,000 Btus (minimum AC capacity)
3,000w x 6 Btus = 18,000 Btus (maximum AC capacity)

At 12,000 to 18,000 Btus, a 1 ton to 1.5 ton air conditioner is required.

The air conditioning system can be a significant capital expense for any indoor garden, so it should not be overengineered. Conversely, an undersized AC is forced to run constant-ly to combat the heat from lights and other equipment. A properly sized air conditioner will be somewhat stronger than the heat loads in a given room. As the temperature rises, the air conditioner will be able to quickly cool the room to the lower set point of the optimal range and then shut down until it is needed again. This will prolong the life of the air conditioner, because it will not have to work as hard or as often to provide adequate temperature control.

Types of HVAC Systems

Stand-alone Systems

"Stand-alone" describes climate control systems where the cooling function is decoupled from the dehumidification function, and integrated systems describe climate control sys-tems where the cooling and dehumidification functions are coordinated, usually with the same pieces of equipment. In general, stand-alone systems have lower upfront costs but provide less precision and fewer energy-related benefits, and integrated systems may be more expensive, but with far greater precision and more energy-saving options.

Surna's grow room climate controller solutions have been developed specifically to address the unique requirements of growing cannabis, including direct temperature and humidity control, CO_2 supplementation, and more. Sensors placed around the canopy provide accurate readings of these crucial limiting factors and maintain the levels set by the grower. All the data is captured and used to optimize the facility and cultivar-specific climate conditions. The SentryIQ system includes the Surna SentryIQ® Central Plant Controller, Room Controller, and Facility Supervisor.

In DX systems with stand-alone dehumidification, the cooling and heating unit is separate from the dehumidification unit, which is usually located in the space it serves. The most common types of standalone DX systems are split systems, mini-splits, and packaged rooftop units (RTUs). Common types of dehumidifiers are stand-alone electric, or desiccant units used in low-humidity applications.

Split DX with Stand-alone Dehumidification

Split systems are made up of two parts: an indoor fan coil unit (FCU) or small air handler (AHU), and an outside condensing unit. The FCU or AHU passes the warm air from inside the cultivation space over cold evaporator coils, which contain refrigerant, absorbs the heat from the air inside the space, and transfers it to the condensing unit outside the grow to be rejected.

Variable refrigerant flow (VRF) systems also fall under this category. While VRF systems are generally very energy efficient in comfort-cooling applications, in process-cooling applications such as cultivation facilities, much of what makes them energy efficient in comfort cooling does not apply. However, they do offer greater redundancy than other stand-alone systems, and there may be some limited energy benefit in smaller facilities compared with standard split systems.

These systems typically supply cooled or heated air to a single zone in grow applications. The typical capacity is from 1 to 10 tons, but they can be larger in some applications.

Pros:

- Low cost.
- Smaller size (split units) common.
- Installation requirements well understood.
- Common, don't require significant building alterations.
- Short lead times.

Cons:

- Lower life expectancy (3–10 years depending on selection), as they are designed for light commercial or residential versus industrial applications.
- Higher maintenance costs, as they are not intended for heavy-duty operation.
- Consistent dehumidification is not available. Requires additional stand-alone dehumidifiers.
- Temperature and humidity fluctuations due to staged on/off operation and tendency for the DX units and DHU to "fight" each other and operate independently.
- Usually less energy efficient than other options
- Many points of electrical connection required.
- Electrical infrastructure costs may be greater due to large HVAC loads being spread throughout the building as opposed to being centralized at the plant.
- Limited free cooling or economization options.

2-Pipe Chilled Water (aka Hydronic Cooling & Dehumidification)

Hydronic cooling is simply the removal of heat and moisture from a space utilizing chilled water as the heat exchange medium. People sometimes confuse chilled water systems with evaporative cooling, which introduces humidity into the space and consumes water to cool, but they are quite different.

Hydronic cooling systems are completely closed loop, meaning no water is added to the space, much like the radiator in a car. In hydronic cooling, water is chilled by a chiller, dry cooler, or cooling tower and circulated via pump through the system into heat exchanger units in the space (air handlers or fan coils) and then back to the chiller to be recirculated again.

Air handlers and/or fan coil units utilize a fan to pull warm air in and over the heat exchanger inside. As warm air in the room moves over the heat exchangers, heat is transferred from the air into the cool water inside the coils, pulling heat and humidity from the room and returning cool, dry air to the space. Since pumps keep water inside the system constantly moving, the warm water leaving the heat exchanger is immediately returned to a chiller, dry cooler, or cooling tower.

These units may sit inside or outside the facility. While indoor chillers are more efficient, for the added cost, complexity, and floor space required, most facilities prefer them outside so that they don't have to give up space inside for equipment.

One of the primary benefits of chilled water systems is that for a minor cost addition,

N+1 redundancy in each space can be built into the design, offering complete redundancy without doubling the equipment cost. These systems utilize multiple chillers organized into a bank and multiple fan coils that are all tied back to the collective chiller bank. This allows for flexibility for the system to grow and cooling capacity to be added as needed.

Built-in redundancy is inherent because indoor gardens use multiple chillers and air handlers or fan coils. Because no fan coil is tied to one specific chiller directly via the chilled water loop, any malfunction of either piece will not cause complete loss of cooling capacity. In this way, facilities can ensure they always have some manner of cooling or even full cooling if going with an N+1 design concept.

In a 2-pipe chilled water system, the fan coil or air handler has only one supply pipe and one return pipe, so the system uses the chiller loop for sensible cooling and passive assist to stand-alone dehumidifiers; the dehumidification is not integral, so there is no direct humidity control.

The 2-pipe chilled water systems provide the ability to economize via a dry cooler in colder climates, saving significant amounts of energy by turning off the compressors in the chiller, which are the single-largest energy consumer in the HVAC system.

Pros:
- Flexible air handling options (ducted, ductless, multiple sizes and configurations available).
- Minimal indoor space requirements.
- Usually results in lower overall electrical infrastructure than DX units.
- Flexible air handling options can result in better room air homogenization.
- N+1 redundancy possible at a minimal cost addition.
- Ability to easily expand operations if phasing plan is identified ahead of time.
- Flexible tonnage.
- Share equipment between rooms without sharing air between rooms (great for flips).
- Lower ongoing maintenance.
- High longevity (~20+ years).
- Significant economization (free cooling) options.

Cons:
- Initial expense can be slightly higher than packaged DX or split units.
- More engineering work is required to design the water piping loop properly than simpler systems.
- More complicated to install than most DX systems.
- Requires a mechanical room in the building.
- Stand-alone dehumidifiers are required.

4-Pipe Chilled Water

The 4-pipe chilled water system is also a hydronic cooling and dehumidification system, as previously described. As the name suggests, four pipe systems have four pipes going to multiple heat exchangers inside the building, with two supply and two return lines. One set is dedicated to chilled water, typically kept between 40 and 60°F (4 and 15°C). Another set of pipes is dedicated to hot water, generally kept between 130 and 200°F (55 and 93°C). The pipes run to terminal fan coils or air handlers, which use chilled or hot water to change the air temperature by cooling, heating, or dehumidifying. The main benefit of using a 4-pipe system over a 2-pipe system is that stand-alone dehumidifiers are not required, as the system provides temperature and humidity control simultaneously in a single unit when controlled properly.

Traditionally these systems utilize air handler units (AHUs) or fan coil units (FCUs), which contain a blower, heating or cooling elements, and control valves (and optionally, filter racks and modulating dampers). AHUs and FCUs can either

a. be connected to a ductwork system that distributes the conditioned air to the area served and reside outside the space, or

b. reside directly in and condition the space served without ductwork.

The 4-pipe chilled water systems provide the ability to economize via a dry cooler in colder climates, saving significant amounts of energy by turning off the compressors in the chiller, which are the single-largest energy consumer in the HVAC system. The most energy-efficient 4-pipe designs utilize heat recovery on the chiller plant to minimize or eliminate dehumidification reheat costs.

Pros:

- When connected to a heat recovery chiller plant, it can recover heat from that process, rather than generating new heat through the consumption of electricity or natural gas.
- Usually among the most energy-efficient options.
- Flexible air-handling options (ducted/ductless, with multiple sizes and configurations available).
- Long life expectancy if maintained properly (over 20 years).
- Very flexible biosecurity options (MERV/HEPA/UV/PCO).
- Ability to economize via a dry cooler in colder climates, saving significant amounts of energy by turning off the compressors in the system.
- When controls are properly applied, flexibility to adjust to changing room parameters and insight into system operation (for perfecting operation and troubleshooting where required) are unmatched.
- Stand-alone dehumidifiers not required.
- Greatest precision of all options in varying conditions.

Cons:
- Controls and installation are more complex than other systems and may increase initial cost.
- Longer lead times for engineering, equipment production, and installation due to the complexity and custom nature of the design and machines themselves.
- Not as common as DX units (usually utilized in true industrial applications).
- More complex maintenance requirements.

Water-Cooled Condensers

In both chilled water and DX systems, water-cooling condensers, either through a dry cooler or cooling tower set up, depending on climate, may offer significant energy benefits. Condensers, where heat removed from cultivation spaces is ejected to the outside, are most commonly air cooled. However, water has a higher heat capacity than air, as well as higher thermal conductivity, so water cooling offers energy benefits over air cooling. But water-cooled condensers also carry substantial upfront and ongoing maintenance costs that are generally only cost effective in large-tonnage systems. Consult with a mechanical engineer and maintenance team to understand the benefits and drawbacks of water-cooled systems.

Using Air-Cooled Reflectors

Because the primary heat load in any grow room is the lights, some growers who use HID lamps use air-cooled reflectors to capture and exhaust grow room heat right at its source. These specialty devices are designed to capture and exhaust much of the heat produced by the lights while allowing most of the light to radiate down into the canopy. Air-cooled reflectors create an enclosed chamber around each lamp using highly reflective metal above and a pane of glass below. They have two duct flanges mounted on either side for connecting to ducting and inline fans. These pressurized systems blow cool outside air through each lighting reflector, picking up heat from each light, which is exhausted back outside via exhaust ducting. Each inline fan can be ducted to a single reflector or to a row of air-cooled reflectors using round, metal ducting.

Sizing Air-Cooled Reflectors

Air-cooled reflector flanges come in four main sizes: 4 inch (10 cm), which has an area of about 12 square inches (77 cm^2); 6 inch (15 cm), with an area of about 28 square inches (180 cm^2); 8 inch (20 cm), with an area of 50 square inches (322 cm^2); and 10 inch (25 cm), with an area of 78.5 square inches (506 cm^2). Larger reflector flanges connect to bigger fans and ducting and have greater cooling capacity. When properly sized, air-cooled reflectors can significantly reduce the amount of air conditioning required to cool a grow room. For air-cooled reflectors to be effective, the reflector, fan, and ducting must be accurately sized. The size of the ducted system limits the volume of air that it can move. Larger fans and ducting cool faster.

Air volume is measured in cubic footage (or cubic meters), and fans and ducts are rated in cubic feet per minute (cfm) or cubic meters per hour (cmh), the volume of air they are rated to move each minute (or hour). Air-cooled reflector systems are designed based on the amount of heat they must combat. Because the heat from the lights is proportional to their wattage, as more and stronger lights are added, larger and stronger fans are required to cool them. Therefore, the rule of thumb when sizing the fan for an air-cooled reflector system is to use a fan with a rating of 0.2 to 0.3 cfm (or 0.34–0.51 cmh) per watt of lighting.

To successfully use this equation, start with the lighting design. Once the number and strength of the lights in the room is known, add up the total wattage of lights in each row. Then the size of fan needed to cool that row of lights can be calculated. Because air-cooled reflectors come with four main flange sizes, the equation is used to determine which of those four sizes will be used for fan, reflectors, and ducting.

For example, if the space is lit with two 1,000-watt lamps in one row of lights:

1. 2 x 1,000w lamps = 2,000w = total lighting wattage per row
2. 2,000w x 0.2 cfm = 400 cfm (680 cmh) = minimum fan rating
   2,000w x 0.3 cfm = 600 cfm (1,020 cmh) = optimal fan rating
   Between 400–600 cfm (or 680–1,020 cmh) of airflow is needed to cool that row of lights.
3. The average six inch (15 cm) inline fan is rated at approximately 435 cfm (740 cmh) and is perfectly sized within the calculated range from step two.

This equation should be performed for each row of lights in each room. If an inline fan is rated within the calculated cfm range, it can be successfully used. Once the fan size is determined, the reflectors and ducting for that row of lights should be sized accordingly.

Root Temperature

The temperature of the plant canopy is critical, but it is not the only area to consider. Root temperature is also important. Cold floors lower the temperature of containers and the planting medium, slowing germination and growth. Cold temperatures also are implicated in encouraging more of the plants to develop as males when growing from seed. When a plant's roots are kept warm, the rest of the plant can be kept cooler with no damage. Ideally, the medium temperature should be 65–70°F (18–20°C). With cold air temperatures, media temperature can be 5°F (~3°C) higher or more as long as roots have access to oxygen. There are several ways to warm the medium or protect it from cold surroundings:

- The best way to insulate a container from a cold floor is to raise it so there is air space between them, using a thin sheet of Styrofoam a half-inch thick (1.25 cm).
- The medium can be warmed using overhead fans to push warm air down from the top of the room, warming containers that are placed on pallets.
- Heat cables, or heat mats, apply heat directly to the root area.
- Heat the water in recirculating systems with an aquarium heater controlled by a

thermostat. If the air is cool, from 45 to 60°F (7–15°C), the water can be heated to 80°F (27°C). At these high temperatures, hydroponic system water should be supplemented with oxygen using hydrogen peroxide or other methods such as nanobubbles, venturi systems, or vigorous agitation. Water holds little oxygen above 80°F (27°C).

In general, water temperature should be adjusted to balance out the air temperature. If the air is warm, over 75°F (22°C), the water should be no more than 70°F (20°C). Should air temperature rise above 90°F (30°C), lower the water temperature from 70 to 65°F (20 to 18°C) to help decrease canopy stress.

Air Filtration/Sanitation

When a closed-loop air system is being used, any infiltration of pests or diseases is brought into the space by humans or imported plants. This can mostly be prevented. The integrity of the structure enveloping the air space is responsible for keeping out climatic variables and airborne impurities such as ash, dust, pathogens, and pests. To prevent them from getting in, they have to be filtered out.

- Media filters slow the air but catch particles.
- Ultraviolet (UVC) lamps kill airborne fungal spores and bacteria as air passes through their field.
- Activated charcoal filters adsorb vapor so that they clear the air of odor. They can be used in the space to keep the air clean and decrease odors.
- Negative ion generators add electrons to the air. These negatively charged particles neutralize positively charged dust and odor particles. Then the particle precipitates out of the air. They should not be used in rooms during the last several weeks of flowering because they neutralize terpenes.
- Ozone generators create ozone (O_3), which is not considered healthy for humans and their pets. However, ozone cleans the air of odors and can be used to treat exhaust air and to sanitize spaces devoid of plants and animals.
- Oxidizers chemically break down compounds, including infectious agents.

Air filtration is used to maintain clean, pest- and pathogen-free air in greenhouse and indoor gardens. Incoming air can introduce contaminants to the growing environment if not properly filtered. For this reason, it is important to seal each grow room as much as possible so that where and how air enters the space is controlled. Similar to how odor mitigation devices are frequently connected to air exhaust systems, decontamination filters are often incorporated into the intake ventilation system. The most common choice is a high efficiency particulate air (HEPA) filter. HEPA filters function by forcing incoming air through a fine mesh that traps bugs, mold and mildew spores, and pollen. By mitigating the introduction of these harmful contaminants, intake air filters greatly reduce the risk of pests, pathogens, and unintentional pollination.

In-room, air filtration and sanitation technologies can also be used to decontaminate

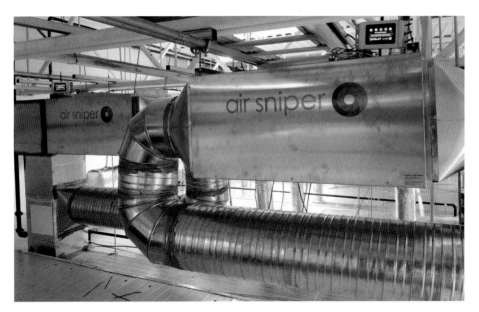

Air Sniper is the industrial-scale solution to air purification. The Air Sniper uses cleanable pre-filters instead of disposable ones and UVC light intensity combined with the highest cfm of air to destroy mobile air pathogens, instead of just capturing them. Air Sniper also includes access to a dashboard system that allows clients to monitor and control the equipment from phones, tablets, and computers.

the air. These devices can filter and/or sanitize the pass-through air, further reducing the frequency and severity of pest and pathogen outbreaks. Each device will be rated for how much air it can sanitize or what size room it can treat. The required quantity and size of these air-sanitizing devices depends on the volume of air in the room and level of contamination to be treated. To improve in-room air sanitation, frequently replace filters used in air conditioning, dehumidification, and other mechanical devices.

Odor Control

Cannabis odors come from the large volume of aromatic terpenes that make up the plant's essential oil. Terpenes are volatile organic compounds (VOCs) that very easily convert from a liquid to a gas and can travel and permeate wherever air travels. The signature odor from cannabis, especially those that are flowering, creates both a risk and a nuisance that can be avoided with proper ventilation system design and technologies.

Negative Ions

Negative ions can precipitate dust, spores, and odors. The air's electrical charge affects plant growth and animal behavior, as well as the strength of odors. The clean, fresh-smelling air that follows a rain is due to the extra negative ions left in the air by falling water. Air in verdant, non industrialized areas and near large bodies of water is also negatively charged; electrons float in the air loosely attached to oxygen molecules. In industrialized areas or very dry regions, the air is positively charged because molecules are missing electrons. Negative ions jump from oxygen carriers to electron-deficient molecules, neutralizing them and causing them to precipitate.

Negative ion enrichment creates a few readily observable effects:

- Plants in negative ion environments grow faster than those in positively charged ones.
- Negative ions precipitate dust particles, hair, and dander from the air, so there are fewer bacteria and fungus spores floating around.
- Negative ions eliminate unwanted odors, which are positively charged particles in the air. Increasing negative ions causes the odor-carrying particles to precipitate. With enough negative ions, even a room filled with pungent, flowering sinsemilla becomes odorless.

Negative ion generators, ionizers, or ion fountain units are inexpensive and safe, use minuscule amounts of electricity, and are recommended for vegetatively growing gardens during the first weeks of flowering. However, when they are used in the garden itself during the last weeks of flowering, they eliminate odors in the garden and the plants.

Most modern ion generators capture the particles they precipitate in a cleanable, re-usable filter. A few cheaper models have no provision for capturing the greasy precipitate. Since the thick film of grime usually lands within a two-foot (60 cm) radius of the ion fountain, placing newspaper around the unit is a convenient way to collect the residue. A precipitator can be made by grounding a sheet of aluminum foil to a metal plumbing line or grounding box. Attach an alligator clip and a piece of wire to the foil and grounding source. When the foil gets soiled, replace it.

To preserve the aroma of the crop, don't use negative ions in the flowering room during the last several weeks of flowering. Negative ions interact with the odor molecules not only in the air but also those present on the plant that are not fully protected by the trichome membrane. The negative ions neutralize them so they are odor-free. The terpenes inside the membrane are unaffected, so a pinched bud still releases a powerful aroma. For best results, use ion generators during the last several weeks of flowering only in the rooms surrounding the garden room, not inside.

Carbon Filters

For indoor and some greenhouse facilities, using activated charcoal filtration is the first line of defense against odor leaks. Carbon filtration captures the terpene VOCs emanating from the plants and significantly reduces the odor footprint of the pass-through air. Using an inline fan, air is drawn through a jacket of activated charcoal, trapping odor and releasing odor-reduced air. The size of the fan and carbon filter depends on the amount of airflow required.

Facilities may have a sizable exhaust system where odor-filled air is drawn through carbon filters before it is exhausted outside. When an active (fan-powered) exhaust system is implemented, a vacuum or negative pressure is created inside the facility. This ensures that odor-filled air cannot escape through door frames and other cracks or wall penetrations. The negative room pressurization creates a system where inside air can only escape through odor-mitigating technologies, like carbon filters.

Carbon filters can also be implemented as in-room "scrubbers" to reduce the odor footprint inside the garden space and in adjacent, enclosed areas. A scrubber system consists of an inline fan outfitted with a carbon filter and is freestanding or mounted to the wall or ceiling. The fan pulls high-odor air through activated charcoal filtration and exhausts the reduced-odor air back into the room. Multiple scrubber systems can be used in targeted areas and can operate 24 hours a day for round-the-clock odor reduction. Over time and use, and depending on air and filter quality, the carbon inside will eventually become ineffective and the filter will need replacement. Higher humidity, above 65%, lowers the filter's efficiency.

Using Ozone Generators and Air Ionizers

While activated charcoal can capture a lot of VOCs and reduce the intensity of odor from the pass-through air, these filters are not 100% effective on their own. Many cultivators add an additional technology to the exhaust system that can neutralize any residual odors that make it past the carbon filter. Ozone generators produce ozone (O_3), a volatile gas that oxidizes and neutralizes VOCs. An inline, ozone generator installed in the exhaust ducting can inject O_3 into the air that has already passed through carbon filtration. This ozone gas oxidizes and neutralizes terpenes, rendering them odorless.

Exposure to ozone can damage the eyes, ears, nose, throat, and lungs and should only be used as part of an enclosed exhaust system or in an empty room. When injecting ozone in an exhaust system, it is recommended that there be a run of ducting at least 15 feet (4.6 m) long post-ozone injection, so that the ozone can fully mix with the air and neutralize any odors before it is exhausted outside.

Ionizers purify and reduce the odor of the air that is treated by adding electrons to air molecules and creating negatively charged particles that attach to free-floating, positively charged contaminants. This neutralizes their charge and causes them to precipitate out of the air. In the process, cleaner, odor-reduced air is created.

Ionizers are safe to use around people and are recommended for use in hallways and other areas adjacent to indoor gardens. While both ozone generators and ionizers can eliminate odors from the facility, they should not be placed inside flowering rooms during the last several weeks of flowering, as they also neutralize the odor of the plants.

Ventilation

Carbon Dioxide Replenishment

During the lights-on period of the day, plants absorb CO_2 from the air surrounding their leaves and flowers. Replenishing CO_2 is one of the most important functions of a grow room ventilation system, ensuring that the plants have access to the levels they need throughout the day and during each stage of development. There are two primary approaches to providing CO_2 in closed-environment agriculture (CEA): air exchange and CO_2 augmentation. Grow room air exchange provides for atmospheric levels of carbon dioxide, while supplementation systems often elevate CO_2 concentrations to much higher than atmospheric levels, to facilitate more rapid photosynthesis and growth.

Open-Loop Ventilation (Atmospheric CO_2)

Atmospheric levels of carbon dioxide are adequate for healthy plant growth during all stages of development. Although it varies depending on geography, planetary CO_2 averages about 420 parts per million (ppm). In CEA rooms, close-to-atmospheric levels can be maintained using what is referred to as "open-loop" ventilation. In an open-loop ventilation system, grow room air is exchanged with outside air to replenish carbon dioxide. Using fans, filters, and ducting, low-CO_2 air from inside the grow room is exhausted and replaced with fresh, outside air that is rich in atmospheric CO_2.

The exhaust components of the open-loop ventilation system are typically mounted high in the room in order to draw on warm, CO_2-depleted air. The active (fan-powered) exhaust is generally hooked up to an odor mitigation system and ducted to the highest exterior point of exhaust in order to achieve the greatest reduction in the garden's odor footprint. As air is drawn out of the room, it creates a vacuum, or negative pressure, inside the room. This is what draws in fresh air, often via a passive (fan-free) intake. This is often a simple wall penetration, mounted on the side of the room opposite the exhaust, and is typically outfitted with a high efficiency particulate air (HEPA) filter.

Exchanging the air at the appropriate rate ensures that as plants use it up, carbon dioxide is replenished and readily available for continued uptake. To maintain close to 420 ppm CO_2 inside the garden, the air in an open-loop ventilated grow room should be exchanged every 5 to 10 minutes. This is achieved using a properly sized exhaust fan, along with intake and exhaust filtration and ducting.

If the exhaust system is undersized, a full turnover of air in the room will take longer than 10 minutes. As a result, the plants may not have adequate access to CO_2 to achieve healthy growth. If the exhaust fan is oversized and exchanges the air faster than every 5 minutes, the in-room climate control equipment, such as air conditioners and dehumidifiers, may not have enough time to function effectively. Incoming air may, at times, be hotter, colder, drier, or more humid than is desired, and HVAC equipment may not be able to keep up and adequately temper this rapidly exchanging air. By consistently turning over all the air in the grow room at the optimal 5–10-minute rate, the plants are ensured to receive adequate carbon dioxide, and the mechanical equipment can, at all times, maintain optimal temperature and humidity.

Closed Loop Ventilation Space

The garden is subject to the vagaries of nature when using ventilation. The temperature of the incoming air is always changing, both daily and seasonally, and can reach such extremes that the stream is harmful to plants. Rapid changes in outdoor temperature and humidity as well as temporary changes in air quality make it difficult to closely regulate air inside a ventilated space. A closed-loop ventilation system is sealed from the rest of the environment. Instead of using air from outside to modify temperature and humidity, the air in the room is constantly adjusted and modified. With a climate-controlled, sealed space, the environment is always conducive to plant health and to optimizing growth and yield.

Since the space is receiving no air from outside, equipment such as heaters, air conditioners, humidifiers, and dehumidifiers are used to maintain the room's air conditions. Carbon dioxide enhancement is used to keep levels high to promote rapid growth. To keep the air sanitized, a carbon filter can constantly filter air in the room. An enclosed UVC light, such as a model often used in restaurants, cleans the space of airborne pathogens.

The advantages are:
- Insects and disease are less of a threat because there is no exchange of air.
- No matter the conditions outside, a closed-loop space creates its own controlled atmosphere.
- With a properly sized conditioning system, there is complete control of air conditions: temperature, humidity, VPD, and CO_2.
- Poor, outside air quality, such as from dust, smoke, and noxious chemicals, is less likely to affect the space.

The disadvantages are:
- The system and installation are more expensive than other systems.
- There is a limited selection of greenhouse manufacturers, builders, and installers who are experienced in closed-loop systems.
- It may take a little longer to dial in the best conditions, especially if they aren't regulated automatically.
- Odor control can become more challenging with the loss of an odor-mitigated exhaust system.

Although closed-loop systems cost more both to install and operate, they can control the air with more precision than a ventilated system. This can increase both yield and quality.

Hybrid Loop Ventilation

For CO_2 enrichment to be successful, the ventilation system must allow for CO_2 to be pumped into the grow room without significant dilution. The rapid air exchange of an open-loop ventilation system dilutes the grow room's CO_2 enriched air with lower-CO_2 air from outside. Instead, cultivators using CO_2 supplementation typically switch to either a closed- or hybrid-loop ventilation system, stopping or slowing air exchange to allow CO_2 to concentrate to more optimal levels.

Traditionally, a closed-loop ventilation system has been used in CO_2-enriched indoor gardens. These "sealed" grow rooms completely eliminate the exhaust ventilation system, allowing CO_2 to be pumped into and saturate each cultivation zone, using a tank or generator. When eliminating the exhaust portion of the ventilation system, the aforementioned negative pressurization, often used for odor control, is lost. The "zero pressure" environment of a sealed room allows odor-filled air to travel freely and potentially escape unfiltered. This could create a significant risk of odor leaks. Using in-room carbon filter scrubbers and negative ion generators in the surrounding nonflowering rooms and hallways reduces but does not completely remove the odors in closed-loop gardens.

To simultaneously minimize the dilution of CO_2 enrichment and maintain negative pressure odor mitigation, a hybrid-loop ventilation system is recommended. In a hybrid-loop room, exhaust ventilation is significantly reduced, but not eliminated. An exhaust system consisting of a fan, carbon filter, ozone generator, and exhaust ducting can be used, but it must be much smaller than the one used for open-loop air exchange. Using the minimum rate of exhaust needed to maintain net negative pressurization in the grow room, control of where and how grow room air is exhausted (and odor mitigated) from the facility is regained.

Hybrid-loop ventilation uses a 20-to-30-minute air exchange rate. Although this is much slower than the open-loop, atmospheric CO_2 approach to air exchange, it is just fast enough to maintain negative pressure for odor control and just slow enough to support CO_2-enrichment efforts. Compared with closed-loop "sealed" grow rooms, using hybrid-loop ventilation will cost a little more for CO_2. However, the cost is generally negligible and well worth the benefits of using CO_2 enrichment while also maintaining 24/7 odor control.

Sizing Exhaust Systems

1. Measure and multiply the grow room's length, width, and height (in feet or meters) to calculate the total volume of air the room can hold (in cubic feet or cubic meters).
   a. L x W x H = volume (in ft^3 or m^3)
2. Divide this volume of air by the range of time in which a total turnover of air should be achieved, in order to calculate the optimal rate of air exchange. This will provide an optimal range in cubic feet per minute (cfm) or cubic meters per hour (cmh).
   a. For open-loop (atmospheric CO_2) ventilation systems, a 5-10-minute turnover is required (0.083–0.167 hour) for air exchange.
   b. For hybrid-loop (supplemented CO_2) ventilation systems, a 20-30-minute (0.333–0.5 hour) air exchange range is required.
3. Find the properly sized and rated fan that fits within the optimal cfm or cmh range calculated in step two.

Example 1: **Open-loop ventilation** in a 10 x 20 x 12 foot (3 x 6 x 3.6 m) garden space.
   1. 10 x 20 x 12 feet = 2,400 ft^3 (3 x 6 x 3.6 m = 68 m^3) = volume of air in the room.

2. 2,400 ft^3 ÷ 10 min = 240 cfm (68 m^3 ÷ 0.166 hr = 409 cmh) = minimum fan rating.
2,400 ft^3 ÷   5 min = 480 cfm (68 m^3 ÷ 0.083 hr = 819 cmh) = maximum fan rating.
3. The average 6-inch (15 cm) inline fan is rated at approximately 435 cfm (740 cmh) and is perfectly sized within the calculated range from step two.

Therefore, to achieve a 5-to-10-minute air exchange using open-loop ventilation in this garden space, a 6-inch (150 mm) exhaust fan needs to be installed. For odor control, odor-mitigating devices (carbon filter, inline ozone generator) and ducting that are also sized at 6-inch (15 cm) in diameter should be installed.

Example 2: **Hybrid-loop ventilation** in a 10 x 20 x 12 foot (3 x 6 x 3.6 m) garden space.
1.   10 x 20 x 12 feet = 2,400 ft^3 (3 x 6 x 3.6 m = 68 m^3) = volume of air in the room.
2.   2,400 ft^3 ÷ 30 min = 80 cfm (68 m^3 ÷ 0.5 hr = 136 cmh) = minimum fan rating
2,400 ft^3 ÷ 20 min = 120 cfm (68 m^3 ÷ 0.33 hr = 206 cmh) = maximum fan rating
3. The average 4 inch (10 cm) inline fan is rated at approximately 200 cfm (340 cmh), which is oversized for the calculated range from step two. However, 4 inch (10 cm) inline fans are typically the smallest available option. Since this fan is oversized for the calculated range for hybrid-loop air exchange, if left running at full strength, it would begin depleting CO_2 from the room too rapidly. To avoid this, connect the 4 inch exhaust fan to a fan-speed controller, a device that can adjust the speed of the fan and reduce its cfm (cmh) airflow. In this case, a 50% reduction would put it back in the optimal range.

Therefore, to achieve a 20-to-30-minute air exchange using hybrid-loop, CO_2-enriched ventilation in this garden space, a 4-inch (10 cm) exhaust fan dialed down to 50% strength by a fan-speed controller is required. For odor control, connect an exhaust fan or odor-mitigating devices (carbon filter, inline ozone generator) and ducting that are also sized at 4 inches (10 cm) in diameter.

Outdoor Temperature & Air Control

Outdoor Temperature

Having evolved outdoors, cannabis appreciates temperate climates and tolerates the extremes of the geographic conditions in which particular cultivars have evolved. For example, tropical sativas can withstand high humidity and are less susceptible to molds and mildews. In contrast, high-altitude indicas cannot and are more vulnerable to molds and mildews than high-humidity varieties. However, both groups can thrive around 75 to 85°F (24–30°C) with relative humidity no higher than 60%. When cultivating outdoors, each cultivar is best suited to climates replicating its geographic origins or appellations. Most cultivars in commerce are not associated with a specific appellation, so it may take a few rotations before the right conditions are dialed in.

Cooling Outdoors

Photosynthesis crawls to a halt when the temperature gets close to 90°F (32°C). In hot weather outdoor plants may be photosynthesizing efficiently during only part of the day. For instance, if the temperature climbs to 90°F (32°C) at 11 a.m. and does not drop below that level until 4 p.m., the plant will utilize only the morning and late afternoon light. High temperatures outdoors during flowering interferes with bud development, making maturing buds airy and lanky. Temperature is a factor when plants are forced to flower in hot areas during the summer.

- Misters that use 5-micron sprayers evaporate water in the air, cooling the space without getting the plants wet. Some systems use rows of emitters, high-speed fans, or a combination of both to create a superfine mist or fog that evaporates instantly, lowering the temperature as much as 30°F (16°C). They work best in dry areas.
- A fine spray of water on the plants keeps them cooler during the hot period. The evaporating water absorbs heat from both the leaf and the air in the micro-space at the leaf surface. Use a water spray only during vegetative growth and the earliest stages of flowering.
- Use cool water to cool the roots. Positive effects will travel up the stem.
- When using planting containers, place a piece of Styrofoam between the container and the soil to stop heat transfer from the ground.
- During the summer when it's important to keep the containers cool, use white or light-colored containers or wrap the containers in white plastic or sturdy paper to reflect the light.
- Cover the ground or raised bed with white plastic to keep the soil cool and slow water evaporation.
- Use a thick layer of organic mulch. It keeps the soil warm when it's cool and cool when it's warm. At the same time, it releases CO_2 to the air and nutrients to the soil as it decomposes.
- Use a 10–20% removable shade cloth to block light during the brightest part of the day. This helps keep the plant canopy temperature lower.

Warming Outdoors

Cultivars differ in their tolerance to cold weather. Most can tolerate low temperatures into the low 50s to high 40s F (8–12°C), and many can tolerate even colder nights. However, lower temperatures set the plants back, and it sometimes takes them several days to continue the growth or ripening.

It's not just the cold that sometimes damages the plants. It's a combination of cold and wind, especially if there is low humidity. The wind causes evaporation, which lowers the temperature of solid objects such as leaves below the air's ambient reading.

When plant roots are kept warm, the plant canopy can withstand cold temperatures more easily and with less damage

Here are a few solutions to cold temperatures and wind:

- Move container plants to a sheltered location such as a shed or other structure. Small plants can be carried. Larger plants can be placed on a cart or dolly. This technique can also be used for light deprivation to induce earlier flowering
- Wrap well-supported plants with polyethylene to shut out wind and preserve heat.
- Use patio-type propane heaters. The units spread heat in a large circle. They can be lined up to provide heat to rows of plants.
- Agricultural gas heaters use natural gas or propane. The heaters are used to prevent frost damage on fruiting plants such as grapes and stone fruit.
- Heat the roots. When they are kept warm, the canopy withstands cool temperatures with less damage. Both electric heat mats and tubing-based hot-water heaters keep the roots warm. Keep roots warm by using black containers or by wrapping with dark plastic to absorb the sun's rays and warmth.
- Place a half-inch (12 mm) or thicker Styrofoam sheet as a barrier between the ground and the containers so that heat isn't drawn down.
- Cover the ground or raised bed with black plastic to keep the soil warm during cooler months.

Greenhouses

Greenhouses provide a defined airspace with opportunities for environmental control and all the benefits of natural light.

There are many types of greenhouses to choose from. Popular greenhouse options include hoop, Venlo, commercial gable, cold frame, gothic arch, and others. There are a number of factors that one should consider when pondering the type and model greenhouse to acquire. Among these factors are:

- Goals: what is the greenhouse to be used for? Is it just to be used seasonally to start plants early in the season? To extend the season for additional crops? Or is it to be year-round?
- Location: the structure and infrastructure of any construction is highly dependent on the environmental conditions (light, temperature and wind) it will be exposed to.
- Financial Investment: greenhouses range in price depending on sophistication.

Environmental Considerations

Along with selecting a greenhouse appropriate to the environment, equipment must be chosen that is capable of regulating temperature, humidity, and CO_2. The selection process will depend on whether the system will be run as an open or closed environment. Both have advantages and disadvantages.

For instance, using an open-loop system, a greenhouse in South Florida may exceed the cooling ability of a pad and fan system, also known as a "wet wall." Another option might be a chiller system.

Forever Flowering greenhouses have been designed around the specific needs of cannabis growers for over 15 years. The G-series are designed for high wind and snow loads and use passive cooling technology through its use of side and ridge vents (single or double).

Closed-loop greenhouses offer many advantages because there is less chance of infection, and it is often cheaper in the long run to maintain the temperature of the same air rather than running an air-exchange system.

Indoor facilities have insulative values or what is commonly referred to as an R-value. R-values represent the capacity of any building material to insulate or resist heat flow. The higher the R-value, the greater the insulating power. Engineers use R-Values and other factors such as location, record highs, record lows, depth of the slab, and internal gains such as lighting to determine just how much HVAC and humidity control is needed for an indoor facility.

Traditional greenhouses have low R-values because they have thin walls. External gains are determined by the outside environment, such as the sun's efficacy through rain, cloud cover, and shadowing from other structures. Expenses and consistency of cannabis will change from day to day and season to season. Newer coverings, sometimes composed of several layers, have higher R-values.

Hybrid greenhouses were developed to increase G-efficiency. They have solid walls on one to four sides. Some only have a northern wall, which never gets direct light. Some have half-height walls. The most extreme are buildings with the only light being let in through the translucent roof. Hybrid greenhouses work well, especially in areas with extreme weather. They use insulation to lessen the external environment's impact, allowing the internal heating or cooling systems to work efficiently.

Standard features of modern-day greenhouses are automated lighting systems that adjust the electric lighting based on the intensity of solar radiation. They also include blackout curtains and chilling and heating systems to accommodate year-round cultivation.

PART III:

SETTING UP THE GARDEN

Moose and Lobsta v2   Photo: Professor P of Dynasty Genetics

GOALS

Cannabis is one of the most useful plants on the planet, but the enjoyable effect on consciousness and gentle nature as a medicine have long been the primary drivers of human fascination and intrigue. Many view it through anthropomorphic filters or as an ally because of its unique characteristics.

A flowering cannabis plant's life span is about 70 days; the life span of humans is about 70 years. It could be said that each day of a ripening plant's life is the equivalent of a year in a human life.

Cannabis, like humans, grows better, healthier, bigger, and stronger with careful nurturing, proper nourishment, and a rich quality of life. Its health, yield, and potency are products of both its environment and its genetics.

Cannabis is rare in that it is an annual dioecious plant. Like humans, there are separate male and female plants. Most other annual plants are monoecious—sometimes growing separate flowers for each sex on the same plant or else having both sexes contained in the same flower.

Like humans, cannabis easily adapts. First it traveled around the world from its origins in the Himalayas. Then it moved indoors and became higher yielding and easier to grow. Gardeners often name individual plants, refer to them by gender, and think of their plants as good friends, although risky ones to hang with (the kind you don't take home to mother).

Why Grow Cannabis?

People choose to grow cannabis for many reasons. The majority grow because they want the satisfaction of smoking the fruits of their own labor. Some are interested in experiencing new varieties with new ranges of aromas, tastes, and effects. Some will grow to make money.

Caregivers cultivate for patients. They perform a needed service that is not provided by traditional medical providers.

Medical patients grow to maintain a fresh reliable supply with specific qualities. In areas where there are no legal dispensaries, patients are simply stuck with what they can get. Some patients grow their medicine because they require a large supply. A personal garden is far less expensive than purchasing a finished product, and it allows growers to be cultivar specific.

Another good reason to begin a garden is just for the joy of gardening. There are few things as satisfying as nurturing a healthy plant. Some people may choose to add cannabis to their kitchen garden. It might be small, on a windowsill or balcony, or larger in a backyard or indoor garden.

Just as with home-grown produce, gardeners often find home-grown cannabis to be the best. Once new growers pick up the hobby, they may wish to experiment. Cannabis is *fun* to grow because it responds quickly to environmental changes and has separate sexes. By regulating the light cycle to force flowering earlier, growers can adjust the plant's growth to better fit in the garden lifestyle and schedule.

Many consumers or new hobby gardeners may have never grown plants for consumption or seen a vital, productive garden up close. Growing produce is a fascinating, awe-inspiring experience. Think of plants as a totally alien life form that are a portion of Gaia—the Living Planet.

After incorporating portions of photosynthesizing bacteria into their cells, photosynthesizers helped transform most of the atmosphere's carbon dioxide to oxygen. They developed cohabitational relationships with animals, which are almost totally dependent on them for food. Without plants, no animals.

One fascinating aspect is how plants adapt to their environment. Animals have a nervous system to sense the environment and mobility to deal with danger. Plants are immobile and depend on a different set of biochemical and electrical cues to sense the environment and react to it. Plants have a much larger set of genes than animals, so they are hardwired with responses to many environmental stresses and opportunities.

One might find it hard to relate to them as living beings, but their reaction to environmental cues can be as instantaneous as a human's reaction to pain. For instance, the moment they receive light, they start photosynthesizing. Step back once in a while to watch the plants and feel the vibrancy of their life and existence.

Some people decide to accept cannabis into their lives quickly after first interacting with it, even so much so that they make it a career. Until recently, guidance counselors could not refer to such a career under penalty of law.

The cannabis industry has flourished since the 1960s, and as a result there are now third- and fourth-generation family members in the business.

And then there are the addicts. No, not those who use the substance, but those who grow it. It bears repeating, "cannabis may not be addictive, but growing it is."

Considerations

Before designing the garden, growers should determine the goal. What is the desired yield? The answer to this question determines the size of the garden and the time, effort, and labor required to manage it.

Yield is based on the convergence of the genetic potential of the plants and the environmental conditions the plant experiences. Indoors, all the limiting factors—space, light, nutrients, water, oxygen, carbon dioxide, and air temperature, humidity, and qualities—are under the grower's control, and each plays a part in determining yield. Outdoors, nature will provide the light and air, but the grower may be in charge of water and will be almost totally responsible for nutrients.

There are important factors to consider, and it is crucial to separate fantasy from real constraints. Every grower should ask:

- Is this affordable?
- Is the location secure?
- Is there a dedicated grower?
- How about the risk/reward ratio?

In Part II, the factors affecting plant growth were described and methods of meeting plant and garden needs were discussed. It's time to put it all together and to give the garden life. The following chapters provide the design basics and step-by-step guides to building noncommercial personal gardens as well as a small-scale indoor commercial garden. It also includes considerations for large-scale commercial farmers as well as unique garden setups from various commercial and home growers around the world.

Growing Indoors

The evolution of indoor cultivation traces its roots to cannabis prohibition. When the War on Drugs started, growers replaced the sun with lights. At first they used fluorescents. The fixtures were inexpensive and produced a fair amount of light (60–85 lumens per watt), and the high output (HO) and very high output (VHO) models, which used more electricity to emit increased intensity, were bright enough to produce respectable yields of high-quality flowers.

As indoor cultivation gained popularity, metal halide and high pressure sodium (HPS) lamps became the favored light sources because they made it easy to increase light intensity, weren't bulky, and produced more usable light per watt than fluorescents.

The newest innovation is LEDs, which are more efficient and easier to use than other lighting options. LEDs are more cost-effective, even compared with a free HPS or fluorescent. Consider that the lamp itself is a one-time fixed cost. The expensive part is the electricity running through the lamp. LEDs produce more usable light and higher yield per watt, making up the cost difference in one to two harvests. For these reasons, no matter the size of the garden, LED lamps are highly recommended. (*See Light.*)

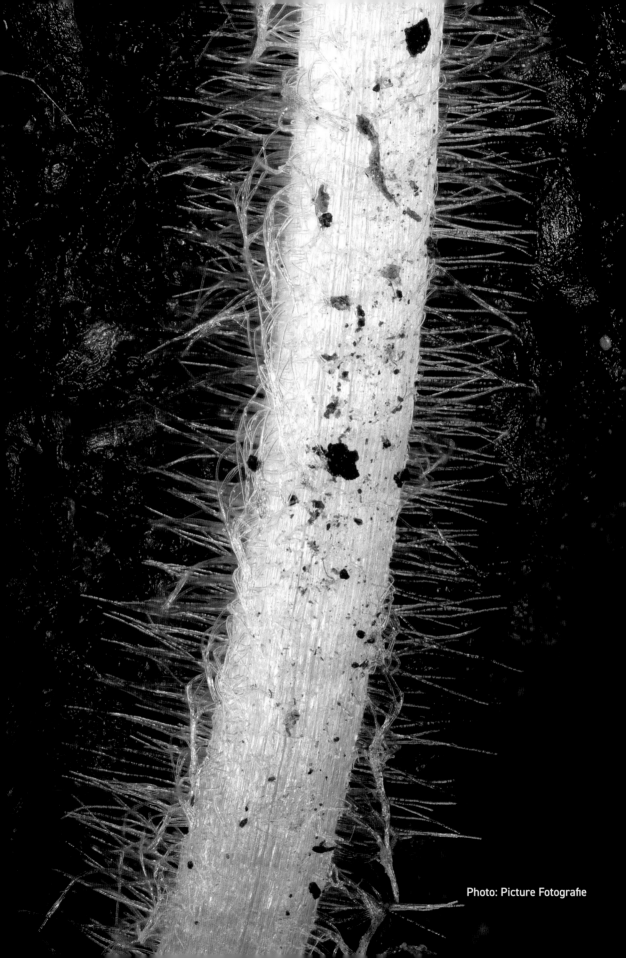

Photo: Picture Fotografie

SOIL

Revised by Brian Malin

The Purpose of Roots

In earlier chapters most of the discussion was about the plant's activities above the soil level. Though hidden, the plant's roots are just as complex as the canopy. The canopy and flower size have a lot to do with how strong the root system is.

It's obvious that roots anchor a plant in place. The network of branched roots forms a tight relationship with the soil that firmly anchors the plant in the ground or its container. Although the canopy may endure winds that tug and pull it, the roots provide stability to the stem, keeping it upright while allowing it to bend.

The roots are the carrier of nutrients and moisture to the entire plant. The root system secretes fluids called exudates into the rhizosphere that help make nutrients available to the plant. Exudates are made up of amino acids, carbohydrates, sugars, other acids, and secondary plant compounds. Exudates help solubilize nutrients and send signals to rhizospheric microbes.

> ### What Is the Rhizosphere?
> The rhizosphere is the volume of soil or growing medium that is in the immediate vicinity of the plant's root system. The rhizosphere is integral to the roots' chemical (nutrient and water absorption) and microbial activities.

With proper oxygen concentration, among a few other conditions, microbial colonies form and thrive. These beneficial microbes help maintain the health of the plant throughout its life cycle *(See Oxygen.)*

Cannabis plants grow roots both vertically and horizontally. The horizontal roots can stretch out to a width equal to the plant's canopy. This means that a plant that is 10 feet (3 m) wide has roots to match. The horizontal roots also grow down to a depth of 9–18 inches (22–45 cm), depending on the soil's moisture. The vertical roots can stretch down to 4 feet (1.2 m) or more in search of water; in moist soil, the vertical roots may be quite short.

Native Soils

Native soil in the northern tier of North America and most of Europe forms layers of decomposed plant material in two distinct patterns. Forest soils develop from the trees' leaf

Bioharmonic Tonic increases root development, plant growth, and yield. This formula of bioharmonically active microbes with Amazonian herbs and gemstone harmonics is a dynamic mix of biostimulants to increase nutrient cycling and available phosphorus during flowering.

drop. Such soil forms by continually adding to the top layer. A typical soil of this kind has an undecomposed top layer. The contents are progressively more decomposed, with the lower portions forming a fine compost. The depth of this layer varies by locale and natural environmental conditions as well as the forest's history. Some native soil is unsuitable for growing in.

Soil that has been covered by grasses and annual plants has accumulated organic matter in a different way. Known as "prairie soils," they may have a thin layer of topsoil near the surface, but the nutrient-rich area is deeper than the topsoil. The root layer of annual plants dies off and decomposes each year, leaving an organic component that provides nutrients, holds moisture, improves texture, and hosts beneficial organisms. This layer, while sometimes shallow, can reach a depth of 10 feet (3 m).

Here are some things to consider when deciding to plant in native soil or to grow in a potting mix in a container:

1. Does the soil have drainage problems? Dig a hole two feet (60 cm) deep, fill it with water, and see if water seeps into the ground. If water is still in the hole one hour later, there will be drainage issues with this soil.
2. Is the soil too rocky? Can a hole be dug without hitting rocks every shovelful?
3. Have toxic or banned fertilizers and pesticides been sprayed on the growing site?
4. Were old vehicles or equipment parked on the site?

If the answer to any of the questions above is yes, the land should not be farmed. Instead, it should be covered with some kind of ground cover and the plants grown in raised beds or containers. Cannabis bioaccumulates everything from nutrients to pesticides to heavy metals and will absorb these toxic chemical residues.

Some native soil is perfect or can be slightly amended to create an excellent environment to grow cannabis.

Growing in native soil has many advantages:
- The earth provides natural insulation against hot days and cold nights.
- Using it is much cheaper than buying soil.
- It takes much less work to use native soil than to prepare imported material.

Soils vary in quality, so there are few generalizations to rely on when discussing soil preparation. Anything done to prepare the soil must be customized to it.

The most important quality of any soil is its texture, which is determined by the size of the soil particles. Cannabis prefers soil that drains well but also holds moderate to large quantities of water, especially in warm dry regions. Depending on the type of soil composition, add materials to improve the texture and nutrients.

When North America was colonized in the 16th century, earthworms were introduced that changed the soils in the eastern half of the continent. Earthworms pull semi decomposed material down into their burrows, which have a depth of several feet. Duff, the large accumulated layer of decomposing organic matter that typified pre colonial forests, has largely disappeared. In its place, there is a smaller layer of decomposing compost soil. The mineral soil, which formed a distinct layer below the compost soil, is now laden with organic material and burrows, so it is more **friable**.

Soil Tips

Growing in soil has many advantages over other methods. It takes less labor and time to prepare the planting area. Adjusting the soil's fertility with nutrients and amending it with additives such as compost, mulch, or fertilizer takes relatively little time and energy as compared with replacing a container's soil.

Roots can stretch out and obtain water and nutrients from a larger area, and, as a result, they can support the needs of a larger plant.

There is no "perfect" soil for growing cannabis; different varieties each grow within a range of soil condition parameters. The soil must be well-drained, nutrient rich, and have a pH between 5.8 and 6.5.

Always test the soil to find out what amendments it may need before preparing for planting. The pH and fertility of soils vary, so there are few generalizations that can be made about preparing them. Only after soil qualities and nutrient values are determined can the correct adjustments be made to optimize the soil's fertility. Also test for chemical residues and heavy metals.

For cannabis plants, the soil should test high in the three macronutrients: nitrogen (N), phosphorus (P), and potassium (K). *(See Nutrients & Fertilizers.)*

Grassland and prairie soils have a different history. The annual dieback of canopy growth deposits a small top layer that decomposes in the same way as in forest soils. However, most of the added organic material develops below the surface, fed by the dieback of annual plant roots. They compost in place, so the organic matter integrates with the mineral content of the soil, creating deep levels of nutrient-rich, composted material.

Soils in warmer climate zones contain much less organic matter and have fewer nutrients because microorganisms, whose metabolic rates increase with the temperature, are more active, so they digest new organic matter faster.

Where the canopy is less dense, and in zones with less rain, not as much decomposing material actually makes it into the structure of the soil.

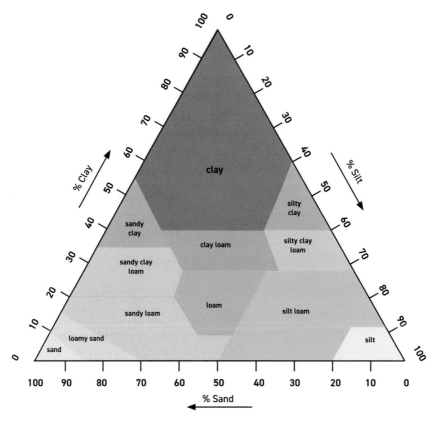

Growers can assess their soil using a soil-texture triangle that classifies the soil based on its percentages of sand, silt, and clay. Most gardens and fields that have been cultivated and have grown good crops fail within the acceptable categories of the soil triangle.

Moist warm tropical soils can contain abundant organic matter and rich microbial colonies; however, the microbes break down dead plant matter and turn it into nutrients for other plant life at a rapid rate due to the warm, wet environment. The quick turnover of organic nutrients is a process called biomineralization, which typically results in soils that are poor in nutrients as they leach out of the soil from the frequent rains.

As soon as vegetation dies, bacteria and other microlife feast and render the nutrients water-soluble. They are absorbed into the soil and almost immediately taken up by the roots of higher living plants or leached out of the topsoil.

Underneath the layer of organic material in forest soils and the mixture of organic matter and minerals in grasslands lies the mineral soil, which contains little organic matter. The mineral portion of soils is usually composed of three main elements: sand, silt, and clay. Each of them lends properties to the mix, and each is needed in order to create a soil that promotes healthy growth.

The relatively small clay particles cling together and form a barrier to water percolation. Clay has a negative electrical charge that binds minerals with positive charges including calcium, magnesium, potassium, and sodium. It releases them in exchange for weak hydrogen ions released by plant roots and microorganisms. Soils that are more than 30–40% clay

SOIL TYPE PARTICLE

Particle	Diameter	Description	Source	Effect
Gravel	2 mm+	Coarse	Broken rock	These larger pieces provide channels for water to percolate in compact soils.
Sand	0.05–2 mm	Gritty	Ground rock	Water percolates freely through sand, leaving large spaces for air. Sand does not stick to other particles so it keeps soil from compacting too tightly.
Silt	0.002–0.05 mm	Floury	Powdered rock	Particles are spaced very tightly, making it difficult for water to percolate through. Water puddles before it drains. Then the small particles trap water molecules, releasing them as needed. Too much silt creates wet soil.
Clay	<0.002 mm	Sticky	Alumino-silicate	The negatively charged molecules in clay cling together to form a barrier in water percolation.

are considered clay soils because the other ingredients are absorbed into the clay dough.

It is challenging to grow cannabis in clay soil. Drainage is difficult when too much clay is present. If the native soil is composed of more than 20% clay, consider growing in a container.

Loams are composed of sand, silt, and clay mixed with organic matter, or humus. As a result, the soil particles vary in size. This creates multiple paths for water to flow and also allows air pockets to remain, even when the soil is saturated.

Clay loams can be silty or sandy but are a little heavy and, in wet weather, can become saturated. Adding organic matter and sand increases porosity, although this may be an arduous undertaking.

Sandy soils leach water and nutrients. They need to be irrigated and fertigated more often because they hold less water and nutrients.

Sufficient amounts of organic compost, worm castings, coir, peat moss, and potting soil can add texture and increase water and nutrient-holding abilities.

Silty soils are composed of very small particles with a high surface-to-volume ratio that makes them chemically active. They hold nutrients in a buffer of charged particles, releasing them as roots draw them out using weak acids and exuded enzymes. This type of soil can be challenging in areas that don't have warm temperatures or receive consistent rainfall throughout the growing season.

These soils become mud with sufficient water. They hold water so well that heavy rains can result in hypoxic or anoxic conditions, so the roots will be unable to get the oxygen they need. When amending silty soils, growers need to "lighten" the soil so that the root zone will not be in a soggy, overwatered environment. Sand and compost help increase soil porosity.

After growers receive the results of the soil test and analyze it for their specific needs, it's time to prepare the soil. There are a few decisions to make, such as whether to plant in holes or rows, amend the entire garden, or use raised beds or containers filled with amended native soil or imported planting mix.

The budget should also be taken into consideration:

1. Amending the hole to plant in is probably the most economical and focused method when trying to grow large plants. The amendments and nutrients are delivered only to areas where they will be used.
2. Rows are a good way to reduce labor and focus the grower's energy on care. Power equipment such as rototillers or tractors can be used.
3. Raised beds are an excellent way to maximize effort and dig less. Imported media or soil can be dumped into a framed-up raised bed if the soil condition is poor. A minimum of one foot (30 cm) deep is recommended for cannabis. This saves the energy of digging. Using raised beds can reduce both water and nutrient requirements.
4. Amending the entire planting area is beneficial because roots grow unimpeded in every direction and can cross paths with other plants' root systems. However, this may require the most amount of material to be added, which increases initial costs.
5. Another option is to use a fabric pot. Fabric pots are available in many sizes. They allow the roots to "air prune," which helps grow larger plants in smaller containers. Container size depends on how large the grower intends for the plants to grow. Irrigation should also be considered. Smaller containers need to be watered more often.

Seed Drilling

If the planting is to take place on soil that has been recently used for agriculture, the seeds can be drilled directly into the ground, at a depth of three eighths to a half inch (9.5–12 mm). Sometimes the ground is disced before the seeds are drilled.

Once the decision is made and the soil is in condition, it's time to break ground. This can be done in several ways: plowing with a tractor, rototiller, hole digger, or simply a shovel.

Whether using a shovel, tractor, or rototiller, it is important to break up compacted soil one to two feet (30–60 cm) deep, more if possible or if bigger plants are desired. Some soils need only to be disced.

As the soil is loosened, amendments are added. These might include nutrients such as plant meals or other organic materials that release their nutrients over the season. If the soil has a bit too much clay, compost, used planting media, bark, and coir all help increase porosity.

Sometimes all the native soil in a hole is replaced. On the West Coast, it is not un-

Smart Pot fabric containers promote exceptional root health and vigorous plant growth. All Smart Pot containers respond to climate conditions; in cold weather Smart Pots warm quickly in the sun. During hot weather, excessive heat is released from the custom-designed breathable fabric. Air flow within the medium prevents plants from becoming root bound, which is common in plastic containers. Smart Pots can be used indoors and out, in both soil and hydroponic gardens. They are BPA and chemical free.

common for growers to dig huge holes one cubic yard (0.75 m³) deep and fill them with a premium potting soil mix. This technique has been proved successful for nurturing giant plants. However, this technique has been replaced for the most part with using raised beds or giant cloth bags, eliminating the chore of digging.

Tilling, or turning the soil over, breaks up compacted soil to make root penetration easier and facilitates mixing in amendments such as compost, worm castings, bat guano, biochar, and fertilizers.

There is some controversy about tilling soil because it chops up earthworms, disturbs valuable microorganism communities, and makes the soil subject to erosion because it has been loosened. (*See Sustainability.*)

Most of the time soils need loosening to a depth of 10–15 inches (25–38 cm). However, soil with loose texture, sandy soils, and soils high in organic matter may have adequate aeration, porosity, and space for roots and may not have to be tilled at all. This is occasionally the case and is most likely to be found in fallow fields.

Texture

Regardless of the particular composition of the soil, its texture is critically important to healthy plants. Texture refers to a soil's density, particle size, and ability to hold together—

all of which affect the soil's porosity, or ability to hold or drain water.

Root health, and ultimately plant health, relies mainly on the soil's drainage ability. If a pool of water develops after rain, the soil is saturated. There are no air pockets, so the roots have restricted access to oxygen; plants fail because pathogens that cause root and stem rot attack roots weakened by the hypoxic conditions. Well-drained soil allows roots to be in contact with both water and air, the ideal condition for healthy growth.

Soils that drain well but can also hold an adequate amount of water are best for cannabis. Loams, silts, and sands drain well and are usually loose enough to encourage healthy root development. Clay is too compacted for roots to penetrate, and when dry, clay soils form hard crusts or clods in which cannabis plants cannot thrive.

There are a few simple tests that should always be done before planting to check both the moisture-holding and drainage characteristics of the soil. For best results, the soil is tested when it is moist but not wet.

A three-foot (1 m) deep hole can be dug so the soil's profile, that is, the composition of its layers, can be examined. The method described in the box "Determining Soil Texture" is used to get a more accurate sense of the soil's relative percentages of clay, sand, silt, and humus, but even a visual inspection of the soil can reveal its profile.

Soils that develop under trees or other overhanging plant cover have decaying plant matter at the top that decomposes into a layer of topsoil. The nutrients the plant needs to grow are found at the topsoil layer, though nutrients also leach to the next lower level.

Topsoil, which can be as shallow as an inch (2.5 cm) or several feet (a meter) deep, is usually the darkest of the layers. It is home to an abundance of life, including a variety of worms, bugs, and microorganisms such as yeasts, fungi, anarchia, and protozoa. If it's easy to dig through the topsoil layer by hand, its texture is right for healthy root growth.

Whether forest or prairie soil, there is a layer of subsoil beneath the nutrient-rich upper layer. The subsoil can be composed of clay, sand, fine mineral particles, and small rocks. Sandy, rocky, and loamy subsoils provide excellent drainage without amending.

Below the subsoil, there may be clay or bedrock; both can create drainage problems, particularly if the area is in a spot with a high water table or where the soil tends to remain wet. If the clay or bedrock is within three feet (1 m) of the soil surface, consider alternatives such as building raised beds or mounds to ensure proper drainage and adequate root penetration.

After a visual inspection of the soil comes the squeeze test. A handful of soil from each layer is squeezed tightly, then released, and then the ball is poked with a finger. If it falls apart easily, the soil is either sandy or loamy. If the soil remains hard and stuck together, or if it feels sticky, there is quite a bit of clay present, and it needs to be amended.

Testing soil for drainage is very simple. The hole that was dug is filled with water. The water is allowed to penetrate the surrounding soil, then the hole is filled again with water. If the moisture drains easily, the soil is sandy. If the water has still not drained through after 24 hours, the soil has very poor drainage.

Types of Soil

Each type of soil has its own unique characteristics that determine how it interacts with plants. Soils can be mainly classified as sands, clays, silts, loams, or mucks. Most soil is a combination of two or more of these. Sand granules, bits of clay, organic matter, and fine silty material can all be found in a random handful of soil.

Sandy Soils

Sand is formed from ground or weathered rocks, including limestone, quartz, granite, and shale. Sand particles have a diameter between 2 and 0.5 mm and will feel gritty when rubbed between one's fingers. Sand doesn't form bonds easily, so little water is trapped. Sandy soils drain quickly, and they don't hold moisture and nutrients very well. Some sandy soils are particularly fertile, however, because they contain significant amounts (up to 2%) of organic matter. This matter also helps the soil hold water.

Sandy soils are rich in potassium (K), magnesium (Mg), and trace elements, but are usually lacking phosphorus (P) and nitrogen (N). Nitrogen, the most soluble of the elements, is quickly leached from sandy soil. Yellow, pale, stunted, or very thin plants growing in sandy soil usually indicate low nitrogen.

Sandy soils are easily prepared for cannabis cultivation. First, clear the ground cover from the soil. Next, treat it with compost, humus, composted manure, chopped plant matter such as small wood chips, mineral powder, and other organic, nitrogen-containing fertilizers. Adding compost, peat moss, coco coir, worm castings, humus, or planting mix increases the water-holding capacity and fertility.

Sandy soil with some organic matter or loam that is supporting healthy plants doesn't usually need to be turned or tilled because plant roots can penetrate easily. The row is hoed immediately before planting. Nutrients and water-soluble fertilizers are provided throughout the season.

If there are concerns about the ability of the soil to hold water, add more compost, worm castings, humus, and peat moss. There are also water-holding polymers that can be added to soil, but they are not organic.

Sandy soil can be amended with more organic matter. In preparation for planting, adding composting green waste on top of the sand will help leach nutrients and microbes into the sand. When the composting process is complete, the organic matter will improve the soil structure.

Silt

Silts are composed of fine particles of minerals such as quartz or other fine-grained rocks. The diameter of silt particles is between 0.05 and 0.002 mm. Dry silt has the consistency and feel of flour. Silty soils resemble a sort of mucky clay when wet and look like dark sand or brittle clods when dry.

Silts are the result of alluvial flooding, created by the deposits that remain after rivers and lakes flood. Alluvial silty soils are most commonly found in the Midwest, in valleys, and along river plains. The Mississippi Delta, for example, is a very fertile alluvial plain.

Silts drain well, but they also hold moisture well. They are rich in most nutrients unless they were leached out by bad gardening techniques. They are simple to work with when damp and are regarded as some of the most fertile soils for planting cannabis. Gardens using silty soils must irrigate frequently. Usually, silts support very healthy and hearty plants because they contain an excellent supply of nitrogen.

> If the soil is clay-loam or compacted, it can be used for making raised beds. First, turn the soil in the whole area. Construct aisles by digging out pathways and adding soil from the aisles to the beds. As the beds are filled, amend the clay-loam by mixing in organic soil amendments and sand. Build the bed to two to three feet (0.6–1 m) tall.

Mucks

Mucks are composed primarily of humus from drained swampland or bogs and are found in areas that get plenty of rain. Though they are often very fertile and normally support dense vegetation, mucks are fairly acidic. They contain little potassium, so this nutrient needs to be added.

Mucks range from very dense to a lighter, sandy soil. Denser mucks need tilling so that healthy roots can develop. Lighter mucks are easily cleared for planting. The dense vegetation that mucks support may be helpful in that, when turned into the soil, the plant material becomes "green" manure.

Soil Tests

The best way to learn about the soil or planting mix is to have a professional laboratory perform a soil test. This is the only way to know exactly how much of each nutrient the soil contains. Using the results, the grower can target the best ways to amend the planting medium.

pH Proper pH is important because outside the range some essential nutrients become unavailable.

Electrical Conductivity A low EC means that there are not a lot of available nutrients. When EC is too high, water, although present, becomes unavailable to the roots.

General Guidelines–Potted Plants in Organic Mixes

pH	5.6-6.5	
Results reported in parts per million of dry soil		
Nitrate Nitrogen (N)	25-50	
Ammonium Nitrogen (N)	10-30	
Phosphorus (P_2O_5)	25-75	
Potassium (KO_3)	100-200	
Calcium (Ca)	2000-4000	
Magnesium (Mg)	100-500	
Sulfate (SO_4)	25-50	
Boron (B)	0.5-1.0	
Zinc (Zn)	2.5-5.0	
Copper (Cu)	1.0-2.0	
Manganese (Mn)	10-20	
Iron (Fe)	20-50	
Results reported in meq/l		
Sodium (Na)	<3.0	
Chloride (Cl)	<3.0	
Results reported in % by volume		
Electrical Conductivity dS/m	1.0-3.0	
Moisture Holding Capacity	>40	
Air Filled Porosity	>15	
Results reported in meg/100 grams		
Cation Exchange Capacity		

Nitrate (NO_3) is the form of nitrogen that plants absorb most easily. Manure has a low nitrate rating. Most of its nitrogen is held in organic compounds and is released over time.

Ammonium (NH_4) is absorbed, to a limited extent, directly by the plants. However, it is used by soil organisms and converted to the more soluble and plant-friendly nitrate. It is not desirable because it is toxic to plants in high amounts.

Phosphorus (P) is one of the macronutrients that plants need. Soluble P is very acidic, so it brings down the pH of the water solution.

Potassium (K) is one of the macronutrients that plants need.

Calcium (Ca) is often considered a macronutrient because plants use so much of it. It is usually adequate in garden soils, but some planting mixes don't contain enough. Coir, pure peat moss, bark, and wood have very little, so it must be added when making a planting mix with them.

There are also results for other plant nutrients including magnesium (Mg), sulfur (S), boron (B), zinc (Zn), copper (Cu), manganese (Mn), iron (Fe), sodium (Na), and chlorine (Cl).

The next two categories, moisture-holding capacity and air-filled porosity, are indications of how well the medium holds each. Media with high water-holding capacity need irrigation infrequently as compared with those that hold less. The roots need oxygen, which is found in air. Media with high air-holding capacity meet roots' needs. Low air capacity leads to anaerobic conditions.

Cation exchange capacity (CEC) is the ability of the medium to hold nutrients. Too low a level indicates a soil or planting medium that has the capacity to hold few nutrients. It will have to be fertilized frequently for healthy plant growth.

A biological soil test will also help determine ingredients to use for amending.

The presence of a diverse microbial population can be the difference between a good and a great crop. Microbes also deter pathogenic microorganisms that could cause problems or even crop failure.

Drainage

No matter how well the soil is prepared, the groundwater level and the permeability of the lower layers are of utmost importance. Soils in areas with high water tables or underlying clay or hardpan do not drain well. In either case, the garden can be grown in raised beds filled with soil from the site that has been amended with additives and nutrients. If the local soil is too poor, use landscape or planting mix.

Clay Soils

Clays are made of fine crystalline particles formed by chemical reactions between minerals. These particles are so small (smaller than 0.002 mm) that they have no structure when wet, but react more like a very viscous liquid. Sticky and easily molded or shaped when wet, dry clay forms hard clods, normally observed as a grid of square cracks along the ground surface. Clays are rather difficult to work with, mainly because they drain so poorly.

Despite their disadvantages, clay soils are often very fertile. The success of a plant in clay soil depends on how well the soil drains. A reddish-colored clay soil (sometimes referred to as "red dirt") indicates proper aeration and good drainage. Blue or gray clays mostly have insufficient aeration for growing cannabis; they must be tilled and amended in order to support healthy growth.

Since cannabis roots (particularly the vertical ones) must penetrate the soil, it is necessary to till clay soils thoroughly to loosen them. The addition of sand, biochar, used planting mix, compost, gypsum, manure, and fresh clippings helps loosen and aerate clay soils.

One method of growing in clay soils is to plow rows of mounds and furrows and plant in the mounds so that the water can drain.

Attempting to plant in clay has led many cultivators to containers or raised beds. Hydroponic systems are a water-saving alternative.

In low-lying areas, with vernal pools or stream banks, for example, the soil often retains too much water. This can lead to rot in both roots and stems. Planting mounds or raised rows and furrows helps the soil drain, so the stem stays dry and the root has access to oxygen in the soil.

Prepare workable clay soil in late autumn before frost by tilling it and adding conditioners such as bark, charcoal, compost, grass clippings, gypsum, leaves, manure, paper and cardboard, used planting mix, and wood chips.

Spread ground cover seed such as clover, vetch, or rye over the top of the soil after tilling. This creates green manure that provides soil texture as well as air and water pathways.

If the soil is still sticky, wait until it dries a bit and then use a tiller to break up large clods.

As the composts and green manure raise the organic level in the soil, it becomes less dense. With each passing year the soil becomes easier to work, and the roots will have an easier time penetrating the soil. After several years, it's likely that the only thing to be done is to use fire to weed or disc the cover crop. No further tilling should be needed.

Loams

Loams are a combination of the soils and humus. They are usually made up mostly of sand and silt with about 20% clay. They are described as sandy silt, silty clay, sandy clay, or organic silty clay. Organic loams are made up of at least 20% organic matter. Loams range from easily worked fertile soils all the way to densely packed sod. Loams with a lot of organic matter produce an excellent cannabis crop with little soil modification.

Loams usually have good drainage, but hold water well. They are packed with nutrients and are excellent garden soils.

Humus & Composts

Decayed organic matter, including plant life, animal manure, and microbes, is referred to as humus or compost. Humus is plant or animal material decomposed to the point it can no longer be broken down any further.

Nutrient contents depend on the original ingredients, but most humus or compost contains bacteria, fungi, insects, worms, and microorganisms that are necessary for a complete conversion of important nutrients. During their life processes, many of these organisms convert insoluble chemicals to a soluble form that plant roots can absorb.

Humus and composts hold water well and are frequently added to condition soils.

Good composts have a rich, earthy smell and a dark brown color.

Humus and compost can be produced naturally as part of the soil's life process, or they can be "manufactured" at the grow site simply by gathering vegetation and piling it up. It takes between one and three months to cure, depending on what type of matter is being used. Decomposition of the humus or compost can be achieved more quickly by chopping up the ingredients, turning the pile, and adding substances high in nitrogen. The art of making compost is not to be taken lightly; it is important to learn about proper composting before adding any material to the garden.

Dr. Elaine Ingham and Jeff Lowenfels have written informative books on DIY compost. A proper compost's pH should be neutral to slightly alkaline and should smell earthy, not rancid or putrid. If compost has a putrid smell, it quite possibly has gone "anaerobic" and could cause more harm than good.

If it isn't possible to make enough compost or there isn't time to make it, there are many resources. When sourcing compost, ask for a copy of the lab report. Check the color, and of course the smell. It should be the color of dark chocolate (black compost has most likely gotten too hot and most of the microbes have been cooked off).

pH

The pH level is a measure of how alkaline or acidic the soil is. The pH scale runs from 0 to 14, with 7 considered neutral: a pH level below 7 is acid, above 7 is alkaline. The pH determines the solubility of nutrients and affects the plant's regulation of its metabolism and nutrient uptake. Slightly acidic soils with a pH range from 5.8 to 6.5 are regarded as cannabis friendly.

The pH of the soil interacts with the soil's composition to affect nutrient solubility. Soils with a high percentage of organic matter contain nutrients that are soluble between pH levels of 5.0 and 6.5. Phosphorus, manganese, and boron are less soluble at pH values above 6.5.

Dry western states have soil that usually range from slightly acidic to highly alkaline. Nutrients tend to be quite soluble in these types of soils, providing that the pH range is adjusted to between 5.8 and 6.5. Use a simple pH meter or a test kit, available at most gardening stores, to accurately test the soil pH. If it is alkaline or near neutral, adjust the soil accordingly before planting.

Adjusting the pH

Always test the pH of any soil before using. The pH of the garden's soil may be different from other soils in the area, so don't simply trust what a neighbor is doing. Developers and homeowners often truck in new soil if the native soil is poor in texture, lacking in nutrients, or both.

Keep in mind that soils vary in the amount of material needed to adjust the pH. San-

Vital Garden Supply's Baseline is full of beneficial microorganisms made from an ancient humus rich in humic and fulvic acids. Baseline will improve the structure of all soil while adding microbes to help break down macro and micronutrients. It can be applied as a top dress, mixed into soil, or used as an ingredient in compost tea.

dy soils require less material to change pH as compared to loam. Clays require the most because of their density and the electrical charge of the soil particles. Whether the soil is excessively alkaline or acidic, there are a number of materials that can be added to adjust the pH.

Something to keep in mind when considering soil pH is that in a 100% organic program, beneficial microbes naturally adjust the pH and the conditions in the rhizome to what the plant needs. Using synthetic salt-based fertilizers will inhibit the natural pH adjuster's ability to help with that.

Adjusting Acid Soils

Limestone, also known as calcium carbonate ($CaCO_3$), is a good way to treat acidic soils. Quarried and powdered limestone contains large amounts of trace elements. It comes in three forms: ground limestone, quicklime, and hydrated and liquid lime (which is the fastest acting).

Dolomitic limestone is a limestone variety high in magnesium as well as calcium. It is a good choice for adjusting the acidic, magnesium-deficient soils often found in the northeast United States.

Seashells and eggshells are composed mostly of calcium, and both raise soil pH. Grind them into a fine powder using a blender. They affect soil pH gradually. By contrast, most wood ashes are alkaline and extremely soluble, so they affect soil pH very quickly.

All commercial lime products list their calcium carbonate equivalent, which is a measure of their neutralizing power, on the bag.

To determine how much lime to use, divide the total amount of limestone required by the pH test by the calcium carbonate equivalent. For example, a field may require 50 pounds (22 kg) of limestone, and the calcium carbonate limestone may have an equivalent of 1.78. If 50 pounds (22 kg) are divided by 1.78, the resulting figure, about 29 pounds (13 kg), is the amount required.

Grade, or particle size, of the powder is also listed on the package. The categories used to define the fineness of the powder are superfine, pulverized, agricultural grade, and fine meal. Finer grades result in faster soil-adjusting action but are more prone to washing away.

Add lime to a depth of one inch (2.5 cm) four to five months ahead of planting so it has time to adjust the soil. It can be watered into the soil. Water well afterward or spread it before a rain, providing that the soil is moist enough to absorb the water and lime, and it does not simply run off.

Adjust the medium in planting holes and raised beds. Soil can be adjusted with lime

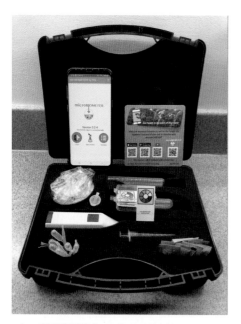

microBIOMETER is an in-field, fully contained testing kit that needs no special training or tools. It reads microbial biomass in soil, compost, compost tea, and compost extract and also provides fungal to bacterial ratio for soil. The phone application includes step-by-step instructions and links to videos. Results are read by the phone and accessible via the phone app or on the web portal. Once the app is downloaded, no internet access is required.

during or after planting, as long as the lime doesn't come into direct contact with the plants. Hydrated or liquid lime can be added to soil with a hose-end sprayer. Lime can also be mixed in irrigation water; however, it can clog up drip lines, hoses, and pumps. Alternately a liquid hydroponic adjuster such as pH Up (usually a potassium salt) can be used to raise irrigation water pH; it has an immediate effect because it's water-soluble.

The best way to adjust pH in acidic soil is to build the microbial population as well as add calcium carbonate. The best way to build the microbial population is to amend with high-quality compost, worm castings, and humus. A good compost tea recipe applied regularly is also recommended.

Adjusting Alkaline Soils

Alkaline soils have a pH higher than 7, outside the range for optimum cannabis growing. Amending alkaline soil with elemental sulfur, gypsum, and compost is a great way to get the native soil's pH where it needs to be. Sulfur lowers the pH even more significantly when used in conjunction with an organic microbial active compost. The bacteria oxidize the sulfur and convert it to an acid that can be absorbed by plants.

Gypsum

Gypsum is a natural mineral composed of calcium sulfate ($CaSO_4$). It's useful as a slow-release form of calcium, or sulfur that doesn't affect the soil pH too much. It should not be added to soils with a pH below 5.5 because it interacts with aluminum (Al) in those acidic soils, making the Al soluble and poisonous to plants. Gypsum is available at garden centers under various local and store brands.

Gypsum is used to break up clay soils. It is a naturally occurring mineral that, like lime, is high in calcium and can be used to address deficiencies. It is important to note that gypsum and lime are different. Gypsum is $CaSO_4$, whereas lime comes in three forms: $CaCO_3$, CaO, and $Ca(OH)_2$. Both are sources of calcium, but only gypsum also provides sulfur.

Gypsum improves soil quality in a few ways:

- It is fairly water soluble, so it improves soil fertility. Both calcium and sulfur penetrate evenly as the gypsum dissolves and seeps deep into the soil.
- It increases a soil's ability to store water. A soil's ability to hold on to water helps prevent erosion, as the soil takes longer to reach saturation before runoff occurs. Adding gypsum to clay-dominant soil helps break up the soil particles, increasing the porosity and the amount of space between them. Additional water is held in these spaces.
- Increased porosity also increases air penetration. Between irrigation events and as the soil loses moisture, air penetrates deeper into the soil, providing better oxygen delivery to the roots, which helps improve overall plant health.

Applying gypsum to the soil can be done through several methods; however, most farmers grind it to a fine powder so that it can dissolve in irrigation solution. It can also be applied as a top dressing before planting or after harvest and can be tilled under or just left alone to soak down as it rains. Although gypsum is fairly soluble, the sulfur delivered from a single application is available for several plantings.

Compost tea or compost extract applications also help speed up the process of lowering the pH in multiple ways:
- Beneficial microbes in conjunction with the plant's roots can adjust the pH to the plant's preferred level.
- Microbes interact with sulfur and gypsum to convert them to soluble nutrients.
- Fish hydrolysate in the compost tea will help lower the pH as well.

Both iron sulfate ($FeSO_4$) and magnesium sulfate, commonly known as epsom salts ($MgSO_4$), act quickly to adjust soils and planting mixes.

Some acidic plant materials that can gradually lower pH include cottonseed meal, which is high in nitrogen; coffee grounds; pine needles; and pineapple and citrus rinds.

Use pH down when alkaline soils are being fertigated. Usually diluted phosphoric acid, pH down is used to adjust the nutrient-water solution to a pH in the low 5s. This will counteract the roots' alkaline environment and create an acidic water-nutrient solution available to the roots.

Adjusting Alkali Soils

Alkali soils have a high sodium content (from sodium carbonate or sodium bicarbonate) and frequently a pH above 8.5. They are usually hard-packed and crusty, sometimes with white powdery salts on the surface. They don't absorb water easily.

Alkali soils such as those found in western Colorado, parts of the US Southwest, Spain, and the Caspian Sea area of Central Europe can be frustrating, energy draining, and time-consuming to work with. Farmers usually prepare alkali soils for cultivation by leaching them of the toxic accumulation of salts.

This is achieved by tilling the soil to a depth of 30 inches (75 cm) and then flood-irri-gating using 6–12 inches (15–30 cm) of water at least once or twice to flush the salt deep into the soil, out of contact with the roots. Next, the soil is tested to determine the amount of amendment needed. Phosphorus and sulpher fertilizers are acidic and quickly bring the pH of these soils down to a more suitable pH.

Another way to adjust alkali soils is to add a thick mulch layer, which interacts with the soil during the winter. The mulch layer should be a minimum of nine inches (23 cm) thick, or about 130 pounds (60 kg) per 100 square feet (10 m^2). Thicker mulch layers neutralize more salts faster. Gypsum is also very effective in these applications, but with all things considered, growing in containers with imported planting soil may be a better option than investing the time to adjust the soil.

Outdoor Water-Saving Techniques

This section is devoted to customizing raised beds, planting holes, troughs, and hydroponic systems.

Plant size and yield are determined to a great extent by the development of the root system. Even plants that are receiving copious quantities of water and nutrients require enough room for their roots to grow and spread out in order to reach their full potential.

When limited by law to growing just 6 or 10 plants, the grower sometimes aims to increase the size of each plant. Creating a large area of prime soil helps the roots penetrate easily and absorb nutrients. Figure that the diameter of the plant is usually the same size to about one-third larger than the diameter of the root ball. A plant with a 10 foot (3 m) diameter canopy will have a root spread of at least a 7 foot (2.25 m) diameter.

With hydroponic systems the canopy diameter often exceeds the diameter of root col-onization by 50%.

In dry areas that require irrigation, providing water to plants this size can be an arduous task that requires a lot of water, so conservation becomes a significant factor. Water that reaches the garden is used in one of four ways:

1. It is used by the plant. Plants use water for metabolic purposes in much the same way that animals do, as well as a raw ingredient in photosynthesis, and plants tran-spire water vapor from the leaves in order to regulate temperature.
2. It evaporates from the earth surface. Heat and sunlight speed the evaporation of water from the top surface levels.
3. It drains from the root level deeper into the earth and becomes unavailable to the roots.
4. It is delivered to the garden, but to areas where there are no roots. It eventually evaporates or sinks, unused.

Water-Saving Strategies

- Organic matter holds more water than the mineral portion of the soil. Adding compost, peat moss, coir, biochar, or other organic matter increases the soil's capacity to retain water. This is especially helpful in fast-draining sandy soils.
- Organic mulch placed on top of the soil layer lowers the evaporation rate: the barrier between the moist soil and heat and light eliminates most evaporation. The topsoil stays moist longer.
- White plastic film placed over the soil keeps it cool and lowers the rate of evaporation.
- Drip irrigation, when installed properly, is a very efficient way to get water to the plants without wasting it.
- Raised beds and containers are water-saving alternatives.

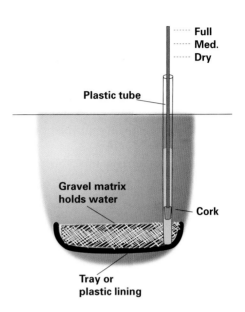

Cannabis grows very well in containers, both indoors and out, but requires more care and attention than plants growing in native soil. Rather than working with the natural environment, or at least a resemblance of it, gardeners can control the space the roots have when plants are growing in containers, as well as the water conditions and nutrients. Container size plays a role in determining the growth, final size, and yield of the plant as well as how much and how often it needs to watered.

Sasquatch Soil Co. specializes in unique blends that naturally replicate the nutrient-rich forest floor. Each batch of soil is alive and ready to be planted with a blend of organic inputs. No chemical treatments or wasteful fillers are added, and all ingredients are sustainable and ethically sourced, with a commitment to regenerative farming.

Premade Soil Mixes

There are two categories of soil mixes to keep in mind: amended and inert.

Amended soil has macro- and micronutrients, minerals, and potentially microorganisms. There are many high-quality amended soil mixes on the market to choose from.

Inert mixes are basic blends that have little or no nutrient value. They are designed for growers who want to control the nutrient program and to have no variables.

Organic certification is another consideration. There are many reasons to choose organic when picking a brand of soil.

1. Organic products are safer for people, plants, animals, rivers, and streams.
2. Organically grown cannabis is more desired by users for health reasons as well as those who embrace organic lifestyles.
3. Organic soil companies tend to choose higher-quality ingredients, which leads to a better-quality finished product.

Enriched planting mixes usually contain compost. This component makes or breaks the quality of the potting mix. Compost varies greatly in quality, and poor-quality compost can kill plants.

Indoors

Indoors, the grower determines what size containers to use based on specific needs. Common sizes for indoor and greenhouse growing are 3–5 gallons (11–19 l) per square foot (0.09 sq. m) of canopy space the mature plant is to occupy. Sixteen of these containers fit in a four by four foot (1.2 by 1.2 m) space. Some gardeners opt to use as few as four 10–20 gallon (38–75 l) containers in the space.

In large commercial cultivation spaces with rolling benches, it is not out of the ordinary for growers to use 2 gallon (7.5 l) containers or even four inch (10 cm) rockwool cubes. Using this technique, the plants are also watered multiple times a day, controlled by a timer or based on sensors to make sure those small root zones don't dry out.

These 3–5 gallon (11–19 l) pots provide the roots with enough space to spread out and down throughout the container without becoming "rootbound," although the roots provide for a canopy of the same width. Sometimes the plant canopy spreads up to a third larger than the diameter of the roots. The plants stay in the container for only a few months because they are forced to flower as soon as they grow into the canopy, a matter of weeks. The plant may live 10–12 weeks after transplanting before being harvested.

Sea of Green (SOG) System

If plant limits are not relevant, plants can be grown close together so that each plant grows a single stem and is then forced to flower. This system, called "sea of green" (SOG), requires very little time spent in vegetative growth. One gallon (~4 l) pots and six inch (15 cm) rockwool cubes are excellent sizes for sea of green cultivation. The plants may require more than one watering/feeding a day. The plants quickly fill the space, increasing harvest frequency.

The advantage of SOG systems is that the plants spend little time or energy in vegetative growth. Rather than a few plants gradually filling out the canopy, in a large group each plant grows a little bit at the same time, so the canopy is quickly filled and the plants can be forced to flower.

Instead of spending months in vegetative growth, with all the energy and labor that goes with it, the plants are forced to flower with only one stem. This decreases time from transplant to flower from 30–45 to at most 10 days.

Another method is to use planting beds rather than containers, which are like raised beds, but indoors. The plants grow directly in the planting mix without the restrictions of containers. Each root system has more total space to explore and grow, allowing it to gather more water and nutrients. Once it's set up, there is no need to pot or unpot the planting mix. Just freshen it up between crops, and it's ready to go again. Make sure there is adequate drainage. Drilling holes in the bottom of the "bed" is important to make sure the soil drains well so it doesn't get too wet and become anaerobic.

Container Facts

- Fabric pots are an excellent choice and are available in many shapes and sizes.
- Rectangular containers hold more than circular containers of the same size.
- Containers must drain well. Avoid containers with holes on the bottom in favor of containers with holes on the side, especially if the containers are to be placed on a solid surface. Bottom holes are easily blocked.
- Unconventional containers are fine to use. Adapt square and rectangular-shaped plastic trays and containers by creating drainage holes.
- Plastic grow bags come in all sizes. They work well indoors and out, and are lightweight and inexpensive. Also, gusseted plastic reusable shopping bags with a rectangular bottom are inexpensive (often free). They'll last at least one season. Drainage holes should be cut on the sides, near the bottom.
- Bags and containers are much easier to move and make gardening much less fatiguing when they are equipped with handles.
- Large containers can be moved with a container handler, hand truck, or heavy-duty wagon.
- There are many potting soil manufacturers who make "perforated" bags, which are meant to be used for growing.
- Large plants require large containers. The desired size of the plant should determine the size of container to be used.
- When containers are on wheels, they are much easier to move around to reorganize a space.

Tips for Outdoor Containers

Fabric pots are excellent for areas that experience warm temperatures.

Boxes built from wood such as cedar or redwood will last a very long time, but even when built from pine or fir, they will last for many years.

Black plastic containers may be a good choice indoors, but in direct sun the roots can get cooked. White plastic containers are an option for outdoor gardens. A solution for black containers is to wrap them in white plastic.

When choosing a potting mix, growers have a few things to consider: quality ingredients, porosity (the soil's ability to retain water and dry out), and texture (how light or heavy as well as how much air the soil holds).

The mixture should drain well so that oxygen, required by the roots, can fill the empty spaces.

The quality of ingredients greatly varies from company to company. Choose a brand with a good reputation. Soil is the foundation of the crop, so choose wisely.

The porosity is a key component in the plant's environment. Some growers like a light mix for young plants and switch to a heavier blend when the plants are larger and more demanding. However, small containers dry out faster than larger containers, so it is important to have a mix that has the ability to hold water but can provide sufficient porosity so that air spaces, containing oxygen, are created.

A moist potting mix with a good texture should form a clump when squeezed into a fist; with a slight poke, the clod should break apart. If it sticks together, it should be amended with ingredients that loosen it up.

These include:

- coir
- compost
- biochar
- mini-sized horticultural clay pellets

High-quality commercial potting mixes almost always have good texture, so they provide plants with high amounts of water and air.

There is an incentive for both home gardeners and commercial growers to use ready-made planting mix. Whether it is a totally non-nutritive or a fortified mix enriched with organic nutrients, the manufacturer has adjusted its pH to ensure healthy growth.

Some mixes perform better than others, so it is worthwhile to test different brands in side-by-side experiments. Although the cost of enriched prepared mixes varies widely, the most important factor is not the cost of the mix but the yield. Although the initial cost might be higher, if the difference in yield or quality is significant, the difference in the cost of the soil will seem insignificant.

Most of the ingredients of planting mixes—bark, coir, and peat moss—are all carbon based and chemically active, so they act as a buffer for fertilizers and nutrients. They catch and hold excess nutrients dissolved in the water-nutrient solution and release them when the nutrient water solution becomes less concentrated. For this reason, they are more forgiving than some hydroponic methods, where there is little or no interaction between the medium and the water.

Another factor is the carbon-based ingredients that anchor the microbial complex found in the rhizosphere, the area surrounding the root and influenced by its exudates.

These organisms solubilize minerals into dissolved salts that are available to plant roots, which sip, but don't eat, solid food. They mediate the peaks and valleys of nutrient availability, acting as buffers.

Perlite

Perlite is a useful ingredient that has been used for many years in horticulture. There is no questioning that its use has made life easier for horticulturalists, commercial growers, and home growers alike.

The problem is that it is extremely lightweight and creeps up to the soil surface, where the small pieces can be carried away with stiff winds. Large pieces also creep up to the top of the soil. Because perlite retains air pockets when it is irrigated, the granules float. These properties make planting mixes containing perlite less desirable when they are recycled.

Perlite is a mined volcanic glass-like mineral, similar to obsidian, that melts at 1560–1740°F (850–950°C). Water held in the rock turns to steam and causes the liquid to foam. It expands up to 20 times its original volume and has a structure with many tiny closed cells or bubbles. The resulting snow-white particles are sterile and inert, and have a neutral pH. The hard pieces remain stable for years. They wick water through capillary action.

The particle surface is covered with tiny craters that create an extremely large surface area that can hold the water-nutrient solution. Passages in the structure also hold pockets of air and promote drainage.

Perlite comes in various sizes, or grades, that range from very fine to pea-sized gravel. The amount of water adsorbed on the surface of perlite is a function of particle size. Coarse perlite particles absorb less water than the finer grades. Generally the smaller sizes are used in smaller containers. Larger sizes are used in larger containers and maintain porous spaces for air. However, various sizes are sometimes included in soil mixes to customize water-holding capacity.

Perlite's bright white color protects seeds by keeping them cool and moist even when placed under bright sunlight. It reflects light back to plant foliage, which further enhances growth.

Propagation and Seed Cultivation: Fine-grade perlite makes a good medium for seed starting and cloning because it maintains a uniform moisture level. Excess water drains, so there is no waterlogging. Since the perlite doesn't form a chemical bond with the water, water tension doesn't increase as long as there is moisture present. This helps young plants overcome environmental stresses.

Perlite clings to roots and root hairs so they can form a root ball. This reduces transplant shock.

Planting Mixes: Perlite is often used as an ingredient in planting mixes. Different sizes are used to adjust water-holding capacity and provide aeration. It keeps the mix lightweight and provides structure, since it does not deteriorate.

Hydroponics: Perlite's capillary action and fast drainage are ideal qualities for hydroponic media. It makes water management self-regulating. It is inert, so it doesn't interfere with fertilizer and nutrient programs.

SOIL

Perlite can be used in a single-ingredient planting medium in many hydroponic systems, including wick, reservoir, drip, and constant flow. Its ability to retain water and provide air spaces, along with its neutral pH and nonreactive qualities, make it an excellent medium. However, because the lightweight granules shift position in ebb and flow systems, plants must be supported using a ScrOG net, staking, or another technique.

Perlite is often used as an ingredient in hydroponic and soil-less media with vermiculite, peat moss, or bark. Part of its usefulness is that it retains its structure, in contrast to peat moss, which deteriorates as it reacts with soil and degrades into compost and vermiculite that gradually loses its structural integrity and collapses.

Perlite can be reused as long as it is rinsed and sterilized and old plant material is removed. It has been used to remediate clay soils, but this is expensive and doesn't work as well as adding organic material.

Peat Moss

Peat moss is an ingredient with an advisory. Peat bogs are nature's natural repository of plant-collected carbon. The world will be better when peat bog mining ends. For this reason, this wetlands-mined ingredient is listed with an advisory. However, the authors would be remiss in not covering it because it is still widely accepted as a media ingredient by the horticultural industry.

Peat moss consists of layers of sphagnum moss that died and were naturally buried in acidic, anaerobic water.

Peat moss is probably the most popular container planting material used in North America. It is a key ingredient in most mixes because it holds 15–20 times its weight in water, has excellent buffering ability, and is inexpensive. It comes in several sizes, or grades, ranging from very fine, which holds more water because the spaces between the particles are smaller, to larger pieces that provide more airspace.

Peat moss is very acidic and must be treated with lime to raise its pH. Most mixes have already adjusted the pH, but the grower should also give it a pH test. Although it has a high buffering capacity, it has no nutrients of its own, so an unenriched mix must be fertilized from the start.

Peat moss has a chemical relationship with water, and as it loses moisture, it holds on to the remaining water more tightly, increasing water tension and making it more difficult for the roots to absorb water and nutrients. For this reason, peat-moss-based media should never be allowed to dry out. Although the medium may feel moist, this water may be unavailable to the roots.

Peat moss is composed of dead plant matter, so it contains carbon. Carbon is used by microorganisms in the soil to build tissue, which degrades the peat moss over time. At the same time, it shrinks as it loses its structure. For example, home gardeners might notice that the soil in a houseplant container shrank over a few months; this happens as the microorganisms use the carbons in the soil. This presents a problem only if the plant is in the mix long-term. The compacted mix doesn't provide enough air to the roots, the roots don't have as much space to spread out, and the plant has less support to hold itself upright. Over a few months this shrinkage does not usually have a noticeable adverse effect. However, it becomes less suitable for reuse without adding structural ingredients to the mix.

Ed Rosenthal Select Blend is coir based for excellent drainage. Designed with Vital Garden Supply specifically for cannabis, it provides nutrients and excellent water-air ratios to promote root health. For use indoors, outdoors, or in greenhouses. It is biodegradable and works well with both organic and mineral fertilizers. Enviroganic, Clean Green, and CDFA OIM certified.

Coir

Coir, or coco peat, is made from the soft fibers and pith that protect the inner kernel of the coconut. Horticultural coir is made from ripe coconuts. As the fruit ripens, the fibers, initially composed mostly of cellulose, increase their content of lignin, which is also found in wood. Lignin resists decomposition better than both bark and peat moss, so it can be used and reused far longer than bark or peat.

Coir holds between five and eight times its own weight in water. The air porosity, the amount of air the material holds, depends on the size of the particles and fibers. The finer the fiber, the more water it holds in relation to air. The larger the particle sizes, the lower the initial water retention.

Quality coir typically also has a medium cation exchange capacity; the fibers not only absorb water but also chemically hold nutrients and buffer nutrient swings. This depends greatly on how well the coir was rinsed and buffered prior to use. Buffering coco is a process used to replace the potassium and/or sodium ions that are bound to the coir particles, with calcium and/or magnesium ions. Soaking with a calcium and/or magnesium solution can help balance the ratio of cations held in the medium and avoid nutrient deficiencies when growing in coco coir.

Another advantage coir holds over peat moss and bark is that it has a higher pH and is in the acceptable range for growing media of 5.8–6.4. It is also a source of potassium as well as iron, manganese, zinc, and copper, which it releases gradually. The finer particles, the pith, can be thought of as organic potassium sources with a sponge-like molecular structure. It is combined with short fibers that act as an anticompacting texturizer.

There is anecdotal evidence that coir possesses fungicidal qualities, which may stem from the lignin or from its surface structure.

There are many grades of coir based on the particle size and which type of tissue is used. Long fibers have granular material, called pith, attached before processing. Sometimes the two materials are left together, but usually they are separated into fiber and pith.

Each coir processor has its own recipe for a particular combination of pith and fiber.

Reiziger® Coco Coir Pith's exclusive Nutricoir® formula will help plants absorb 50% more nutrients than ordinary coco peat to protect against over- and under fertilizing while minimizing uneven growth and stunting. It is ready-to-use out of the bag and the homogeneous texture maintains an optimum balance of air and water, resulting in rapid root development to grow strong plants and high-quality flowers.

The more pith that it contains, the better its water retention, but the less air it holds.

Coir chips are pieces of coir sliced into cubes. They range from 0.25–0.75 inches (6–20 mm). They are used in place of bark in some soil recipes, as a planting medium for orchids and as a hydroponic planting medium.

Bark

Bark is a filler ingredient and can cause issues if used in too high of a concentration. Chopped or ground bark is often used as an ingredient in planting mixes. Bark's qualities, such as its water-holding capacity and pH level, differ by tree variety. The grade of bark and the size of the pieces affect water-holding capacity. The smaller the pieces, the more water they hold and the less airspace between them. Bark contains carbon, so it is subject to microbial disintegration. However, this occurs at a slower rate than with peat moss. It also buffers the water nutrient mix, absorbing some excess nutrients and releasing them when the solution becomes less concentrated.

If planning to grow a plant that will be kept for five months or more, select a bark or coir-based soil rather than one made from peat moss.

Bark is not usually used in hydroponics except in fertigation systems such as capillary mats.

Worm Castings

Worm castings are often an ingredient in a high-quality amended potting soil. Worm castings are the excrement of earthworms. Worm castings are packed with macronutrients, humic acid, beneficial microbes, and micronutrients.

Worm castings also improve the structure of the soil. Castings hold water well, and the roots weave around the little balls, which are filled with soluble nutrients and microbes.

Mycorrhizae

Mycorrhizae are fungi that live in soil in various forms and share a symbiotic relationship with plants. They are found mostly in the rhizosphere, the area surrounding the roots where plants absorb water and draw nutrients.

They benefit plants in a number of ways;
1. Increase nutrient uptake
2. Exchange of fungal hormones and other manufactures to plants
3. Protection from pathogens and root predators

4. Better water relations, including reduced drought stress

This results in increased root vigor and growth with more resistance to disease organisms and drought. Bud quality and yield also increase.

Types of Mycorrhizae

Mycorrhizae are divided into two groups, endomycorrhizae and ectomycorrhizae. The latter is associated with forest trees in temperate climate zones and probably has no effect on cannabis growth.

There are several groups of endomycorrhizae, but cannabis growers are interested primarily in the arbuscular mycorrhizae (AM fungi, named for their "tree-like" structure). Their hyphae, the center of new growth in AM fungi, are root-like or branch-like structures. Hyphae grow through the root cell wall and position themselves between the cell wall and the cell membrane. The string-like structures, the arbuscles, colonize new space through growth. As the hyphae mature, vesicles containing stored lipids saved for leaner times develop along their length.

Once it has grown into the cell, it has parts both inside and outside the roots. Outside it grows a fine network of filaments that serve as an extension of the root hairs. They use electrochemical reactions to dissolve nutrients, especially phosphorus (P), but also the micronutrients, and bring them into the cells. Nutrients get delivered to plants inside the roots and absorb sugars and other plant products released by the roots.

The AM fungi produce and release abundant amounts of the glycoprotein glomalin.

ARBICO Organics Root Build 240 provides a mixture of mycorrhizae that aids plants as they establish themselves. The blend of ectomycorrhizal and endomycorrhizal fungal species in Root Build 240 is carefully mixed with other organic components and is suitable for use in a wide variety of soils and climates. The result is a replenished natural microbial system on the roots of inoculated plants that increases crop productivity, quality, and sustainability. In addition, Root Build 240 helps reduce the effects of transplant shock while promoting extensive root growth.

A glycoprotein is a molecule that combines protein and sugar, which gives it many unique properties. Glomalin is almost 40% carbon, and with that much carbon it can host a lot of microorganisms and supply them with one of their needed sources of food.

Glomalin permeates all the ingredients of soil and organic matter (sand, silt, and clay) and binds them together so that they form little clumps of soil granules called aggregates. This adds structure to the soil and is the first step in nature's erosion control program that keeps stored soil carbon from escaping.

Mycorrhizae increase absorption in two ways: physical and chemical. Mycelia are smaller in diameter than even the smallest root, so they examine the soil more closely, providing a larger surface area for absorp-

Great White® premium mycorrhizae formula contains 16 different species of mycorrhizal fungi, 14 different species of beneficial bacteria, and two species of Trichoderma, which ensures optimum colonization of root systems by the fungi. The powder dissolves easily, delivering the spores directly to the roots, where they immediately germinate. Expect rapid root growth, increased nutrient absorption, and enhanced fruiting and flowering, resulting in larger yields.

tion. Fungi use different methods than plant roots to make soil nutrients available. Their work is most beneficial in nutrient-poor soils.

AM fungi protect plants from microbial soil-borne pathogens by forming a protective shield around the roots, which keeps them healthier. They also produce warning chemicals that stimulate the plant to prepare for an attack, possibly with protective chemicals, making the roots more resistant to disease organisms and drought because of improved water and mineral uptake.

Plants grown in sterile soils and growth media don't yield as much as compared with enriched planting media and inoculated soils. Add an AM fungi mix to new soils and planting media. AM fungi take several weeks to colonize a container holding a large plant. However, if the plants are inoculated when they are small, the microlife will grow with the roots and fill the rhizosphere with organisms that ward off pathogens.

AM fungi and other beneficial organisms may be present in soil or planting mixes that have been used to grow plants for a crop, especially if it was inoculated and the organisms had time to colonize the roots.

That is why uninfected, inoculated planting mix usually yields a larger harvest on the second and third crops. To change the planting mix, mix some of the old mix into the new medium to inoculate it with the microbes.

In soil and planting mixes, most of the phosphate is bound in water-insoluble minerals. The soil water contains very low concentrations, and roots often have a hard time obtaining enough of it. The root hairs and associated mycorrhizae have an active transport system to supply the canopy with orthophosphate (H_3PO_4). Most plants enhance their nutrient uptake capacity using AM fungi to extend the surface area of the roots by proxy. This increases the plant's ability to transport nutrients and to obtain phosphate.

Trichoderma

Trichoderma fungi are found in nearly all soils. Some species live freely, while others colonize the roots. They are variable because cells often contain more than one nucleus and there is a lot of gene mixing, resulting in many unique combinations.

The fungus grows long filaments, or arms, in the search for food. *Trichoderma* attack, parasitize, and otherwise gain nutrition from other fungi. They use numerous mechanisms to attack other fungi and to enhance plant and root growth. Different strains of *Trichoder-*

Miicrobial Mass is specifically developed for cannabis and hemp production. It is made up of five targeted bacterial strains that work to unlock phosphorus, calcium, and iron, which increase root development and plant vigor, accelerate growth, and maximize yields. Miicrobial Mass is a safe, clean, and certified organic way to bring out the full genetic potential of any indoor, outdoor, or greenhouse crop.

ma control almost every pathogenic fungus for which control has been sought. Each *Trichoderma* strain has its specialty and controls some pathogens better than others. A particular species may be ineffective against some fungi.

Some species such as *T. harzianum* are used in bioprotectants such as RootShield. Mixed species are often included in endo/ectomycorrhizal mixes.

There is some controversy on whether mycorrhizae and *Trichoderma* can cohabitate. Many growers only inoculate with *Trichoderma* if a root disease or pathogen is threatening the health of the plant. After the *Trichoderma* inoculation, they reapply mycorrhizae.

The mycorrhizae will not harm the *Trichoderma*'s ability to eradicate root-borne pathogens. Trichoderma are known to be a stronger species of fungi and kill most microorganisms. Many organic growers will also apply compost tea or extract after using the *Trichoderma* to help the microbial population get stronger.

Beneficial Bacteria

There are many theories about beneficial bacteria in soil. One thing is certain: there is a shortage of bacteria in most native soil as well as heavily farmed agricultural land. Inoculating a beneficial bacteria blend is a good way to water the garden and introduce new species of bacteria to help with plant health. A nitrogen-fixing bacteria helps make nitrogen more available, and a phosphorus-solubilizing bacteria helps break down phosphorus and make it more soluble to plants.

VOLUME OF SOIL EXPLORED BY A 1 CM LONG ROOT WITH AND WITHOUT VAM MYCORRHIZAE

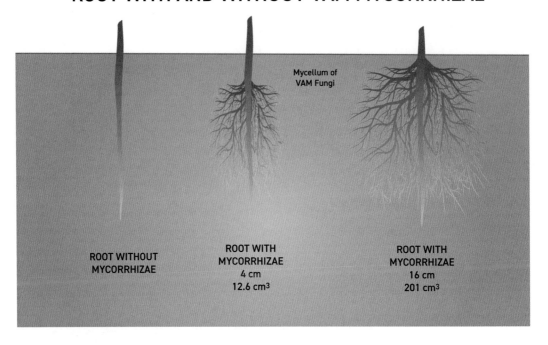

Mycellum of VAM Fungi

ROOT WITHOUT MYCORRHIZAE

ROOT WITH MYCORRHIZAE
4 cm
12.6 cm3

ROOT WITH MYCORRHIZAE
16 cm
201 cm3

Beneficial Microorganisms

Inoculating growing media or soil with beneficial microorganisms, sometimes referred to as plant growth-promoting bacteria (PGPB), benefits the productivity of plants through a number of methods (Souza et al. 2015):

- Increasing efficiencies through reducing production costs and environmental pollution
- Tolerance toward abiotic stress through modulation of ACC deaminase
- Soil microorganisms that produce the enzyme 1-aminocyclopropane-1-carboxylate (ACC) deaminase promote plant growth by sequestering and cleaving plant-produced ACC, and thereby lowering the level of ethylene in the plant. Decreased ethylene levels allow the plant to be more resistant to a wide variety of environmental stresses (Bernard et al. 2005).
- Microbial protection against disease and pests
- Inducing a systemic acquired response in the plants so they are better equipped to protect themselves against pathogens (e.g., beneficial siderophore production, which induces the plant's natural defenses)
- Predation or hyperparasitism, aka beneficial microbes preying on pathogenic microbes
- Competitive exclusion or antagonism, which is best described as the beneficial microorganisms' ability to outcompete pathogens for nutrients and/or producing compounds that either kill pathogens or make them less viable in the environment

Left: untreated roots. Right: Roots treated with DYNOMYCO®, a mycorrhizal inoculant developed specifically for cannabis. DYNOMYCO® is highly concentrated with unique strains of *Glomus intraradices* and *Glomus mosseae*, both known to have a symbiotic relationship with cannabis.

- Rhizospheric competency, or the physical blocking of access to the roots by the beneficial microbes
- Increase of access to nutrients and increase of plant productivity
- Microbial biological nitrogen fixation (BNF)
- Microbial Indole-3-acetic acid (IAA) production
- Increase of phosphate solubility through microbial activity in the root zone

Examples of Commercially Available Beneficial Microorganisms & Modes of Action

Examples of organisms that have been shown to be effective in field studies (Gaskin et al. 2013).

Organism	MOA	Crops	Persistence
Biofertilizers			
Rhizobium spp.	Form nitrogen-fixing nodules on roots of legumes. Specific strains are used for each crop species.	Peas, beans, clovers	Several years if legumes are regularly grown.
Specific strains of *Azospirillum*, *Azotobacter*, *Bacillus*, and *Burkholderia*	Rhizosphere (free living) bacteria that fix nitrogen.	Corn, rice, wheat	Occur naturally in many soils. Can persist for years depending on soil conditions.
Mycorrhizae fungi	Increase uptake of phosphorus, other nutrients, and water. Increase disease and drought resistance.	Most crops except spinach and brassicas such as broccoli and cabbage	Several years if host plants are grown.
Pseudomonas spp. *Bacillus* spp.	Increase root nodulation by *Rhizobium* spp. in some legumes.	Clover, soybean, alfalfa, bean	Ubiquitous soil inhabitants. Years depending on soil conditions.
Biopesticides			
Bacillus subtilis: specific strains and other *Bacillus* spp.	Release inhibitory compounds and activate plant resistance against numerous plant diseases above- and belowground.	Cucumber, melons, squash, leafy vegetables except brassicas, peppers, potatoes, tomatoes, walnuts, cherries, grapes, cotton, legumes	Must be reinoculated as seed treatment or drench with each crop to maintain high numbers on the roots. Populations decrease over time to low numbers in the soil.
Bacillus thuringiensis: specific strains	Kills larvae of butterflies and beetles, fly larvae, and nematodes.	Most crops	Less than four days on foliage, three months in the soil.
Trichoderma spp.	Rhizosphere fungi that release antipathogen substances and promote plant growth.	Flowers, ornamentals, vegetables, root crops, hydroponic crops, fruits, nuts, transplants	Generally incorporated as granules at planting time. Survives indefinitely in lower numbers in most soils.
Pseudomonas spp.	Release antifungal compounds and are a plant growth promoter.	Greenhouse ornamentals, nursery crops, vegetable transplants	Applied at planting as drench. Can be repeated after two to three months. Soil inhabitant.
Streptomyces lydicus, *griseoviridis*	Releases antifungal compounds and is a plant growth promoter.	Many crops	Applied at planting as drench or on seed, can be reapplied every two to six weeks. Natural soil inhabitant at lower numbers.
Gliocladium sp.	Antifungal activity.	Ornamental, vegetable, and tree crops	Applied as drench prior to seeding or transplanting. May be reapplied every one to four weeks. Natural soil inhabitant at lower numbers.

Regenerative Growing

By Jeff Lowenfels

Given the state of the environment, it makes sense to grow cannabis in a regenerative manner, one that aids the environment. Most important, regenerative techniques build up farmed soils instead of depleting them.

Indoors and outdoors, there are two mainstays to rebuilding soils: the addition of organic matter and establishing and maintaining soil biodiversity.

These strategies can be implemented in a number of ways. Primary among them is the use of living soils. Conventional farming practices such as tilling and the use of synthetic fertilizers and pesticides results in soils with reduced microlife and diversity. Living soils contain thriving microlife communities composed of diverse populations of beneficial microbes. In sum, living soils are regenerative. Because they are alive and thriving, they add to the system while supporting plants.

By its very nature, farming anything can be detrimental to the environment. At the very least, cannabis growers violate the Law of Return: plant material that falls to the soil should be left so it decays, adding back to the soil.

Growing cannabis regeneratively requires adding life and organic matter to the soil as it is farmed. This is accomplished by sheet composting and adding composts, compost teas, and living and static mulches. They add organic matter and microbes to the soil in quantities that replace or improve what is removed at harvest.

Sheet Composting

Sheet composting, or "composting in place," is a method that mimics the natural layers of decay found in soil from the forest floor. Sheet composting is spreading a layer of compost directly over the soil with a top layer of mulch. As the compost breaks down, it releases usable carbon dioxide to the plants.

Living Soil

Many cannabis growers, indoors and outdoors, have discovered the benefits

Teaming with Microbes is the must-have guide for everyone who wants to understand and utilize the soil food web, from those devoted to organic gardening techniques to weekend gardeners who simply want to grow healthy plants without resorting to chemicals.

A regenerative farm. Photo: Ed Rosenthal

of growing in soils that are full of beneficial microbes. These microbes support a healthy and functioning soil food web. They sequester carbon in their bodies, make nutrients available when they are consumed and excreted, and build soil structure by producing glues and threads and more.

Simply put, compared to hydroponics, living soils substitute compost for coco coir and other substrates, and microbes for chemicals. Living soils allow a grower to produce cannabis as nature does, naturally, organically, and with odors and tastes that are universally considered better than chemically grown products.

Best of all, using living soils is easier than maintaining a hydroponics system. A properly made living soil only needs the addition of water during the life of the crop. The balance of microbes and the metabolites they produce helps keep pathogens in check while feeding the plants.

As the name suggests, there are two obvious aspects to living soils: the soil part, of course, and then the microbial component. Each brings specific attributes to the mix.

Soil

Soil is very different from hydroponic substrates in lots of ways. Properly made, it contains all the nutrients plants need. All that is required is to add water as the plants grow.

The reason is clay and organic particles in soils hold negative electric charges. These negative particles are known as ions, and they attract and hold positively charged plant nutrients known as cations.

These positively charged cations include potassium ($K+$), calcium (Ca_2+), magnesium (Mg_2+), ammonium (NH_4+), sodium ($Na+$), hydrogen ($H+$), aluminum (Al_3+), iron (Fe_2+ or Fe_3+), manganese (Mn_2+), copper (Cu_2+), and zinc (Zn_2+). All of these are essential plant nutrients. They move from the soil to plants in a process known as cation exchange. Cation exchange potential can be measured and is known as cation exchange capacity. The higher the number, the better the soil's ability to hold and transfer needed nutrients. (*See Water.*)

Soil Food Web

The second part of living soils is microbes, specifically bacteria and fungi that form the base of the soil food web. This is a complex population of diverse organisms that live in the soil and interact with each other.

Plants grown in living soil produce substances called exudates that are released out of roots to attract these microbes. Root exudates are full of carbon, which is needed by the bacteria and fungi. The fungi and bacteria, in turn, attract their predators, mostly nematodes and protozoa (think paramecium and amoebas).

Nematodes and protozoa graze on the bacteria and fungi attracted to the roots by the exudates, which include sugars, carbon, and other phyto products. The bacteria and fungi use these exudates as food because they cannot produce it themselves. Only chlorophyll-containing organisms can fix carbon using photosynthesis.

What is most important is that wastes produced as a result of this microbial grazing contain nitrogen in electrically charged forms that can move into plants. This is one way microbes help feed plants.

The second way is via specialized mycorrhizal fungi that enter roots and form a symbiotic relationship with the plant. Once these fungal-plant mycorrhizae are established, the fungi feed phosphorus, nitrogen, zinc, copper, and even water to their plant partners. In return, the fungi receive plant exudates.

The microbial diversity attracted by exudates results in a balance of populations, including pathogens, which keep each other in check.

Bacteria attracted to exudates produce a slime as a protective covering, which also glues soil particles together. Then they are literally woven together by fungal hyphae. What results is an aggregate of soil particles replete with pores in which microbes hide from predators and nutrients accumulate and are reservoirs for water and air.

Finally, the microbes attracted to the root system by the exudates in turn attract other, bigger life forms looking for a meal. These keep populations in balance while they travel through the soil and create more structure and excrete substances that are useful to plants.

Benefits of Living Soil

There are several benefits to using living soils to grow cannabis. First, and perhaps most important, the grower does not have to add chemical fertilizers. If made properly, all the nutrients that plants need will be in the soil, and there will be ample life to ensure these nutrients are made available to the plants.

Since it is the microbes that make the nutrients available to the plants, as long as there are microbes and there is enough organic matter for them, living soil can continue to be used from grow to grow.

This is quite an advantage. The addition of a bit of compost to refresh things between several grows should be all that is needed with a good living soil.

A second benefit to using living soils is that the soil food web tends to police itself. The diversity of microbes and micro and macro arthropods results in a delicate predator-prey balance. This is impossible when using synthetic chemicals, which alter or destroy the soil food web and thus its natural protections, leading to the use of more, and often more dangerous, chemicals.

A third benefit is that the gardener knows where the soil comes from and what is in it. When it's made on the premises, the blend's quality is assured.

Fourth, living soils should contain the proper fungi to form mycorrhizae with cannabis. Fortunately, there is only one, currently known as *Rhizophagus intraradices*. If purchasing living soil, make sure this is included. If it has not been added by the manufacturer, it can be added by the grower.

Fifth, cannabis grown in living soil smells and tastes better than that grown using nonsoil methods. Many claim they can taste chemical fertilizers. Others insist these affect the quality of the smoke. Not so with cannabis grown in living soils.

How to Get Living Soil

Living soils can either be made on the site or purchased. Each has its advantages and disadvantages. The end products should be pretty similar.

Obviously, buying living soil is the easier of the two. There is no need to expend time or energy sourcing ingredients and mixing them, just open the bag and use.

Making living soil requires ingredients in well-made compost to provide the living component, an additive such as biochar, coir, or pumice to provide drainage, and nutrient ingredients to feed the microbes so that they can feed the plants. These include alfalfa, crustacean meal, gypsum, kelp, rock dust, ground sea shell, and soy meal. All these ingredients should be organic; one reason to source materials is to know what is in it.

A Recipe For Living Soil

There are myriad recipes on the internet for making living soils. Some growers insist that indigenous microbes from locally sourced compost are better.

Composts are great for use in living soil mixes. Worm compost is even better. In fact, comparing vermicompost, as worm compost is called, to thermally made compost is like comparing cream to skim milk when fat is desired. Up to 30% of compost used for making living soil should be vermicompost. It complements the thermal compost. Why? Because vermicompost has higher concentrations of nutrients than regular composts. Properly made, it contains 10 times more potash, 5 times more nitrogen, 7 times more phosphate, 1.5 times more calcium, and 3 times more magnesium.

Vermicompost is made by feeding worms organic matter in specialized containers. They ingest it in their search for fungi, bacteria, and protozoa, their real food sources. Added to regular compost or soils, it enriches them.

Worms can also be added to regular compost piles, where they will add their excrement to the mix. One reason many recommend composting systems with bottoms open to the ground is to allow worms to move up into the pile when it cools. It also allows them to move away from too hot areas.

Many growers swear by putting worms into their living soil mixes. Worms eat mostly bacteria like those attracted to plant roots by exudates. They do not eat roots. They help create and maintain soil structure, which ensures aeration, water filtration, and water drainage. They also help feed the plant through their droppings.

DIY Living Soil

Before planting, let this mix sit for at least two weeks to enable the microbes in the compost to start cycling the nutrients.

Start by mixing:

　　1/3 sphagnum peat moss or coco coir
　　1/3 pumice, perlite, or lava rock
　　1/3 compost

For each cubic foot (0.02 m³) of the above, add:

    1/2 cup (118 ml) organic neem meal

    1/2 cup (118 ml) organic kelp meal

    1/2 cup (118 ml) crab meal

    1 cup (237 ml) glacial rock dust

    1 cup (237 ml) gypsum (calcium sulfate, $CaSO_4$)

    1 cup (237 ml) oyster shell flour

    1 cup (237 ml) basalt flour

This recipe can be adjusted to suit local prices and material availability. A vegan alternative to crab meal is alfalfa meal, and dolomite instead of oyster shell flour.

Keep Living Soil Alive

It is easy to kill life in the soil. The most obvious ways to accomplish this would be activities that deprive the soil life of oxygen, like compacting the soil or letting it get waterlogged. Much less obvious are the impacts of rototilling an outdoor grow or disturbing the soil of an indoor one.

The rule is to disturb the soil as little as possible. When the soil is tilled, the network of fungi that feeds plants and provides soil structure is broken and destroyed. The burrows and passages used by micro and macro arthropods and worms are also destroyed. Soil food web organisms are severely displaced and moved into new environments that are often not suitable for them, where they may miss symbiotic partners and proper foods. Most important, tilling can kill worms.

Once a garden bed is established, there is no good reason to till it. Nutrients and organic materials placed on the surface will be moved into the soil by members of the soil food web. Plants have no trouble moving roots through non tilled soil, which is why it is common to see plants growing up through pavements and driveways.

The same is true with container soil. The least amount of disturbance possible is the rule here, too. Having built up exudate carbon in it, having established good soil structure, and having the old roots serve as organic material all make sense. Not only should it be reused, but if possible, simply replant without disturbing the remnants of the last grow. New roots will find it easier to grow in the old root channels, and the right bacteria and fungi should be nearby in the old rhizosphere.

Mulches

Mulches do several things. They provide cover, which helps conserve water use. More important, they provide organic matter to soil and serve as a food source to the soil food web.

There are two kinds of mulches to use for growing soils indoors and outdoors: living and static mulches. Each adds to the soil to help grow better cannabis.

Living Mulches

Plants can serve as mulch. There are two kinds that make the best living mulches. The first, nitrogen-fixing mulches, or legumes, are mulches that take nitrogen from the air, which cannot be used by plants, and fix it so that it is available through the roots. When growing cannabis, nitrogen-fixing legumes shouldn't compete for light with the plants they are helping, so they should be pruned to stay out of the path of the crop plant's direct relationship with the sun.

Dutch White Clover

The second kind of living mulches is known as bioaccumulators. These plants can draw nutrients from the soil. These are released back when the plant dies and is decayed by the bacteria and fungi in the soil. The regenerative impact is obvious.

There are many plants a grower can use as a living mulch, but the most popular (especially for indoor gardens) and the easiest to obtain is Dutch white clover (*Trifolium repens*). This nitrogen-fixing legume is a very low grower. It forms dense mats of very low green growth so it does not interfere with cannabis growth. It acts as an annual indoors and a perennial outdoors.

There are reports that *Trifolium repens* is a bioaccumulator. It is said to accumulate phosphorus, one of the necessary elements for growth. Bioaccumulator or not, when it does, the accumulated nutrients that grew the clover are returned to the soil.

Every area is different in terms of invasive plants. For this reason, outdoor growers should consult their local agricultural agents to ensure a proper living mulch is used. Cannabis has enough problems, and there is no sense in being blamed for introducing an invasive. Some other common living mulches include alfalfa, cow peas, and vetch.

Outdoors, living mulches also serve as green manure. When the season is over, they are cut and left on top of the soil as fresh sheet compost or worked back into the soil, where they feed the food web microbes.

Static Mulches

Static mulches are not alive per se. They just used to be alive. They include things like straw, leaves, or stalks. Static mulches support soil food web life, slow water from evaporating, and sometimes act as barriers to pests. Static mulches are also great at keeping weed growth in check when applied thick enough.

Straw is covered with protozoa, which work their way into the soil and consume bacteria, ultimately releasing usable nitrogen. Thus straw is a great static mulch for growing cannabis, indoors or outdoors. Straw is available at feed stores as well as many grow supply stores. Just make sure to use straw and not hay, which contains seeds.

Composts, Compost Teas & Extracts

The same compost that is used to make living soil can also be used alone to freshen soil. Adding vermicompost makes it an even better mulch.

Compost mulch is so useful because it has a tremendous population of bacteria and fungi that solubilize the basic nutrients needed by plants. Compost also contains ample numbers of nematodes and protozoa. These consume the bacteria and fungi in the compost, thereby releasing and making available the nutrients that the bacteria and fungi held.

Compost can be made into living soils or mulch. There are many great books that discuss how to do this. Good composts can also be purchased, but it is important to know what's in them.

In either case, compost is used as one would use living and static mulches. Layer an inch (2.5 cm) or so onto the surface of the soil after each crop cycle. Both the life in the compost as well as the organic matter in it will be worked into the soil by the soil food web that utilizes it.

Compost Teas

Compost teas are liquid compost mixes. They are made by putting a relatively small amount of compost into water and growing the microbes, feeding them, and allowing them to grow over a few days.

The mixture is kept aerobic if properly made. The nutrients are designed to feed the compost's microbes released into the tea. The mixture is fermented using heavy aeration for 24 to 48 hours.

The Vital Garden Supply Tea Kit is a five gallon (19 l) plug-and-play brewer that comes with everything needed to make Vital Tea. The kit includes a five pound (2.25 kg) pouch of Vital Tea, one quart (1 l) of Vital Fish, and one pound (0.5 kg) of Vital Roots mycorrhizae, as well as an extractor bag and a pump to add oxygen to the brew.

The aeration of the tea provides the energy to strip the microbes from the compost. The oxygen should keep the mixture aerobic and free of harmful pathogens that live under anaerobic conditions. The added nutrients keep feeding the microbes as they multiply or grow.

The final brew should smell sweet, not sour, which would indicate unwanted anaerobic microbes. It is best to use within 24 hours because the microbes use up the oxygen and quickly turn it anaerobic. One gallon (3.75 l) of compost tea can be diluted up to five times or used straight.

The tea can be applied as a soil drench or sprayed on leaves. The microbes become part of the soil microbial biomass and coat leaves to outcompete pathogens for food, space, and entry locations.

DIY Compost Tea

Fill a five gallon (19 l) bucket with non chlorinated water or allow the chlorine to evaporate over 12 hours. Then add:

  1 to 2 cups (128 to 256 g) compost
  1 tablespoon (15 g) unsulphured blackstrap molasses*
  1 tablespoon (15 g) liquid kelp

There is no such thing as applying too much compost tea; it is not like using fertilizers and will not burn the plants. Instead, the process adds beneficial microbes to the soil. *Molasses can become pathogenic. Good alternatives include honey, refined cane sugar or syrup, and beet juice.

Compost Extracts

Compost extracts differ from compost teas. They are made by stripping the microbes from compost as one does when making tea, but nutrients are not added, and the process takes about 15 minutes.

These extracts don't have as much microbial life, but they are much quicker to make. Good compost will provide great benefits, and extracts will help keep soils alive and functioning.

Compost extractors can be made at home or purchased. A simple method is to wrap up compost in cheese cloth and knead it into the water for 15 minutes, or let it soak like a teabag for half an hour.

SOIL

A deep water culture system.   Photo: Courtesy of Current Culture H$_2$O

HYDROPONICS

Revised and expanded by Neil Mattson, PhD

Planting Mix versus Hydroponics

Both planting mixes and hydroponics have advantages and disadvantages. Both are capable of producing a high yield. Importantly, both provide a satisfying gardening experience.

Organic media such as bark, coir, compost, and peat moss all contain carbon, which can retain nutrients and make them available to the plant when they become less plentiful. This buffering action softens peaks and valleys. Many planting mixes are already enriched with nutrients using slow-release fertilizers or natural organic nutrients. If there is a large-enough space for the roots to obtain adequate nutrients for the plant, caretaking the garden is a more passive endeavor, save irrigation.

Once the plant runs out of nutrients and indicates a hint of deficiency, or if it is detected using tissue sampling, it is most likely that the nutrients will be supplied using nutrients dissolved in the irrigation water. This is called fertigation.

Fertigation (fertilizer + irrigation) is a hybrid between planting mixes and hydroponics, providing the advantages of both systems. Fertigation system containers are filled with non-nutritive media. The plants receive dissolved fertilizer every time they are watered. The media buffer the peaks and troughs, but provide little or no nutrients.

Hydroponics is a method of growing plants that supplies dissolved nutrients through the irrigation water, rather than the growing medium. Plants are either held anchored by their roots in an inert (chemically inactive) medium or held using a collar that supports the stem.

Hydroponic culture is a bit more exacting than using a planting mix because there is no organic media, which helps buffer nutrient imbalances and takes the edge off the peaks and troughs. Since hydroponic systems don't have this buffer, it is up to the gardener to keep the root conditions in a narrow range through more frequent monitoring and adjusting.

Hydroponics offers some advantages over planting mixes.

The systems usually take less physical labor to set up, and plants can be grown in smaller containers.

Plants grown hydroponically often produce higher yields, faster than those in planting media. This is the result of a more consistent root zone environment and high fertility conditions that make it easier for the roots to obtain nutrients.

Postharvest labor, such as removing the planting mix, cleaning, disinfecting, and replanting, are much easier.

Soil problems that sometimes affect container gardens such as overwatering and soggy conditions (poor air porosity) do not occur.

Nutrient and pH problems can be eliminated quickly in hydroponics, since the grower maintains tight control over the water-nutrient solution. When the solution is kept within the acceptable range, there is little chance of nutrient lockup.

Bio Harmonic Tonic is a bioharmonically active microbial mix in an easy-to-use odorless liquid ready to go to work for growth and bloom. This mix of biostimulants can be used indoors, outdoors, in greenhouses, soil, coco, hydroponics, and in conjunction with the grower's preferred nutrients. Bio Harmonic Tonic will run through any standard irrigation or drip system.

Many hydroponic systems reuse water in a recirculating loop. These systems are far more water and fertilizer efficient than planting mix or drip-to-drain systems. The nutrient solution drains from the root zone or containers and is captured in a reservoir and recirculated.

Many hydroponic systems reduce the amount of media required because after transplanting, much of the root system is suspended in water, mist, or reusable substrates such as clay beads, perlite, and rockwool.

Modern planting mixes are made with organic plant-based ingredients including peat moss, bark, coir (coconut husk), and rice husks as well as inert mineral-based components such as vermiculite and perlite. All these ingredients can also be used as planting media in fertigation and hydroponic systems.

Higher-quality planting mixes often include biologically active ingredients such as compost or vermicompost (worm castings and other worm-worked material), guanos, seed meals, ground rock, and animal by-products such as blood, bone, or feather meal. These mixes support plant growth for a month to six weeks or more with no additional fertilizers, depending on whether the roots have a sufficient area to grow and gather nutrients.

Some mixes are enriched using inorganic fertilizers. A few brands contain time-release fertilizers designed to support plants for several months. They require little or no additional fertilizer as long as the plants are grown in a large-enough container. For long-term vigorous-feeding crops such as cannabis, additional fertilizer supplementation is usually required over time to achieve highest yields.

Hydroponics is the method of gardening in which plants are supplied with nutrients through the water solution. Gardeners have a choice of systems to accomplish this.

Deep-water culture (DWC), drip, ebb and flow, nutrient film technique (NFT), and reservoir and wick are easy to construct, and most methods are also available as commercial units. Another kind of system, aeroponics, is also discussed here.

Systems vary in their complexity and the amount of care that they require. However, the simplicity of construction or difficulty of maintenance does not infer that the crop will be larger or of higher quality. The systems will be discussed in order of complexity.

Systems fall into one of two broad categories: passive or active. Passive systems such as reservoir or wick setups depend on capillary action to make water available to the plant. Active systems, including ebb and flow, nutrient film technique (NFT), and deep-water culture, use a pump to provide the plants water and nutrients.

Hydroponic Planting Media

Gardeners have a choice of hydroponic media (substrates). Substrates may be inorganic, meaning that they do not contain carbon molecules, do not deteriorate quickly, and have no buffering ability. Examples of inorganic/inert materials include perlite, vermiculite, or lightweight expanded clay aggregate (LECA), and rockwool.

Perlite and LECA are desirable materials because they can be used for long periods without breaking down. Nutrients must be continually supplied because these inert materials do not have many buffering/nutrient-holding properties.

Some substrate components are organic (carbon-based) materials like peat moss, coconut coir, aged bark, and wood chips. These organic substrate materials react with nutrients, retaining and releasing them to the plant. They deteriorate over time, compact, and become poorly drained. This breakdown usually takes a minimum of six months to a year, so it has virtually no impact on cannabis plants, which only grow three to six months.

Material in order of deterioration:
- Peat moss
- Pine bark
- Hardwood chips
- Coir
- Redwood bark

All these materials need to be replaced over time. In planting mixes, two or more substrate components are blended to ensure a good balance of water and air retention. The materials can also complement each other, for example, one common mix contains peat and perlite/vermiculite. Peat has good nutrient retention properties but not enough air porosity. The perlite ensures good air porosity even if the peat and vermiculite breaks down structurally over time.

Lightweight Expanded Clay Aggregate (LECA)

LECA is used as a medium in all types of hydroponic systems: reservoir, wick, deep-water culture, nutrient film, aeroponic, ebb and flow, and drip.

It is made by baking pure natural clay at 2200°F (1200°C) for three hours. The pellets expand into a lightweight, semi porous medium. It is pH neutral, so it doesn't affect the water-nutrient mix. The clay surface provides some retention of nutrients.

LECA provides both moisture and air to the roots using capillary action. The water-nutrient solution is wicked up along the pebble surface. Overwatering and root rot are eliminated due to the high air porosity that is provided by the space between the pebbles, which allows oxygen to get to the roots.

This planting media is permanent. It can be used for many years and is easy to clean and sterilize.

Grodan Improved stone wool growing media features an advanced wetting agent and optimized wool structure for uniform water content and EC distribution throughout the entire block, higher water-holding capacity, faster rooting in, improved steerability, and increased yield. They are available in all block sizes including the new Uni-Block.

Rockwool

Rockwool (also known as stone wool) is sterile and convenient to set up and remove. It holds together well and is easy to handle when following basic precautions. It is made by melting basalt and chalk and then spinning the molten rock mixture in a process very similar to making cotton candy. Long strands are formed and then processed into different shapes, textures, and sizes that vary from 1 inch (2.5 cm) propagation cubes up to 3 x 12 x 36 inch (7.5 x 30.5 x 92 cm) slabs. They are very lightweight.

Standard rockwool is constructed so that 18% of the space is reserved for air, even after the blocks have been irrigated to saturation. Water tension doesn't rise as the material becomes drier, so it is easy for the plant to absorb moisture until it is used up. These two characteristics mean that rockwool retains both water and air, so the roots' needs for oxygen and water are easily met. Rockwool is also made with different air- and water-holding properties.

All rockwool must be steeped in highly acidic water before use. Follow the manufacturer's instructions; some will only require a soak in pH 5.5 water. Adjust the water using pH

Down. Then flush the cubes or slabs with pH'd water or nutrient-water solution. They are now ready to use. From this point on, the rockwool has only a slight alkaline value. Adjust the pH of the nutrient-water solution so that it is no higher than 6.1 to buffer the medium's alkaline qualities.

Cubes range from 1 to 6 inch (2.5–15 cm) cubes. The two sizes of "starter cubes" used for cannabis propagation are the 2 x 2 x 1.5 inch (5 x 5 x 3.75 cm) unwrapped cubes and the 1.5-inch-square (3.75 cm) plastic-wrapped cubes that slow evaporation. The starter cubes can be used for rooting stem cuttings or starting seedlings. After rooting, they can be transplanted into larger rockwool cubes or other substrates. The 4-inch-square (10 cm) cubes are large enough to support small plants. For larger plants, 6 inch cubes can be used, or place the starter cubes on top of rockwool slabs or into other growing media.

Slabs are all 3 inches (7.5 cm) deep and 36 inches (91 cm) long and come in widths of 6, 8, 10, and 12 inches (15, 20, 25, and 30 cm). The 6 inch (15 cm) and the 8 inch (20 cm) wide slabs are by far the most popular sizes and are large enough to grow a 2 foot (60 cm) or larger diameter plant.

The slabs come wrapped in plastic, which should be left on to prevent algae and other infections. To allow for easy drainage, cut one-inch-long (2.5 cm) slits along about a half inch (1 cm) above the bottom of the slab. Slits should be made about every one foot (30 cm) on both sides of the slab. To transplant a cube to a slab, cut an X the size of the cube in the plastic on top of the slab. Fold up the corners of the X, and place the cube directly on. If needed, use kabob skewers to hold the cubes in place temporarily. The roots quickly grow into the slab and lock the cube in place. Drip irrigation emitters can be placed in the cube, about one inch (2.5 cm) from the plant stem.

Loose rockwool is another option. It is available with either water absorbent or repellent qualities. Using loose rockwool enables pots or other containers to be filled with the growing medium. Another benefit of using loose rockwool is that it can be customized to the medium to retain just the right amount of water for the setup.

Small, half inch rockwool (pellet) cubes are an easy-to-use alternative to loose rockwool. They can be poured into containers to provide a very root friendly medium.

Use care when working with rockwool. Its dust and fibers pose health risks. They can cause skin rash or lodge in lungs, causing temporary micro-ulcers. First, wet it down so fewer fibers become airborne. At the very least, wear a mask, long-sleeved clothing, and rubber gloves when working with dry rockwool. When working with loose rockwool, a bodysuit with a ventilator is the best protection. Wetting the rockwool before handling reduces dust substantially.

Historically, rockwool has been difficult to dispose of because it does not decompose, even when buried. Fortunately, rockwool is easy to reuse, and recycling programs for rockwool are emerging. The used rockwool can be recycled by being added to asphalt, pavement, commercial landscaping media, and so on. Although most home gardeners use it only once, commercial greenhouses growing roses and tomatoes often use the material for one to two years, until it starts to fall apart.

To prepare rockwool for reuse, it's best to let it dry out a bit, so plan on alternating two sets of blocks between crops. Cubes are easily removed, but it's easier to work with slabs while they are in place. First, pull out stems and roots or cut them off. Then sterilize the rockwool by irrigating it with a 3% hydrogen peroxide solution for 24 hours, using drippers or ebb and flow to deliver the solution to the material. After treating with the hydrogen peroxide solution for 24 hours, rinse the rockwool thoroughly. Any residual peroxide breaks down in water and oxygen.

Used rockwool is sometimes collected commercially to use for conservation and to prevent erosion. It is washed and chopped. This material can be used in containers or in trays. Rockwool is mostly used by cannabis growers only once, which is a waste, since it can be reused once it is chopped up for general gardening and conservation purposes. The roots thrive in the material, which is composed of different-sized pieces ranging from pebbles to about an inch (2.5 cm) long.

Perlite

Perlite can be used as an inert substrate in wick or Dutch bucket systems or as a component in planting mixes. Perlite is made by crushing volcanic rock into small particles and heating at high temperatures to create a lightweight expanded particle. Different-size classes of perlite can be purchased; coarse perlite is commonly used because of its high air porosity. Perlite is inert; it doesn't contribute to the substrate pH or nutrient retention. Perlite doesn't degrade over time, which makes it a useful addition to planting mixes to help maintain air supply to roots. Perlite can be reused by removing roots and debris and disinfecting. There are several methods that can be used:

- Place perlite in a shallow oven-safe container in an oven at 200°F (93°C); make sure the inside of the perlite heats up to 180°F (82°C) and holds that temperature for 30 minutes. Similar to rockwool, care must be taken with using perlite so that dust is not breathed in; wet down the perlite to reduce dust and wear a face mask when handling.
- Steam perlite for 15 minutes.
- Rinse with 3% hydrogen peroxide solution.
- Place in boiling water for 5 minutes.

For more information on perlite, see Soil.

Vermiculite

Vermiculite can be used as a substrate for cloning or as a component in planting mixes. Vermiculite begins as a flaky, naturally occurring mica-like mineral (hydrated magnesium iron aluminum silicate) that is ground and heated, which expands the layers to turn into a lightweight material. The alumina layers can retain some nutrients and also adsorb water. Unlike perlite, vermiculite has relatively high nutrient- and water-retention properties.

Coarse vermiculite can be used to increase the air porosity of substrates (though it will retain more water and less air than perlite). The layers of vermiculite compress over time, so it is not recommended to reuse. Before vermiculite is worked with, it should be wet down to reduce dust and a face mask should be worn.

For more information on vermiculite, see Soil.

Hydroponic Methods

Fertigation

Fertigation is the simplest form of hydroponics. The plants are grown in regular planting containers. They are filled with planting mix and watered by hand, through a drip system, or with a capillary mat. Nutrients are supplied using a nutrient-water solution that is usually applied at each watering.

Fertigation systems are frequently used in the nursery industry to grow potted plants. They are simple to construct and maintain and can easily be upscaled. Any medium can be used, but blends with organic components such as bark, peat moss, or coir are favored because they are inexpensive, have good buffering ability, and have good capillary action.

Potting-mix blends with bark, coir, peat moss, or vermiculite-perlite require less irrigation than other hydroponic media because they hold more water. If LECA or coarse perlite are used as the sole substrate, more irrigation cycles per day are required, and due to the lack of buffering, more careful attention to the pH of nutrient supply is necessary.

Passive Hydroponics Systems

Passive systems (reservoir, wick, and capillary mats) use capillary action to draw water up from the bottom of the container through the planting medium. As water is used, it creates "tension," which pulls water molecules up into the narrow spaces between substrate particles. It supplies plants with as much water as they need. These systems don't use pumping, so they are less susceptible to leakage.

The advantages of reservoir and wick systems over traditional raised beds or containers outdoors cannot be overemphasized. They save tremendous amounts of water because none is lost draining below the root level and very little is evaporated from the unit, unlike uncovered systems. This leaves the environment without fertilizer overload and inappropriate hydration in some areas.

No fertilizer is lost by draining into the environment, since it is provided in the water solution. This represents a tremendous financial saving while doing less harm to the environment. Units like these might be the most sustainable solution when growing in forests, deserts, or other non agricultural areas.

Active Hydroponics Systems

Active systems use pumps to move water-nutrient solutions to the plants so that the root zone environment is refreshed by a solution that hasn't been depleted of nutrients and oxygen. There are many types of active systems, but most of them fall into one of five categories: deep-water culture, drip, ebb and flow, nutrient film, and aeroponic systems. These systems require pumping water, and some can be more prone to leaking, so they must be monitored.

When selecting which type of hydroponic system to set up, one should consider several factors: cost, yield, space use efficiency, and level of maintenance. Some systems are easier for smaller plants at higher density, while others are more appropriate for large plants. The choice of substrate and system will also influence what type of fertilizer is used.

In systems that use planting mixes with good nutrient retention (peat, coir, or compost), both conventional and organic fertilizers may be used, as the substrate offers good buffering and can foster greater microbial activity. In hydroponic systems it's difficult to use organic fertilizers because they lead to the development of biofilm (sludge coating surfaces from microbes feeding off the carbon sources), which coats roots, clogs tubing or emitters, and complicates microbe-mediated breakdown of complex organic compounds, turning them into plant-available nutrients.

Passive Systems
The Reservoir System

The reservoir system is a passive system that is by far the easiest system to set up and maintain. Plants are grown in ordinary plant containers of the chosen size. The containers are placed in a tray-reservoir that has walls 4–6 inches (10–15 cm) high.

The containers are filled with clay pellets, called lightweight expanded clay aggregate (LECA), also sometimes called hydroton. Or the bottom third of the container is filled with LECA (to ensure good drainage) and the top portion is filled with a hydroponic mix such as vermiculite-perlite, or planting mixes with coir or peat moss, or even a non hydro– planting mix. The container is placed in the tray and sits directly in a hydroponic nutrient-water solution, with about 20–25% of the container immersed in the water. A one foot (30 cm) tall container should sit in 3 inches (7 cm) of water.

The water in the system is circulated using a small pump or aerated using an air pump or bubbler. This prevents stagnation of the water. The water temperature is maintained at about 72°F (22°C) using an aquarium heater, which ensures strong root and plant growth, even if the air temperature is a bit cooler. Some experts recommend lower temperatures to maintain higher dissolved oxygen levels 64–68°F (18–20°C).

This may be the most inexpensive system and the fastest one to set up, and is an excellent technique for use indoors as well as outdoors. The container has its own limited reservoir but can be attached to a remote reservoir as well. The water level is maintained using a float valve.

Make sure to use a light-colored, opaque, plastic cover over the tray to prevent rain from entering and to keep the roots cool. The cover is also important to exclude light, which encourages algae growth.

This technique can be adapted so that containers have their own internal reservoirs, rather than external trays. A reservoir overflow drain can be made in a container without holes by drilling holes about 20% from the bottom.

Buckets with gauges are available commercially and are the better option if just a few are being used. To make them, holes are drilled in a plastic tube to allow water to enter and exit freely. It is placed vertically in the container and affixed with silicon glue. Or pebbles can be placed around it to hold it vertically. A thin wooden or plastic rod with a cork on the bottom is affixed using silicon glue. A bamboo stake works well for this. The stake is placed in the tube. The cork will float, pushing the rod up to indicate water level. Mark the rod so it shows maximum desirable levels. A small tube attached to a pump or siphon is inserted to drain water from the pot.

A different version can be made using a piece of transparent flexible plastic tubing. The tubing is inserted into a hole near the bottom of the container and silicon glue is used to prevent leaks. The tube is attached vertically to the side of the container so that it indicates its water level. To drain water, change the tube's position. With tubing, several containers can be connected to a single reservoir regulated by float valves.

Setting Up a Reservoir System
Equipment
- LECA
- pH test meter or pH test paper
- EC or ppm meter
- Planting containers
- Styrofoam board heat barriers
- Tray with walls of the appropriate height (4–6 inches, 10–15 cm)
- Hydroponic nutrient solution
- Tiny submersible pump
- Air pump and bubbler
- Aquarium heater
- Tray cover
- Remote reservoir (optional)
- Float valve (optional)

Steps
1. Enough clay beads (LECA) or large-size perlite is obtained to fill the containers.
2. A Styrofoam board is placed under the tray to provide a temperature barrier between the floor and garden.
3. The tray is positioned.
4. The containers are placed in the tray.
5. The LECA is poured into the containers.
6. The containers are watered from the top to get started, making sure the planting medium is thoroughly moistened.
7. The nutrient-water solution is mixed and adjusted using meters to test the EC or

ppm and pH of the solution.

8. A small air pump with a bubbler is used to add oxygen to the water.

9. If the room temperature gets cool, it may cool the water too much. If this happens, an aquarium heater is added to the tray.

10. Outdoors, use a sheet of white/black polyethylene (white on the outside and black on the inside, often called "panda plastic") or other opaque cover to place over the tray. The cover keeps light from getting into the nutrient-water solution, where it would promote algae growth. The white cover also keeps the roots cool. The cover can be reversed to passively heat the reservoir with sunlight.

11. Optional accessories: water reservoir regulated by a float valve. The water level of this system should be maintained at a fairly stable level. As the plants grow, they will use larger quantities of water, so it will have to be replaced more frequently as the garden proceeds to flowering. With an external reservoir, the system is automated and does not have to be serviced as often.

The Wick System

The wick system is inexpensive to construct and easy to set up and maintain. The planting container is held above a reservoir. Both ends of braided nylon rope hang from holes in the bottom of the container into a reservoir filled with water-nutrient solution.

The principle that drives this system is capillary action, the same chemistry that draws water up a napkin. As the water is removed from the wick, the water molecules above draw neighboring molecules toward them to maintain the electrical charge and ultimately equalize water tension. As a result, the wick maintains moisture by drawing up water as needed.

The wick is made from braided nylon rope. The diameter of the rope increases with the size of the container.

An ordinary nursery container, a bucket,

The bottom of a kiddie pool wicking system.
Photo: George Bianchini

Container diameter	Rope diameter
Up to 6" (15 cm)	1/4" (6 mm)
8–9" (20–22 cm)	3/8" (1 cm)
12–15" (30–38 cm)	5/8" (1.5 cm)
15"+ (38 cm+)	¾–1" (2–2.5 cm)

or even a soil bag can be used. Install the wicks before the container is filled with planting mix. They should be long enough to stretch from the bottom of the reservoir through the bottom or side hole of the container, then exit the hole on the other side and run down to the bottom of the reservoir. Each container should receive two wicks at 90° angles.

Keeping the holes in the container small makes it difficult for roots to penetrate to the reservoir. Keeping the roots from growing down the wick into the reservoir may be a matter of convenience (makes clean-up easier at the end). However, once the roots hit the water, both their growth and the growth of the plant spurts because the roots now have free access to water and nutrients.

The wick system is self-regulating; the amount of water delivered depends on the amount lost through evaporation or transpiration. With the wick system, the reservoir is the most important to check; there is no need to monitor the containers for moisture. As long as the reservoir has water, the plants are being watered. Individual containers should be inspected as well.

A number of different media can be used as planting mixes for wick systems, but virtually any planting mix can be used, since the particle size is generally small enough to draw water through capillary action. Using an enriched planting mix has the advantage of providing the plants with a nutrient-rich base that can be supplemented with a water-nutrient solution. If the medium does not seem to be drawing water and is too dry, adding 20% vermiculite to the mix will add drawing capacity. Media such as LECA or coarse perlite cannot be used, as they will not allow for enough capillary action to draw water from the wick.

A mix consisting of half each vermiculite and perlite provides a non-nutritive medium that is easy to work with, has a nice consistency, and draws water well. The fine grades of both ingredients do not allow the roots as much air, especially in large containers. Use coarser grades of both. Using vermiculite-perlite allows the grower to have complete control over the nutrients being supplied to the plants. Adding 10–20% worm castings or compost increases the microbial life and provides a substrate for them to thrive. Their symbiotic relationship with the roots increases plant vigor and growth.

Each medium has a maximum saturation level (which is simply a function of the particle size of the planting mix or substrate). Beyond that point, an increase in the number of wicks does not increase the moisture level.

Wick systems are easy to construct. The wick should extend from the container to the bottom of the reservoir. Supports keep the containers above the level of the water in the tray. Cement, untreated wooden blocks, plastic pallets, or other plastics make good supports.

The containers are placed on the supports, with the wicks touching the bottom of the tray. The tray is filled with nutrient-water solution. It is replaced as it evaporates or is absorbed by the medium through the wick.

It is easy to construct variations of wick and reservoir systems using two planting containers such as five gallon (19 l) buckets. One container should fit inside the other. The bottom outer container, which has no drainage holes, will be the reservoir. It is fitted with a support on the inside bottom that keeps the upper container from fitting tightly into the lower container, creating a hard-to-release vacuum. It also allows for an ample water reservoir size. A block of wood or Styrofoam can be used for this purpose.

If the unit is to be used outdoors, holes are drilled in the outer container just below the level where the inner container will rest. These overflow holes prevent waterlogging of the upper container from overwatering should it rain. Placing a cover (such as panda plastic) over the container also prevents rainwater from entering.

The inner container is fitted with wicks, placed in the reservoir container, and filled with planting mix. Using these closed systems rather than containers with bottom drain holes that let water escape conserves water and requires less frequent irrigation. The unit can be fitted with a water-level gauge, described above.

It is easy to automate individual buckets so they are self-watering. On a level surface tubes connect several bottom containers to a reservoir regulated by a float value. The valve is adjusted to close when the water reaches a height about half an inch (1.25 cm) below the bottom of the growing (inner) containers. On a hilly or terraced surface each container is fitted with a float valve.

The automated wick system requires no power. Water siphons into the growing buckets as needed. To get the siphon started, the valve container is primed and raised above the level of the individual trays. Water flows from the valve to the plant trays as a result of gravity. Once the containers have filled and displaced air from the tubes, the water siphons automatically.

If the containers are not getting a sufficient supply of water, either the substrate is too coarse, wick diameters are too small, or the water level in the reservoir is too low.

A simple solution might be to add a tiny water pump to each outer container that periodically delivers water to the top container. Timing and duration depend on how long the planting media stays moist.

A simple system can be devised using a plastic kiddie pool, flexible planting bag, and a shipping pallet or plastic trays. Untreated wood, cement blocks, or plastic racks can also be used. Shipping pallets should be made from untreated wood or not used.

The pallet is placed in the pool. Wicks are installed in the container(s) and placed so that they sit firmly on the pallet. The pool is filled with a water-nutrient solution to just below the bottom of the pots. The wicks move the water to the containers automatically as needed.

Options to supercharge this system are aerating the reservoir water using air pumps for bubblers and a small circulation pump. To get more water to the container, a small pump drawing water from the bottom container is set on a repeating timer to provide small amounts of water periodically.

Another iteration of this is to use either a large-diameter grow bag installed with wicks or a second plastic kiddie pool filled with planting mix.

Reservoir and wick systems are available from several manufacturers. They require no moving parts and are reliable, although much more expensive than homemade ones, which are simple to make. Although these systems are denigrated to an extent by industry because they are so simple to construct and maintain, they supply all the plants' needs and are efficient producers. In addition, they are much easier to care for than systems that move water from one container to another.

Setting Up a Wick System

Equipment

- One tray
- Support for containers: untreated or heat-treated wood (not pressure treated), bricks, concrete blocks, or wood block wire trays
- Appropriate diameter nylon rope
- Planting containers
- Tape or glue
- Planting mix
- pH test meter or pH test paper
- EC or ppm meter
- Hydroponic nutrient solution
- Submersible water pump or aquarium air pump and bubbler(s)
- Aquarium heater
- Tray cover
- Remote reservoir (optional)
- Float valve (optional)

Steps

1. The tray is placed in the grow space.
2. The containers are raised about four to six inches (10–15 cm) from the bottom of the tray. Plastic shipping pallets, untreated wood blocks, bricks, and concrete blocks all work well.
3. The distance from the bottom of the tray through the container and back to the tray bottom is measured. The nylon rope is cut and the ends sealed.
4. The rope is placed into containers and taped or glued in place. Once the medium is added, it won't move.
5. The containers are filled with planting medium.
6. The containers are placed on supports. The wicks are checked to make sure that they hang down to the bottom of the water tray.
7. The tray is filled with nutrient-water mix and adjusted using meters to test the EC or ppm and pH of the solution.
8. The containers are watered from the top to get started, making sure that the planting medium and wicks are thoroughly moistened.
9. A small submersible pump is placed in the water tray for circulation. Or an aquarium air pump can be used to bubble air to prevent stagnation.
10. If the room temperature gets cool, it may cool the water too much. An aquarium heater is used to keep the water at 72°F (22°C).
11. A sheet of white/black polyethylene or other opaque cover is placed over the tray. The cover keeps light from getting into the nutrient-water solution, where it would promote algae growth.

12. Optional accessories: water reservoir regulated by a float valve. The water level of this system should be maintained at a fairly stable level. As the plants grow, they will use larger quantities of water, so it will have to be replaced more frequently as the garden proceeds to flowering.

Capillary Mats

Capillary mats are about a quarter inch (6 mm) thick. They are made from soft polyester covered with opaque polyethylene perforated with small holes. They have great wicking ability and are used in subirrigation systems. When containers are placed on the mat, it compresses. This indent is below the level water travels, creating a little puddle in which the bottom of the container sits.

A table is covered with polyethylene plastic to create a water barrier. It has a slight slope, about 2.5%, 1 inch per 40 inches (2.5 cm per 100 cm). The capillary mat is placed over it. The water in the mat puddles around the depression made by the container and is drawn through the media by capillary action, in the same way a tissue draws up water. Containers draw water only as it is needed so that plants are neither over- nor underwatered. Only containers with drainage holes on the bottom should be used.

The mats are kept filled with water. A small pump delivers water from a reservoir. The water flows through the mat and drips back into the reservoir.

Capillary mats are effective in irrigating containers up to about 10 inches (25 cm) high. They are simple to maintain and a very efficient method of using both nutrients and fertilizers.

Active Systems

Ebb & Flow Systems (Flood Systems)

Ebb and flow are the systems that most people think of when hydroponics is mentioned. The containers, rockwool cubes, or just the medium is held in a tray. Its depth depends on the height of the planting beds or containers.

A pump is used to flood the tray with nutrient solution to a depth of half the height of the media and then allowed to drain back to the reservoir. The planting media holds enough moisture between irrigations to meet the needs of the plant.

Ebb and flow systems are easy to construct and promote vigorous growth, and their maintenance is fairly low. They can be used to irrigate rockwool cubes or any of the hydroponic planting media.

Equipment
1. Tray to hold rockwool, media, or containers
2. Rockwool or planting containers
3. Planting medium: rockwool, bark, coir, LECA, peat moss, perlite, planting mix, or vermiculite-perlite
4. Short-term timer

5. Float valve to maintain water level (optional)
6. Submersible pump
7. Tubing
8. Additional reservoir servicing the tray(s) (optional)

Several ebb and flow gardens can be plumbed to a central reservoir using a pump for each garden. The lost water is automatically replaced from a reserve reservoir or plumbing line. Fertilizer can be added automatically using a controller.

Steps

To construct a simple four by four foot (1.2 x 1.2 m) manual ebb and flow system, use a tray with sides six inches (15 cm) or higher.

1. A flexible one half to one inch (12–25 mm) tube is attached to the bottom of one side of the reservoir to drain it. It should be on a side that will be easily accessible. Another flexible tube is connected near the top of the tray, draining to the reservoir. This is the overflow protection tube that prevents flooding caused by a malfunctioning pump or a jammed drain hose. This is a necessity.

2. Eight inch (20 cm) tall planting containers are filled with one of the recommended hydroponic media and placed in the tray. Or the tray itself can be filled with planting media. Loose or cubed rockwool can also be used. Small plants use four inch (10 cm) cubes. If the plants are to be larger, six inch (15 cm) cubes can be used, or a rockwool slab can be laid down first and the cube set on top.

3. Garden irrigation requirements differ because of planting medium, garden temperature, and size of the plants. It is hard to overwater with LECA, bark, perlite, and rockwool, so the garden can be scheduled to irrigate several times a day. Each time the water creates a vacuum in the media, drawing in new oxygen-laden air. Peat moss and planting mix do not require as much irrigation because the media hold larger quantities of water. The scientific way to determine whether the plants need irrigation is with the use of a soil moisture meter. It can measure water availability at different heights in the container.

    a. LECA should be soaked in water to moisten before first use. LECA doesn't hold much water, but it readily wicks it up as needed.

    b. For other media being used for the first time, fill the tray to half the height of the media. Add more nutrient solution to maintain the level until the medium is saturated. Drain it into the container, using the flexible tube. Aim for half the height during standard watering. Not as much drains back in as was poured out; some water is retained by the medium.

4. Automating ebb and flow systems is not difficult. The garden is raised above the reservoir. A tube attached to a submersible pump in the reservoir lifts water into the tray. The pump is controlled by a short-cycle timer. The timer should be set to fill the tray with the desired amount of water. A float valve protects against overflow. A float

valve should be preset to stop the flow at the desired depth of the water. The tray's drain hose returns the water to the reservoir.

5. When the pump turns on, water should flow into the tray faster than it drains. This is accomplished by using a hose that drains slower than the pump fills the tray. The recirculating water dissolves dried salts and freshens the water in the medium. When the pump turns off, the water continues to drain back into the container from the tray. Establish the "on" time for the repeating timer by observing how long it takes to reach half the height of the planting mix.

Ebb and flow system kits and components are readily available commercially. The ready-made systems are convenient and reliable and have ironed out all the kinks that a home grower is likely to encounter. Components to make a DIY system are available at hardware stores and indoor garden centers.

Drip Systems

Drip irrigation works by delivering water-nutrient solution slowly to the planting medium or soil using irrigation tubing and drip emitters installed above the root zone of each plant. Emitters are manufactured to deliver water at a set rate, such as one half to one gallon (2–4 l) per hour. The system consists of a submersible pump that delivers water from a reservoir to an irrigation tube that stretches the length of the garden. Quarter inch (6 mm) spaghetti tubing is connected to the central tubing using connectors that are punched or drilled into the main line. Emitters are connected to the end of these smaller tubes and staked above the planting medium. Each container or rockwool cube is serviced by its own emitter(s). Different-sized plants can each get the appropriate amount of water by using drippers with different flow rates or a different number of emitters per container.

Drip rings deliver water in a circular pattern rather than in one spot. They are a more efficient way to irrigate and are especially useful with LECA, large-sized perlite, and other media. With the large particle size of LECA and other media, there is less horizontal movement of water in a container, so with a simple dripper the water does not spread evenly in the container. Almost all hydroponic drip systems recirculate the water and include a reservoir that catches the drain water.

A submersible pump is placed in the reservoir. A tube carries the water up to the planting tray. Spaghetti tubing, one for each container, is attached to the larger tube. The steady stream of water is released and forms a film as it trickles through the rocks. The roots receive plenty of oxygenated water, and the spaces between the rocks provide ample contact with air.

Drip emitters are used with soil, bark, coir, LECA, peat moss, perlite, planting mix, rockwool mini cubes, and vermiculite-perlite.

Constructing a Drip System (Method One)

Equipment
- Table or frame with sturdy top such as half inch (1.25 cm) plywood
- Corrugated plastic such as polycarbonate roof panels (available in home improvement stores)
- Trough to catch drain water from corrugated plastic, made from a rain gutter
- Rockwool
- Planting containers
- Bucket for use as a temporary reservoir
- Submersible pump used to supply water to the drip emitters
- Distribution tubing (often half inch [1 cm] inner diameter) to distribute water from the pump to the garden area
- Spaghetti tubing (often about a quarter inch [6 mm]) to supply water from the main distribution tube to each container
- Drip emitters
- Quarter inch (6 mm) barbed connectors from main distribution line
- Hole punch tool
- Reservoir or catchment bucket
- Sump pump
- Short-term timer
- Pressure regulator (optional)

Steps
1. A drip emitter system is easy to make using a sturdy table or by building a wooden frame such as two sawhorses. Frames can also be made using steel shelving or PVC pipe. When using a frame, place a piece of half inch (1.25 cm) thick plywood for use as the top. Arrange a slight slope of 2.5 inches (i.e., 1 inch in 40 inches, or 2.5 cm in one meter), so the water drains easily from one end.
2. Place a piece of corrugated plastic (such as polycarbonate roof panels) over the tabletop, so the water runs along the troughs to drain. Install a drainage trough along the side of the table or frame. The trough is made using plastic rain gutters. Place a holding tank at the end of the trough to catch the draining water.
3. Place the containers or rockwool on the corrugated plastic.
4. Set up the drip system using a temporary reservoir such as a plastic bucket.
5. Attach tubing to the submersible pump.
6. Place the pump into the temporary reservoir and install the distribution tubing across the center of the garden. Typically a half inch (1.25 cm) inner diameter distribution tubing is used. Installations with a very large number of containers may need wider-diameter tubes or multiple distribution lines connected to a larger-diameter PVC.

7. Install the spaghetti tubing. First measure the length of spaghetti line required, and cut the piece off the roll. Push the connector into the spaghetti tubing. Push the emitter into the other end of the line. Punch a hole in the main tubing using the tool sold with the drip equipment, or drill an appropriately sized hole. Push the connector into the main distribution tube and place the emitter into the rockwool or container. Repeat with each cube or container.

8. More sophisticated systems use pressure regulators to ensure uniform flow rate and filters to remove sediment, which can otherwise clog drip emitters. These options are highly recommended.

9. Automated systems continually measure water pH and nutrients and make adjustments as needed (dosing in acid if pH goes above a threshold or adding concentrated fertilizer stocks if EC dips). If not done automatically, EC and pH should be measured three times a week.

10. To determine how large a reservoir is required, run the system with the emitters draining directly onto the plastic. Measure how much water is emitted in one minute. If possible, use 100 times that amount. If that is too large a reservoir for some reason, use the biggest reservoir possible. The smaller the reservoir, the more maintenance that is required.

11. Place a catchment bucket at the end of the table to hold water that pours from the drainage gutter. Place a sump pump in the catchment bucket. Or devise a drain system that can return the water directly to the reservoir.

12. Place the pump in the reservoir. Use a short-term timer to turn the drip system on for several minutes at a time multiple times during the day. The system is ready to go.

Constructing a Drip System (Method Two)

Equipment
- Sturdy table or frame with top that will hold a four by eight foot (1.2 x 2.4 m) tray
- Five plastic gutters with caps, four cut to eight feet (2.4 m), one cut to four feet (1.2 m)
- Silicon glue and/or fasteners
- Reservoir (30–60 gallon / ~100–225 l)
- Submersible pump (up to 100 gallons / ~400 liters per hour)
- Day timer
- Short-term timer
- Main tubing
- Spaghetti tubing
- 33 connectors to spaghetti tubing
- 33 drip emitters (one gallon / four liters per hour)

- 32 rockwool cubes measuring 4 x 4 x 4 inches (10 x 10 x 10 cm)
- Large measuring cup

Steps

This is a design for a system that is on a four by eight foot (1.2 x 2.4 m) table.

1. Use a table or frame with a sturdy top.
2. Raise one end of the table one and a half inches (13 cm) or three quarters of an inch (2 cm) of width to facilitate drainage.
3. Outline each foot (30 cm) of the table's four foot (1.2 m) width. Position an eight foot (2.4 m) gutter in the middle of each marked foot. Or use eight four foot (1.2 m) gutters that cut across the table's width.
4. Fasten the gutters to the table using silicon glue. If that isn't sturdy enough, use metal fasteners and then seal the fastening with silicon glue. Close the upper end of the gutters using caps.
5. Attach a gutter to the table or frame to catch drainage.
6. Place the submersible pump with a tube attached into the reservoir and bring the tube up to the garden.
7. Attach pump to the timers. Set the day timer to turn on at the same time as the lights. Plug the short-term timer into the day timer. Set the short-term timer to initially turn on every three hours for 15 minutes. As plants require more water, increase the frequency of irrigation.
8. Place eight rockwool cubes in each gutter. This allows for spacing of one plant per square foot (0.09 m²).
9. Measure drip line length, and cut the lines.
10. Attach connectors and emitters to each of the 33 spaghetti drip lines, and connect them to the main line.
11. Attach an emitter to each of the cubes.
12. The spare emitter is placed in the system to monitor the irrigation system. Place it in a large measuring cup or pitcher to get an exact reading of how much solution is being emitted each day. This water (or the reservoir) can also be used to monitor nutrient solution pH, EC, and temperature.

Nutrient Film Technique (NFT)

The nutrient film technique (NFT) uses a film of water that is constantly moving around the roots. This technique is used in many commercial greenhouses to cultivate fast-growing vegetables such as lettuce and basil, with little to no planting medium.

Most cannabis NFT systems use net pots sitting in covers over flat-bottomed, ribbed, heavy plastic trays that are 4 to 6 inches (10–15 cm) wide and tall. A film of water passes slowly over the flat bottom. A slight slope to the tray of 1 inch per 40 inches (2.5 cm per one meter) ensures sufficient water movement and that the roots stay bathed in a freshly oxygenated nutrient solution. The roots dangle from the containers and thrive in the moist air created by the closed environment. The plants may need occasional top watering until the roots reach the water at the bottom of the tray. Within a short time the roots reach the water in the bottom of the gutter and thrive in the flowing oxygenated nutrient solution.

The roots grow in a covered tray irrigated by a shallow, slow-flowing nutrient solution, so good aeration is essential for fast healthy growth. Aerating the water in the reservoir is achieved by using water circulation, air bubblers, and water sprays that come in contact with air.

NFT systems can be enhanced with misters that spray water in all directions. The highly oxygenated spray keeps the humidity high in the air space above the flow of nutrients. Some growers will place air stones in the NFT trays to be sure that the roots can have an adequate supply of oxygen for gas exchange. Remember that good air in the root zone helps plants take up nutrients faster and easier.

Reservoirs that hold large volumes of water keep the pH and nutrient levels more stable than small reservoirs.

NFT systems are best for growing small plants rather than large ones. Large plants have prodigious root growth that tends to eventually block the water channel. They don't supply a lot of support for the stem. With small plants this isn't a problem, but it causes large plants to tip and fall over if they are not supported.

Another type of NFT system uses planting containers that are filled with LECA. The containers are placed either in a planting tray or in channels wider than the containers. The recirculating system uses a drip hose with no emitters attached to deliver a continuous stream of water from a reservoir to the tops of the containers. The water flows over the pebbles in a thin film so that the roots have access to both water and oxygen. Should the roots grow out of the containers, they are embraced by a stream of water flowing in the channel with a drain placed at a depth of one or two inches (2.5–6 cm).

Aeroponics

Aeroponic systems spray an atomized mist of water-nutrient solution directly on the roots. The tiny droplets of fast-moving water are well aerated, so they constantly replenish the roots with oxygen. The nutrient-water spray also delivers nutrients in an absorbable form that encourages extremely fast growth.

Aeroponics systems are commonly used for cloning, and many cloning machines that use this technique are available. However, larger aeroponic systems are sometimes used to grow plants through ripening.

In both cloning and larger aeroponic systems, the plants are sometimes held in small baskets, usually two and a half to five inches (6.5–12.5 cm) in diameter, and filled with rockwool or LECA. With other versions a neoprene plug holds the stems. The roots hang free. The roots or containers are set into a tube or tray inside with a pump, which produces a high-pressure 50–60 micron mist that covers the roots.

Aeroponic systems spray a mist of water-nutrient solutions directly on the roots.
Courtesy of AEssenseGrows

A plastic storage container with cutouts in the cover can be modified to use as an aeroponic unit.

Use a pump that puts out enough pressure to produce a fine spray. Less powerful pumps result in a coarser spray. Use a short-term timer to set the pump to spray for a minute and then rest for three.

The roots grow down to the bottom of the container and then continue growing. For the water to drain, place the tube or container at a 2.5° angle, or 1 inch per 40 inches (2.5 cm in one meter) of length. If the root growth is too prolific and clogs the water so that it has trouble draining, increase the angle.

The drain can be raised up from the bottom of the container two to three inches (5–7.5 cm) so that roots have a water reservoir in case the electricity goes out or mist nozzles clog.

Aeroponic gardens can produce large yields and speed up growth and maturation time. The problem is that there is little room for error. Should the spray stop or the misters malfunction (they can clog easily with accumulated salts and need to be periodically checked and cleaned with a weak acid), the plants go down in a matter of hours. For this reason, gardeners use small, reliable aeroponic clone units, but few venture to grow plants to maturity using this technique.

Deep water culture systems encourage prolific root growth and can produce high-yielding plants. These roots were grown using a Current RDWC system from Current Culture H₂O at High Latitude Farms in Hood River, Oregon. Photo: Courtesy of Current Culture

Deep-Water Culture (DWC)

DWC systems keep the roots bathed in an oxygenated water-nutrient solution. The system consists of a submerged container that holds the plant stem in place above the water level. The roots hang down into the oxygenated water. The roots have total access to water, nutrients, and oxygen, which is dissolved in the water. This promotes extremely fast growth and high yields.

DWC systems require sensitivity to the plants on the part of the grower. Unlike planting mixes that buffer nutrient imbalances, the DWC environment is instantly affected by changes to the water. The result of these changes, helpful or harmful, become apparent very quickly. The pH/EC should be monitored and adjusted several times a week, as these conditions can change quickly. DWC systems with a larger volume of water per plant will add some buffering in rapid pH/EC and temperature changes simply due to the large volume of water. Experienced gardeners can "read the plant" to determine its health and needs.

The common denominator of all DWCs is a container that holds water that the roots hang down into. A container (such as a net pot, or plastic container with numerous holes for roots to grow out) nests snugly into a hole in the lid/float, which holds a hydroponic planting medium such as clay pellets or rockwool cubes over the water.

The reservoir water-nutrient solution is aerated using an aquarium pump connected to air stone bubblers, circulating water, or creating a waterfall.

DWC systems are manufactured as stand-alone containers, as well as sets attached to a central reservoir. Other models circulate the water using tubes that connect the containers to each other. The plants are held in small open-grilled containers partially above the water. However, if the grower is only planning to make one piece or even just a few, it is easier, more convenient, and often cheaper to buy the ready-made. Of course, some people enjoy tinkering, and for those people this project yields tangible results.

Outdoor Hydroponics

Plants grow very well in hydroponic systems outdoors when there is ample sunlight and not extreme temperatures. Unlike soil systems, where the roots are in a dynamic environment that sometimes limits their access to water and nutrients, the hydroponic environment ensures access to adequate quantities. Hydroponics also allows growth where the soil is not good for crops; poorly drained, too rocky, too alkaline, or poisoned.

Hydroponic systems are water savers because water does not seep below the root level and drain away, taking it beyond useful bounds. Also, virtually no water is lost to evaporation, since the growing units are enclosed on top. The plant utilizes almost all the water going into the reservoir.

Hydroponic units can also be used to control root temperature, which can compensate for poor air temperature. A water heater keeps the roots warm during cool weather. Water chillers are used to cool the water during hot weather.

Plants can grow quite large outdoors if grown when there is not a short day length to initiate flowering. To grow a large plant hydroponically, a large container is required. The largest commercial container is 16 gallons (60.5 l). It supports a plant with a diameter of about eight feet (2.5 m). Larger units can be made using plastic storage containers, tarp-lined soft containers, kiddie pools, water troughs, or tanks.

Most hydroponic systems can be used, including wick and reservoir systems, which need no power.

The pumps for recirculating drip, deep-water culture, and ebb and flow systems can be powered using a small portable solar panel. The panel supplies the pump power during the sunny part of the day when the plants require more water (plants transpire little water at night).

Smaller hydro units can also be used outdoors. Even a five gallon (19 l) unit can support a large plant. The problem with smaller units becomes apparent when the plants grow larger. On warm sunny days they quickly use all the water in the reservoir. This water must be replaced as needed, or the roots and plant will suffer irreparable damage.

One solution to this problem is an auxiliary or central reservoir that feeds the hydroponic unit(s) on demand. In a homemade system this could be a 55 gallon (208 l) barrel. Many commercial units have integrated reservoirs into the system.

Plant support often becomes a problem with smaller hydroponic units. The root system is held in a small amount of planting medium, leaving the unit top heavy.

Planting holes are easily converted into hydro units using a pool liner to hold the water. The walls will need to be braced so that they don't collapse.

Pea-sized lava chips or inexpensive gravels available locally are often good choices as planting media for outdoor hydroponic systems. They are low cost and heavier than clay pellets, so they provide more mass to support a heavy plant. The lava chips often have irregular surfaces, cracks and crevices that hold the roots tightly, are reusable, and have capillary action. To increase the capillary action of the planting medium, add peat moss or vermiculite at the rate of about 1 part to 10 by volume. This coats the rock with absorbent material that wicks water.

Outdoor Irrigation & Hydroponics

Water is one of the six limiting factors. Plants react to the environment by adjusting their growth. The difference in growth between a plant receiving adequate water and one that has limited access may not be immediately apparent, especially if they are in different gardens. The adequately irrigated plant grows larger faster and yields more, but matures slightly later than the plant on water rations.

The water needs of plants vary widely because of plant size, climatic conditions, and the temperature, rainfall, and water-holding capacity of the soil.

In areas where rain falls during the summer or where there is a high water table, there may be no need to irrigate outdoor plants at all or to use it as just a supplement to natural sources.

In areas where there is a summer drought, irrigation is required or the plants will die.

Outdoor plants and gardens can be irrigated by using a hose that fills a trough reservoir, by using a gravity-powered canal that delivers water to a group of plants, or more efficiently by using a drip system.

Overhead watering is very inefficient because of loss to evaporation and the shotgun approach of delivering water in areas where there are no crop roots. Once the plants are flowering, overhead water is dangerous to the buds, which are susceptible to attack by mold when moisture is present.

Drip Systems Outdoors

Drip irrigation is a 90% more efficient method of delivering water to plants outdoors than other methods such as flooding an area using a hose or overhead spraying. The result is more water delivered to the root zone than any other watering system. Drip irrigation has other benefits that make it useful. It is inexpensive and easy to design and install.

Drip systems use pressure from the public water system, gravity, or a pump to deliver water where it is needed. Drip systems usually operate at about 25 pounds per square inch (1.75 kg per m²); 10–30 pounds (4.5–14 kg) is a common range, whereas municipal water is delivered to households at more than 30 psi. A 25 psi pressure regulator can be used so that excess pressure doesn't damage the drip system. Spaghetti lines tap off a main delivery line that is connected to the water source. An emitter on the other end of the spaghetti line controls the rate at which water flows. (Follow the instructions for constructing a drip system earlier in this chapter.)

As with other plumbing systems, there are all kinds of accessories to deal with problems that may be encountered by plants or gardens. Some of these are gardens located on different levels, remote gardens, and different-size plants with varying water needs. The plants can be fertilized using a fertilizer siphon or injector placed in the water line.

Irrigation systems vary tremendously in their complexity depending on the tasks they are designed to accomplish. Store-bought kits are suitable for most backyard gardens. Even simpler is the pinhole pail or bag irrigation. A container is filled with water. The water drips to the desired area through small holes drilled or pierced into the reservoir. It delivers water slowly to the plant so that little is lost.

Hydroponic Sanitation

Aeroponic, deep-water culture, and other hydroponic systems require regular sanitation to prevent bacterial and fungal growth and the development of biofilm. This can be achieved by increasing the oxidation reduction potential (ORP) of the nutrient solution. ORP is a measurement of a solution's tendency to either gain or lose electrons and can reflect the antimicrobial potential of the solution. Measured in millivolts (mV), recirculating hydroponic solutions are generally recommended to be kept above 250 mV, optimally between 300–420 mV. The ORP can be raised above 680 mV for flash treatments, to quickly kill root pathogens.

To prevent bacterial infection, hypochlorous acid, peroxyacetic acid, and/or hydrogen peroxide additives can be used.

Another way to prevent disease in recirculating hydroponic systems is to use a UVC water-sterilizing light. It damages microorganism DNA that passes through in the water stream. However, UVC breaks down chelated nutrients; more chelated micronutrients must be added, non chelated forms must be used, and the pH must remain between 5.5–6.0.

Commercial products that use natural enzymes to break up biofilm are also available. Extracted herbal oils such as garlic, oregano, cinnamon, and curcumin perform the same function.

VERTICAL GARDENS

Historically, the size of a garden is has been measured by area, or length times width. This has been appropriate for almost the entire history of agriculture because sunlight reaches only the top layer of opaque canopy before it is converted to heat. The understory receives virtually no light.

By contrast, the size of an indoor or greenhouse garden is measured in terms of cubic space rather than area. By developing several levels of gardens, or growing vertically, the space is utilized more efficiently.

There are two different approaches to 3D cultivation: produce a single garden that grows vertically, or create separate horizontal gardens on several levels.

Multi-level gardens are commonly used during certain phases of the growth cycle. Cuttings rooting into clones are frequently grown in 10 by 20 inch (25 by 50 cm) trays placed on steel racks that have three or four shelves, each lit by strip-light LEDs or fluorescent tubes.

Coliseum Structures

"Coliseum" structures, which have declined in popularity due to the shift from HID to LED lights, make excellent use of the omnidirectional light path emanating from the bulbs. With HID lamps, especially in a small garden, much of the light is lost inside the reflector or falls outside the plant canopy. Larger gardens are more efficient but still emit light that is lost.

The Coliseum structure holds containers or rockwool padding on a frame six to eight feet (1.8 x 2.4 m) in diameter. It makes a complete circle when closed, but opens to reveal spaces to plant or attach plants at regular intervals and at heights of about two feet (60 cm).

When the bare lamp is hung inside a Coliseum all the light goes directly to the walls and the floor, which may also hold some plants. The only reflector that might be required is on the top of the lamp to prevent light from drifting up and out.

Left: Grow Glide premium racks are designed by cannabis growers for cannabis growers. This vertical racking system optimizes both horizontal and vertical space in the garden that allows indoor growers to truly maximize use of the entire space. Grow Glide racks are set on tracks that easily open up mobile aisles as needed to tend to the plants and optimize workflows. Each tier can be connected to electric and plumbing/watering systems. They are designed to easily run power to every level, and holes drilled into the racks (which are e-coated and powder coated for premium protection) make installing lights a breeze. The low-profile drainage system is easy to clean and optimized for airflow.

Coliseum structures are sometimes designed taller, using two lamps, each held vertically at the center.

Stadium Structures

Another version of a multi-level garden features "stadium" structures. Rather than placing the plants in a circle, they are placed on steps, like bleachers in a stadium, that can stretch to a desired length. Each step is about a foot (30 cm) higher than the next. With the steps on either side they form a "V" that can be constructed with up to 10 steps, each about a foot taller than the next. HID lamps are placed in the middle of the V. Two lamps are used for taller stadiums. Lamps are placed on centers close enough to maintain proper light intensity.

Vertical Shelf Gardening

With the use of LED lighting, shelf gardening has become more popular for three reasons, light, heat, and space.

No matter what appliance is used, it produces the same amount of heat per watt. However, HID lamps produce intense light from a small point or line and it must spread out, requiring a three foot (1 m) space between lamp and plant canopy. Some LEDs emit their light over a large area so they are ready to use as emitted, reducing the space between the lamps and the plants.

The light from LEDs is distributed over a wide area, which is preferable to having intense heat that must be dissipated from a small area using HIDs. Much of the LED heat is drained in some units by heat sinks of one kind or another. This allows the lamps to be spaced closer to the plants.

The third reason relates to space, which becomes available with the use of LEDs. Instead of five or six foot (1.5 or 1.8 m) shelves, a shelf from bottom of container to top of light can be just four feet (1.2 m) high. This creates room for multiple shelves.

Lighting and irrigation are easily dealt with. Two important considerations that are more difficult to deal with in all duplex or triplex systems are safety and the different air conditions on each level.

When working above floor level, safety must be primary. How will workers access the plants? How will equipment and tools rise to the appropriate level? Guardrails, secure stairs, to-code dumb waiters and elevators, and non-slip materials are necessary to address safety issues.

Heat rises and humidity accumulates, so each level's air conditions will differ and so each level must be treated separately. These environmental concerns are best addressed before building or purchasing a system.

With some installations it will be easier to meet code using industrialized systems that have been designed taking both OSHA and air conditions into consideration. A well made system created by professionals could be far cheaper in the long run than a less costly home-made unit.

This is a vertical garden using shelving so that there are four levels of plants. It is lit by two double-ended ceramic metal halide lamps with no reflectors so that the light shines directly on the plants.

Photo: Courtesy of Guy Holmes

Photo: Dr. Robb Farms

SIEMENS

ELECTRICITY BASICS & LOAD CALCULATION

by Joey Ereñeta

Electrical Service Equipment

All work should be done by a licensed, bonded electrician. No one should attempt to do any electrical work without one. It is important, however, for indoor cultivators to understand the makeup of their electrical system and to recognize potential hazards. Whether assessing and upgrading an existing operation, or vetting the scope and cost of establishing a new one, it is essential for cultivators to be able to roughly calculate their needs, coordinate with electricians and electrical engineers on proper design, and troubleshoot potential issues if and when they arise.

Electrical power travels along a network of high voltage wires and is broken into grids based on geography and commercial or residential demand. The amount and type of power allocated to each customer is based on the service contract, equipment, and infrastructure tied to their property.

Along the grid, the power company installs transformers which convert high voltage electricity to the lower voltage service supplying each location. This transformer feeds the electrical wires that carry power to each property, typically referred to as the "service drop." Each cultivator and their electrical contractor will need to know the capacity of their existing electrical service, as well as any unused capacity from nearby transformers, in order to determine the potential size and scope of the operation they can design and implement.

The service drop passes through a meter and terminates at the main service panel. The utility meter measures the kilowatts of electricity consumed in order for the power company to bill for usage. After the meter, there is a service disconnect that can cut all the power to the facility. The main service disconnect may be a special breaker switch housed in an exterior box enclosure, or it may simply be the main circuit breaker inside the main service panel. The electricity coming through the main panel can be distributed to sub panels throughout the property. Each panel or sub panel then distributes electricity via circuits that power outlets in different locations throughout the facility.

In the past, some growers in the unregulated market would bypass the meter and service disconnect in order to steal unmetered electricity from the grid. Not only is this a serious crime, but it puts workers in the facility and first responders during an emergency in serious danger. In the case of a fire, the service disconnect is typically switched off before the fire is doused with water. If the stolen power bypasses this essential safety mechanism, it can lead to electrocution and death of a first responder. *Never bypass the main service disconnect.*

Circuit Breakers

Circuit breakers are safety devices installed in each panel which control the flow of electricity to, and limit the overloading of, each circuit. Breakers have an on, off, and tripped position. "On" and "Off" positions are typically labeled, while the tripped position falls in between the two.

A circuit can be overloaded from plugging in equipment that pulls too much power or by plugging in too many devices into its connected outlets. When 100% or more of the rated capacity of the circuit is used, the breaker will flip to the tripped position, stopping the flow of electricity to that circuit. The breaker should never trip when using the 80% Rule. The number located on the end of each breaker is the electrical capacity of the circuit, rated in amperage. (The number "20" signifies that the rated capacity of that circuit is 20 amps.) The bigger the number, the greater the circuit's capacity.

The panel should have a schedule or map that lists which rooms/locations each breaker (and its circuit) powers. If any panel in a facility has not already been mapped, it should be before use. This is done by plugging an electrical device into each outlet and flipping circuit breakers off at the panel, one at a time. Since the panel may be located far from some of the outlets being mapped, this should be done with a partner. If solo, plugging a loud radio into each outlet can help determine when a breaker turns power on and off, as the sound will go on and off with the breaker. The process can be repeated until each outlet and the entire panel of circuit breakers is mapped. This map is typically kept inside the cover of the electrical panel.

Amperage, Voltage, Wattage & Load Calculations

The amperage, voltage, and wattage of a circuit are electrical concepts that may be easier to understand by using the analogy of water in a pipe. Amperage would be the volume of water flowing through the pipe. Voltage is the water pressure. Wattage is the amount of power that water would generate if it were powering a watermill. Too much water being pushed too quickly through too small of a pipe will increase pressure and resistance and eventually cause the pipe to burst. Similar effects can occur when overloading a circuit, such as overheating, melting, shorts, and fires.

Power service voltages come in a variety of sizes. Most home and commercial cultivators make use of low and medium voltage systems and equipment.

Low voltage is typically under 50 volts, often available in 12v, 24v, or 48v. Examples of low voltage applications in commercial and residential buildings are network data, telephone, Wi-Fi, HD video, audio, and computer networking systems such as phone, internet, security cameras, and alarms. All of these components require a low voltage wiring network that is separate from standard electrical wiring. Low voltage wiring does not require an electrician but does require a certified technician who specializes in installing low voltage networks throughout a building.

Medium voltage options vary depending on the location and application. Residential voltages range between 110v to 240v. Commercial/industrial voltage options range from 110v to 480v. Lower voltages in this range are typically used for powering low wattage devices, such as fans, small pumps, low intensity lighting, and small dehumidifiers. Higher voltages in this range are reserved for powering high wattage devices, such as large air conditioners and dehumidification systems, high-intensity lighting, plant waste shredders, soil sterilizers, and large water-system pumps. Each device will be rated to run at certain voltages.

Certain higher wattage devices in the garden may be rated to run at multiple voltage options. To maximize the efficiency, longevity, and integrity of electrical systems and grow equipment, the rule of thumb is to run high wattage devices at the highest available voltage for which they are rated. Using lower voltages with higher wattage devices creates inefficiencies that affect the quality and yield of plants.

Cultivators must familiarize themselves with the voltage options available from their power service. Electricians can create different voltage circuits using the available electrical "legs" or wires running from the power grid to the main service panel.

Load Calculation (Ohm's Law)

There is a basic equation in electrical engineering that explains the relationship between amperage, voltage, and wattage. It is called "Ohm's Law." It states that amperage is equal to

Ohm's Law:

Amps = Watts ÷ Volts

Watts = Amps x Volts

Volts = Watts ÷ Amps

wattage divided by voltage. Alternately, it also states that wattage is equal to amperage multiplied by voltage. The third part of the equation can be calculated with the other two;

Ohm's Law can be used to perform a "load calculation." This is a way to determine what can safely be plugged into the outlets on any circuit without overloading it. The circuit's amperage capacity (the number found on the circuit breaker) is converted to its wattage capacity, and then the maximum number of total watts that can be safely plugged into the circuit can be determined using the 80% rule.

Example: What can safely be plugged into all the combined outlets of a 20 amp 120 volt circuit?

20 amps x 120 volts = 2,400 watts (100% of the circuit's rated capacity)

2,400 watts x 80% = 1,920 watts (using the 80% Rule)

Therefore, according to the 80% Rule, the total combined wattage of all devices plugged into the outlets of that 20amp/120v circuit should never exceed 1,920 watts.

Photo: GrowWeedEasy.com

DESIGNING PERSONAL GARDEN SPACES

by Bill Faulconer

Grow tents are a great place to start for hobby gardeners, home growers with limited space, and experimenters who require a controlled space, isolating for breeding, or quarantining newly acquired or sick plants. They can also be used for small plants grown to ripening.

This garden is in a tent, but these are basics that can be applied to small rooms or outbuildings as well.

Setting up a 4 x 4 x 6.7 foot (1.2 x 1.2 x 2 m) Vegetative Grow Tent

This tent is four feet (1.2 m) deep, four feet wide, and six feet seven inches (2 m) tall. This model tent has clear windows so that the grower can enjoy the plants visually while maintaining temperature and humidity control.

A few plants and a light are all that is needed to get started. When it's time to flower, either move plants to a larger space with a bloom light or close the light-blocking doors during each day's dark hours and add a fan to draw fresh air through the tent.

Lighting: depending on vegetative photoperiod used and the cultivars' DLI requirements, the 16 square foot (1.4 m²) area is best lit with a dimmable lighting fixture that produces a PPF range of 600–900 μmol/s.

Climate: a four inch (10 cm) 150–200 cfm inline ventilation fan can be connected to a thermostat or to a humidistat to automate exhaust for climate control.

Odor Control: a four inch (10 cm) charcoal filter can be connected to the exhaust fan when flowering plants become pungent.

Step 1: Gather Equipment
- 4' x 4' x 6'7" (1.2 x 1.2 x 2 m) tent with gear board
- Light that provides 600–900 μmol/s
- Ratchet pair for light suspension
- 4 inch (10 cm) 150–200 cfm inline fan
- 4 inch (10 cm) charcoal filter (optional)
- Fan speed controller
- Flexible 4 inch by 25 foot (exhaust) and 4 inch (25.5 cm) by 25 foot (intake) (optional)
- Strip timer/thermostat/humidistat
- (2) Clip-on circulation fans

Step 2: Assemble Frame

No tools are required for assembly. Well-made tents provide simple and accurate assembly instructions, and each framing component will be labeled alphabetically. All corners and connectors are made of steel, not plastic. When plastic connectors break, they are rarely replaceable. All fabric is heavy duty and well stitched. Zippers are high quality, and numerous large duct openings are provided. Clear windows permit viewing without opening the doors.

Step 3: Install Roof

An installed roof must be pulled over the top of the frame incrementally. If the process is rushed and one corner is pulled down all the way before the other corners have been started, the task will be difficult and the product could be damaged.

After the roof installation, the ceiling support poles are installed under the roof to support equipment such as lights and fans. It is important to note that there are upper and lower support poles; heavy equipment should be suspended from the upper load-bearing poles. If the upper supports begin to sag, the lower poles will offer additional support.

Step 4: Install Walls

Once the walls are zipped to the roof and floor, the tent will become structurally sound and rigid. With the quality tight-fitting fabric, there will no longer be any flex in the frame, just as with a camping tent. The tight covering ensures that the frame is more than sturdy enough to support relatively heavy lights, fans, filters, and any other accessories.

The tent is equipped with a removable floor "puddle catcher" to avoid water damage to the frame and tent fabric. This will be the last part installed in the tent. It can be removed easily for cleaning.

Step 5: Install Ventilation Equipment

Ventilation equipment is used to remove air heated by the lighting and to ensure that fresh, dry air and CO_2 are supplied to the plants. An intake duct is installed to ensure that the duct port remains open. A four foot (1.2 m) length of four inch (25 cm) lightproof ducting is installed so that a 90° bend will allow fresh air in but not let light in or out. Keeping light out will become critically important if this tent is used for flowering. A four inch (10 cm) duct is installed to exhaust hot and/or damp air from the tent. The exhaust duct can be routed into an attic, out through a window, or back into the room where the tent is located.

A four inch (10 cm) inline fan is installed near the ceiling to pull out the hot air that naturally rises. When the fan is operating, it causes negative pressure. This fan is rated to move 150–200 cubic feet (4.2–5.6 m^3) of air per minute. In a four by four foot (1.2 by 1.2 m) space that is six feet seven inches (2 m) high, there is 106 cubic feet (3 m^3) of air space, which indicates that the air will be exchanged every 32–42 seconds. When the doors are closed, fresh air is drawn in through the intake duct.

Sometimes growers use an underrated fan, relying on general construction guidelines that state (in toilet rooms, for example) a complete air exchange every 10 minutes is adequate. The difference between the spaces is that grow spaces generate a lot of heat from the lights. Without air conditioning or other cooling technologies, a faster rate of exhaust and air exchange is needed to combat the heat.

If the tent implodes from too much negative pressure, a fan speed controller can be used to adjust the rate of air exchange. Another solution might be to install an intake fan in the intake duct.

Step 6: Install Grow Light

To keep the lights at the right distance from the plants, a pair of light ratchets is installed to easily move the light up or down when feeding or when the plants grow taller.

The lamps and fixtures should be dimmable to avoid giving young plants too much light. The fixture shown is equipped with a "daisy chain" outlet so that additional lights, circulation fans, and other power users can be plugged into the light without having to run an extension cord to an outlet.

Step 7: Set Up Electrical Connections

Many tent manufacturers offer a gear board to neatly and effectively install equipment such as timers, ballasts, fans, and controllers at an optimal height and location to easily access controls. The gear board keeps high-powered electrical equipment off the floor (an absolute "no-no") and away from potential spills.

This tent has been equipped with a "strip timer" that provides timer function to the bottom four outlets while providing continuous power to the top four outlets. A fan speed controller is used to moderate the fan speed. A high temperature limit controller is used to disable the grow light if the temperature exceeds a preset limit. This prevents the plants from overheating if the cooling system fails.

Step 8: Basic Operations

When the plants get larger and need support, the grower must either install bamboo stakes with ties or use a "bungee" net or screen.

If additional air movement is needed to maintain temperature control, a second inline fan or booster fan can be installed at either end of the intake ducting to blow air into the tent. When using a carbon filter to mitigate the exhaust air, be sure to use a fan speed controller to slow down the rate of intake air so that it is less than the rate of exhaust air. This maintains net negative pressure inside the tent and ensures that better odor control is maintained.

During the vegetative stage the plants are accustomed to 18 hours or more of light, but because they are in a vegetative stage, it is not a problem for ambient light to enter during the lights-off hours. A grower can provide a better plant environment by simply leaving the doors open if the light and odor escaping isn't a problem. If the doors remain open, the exhaust fan can be eliminated or disabled because the heat from the light will escape naturally.

If the grower lacks the space, budget, or need for a bloom space, this tent can easily become a "hybrid tent," allowing a "cradle-to-grave" grow cycle. To accommodate that objective, simply add a roof extension to ensure adequate clearance from the top of plants to the higher intensity bloom light if needed, and add a charcoal odor filter.

Building a 4 x 8 foot (1.2 x 2.4 m) Bloom Tent
Equipment Needed

1 - 4' x 8' x 7 '7" (1.2 x 2.4 x 2.3 m) bloom tent with roof extension and gear board

2 - Lights that provide 1,200–1,500 μmol/s each

2 - Ratchet pair for light suspension

1 - 6 inch (15.25 cm) 400 cfm inline fan

1 - Fan speed controller

2 - Flexible 6" (15.25 cm) x 25' (7.62 m) (exhaust and intake)

1 - 6 x 24 inch (15.25 x 61 cm) 400+ cfm charcoal odor filter

1 - Strip timer/hygrometer

2 - Clip-on circulation fans

The basic process for setting up a grow tent is described in the previous section.

Because this space will be used as a bloom room, the tent has been equipped with an optional height extension, which raises the height from 6 feet 7 inches (2 m) to 7 feet 7 inches (2.3 m). The benefits are as follows:

- Heat rises, so the trapped heat will be farther above the plants.
- When the plants get taller, they won't be stressed by intense grow lights.
- More space will be available for ceiling-mounted exhaust fans and filters.
- Using autoflowering cultivars, the tent can be modified with a shelf to flower short plants on one level and have a vegetative garden on the other level.

Ventilation versus Contained Space

The best way to cool the tent is to use an air conditioner so that the air in the tent is not exchanged, which makes it easier to maintain high CO_2 levels. This reduces the risk of diseases and pests riding on the incoming airstream from outside. Using recirculating air, all the ventilation equipment and setup described in the following paragraphs is eliminated. This information is only for gardens cooled using air exchange.

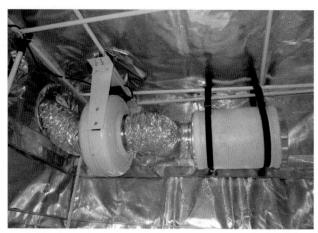

An exhaust duct can be routed to another space, out a window, or simply into the room the tent is located in.

The Grobo Grow Box makes it easy for anyone to start growing cannabis at home regardless of space constraints and experience level. The Grobo Box is a deep-water culture hydroponic automated system that uses smart notifications to indicate potential issues in the system. The grow process is automated and customizable: choose from over 1,500 grow recipes to automate nutrient dosing, adjust pH, and regulate light cycles. Simply change the water weekly.

Ventilation

A 6 inch (15 cm) duct is installed to exhaust hot and/or damp air from the tent. The exhaust duct can be routed to another space, out through a window, or just into the room where the tent is located.

A fan speed controller can be employed to balance the air flow. Or a second inline fan can be added at intake to push more air through the ducting. A charcoal filter is connected to the exhaust fan intake with a section of flexible ducting to remove odors from the extracted air. To maximize airflow, the filter has been sized to ensure that the cfm rating of the filter is at least equal to the cfm rating of the fan. To prolong the life of the filter, the duct is removed during early flowering and reconnected when the plants become pungent.

If additional air movement is needed to maintain temperature control, a second inline fan or booster fan can be installed at either end of the intake ducting to blow air into the tent. When using a carbon filter to mitigate the exhaust air, be sure to use a fan speed controller to slow down the rate of intake air so that it is less than the rate of exhaust air. This will help maintain net negative pressure inside the tent and ensure that better odor control is maintained.

Lighting

Using the more efficient LED lamps, gardens can achieve high yields, as well as increased cannabinoids and terpenes. For a tent this size, use two LED fixtures that each provide 1,500 µmol/s. Install a pair of light ratchets to easily move lights up or down when feeding or when the plants grow taller.

Environmental Equipment Options
Installing a Dehumidifier

Humidity levels increase significantly once the plants get larger and transpire more water. The environment outside the tent also affects the humidity inside. Excess humidity must be controlled to avoid problems with mildew, mold, and bud rot. (*See Air Temperature, Humidity & Qualities.*) If the air conditioner or ventilation system cannot keep the humidity low enough, the best way to control it is to employ a dehumidifier.

A 40-pint dehumidifier is designed to extract 40 pints of moisture daily. Many will overstate their capacity by rating the unit to meet its stated capacity at high temperature and humidity levels (over 85°F [30°C] and 80% RH). Dehumidifiers remove more water at higher temperatures and higher humidity levels, but accurately sizing the units requires a knowledge of capacity at desired grow tent temperature and humidity levels (about 75°F [24°C] and 55% RH).

The condensate water drained from the dehumidifier is safe for use in the garden. (*See Sustainability.*)

The Armoire makes home cultivation easier for the casual consumer through its high-tech, organic gardening system that blends seamlessly into living rooms, bedrooms, or anywhere in a home or small apartment. It comes in either cherry, modern black, or rustic barn board wood veneer finish styles and makes growing at home as easy as plugging in and watering once a day; it comes as a complete system with all internal and exhaust fans, odor filtration, and more, and is powered by an included LED light. The Armoire can produce a quarter pound or more of flower every other month.

Installing an Air Conditioner

Controlling heat can be a major problem when the tent is in a warm environment. To keep outside heat from invading the tent, it can be lined with Styrofoam sheets.

Even with insulation, an air conditioner is required to keep the temperature cool in high-temperature environments. A portable AC with intake and outflow is the easiest type of unit to install because it can simply be rolled into the space and connected to the intake and exhaust ducts through a window or vent or into an attic. The inflow-outflow ducts act as a heat exchanger; no air is exchanged.

The unit can be placed outside the tent to provide more space for the plants. When placed outside the tent, the thermostatic control on the AC is unable to measure the temperature inside the garden. Instead, the AC is plugged into a separate temperature controller, that is equipped with a remote thermostat placed inside the tent.

To use a remote controller, the AC unit must be equipped with an "auto restart." When the controller switches to "on," the AC turns on automatically.

At about 12 amps of power consumption, an air conditioner probably will require a separate circuit than the grow tent equipment. (*See Electricity Basics.*)

Example of Poor Garden Design

- The electrical system is haphazard and dangerous. The wiring is a series of extension cords, some of which are lying on the floor. The wire jungle could be used as a net trap.
- The light is unprotected and can burst if it comes into contact with a drop of water.
- Without a reflector to direct the light, much of it never gets to the garden, so it is wasted. The lamp is illuminating an area of about 60 square feet (5.5 m²).
- The fan is pointed directly on the light and blowing the hot air over the plant canopy.
- An old-fashioned magnetic ballast powers the light; however, electronic ballasts use less power and would have saved about 8% in electrical costs. This is an outmoded system. Switch to LEDs.
- The ballast and tools are on a high shelf, which makes them hard to reach.
- There is no indication of ventilation, heat exchange, or CO_2 enrichment.

Hygro Humboldt in Eureka, California.
Photo: Angela Bacca

DESIGNING MEDIUM & LARGE SPACES
by Bill Faulconer

Medium-Sized Rooms: Setting Up a 20 x 20 x 8 feet (6 x 6 x 2.4 m) Bloom Room

Equipment

- Lights: (12) LEDs that each provide 1,550 µmol/s or (9) double-ended HPS lights that provide 2,100 µmol/s
- Ratchet pairs: one per light
- Light controller
- High-limit controller
- CO_2 supplementation
- CO_2 tank and tank controller
- Or CO_2 generator and controller
- Strip timer
- Reverse osmosis system if indicated by tests
- 55 gallon (208 l) barrel with float valve
- (2) neoprene light socks (algae black)

If the space will not be ventilated:
- Air conditioning

If the space will be ventilated:
- 1700 cfm charcoal odor filter
- 12 inch (30 cm) 1,700 cfm inline, exhaust fan

Construction

Seams are covered with aluminum tape. The base of the walls is protected using black rubber cover base. This makes regular mopping easier, seals out bugs, eliminates drafts, and traps water, preventing grow room leaks should a flood occur.

Ventilation

Skip this step if the space will not be ventilated.

Toward the right side of this room is an exhaust system designed to ventilate the space. The fan pulls fresh outside air from the opposite side of the room. The system consists of a charcoal filter with a dust sock (sitting on floor), a 12 inch (30 cm) 1700 cfm (48 m³/m) inline fan (sitting on the filter) and a 12 inch duct connection to the ceiling. A replaceable dust filter is installed at the ceiling, and a duct elbow is installed above the ceiling to direct the exhaust toward the exterior vent. The fan is connected to a timer set to run during the dark hours (when CO_2 is off) and pulls air out through the charcoal odor filter for about 15 minutes every few hours. The charcoal filter is necessary to avoid exhausting strong odors outside. The fan has a built-in silencer. The main purpose of this system is to provide fresh air periodically, but it can also be used to purge the room after activating bug bombs (when no plants are in the room) or, if necessary, to cool and ventilate the room during air conditioning failure.

Light, air qualities, and other limiting growth factors should be addressed before moving in plants. Photo: Bill Faulconer

Plant Support

Trellis netting supports plants without installing and removing stakes and tie wire each cycle. In addition to providing support, trellis nets are used to spread the branches to increase light penetration.

A "floating net" trellis designed by the author has the advantage that the front of the net frame can be lifted up while the back is left in place, making it much easier to harvest and replant.

Rather than building legs for a PVC frame at a set height above the floor, the net hangs from ceiling hooks with rope ratchets that are easily raised and lowered. The adjustable height makes it easy to customize for different cultivars. The second layer of netting usually hangs about 10 inches (25 cm) above the first net. Half inch (1.25 cm) electrical aluminum tubing is used because it's lightweight and inexpensive. The tubing is attached to the ropes, holding up the one and a quarter inch (3 cm) PVC frame with zip ties. Don't cut the ends off the zip ties and don't over tighten them. With just enough zip-tie tension, the tubing can be slid up and down and still hold firmly where it is positioned.

Circulation

Circulation refers to how the air moves through the space rather than in and out of it. The mounted wall fans were installed just above the base of plant containers to ensure good air circulation. Note that all cords are securely installed and not lying on the floor or the plants. Good circulation minimizes potential for mold and helps ensure that the temperature, hu-

Trellis netting supports plants without installing and removing stakes and tie wire each cycle. Photo: Bill Faulconer

midity, and CO_2 levels are consistent throughout the growing environment. Fans are disabled until the plants are tall enough to have been bottom-pruned to avoid blowing directly on lower leaves. Breathable fabric pots and plastic saucers have been chosen for this garden. Plant roots like to breathe. Movable saucers are easier to move around and clean than large plastic trays. Saucers are also less expensive than larger trays.

However, using trays or plumbing and tubing, water can be drained automatically while avoiding spills, which are much more likely when using saucers.

Cleaning & Maintenance

A garden can be cleaned and maintained more easily using the right surface materials. Drywall is acceptable, but foam board is mold resistant, has high reflectivity, is easy to install, is lightweight, has a moderate cost, and is easy to clean thoroughly. Polyethylene plastic can be easily installed over other surfaces and can be washed. Epoxy-coated floors are easy to install, incredibly durable, and easy to clean, and they make the whole room seem more like a laboratory.

Air Conditioning

This space is cooled using a four ton (900 kg), 48,000 Btu air conditioner. A frame was built to support the air conditioning unit and to provide a filter frame for the return air being pulled from the room near the floor.

This unit has a quick connect feature, allowing someone who is not an AC technician to install the flexible copper refrigerant lines from the indoor unit to the outdoor unit without having to charge them.

The unit also has a grower-friendly feature called low ambient control. The low ambient feature diminishes or disables the cooling fan on the outdoor unit. Mainstream (as opposed to cannabis horticulture specific) AC units are not designed or warranted for operating in cold temperature. This unit is designed to automatically restart if the power fails and then restores. Mainstream units require a button to be pushed to power them back on after an outage.

All electrical devices are connected through the smart panel and controlled through timers and digital applications.

Control Equipment

For most projects, a painted plywood backboard, usually two by four feet (0.6 x 1.2 meters) is mounted to the wall so that all controls and wire supports can be securely and easily mounted. Half inch (1.25 cm) plywood was installed under the foam board so that anything could be mounted anywhere.

Power wiring from the main electric panel has been installed in flexible conduit. All wires are labeled, and each light is numbered. At the top of the image is an electrical sub-panel to distribute power to individual circuit breakers for light controller (45 amps), AC (30 amps), and wall outlets (20 amps). Breakers are labeled.

Lighting

The lighting regimen is managed using a controller. It can accommodate sixteen lights.

The 240 volt power supply enters the bottom of the controller via flexible conduit connected at the other end to a 50 amp, 2-pole, 240 volt circuit breaker in the main panel, using three #8 gauge wires.

No power is provided to the light receptacles until the "trigger cables" receive 120 volts of power from a timer. A high-limit controller is connected between the timer and the light controller to disable lights if the room overheats. A trigger cable controls power to the controller. In an emergency, it can be turned off, eliminating all power to the lights.

High Limit Controls

The wall-mounted device is connected to a timer to activate the lights. This device can avert a costly destruction of the entire crop. The light controller trigger cords are plugged into the controller. The maximum temperature is set so that if the room temperature exceeds 90°F (32°C), due to AC failure or any other cause, the lights are disabled to avoid excessive temperature.

In each room at least one recording thermometer and hygrometer (RH meter) and a surface temperature thermometer aimed at the canopy are used to check plant temperature, rather than just where the display is placed.

Humidity

The humidistat is mounted on the wall, but the humidity sensor is positioned in the canopy to measure humidity in the plant zone. The controller is connected to the ceiling-mounted dehumidifier. Another humidistat controls a humidifier that turns on should the humidity level dip below 55% RH.

CO_2

The CO_2 controller is connected to a timer or photocell so that the system operates only during the light cycle.

The CO_2 tank is plugged into the controller and activated when CO_2 levels fall below 1250 ppm during the lit period.

Fuzzy logic is only recommended for CO_2 bottle systems as opposed to CO_2 generator systems because gas generators cost so little to operate that fuzzy logic is unnecessary and the function simply causes the generator to be ignited too frequently. Aluminum tape was installed over the LCD display to minimize the potential for the display to emit light and disrupt the light cycle during dark hours.

In addition to having a CO_2 controller to monitor levels, a second monitor can be useful to check the controller's accuracy and to check CO_2 levels in various areas in the space.

Timers & Timer Strips

There are two wall-mounted strip timers. The top row of four outlets is controlled by the timer, and the bottom row of four outlets is always on. For this project, the light controller and the CO_2 controller are connected to timer outlets; the humidity controller, the music box, and wall fans are connected to the hot outlets. Timer strips are handy for eliminating multiple timers, cords, and adapters. The timer is a simple thermostat for control of room temperature.

Drainage

This is an effective drainage system for excess water. The blue tubing on the left is discharge water from the reverse osmosis water purifier runoff. The white tubing in the center is condensate water from the air conditioner. The clear tubing toward the right is condensate water from the dehumidifier mounted above. The black tubing drains to the sewer system and has a P-Trap to prevent sewer gas from entering the room.

Ducting

An innovative fabric duct was selected to supply cooled air into this room. The 16 inch by 20 foot (40 x 60 cm) duct is connected at one end to the air conditioner and is capped at the opposite end. The duct is supported by a steel cable fastened to the ceiling. Moderate bends can be made. The duct clips attach to the steel cable to suspend the entire length. Because the entire length of ducting is perforated along the sides, the cool air is evenly distributed throughout the entire growing space and all the leaves flutter gently. The AC thermostat is set for the blower to be on 24/7 to maximize circulation.

Convenience Lighting

Several ceiling lights (white bulbs) enable the gardener to work in the room (light schedule permitting) without having to turn on the cultivation lights. Working in the garden with thousands of watts of firepower can be unpleasant or unnecessary when pruning, inspecting, spraying, building or taking down a space, or just checking.

Toward the rear of this room is a three-bulb green LED fixture. Green lights provide a working light that can be sparingly used during the "lights off" hours. Without a green light, the bloom cycle is disrupted when lights are turned on during dark hours.

Convenience Light Controls

These old-fashioned yet clever devices prevent serious problems in the garden. Similar to the devices seen in gas station restrooms, these "ticker timers" can be used to turn on white or green convenience lights. In most gardens a wall switch can be accidentally left on, but this does not happen with these ticker timers.

Door Seals

Doors are a notorious source of unwanted light leak, bugs, dust, and contaminants. This door is sealed at the edges with a one inch (2.5 cm) wide and one quarter inch (6 mm) deep felt strip stapled to the door. The door bottom is sealed with a rubber sweep that works like a squeegee and is fastened to the door with screws. To moderate temperatures in the entry room, a vent was installed. The vent is protected with a washable bug screen, and it is protected from light leak with a rooftop rain vent behind the door.

Secure Entry

An entry room or "vestibule" allows the operator to keep unwanted light from entering the bloom room and possibly disrupting the light cycle. It also allows the operator to keep light from escaping and minimizes the potential for contaminants to enter the bloom room.

Nutrient Test Meters

This meter remains in the solution, constantly monitoring the nutrient pH level, temperature, and nutrient strength. The grower can see the levels change as products are added.

Water Purification

A reverse osmosis filter is needed if the source water exceeds 150 ppm dissolved solids (0.6–0.8 EC). Reports are available from the local water company or agency.

Rainwater is a good source because it contains low ppm of minerals. Adjust it to 100–125 ppm prior to adding any supplemental nutrition using CalMag. (*See Nutrients & Fertilizers.*)

This reverse osmosis purifier can provide up to 150 gallons (568 liters) per day of pure water. The water supply is connected at the pressure gauge. A minimum of 60 psi is needed. Higher pressure results in higher flow. The discharge tubing is connected to a drain.

The purified water is connected to a barrel that has a float valve to stop water flow when the barrel is full. When the inexpensive pre-filters look dirty, they should be replaced. When the purified output exceeds 100 ppm, the costly filter membrane should be replaced.

Water/Nutrient Reservoir

This reservoir barrel is a 55 gallon (208 l) food-grade, high-density polyethylene reservoir. Non-food-grade, low-density polyethylene reservoirs (trash cans) are made from low-density plastics, which degrade and leach petrochemical polymers into the water.

Here the test meter is wall mounted above the reservoir. An air pump is installed outside the reservoir with an air stone inside it to oxygenate and circulate the nutrients.

A submersible water pump in the barrel is connected to a garden hose with a long wand attached to minimize the need to bend over when watering plants. A hose support wheel is mounted above the barrel to store the hose and prevent it from kinking.

Large-scale farms require detailed planning. Every farm is different and requires different considerations for scaling. Photo: Stinkbud

Considerations for Designing Large Cultivation Spaces
By Justin Arriola

- Designs must be up to code and must comply with all regulations, legal limitations, and requirements of all aspects of the project. Style and design must also be considered.
- Owners of large-scale commercial gardens often have already chosen a "head grower" or "cultivation supervisor," sometimes referred to as a "master grower." This individual has usually already chosen cultivation methods and the cultivars that will be used in the facility. Serious consideration must also be made on whether the grower's knowledge base and experience is up to the challenge. It is better to decline a project than work on one whose success is not probable.
- The space may be designed to adapt what the grower is already doing and to make it more efficient at a larger scale. On the other hand, scaling up a method that has inherent flaws can lead to disaster. New approaches may be considered.
- Efficiency is achieved using data capture and automation, which allows for continual improvements on quality and consistency while reducing inputs including labor.
- For the most part, growers are moving toward automated light-deprivation greenhouses because they are the best of both worlds: the climate variables are as controllable as a large-scale indoor facility, but with no-cost sunlight.

Getting Started: The Limiting Factors

Start the design by addressing the two most significant limiting factors on the operation: local regulations and harvest style.

Laws regulating cannabis vary widely by jurisdiction, and compliance needs to be factored first. Designing around compliance means planning for security, zoning, local ordinances, interactions with regulators and/or law enforcement, and all other applicable building requirements and regulations.

Compliance to cultivation space size requirements varies by jurisdiction. In some places the cultivation space is measured by square footage of canopy, and in others, by plant count. When limited by plant count, the goal is to grow very large plants. In that case, the design focuses on maximizing the yield per plant. When the cultivation space is measured in canopy area, it really comes down to filling that space with as much plant canopy as possible, usually using a SOG technique. (*See Vegetative Growth.*)

Although planning for harvest is a crucial step in large cultivation space design, it is very often overlooked. Harvesting involves a lot of logistics and often more labor than the day-to-day operation. Dedicated climate-controlled spaces for processing, drying, curing, and manufacturing should factor heavily when designing the space.

There are several details that must be worked out about the harvest before designing. How often will the operation be harvesting? Traditional outdoor farms will have one to three harvests a year. Many indoor cultivation spaces are designed to harvest smaller batches perpetually. What is the end product? If flowers will be sold as top-shelf dried buds to a final customer, hand trimmers are likely to process the crop. In a large-scale outdoor farm, or in the case of flowers that are being harvested for processed or manufactured products, trim machines and industrial drying equipment may be necessary.

Defining the Operation's Goals

Some cultivation licensees are vertically integrated, so goals may be driven by the need for product diversity. Decisions must be made on whether the in-house brand will be a value-provider or a top-shelf producer, and what sort of end products the operation needs to produce to satisfy its market. Work backward to design the space with these end goals in mind.

Postharvest manufacturing presents logistical challenges: the need to provide space and electrical capacity for large industrial equipment. Planning and management of workflows is imperative to minimize overhead costs in a complex operation that is vertically integrated. If one or two thousand steps are taken out of a worker's daily routine, or a faster or easier way to accomplish a task is introduced, then efficiency goes up, with more time spent on tasks. A 10-minute savings daily adds up to 41 hours, a full work week.

Automation & Data Acquisition

If it can be measured, it can be managed. Using data acquisition and automation, every piece of data can be used to reduce time spent on menial tasks and making all inputs consistent. Data are used to quantify inputs resulting in consistent outputs.

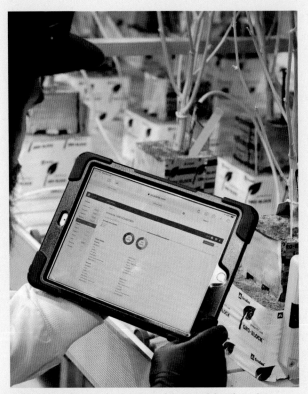

e-Gro from Grodan is the data-driven cultivation platform that integrates the Grodan GroSens Root Zone and Climate sensors for deep insights of the entire facility. With e-Gro's easy-to-understand dashboard and graphs, growers are able to optimize crop steering and climate strategies, track individual batches, including mother plants, from cloning through to harvest, and be notified instantly when readings go out of range. e-Gro combines Grodan's 50+ years of proven crop steering advice with leading-edge data science and technology to give growers the data needed to control and maximize their production, plant quality, and profitability.

For instance, positive pressure emitters can be set for consistency in watering so that plant 1 and plant 200 down the row are getting the exact same amount of water for the exact same amount of time.

Another piece of equipment tracks when the pumps are turned on and off and how long they run, and translates that to the amount of water delivered to each plant. From there, day 1 to day 25 can be compared to determine whether all the pumps were working correctly. The pumping sequence from the last three harvest cycles can be compared. If there is a difference in yield between cycles, data can help determine the cause.

Refining and analyzing the microdata around the facility is crucial to operators who want to make sure GG #4 vape pens purchased in a California store are uniform with the ones sold in Massachusetts.

Although many day-to-day gardening tasks can be automated, there is still a need for people on the ground to manage the operation. If not using monitoring equipment, staff members must be assigned to actively scan for signs of disease or pest infestation to assess plant quality.

Once methods and settings have been selected, quantifying what went into that production makes it a lot easier to repeat.

Growing Zones

Some greenhouse and indoor cultivation spaces are large but are broken up into smaller rooms, or climate zones each with different plants in varying stages of growth for a perpetual harvest. Each space's environment is customized to each cultivar's preferences and growth stage.

Climate zones are great for large-scale growers who have been using the same cultivars for a while and have perfected a "recipe," or protocol, because they know its idiosyncrasies

Whether in a single-tent garden or a multiroom commercial facility, Pulse Grow enables remote monitoring of the garden's complete environment. The Pulse Grow monitor will send mobile notifications the moment something goes wrong. Real-time data collection and analysis allows growers to customize to their cultivars and operations. Easy-to-add wireless sensors make for easy scaling in large operations.

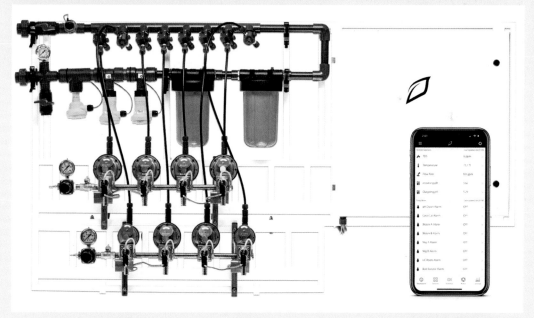

Growlink's Fertigation Skid is a smart, preassembled drop-in fertigation skid that continuously measures the actual EC and pH of the flow-through and precisely adjusts the concentration of fertilizer into the system based on preprogrammed recipes. It improves both crop yield and quality by throttling up and down to hit precise EC and pH targets for each recipe. This single system injects nutrients and minimizes energy consumption while conserving labor, water, and fertilizer.

such as growth patterns, height, and ripening time. This sort of "zoning" is also important for pest and disease management: infestations are more easily contained in the smaller spaces. These climate zones can be designed in a variety of ways, such as creating walls and other physical separations or sophisticated light-deprivation systems programmed to the different zones.

In larger spaces with separate climate zones, each zone is programmed and monitored, controlled, and adjusted through a tablet or mobile application that uses data to remove the variability of decision making from workers. Instead, the decisions are based on data that the cultivation supervisor interprets.

Although these smaller spaces have several advantages, such as smaller, more frequent harvests, isolation from infections, and customized conditions for specific varieties, they preclude the introduction of automation and robotic controls. Having a large, automated space, unimpeded by walls and barriers, can become far more efficient in every phase of cultivation and harvesting.

The advantage of this is that it's easier to attend to plants that have the same requirements rather than dealing with each space's particular requirements. Single-harvest operations are less likely to have infections because the entire space can be cleaned after each crop, leaving no residual pests on living plants.

Future Goals

A lot of new licensees want to start small and generate revenue without taking on too much investment. If growers are planning to start small and scale up, they should think about where they want to be in three to five years. If the key components are built with expansion in mind, a lot of headache (and money) is saved down the road.

Labor, Staffing & Workflow

When designing the space, it is important to look at all the processes in the growth of the plants, from seed to harvest, and the labor and equipment involved.

Before design begins, there are some important decisions to make.

Where will propagation take place?

- Will the operation make its own clones, or will it purchase them?
- If clones will be made in-house, will they be from "mothers" or clippings from plants about to enter flowering?
- Will there be a separate research space where controlled cultivation experiments are performed?
- Will there be space for a dedicated breeding program, including isolation of males and pheno-hunting?

After propagation comes the vegetative growth stage. What will that space look like? In cultivation spaces with high ceilings, climate-controlled stackable shelf trays are used so that the area of the space is maximized vertically as well.

Growing sea-of-green (SoG) also changes the needs of the vegetative space. Vegging for SoG takes a maximum of two weeks, so there's quicker turnaround for many more plants. A conventional style of production requires fewer plants, but the vegetative growth time takes much longer.

In climate zones, vegetative spaces can become flowering spaces by simply altering the photoperiod in that zone.

Large outdoor farms that harvest once a year will most likely need to work with a cannabis-friendly staffing company to provide the extra workforce needed to process the crop. Extra people on-site means a need for extra accommodations such as restroom facilities and break spaces. Spaces for bucking and shucking the plant and trimming the buds must be designed. It should be an organized workspace, with designated spaces for each task and an open design so that managers can easily see the product as it moves through processing.

By focusing on efficient organization and workflow, strategy, and labor-saving devices, fewer people are needed, less total labor is required, and a smaller investment in equipment and space is needed. (*See Automation.*)

Additional climate-controlled spaces for drying and curing must be planned too. (*See Drying, Curing & Storing.*)

Security

Monitoring tools are an important piece of security and cultivation plans. Usually cameras are required to cover the entire inside and perimeter of the space, and footage is to be stored on-site for up to 60 days. Through seed-to-sale tracking software and security systems, regulators have access to yield and harvest data as well as detailed logs of who is provided access to the facility.

"Geofencing" is an efficient way to secure the site. Using sensors in key cards, the grower can see and restrict how people move through the zones in the space. High-value inventory can also be tagged and traced in the space. If a container is moved out of its designated space—or even around it—programmed alerts will go to the appropriate people. This is an effective way to prevent diversion and theft.

Pest Management

Sanitation is the best way to manage pests and disease. It is especially important in large operations that are constantly cycling crops through the space. Rolling benches, racks, and other equipment must be sanitized in between cycles. A lot of construction is designed around easy cleaning, as sanitation is really just diligence.

It is critical to have a good protocol regarding access to the cultivation space for security and pest management. Guests to the site such as investors, members of the media, legislators, and friends may want to tour the space. Sometimes groups will tour multiple cultivation sites on the same day, potentially spreading pests from one site to the other.

A staging area outside the cultivation space entrance is effective at maintaining hygiene. Guests remove coats and put on protective gear such as booties, hair and beard nets, and Tyvek suits or lab coats. Also included are hand-washing stations, and in some spaces sophisticated blowers that "dust" people as they enter the space.

Planning for Electricity & Equipment

One of the biggest concerns is making sure that there is adequate power. Increasing power may require working with the electric service provider to upgrade equipment. This requires time and perhaps a costly investment.

Prepare for the possibility of losing power by having a generator set to start should the power from the grid fail. Solar batteries can be used as a main source or a backup. This can save a crop.

A CoGeneration (CoGen) system based on the co-generation of power is a good option for a large-scale cultivation facility. CoGen systems use a proven natural-gas-fueled engine to generate electricity. Electricity is fed into the building, thereby reducing the facility's electrical consumption and utility bill significantly.

At the same time, free "waste" heat is recovered from the CoGen system's engine oil, jacket, and exhaust heat. Captured heat is then used to offset fuel that would otherwise have to be burned in the site's water heaters and boilers. This allows the site's boilers to not have to work as hard, so the gas bill is also reduced. The space heating, domestic hot water, process hot water, pool heating, and more run on gas. "Waste" heat captured from the CoGen system can also be fed into a device called an absorption chiller, which is able to convert the "waste" heat into cooling, relieving the site's electrically powered chillers from having to do as much.

Carbon Dioxide & Climate Controls

Climate controls in large-scale cultivation spaces, whether one large space or several climate zones, are best managed with sensors and automated controllers.

Automation and data capture can now literally tie into everything. Fans and air systems, temperature, humidity, heating, cooling, and carbon dioxide can be dialed in with precision. Although these systems can be expensive, they are incredibly valuable. They provide consistency, reliability, and usable data to refine processes. If there is a problem in the cultivation space or facility, those who need to know about it will get an automatic alert.

Sensors and automation tools in the cultivation spaces allow growers to maintain exact concentrations of carbon dioxide in the space and automatically shut off and air out the room prior to workers entering the space. It is not recommended that workers are exposed to high concentrations of carbon dioxide, as studies suggest that it may be unsafe.

Lighting the Space

One of the nice things about LED lights is that with certain fixtures the light spectrum can be controlled by the grower. Varying light spectrums directly affect the plant. LED lights produce far less heat than an indoor or greenhouse system full of HPS lamps.

Light manufacturers may aid directly with design as it pertains to lighting efficiency. Usually the companies will provide access to software that will calculate the lamps needed to achieve a specific light level over the canopy. Often manufacturers will provide assistance in the lighting plan, especially if it helps them make a large sale.

FEATURED GARDENS & GROWING STYLES

Dennis Peron examines some of the plants recently forced to flower
in his personal garden, San Francisco, California,1994.

Dennis Peron's Revolutionary Balcony Garden

by Ed Rosenthal

In 1969 Dennis Peron disembarked from a troop carrier from Vietnam to San Francisco. He decided to stay, found housing, and opened his duffel bag to start dealing the kilo of Southeast Asian cannabis he brought with him. From those beginnings, Peron became the founder of the first medical cannabis dispensary in the United States, offering a revolutionary model of compassionate care that included providing free cannabis to those who could not afford it. He was a leader in the cannabis reform movement, and he also was a friend of mine. Dennis died on January 27, 2018. His loss is felt greatly, and this edition of the *Cannabis Grower's Handbook* is dedicated in his memory.

Dennis was one of the first medical cannabis activists in the United States. The medical community and cannabis industry worldwide owe a debt of eternal gratitude to Dennis, who saw the unfairness of making sick people endure pain when there was medicine to relieve their suffering, and who did something about it.

Originally from the Bronx, Dennis grew up in Long Island and served in the US Air Force during the Viet Cong's Tet Offensive in 1968. Dennis chose to move to San Francisco because of the freedom he found there. At that time, homosexuality was widely discriminated against all over the country, and San Francisco had a large gay population that has had a profound effect on the area's attitudes, politics, and culture.

Within a few years he opened a café, The Island, downstairs from his cannabis shop, located on the second floor. The Island had a cozy atmosphere, and cannabis use was policy. In 1973, I signed the contract for my first book, *Marijuana Grower's Guide*, on the premises.

In 1978, Dennis wrote San Francisco's Proposition W, gathered signatures to get it on the ballot, and 63% of the voters agreed, approving the demand for a ceasefire in the war on cannabis and making San Francisco the first city in the nation with a "lowest priority" enforcement law. It read, "We the people of San Francisco demand the chief of police and the district attorney stop the arrest and prosecution of people for possessing, transferring, or growing marijuana."

Harvey Milk, the first openly-gay elected official in California, was a good friend to

Dennis. He started his political career collecting signatures for the initiative. He would continue as a San Francisco supervisor before he was shot dead by another supervisor who was a crazed right-wing, antigay terrorist.

In 1993, Dennis's life partner, Jonathan West, died of AIDS. Dennis had seen the relief that cannabis provided Jonathan as the virus ravaged his body. It helped with the nausea, the anorexia, and the pain in his joints and nerves.

After seeing how much cannabis had helped Jonathon as he was dying, Dennis opened the first medical dispensary in the United States, the Cannabis Buyers Club. It was located on Church Street in the heart of the Castro District, the most ostentatiously gay area of the city.

Dennis knew he was taking a risk, but the establishment was an immediate success, and within a few months over 5,000 medical patients had joined the club. Dennis was considered an angel by many of the patients he served, providing respite and comfort to the sick and needy.

Not only did the Cannabis Buyers Club provide patients with cannabis, it also served as a community center and living room for many of the patients who lived in SROs and had lost their jobs, and often their friends, when they became ill.

Tom Ammiano, then on the San Francisco Board of Education, cut the ribbon at the opening of Dennis's club. He went on to become a California assembly member and remained an advocate of legalizing cannabis.

In 1996, Dennis coauthored Proposition 215, California's medical cannabis initiative

Clients socializing at The Cannabis Buyers Club, San Francisco, California, 1994

that, for the first time in the nation, allowed patients with a written recommendation from their doctor to possess and grow cannabis.

The Cannabis Buyers Club was closed in 1996 by then California attorney general Dan Lundgren. Lundgren was another ultra-right-wing zealot; however, the dam had broken, and dozens of new medical dispensaries were opened by former workers who were trained at Dennis's dispensary. Now, there are tens of thousands of dispensaries in countries all over the world.

Dennis never reopened his dispensary. He was more of a social worker and social innovator and just didn't have the ambition to be a merchant.

He lived in the Castro District of San Francisco in the house that came to be known as the Castro Castle. He converted the space to an oasis of greenery, comfort, and hospitality.

Dennis was always a big supporter of homegrown cannabis and of letting patients grow their own medicine.

One would think that Dennis would depend on the largesse of medical dispensaries and growers for his medicine, but that wasn't the case. He grew his own.

Dennis's garden was one of my favorite gardens to visit even though it was not the most efficient or productive. I enjoyed it because of the diversity of the plants. Dennis would often get clones from friends, and he chose to grow small plants in a constant rotation.

Dennis started his clones in rockwool in a small room to the side of the house. Once they got large enough, he transplanted them into containers that range in size from about 1.5 gallons to 5 gallons (6–20 l).

He liked to grow in containers that could be moved around so that he could manipulate their flowering cycle by moving them into darkness, and also because they were easy to move into sunny areas of the deck. The sun's angle, and thus the sunny areas, changed with the season and the time of day.

When I visited Dennis in 1994, the plants were basking in the early afternoon sun. One group was on a specially constructed shelf along the deck fence and another group was sitting on a table on a sunny deck.

Each evening he placed his plants in a small room or in an outdoor shelter covered with opaque plastic to protect against both stray light and the cold night air of San Francisco, which can drop from a daytime temperature in the high 70s (~25°C) down into the low 50s (~11°C) or even 40s (~6°C) at night.

All the plants were forced to flower when they were small so that they remained manageable, under two feet (2.4 m) tall. The fertilizer and soil brands varied because friends often donated material.

San Francisco is cool during the summer because the cold air from the sea meets the warm inland air there, creating fog. The winds change around Labor Day, which means that the sun can penetrate. September is the warmest month of the year in the city, with warm, clear weather. The cool summer weather delays growth and maturity, so varieties take 20–30% longer to grow and mature there.

The cool weather does have its advantages. The mild conditions make it much less likely

Dennis Peron Garden, San Francisco, California, 1994.

to suffer environmental damage. There are few problems with insects. Also, the plants don't suffer from container burn (containers getting hot from strong sunlight and harming roots), and their water needs are much lower than plants growing in hot conditions.

When I visited, Dennis's plants were in all stages of growth, from close to harvest to clones growing into young plants, attributable to San Francisco's mild climate.

Throughout the year the daytime temperature rarely dips below 40°F (4.5°C), and even in winter the temperature can rise into the mid-70s F (mid-20s C). Plants can be grown year round, especially in this situation, where plants get sunlight during the day and protection from the cold air at night.

In late September, plants would start flowering immediately unless they were given supplemental light to break up the long dark period. Then, once they were tall enough, they were moved outside to flower under the long night regimen of uninterrupted darkness.

Dennis's garden was not only full of healthy plants; it was rich with historical meaning and a small reflection of Dennis's significance in the fight to end marijuana prohibition.

I miss him.

KISS Garden (Keep It Simple System)

By Dan Vinkovetsky, formerly Danny Danko of *High Times*

If a grower is seeking an affordable and easy way to procure a pound (~0.5 kg) or more of pristine cannabis flowers every three months, look no further than this uncomplicated and manageable system for less than a $1,000 initial investment.

Grow Tent

Get a light-tight unit that's easy for one person to set up and take down. Choose a tent sized appropriately for the available space. This one is a 5 x 3 x 6.7 feet (1.5 x 0.9 x 2 m) UltraGrow tent unit, but there are plenty of similar options available. Make sure it comes with sturdy metal supports for the lighting and has holes for intake and outtake fans as well as flood protection. Many tents come as grow kits with lighting and fans included, but it is not necessary to pay extra for a complicated hydroponic system when it is far more simple to just hand-water the plants in containers. Once the tent is set up, go inside it with the door closed and the lights off to check for any possible light leaking in from outside.

Buckets

I recommend the cheap 5 gallon (19 l) buckets that are readily available. Be sure to drill holes in the bottom for drainage and use trays underneath them to contain overflow. Never allow plants to sit in stagnant water. Remove any overflow to prevent complications. Buy a 1–2 gallon (3.75–7.5 l) watering can and a spray bottle from the hardware store. Start with 1 gallon (~4 l) containers, which are about 8 inches (20 cm) in diameter at the top, and transplant into the 5 gallon (~29 l) containers before the flowering stage.

Soilless Mix

I fill the buckets with a soilless mix that already contains coco coir or mini-sized LECA and other amendments. I recommend Pro-Mix BX as a base and then add dry supplements. These include additional perlite, bat, or seabird guanos, greensand, beneficial microbes, bacteria, and more. I use a quarter to a half cup (34–68 g) of each supplement per 5 gallon (19 l) bucket. Different supplements are concentrated at different levels, so this is just a basic guideline. The important thing is that it's light and airy.

Lighting

I try not to overwhelm myself with too much light for the space. The one in this tent is a 1000-watt Plantmax high pressure sodium lamp driven by a Quantum Blitz digital ballast. The six inch (15 cm) reflector by Sun System spreads all available light efficiently to the canopy below. The light raises the temperature dramatically, so I have to set up an air conditioner in the room outside the tent and use a strong window fan to exhaust the air. Next time, I'll install an efficient LED lighting system. It uses much less electricity and produces much less heat.

Nutrients

The plant food that the grower chooses will determine how often to fertilize and how much

High yield plants have healthy root systems.
Photo: Dan Vinkovetsky

to add to the nutrient solution. I love the line from Suite Leaf because it's clean, straight-forward, and almost 100% vegan. Whatever feeding system is chosen, be sure to feed lightly at first and bump up the nutrients as the plants grow larger.

Fans & Filters

It's important to move cool fresh air in and hot spent air out at the proper rates, so be sure to use an outtake fan that can clear out the tent in less than five minutes. The one for this tent is rated at 435 cfm. It's attached to a six inch (15 cm) in-line duct fan by Grow1 attached to a six inch DL light-proof ducting exiting the tent. The intake fan uses an eight inch (20 cm) UltraGrow light-proof ducting inside the tent. Always keep at least one oscillating fan inside the tent to move air around as well. Ours is a Monkey Fan from Secret Jardin.

Monitors

There are a few items it would be foolish to do without. A digital thermometer with a built-in hygrometer keeps track of the temperature and humidity inside the tent, even when I am not there.

I use the Wireless Weather Station by Grow1 unit. It alerts me the moment that the tent environment strays from preset limits. I also measure the pH of the nutrient solution after I've mixed in the plant food before watering. The inexpensive chemical test kits for aquarium water provide a rough idea of pH, but there are inexpensive electronic meters that indicate more precisely. A timer keeps the light schedule whether I'm home or not.

CO_2 Supplementation

I use different cheap and effective ways to increase carbon dioxide (CO_2) levels and thus plant yields. I've used mushroom buckets and CO_2 production bags. These units produce CO_2 gas as a result of natural biological processes. They continue producing gas for the entire 65 days of the flowering stage. In this tent, I used Green Pad CO_2 generators that are doped cloth pads activated by simply hanging them up and occasionally misting with water.

Harvesting Materials

I use a clean table and a comfortable chair in a cool room with decent lighting for proper trimming. I also use a magnifying glass to closely examine the flowers to determine ripe-ness. For trimming, I use small clipping scissors or snips, rubbing alcohol (for cleaning scissors), string or coat hangers for drying branches to hang from, and a fan to move the air around in the drying area (not pointed directly at drying branches). Finally, I use glass jars for curing and storing buds.

Other Useful Items

I use a step stool to sit on while I'm working in the tent, a notebook pad and pen to keep track of everything, and a calendar to keep track of and dial in the timing of every grow.

Once my tent is set up and my plants are growing, I hand-water them as needed, alternating between using nutrient solution and plain water. Once they have three or more sets of leaves, it's time to start training them in order to increase their yields. In this tent, I'm using the Screen of Green system (ScrOG), Trellis Netting from Grow1.

I also employ strategic defoliation of some fan leaves and lower branches during the vegetative stage to stimulate growth and aid in the circulation of air below the canopy. This keeps fresh air moving throughout the tent and helps avoid mildew, mold, and bud rot from stagnant air pockets.

I lower the light to the proper distance from the canopy level and raise the light as the plants grow taller. This keeps them from stretching for the light and growing long and lanky instead of short and stocky.

Danny is the author of *Cannabis: A Beginner's Guide to Growing Marijuana*, host of the Grow Bud Yourself podcast, and editor at *Northeast Leaf Magazine*.

Danny uses Suite Bloom nutrients and Ed Rosenthal's Zero Tolerance to prevent and manage pests.
Photo: Dan Vinkovetsky

Photo: Tyler LeBlanc

Big Floating Buds: Tyler's Aquaponic Garden

By Felisa Rogers

"I'm in the room. You wanna see the girls?" asks Tyler Leblanc. He's standing above a uniform forest of giant buds. Each plant consists of one stem that's grown up into a spiral. The tightly packed flower is the shape of the club a cartoon caveman might carry. "See how it just grows one bud straight up?" he asks. "These buds gotta be about 30 grams." To demonstrate the size of the clusters, Tyler holds up a wine bottle, which is dwarfed by the cola. "They're just rock hard," he says happily.

The key feature of this unusual garden is difficult to see at first. But the two foot (60 cm) tall plants are floating in a single pond, stabilized by styrofoam rafts. Tyler says it's possible to grow between two and four plants per square foot (0.09 m²). By putting small plants immediately into flower, he saves a month's worth of energy.

The obsession with growing giant plants was of course spawned by maximum plant counts for medical grows, but giant plants aren't energy efficient. "You only harvest the top foot or two [30–60 cm] of the plant, right?" Tyler points out. "With these tiny plants, you save a month of vegging, and the pruning, the labor, everything is less because it just grows so quickly," he explains. "Even trimming—it's just one big rock solid bud. The dream, right? You can just push these floats down the pond like they do with lettuce and that's your automation."

This floating garden of dwarf plants was inspired by Ed Rosenthal's theories on best practices for minimizing labor and maximizing energy efficiency. The arrangement is a fraction of the hassle of a traditional hydroponic grow. Filling the pond with water requires little effort, and the waterway makes it easy to move the plants around. There's no hauling of buckets, no solid grow media, and no drip lines. By simplifying the process, he's created a method with fewer potential breaking points.

This is only Tyler's second time growing using this technique. Once he tweaks it a bit, he envisions a larger operation. "The idea of using this on a commercial scale is that it is easily automated so we wouldn't touch anything and the plants would just float down the pond while growing into massive buds."

For now the pond is only nine by four feet (2.7 x 1.2 m). Four floats measuring two by four feet (0.6 x 1.2 m) are home to 108 plants. To prevent algae growth and protect the roots from light, Tyler uses garbage bags to cover the narrow channels between the edge of the floats and the side of the pond. This floating forest requires minimal intervention. In fact, Tyler says that it can go unattended for a week at a time.

The garden requires no unusual strategies for lighting, water, or nutrients. The water is from the well. Tyler uses an $18 Venturi adapter meant for a dishwasher hooked in-line for the water chiller output in addition to an air pump with tubing to 10 air stones that he places around the pond.

The lights are high pressure sodium. Tyler feeds the plants every day with a diet of Current Culture nutrients: Veg A&B, Cal Roots, and UC Roots, an optimization and sterilization agent. He thinks that UC Roots is a vital component to his success.

It might be possible to use a little rooting gel and put the clones directly into the raft, but this time around Tyler started out with aeroponic cloners. "When they get a nice white root, I take them out of that and put them in the pond," he says. Using this method, he cuts out the vegetative stage almost entirely. Once they are planted, he keeps indica-looking plants in vegetative growth for 3 to 10 days, but starts forcing the sativas to flower immediately.

The pond garden is an experiment using two cultivars. The Moby Dick looks a little leggy, but the OG Mendo Grape is stout and sturdy. Indicas are likely the better choice for this style of growing because they stay fairly short and stout. Tyler occasionally had to prune to prevent branching, but if the plants had been placed a bit closer to each other, it is possible to create an even canopy that would naturally stop a tendency toward branching. "With the right cultivar you can leave it untouched and it'd grow straight up," Tyler says.

Like any garden, there have been some problems to solve. Tyler relies on help from his uncle, a talented local gardener. "I couldn't have implemented this without the dedicated support of Uncle Ribinski," Tyler says.

Originally he started the water at a pH of 5.8. "The plants had explosive root growth but the tops shriveled and died," he says. He upped the pH to 6.2 and got happy plants. At another point in the grow, he realized that the roots were getting too much CO_2 from the air pump. He moved the pump out of the grow room so that it wasn't sucking air enriched with CO_2. The problem disappeared.

Calibrating water temperature and pH is essential to this style of growing. Both need to drop as the plants grow. "When you put them in the water it should be between 70 and 72°F (21 and 22°C). The target pH until they acclimate should be 6.2," he says. "As soon as it takes and you get a little new growth you can drop the water to 70°F (21°C) and the pH to 6.1," he instructs. "Once you trigger flowering, you drop the temperature to 68°F (20°C) and the pH to 6 and keep it that way for two weeks. By the third week, the pH is reduced to 5.9, while keeping the water at 68°F (20°C). Maintain for three weeks. For the last three weeks of the flower cycle, the pH should be 5.8.

The current crop was in flower for 56 days. He estimates that the typical cycle for this type of garden is about seven or eight weeks, maybe a little more for some cultivars. He expected about 30 grams per plant, though the plants yielded a fraction more, averaging 31 or more. His biggest plant from the grow yielded 42.5 grams. "It was one bud, straight up!" he says, adding that the flowers were aromatic, covered in trichomes. "Smokes smooth and hits hard," he says with a smile. The total yield was 3,240 grams, or 7.1 pounds (3.24 kg).

Processing is simple. He just picks off the bigger leaves and hangs the entire plants, using traditional good practices for curing. There are no larfy branches, so the final product requires very little trimming. Starting over is also simple and waste free; he just drains and refills the pond and reuses the rafts. He estimates he can do five or six gardens a year.

Clones are installed to float over the reservoir.
Photo: Courtesy of Tyler LeBlanc

Plants grown in this aquaponics system grow long, dense colas. Photo: Courtesy of Tyler LeBlanc

Oklahoma Sungrown:
Localized Breeding with
Fungi & Hügelkultur

Photo: Andy Unruh

In 2018 Oklahoma voters passed State Question 788, which legalized medical cannabis use and possession, solidified the right of patients to maintain home gardens, and created a free market for commercial cultivation with low barriers to entry. The result has been a robust industry full of locally owned and operated businesses that thrives off constant innovation and community breeding.

Friends and farmers Jeremy Babbit and Andy Unruh are both licensed growers under the Oklahoma Medical Marijuana Authority (OMMA) and work together to explore and improve on permaculture practices adapted to the unique microclimates they live and garden in. Through a combination of regenerative agriculture techniques, including hügelkultur, and cultivating several strains of carbon-dioxide-producing mushrooms, they are producing localized varieties of high-quality sungrown flowers for premium single-source ice hash rosin.

Hügelkultur translated from German means "hill culture." It refers to a method of permaculture that involves burying wood in mounds or raised beds. As the wood rots, it becomes a sponge that retains moisture, thus reducing or eliminating the need for irrigation. While compost is typically broken down by bacteria, wood is digested by fungi. The use of both the rotting wood and compost creates a thriving living soil ecosystem filled with earthworms that reduces or eliminates the need for fertilizers.

Andy says that he decided to use hügelkultur because the soil on his farm was really compacted and full of clay. He had cut down oak trees six months prior, and the logs and sticks were in varying states of decay. He created a circular pattern around a post hole to create mounds as well as a traditional hügelkultur trench.

Andy and Jeremy have combined the use of the wood with helpful fungi that thrive in it as it rots: mushrooms. While some of the mushrooms grown in the gardens arrived on their own, others have been brought in by adding spores to compost tea to encourage the soil diversity and provide an ongoing source of carbon dioxide directly underneath the cannabis plants.

Andy says the wild mushroom strains in his garden include bird's nest, ink head, puff balls, and rose guild mushrooms, which seem to thrive in the iron-rich native "red dirt" soil in his garden that Oklahoma is famous for. As he forages in the woods around his farm, he picks mushrooms and places the fresh caps in the compost tea he feeds the plants.

"By placing the spores, caps, and mycelium into the compost tea before feeding, I am able to introduce local native fungi directly to my plants. My best results so far have been with Stubble Rosegill (*Volvopluteus gloiocephalus*) and Bird's Nest Fungi (*Nidulariaceae*). I have begun introducing porcini (*Boletus Edulis*) mushrooms, which form mycorrhizal partnerships with plants, but I have not seen any fruiting bodies to date."

To encourage the growth of bolete mushrooms near the cannabis plants' roots, he has thrown spores into the compost heap.

"I knew I had to get my soil mixed with more fungi because it is clay, dense, and anaerobic, and I want it to become aerobic. Fungi is one of the ways to loosen up the soil without tilling. The hyphae build pathways for oxygen, develop soil structure, decompose organic matter, and extract and hold nutrients," Andy says.

Andy warns that not all the mushrooms are edible, and many are dangerous if consumed, but his work with the fungus has inspired him to cultivate beneficial mushrooms that are also edible, such as reishis and shiitakes, which he plans to add to the hügelkultur beds under his cannabis plants by first inoculating the logs with the spore plugs and then burying them in the beds.

Together Andy and Jeremy focus on permaculture methods and localized breeding programs with two end goals: creating thriving sungrown varieties acclimatized to the microclimates of eastern Oklahoma, and especially those that produce high-quality resin-rich flowers for Jeremy to process into single-sourced ice water hash, for both their farms as well as others using similar methods.

"I need the right resin, the right trichome heads. That is what I am growing for," Jeremy says. Unlike Andy's farm, Jeremy's property doesn't have the famous "red dirt" Oklahoma is known for, but instead clay and sandstone. Jeremy uses traditional hügelkultur beds amended with compost, coco coir, worm castings, and spore-rich wood chips produced from trees cut down on his own property.

Andy's and Jeremy's farms are about an hour away from each other in the greater Tulsa area. Jeremy's farm, 918 Oklahoma Grown, is just northeast of the city in Collinsville; Andy's is Sticky Flower Farm, to the southwest outside Depew. They are quick to point out that the State of Oklahoma has many diverse microclimates, from the wetter and greener rolling hills in the east to the dry, arid land in the western panhandle sandwiched between

Andy Unruh next to the beginnings of a hügelkultur mound. Photo: Jeff Hooten

Texas to the south and Kansas and Colorado to the north.

While the goal of Jeremy's garden is to produce high-quality solventless concentrates with locally bred varieties, Andy says the goal of his garden is to work with farmers and breeders throughout the state to create a community around producing genetics specialized to the region.

"The community here in Oklahoma is really good, State Question 788 has given everyone the opportunity that wants to put in the effort, do it legit, do it right, and not put out a half-assed product," says Jeremy. "I want to find genetics that grow well outdoors and produce the best hash rosin I can make."

Most commercial cannabis varieties available in Oklahoma and other states in the East, Midwest, and South were the result of breeding programs and alliances that originated on the West Coast. While most states east of the Rockies have strictly limited the amount of grow licenses and the qualifications to grow, Oklahoma's free market approach has resulted in thousands of small farmers like Andy and Jeremy, with the ability to breed and grow new plants that are more appropriate to the region.

Andy says, "Oklahoma is absolutely incredible for having a local breeder community. If we work together as a community on cultivars and methods that work best in our state, we will find cultivars that Californians wish they could grow as well as we do, just like we wished we could grow specific cultivars as well as they do."

Neither Jeremy or Andy refers to himself as a "master grower," but as farmers. Both seek to transform the region's current farming practices and have integrated permaculture and regenerative techniques into their gardens.

"I am just a farmer. I don't know anyone on my dad or mom's side of the family who wasn't a farmer. I am just going back to my roots. I saw too many people using 'traditional' commercial agriculture practices but always struggling and always fighting something," Andy says about the decision to transition to using natural techniques.

Both farms produce one yearly annual harvest under natural light. Although neither plans to use light deprivation, they have gotten creative with planting seasons and using autoflower varieties.

Jeremy's garden is 40 by 72 feet (12 by 22 m) and enclosed in a state-mandated 8 foot (2.5 m) fence. It contains 100 plants of 12 varieties. He is growing some for the first time and others that are reliable hash plants. He started some from seeds and others from clones obtained from local breeders. He has a preference for sativa varieties but tends to grow more hybrid and indica-dominant plants because they are better hash producers, as are most Diesel varieties. Currently he's growing Killer Cupcakes, Sundae Supreme, Watermelon Zum Zum, Glue Ball, Thunder Diesel, Durban Kush, Orange Mac, MorningWood, Strawberry Diesel, Cornbread, and Island Mimosa.

Andy's garden is smaller than Jeremy's and includes a personal home garden where Andy does most of the breeding and experimentation. Unlike Jeremy's, Andy's is a seed garden. Its purpose is breeding and storing local-specific varieties.

He has propagated feminized seeds from Morning Wood, a cross of Sour Diesel and

Jeremy Babbit's outdoor farm contains 100 plants of 12 different varieties. Photo: Jeremy Babbit

Alaskan Thunderfuck produced by local breeder Pac-a-Punch. Both he and Jeremy say it produces great hash. Morning Wood was crossed with Green Crack, which will eventually be released as "Pepe Depew." Local breeder Oklahoma Kush Collective has provided an Athena's Wisdom that he is experimenting with. He has crossed two of these plants with Thunder Cheese from another local breeder, Shaggy Roots, which was crossed with Purple Urkle. There is also a cross of Green Crack and Purple Urkle and a new unique variety from out west: Freak Show, which looks more like a fern than a traditional cannabis plant.

Jeremy must contend with all four seasons. It gets hot and humid in the summers. He irrigates the plants with just enough water to keep them from wilting. They are supported using netting and cages when the plants grow large. Beyond the heat, the biggest challenge is dealing with grasshoppers and caterpillars, which like to burrow into nugs and destroy them from the inside.

Andy's farm is a lot wetter, so he breeds for mold resistance and, when necessary, uses an indigenous microorganism (IMO) spray to keep mold at bay.

Andy's gardens are irrigated using a drip system. Jeremy uses several methods, including soaker hoses and gravity beds.

Both farmers seek natural methods of pest and fungal control. Jeremy has attempted to rely on his turkeys and guineas to eat up grasshoppers and caterpillars, but they haven't been too reliable. Both use natural foliar sprays to control pests and fungus including Dr. Zymes and IMOs. Both gardens are abundant with beneficial predators including ladybugs, praying mantis, assassin bugs, and spiders.

When it is time to harvest, Jeremy is focused on preserving the high-quality trichomes that he will make into hash. He takes the plants into a freezer room immediately after harvest, chops off the nugs and prepares them to become ice water hash.

Both use traditional drying and curing methods to harvest flowers: hanging the branches to dry in a temperature- and humidity-controlled space before burping in jars as they cure.

Mushrooms are encouraged to grow in the dirt as both a source of CO_2 and below-the-surface fungal life. Photo: Andy Unruh

Creswell Oreganics
Octagon Gardens

Growing vertically has several advantages, but the reason why this grow method is so efficient is it maximizes all the energy produced by the HPS lamp and minimizes the space and power needed for rooms dedicated to vegetative growth. Rather than lighting a horizontal garden with overhead lights and reflectors, the canopy is literally wrapped around the bulb, absorbing all the output produced by the lamp and doubling the canopy space that the lights are covering.

Trent Hancock of Creswell Oreganics designed two "octagons" for vegetative growth and flowering. The octagon for vegetative growth has six shelves evenly spaced, with three containers per shelf. It is capable of holding 128 plants and supplying four flowering octagons.

The flowering octagon is 12 feet (3.65 m) in diameter and has eight sides with four levels of shelves that each hold two plants around four vertical HPS lights. Each level is spaced evenly, with the top shelf at 6 feet (15.25 cm). Each shelf holds two containers.

As the plants grow up and out toward the lights at a 45° angle, they cover the containers on the shelf above them. The flowering octagon holds 64 plants that produce up to four ounces (113 g) of flower each. Although the plants stay relatively small, between 3 and 3.5 feet (0.9–1 m), the yield is higher and the density is spread throughout the entire stalk, not just the top cola.

The goal of Creswell Oreganics is to produce connoisseur-quality flowers in the most cost-effective and natural ways possible: to have "all the quality of indoor with the efficiency of outdoor" growing. Creswell has focused on vertical efficiency and using rapid-fresh air exchange as a method to control pests.

The air inside the octagons is rapidly exchanged. This creates a hostile climate for bugs; they are blown off by wind gusts and cannot move or reproduce in cooler climates. Hancock designed the garden so that the air could be fully replaced every 20 seconds in order to simulate a high-altitude climate that is inhospitable to pests. The gusts and warm air in the daytime prevent the proliferation of mold and mildew spores, and cool temperatures in the night cycle prevent proliferation of pests. Air is exchanged rapidly using three air plenums that interact with each other. Temperatures are kept at 75°F (24°C) during the day cycle and lowered to 48°F (9°C) during the night cycle. The heat bursts during the last five minutes of the day cycle at 94°F (35°C).

The company grows with one solid philosophy: they won't grow it if they wouldn't smoke it. This means dedication to pest-free climates and never using sprays of any kind, even certified organic pesticides.

Creswell produces a regular supply of cannabis flowers for dispensaries in the Portland and Eugene, Oregon areas. Trent got his start as a teenager in the 1990s working on small indoor gardens in Oregon. He relocated to Montana, where he ended up with a felony cannabis charge in 2004. While he was on probation, he studied political science and started consulting. When Montana legalized medical cannabis by ballot initiative, also in 2004, as a felon Trent was barred from being a provider in the industry but became a consultant to legal medical gardens and helped design many that reached commercial success.

Trent produced well-known cultivars in Montana including Big Sky Kush and Blue-

Photo: Guy Holmes and Grow Magazine

berry Silvertip. After a ruling in the Montana Supreme Court shut down legal cultivations in 2016, Trent and head grower Shayney Norick relocated back to Trent's home state of Oregon and founded Creswell Organics.

Creswell usually grows about seven varieties at once. They specialize in their own cultivars, Grapefruit Crater and Crater Kush (White Widow x Obama Kush), but grow other regional favorites like Purple Punch, Kashmir Kush, and White Tahoe Cookies.

When Shayney and Trent are pheno-hunting, they start with up to 5,000 non feminized seeds and whittle them away through a series of stress tests. The 300 best structured plants with the best immune systems are cloned and numbered. They go in the flower room in a soil-coir mix. After the seedlings flower, the best three versions of the cross are saved in the clone room and the other clones destroyed. The final phenos are determined by aroma, effect when smoked, aroma after smoking, trichome production, immunity to mold and disease, structure, root structure, and speed of vegetative growth and flower ripening.

The plants are fed just enough liquid nutrients to not be deficient, customized to each variety's preferences. Water is mixed in tanks and plants are watered by hand.

"We never have to spray, so it's the only time we have interaction with the plants. I use it as time to check on them," Trent says. "The best crops I ever had was when I was a small grower. Shayney and I try to do as much as we can to repeat that high quality on a commercial level."

After harvest, plants are dried using a negative air pressure dry rack that pulls air from the center; the shelves each have their own intake drawing evenly at the edges. Once buds dry to the touch, it is sealed up and opened every day until the stems snap.

Autumn Brands: Dutch-Style Flower Farming

Courtesy of Autumn Brands

Courtesy of Autumn Brands

Autumn Brands provides hundreds of dispensaries in California with a variety of pesticide-free cannabis flowers and pre-rolls grown using a unique integrated pest management program and the wisdom of six generations of Dutch-style cut-flower farming.

"We don't spray anything, not even organic pesticides," says Hans Brand, who oversees the greenhouses with his son Johnny.

The goal at the garden is to meet market demand while also being sustainable, contaminant free, and cost efficient. To control pests, for the last three years the farm has relied on a sparkling clean facility and local beneficial insects that have moved in and made the greenhouses their breeding grounds.

As no-spray cannabis farmers, they search for and develop resistant varieties that thrive in the "sun grown indoor" climate provided in their greenhouses in Carpinteria, California. Year-round high temperatures in this coastal southwestern town range between 70–88°F (21–31°C), with 280 days of sunshine annually and 60–65% relative humidity.

Once Johnny determines that a variety is not hypersensitive to the humid climate, he tests 10 plants, observing each one's unique growth patterns through three distinct stages. First, he observes how quickly and easily cuttings grow roots. Next, he observes how fast they grow and mature. Finally, he looks for plants that swell quickly and finish with strong and dense trichomes.

The full process takes around six months, and Johnny is constantly searching for new varieties to test and grow. The family has grown in the same greenhouses for more than 27 years, using techniques and knowledge accumulated by his father and grandfather that were passed down to him.

"Growing quality flowers is more than the right [genetics], plants, and technology. It's a feeling for the flowers. You can't get it from a book or from a school. It's in your fingers . . . it's in your blood," says Hans.

The Brand family began farming flowers in Holland more than a century ago, and today Johnny carries on the family's flower-growing tradition as a sixth-generation flower farmer, although he is the first to specialize in cannabis.

Johnny grew up in his father's greenhouses when they were still producing tulips and gerber daisies. Like other cut-flower farmers in the region, the Brands' business started declining in the late 1990s after Congress enacted the Andean Trade Preference Act (ATPA), which encouraged South American countries like Colombia, Peru, and Ecuador to transition coca production to cut flowers.

California flower farmers couldn't compete, and a steady decline in the business continued through the early 2000s, with nearly half the state's cut-flower farmers out of business by 2012. That's when the region's farmers increasingly started to look to producing another kind of flower.

The Brand family began that transition in 2015 under California's medical cannabis law. At first, Hans was not a cannabis proponent and was skeptical when a cannabis grower asked to rent space in one of his greenhouses.

It didn't take long for Hans to recognize the financial opportunity in growing cannabis flowers, and so in partnership with Johnny, daughter Hanna, and partner Autumn Shelton, who had worked with the farm when it was still producing flowers, Autumn Brands was born.

The greenhouses deliver a steady stream of pre-rolled joints and flowers to popular dispensaries in Los Angeles, San Francisco, and other parts of the state where adult-use retail sales are legal. In order to maintain the quality and product integrity, the garden was designed with the same efficiency as when it produced cut flowers.

"We have developed our systems to be lean and mean. I used to battle over pennies in the flower business, and I am taking the same approach in this business. We don't throw around hundred dollar bills. We try to be frugal and smart and to keep the overhead low at all times," Hans says.

Each greenhouse produces six harvests a year of a dozen "mainstay" varieties, including Chocolate Hashberry, Dream Walker, GG #4, Orange Crush, OG Kush, Purple Punch, Shark Shock, Sour Diesel, and Strawberry Banana. The Brands often experiment with other varieties as well, including CBD cultivars such as Blue Dream CBD.

Plants are started as clones and

Courtesy of Autumn Brands

387

grown hydroponically using a coco coir medium. They are constantly watered through a closed loop system that irrigates 12 times a day with nutrient-adjusted water that is looped and blended with fresh water for the next watering.

Once plants have rooted, they are placed on rolling trays for efficiency. Each tray contains 128 plants that move together on the rollers as needed throughout the greenhouse. Two layers of trellising are placed to support the plants, once in vegetative and the second time as the plants enter flowering and the buds become heavy.

Autumn Brands does not use supplemental lighting, since it's so sunny year-round. The greenhouses' climate is controlled using software, but generally the overnight low in the rooms is 59°F (15°C) and daytime highs are between 80–86°F (27–30°C). Occasionally in the winter, heating is used to keep the rooms from freezing, but the biggest concern is humidity control.

Humidity is maintained in the low 80s at night using climate controllers that measure and adjust the climate based on the current dew point, relative humidity, humidity deficit, temperature, and available light.

Plants are harvested by hand and dried in a large temperature- and humidity-controlled cooler. After drying, the harvest team begins the bucking and trimming process, removing flowers from their stems by hand with extreme care. Next, plants enter the two-week curing phase, in which they are kept at a low temperature and medium humidity level to help preserve their unique potency and ensure a smooth, flavorful toke. Then, they are placed in eco-friendly glass jars or rolled into joints.

Plants are moved around the facility using electric go-karts. Courtesy of Autumn Brands

The California Appellation of Origin Garden

by Kristin Nevedal

Geographical indications (GIs) and appellations of origin (AO) are internationally recognized intellectual property systems that offer significant opportunity to protect valuable traditions and genetic resources for peoples throughout the world.

A GI is a sign used on products that have a specific geographical origin and possess qualities or a reputation that is due to that origin. Appellations of origin are a special type, or subset, of a GI in that the qualitative links between product and place must be stronger than that of GIs.

In the case of an appellation of origin, the distinctive quality or characteristics of the product must result essentially or exclusively from its geographical origin. Terroir, a French term, is commonly used to describe the combination of factors including soil, climate, and sunlight that gives the product its distinctive character.

Happy Day Farms grow both commercial cannabis and vegetables according to California's appellation program in the Bell Springs Appellation of Northern Mendocino County. Photo: Amber O'Neill at Happy-Day Farms

These standards-based regulatory systems act to codify traditional knowledge and traditional agricultural practices, as well as protect valuable genetic resources, resulting in the harmonization of respective intellectual property standards, values, and technologies between countries engaging in the trade of AO products.

How Might These Systems Be Applied to Cannabis?

Recognized by farmers as a highly adaptable plant, cannabis is heavily influenced by the environment in which it is grown. As cannabis seeds spread throughout the world, the plant was bred for different uses and adapted to a multitude of natural environments, resulting in the development of countless cultivars with distinctive variations.

There are many regions known for unique cultivars that produce high-quality inflorescence with distinctive characteristics attributed partly to the original environment where the cannabis was grown and bred. This includes geographical regions known for modern breeding such as California's Emerald Triangle and regions of Spain, but especially the many regions in Central and Southeast Asia where the plant evolved. This includes countries such as Afghanistan, Bhutan, India, Nepal, Thailand, and Vietnam as well as many areas in Central and South America and the Caribbean.

Despite decades of international cannabis prohibition, the most well known of these regions established global brand-name recognition among patients, consumers, and the public. As regional recognition increased, so has the demand for cannabis products from these regions.

However, as regional fame grew and product value increased, so did the number of products branded with regional names grown or manufactured outside the named region.

Developing the World's First GI & AO Programs for Cannabis

In 2015, nearly 20 years after the passage of the Compassionate Use Act, the California Legislature established the Medical Cannabis Regulation and Safety Act (MCRSA). MCRSA created a statewide framework to regulate medicinal cannabis and established two very important geographical indication programs for cannabis: County of Origin and Appellation of Origin. Subsequent legislation was passed in 2019 that strengthened the appellation of origin statute.

In 2020, the California Legislature passed Senate Bill 67, which expanded the County of Origin program to also include city and county of origin indications based on political boundaries. It allows cannabis and cannabis goods produced 100% within the boundaries to bear the name of the county, city, or city and county.

Additionally, and maybe even more important, Senate Bill 67 established terroir-driven baseline standards for California's Appellation Program (CAP), which requires that for cannabis to qualify for an appellation of origin seal, it must be grown in the ground, without the use of a structure, and without the use of artificial or supplemental lighting in the flower stage.

Pathway to Establishing a Cannabis Appellation of Origin in California

To establish an appellation of origin, a group of licensed cultivators, located within the proposed appellation region, must prepare and submit a petition to the California Department of Food and Agriculture for review and approval. Consistent with appellations of origin for products such as wine, Champagne, and cheese, California's cannabis Appellation of Origin program requires the petitioner to, among other things:

1. Show evidence of historical name use;
2. Describe each geographical feature affecting the cannabis produced in the geographical area of the proposed appellation of origin, including:
   a. Climate information, which may include temperature, precipitation, wind, fog, solar orientation, and radiation;
   b. Geological information, which may include underlying formations, landforms, and such geophysical events as earthquakes, eruptions, and major floods;
   c. Soil features, which may include microbiology and soil series or phases of a soil series;
   d. Physical features, which may include flat, hilly, or mountainous topography, geographical formations, bodies of water, watersheds, and irrigation resources;
   e. Cultural features, which may include political boundaries associated with a history or reputation of cannabis cultivation, the distribution of a specific set of cultivation practices, and anthropogenic features; and
   f. Minimum and maximum elevations.
3. Provide substantial evidence that the geographical area is distinctive when compared to areas outside the proposed boundary and to other relevant areas that produce cannabis for sale in the marketplace;
4. Provide an explanation of how the geographical feature is considered intrinsic to the identity or character of the area by means other than being required by local or state law, regulation, or ordinance;
5. Provide a description of the quality, characteristic, or reputation of the cannabis that is **essentially or exclusively caused by the geographical feature**, including an explanation of how the geographical feature causes the cannabis to have that quality, characteristic, or reputation; and
6. Identify at least one specific standard, practice, or cultivar requirement that acts to preserve the distinctiveness of the geographical feature and maintain its relevance to the cannabis produced within the appellation region.

Planning for and Setting up an Appellation of Origin Cultivation Site
The Cannabis Must Be Planted in the Ground.

Planting the cannabis in the ground ensures that it is produced within the appellation region and is influenced by the native soil and microbiology unique to each appellation region. Various methods of planting in the ground may be used, including tilling, or turning the native soil, sheet mulching, and mounded beds. The type of amendments, or soil additives allowed, as well as the method(s) allowed for planting in the ground, must be in accordance with any relevant standards and/or practices established by the appellation.

The Cannabis Must Be Grown without the Use of a Structure.

Cannabis produced within the appellation region must be grown in an open-air setting without the use of a greenhouse, hoop house, shade house, or other structure that might alter the natural temporal environment of the appellation region. The use of light-deprivation techniques is also prohibited, as this technique not only manipulates the temporal setting where the cannabis is produced but also alters the natural sunlight hours the plant would otherwise receive.

Producing cannabis without the use of a structure additionally prohibits the use of coverings temporarily to protect from natural conditions such as early frost, rain, and/or smoke particulate from nearby wildfires.

Cannabis Must Be Grown without the Use of Artificial or Supplemental Lighting.

While artificial or supplemental lighting may be used for supporting the growth of mother plants and for other propagation activities, artificial or supplemental lighting shall not be used once the plants are taller or wider than 18 inches (46 cm). This baseline standard ensures that the cannabis is grown utilizing natural sunlight, subjecting it to the appellation region's natural daylight hours and sunlight intensity.

Irrigation Water and Water Sources

In addition to the terroir-driven baseline standards established for California's Cannabis Appellation Program, the water used to irrigate the cannabis must be sourced from within the appellation region and in its source form, or otherwise "untreated." Such water sources could include permitted surface water such as streams, creeks, rivers, and springs, or groundwater sourced from a well or aquifer, as well as rainwater captured and stored within the appellation region.

In some appellation regions, natural environmental conditions eliminate the need for irrigation altogether, allowing farmers to utilize dry-farming techniques. Rich alluvial floodplains such as the Holmes Flat area in the Eel River Valley in Northern California, where historic flood cycles have deposited layers of silt and forest mulch on the valley floor, and the water table is naturally high, are perfect for dry-farming a multitude of agricultural crops, cannabis included.

The Benefits of GI and AO Programs for Consumers

Both geographical indication and appellation of origin programs offer consumers an opportunity to verify the origin of the products they purchase and to directly support the economy of the originating community.

Appellation of origin products offer consumers additional opportunities including the ability to verify the standards by which the products were produced, as well as the unique ability to experience the taste of a place and the subtle differences between a cultivar produced in different appellation regions.

Planting by the Moon:
The Martyjuana™ Garden

The Martyjuana garden goal is to provide organic sun-grown, small-batch cannabis using the natural methods used to produce the best organic foods.

Each annual crop is cultivated using biodynamic methods, although the farm is not Demeter-certified biodynamic. Planting and harvesting are done by sun and moon cycles using systems that are sustainable from start to finish and work with seasonal rhythmic flows. Martyjuana plants seeds in spring and picks the flowers around the autumn's harvest moon.

Batches of seeds are planted at every new moon during the spring, starting in March and ending in May or June. The dates fluctuate from year to year depending on when the new moons fall in relation to the spring equinox.

The plants declare their sex around the summer solstice and mature in time to harvest on or around the full moon in September or October. Martyjuana believes these are the elements that cannot ever be exactly re-created with indoor cultivation, which mimics sunlight but not the moon phases that change nightly. Martyjuana operates under the theory that the full spectrum of effects are more diverse when grown in the full sun and under the moon and stars for the entire life cycle of the plant. There is a natural magic in allowing the seeds to start growing along with the waxing moon as well as harvesting at the full to waning moon.

Martyjuana methods have earned awards and accolades in California's cannabis industry. Martyjuana was the winner of the 2012 Sonoma County cannabis cup for solvent-free concentrate (hash) and featured in the mainstream *Sonoma Magazine*. Marty Clein, Byron Kohler, and the team at Martyjuana are longtime advocates for cannabis law reform. Marty and Byron emerged from the early medical markets of Northern California in 2004 as Big B's Martyjuana Farm, one of the first commercial medical cannabis farms to become regionally legal and regulated. Since California legalized cannabis for adult use in 2016, these traditional methods have made them a standout craft cannabis farm in the region.

The farm is located on a pristine mountaintop in Covelo, California, a remote community in the Round Valley region of Mendocino County, the heart of the Emerald Triangle. The garden is 10,000 square feet (930 m²). Finished dried buds are distributed throughout the state in branded jars. The trim is white labeled and used by other regional brands for pre-rolls, concentrates, edibles, and other extracted products.

Plants are grown in living soil in recycled redwood planter boxes and provided nutrients only through certified organic amendments. They are watered with artesian well water sourced on-site.

The integrated pest management plan precludes the use of pesticides or any sort of spray or foreign chemicals. Instead, companion planting creates an insectary of food and flowers. California poppies, roses, lavender, chrysanthemums, tomatoes, zucchini, pumpkins, squash, and other bee- and pollinator-friendly plants are grown around the cannabis garden. Beneficial predatory insects including ladybugs, praying mantis, green lacewings, and nematodes are released to combat pests like aphids and mites.

Plants are grown from seed and bred on the farm or from neighboring farms. The original Supreme, Northern Lights #4, and Super Skunk #1 seedstock was sourced through Canada's Cannabis Culture Magazine around 2000. Over the years, Martyjuana has crossbred a variety of cultivars by trading seeds with other farmers in the community. Preferred cultivars include old school kushes and OGs as well new cultivars like Skittles, Jelly Roll, and Gelato.

Almost all the processing is done on-site. Plants are harvested branch by branch as they ripen and hung to dry and cure in the barn to make them ready for long-term preservation and storage that protects the integrity of each flower.

Photo: Martyjuana Farms

Dry Farming with Sunboldt Grown

Photo: Phil Emerson

"Dry farming is not for the faint of heart," says Sunshine Cereceda of Sunboldt Grown Farms.

Dry-farmed plants receive no irrigation and instead pull what they need from the soil or the atmosphere. Sunshine says that she switched to dry farming cannabis and other crops because the buds and other produce have stronger, more pronounced flavors and a clean long finish. Just as important, it's more sustainable.

At first it is nerve-wracking for a grower to watch the plants suffer the stress of being transplanted into a dry environment, but they do adapt. Many other cultivated crops are dry farmed. Dry-farmed grapes and tomatoes, in particular, are prized for their flavor, which is thought to be richer and more concentrated in the absence of water dilution. "Natural wines" or "low-intervention wines" are dry farmed in native soil and are thought to be a truer expression of terroir, the unique location where the grapes were grown, from its soils to all the elements of its microclimate. What Sunboldt produces is "low intervention cannabis."

Sunshine was introduced to dry farming by a neighbor farmer in Shively, California, a community on the banks of Humboldt County's Eel River. It winds through the Avenue of the Giants, a road tour through the largest and oldest redwood trees the region is known for. Many other gardeners in the community are dry farming in the rich alluvial soil. One by one, they found that dry farming produces high-quality cannabis flowers that are dense, pungent, and flavorful. Cannabis is likely to express more of that terroir when grown "naturally."

When the soil is tilled, the roots do not need to reach down into it to get to the water, because the water actually works its way up to the roots using capillary action. At Sunshine's farm, the native soil is clay loam that has some of the holding capacity of clay but also allows the water to drain easily.

"Plants prefer less water and fertilizer. They prefer to be on their own. The growth is better overall. Water is an addiction for the plants," she says.

Traditionally, dry farming relies on tilling the soil to loosen it a bit for better percolation. Instead, she uses a rotary spade that mixes her cover crop into the upper four inches (10 cm) of soil. She adds some amendments: aged redwood sawdust, biochar, and soluble calcium.

The practice of dry farming is a return to ancient traditional farming methods. Native Americans have been dry farming the deserts of the Southwestern United States for thousands of years, as have other communities around the world. These practices are still used today, which include tilling the soil to aerate it and planting seeds deeper beneath the topsoil.

Sunshine observed dry-farmed crops on the Navajo Reservation when she traveled there as a child with her mother to protest the Peabody Western Coal Company from mining on Navajo land.

"As a goal for my garden I wanted spiritual healing for people, and to grow the plant to its fullest so that I can experience everything it has to offer. I want to taste the land where my bud was grown."

Photo: Phil Emerson

Sunshine's garden is in a coastal climate, and the ocean has a profound moderating influence on the weather, keeping the temperature in the 80s Fahrenheit (approx. 26–31°C) during the summer and experiencing few frost days in the winter. Because it never gets too hot, the plant's metabolism is never stressed. Nights are cool and humid, with dew drop providing moisture to the dry-farmed crops.

Sunshine R&D's new crosses and maintains a library of cuttings in a mixed-light greenhouse in her personal noncommercial garden. After harvesting the light-deprivation greenhouse in May, the plants are moved outdoors and planted in the ground. They go back to vegetative growth because of the lengthening days and are harvested in the fall.

Clones for the commercial garden are planted in a cold frame either directly in a rockwool cube or sometimes with soil in a 3 inch (7.6 cm) pot. Once the plants have rooted in the cold frame, they are planted directly into the field in the rockwool cube or from the 3 inch (7.6 cm) pots. They will be planted in waves between May and June.

The plants may be watered once, after transplanting into the soil to encourage the roots to search for water. She dips the root ball of large plants in a bucket of water to give them a good soak before putting them in a hole deep enough to bury the stem below the topsoil, closer to the moisture.

"It was initially hard to watch the plants suffer when they were first transplanted into the ground. When new growth appeared, I was confident the roots had found water beneath the soil surface. By the third week, the plants were no longer in a stress state, but one of rapid growth."

For the most part, the rest of the gardening process is hands off, other than monitoring for pests. As part of an integrated pest management (IPM) plan, many varieties of flowers and herbs are used as companion plants to attract beneficial insects.

Buds ripen in the field and are harvested in small batches and handled gently, just like high-end wine grapes, which are never stacked or compressed during harvest.

They are put into a room that is heated to 90°F (32°C) for the first 24 hours to release moisture into the air, which is collected by a dehumidifier to keep the RH low.

After 24 to 36 hours, the drying is slowed by increasing humidity to about 75–80% for a minimum of seven days. The climate is controlled to 60% RH and 65°F (18°C) or cooler. After the stems and leaves are evenly dried, the buds are ready for a six-month cure. Both buds and branches go into the cure; the buds go into unsealed but partly closed paper bags, and the branches are placed in cardboard boxes.

After six months, the buds are vacuum-sealed in jars and released to the market.

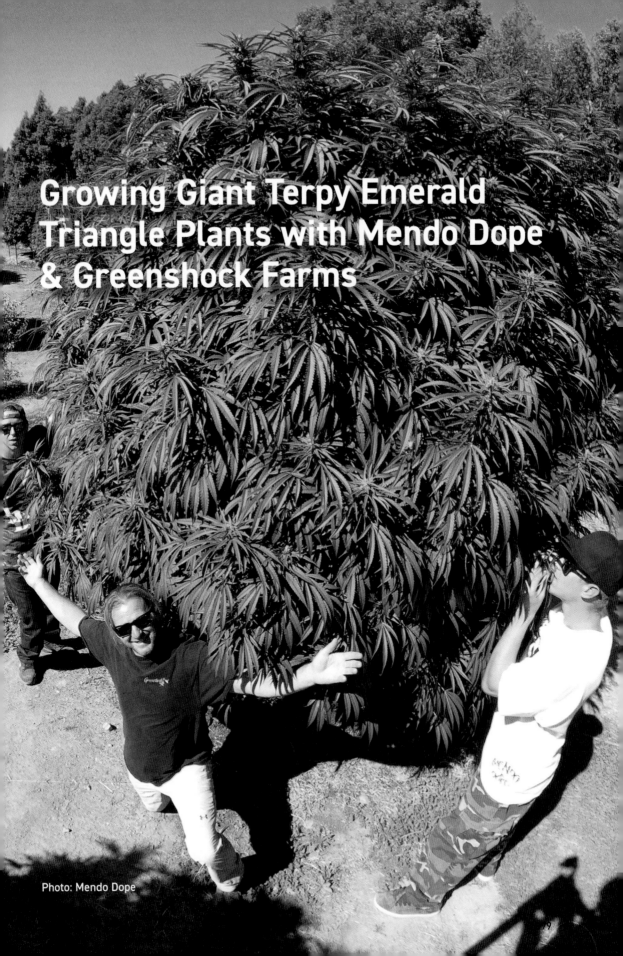

Growing Giant Terpy Emerald Triangle Plants with Mendo Dope & Greenshock Farms

Photo: Mendo Dope

Greenshock Farms and Mendo Dope grow the massive tree-sized cannabis plants the West Coast has become famous for. Their award-winning flowers have rich scents and high terpene content, which they attribute to their back-to-nature volcano-mound soil method and diligent work in breeding cultivars that thrive in the garden's microclimate.

Greenshock produces one sun-grown harvest a year. Clones and seeds for the pheno hunt are started indoors in January and February under basic fluorescent fixtures. The plants root and grow vegetatively indoors in the winter and are then transplanted to one to two gallon (4–7.5 l) pots before being placed in a greenhouse in the early spring. By April they are planted directly in the ground and have grown 2 to 3 feet (0.6–1 m) high. When they are harvested in October, they will be up to 12 to 14 feet (3.6–4.25 m) tall and wide, producing an average of 8 to 10 pounds (3.6–4.5 kg) of finished dried buds each.

Each root system is planted in a volcano-shaped mound that rises about three feet (1 m) from the soil's surface. Without the mounds, the plants would not grow as healthy or large. Mark Greyshock of Greenshock Farms says the practice is common with giant pumpkin farmers because it secures the roots in the ground, manages moisture, and increases oxygen at the root level while preventing root rot and providing the plant nutrients through layers of natural amendments to the native soil ecosystem.

The mounds are formed, amended, and replanted each year and throughout the plant's growth and flowering through top dressing of dry amendments, including alfalfa straw, compost, manures, kelp, guanos, lava rocks, and trace mineral sand. Once planted, the soil will not be disturbed again. The goal is to provide a healthy root environment thriving with microlife to fuel the massive growth and flowering of the giant plants.

Cover crop seeds such as red clover and Dutch white clover are tossed into the top layers of the mounds early in the planting season. The rows of plants are interspersed with native plants, a technique Mark Greyshock learned in the 1990s while tending clandestine gardens in Southern California's Santa Ana mountains.

At the time, blending the native plants in the garden was a technique used to help evade law enforcement, but Mark fell in love with the native plants and the bees, butterflies, and hummingbirds they attracted to the garden. He attributes the quality of the finished product to the garden's healthy soil ecosystem.

Growing in Mendocino, they use regenerative farming practices that do not disturb the native redwood forest or damage the local native soils. Alongside every year's "Avenue of the Giants," or the massive plants grown from clones to harvest their flower, is a "pheno patch," where more mounds are utilized to test the seed-plant variations of new cultivars they are experimenting with.

The Greenshock Mendocino farm is a partnership between longtime grower Mark Greyshock and brothers Daniel and Bryan Eatmon, aka Old E and Bleezy of Mendo Dope. Mendo Dope is known for its music and YouTube videos that celebrate the culture and communities of California's Emerald Triangle.

Old E and Bleezy started working as cannabis trimmers in 2007. Gradually their home garden grew larger, which culminated in a raid by the Mendocino County Sheriff's Office

Photo: Mendo Dope

in 2013. Although the garden was within the legal plant count limit of 25, they were very large, which the sheriff claimed meant they were no longer legal. The garden was destroyed.

Shortly after California legalized cannabis, they paired up with Mark Greyshock to produce a range of new cultivars that could grow as giants through Greenshock farms using the Mendo Dope brand. The most popular cultivar of the moment is the Tropical Sleigh Ride, a winner of the highest-terpene flower and most interesting terpene-cannabinoid combination at the 2019 Emerald Cup. Their Passion Orange Guava "POG" took second place.

Other favorites in the garden include The Mendo Dope, a collaboration between Mendo Dope and legendary breeder Subcool, who passed away in February 2020. The Mendo Dope is a cross between Subcool's Querkle and Locomotion. They have also produced several Tropical Sleigh Ride crosses: Peppermint Sleigh Ride, Trifle (Tropical Truffle x Tropical Sleigh Ride), and Spumoni Kush, a cross of Tropical Sleigh Ride and a legacy version of Barney's Farm's Vanilla Kush that Mendo Dope has nurtured for nearly a decade.

They have recently started breeding with CBD flowers. Results include two cultivars, Dr. Greenshock, described as a "perfect 1:1 ratio" of THC to CBD, each testing about 10%, with a high terpene content of 3.8%, and the flavorful G Lime Burst, testing at about 5% THC to 18% CBD. They hope the high-CBD sun-grown flowers will be a gentle introduction to cannabis for new users.

Pollen is collected and stored to pollinate selected plants in the pheno patch in late summer. The phenos must be able to adjust to the specific microclimate about 2,000 feet (610 m) above sea level near Willits, California. Just 20 miles (32 km) from the Pacific Ocean, the region is a coastal mountain range covered in redwood forest full of microclimates that range from hot and dry to moist and cool. In the Greenshock garden, summers are hot and sunny, but sometimes rain and even snow come early in fall, making it a challenge to harvest before the buds are damaged. This is why the pheno hunt focuses heavily on mold-resistant cultivars and why mold problems are rare outside the pheno patch.

At the start of the grow cycle, the plants are hand-watered. Once transplanted to the

The growth of native plants between the mounds is encouraged. Photo: Mendo Dope

Wire cages are buried around the root ball to protect it from gophers and voles. Photo: Mendo Dope

mound, they are watered using a drip system that rings around the top of the mounds and guides water away from the plant stems, keeping them dry to prevent mold as they grow as thick as tree trunks.

Before the plants are placed in the ground, the hole is lined with wire cages to prevent gophers and voles from destroying the heart of the root ball. Another advantage of using wire cages is that they help the root system support the top-heavy plants from wind. Wire cages are placed around the plant to support the branches and spread them out so that they capture more light. As the plants grow larger, the supports are adjusted.

To control pests in the garden, they utilize integrated pest management (IPM) techniques like predators and traps. Dyna Traps are used to control caterpillars by capturing moths that lay eggs on the plants. The Dyna Trap has a small light and a fan that attracts and catches moths and little bugs.

The crop begins to mature around October, and colas and branches are cut from the plants as they ripen. The plants are dried in a dark room with dehumidifiers and fans to regulate the climate. After drying for one to two weeks, they are broken down into buds and put in a temperature-controlled room to cure.

Remo's High-Tech, High-Yield & High-Efficiency Indoor Garden

Remo has been growing indoors since the late 1980s and likes to experiment with the newest technology in indoor cultivation. He documents his garden and postharvest processing on his popular YouTube channel UrbanRemo, where viewers get an inside look at the experiments he conducts in the personal medical garden he uses to explore and promote his Remo Nutrients line. Manufacturers send him new products to play with—sometimes even before they hit the market. The result is a high-efficiency, high-yield, high-tech personal indoor garden with a wealth of bud, hash, and other fun DIY by-products.

The Garden Space

Remo is permitted to grow up to 98 plants for personal use under Canada's medical cannabis regulations. The entire garden is approximately 534 square feet (50 m²). The grow area is divided in two separate spaces; one space for propagation and vegetive growth and the other for flowering. The height of both rooms is 12 feet (3.6 m). The vegetative room is 8 by 20 feet (2.4 by 6 m), and the flowering room is 17 by 22 feet (5.1 by 6.7 m).

Lighting

Overall, Remo has experienced a 21% savings and a 50% increase in overall yield by switching to high-efficiency LED lights.

Both the vegetative and the flower room are exclusively lit by the latest technology in LED lighting. The vegetative room is lit with 8 Aelius Matrix 420 LED lights. The flowering space is lit by 20 Aelius REDDs. These lights are dimmable from 0 to 100. By replacing 7800 watts of mixed traditional lighting with 3360 watts of high-efficiency LED light, power usage has been cut by more than half.

Opposite: Remo eliminates pest and disease problems before they start using a combination of preventative measures and the Air Sniper. The Air Sniper effectively kills airborne pathogens using UVC light. Air Sniper equipment is easily integrated into indoor cultivation spaces of all sizes, from a personal garden like Remo's to a large-scale industrial facility. A combination of stand-alone, in-line (integrated with HVAC systems), and hybrid units means Air Sniper has the right solution for the needs of any space.

The lights are affixed to automatic lifters controlled through the Stratus Control Unit and can be quickly and easily adjusted up and down with a touch of a button to adjust to plant growth.

Climate Controls
Closed Spaces

Remo practices closed environment agriculture. His gardening space is completely sealed, and there are no intake or ventilation fans of any sort. A good-quality charcoal filter is used to help control smell.

The air in the room is treated and sterilized by a UVC-light unit called the Air Sniper. The UVC light kills any airborne pathogens.

Stratus Controller

The Stratus Controller controls the entire grow room. All electrical equipment including lights, air-conditioning, dehumidifier, and CO_2 system are powered through the controller and managed through a mobile application and sensors placed around the garden. The controller has sunrise and sunset capabilities, which prevent the spike of humidity and temperatures that can happen with regular on/off timers. In this way it better mimics nature.

Vapor Pressure Deficit (VPD)

Remo follows a VPD chart to keep the space similar to hothouse conditions, which he says has also contributed to the increased yield from his rooms. Since he began using these techniques, Remo says he doesn't have mold or mildew problems. Remo stresses that understanding VPD is critical to increasing yields. He aver-

Remo Nutrients provides a complete nutrient system with a total combined 52 ingredients that provide macro and micronutrients plants require for growth.

ages over four pounds (1.8 kg) per light. (*See Air Temperature, Humidity & Qualities.*)

The vegetative space is set to 85°F (29.5°C) with 70% RH. The flowering space starts out at 84°F (29°C) and about 65% RH. Each week the temperature is lowered by 1°F (about 0.5°C). By the end of week eight the temperature is reduced to 76°F (25°C). Each temperature adjustment is accompanied by an adjustment in RH as well as adjustments for the three different rates of transpiration the plant will experience between the beginning and early flowering to midflowering and late flowering.

Closed Loop Air-Conditioning, Dehumidifier & Water Purification System
Both the air conditioning and the 310-pint Anden Dehumidifier recapture moisture from the air and transfer it to a water purification system attached to the wall in the flowering space. Here the water is purified using UVC lighting and fed back to the plants. Although a little additional water is used in the beginning and sometimes in the middle, the garden otherwise operates on 100% recycled water. Remo has been using this process for so long that he has used the same water for years at a time.

CO_2 Supplementation
Sensors on the wall trigger the release of CO_2 over the canopy. Remo sets the levels to 800 ppm over ambient levels or about 1100 to 1200 ppm. A 20 pound (9 kg) tank supplies the flowering space with ample CO_2 for about 7 to 10 days.

Media, Nutrients & Fertilizer
Remo uses coco coir and Proterra growing media in six gallon (22 l) square pots. Plants are fed exclusively by Remo Nutrients, as the garden is designed for experimenting with new popular varieties and Remo's line.

Remo saw a need in the marketplace to create a more efficient line by "stacking" ingredients to create fewer bottles for the whole grow cycle. Remo Nutrients are easy-to-use blends of premium synthetics and high-quality organics that are designed to work with probiotic systems. Remo Nutrients is a vegan line, with no animal by-products.

Remo Nutrients provides a complete nutrient system. In addition to the two-part micro and macronutrient base provided in the Grow and Bloom formulas are four other additives with a total combined 52 ingredients: Velokelp, Magnifical, Astroflower, and Nature's Candy.

Velokelp combines two types of cold-pressed extracted kelp, B vitamins, humic acid, fulvic acid for mineral uptake, and 0.6% orthosilicate. Magnifical is a Cal-Mag supplement with an N-P-K ratio of 3-0-0. Astroflower is a phosphorus-potassium booster that helps develop bigger, denser buds.

Nature's Candy is a carbohydrate-loading product full of sugar, specifically inverted cane sugar and blackstrap molasses for terpy pungent flowers, along with 14 amino acids that are natural building blocks of life.

Visit RemoNutrients.com/Calculator for customizable feeding schedules. Photo: Remo

Cultivars

Remo has a genetic collection of over 500 cultivars, mostly seeds. Most genetics were acquired from other growers and breeders he met at cannabis events over the last 15 years. Some viewers of his YouTube channel have even sent branches in the mail, which is how he started growing one of his favorites: Frosted Fruitcakes. He tends to grow current popular varieties to experiment with the nutrient line. This garden features Zombie Kush, Girl Scout Cookies, Fruity Pebbles OG, Sin Mint Sorbet, Wedding Cake, Oreoz 1 and 2, GMO, Sour Tangie, Strawberry Banana (both from DNA Genetics), Lemon Kush, Blue Jelly, and Island Pink.

Pest & Disease Management

Pest and disease problems are eliminated from the start by using the Air Sniper in the sealed environment combined with preventive measures. Remo doesn't like to use sprays on the plants and instead will use sticky cards and predator bugs such as cucumeris, persimilis, and/or nematodes as a regular preventative program every six weeks.

He doesn't spray for powdery mildew; instead, he uses high heat to kill the mildew. Temperatures above 77°F (25°C) with matching humidity set according to the VPD chart will eliminate the problem.

Harvest & Processing

Fan leaves are removed as the plants are harvested. Deleafed branches are hung to dry before manicuring. The vegetative room converts into the drying space by adjusting the climate settings; the temperature is lowered to 60°F (15.5°C) and RH set to 60%. After two weeks drying on the string lines, the sugar leaves are crisp enough to snap off. Remo finds the flavor and quality of the buds are far superior when dry trimmed rather than tightly manicured while they are still wet. The dried buds are delicately trimmed and will cure in storage.

The large top colas of the plants are harvested for bud and the rest of the smaller nugs and leaves are used to make all manner of extractions: hash, shatter, rosins, diamonds, and sauce, and butter for edibles.

Buds are trimmed by hand using a Trim Bin, which has a kief-catching screen. Hash is hand-rolled into balls; sometimes it is further pressed using the Frenchy Cannoli hot water bottle method.

Trim is tossed in a Pollen Master, which further extracts more kief to be pressed into hash or infused into foods using the Magical Butter Machine. Sometimes the trim is used to make bubble hash using BC Bubbleman's Bubble Bags.

Curing & Storage

Remo prefers to store his buds in stainless steel C-Vault containers. They are smell proof, light proof, smash proof, easy to clean, and reusable.

Photo: Wendy Kornberg

Korean Natural Farming

by Wendy Kornberg and Chris Trump

Sunnabis Farms in Humboldt County, California, produces all of its cannabis outdoors under natural sunlight using Korean Natural Farming (KNF) methods. Although widely practiced in Asian countries for hundreds of years, KNF methods are starting to be used in Western countries as well. It is notable that most of the world simply calls this methodology Natural Farming.

At the heart of this style of farming is the practice of learning how to make all the nutrients, or inputs, that one needs for a successful crop. Most of the ingredients for these inputs can even be found around the garden. The reason this is important is threefold: (1) The cultivator can control what goes on the crop and knows exactly where everything came from, so there are no surprise pesticides, poisons, or test failures; (2) the environmental impact is extremely low when sourcing and making one's own nutrient line; and (3) the cost to make a year's supply of KNF nutrients is pennies on the dollar compared with traditional fertilizers that are purchased at a grow store.

KNF improves the fungal diversity and density in soils. Cannabis loves a 30+:1 fungal to bacterial ratio, and with natural farming this is achievable. Properly balanced living soil produces a very high quality product, as plants with symbiotic root relationships are able to thrive in environments with greater nutrient density, and thus express the full range of the biochemicals that the cultivar is capable of expressing. This full expression of biochemicals provides the best experience possible to the consumer, as opposed to a narrow expression of one or two biochemicals in high percentage.

KNF uses the micronization achieved through fermentation to provide a full suite of highly available plant nutrients. The method is, in part, a bringing together of enzymatic theory from Japan, long-used traditional agriculture, and methods developed by Master Cho Han-Kyu in the last 60 years. Some of his students in the States have further adapted the methods for America.

One of the greatest strengths of KNF is in the cultivation and application of indigenous microorganisms to condition soil and add indigenous microbial diversity. Soil that has high density and diversity of indigenous microorganisms helps plants to be resistant to disease. At the same time, the nutrient cycling that occurs in these systems gives plants access to nutrients through symbiotic exchanges in the root zone.

One of Master Cho's first teachings is "the farmer must first farm himself." This means if farmers are not taking care of themselves, then the farm will eventually suffer; it isn't sustainable.

Another core philosophy of Master Cho is, "A farmer should have parental love towards their crop and livestock. This is the heart of a true farmer." This links to the psychology of animals and has a direct connection to the yield/profitability and health of a livestock farm, with some implications for plants, that is, a happy chicken produces more with the same inputs than an unhappy chicken.

A third core philosophy of Master Cho's is the concept of nutrient application/fertilizing and the three rights of natural farming: right nutrient, right time, right dose. With the high availability of homemade nutrients, farmers are able to increase yields while using far less total amounts than other agricultural systems.

There are five core principles of KNF.
1. Follow the laws of nature.
2. What you need is what's around you.
3. Enjoy the process.
4. Start with an empty mind.
5. A farmer is to foster a healthy relationship between all beings.

Practitioners agree that learning from experienced natural farmers is the most effective way to acquire proper technique that leads to success; the system works, but there can be a learning curve, as it is a skill-based system. Natural farming has a pesticide suite in an iteration called JADAM, a natural farming offshoot developed by Cho Youngsang. In large-scale production an effective liquid indigenous microorganisms (IMO) application was developed in Hawai'i (where natural farming first landed in the United States) that reduces costs while remaining highly effective, and this solution has proved highly beneficial in creating a strong plant that can better withstand attack from pests and pathogens.

Overview of Basic Inputs
Indigenous Microorganisms (IMO)
Natural farming is all about IMO collections. They are used to make true living soil by inoculating the ground with diverse microbes, including fungi. The microlife is collected for propagating.

Most crops prefer a soil that is mostly colonized by fungi rather than bacteria, with the possible exception of the brassica family. The relationships that the plants build with the microorganisms in the soil are complicated, but as a group they work together synergistically to provide the needs of all the organisms. A simplified view of this is that the plants send out signals to the microbes when a specific nutrient is in need, and the microbes go and gather it for the plant. In exchange the plant feeds the microbes sugars and carbohydrates created through photosynthesis.

Cannabis prefers a highly fungal-dominant soil with ratios above 30:1 fungi to bacteria. To achieve this balance, the soil is inoculated with a diversity of fungal propagules, or spores that capture the diversity of undisturbed nature and bring it into grow spaces.

The best places for an IMO collection are the places that are undisturbed by human interactions. Sometimes we're lucky enough to own such land, but sometimes one has to get creative and go for a drive to a pristine forest or wild open space. These areas are ideal to place an IMO box to capture the diversity that is there. This must be done more than once a year. The ideal IMO collections will include at least three different habitats taken during at least three seasons.

Photo: Wendy Kornberg

This ensures that IMO2 to IMO3 will have incredible diversity of fungi that will sporulate into the substrate. As this is broadcast into the garden or grow space, all those fungal species will be spread out over the soil. Because of the diversity, several fungal species will thrive in their new environment regardless of the heat, humidity, or light.

Traditionally a wooden IMO collection box or basket is filled to two thirds with short-grain undercooked white rice, covered with a cloth or paper, and placed in the pristine area for five days. Then the box is collected. If properly inoculated, it will be full of fluffy white fungal bodies. This is mixed 1:1 by weight with raw or brown sugar to create a shelf-stable product, called IMO2, that can be used to propagate out into IMO3–IMO5.

The ideal IMO3 pile is made up of a few small IMO2 samples and a balance of carbon and carbohydrates such as whole or milled rice, wheat, oats, or barley, and hardwood wood chips. The fungi will sporulate and inoculate the entire pile when kept below 120°F (50°C), which is generally achieved by consistent turning, much like a compost pile. IMO4 takes the process one step farther by utilizing IMO3 and the garden soil, and IMO5 brings it to the final step by incorporating a high nitrogen source, such as an animal manure.

Fermented Plant Juice (FPJ)

FPJ is used throughout the plants' life cycle. This is one of the staples of natural farming inputs. It's made from the fresh, young, growing tips of different plants. While it can be made from almost any nontoxic plant material, FPJs are full of growth hormones, nutrients, and microbial life, which are found predominantly in the fresh growing tips of plants before sunlight hits them. The microbial life that is present on the leaf surface of the plant then breaks down and ferments the nutrients, making them bio available.

FPJ is generally used at a 1:500 ratio, and it's shelf stable for up to six months when properly stored. This is one of the inputs that should be made fresh, stored with a breathable lid to protect microbial life, and utilized on the farm where it was made. Fermented plant juice should never be used alone, but always in conjunction with brown rice vinegar and oriental herbal nutrient (OHN). All KNF recipes start with these three inputs as a base.

Oriental Herbal Nutrient (OHN)

OHN is a tincture composed of five herbs: angelica, cinnamon, licorice, ginger, and garlic. OHN is one of the staples of natural farming and is used in every recipe. The blend is based in Chinese medicine. The five herbs were chosen because of their warming properties as well as how they work synergistically. If one of the herbs is unavailable it can be left out, but the addition of any other herb creates a tincture that is not considered OHN.

This input is an immunity booster and has antipathogenic properties that support and increase the health of the soil, plants, and animals. It is generally used at a 1:1000 ratio. However, the older the tincture, the more diluted it can be while still maintaining efficacy.

Fish Amino Acid (FAA)

FAA is the natural farming solution to provide nitrogen that plants need during vegetative growth. It is made from fish waste, including heads, fins, guts, and other refuse. It becomes a high-quality fish fertilizer that is used at a ratio of 1:1000 to 1:500.

FAA takes time to create. The fish refuse is mixed with an equal weight of brown sugar, and ideally a skosh of OHN and a sprinkle of IMO4. After mixing thoroughly, it is left to ferment for six months to a year.

Because cannabis is a heavy feeder, FAA can be used at higher ratios, but first it should be tested for phytotoxicity using a plant or as a foliar spray on a single branch.

Water Soluble Potassium (WSK)

WSK is made by charring plants that are potassium accumulators. Sunflowers are an excellent example. Traditionally, it's been made from tobacco stalks, but any plants that make a good biochar and are high in potassium will work well.

This input is very simple to make: biochar from the plant material is added to water at a 1:10 ratio and left to sit for a couple of weeks before it is strained and diluted at approximately 1:1000 ratio before use. As with all other inputs, this should not be used alone but in conjunction with FPJ, OHN, and BRV.

Water Soluble Calcium (WCA)

WCA is a solution made from charred eggshells and vinegar. The charring of the egg-shells efficiently breaks down the calcium, and when added to an acid such as vinegar, the resulting solution is an easily absorbed form of calcium. This input is usually used during blooming, but can be added whenever the plants need a calcium boost. It is generally used at a 1:1000 ratio in conjunction with FPJ, BRV, and OHN.

Water Soluble Calcium Phosphate (WCAP)

WCAP is created using charred bones and vinegar. Much like WCA, WCAP utilizes acidic vinegar to break down bones into bioavailable calcium phosphate. Once large animal bones have been charred to charcoal that is blackened all the way through, they are added at a 1:10 ratio to vinegar and soaked for a week to 10 days. The calcium phosphate is dissolved by the vinegar. This solution is used as a foliar spray at a 1:1000 ratio. The spray should also include FPJ and OHN. It is primarily applied during the transition period, one week before the light cycle changes and one week after.

Fermented Fruit Juice (FFJ)

FFJ is one of the least-used inputs by cannabis farmers. It consists of one to three types of ripe fruit fresh from the farm, mixed with an equal weight of brown sugar, and left to ferment in a dark location for 7 to 10 days. The ferment retains high levels of enzymes and is used for enhancing fruit ripening. Because cannabis is sinsemilla, or without seeds, the jury is still out whether FFJ actually enhances the cannabinoid or terpene profile of cannabis.

Seawater

Seawater is an important part of natural farming. It's the source of micro nutrients and minerals. It can be collected from the ocean and stored in a reservoir tank. This can be added to the other inputs on a 1:30 ratio and included in any or all foliar or soil drench applications. If one does not live near the ocean, then sea salt can be substituted. Sea salt is added to the final solution at the rate of 1 g/L.

Lactic Acid Bacteria (LAB)

This input has probiotic qualities and is helpful in creating healthy human and animal intestinal tracts. It is also beneficial when added to soil or leaves. It is made by collecting the LAB that is naturally occurring in water that has been used to rinse rice. The rice water wash is left in a container loosely covered with paper or cloth to collect the initial LAB and then added to milk, which provides a source of food for the bacteria. After 3–5 days the milk solution will separate into curds and the LAB serum. The solids are separated off. They can be seasoned and eaten or fed to animals. The serum is used in conjunction with the other supplements at a 1:1000 ratio.

Photo: GreenSourceGardens

SUSTAINABILITY

By Dale Sky Jones and Oaksterdam University Faculty

Sustainability isn't just the practices used on the farm or in the garden; it is a mindset, but as a concept it is simply meeting the needs of the present without compromising the ability of future generations to meet their own. The three pillars to consider are economic, environmental, and social, informally referred to as people, planet, and profits. Small decisions made every day add up to a larger-sum impact over time. The decision to be more sustainable does not need to be tremendous, sudden, or a costly lift.

Is cannabis cultivation sustainable? Like all agriculture it can be, but it also can be incredibly destructive. Many "old-school" practices were focused on executing a fast harvest and not getting caught in the process. Illegal grow operations and law enforcement abatement actions taken to cripple and destroy illegal grow sites would often release diesel, harsh poisons, and chemical fertilizers directly into the ground and water supply.

In the past, sustainable practices like utilizing solar energy often resulted in enhanced criminal charges for operating a sophisticated illegal operation. The reality of operating under prohibition forced cannabis cultivators into a linear economy, which has a "take, make, dispose" model of production, rather than a circular economic system designed for longevity. The circular concept is simply minimizing the use of resource inputs and reducing waste, pollution, and carbon emissions.

Some elements of the legal commercial cannabis industry have become unsustainable by law, such as excessive packaging requirements and mandated indoor-only cultivation. The influence of the unregulated market is the root of unsustainable implementations in many commercial cultivation regulations worldwide.

The unregulated market ethos was and still is, get in and get out quick. The basic cultivation and manufacturing systems and standard operating procedures utilized today reflect that illicit market approach. This is an indicator that this market is still in its infancy due to immature regulation, production systems, and the operators' approach to cannabis cultivation.

Sustainable cultivation of legal cannabis means growing responsibly outdoors or in controlled environments and bringing a focus on renewable energy sources, localized production, conserving land, using polyculture and permaculture techniques, preventing soil erosion, conserving water, preserving natural land, conserving resources, using alternative energy sources, responsibly disposing of waste, and reducing the farm's overall carbon footprint.

From an outdoor farming perspective, there are three concepts at the core of sustainable cannabis production: no-till soil, wildlife-friendly farming, and land sparing.

No-Till Production

"No till" means avoiding any sort of disturbance to the earth. Anything from putting a shovel in the ground to the large-scale evisceration of an entire field is considered "tilling." No-till production is important because it preserves the soil microbiology. There is a whole living system in the soil that is disturbed every time it is moved.

Prepare soil for winter by continuing not to till and using mulches and cover crops to protect it. It is important to use cover crops because when the plants are removed and not replaced with cover crops, the topsoil is vulnerable to wind erosion and can cause damage to watersheds.

It is important to reinvigorate the soil because cannabis will remove a lot of nutrients, especially nitrogen. Reinvigorate the soil without disturbing it by using dry-crumble fertilizers and amendments as top dressing. When pelletized or dried nutrients are used, they slow release as the plants are watered, and they are broken down in the soil. Fertilizing this way avoids the use of synthetic liquid nutrients or the necessity to till the soil.

When plants are cultivated in nonagricultural zones such as forests, strong nutrient-water solutions invariably seep into the ecosystem. One way to eliminate this is to grow in a "closed system" so that the water never gets into the water stream. Wicking systems and hydroponic systems use water without letting any of it leave the system.

A polyculture cannabis garden. Photo: GreenSourceGardens

Wildlife-Friendly Farming

Wildlife should not be shot and killed simply for being on the farm property. Use fencing and disruptive stimuli to scare the animals away to keep them from disrupting the farm. Practicing conservation agriculture means minimal disruption to nature and wildlife. In the United States, Second Amendment rights do not apply to those who use, consume, or are in possession of cannabis. Consult an attorney. Be thoughtful and cautious about choosing to have guns on the farm or at the grow facility.

Land Sparing & Permaculture

Land sparing means preserving as much of the land that is not being cultivated as possible. This means not disrupting the natural ecosystem and not taking too many resources from the land. Never clear-cut trees to set up a farm. Choose a site where the farm will have the least impact on the land as well as the creatures and plants that live on it.

Sustainable commercial and personal growers are adopting permaculture and other regenerative techniques to not only preserve the land but increase the quality of the crop.

Permaculture is a growing method that is not specific to cannabis. The term means "permanent culture" and refers to practices that mimic nature to preserve its biodiversity while cultivating crops needed to sustain human life. In nature there is a balance and natural systems of nutrition, companion planting, and soil biodiversity. Nature has its own cycle of regeneration. Permaculture is really about the diversity of life in the garden environment. Crops are cycled through the fields, and each adds to the biodiversity of the soil.

Permaculture is opposed to monocropping. Monocropping is growing the same plants, often genetically identical, on the same space year after year. Doing so depletes nutrients and diversity in the soil and makes the plants themselves more susceptible to disease.

Growers who pursue land sparing and permaculture styles of production must work with the weather and terroir of the garden space. Outdoors there are a lot of different types of climates to plan around. Growers must design to work with the land and its microclimate.

Landsparing relies heavily on companion planting, which means planting different types of plants next to each other to increase the health and vitality of the whole garden. Marigolds are commonly used companion plants to cannabis and are used both as indicator and trap plants because thrips preferentially feed on their flowers, indicating an impending infestation.

Hot peppers are another great option for companion planting. The same capsaicin that gives peppers their spicy flavor and sensation is released by the roots and is found in the rhizosphere, where they are planted. As ground-dwelling rodents are chomping away and taste the capsaicin, they turn and dig the other way.

Many growers plant flowers and herb crops that repel herbivores or attract beneficial insects. In addition to indicator plants, growers can simultaneously cultivate banker plants that act as natural habitats and breeding locations for predatory insects that will also assist in pest mitigation in the canopy (Miller & Rebek 2018).

The more synthetic sprays are eliminated in the garden, the more sustainable it is.

What about the Bees?

Cannabis is a wind-pollinated plant and does not rely on insects for pollination, so it produces no nectar, which is what bees use to produce honey. However, bees do collect cannabis pollen to produce bee pollen. There is concern because honeybee populations have dwindled. Being bee safe means not using sprays that impact beneficials and preserving their natural habitats.

Soil Erosion

Soil erosion has major impacts on daily human life. A good example is the Dust Bowl. Settlement policies tied to the American policy of "Manifest Destiny" encouraged the mass tilling and monocropping of the Great Plains. Settler-farmers created the perfect disaster conditions through heavy tilling and the removal of the natural grasses that held the topsoil in place. A single dry year coupled with a wind storm created huge black clouds of dust that traveled as far away as New York City and contributed to the largest economic depression in US history. The Dust Bowl was a completely human-made crisis that wouldn't have happened if the settlers hadn't removed all the native plants that held down the topsoil.

There are huge consequences for disturbing the environment; using no-till farming and permaculture methods, topsoil is preserved and the damages of soil erosion are mitigated or prevented. Mulching and cover crops are a natural regenerative way to avoid soil erosion.

Growing on Slopes

It is not sustainable to develop farmland on hillsides or steep grades. The only way to do it is to cut into hillsides and create flat areas. This often involves burning or tilling the space where the cultivation will take place and is an unsustainable practice that contributes to soil erosion and damage of waterways. Preferable grade for cultivating cannabis, as mandated by many state regulations, is 5%.

Water Conservation

Water conservation entails rainwater harvesting, reducing and reusing water, using hydroponics production, reusing condensate from dehumidification, establishing ponds, and employing permaculture techniques. Proper companion planting assists in soil moisture retention.

Depending on climate, rainwater can be difficult to rely on as the sole water source. It takes 80,000 to 100,000 gallons of water or more to cultivate a quarter acre (10 hectares) of cannabis. One way to collect rainwater is to establish a pond that rainwater on the property is directed to.

The two best water-conserving techniques are to use a hydroponic system or a "reservoir" system. Both systems have less impact on the land than planting in the ground or in drain-to-waste, raised beds, in which much of the water sinks below root level.

Most hydro systems do not release water. Instead, they contain it in the system so it never or rarely interacts with the surrounding environment. The reason the plant is placed in position is to enjoy the sun, not the soil.

Reservoir systems often use planting mix in containers, but capture the water underneath in a tray that serves as a reservoir. No water leaches into the ground. Instead, the water uses capillary action and wicks to hydrate the planting mix, and/or the water irrigates the top of the mix using a very small water pump.

Recapturing Condensate

Efficiency and sustainability are synonymous in horticulture. Indoor water use efficiency is increased using recovered condensate, which captures moisture from the air using dehumidifiers or air conditioning (AC) units.

Every time plants are irrigated in a relatively closed environment, RH increases as water evaporates from the growing medium and drainage system and as the plants transpire. This humidity can be controlled by changing irrigation methods so not as much water is delivered to the top of the container, which increases water gasification, air exchange, air conditioning, or running a dehumidifier.

Both dehumidifiers and AC units remove water from the air through condensation. Although they have different purposes, both units use the same fundamental principle. Dehumidifiers and AC units intake warm air that moves across cold radiator coils. As the air cools, its ability to hold moisture decreases and water will start condensing on the coils. That drier air is then exhausted back into the grow room. The condensate can be collected and reused as irrigation water.

Recovered condensate is essentially distilled water; however, it is important to confirm the cleanliness of the water. Most coils in dehumidifiers and AC units are made from copper, which is perfectly fine. However, the solder used to join the copper pipes is usually made from a tin or lead alloy. There is potential for lead to leach into the condensate, which if applied to the plants as irrigation water can cause an accumulation of the heavy metal in the plant. Make sure to use a food-quality dehumidifier that does not leach heavy metals into the water.

Energy Conservation

Energy conservation is key to reducing the carbon footprint of any cultivation operation. The carbon footprint of the cannabis industry is massive because of specialty agriculture products, widespread indoor cultivation without renewable energy sources, and mass export from growing regions.

Alternative energy sources such as wind turbines and solar panels make a farm operate more sustainably. Although the cost of installation can be prohibitive, in the long run the returns are much greater by not having to pay for or rely on a power utility for energy.

The first way to conserve energy is to analyze it. What can't be measured can't be managed. After reducing, energy usage efficiency can be improved. Replace energy-intensive infrastructure and switch to solar panels.

Coco coir is a by-product of palm trees that are heavily farmed and processed in India, Thailand, and other parts of Southeast Asia. It is most likely being farmed and harvested by leveling natural ecosystems, processing, and shipping it around the world. Try to purchase coco coir from trusted and sustainable sources.

Types of Alternative Energy Collectors

There are three main sources of alternative energy that can be produced on the farm: solar, wind, and biomass.

Solar panels are commonly used in cannabis production. Wind turbines are heavily utilized by the Dutch to harness wind energy and are starting to be used in more and more parts of the world. Passive regeneration produced by biomass energy is newer, but a great option because it harnesses the energy produced by decomposing trash. The cost of producing biomass energy is still prohibitive.

Planting Mix

Planting mix can be reused many times. With each use it shrinks a bit as the structure changes and some is used by microorganisms. Renew it with new ingredients that lend structure and organic matter to it.

Responsible Waste Management
- Reuse: water, resources, soil, nutrients
- Reduce: water, resources, energy, waste
- Recycle: water, plastic, paper, glass, etc.
- Compost: soil, leaves, stems, food wastes

It is important to not only reuse, reduce, and recycle but to close the consumption loop by composting food and garden waste.

PART IV:

THE PLANT LIFE CYCLE

Photo: Ed Rosenthal

GETTING STARTED

Indoor

The lights are in position. The growing unit, hydroponic system, or planting containers are in place. Fans are installed in the space as appropriate to provide air circulation. A CO_2 enrichment or ventilation system is set up to provide a continuous supply during the lit period.

Temperature and humidity are controlled with sensors and automatic systems using air conditioners and dehumidifiers in either a closed-loop system or a ventilation system using filtered outside air.

The nutrient solution is monitored by measuring either parts per million (ppm), electrical conductivity (EC), or total dissolved solids (TDS). (See *Water* and *Nutrients & Fertilizers*.) A pH meter or test kit is used to measure pH. A surface temperature thermometer and a light meter are also useful.

Greenhouses

The greenhouse is in working order. Vents, openings, evaporative coolers, or other cooling methods are operable using an automatic system controlled by a thermostat and humidistat. If soil is being used, the planting beds or containers have nutrients and soil amendments mixed in. If a hydroponics unit is being used, it has been set up and is ready to plant.

Any supplemental lighting is in place to increase the intensity of the light during low-light periods and/or, when needed, to extend day length during the shorter days of the year. Blackout curtains are used to shorten the day length inside the greenhouse and trigger flowering during the longer days of summer.

Outdoors

The ground, planting holes, or raised beds are prepared and ready to be planted. In dry areas where there is little rainfall during the summer, irrigation is required to grow crops, so the water is sourced and ready to flow. If the plants are to be forced to flower early, the frames and blackout curtains have been installed.

Everything is set.

It's time to give this garden life!

Seeds or Clones?

There are two ways to start a garden: using either seeds or clones.

Seeds

Seeds have several advantages. Only plants grown from seed develop a taproot. The taproot is the underground equivalent of the main stem. The taproot on plants grown from seed is an extension of the stem, so it anchors the plant and holds the canopy securely. It grows straight down with lateral roots branching out along its length, providing the plant with a network that occupies a larger three-dimensional area. A deep taproot can reach the water table or moist layers of penetrable subsoil. The taproot and main stem form a single column, so water and nutrients are drawn easily up to the plant canopy. The result is that there are more roots in several layers of soil that can obtain more water and nutrients to support the plant's growth.

The depth and vigor of a root system are also essential for the stress tolerance and resilience required to optimize sun-grown cannabis.

Seeds are less likely to carry and spread pests and pathogens, while clones can transfer them readily.

Seeds are the product of sexual reproduction, so they inherit genetic characteristics from both parents. Plants from the same seed stock exhibit different characteristics due to genetic variation, so growers can choose the best plant, or the one they like best, and reproduce it using cloning. Growing from seed is more adventurous, because there is no way to know exactly how the plants will turn out. (*See Basic Breeding.*)

Seeds are very portable and easy to store for long periods of time.

Seeds of many varieties are readily available in shops, dispensaries, by mail, and over the internet. It is easy to verify the variety when it comes from a seed company. Investigate and select carefully. First investigate the company and then read reviews of the selections. How long has the company been in business, and what is its reputation? Has the cultivar won awards, and in what categories? Reach out to the vendors if there are questions. Many times their response influences purchasing decisions.

Seeds have several disadvantages. Cannabis has separate male and female plants. Unless they are used for breeding or hemp for seeds, males are of no use and will become pollinators that endanger the potency and yield of seedless, cannabinoid-rich, female flowers.

Usually, about half the seeds produce males, which must be detected and removed. This can be an arduous task, and the consequence of missing one can be seeded buds throughout the garden.

Seeds take longer to germinate, grow, and be ready to flower because rooted clones are already biologically mature, so they are 15–20 days ahead on root development.

Plants from seeds don't exactly reproduce their parents' traits. Seeds from a finished bud will not grow to be exactly the same as their mother, though their morphology may be a close approximation. This is just how different siblings from the same parents are genetically and physically unique from one another, unless they are identical.

Because roughly half of the plants will be discarded once they are sexed, growing from seeds is more likely to result in fewer plants than anticipated.

Feminized Seeds

Feminized seeds have been bred to produce only female plants. They are the solution to the problem of sexing males, since virtually all the feminized seeds will grow to be female plants.

Feminized seeds are created by treating a flowering female plant with a chemical catalyst, such as colloidal silver, silver nitrate, or preferably silver thiosulfate. This induces female plants to grow pollen-producing male flowers. Because the mother plant has only female chromosomes, it contributes only female genetics to any seeds produced. The result is that virtually all the plants will be female. (*See Basic Breeding: Feminizing Seeds.*)

Clones

Cloning is the asexual reproduction of another plant. No pollen or seed is needed. Rather than being a genetic mix, a clone is the exact genetic reproduction of the plant from which

The Mondi Mini Greenhouse Propagation Kit includes the Black and White Premium Tray, seven inch (18 cm) Mini Greenhouse Dome with easy vents, and an attachable thermo-hygrometer. The patented Black and White Premium Tray is designed to be strong while using less plastic in order to minimize the environmental impact. Its interior white plastic increases light reflectivity, while the black base prevents light penetration to the root zone, reducing the chance of root disease. It is easy to clean and very durable. The seven inch (18 cm) Mini Greenhouse Dome is made from premium proprietary plastic that does not off-gas and is safe for food production. It is designed to tightly control temperature and humidity through adjustable vents. The patented thermo-hygrometer has a unique mounting, allowing easy access to accurate measurements inside the controlled environment.

it was taken. There are other methods of asexual reproduction, including tissue culture. (*See Appendix A: Cloning* and *Appendix B: Tissue Culture*.)

There are many benefits to working with clones. Because they are taken from female plants, they are also female with no males or hermaphrodites to mess with the buds. Clones get the grower past the germination "hump" seeds present. Seeds take 15–20 days to catch up to a rooted clone, which is ready to be transplanted and start vigorous growth.

Commercial clones come from stock that has already proved itself vigorous and potent. Rather than having to select the best from a group of plants grown from seeds, the arduous selection process has already been done.

Clones from a single mother are genetically identical because they are the result of asexual reproduction. Growing a uniform crop is easier than growing different varieties or even different plants of a single variety.

Clones make it easier to limit the number of plants in the garden because they can be obtained or cut to replace plants as they are placed into flowering.

There are disadvantages of clones. Clones are only available commercially in regions where cannabis is permitted for home cultivation. Not all varieties are always available, even when they are legal. Clones can carry diseases and pests that infect the whole garden. Clones from friends are more likely to be infected than professionally grown clones.

There are major disadvantages starting from clones for outdoor growers. Clones do not grow as vigorously as seed-grown plants, especially outdoors, because clones do not grow a taproot, only secondary roots from the stem, and therefore do not develop as deep or vigorous of a root system as plants grown from seed. When grown in the ground or large planting beds, they generally do. Clone plants have a single layer of lateral roots. The stem ends close to the soil line, where it was cut. This doesn't provide as much support as a plant with a taproot.

Subsequently, some of their growth is lateral rather than downward, which may not provide access to optimal moisture found in deeper soils and limits the plants' resiliency during stressful weather conditions.

This doesn't affect plants grown inside in the same way because the plants don't grow as large and the taproot isn't as important in a container environment.

Selecting Seeds
by Professor P

Selecting viable seeds isn't difficult and can be done mostly by a brief visual inspection. Is the seed fully formed without indentations, cracks, holes, or have a white/green tint? Do the seeds sink or float? Seeds that continue to float after 12 hours are possibly not viable, but seeds that sink are more suitable candidates for germination and generally have a high percentage of success. Green seeds, undeveloped seeds, and cracked shells are highly unlikely to sprout, but some may miraculously do so at a much lower percentage.

Seed color is another indicator. Although darker seeds tend to be more mature, a few cultivars produce fully mature light-colored seeds. This is the result of the plant's adaptation to its environment.

After a visual examination, a further inspection is performed by squeezing the seed firmly. If it crushes with minimal pressure, it's a dud. If it doesn't crush with continued pressure, it is viable no matter its color.

Photo: Professor P of Dynasty Genetics

Overripe seeds present another problem. The embryo bursts the seed shell open, creating a split along the seed hull. Split seeds may be viable for a short amount of time before the embryo dries out and dies.

Viability of aged seeds is affected by storage conditions. For long-term storage, they should be kept frozen until shortly before use. To extend their life, keep them refrigerated in a sealed container. Seeds stored at room temperature start losing vitality after about a year. Some may survive up to three years.

Shells of poorly handled seeds often have small blue specks. A quick dip in 3% hydrogen peroxide eliminates the mold, fungi, and some bacteria. After the hydrogen peroxide dip, soak in a diluted microbial solution such as Bioharmonic Tonic or *Trichoderma harzianum* (URB), which promote plant biology.

Healthy, fresh cannabis seeds do not require scarification to naturally germinate, but it increases the germination rate of challenged seed. It is done with a few strokes of the seed against a nail file or sandpaper. Scraping away part of the shell assists in introducing water into the seeds, which signals them to germinate.

Cold "stratification" is sometimes used for germination of older seeds from cold climate cultivars. Although cold climate seeds readily germinate soon after dropping from a plant in autumn, the embryo may be stimulated after experiencing a cold spell, depending on the genetics. A visit to the freezer for 24–48 hours is suitable. Again, this is not necessary for most cannabis seeds to properly germinate, but some stubborn seeds may need a little extra nudge. Sometimes feral varieties from cold climates germinate sporadically and require several freezes and thaws.

There are many ways to navigate the realm of seed viability, but it all starts with proper storage. To store seeds properly, three environmental factors must be addressed: light, humidity, and temperature. Cannabis seeds retain their viability longest when they are stored in cool, dark, and fairly dry conditions. Seeds stored in a jar in a dark space at room temperature start to lose viability after two years. They may remain viable for four years or more in a refrigerator with low humidity. Seeds packaged properly can remain in a freezer for an extended period. The biggest threat to seed viability is high humidity and warmth. Humidity between 20–30% and temperature of about 41–45°F (5–7°C) is ideal for most situations.

Bioharmonic Tonic is a bioharmonically active microbial mix derived from all-natural ingredients. A fermentation and enzymatic process is used with a special blend of Amazonian herbs and gemstone harmonics. This easy-to-use odorless liquid is a dynamic mix of biostimulants ready to invigorate growth. Professor P has used it over several tests and found that it increases germination on older seeds and accelerates early growth.

Starting Seeds

Fresh seeds are usually viable, with high germination rates. Seeds more than two or three years old may not germinate as well. Older seeds may have a higher percentage of weak plants, and slower germinating seeds are more prone to attack from molds and bacteria.

Intact, dark brown, or gray seeds are most likely to germinate. Whitish, light tan, or cracked seeds are usually not viable. Most grow books suggest selecting the largest seeds in a batch for planting, but the size of the seed is genetically as well as environmentally determined and does not necessarily relate to its germination potential.

Cannabis seeds germinate best in a warm room temperature range of 70–80°F (21–26°C). At lower temperatures, germination proceeds slowly, and seeds are subject to attack by fungi and bacteria.

There are multiple methods of germinating seeds.

Planting in Place

The easiest method of germination is by planting directly in the ground or planting medium, in small cups or containers using soil or planting mix, peat pellets, rockwool cubes, or other germination media.

Pasteurized or sterile planting media or substrates such as rockwool and most indoor planting mixes are excellent for seed starting. Keep the water pathogen-free by using a 0.5% solution of hydrogen peroxide or protect the roots using compost tea or root-protecting organisms such as mycorrhizae. Do not use the hydrogen peroxide concurrently with the mycorrhizae, or they will be killed.

Paper cups (not plastic) are convenient germinating containers, but they must be removed or well scored before planting. Lightweight horticultural cups made from peat moss, straw, rice, paper, or other natural materials are ideal containers for germinating plants that are to be transplanted. They can be placed directly in the ground or into a larger container without disturbing the roots.

(1) The seeds have germinated. Photo: Picture Fotografie **(2-3) The stem is emerging.** Photo: (2) Phil Sullivan / Team Terpene (3) Picture Fotografie **(4) The cotyledons are opening.** Photo: Phil Sullivan / Team Terpene **(5) The first true leaves have appeared.** Photo: Phil Sullivan / Team Terpene **(6) Seedling are labeled and will carry IDs until harvest.** Photo: GreenSourceGardens

Germinating in rockwool blocks, Oasis cubes, or bonded peat cubes also avoids having to remove rooted plants from the container. Starter sheets fit in standard 10 x 20 inch (25 x 50 cm) horticultural trays and are divided into either 30, 50, or 72 cubes. Seedlings should be attached to growing blocks, planting mix, or soil soon after germination. The 30s can usually remain 15–20 days, the 50s 10–15 days, and the 72s about 7–10 days.

Four inch (10 cm) diameter cubes can hold the plants for two weeks to a month without inhibiting growth. Six inch (15 cm) containers can keep plants comfortable for four weeks or more, and even through flowering for small plants.

Germination Techniques
There are many methods of germinating seeds. Germinating in a wet paper towel is among the most popular.

Moisten the paper towel or cloth with water until it is almost saturated. Place the seeds on the towel and fold it over. Put the folded towel or cloth on a bowl or plate and cover it with plastic wrap. Check the seeds once or twice a day for signs of germination. When it is apparent that the taproot is emerging, place the seed in the prepared sterile or pasteurized growing media at a depth of about a quarter of an inch (5 mm). Be careful not to injure the emerging root when planting. Keep it moist.

Seeds can be germinated in place in rockwool blocks or cubes, peat plugs, or other media starts. These are very convenient to use because they come ready to plant. Place the seed about three eighths of an inch (9.5 mm) deep in the block or cube and keep the seeds and seedlings moist.

To keep the environment disease-free, treat the water with a 0.5% solution of hydrogen peroxide (H_2O_2). Drugstore hydrogen peroxide is 3%, so mix one part hydrogen peroxide for every five parts water to create a 0.5% solution.

Compost tea also protects germinating seeds and seedlings because it contains living microorganisms that may outcompete pathogens and aid root growth. Before adding it, make sure to rinse out the H_2O_2 because it will kill microorganisms.

Whether seeds are germinating indoors or outside, the planting medium must be kept moist during the entire period. Seeds dry out quickly during this process, and dry medium results in dead seeds. If possible, place a cover or clear plastic film over them. The sun can dry the surface of the soil very quickly, so it is best to plant outdoors when the soil will remain moist for a few days. Otherwise, it may be more successful to germinate indoors

IHORT Quick Start® plugs are made from a custom proprietary blend of peat moss, coco coir, and biochar to create the ideal propagation conditions. They are expertly designed for the optimum amount of moisture and aeration and come predrilled for enhanced stem-to-media contact. All plugs come pH balanced ready to use right out of the box. IHORT plugs promote more fibrous root growth to aid in water and nutrient uptake and increase the amount of branches per plant and stem caliper, providing more tips on mother plants or increasing yield.

or in the shade outdoors and then transplant. This is more of a problem in the late spring and summer, when the light becomes more intense and high temperatures increase evaporation.

Seeds usually germinate in 3 to 10 days. Germination time is affected by media temperature as well as the seed's age and health. The best temperature range for germination is in the high 70s Fahrenheit (mid-20s Celsius). At lower temperatures germination is prolonged.

First the root emerges. Shortly after, the stem emerges and orients itself perpendicular to gravity. Folded on top of the stem, a pair of embryonic leaves called cotyledons unfold and begin to supply the plant with the sugars it needs for growth and respiration. Cotyledons are rounded single blades and look nothing like mature cannabis leaves.

The elongated stems of these seedlings are the result of too dim or too little light, or too high a temperature.

As soon as plants germinate, they require light. If the light is not intense enough, the stem stretches, reaching for it. If the lighting creates too much heat, the young seedling's leaves may burn. This could also dry out the planting medium, adding to the seedling's stress. Depending on the intensity of the lighting fixture, the distance between the light and newly germinated seedlings must be adjusted.

Plants can be started under LED panels, kept at least 24 inches (50 cm) above the surface of the grow media. Seeds can be started under either standard T-8 or T-5 fluorescents or under CFLs. Place fluorescents about 2 to 12 inches (5–30 cm) above the canopy. Space high-output T-5s and high-watt CFLs about a foot (30 cm) above the plants. The plants can also be started under metal halide (MH) or high pressure sodium (HPS) high-intensity discharge lamps or place the seedlings under them soon after germination.

HPS 600-watt and 1000-watt lamps should be placed about one and a half to three feet (45–90 cm) above the canopy if they are air cooled, and about three to four feet (90–120 cm) if not. Seedlings can be germinated under HPS or MH lamps or can be placed under the lamps shortly after. They can also be moved outside.

Outdoors, the sooner after germination the seedlings are planted, the faster they adapt to the environment. Place them outdoors at the same time of the season as tomatoes and corn are planted. However, depending on the latitude of the garden, the dark period may be too long early in the spring, forcing some varieties to flower prematurely. (*See Flowering.*)

Seedling Vulnerabilities

Seedlings are at their most vulnerable stage immediately after they germinate. Stem rot, a fungal infection, attacks when the medium is kept too moist or when roots are deprived of oxygen. (*See Oxygen.*) This can happen when the soil or planting mix is too fine or compressed and holds too much water but not enough oxygen. Seedlings don't need to be watered as often as media with more porosity. As with germinating, use compost tea or a 0.5% hydrogen peroxide solution to prevent both fungal and bacterial infections in seedlings.

Dry media damage both roots and canopy leaves. The time between first signs of wilt and irreparable damage from dehydration is very short for young plants, which don't have much of an infrastructure reserve. Dry conditions cause the leaves to wilt as they use the available water in the cells and lose turgidity. If the conditions are caught in time, the plants recover soon after they are irrigated. This situation is time sensitive and should be corrected immediately.

Deer, mice, birds, dogs, and cats have all been noted to have a fondness for cannabis sprouts and young plants. These animal friends should be protected from temptation by installing barriers. Another problem with pets, especially those that live both indoors and outdoors, is that they may carry insects and pests into the indoor garden.

The goal is to grow a stout stem that has the strength to support the canopy. Stem height is mostly determined by a combination of temperature and light intensity. The warmer the temperature, the more light the seedlings require. Stretch is often an indication of too little light for the temperature. The long, slender "pencil neck" shoots subsequently have problems supporting the canopy as it gains weight. This can be resolved either by providing more light or by lowering the temperature. Use fertilizers with relatively low amounts of phosphorus to prevent stretching (Nelson, Song, and Huang 2002).

Minimizing what is referred to as "DIF," the drop from the daytime temperature high to the nighttime low, can also reduce stem elongation. Although cultivar selection will have the greatest effect on stem length and internodal spacing, limiting diurnal temperature shifts can reduce stretching. Plants are especially sensitive to temperature in the first few hours of daylight. Research shows that using a "morning temperature dip" can achieve the same effect as reducing overall DIF throughout the day and night. This can be achieved by dropping the temperature slightly during the first two to three hours of daylight and then allowing temperatures to reach their normal levels for the rest of the period when lights are on.

To correct stretch that has already occurred, support the seedlings using toothpicks, chopsticks, skewers, or thin bamboo stakes. Once the situation is resolved, the stems will develop more girth.

Too little sun can be a problem for young plants, but so can a withering sun. Seedlings have more problems with this when they are set outside in late spring or during the summer, especially if they have been under lights for a while. To prevent damage from sunlight that is too intense, plants are placed under screening or partial shade when they are first brought outdoors. They are moved to full sun gradually, over five days or so. Plants can also be protected by spraying **anti-transpirants** on them before they are placed outdoors. These substances place a screen between the leaf and the sun and slow transpiration so the plants won't wilt.

Seedlings started outdoors or acclimated to direct sunlight will easily adjust to the bright sun. New leaves that grow in the sun will grow longer palisade cells that absorb more light before it reaches the chlorophyll. They position the chlorophyll so it receives less light, protecting it from the more intense environment. In addition, new leaves will not have the sensitivity to UV light that destroys indoor-grown leaves placed outdoors.

> If it is inconvenient to plant at the moment, unrooted cuttings can be placed in the refrigerator, not the freezer, to stop their growth. Store them in the vegetable crisper of the refrigerator for a week or more. Keep them in a moistened plastic bag with the temperature above 40°F (4°C) to prevent cell damage. This treatment does not adversely affect the plant's later growth and, in fact, is an easy way to harden up plants that are placed outdoors later. Rooted clones and larger plants can be kept in stasis under a regimen of low light, dilute fertilizer, and a constant temperature of about 55°F (13°C).

Reiziger® Root Booster contains the purest Arctic marine extracts, bioactive compounds, nutrients, and B vitamins to aid overall plant growth, assuring a larger, more vigorous plant. This nutrient-rich, organic root stimulator has the power to save, revive, or help newly potted plants and transplants grow early white healthy roots, create more uniformity, and improve survivability, resulting in greener, vigorous plant growth and abundant new flowers.

Planting Seedlings & Clones

After cuttings have rooted, the clones grow stems and leaves, starting at the apical meristem, the very top of the growth tip. After seeds germinate, they develop a taproot, and the first true leaves emerge. Seedlings and clones are ready to transplant when they have developed a network of roots and several sets of leaves. In both clones and young plants, the new growth indicates that they are ready to develop under full light indoors. Once placed in the garden, the new growth adjusts to the light intensity.

If the plants are being transplanted into soil or a planting mix, place the entire root ball in the medium just slightly deeper than the root ball's height so that it is covered with soil, without burying the previously exposed base of the stem. The roots will grow from the root ball in all directions, downward and outward.

Roots concentrate their growth in permeable areas of the growing medium that contain water, nutrients, and oxygen. Whether nutrients are held in the soil or provided using a nutrient-water solution, roots absorb them as simple dissolved salts.

Microorganisms in the planting media digest complex organic nutrients and then release them in a water-soluble form available to the plants. As the plant draws up the nutrients from the water, the planting medium gradually releases more that dissolve in the water. Enriched planting media and soils contain high levels of organic amendments or compost that support seedling growth and will not need supplementation for at least one to two weeks. Some commercial planting media support plants longer. A few are made with time-release formulas that last the entire growing season.

The length of time that a planting mix or soil can support growth depends on several factors. The most important ones are the volume of planting media, nutrient levels of the mix, and growth rate of the plant.

If two plants are growing under identical conditions, except for the container size, the one in the larger container will yield more. Contrary to myths, there is no harm done in growing a plant in a container larger than is required. However, growing plants in containers that are too small slows growth and stunts the plant.

With many cultivars grown in soil or planting mix, the canopy of the plant will typically grow in proportion to the diameter of the roots. A plant with a 10 inch (25 cm) diameter canopy will generally have a root system 6 to 10 inches (15–25 cm) in diameter. The same ratio applies to a plant with a canopy 2 feet (60 cm) in diameter; its root system will typically range from 15–25 inches (38–63 cm).

In contrast, hydroponic plants can grow considerably larger than the size of the root zone because easy access to water and nutrients encourages roots to grow much more densely. As long as the roots have access to water and air, they will colonize the growing medium very densely. The canopies of hydroponically grown plants can cover an area several times the diameter of the container, depending on how well supplied the plant is with its essentials.

Plants probably grow more vigorously without being transplanted from container to container, although using containers that can be transplanted directly minimizes transplanting shock.

The ideal conditions for young seedlings and newly transplanted clones is an environment with ambient temperatures between 72 and 78°F (22 and 25°C). Do not leave the plant containers directly on the floor: cold floor temperatures cool the grow medium and slow plant growth. For the first one to two weeks, use low- to medium-level lighting with an average PPFD of 200–400 μmols, after which the plants can be acclimated to higher levels. Higher-output lights can be used, but should be distanced farther from the canopy. LEDs and other dimmable lamps can be adjusted accordingly and placed closer to the tops of the new transplants.

During early growth, cannabis plants need little special care. The plants adjust to their environment and grow at the fastest pace that limiting factors allow. When provided with optimal conditions, seedlings and clones survive the perils of early growth and, within a matter of weeks, develop into vigorous young plants.

Plant & Container Size

Indoors and outdoors, the size of the container helps determine the size of the plant and its yield. If two identical plants are given the same conditions except for container size, the plant in the larger container will produce more. For this reason, it's wise to give roots as much room as possible to spread out. Indoors, the container size should be limited only by the space each plant has in the canopy.

Container Sizes

In a garden space of 16 square feet (1.5 m²) the following configurations apply.
- A single plant can be grown in a container 30–50 gallons (113–190 l).
- Two plants can be grown in two containers 20–30 gallons each (75–113 l).
- Four plants can be grown in four containers 15–20 gallons each (56–75 l).
- Eight plants can be grown in eight containers 7–10 gallons each (26–38 l).
- Sixteen plants can be grown in 16 containers 3–5 gallons each (11–19 l).

Sexing the Young Plants

Sexing is the process of identifying whether the plant is male or female. There are few things more important to careful gardeners than being sure that their crop is protected from unwanted pollination. The plants are sexed as early as possible, even during the seedling stage.

Plants grown from standard seed are either male or female, in a roughly 50–50 ratio. Plants grown using feminized seeds are almost all female, but they still have to be sexed. Unless the grower intends to breed, males have no use in the garden and are detrimental to the crop if their flowers are allowed to open and pollinate the female flowers. Pollination not only creates seeded buds but lowers the effective potency and usable weight. By eliminating males early, fewer resources are spent caring for plants that are to be discarded.

Rather than wait until late in the season to determine sex, there are methods that can be used to sort the plants much sooner. Male plants are likely to be taller and more vigorous than females early in life, so gardeners are often disappointed when their favorite plant turns out to be male; however, plant morphology is a difficult way to figure out the sex.

Two good ways to determine sex are as follows:
- Look at the nodes of the young plant where the leaf petioles and the stem are joined. Sometimes a small, single male or female flower grows at this point. The plant is the same sex as this single flower. Some varieties indicate more than others, so while this method can be helpful, it cannot be used to determine every plant's sex. Using a magnifier provides a clearer view.
- Early flowering is induced by adjusting the photoperiod. However, forcing the whole plant to flower requires 10 days as it switches to flowering cycle and 10 days to switch back to vegetative growth. Instead, cuttings are taken to deter-

mine sex without forcing the whole plant into flowering. Cuttings are placed in a planting mix or a cup with water under a flowering light regimen of 8 hours on, 16 hours off. Cuttings will begin to flower and indicate sex within 7 to 14 days. They will indicate faster if kept in darkness for 3 days before placing them under a reduced light cycle. The cuttings and the plants from which they came have the same sex.

Left: early flowering on a female plant. Right: flowering on a male plant. Photos: Ed Rosenthal

Once the cuttings have indicated, remove the male plants from the garden and destroy them. Sentimentality should play no part in the decision. The indicator cuttings are not worth saving.

(*For more on sinsemilla and plant sexing see Flowering.*)

Plant Sex Tests

DNA-based sex testing is now available commercially. After blade leaves have emerged, sanitized tweezers are used to remove a cotyledon leaf from the plant to be sexed. The leaf is then smashed with the cover closed on the sample collection plate. A portion of the plant's DNA is sequenced in a lab. Like humans, genetic females have XX sex chromosomes and genetic males will have XY. The test itself is quick. Commercial labs will deliver results in one to three days.

Early Plant Growth

In a few weeks, the plants grow a foot (30 cm) or more in height and develop branches typical of their variety. By now, plants from standard seeds should be sexed, leaving only females in the garden. Depending on desired size and plant spacing, they should be transplanted to their final containers or into the ground.

Seedlings and clones that are transplanted into hydroponic units or an unenriched planting mix need fertilizers to supply them with nutrients. Both clones and young plants require fertilizer; see *Nutrients & Fertilizers* to determine the right ratio of N-P-K to use.

After transplanting, keep the temperature in the low 70s F (low 20s C), if possible. Photosynthesis is limited when the air is kept cool. Since less water and nutrients are required with slower photosynthesis, the roots don't get stressed and there is less chance of wilting. Keep the CO_2 at 500–600 ppm, giving the plants easy access to the gas.

About three days after transplanting, the light intensity is increased and the plants enter rapid vegetative growth. The CO_2 is increased to 1200 ppm, and the strength of the water-nutrient solution is raised to midrange. The temperature is raised to 80°F (26–27°C). (*See Light* to help determine photoperiod.)

If the young plants are destined to be grown outdoors, and they are started under continuous light indoors, they may be shocked into premature flowering when placed outdoors, even in early summer. To prevent this, cut the light regimen to 16–18 hours of light and 6–8 hours of darkness. Indica varieties are especially sensitive.

Photo: Stinkbud

VEGETATIVE GROWTH

As soon as the roots have adjusted to the new environment, it is time to increase the light and nutrients. Firm, turgid leaves and new growth are indications that the plant is ready for rapid growth. The plants should be kept on a high N fertilizer regimen until they are put into flowering. "Grow" formulas that include micronutrients support rapid vegetative growth. (*See Nutrients & Fertilizers.*)

Indoors

Vegetative growth can be started indoors any time it's convenient because the grower determines the plant's environment and simulates seasonal variations by adjusting the periods of light and darkness.

Outdoors & Greenhouses

To prevent burning, slowly acclimate plants rooted indoors to higher light. Plants rooted indoors to be planted outdoors should be shaded as they acclimate before being placed in the full sun. Seedlings can be started in full sun as long as care is taken that they do not dry out during germination. Gardeners using natural light as either a primary or a secondary source must take the seasons into account. Planting time and strategies vary depending on the environment.

The earliest that seedlings or clones should be planted outdoors is when the soil temperature three inches (7.5 cm) below the surface reaches 60°F (15.5°C) in the afternoon and slips no lower than 45°F (7°C) at night. They can be planted when ground temperatures are lower, but growth will be slow until the ground heats up. In areas where there are four distinct seasons, clones or rooted cuttings should be planted outdoors at the same time as tomatoes. Almanacs can be checked for optimal planting times based on local microclimate zones. Light deprivation may be needed to prevent flowering.

No matter what time plants are transplanted outdoors, they will flower in the fall, although ripening times differ by cultivar, except for autoflowering plants. No artificial light is needed as long as there is plenty of sunshine.

At higher latitudes, the intensity of light that plants receive from the sun in early fall is a fraction of the light in early summer. The available amount of UV light also decreases the farther away from the equator one cultivates. As discussed in more detail in the Lights chapter, artificial light can be used to supplement the plants' lighting needs in the fall.

The sun's angle changes over the growing season, so plants that were in direct light in spring and summer may be shaded in autumn. Strategic planting will anticipate where the sunny areas will be during flowering, growth, and ripening.

Plants in containers can be moved, following the sun either daily or seasonally to provide them with more direct sunlight. Plants in the ground that are shaded require supplemental light to grow and ripen properly.

On overcast days, clouds absorb most of the light, so they delay ripening. Even sunny gardens receiving direct but weak sunlight may require more light for the buds to develop well.

Providing plants with supplemental light during the brightest part of the day may be all that is needed to help the buds mature in early fall. (*See Light.*)

Gardeners in lower latitudes, such as Mediterranean and subtropical regions, can grow outdoors virtually the entire year. These areas include the southern tier of Europe, the southern tier of the United States, and all of Mexico and Central America. Therefore, in these zones day length and light intensity do not vary as much between summer and winter as in higher latitudes.

Most indica and indica-dominant hybrids are early ripening, because they require the least amount of uninterrupted darkness to flower. Depending on latitude, some varieties trigger almost immediately when placed outdoors; for them, the night length is long enough in summer to promote flowering.

One strategy for taking advantage of this is to grow plants indoors until they reach the desired size, then set them outside to flower. Indica-dominant varieties slow their rate of vegetative growth quickly once they start to flower. They may grow only 25 to 100% of their size in this period. Sativa-dominant varieties may continue to grow vegetatively for the first several weeks of the flowering cycle. They can triple or even quadruple in size. Other strategies include keeping small plants in vegetative growth by interrupting the dark period. However, to grow larger plants without effort, growers choose more dark-tolerant cultivars.

Sativas and sativa-dominant hybrids are usually late-season varieties that require a longer dark period to flower. Some equatorial sativa varieties do not start to flower until early fall and don't ripen for two to three months. In winter, flowering is induced quickly, but the plants may continue to grow vegetatively for a month or more before they concentrate their energy on flowering. The result is that they can be planted anytime of the year. Sativas set out between late summer and midwinter will ripen within 120 days. Plants transplanted outdoors in the spring and summer flower in late fall in warmer microclimates.

Dedicated flowering greenhouses can be used to grow up to six crops a year using supplemental light, with a separate vegetative area. The determining factor is root and air temperature. Plant growth is slow when air temperature is below 60°F (15°C). It quadruples with adequate light as the temperature increases from 60 to 80°F (15 to 26°C). At the same time, ground temperature below 65°F (18°C) hinders root function, which affects the supply of water and nutrients to the canopy. Supplemental heating of containers will ameliorate the problem. With this in mind, the garden plan should be based on average temperature for the zone, which can be found in almanacs or on the internet. If the plant roots are kept warm, the plant canopy does better in cool weather.

Outdoor subtropical zoned gardens can be planted all year. In other warm areas, where spring comes early, gardens can be planted in mid to late winter, as the sun's intensity starts to increase. In areas that are in zones that are cooler, row covers can be used to keep the plants warmer.

Row covers keep the garden warm and sheltered from the cold, wind, and rain. Photo by Brian Walker Courtesy of Central Coast Agriculture

Young plants placed outdoors immediately start to flower, because the night period is still longer than 12 hours. Indicas and indica-dominant hybrids continue to flower as the days get longer. However, sativas and sativa-dominant hybrids revert to vegetative growth unless light-deprivation techniques such as blackout covers are being used.

In some areas, it's just too cold to plant in late winter or even in early spring, but passively heated greenhouses move the planting period forward three weeks or more. A heated greenhouse can overcome inclement and cold conditions, but cloudy spring skies may not provide quite enough light to the plants. LEDs or HID lamps can be used to supplement the light for five or six hours during the brightest part of the day and to increase the number of hours of light during the winter. Systems that measure sunlight and adjust lamps keep the light levels constant and the greenhouse running at top efficiency.

Removable tunnels, often called row covers, are another way to get a jump on the season. They keep the outdoor garden warm and sheltered from the cold, wind, and rain.

Row covers are easily constructed using rebar or metal pipe covered with (6 or 8 ml) clear polyethylene. The plastic is removable, so it is placed over the plants only when there is cold or inclement weather. In early spring, it might be used nightly. The tunnels should be constructed about 6 feet (1.75 m) high so they can be used for forcing flowering with blackout covers later in the season. This process is known as light deprivation and is covered further in the Flowering chapter. They are often 10 feet (3 m) wide, but can be designed for any width.

One design has two sheets of polyethylene, one on either side of the frame. The first sheet is clear plastic and is used to cover plants in cold or inclement weather. The other is panda plastic, which is white on one side and black on the other. Panda plastic is used as a blackout curtain for light deprivation. It is placed white side out to reflect sunlight so the air inside the tunnel doesn't heat up.

Using a tunnel or a greenhouse, it's possible to manipulate the light cycle to either prolong vegetative growth or to force the plants to flower. Using these techniques, a crop can be produced in 90 days or less.

One greenhouse strategy is to plant in early spring. The plants will ripen in the late spring or earlier. Immediately after harvesting, the next crop is planted and will ripen by late summer or early fall. A third crop is then started. It will flower immediately and is ready by midfall. The second and third crops could be started in a smaller area while the current crop is still growing. They could be in the "flower field" for a shorter time, increasing the number of harvests annually.

There are several advantages to forcing an early harvest other than trying to produce multiple crops:

- The crop is less vulnerable to thieves, who look for gardens primarily during the fall harvest season.
- Plants harvested in summer are less susceptible to mold or the vagaries of weather that plague farmers in the fall.
- Total light intensity is lower in the fall than in summer, so the buds are not as large or potent.
- The bud quality is higher when plants flower and are harvested under the strong UV rays of summer rather than in autumn, when UV light is declining. High UV light increases potency.

During early spring, plants usually require an interruption of the night cycle (or extension of the light period), so they do not go into the flowering stage prematurely. Lights on a timer are used to interrupt the dark period briefly during the night.

A 400-watt HPS covers an area of about 600 square feet (55 m²) with enough light to stop flowering. HPS reflectors are available that oscillate a 1,000-watt lamp, which covers 1,500 square feet (130 m²). HPS lamps and warm white fluorescents emit a high percentage of red light, the spectrum used by plants to prevent flowering.

String or strip red LED lights that produce this spectrum are used but need to be rated for outdoor use (IP65 and above).

Compact fluorescent lights (CFLs) can be set out at a rate of one 24-watt bulb per square yard (0.8 m²). Flash the lights on for a minute using a timer at least once during the middle of the dark period. Several light interruptions may be more effective. Gardeners with large spaces sometimes stagger the timing of the night lights.

Indoor Greenhouse Manipulation

Growers can use a combination of indoor and greenhouse or outdoor gardening. Plants are started and initially grown indoors to get a head start, then moved outdoors. By starting early with large plants, the grower can get a jump on the season. This is how growers on the West Coast of the United States grow giant outdoor plants; the plants are started indoors as early as midwinter and may be six feet (1.8 m) tall by the time they are transplanted outdoors into raised bed or soil.

Another strategy is to start plants early indoors using autoflowering varieties. When the weather becomes favorable, they are moved outdoors. Meanwhile, another crop is started outdoors and is transplanted after the first crop is harvested. Use a standard variety if the season is short, or an autoflower if the season is longer. Long-season growers can plant a third crop that will mature in the fall.

Plants grown indoors that are placed outdoors during late spring and summer usually need to adjust to the harsh UV rays by being kept in the shade at first, using an antitranspirant, or covering the canopy with shade cloth. New growth will adjust to new conditions.

The Missing Link by Bionova stimulates the natural immune defense system of any plant, prevents most deficiencies, and leads to both higher-quality and higher-yielding crops. Growers apply it on the roots or as a foliar feed during vegetative growth and early flowering, on mother plants when clones are cut, and on seedlings and cuttings to prevent infection and disease.

Bionova Silution is a plant-strengthening liquid stimulator based on mono-stabilized silicic acid and fulvic acid that stimulates nutrient uptake and defense against viruses and infections, resulting in more dry weight. Silution helps crops develop a higher resistance to the negative impact of stress and temperature extremes, as well as stronger cell walls, stronger defense against plant infections and pests, and a higher weight at yield.

Nutrients for Growth

Cannabis grows very quickly when supplied with ample amounts of all its requirements, including nutrients, during the vegetative stage. If the soil or planting mix cannot meet the plants' nutrient needs, the plants require fertilizers.

If the plants are suffering from a particular nutrient deficiency for a short period of time, supplying that individual nutrient puts them back on track. There are many brands of organic and mineral nutrients available. Most of them have been on the market for many years and have a long successful history of providing quality products.

Always use a control when testing a new product. Friendly garden "mavens" and garden shop employees are always suggesting mixing recommendations or odd combinations of products. The grower may also wish to compare two fertilizers and see how their performance in the garden differs. A wise gardener tests the suggestion on just a small group of plants first to see if the recommendation is beneficial or perhaps harmful.

Plant leaves catch dust. So even if the plants are not being fed foliarly, it is a good idea to mist them every two weeks with a fine spray, letting the water drip off the leaves. Do this at the beginning of the light cycle so the leaves are sure to dry completely and the lights are not yet hot. Be careful not to direct the spray near the lights. If the reflector does get sprayed, clean the glass plate so light is not obstructed. Don't spray when HID lights are on if there is any chance that the spray will get near the bulbs. There is a real possibility of the bulb exploding when the cool water hits the hot glass bulb.

LED lights that are rated at IP66 are water resistant and not affected by direct spraying.

These clones were planted at the same time and received identical inputs, except the plant on the right was treated foliarly with PowerGrown's Triacontanol and Brassinolide Cannabis Kit. When used correctly, triacontanol can significantly increase the amount of chlorophyll in leaves, improving the rate of photosynthesis as a result. It can also destress plants. Triacontanol can also be used to help fight disease in plants, ward off potential disease, and act as an anti-aging agent. As a nutrient uptake enhancer, it can also aid plants suffering from poor nutrient intake or other growth deficiencies. For R&D use only.

Watering & Irrigation

Cannabis is a water-loving plant. It thrives in moist soil and responds to dry conditions first by slowing and then halting photosynthesis. As dry conditions continue, the leaves lose turgidity and wilt. Then they dry up. Even a short period without water can result in a dead plant unless the plant is "dry farmed" or other measures are taken for it to thrive in a low-water climate. (*See Dry Farming with Sunboldt Grown.*)

Cannabis that has easy access to water can grow to its full potential. This translates to maintaining a moist, but not waterlogged, growing medium. As the growing medium dries, the plant's ability to move water into the roots becomes more difficult. The water tension increases as a result. Water moves from the growing medium into the roots, up the stem, and finally out the stomatal pores in the leaves. If the growing medium dries too much, the increased water tension disrupts water movement into the plant and up to the leaves. When there is a continued water deficit, the first thing the plant does is close the stomata on the leaves. With the stomata closed, the plant cannot absorb CO_2, resulting in the cessation of photosynthesis. At the same time, it transpires water to keep cool. This results in loss of water and turgidity, causing the leaves to wilt.

WATER USE ON HOT DAYS

Plant Diameter	Area	Water Requirement
4 feet (1.2 m)	12 square feet (1 m²)	4 gallons (15 l)
10 feet (3 m)	78 square feet (7 m²)	25 gallons (95 l)

Outdoors

Under natural growing conditions, cannabis planted outdoors uses between 20 and 30 inches (50–75 cm) of water over the season. Most of it is used in the summer, when the plants are in the vegetative stage and growing rapidly. This is also the period of peak temperature, so the plants' use of water increases dramatically because it is used for both photosynthesis and transpiration. Photosynthesis increases in relation to higher light intensity and rising temperature. At its peak, this process uses large amounts of water. Transpiration increases with more light and heat, as it helps cool plants through water evaporation and draws more water from the roots.

> Much like humans, plants cool themselves off by "sweating." "Plant sweating" is known as transpiration. As the water evaporates from the leaf, it cools off the leaf.

Many factors affect how much water is available to an outdoor garden. In areas where there is regular rainfall or a high water table, plants may need no irrigation. However, areas with a Mediterranean or desert climate, where there is very little rainfall in the summer, cannot support plant growth without irrigation. Water availability also varies by soil type. Clays, mucks, and loams with high content of organic matter hold more water than sandy soil.

Water loss to soil evaporation can be eliminated or slowed using mulch, pebbles, or plastic sheeting to keep soil cooler by protecting it from the sun. Container systems that catch and recycle the excess water that would otherwise drain past the roots also conserve water.

Plants growing in soil or soilless mixes should be watered before the medium dries out, but only after the top inch or two (2.5–5 cm) has lost a bit of its moisture. If the soil or mixture drains well, overwatering does not create anaerobic conditions because the excess water drains. However, soluble nutrients are leached out by overwatering, and unnecessary water use can be costly and environmentally unfriendly.

Roots require oxygen to function and thrive. They have problems with some soils not because they are too wet but because they have too fine a texture and do not hold air between the particles. When roots have no access to air, they become stressed and susceptible to attacks by pathogens. Interestingly enough, sometimes too much water will look like too little

Drip irrigation is an effective way to conserve water outdoors. Photos: Mendo Dope

water because too much water can cause an oxygen stress that results in leaves wilting. Wilting leaves as a result of prolonged root oxygen stress can usually be relieved by letting the growing medium dry out, which seems counterintuitive when the leaves are wilting. (For more on this, *see Soil*.)

Hydroponic Water Use

Hydroponic gardens typically use one half to two thirds the amount of water that plants grown in the ground require because almost all the water in a hydroponic system is used directly by the plant.

Gardeners using hydroponic systems just add water to the reservoirs, replenishing water that is either lost to evaporation or used for transpiration, photosynthesis, and general metabolism. Before adding water, it is necessary to check the nutrient levels of the water-nutrient solution remaining in the reservoir. The nutrients in the water to be added are adjusted so that when they are combined with what remains in the reservoir, the pH and nutrient levels are within an acceptable range.

Growers using active hydroponic systems, such as drip emitters or ebb and flow, should adjust the watering cycle so that the medium never loses its moisture. Each type of medium retains a different volume of water, but media for active systems should drain well so that the roots are always in contact with air. The plant's size and growth stage, as well as the ambient temperature and humidity, all affect the amount of water used, so adjust the cycling schedule accordingly.

Indoor Watering

As with plants growing in the ground outdoors, plants growing in soil or soilless mixes indoors in containers need water once the top layer is no longer moist but before the soil in the root zone dries out. Overwatering is not a problem so long as the soil or planting mix is porous and drains well. Additionally, overwatering in well-draining hydroponic growing media is nearly impossible as long as the nutrient solution is thoroughly oxygenated.

Roots remain healthy as long as a medium allows both air and water to penetrate. If the roots do not have access to air, they grow weak and are prone to attack by bacteria. Planting mixes vary greatly in both their water- and air-holding capacity, so the watering regimen must be developed based on the medium and plant size and growth stage.

When plants are small, they use less water. As they grow, their water needs increase, so the watering schedule should change. In general, plants require more water during vegetative growth than during flowering; however, even during flowering, plants are most productive when they have easy access to water. During the last two weeks of flowering, plants grow more slowly, use less water, and need fewer nutrients.

Some growers withhold water for several days before harvesting. This results in a slightly smaller yield but may slightly increase potency. A better practice is to limit fertilizing to improve bud flavor.

Spray-N-Grow Micronutrients® is formulated with the full spectrum of 16 naturally occurring micronutrients in a single foliar spray. Used in conjunction with a macronutrient solution it optimizes plant growth and bud production, and increases yields, flower size, and root mass. In studies conducted on lettuce, tomatoes, snow peas, and strawberries, it increased fruiting, yields, and weight of the finished harvested crop.

Maximize absorption and improve the efficiency of any nutrient by using Coco-Wet Wetting Agent. Coco-Wet is a natural wetting agent with a nonionic formula that makes it compatible with any nutrient product. Whether in a foliar spray or in the reservoir, improve the absorption of nutrients and achieve optimal results with Coco-Wet.

Foliar Feeding

Plants can absorb both water and nutrients through their leaves, so the nutrient-water solution supplied to the roots can be misted on the foliage as well. Leaves have stomata that serve the same purpose as pores: They open and close as needed to regulate the absorption of CO_2, water, and nutrients. Foliar-fed plants grow faster. Foliar feeding also saves fertilizer compared with soil; a higher percentage of the fertilizer is more quickly absorbed than with conventional methods.

Foliar spraying should be done at least an hour prior to lights on or after lights out. Be sure to spray generously, in particular the underside of the leaves. To help the foliar spray stick to the leaves, use a few drops of a wetting agent or liquid soap such as Dr. Bronner's Hemp or Castile soaps.

Foliar feeding is especially helpful when plants are suffering from a deficiency, because the needed nutrients are delivered directly to the leaves.

Foliar feeding can be started as soon as the seeds germinate. Once they have roots, clones grow faster when they are misted with a water-nutrient solution. Since the ability of young plants to absorb water is limited, a dilute nutrient solution spurs growth. Continue foliar feeding during vegetative growth and early flowering. Stop spraying once the flowers are three to four weeks old and are beginning to develop water-trapping crevices. Buds at this stage are susceptible to mold and infections promoted by excess humidity.

In a sea of green garden, each plant only has to grow a small fraction of space to fill the canopy. Photo: Angela Bacca

Sea of Green (SOG)

In traditional planting a high proportion of the plant's life cycle is spent by growing infrastructure to fill space in the canopy. For instance, a plant that is to occupy a four by four foot (1.2 by 1.2 m) space may take 45–60 days to fill the canopy. A three by three foot (90 by 90 cm) space can take 60–90 days. During that time it is occupying space and growing vegetation that will never be harvested.

Instead, using the sea of green (SOG) method, each plant in the canopy is assigned a space of six by six inches (15 by 15 cm) to one by one foot (90 by 90 cm). Each plant has to grow only a small fraction of the space to fill the canopy. The time the plant spends in vegetative growth producing infrastructure is reduced to a fraction of the time it takes to fill a larger space, and only a fraction of the energy required to build a larger infrastructure. As a result, less time and space is spent in growth that is not producing harvestable material. That is the essence and efficiency of the SOG.

In a SOG garden, plants are placed together very closely so that each plant needs to grow a little bit to fill the canopy. Plants are forced to flower by switching the photoperiod to bloom. The timing of the lighting regimen change ranges from zero time in vegetative to about two weeks depending on the cultivar and the size of the assigned space.

SOG has a lot of advantages and a few disadvantages over traditional cultivation:
- The number of crops per year is increased because little time is spent in the vegetative cycle. Almost all the plant growth is used to produce flowers.
- Because the plants are close together, the number of top buds is increased. This short-cropping method produces approximately the same yield per crop as with larger plants. Same yield, shorter time.
- The plants remain short, usually no higher than 3.5 feet (1 m), so a grow area can be stacked with two, three, or more layers, taking advantage of the vertical space.
- This method can be used with either seeds or clones, but for best results the plants should be uniform so that no single plant dominates an area.
- Very little time is spent tending plants because the plants don't have time to develop extraneous growth. They need little support, but sometimes netting is used to keep the plant tops in place. Usually the plants need little pruning, which goes faster, since the plants all have single stems.
- Although the plants are very close together, there is less opportunity for pest damage because the plants are in place for a much shorter time, giving the pests less time to build up harmful numbers. It's easier to contain the infection, because they are in plain sight rather than hidden in dense foliage.
- This method is well suited mostly for commercial growers because home growers often run up against plant number restrictions.

Eliminating the vegetative growth stage decreases turnaround time. SOG gardens hold one to four plants per square foot (0.09 m²). Spacing depends on several factors:
- Number of clones available: A shortage of clones can be a key limiting factor in determining spacing. Divide the space by the number of clones to find the best available spacing.
- Cultivars differ in their growing pattern: Plants with less side branching can be placed closer together than plants that side branch. Trim off the side branches to place side-branching plants closer together.
- If growing in containers, choose the maximum cubic space possible: For instance, plants being spaced at 12 inches (30 cm) should be planted in 12 or 10 inch (25 cm) containers. Plants spaced at 6 inches (15 cm) should be planted in 6 inch square containers if possible. Square containers hold more medium than cylindrical.
- Space: A raised bed or soil-filled tray, rather than individual containers, is used to provide the most planting mix in the space. Rockwool 6 inch (15 cm) blocks are often used because they are easy to set up and provide adequate space for the roots.
- Plants mostly forgo side branching when placed close together.

SOG Tips

- Lower leaves can be trimmed off. However, if there is good air circulation in the garden, there is no reason to spend labor trimming them. They won't interfere with the top buds, so most of the lower leaves can be left on.
- Although breeders recommend certain varieties, most varieties can be used because when plants are placed close together, they tend to grow vertically rather than spread out with side branching.

Clones versus Seeds: Which Is Better for SOG?

As the name of the growing method suggests, the goal of SOG truly is to achieve a sea of uniform, as close to identical as possible plants. SOG production has many advantages as previously stated; however, the choice of sourcing plant material strongly leans toward using clones as opposed to seeds.

Seeds result in more heterogeneity than clones simply because seeds are the result of sexual reproduction. Large-scale seed production requires two separate parents to hybridize. The resulting seeds will have genetic variability, which manifests as slightly different phenotypes with differences in cannabinoids, potency, flower development, height, or flowering time.

Having plants develop at different rates is detrimental to any large-scale production, but especially SOG. Since there are so many more individual plants to harvest, the chances of differing ripening times are greater. Additionally, if a few plants here and there are taller than the rest of the canopy, they will shade the plants immediately surrounding them. Uniformity is very important in horticulture in general, but its need is amplified in SOG style of production.

On the other hand, clones are genetically identical, so there is more uniformity. Growing with clones removes a pretty significant obstacle to achieving a uniform canopy: different genetic makeup of the individual plants in the canopy. Since SOG does better when the canopy is uniform, clones are the preferred method of obtaining genetic material for production. Although it is not impossible to grow in SOG fashion with seeds, it is better for a more uniform canopy to use clones.

SOG Sativa Tips

SOG is a good method for growing sativas. Whether starting from seed or clone, the plants are set on flowering cycle (12/12) light-dark from the very beginning to keep them as short as possible. After the first six weeks the lights can be turned down to 10 hours on and 14 hours off to induce faster ripening. Keep the lights on their brightest setting. A UV light such as the EYE Hortilux PowerVeg fluorescents may encourage stouter growth.

The EYE Hortilux PowerVEG FS+UV (full spectrum plus ultraviolet) is a fluorescent T5 lamp that provides plants with a well-balanced spectrum and UV light. The spectrum closely mimics natural sunlight and promotes extreme photosynthesis for faster growth, creates a stronger root system, enables easy transition from indoor veg to outdoor flowering, helps to develop stronger, healthier vegetative plants that will produce higher yields and higher-quality crops, vivid colors, more flowering, and better-tasting crops.

Screen of Green (ScrOG)

by Royal Queen Seeds

Screen of Green (ScrOG) is a training technique that forms an even and horizontal canopy. There are myriad benefits to creating this botanical structure.

Left to their own devices, cannabis plants grow taller than they do wide. The ScrOG technique aims to bring the lower branches up and the upper branches down, stretching them across an evenly distributed plane. By placing a screen above the growing medium, cultivators weave branches through the mesh as plants grow and mature. By redirecting individual branches and running them lengthwise across the screen, growers achieve a flat horizontal canopy.

But why ScrOG in the first place? Well, the technique offers plenty of advantages, including:

- **Light exposure:** A ScrOG canopy receives even light exposure. Untrained cannabis plants feature one main cola that rises above the rest of the plant, resulting in uneven light distribution. In contrast, there is no shading because no plants are taller than others.

- **Yield:** Because all bud sites receive adequate light, they maximize their photosynthetic potential, leading to an increase in size and resin production. This level of training also transforms the main stem and central cola into a multitude of both.
- **Aeration:** The horizontal screen of green receives adequate airflow above and below the canopy. The addition of a fan further enhances this benefit, reducing the risk of fungal pathogens.

A Screen of Green system utilizes light and space to increase yield-per-plant.
Courtesy of Dutch Passion Seeds

When to ScrOG

Guide plants through the screen as soon as they start making contact with it. Position the screen about eight inches (20 cm) above the base of the plants so that their growth rate will determine when it is time to ScrOG.

Start the "tucking" process as the apex of each plant begins to grow through the screen. Wait for each tip to grow about two inches (5 cm) above the screen. Proceed to tuck each individual shoot under the screen and direct them through the next square away. Tucking will lay the foundation of the ScrOG process, so be mindful of the direction each branch will grow.

Continue this process throughout the vegetative phase. Induce flowering when the screen becomes mostly filled. Continue to tuck and weave each branch over the next two to three weeks as plants begin to stretch.

Avoid tucking and weaving plants too early. It might be tempting to rush ahead, but they'll only grow well beyond the screen. Training plants into the mesh too early—during the early vegetative phase—will lead to extra work.

Select the Correct Pot Size

Select the correct pot size to optimize the garden space. This variable will shift depending on how many plants are to be incorporated. Consider the following factors:

- **Multiple plants:** Consider spacing when growing several plants in a smaller space. Each plant requires a smaller pot. Three gallon (11 l) pots make the most of the space while optimizing plant growth.
- **Single plants:** Increase the pot size when using a single plant in the ScrOG setup. A 6.5 gallon (25 liter) pot gives the plant enough room to establish a substantial root system and large canopy.
- **Fabric pots:** The ScrOG technique greatly improves aeration of the canopy. Using a fabric pot increases aeration of the growing medium.

Correct spacing will minimize mold formation while encouraging the best yield possible. The goal is to fit as many plants as possible into the space while keeping them far enough apart to increase light exposure and aeration.

Pruning & Training

There are probably as many theories about pruning and training and their effect on crop yield as there are cultivators. Pruning and training theories are complicated by the many varieties of cannabis, which have different branching patterns and growing habits. The intent of pruning and training plants is almost always to increase yield.

Traditionally, gardeners have been more interested in the total yield of their garden space, rather than each plant. Growers have become concerned with the yield per plant primarily because of regulations regarding the number of plants. Most home growers are limited to only a few plants, so each plant is nurtured to produce the highest possible yield. Only when the regulations limit canopy space rather than plant count does it make sense to be concerned about total yield of the space rather than the yield per plant.

Pruning Techniques

Some pruning techniques increase yield in a given area. In addition, pruned plants usually occupy more space than plants left unpruned, so yield per plant may increase substantially with pruning.

Cannabis adjusts well to many kinds of pruning techniques. It can be pruned to become bushy rather than tall, trimmed to only a few branches, cut to fit a space, or stretched out to promote branching. Flowering plants can also be pruned to increase flower production. (*See Flowering.*)

To make a plant bushy, clip the tip of the growing shoot after the third set of leaves has developed. The branches surrounding the top branch are no longer inhibited from growing and create a rosette of three or four branches. Meanwhile, the two top shoots that have been hanging out at the pair of top nodes begin to grow. Other lower branches grow a bit as well. After the plants have grown another three or four sets of leaves, clip the tops again to make the plant grow even bushier. Sometimes the plants are topped once or twice more during the vegetative stage. Cutting the tips encourages plants to spread out rather than to grow vertically.

Indoors, the canopy absorbs virtually all the light, leaving little in the shadows below. For this reason, the understory below the canopy contributes little energy to the plant. Instead, it costs the plant nutrients, increases humidity, and stops airflow.

Pruning the lower limbs creates more airflow under the plants and cuttings for cloning. It also forces the plant's growth to the top limbs that get the most light, maximizing yield. These lower leaves and branches should be removed to create an open airspace.

Flat Plants

Selective pruning creates "flat," two-dimensional plants that can be placed against walls, positioned close to each other, or used in unusual configurations.

Cannabis typically grows leaves in an alternating pattern along the stem, with each set of leaves perpendicular to the next. Each leaf is attached to the stem at about a 90° angle, parallel to the ground, positioned to catch light. Opposing branches develop at the nodes in the axils between the leaf and stem, hence the name axillary buds. This growing pattern results in a plant that basically has four corners.

Removing the branches from every other set of leaves creates plants with branches that are opposite each other in two dimensions. This technique can be modified to remove only one branch from every other set of leaves, so one set of branches juts out at a 90° angle from the opposing pairs, creating a more triangular shape. This way, the flat side can be placed against a wall, while the others project into the space.

Floribunding (Fimming)

Trim the top 80% of the apical growing tip, leaving about 20% intact. The tip develops multiple tops, creating a bushy plant laden with heavy branches. Topped branches usually develop two to four new tops for each one cut. Using this technique, a single branch produces six to eight tops.

Sunleaf (Fanleaf Removal for Light)

Contrary to myth, most sun or fan leaves should not be removed from the plant during the vegetative stage. These leaves are costly for the plant to produce, and they are sugar factories that turn light into chemical energy. These sugars are used to power metabolism and for tissue building by combining with nitrogen and phosphorus to make amino acids and proteins. When a leaf is removed, the plant loses a source of energy and its rate of growth slows. Gardeners who routinely remove the fan leaves from their plants outdoors slow growth and lower yields.

To test this, try an experiment. Use a plant that has two sun leaves opposite each other with a small branch growing from either side. Remove one of the leaves and see which side branch develops faster.

Sometimes a few fan leaves block light from a large section of a plant. These leaves can be removed if, on the whole, the plant receives better distribution of light.

Similarly, leaves that are constantly in shadow, such as leaves below the canopy indoors, are not contributing to plant growth, so they should be removed. Similar to "lollipop" pruning, this eliminates the risk of infection, improves air circulation, lowers humidity, and reduces the demand for nutrients.

Leaves that are directly blocking light from getting to buds or the cola should also be removed. This becomes more apparent as the buds grow and become more prominent. However, leaves near the buds but not blocking light should be left in place.

Remove yellow leaves, as well as any infected or infested material.

Single-Bud Plants

Plants can be put into the flowering cycle when they are only a foot or two (30–60 cm) tall, before they have developed branches. They grow into plants with only one bud. The main stem becomes swollen with flowers, but there is little to no branching. These plants are useful for compact gardens because they require only one quarter to one square foot (7–30 square cm) of floor space.

Another advantage is that the plants spend little time growing vegetatively, instead spending most of their time growing flowers. The canopy fills quickly when plants are placed close together and then the garden can be flipped into flowering.

Bending & Crimping

Proceed carefully when bending to avoid breaking the stem or branches. The plant will repair damaged stems if there is some snapping or pinching, so long as the stem is not severed or split. Young branches that are still green are more flexible than older ones that are woody and have turned tan or brown, which cannot be bent much before they snap.

One method of bending the branch is called crimping. The goal of this technique is to stress the branch by twisting top stems so the plant will reinforce the damaged area. The plant repairs the damage quickly. The stem remains bent, and the repaired area is stronger than it was before it was treated.

To crimp a stem or branch, use one hand to hold the stem in place. With the other hand, gently twist the stem back and forth by rolling it between the thumb and forefinger until tissue crunching or snapping is felt. On larger branches, an audible break indicates that the twisting has damaged the stem. Smaller branches can be pinched rather than twisted.

Tomato Rings

Plants can be "opened up" to allow more light to reach lower branches in the interior. This usually entails positioning branches so they don't shade the interior or so that they get more light themselves. String, rope, cloth, gardener's tape, twist ties, stakes, and braces are all useful for bending branches to the grower's will. Also, plants can be controlled by keeping all branches inside the cone. This way they are kept within a designated canopy area.

Tomato trellises (the metal cones) can be used to open up the plants when they are still young. The branches all get more light from the opening and respond by growing bigger buds. Position branches around the outside of the cone, and tie them to it using twist ties or plastic gardening tape. Indoors, these conical trellises can be used to contain unruly plants. A canopy of sativas and other large plants can be confined so they don't infringe on their neighbors using the four or five foot (1.2–1.5 m) cones.

Plants can also be trained with a trellising technique commonly used by grape growers. Stretch ropes at one foot (30 cm) spacing between posts. Tie the plant branches to the ropes. Stretch each branch horizontally so the plant has virtually no depth.

Alternatively, use chicken wire attached to a frame as a trellis. As the plants grow, use twist ties, gardener's tape, or soft string or cloth to attach them to the wire.

Inverted Tops, Supercropping, Bending

Removing the top bud stops auxin production in the shoot apex (high auxin concentrations will keep the lower axillary buds dormant), so the lower branches begin to grow. A way to achieve this result without the loss of the top bud is to bend the top bud down. When

it is positioned at a height below the side buds, auxin movement down the stem is inhibited. The side branches are no longer inhibited, so they start growing. At this point the main bud can be released and will start to grow again. This results in more very large buds.

Supercropping is a similar technique of training top branches to grow horizontally so that the primary bud is exposed to more light. With more areas exposed, the bud grows larger than normal. This technique can also be used when one bud is growing taller than the rest of the canopy. Position the

These supports guide the branches in the desired pattern.   Photo: David Downs

A single large plant can produce 15 pounds (6.8 kg) of flowers. The perimeter fence helps keep plants upright. Photo: David Downs

branch by bending, tying down, or gently snapping it. Supercropping is also used to control vertical growth, especially if the garden has height limitations.

There are several ways to tie the top bud. The top of the stem near the growing tip is composed of flexible soft green tissue, so it can be gently bent down or sideways. To secure the stem and branches, use soft string or cloth, gardener's tape, twist ties, or stakes. Keep any knots loose to minimize damage. The branch may have to be supported by splinting with a skewer or bamboo support.

The top branch is then bent so that it is positioned at the height of or lower than some of the side branches; the side shoots grow as if the top branch were cut. After the side branches have started growing, release the top branch so it can grow upward again. Branches produce more growth than they would with the top branch dominating. The plant with a group of branches produces more bud weight than top-dominant plants.

'Dough Girl' Photo: Théo Oldfield Photo

FLOWERING

Most cannabis varieties are referred to as short-day plants. They determine when to flower based on the number of hours of uninterrupted darkness they receive. When the plant receives the critical period of uninterrupted darkness, the plant flowers.

The plant measures the length of the dark period using the hormone phytochrome, which has two states. The hormone's inactive state, P_{fr}, occurs when it absorbs a red spectrum of light at 666 nanometers. It also has a slight sensitivity to blue light. When the plant is in darkness, the hormone changes from its inactive form, P_{fr}, to its active form, P_r, over two hours. A far-red light at 730 nm after lights out converts P_{fr} to P_r instantly. Unfortunately, it also induces some stretching. When the P_r flowering hormone levels remain high for a critical period of time each day for several days, the plant initiates flowering.

The number of hours of darkness that plants need to initiate flowering differs by cultivar. Sativas require a longer period of darkness than indicas because they developed near the equator, where the length of the growing season is much longer and there is less variation in daylight as compared to indicas, which developed in the northern latitudes. Some sativas continue to grow vegetatively with 10 or 11 hours of darkness, which usually cues most plants to flower.

There are two notable exceptions to light sensitivity regarding flowering. Autoflowering varieties have a programmed chronological strategy, that is, they start flowering soon after germination.

Many sativas initiate flowering only when the dark cycle increases to 12 hours or more, which occurs when fall begins.

By contrast, most indicas flower with 8 to 11 hours of uninterrupted darkness (13 to 15 hours of light). In lower latitudes a few indica varieties flower as early as summer solstice, the shortest night of the year. For this reason, outdoor growers in these zones should consider sativa-indica hybrids and sativas. In mid and higher latitudes, indica and indica-sativa hybrids usually start flowering in late summer and are ready to harvest in early fall.

Some sativas and sativa hybrids require a longer dark period at the end of flowering to fully ripen their buds. Outdoors, this happens in due course as the nights lengthen in the fall. Indoors, change the lighting regimen to 14 hours of darkness/10 hours of light to promote ripening. This is especially helpful in finishing low latitude varieties that don't reach maturity in their native lands until extremely late in the season.

Indoor Flowering

Flowering time of female cannabis plants is regulated by the length of the uninterrupted dark period, so gardens under lights can be forced to flower at any time with the flick of a timer switch.

In general, to determine when to flower the plants, look down at the canopy. When two-thirds of the floor space is hidden by plant canopy, it is time to start the flowering process. The remaining space will fill in during the flowering stage. The breadth and height of the plants may also need to be considered. If the garden has height limitations, the plants should be forced to flower before they get too tall.

To force flowering, lights must be turned on and off in a consistent manner, and the darkness must be uninterrupted. For that reason, it is essential to use a timer to regulate the lights. The timer is set so the lights stay on for 12–13 hours and then remain off for 12 or 11. Within a week, growth slows. The plants are responding to the new light regimen and are beginning to flower.

The light change does not need to be tapered. Reduce light from 18 hours daily (or continuous) down to a flowering cycle of 12 or 13 hours of light and 12 or 11 hours of uninterrupted darkness, with no intermediate steps. The change in the light regimen does not shock the plants.

Sinsemilla & Sexing

Cannabis users prize seedless female flowers, known as sinsemilla, because they are more attractive and far more convenient to use. Cannabis seeds have a noxious oily odor when they burn, so they need to be removed before smoking. Sinsemilla buds are seedless, so there are no seeds to remove. In addition, no energy is wasted on seed production.

"Sin semilla" means "without seed" in Spanish.

In order for female flowers to ripen without seeds, they must remain unpollinated (unfertilized). Because cannabis is dioecious, male and female flowers appear on separate plants and the males must be separated.

If the garden is started using nonfeminized seeds, roughly half the plants will be male and must be removed from the space as soon as they are identified. This culling should be done early in the male plants' development, before any large flower clusters appear. Even a single open male flower can release enough pollen to fertilize dozens of neighboring female buds.

Cannabis can be sexed early. There are two basic methods:
1. Identifying early, premature flowers
2. Forcing plants to flower by altering the light regimen

There are several ways to use the forcing method, each with pros and cons.

Visual identification of the plant gender is easiest, since it requires no intervention. Sometimes, while a plant is growing vegetatively, a single, small flower appears at the space where the leaf joins the stem (node) two to four pairs of leaves from the top. The sex of the plant is the same as that flower. Identifying the tiny, premature flowers can be challenging, and not all plants produce them. A magnifying glass or photographer's loupe is often employed to get a clearer image.

Forcing plants to flower is a more certain method of determining sex. Flowering is regulated by the number of hours of uninterrupted darkness plants receive each day, and so it's easy to manipulate plants to reveal their sex. Establishing a long-night regimen for a week forces them to indicate. Once this has occurred, remove the males from the garden, or separate them if they will be used in breeding, and return the garden to the vegetative growth cycle by changing the light regimen back to the long day/short night.

A better alternative is to take a cutting from each plant and force it to flower. Each cutting is carefully tagged to identify which plant it came from. Set the clones in a grow medium and provide a light regimen of 16 hours of darkness/8 hours of light. Within a few days, the clones will indicate. Each clone has the same sex as its parent, so the parent's sex has been identified without taking it out of the vegetative stage and disrupting growth.

The female clones can be kept under the flowering regimen to get a tiny taste of the parent's future buds. Be careful to label cuttings and plants so they can be matched up accurately once they've been sexed.

Blue Light

Blue light is another option for sexing. As mentioned earlier in this chapter, cannabis flowering is very sensitive to red light of specific spectrums. Any interruption of the dark period with light that contains the red 660 nm spectrum returns the flowering hormone P_r back to P_{fr}, its inactive state. This prevents flowering.

Blue light at 400–450 nm also has an inhibitory effect on flowering, but its effect is weaker than red light. Plants grow some flowers when blue light is kept on during the dark period; however, they continue to grow vegetatively as well. With blue LED or fluorescent lights to provide the plants with nothing but pure blue light, they will get enough stimulation to produce some flowers for sexual identification but not go into full flowering mode.

This is a good sexing technique to use anytime, but especially when a large number of plants are involved. No cuttings need be taken and matched to their mothers, so there is no chance of a mix-up or dead, non indicative clones. As soon as a plant produces male flowers, remove it from the space. Once all the plants indicate, replace the blue light with a full-spectrum light to keep the plants growing vegetatively.

Plants use blue light to regulate flowering as well as for photosynthesis. Blue light is not as efficient a source of energy for photosynthesis as red light indoors because blue light has a higher energy value than red light and requires more energy to produce. The plant obtains the same amount of energy from both of them, however. When blue light is turned on during the dark period, plants photosynthesize, but the growth from the blue light is not significant. The stems grow a little more stocky.

The effect of blue light on flowering is more important to cannabis growers. See the Phytochrome Response chart, which shows phytochrome P_r-P_{fr} sensitivity across the light spectrum. The red and far-red portion shows high activity. The blue spectrum shows just a little bump. This indicates a slight activity. The result is sporadic flowering on all the plants.

Pure blue light (400 nm) can be created with LEDs and blue CFLs. Use about 10% blue light per watt of regular light. (*See Light.*)

ABSORPTION SPECTRA OF PHYTOCHROME

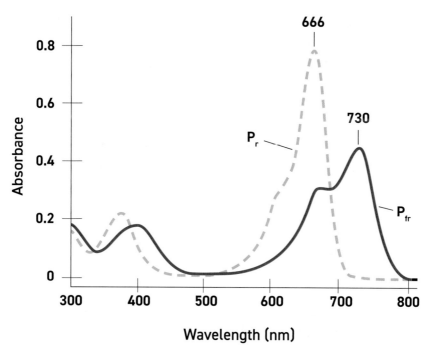

Absorption spectra of phytochrome in both its active (P_r) and inactive (P_{fr}) forms. P_{fr} is the form of phytochrome that optimally absorbs far-red light (~730 nm). P_r optimally absorbs red light at ~666 nm.

Male and Female Flower Anatomy

Identifying the sex of cannabis flowers is easy once their characteristics are known. Male flower buds look like balls dangling from thin stems, with a curved protrusion at the bulb's end that comes to a blunt point. As the male flower ripens, the head's position moves from hanging down to upright. The petals that formed the bulb open, revealing five simple petals that range in color from cream to yellow. Each has a stamen in the middle that releases pollen to a breeze, or wind, or when touched.

Female flowers have no petals, but they are identifiable because of their pistillite structure. Each flower has noticeable stigmas, two white or sometimes pastel pink or lavender antennae-like protrusions, attached to a pistil, which is an oblong pod-like structure.

The males release wind-borne pollen. Each pollen grain contains two sperm. The stigmas capture pollen from the air and then transfer the male gamete cells via hollow tubes down to the ovary. In the ovary, the pollen tube from one stigma fertilizes the egg to form an embryo. The pollen from the other stigma is combined with portions of the ovary to form a food source for the embryo within the seed. The stigmas of fertilized flowers then dry up, beginning at the tips. Each fertilized flower produces one seed. Seed development starts as soon as the female flower is fertilized. The ovary at the base of the flower swells as the new seed grows inside it. This is typically visible within three days after fertilization.

Pollination is avoided in cannabis gardens that are well cared for. The females' stigmas search in vain for pollen because the males have been removed. Eventually the stigmas dry up and become part of the ripe, unfertilized flowers. The leaves start growing closer together as the plants form strong stems that will hold clusters of flowers along a branch. These branches of tightly packed, ripening buds are often called "colas."

As flowering proceeds, any plants that have not clearly indicated their sex must be closely watched. Males usually indicate earlier than females; they are less likely to be encountered later in the season.

(1) A hermaphrodite bud. Both male and female flowers are apparent. (2) Male flowers sometimes appear just as a bud is maturing. They are an indication that the bud is ripe. (3) Older male flower. These are useful breeders. Photos: Ed Rosenthal

Hermaphroditism

Some plants that are primarily female become hermaphrodites and grow male flowers in addition to female ones. This can happen indoors and outdoors; some varieties are more prone to hermaphroditism than others. Stress plays a role.

A hermaphrodite's male flowers may be interspersed among its female buds; they may appear in clusters; or they may occupy one or more separate branches.

For obvious reasons, hermaphrodites are dangerous in any sinsemilla garden; even a single male flower can ruin many neighboring buds. Any plants with male flowers should be removed from the garden before the flowers open. This is the only safe course of action.

Trying to control a hermaphroditic plant by removing just the male flowers is an extremely difficult task, and one mistake, lapse in monitoring, or hidden flower can cause serious damage. Even if the plant seems like a winner, it is not worth risking the rest of the buds in the garden.

There are several reasons why a plant becomes hermaphroditic. It may have a genetic predisposition to be a hermaphrodite. For instance, French hemp breeders have developed monoecious varieties; all the plants have both male and female flowers.

Female plants sometimes develop male flowers as a result of stress, including irregular light cycles and heat stress during flowering, or other drastic changes in the environment.

Some plants develop male flowers just as they ripen. This is an indicator of ripeness and is not a danger to the garden, since the plants are to be harvested shortly.

Flower Growth

Within a few days of establishing a long dark period, the plant's growth pattern changes. First, its rate of growth, which might be as much as two inches (5 cm) a day during the vegetative growth cycle, slows. Under a flowering light regimen, indica varieties usually grow anywhere from another 25–100% taller and wider. Sativas can double, triple, or even quadruple in size before growth stops. Hybrids have growth patterns that vary between these two extremes. If the intent is to produce seeds and there are both male and female plants growing, they begin to differentiate and become dimorphic.

The males elongate and grow new shoots that hold the flowers, or they develop flowers along their existing branches. Upon ripening, the male flower sacks, which contain copious amounts of pollen, tower above the females. This difference serves the plant well, since cannabis is normally wind-pollinated, and the pollen from a tall male plant is more likely to catch the wind for a ride and drift down onto an obliging female stigma below.

Within the first week, females start to grow stockier stems with shorter nodes between the leaves. The number of fingers on new leaves decreases, and the plants no longer form leaves on opposite sides of the stem but now alternate sides. Most important, the first stigmas appear.

By the second week, the first stigmas are joined by a cascade of flower growth. The plant is now spending most of its energy on flower development.

The flowering pattern changes as the stigmas begin to wither, dry, and turn red, purple, or even a light brown, similar to the pattern of fertilized flowers. In the third week, a large number of stigmas form along the stem and on the tops of the branches. As long as it remains unfertilized, the plant continues to produce new flowers.

Flowers develop capitate trichomes all over their outer surfaces. They also develop along the small leaf parts surrounding the flower. Capitate trichomes differ from the sessile trichomes that grow on the sun leaves and stem.

Sessile glands are much smaller than capitate trichomes and are either directly connected to leaves or stems or rest on a one-cell stalk. Capitate trichomes have a much longer, four-celled stem with a large, bulbous cap at the end. When they first start growing, the caps on top are small. They swell as the resins are produced and stored. By the time they are ripe, the caps look like balloons so overinflated that they might burst. Given any stress, such as wind, rain, or touch, many of them will detach from the trichome. They are semi porous, so the terpenes evaporate. Evaporation increases with increasing temperature and vapor pressure deficit.

Over several weeks, the clusters grow thick with unfertilized flowers forming at each leaf node along the branches and main stem. The buds fill out with supporting fresh, moist stigmas reaching out for pollen. Just as the cluster looks like growth is finished, a new wave of flower growth begins, usually concentrated in a relatively bare spot. Successive waves of flowers may grow for weeks.

With most commercial varieties, flower ripening starts between the fifth and eighth week. The bracts (ovaries) start to swell. These are false seed pods, the flowers have not been fertilized and no seed can develop. The swollen bracts and underlying flower parts is one indication of ripeness. It begins about two weeks before maturation, so the timing depends on the variety.

The stigma's color is a factor of genetics and temperature. Many indicas and most sativas develop a red color; however, the color may change to purple or become more pronounced, particularly if the roots are subjected to a cool environment, below 55°F (12°C).

Capitate trichomes, the tiny stalk-like resin glands that fill with THC, terpenes, and other cannabinoids, start to grow on the leaves surrounding the flowers. The flower areas will become totally covered with resin glands.

For the first 5 to 10 days after the light regimen changes to support flowering, vegetative growth slows and may stop as the plant enters the reproductive stage. Then the buds start explosive growth that lasts from four to six weeks, depending on the variety. Varieties that ripen in seven weeks usually spend about four weeks in this period of heavy flower growth. Long-maturing varieties linger in this stage for five weeks or more, maturing nine weeks after flowering is initiated.

During this time, trichomes become more prominent and stand more erect. The cap that tops each one swells with resin. The viscous, sticky liquid contains terpenes and cannabinoids such as THC, which are produced on the inside membrane of the trichome cap. As the resin accumulates in the cap, the flowers' odor becomes more intense.

The explosive growth slows and then ends as the buds begin to ripen, that is, change form rather than grow during the 10–15 days before ripening. The buds contain the most THC and some other cannabinoids at this point, although the terpene content is probably still climbing. If the plants are being grown primarily for concentration or extraction of cannabinoids, this is the best time to harvest.

As the buds continue to ripen, the odor reaches a peak at the same time the trichomes begin to fluoresce in the light, twinkling like little crystals. In some varieties, they are so prominent that the whole bud sparkles.

Using a magnifying glass, a jeweler's loupe, or a microscope, the buds' progression is monitored to the peak of ripeness by watching the resin in the gland tops. Under magnification, the individual glands are visible as they mature and turn from clear to cloudy white to amber. When they begin to change from clear to amber or cloudy white, the buds should be harvested. This is the peak moment.

With the increase in popularity and use of cannabis concentrates, both solventless processed extracts and those made with butane, propane, and other solvents, the peak harvest times for specific uses of the plant may differ. (*See When & How to Harvest.*)

Research conducted by David Potter at GW Pharmaceuticals is instructive. Potter found that in plants that ripen at nine weeks, peak THC occurred between weeks six and seven. High THC potency rather than terpene production is sought by producers of distillates, so harvesting at seven weeks is more productive than waiting for ripening.

After week seven the plants continued flower production and weighed a slight bit more at nine weeks after inducing flowering and had a much higher terpene content. For growers of cannabis bud for medical or recreational use, the nine-week marker for peak terpenes is important.

Variations on Light and Flowering Regimen

The flowering response to different light cycles is a graduated one. Plants that initiate flowering at a particular light-to-darkness ratio put more energy into flower growth when the length of darkness is increased. This response is more pronounced in plants such as indicas that originated at higher latitudes where the light cycle has more seasonal variation.

All varieties respond to a longer dark period by hastening ripening. Shortening the light regimen down to 10 hours of light and 14 of darkness forces all plants, indicas as well as long-flowering sativas, to ripen faster.

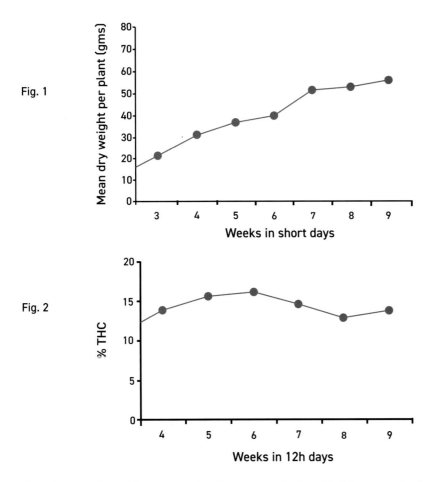

Fig. 1

Fig. 2

Fig. 1 Average flower biomass per plant between weeks 3 and 9 of flower production. Fig. 2 Average THC concentration between weeks 4 and 9 of flower production. Weeks 3 through 6 of harvesting show a steady increase in yield with the final three (7, 8, 9) weeks not showing substantial increases. The THC % is not substantially different between weeks 6 and 7. According to these data, the optimal time to harvest this 9-week cultivar is at 7 weeks, when THC content and biomass production are no longer increasing.
SOURCE: David Potter, *Handbook of Cannabis*, edited by Roger G. Pertwee

A consistent, uninterrupted dark period is key to good results for cannabis and other long-night flowering plants. Chrysanthemums and poinsettias are examples of plants with similar growth patterns and flowering behaviors that have been studied extensively by the greenhouse industry. Researchers found that the largest flowers with the highest total weight are grown when the dark-cycle routine is provided each night. When the plants were in darkness only six nights a week, there was a slight diminution of flower size and total weight. With each additional lost night, flower size and weight dropped.

Without consistent dark periods of sufficient length, cannabis buds elongate and grow looser. Every time the dark period of the flowering cycle is interrupted, there is a slight loss of flower-growing time and thus of yield. A spate of irregular start and finish times may also stress the plant to the point that it becomes hermaphroditic.

FLOWERING

Some cannabis varieties have a flowering trigger that they respond to under normal growing conditions, but when they are accustomed to an unusual light regimen, they may respond to the change in the light conditions in unusual ways. For instance, early-flowering indicas normally trigger when they receive a minimum of 10 hours of darkness, but when they are grown under continuous light, a regimen of just 8 hours of darkness, they initiate flowering.

Once indicas are triggered, the light cycle has little effect upon them. The developing flowers are not as sensitive to occasional interruption of the dark cycle. Indica-sativa hybrids, early-flowering indicas, and South African varieties react similarly. These plants don't revert to vegetative growth as easily as some sativa-indica varieties, so the plants are harder to regenerate.

Cold may hasten sexual expression but not flower development of some northern varieties. Cold weather slows growth, lowers yield, and delays ripening. In autumn, gardeners often protect their northern-variety plants from bad weather, waiting for a few days of warm, sunny weather so the buds will ripen.

Males of most varieties indicate under continuous light in three months. Some equatorial sativa males are exceptions and require a dark period to flower. Most cultivars will show male flowers sooner than their female counterparts, given the same light schedule.

Cannabinoids and terpenes are costly for the plant to produce, but they do so because they serve a range of important purposes, such as
- Acting as antibacterial agents.
- Repelling or trapping insects.
- Repelling birds and mammals; the psychotropic effects probably cause mental discomfort or disorientation to birds and mammals that eat it.
- Protection; THC levels increase as UV exposure increases, so THC protects the plant from UV light. This is not an uncommon use of chemistry by plants.
- Even more protection; to ensure that the flowers and seeds are not consumed before they mature, plants produce a powerful array of chemicals to thwart predators.
- Proliferation: Once the seed matures and drops out of its resin-coated pod, it is far more palatable to animals that were repelled by the resin. Small mammals and birds eat the seeds, some of which pass through the animals' digestive systems and remain viable. As animals excrete viable seeds on suitable ground, they spread the plant to new locations.

Autoflowering Plants

Males and ruderalis varieties from the far north are not photosensitive at all. Both age and development play a role in determining when these plants flower. Ruderalis develops flowers under continuous light within a few weeks of germination.

This trait has been bred into several varieties that are available commercially as "auto-flowering" plants. No matter what light regimen they are growing under, they will germinate, grow, and flower in a predetermined pattern. Flowers ripen between 60 and 100 days from germination. For the most part, these varieties produce small plants. They are very difficult if not impossible to treat as clones, so feminized seeds are helpful when growing a garden of autoflowering plants. Clones are set to flower at the same growth stage as the mother plant they were cut from, and ruderalis plants have already initiated flower when they are large enough to take cuttings.

Critical Light Period

The 12/12 light-dark period formula has been accepted without question by growers all over the world. Probably one of the reasons was that this advice was common to most early grow books, including *Marijuana Grower's Guide* (1974), the first serious cannabis cultivation book ever published in the US, written by Ed Rosenthal and Mel Frank. Subsequent books adopted this advice over the decades since. The 12/12 regimen was arrived at based on the reasoning that no matter what critical period a specific variety might have, 12 hours of darkness was sufficient to induce flowering. It was an easy and reliable heuristic; however, most cannabis varieties need fewer than 12 hours of darkness to initiate flowering.

If cannabis plants grown outdoors required a 12-hour dark period to flower, they would not be induced to start flowering until the autumn equinox, when day and night are of equal length. They would ripen six to eight weeks later. Most modern varieties ripen in the early fall. Budding was triggered six to eight weeks earlier.

For instance, under natural light an eight-week variety that requires 55 days from forcing to maturity starts flowering in late summer and ripens in early fall. In San Francisco on August 5, sunrise occurs at 5:14 a.m. and sunset at 7:18 p.m., a total of 14 hours 4 minutes. Dawn and dusk add another 15 minutes of red light. Plants use the absence of this spectrum to measure the dark period. The total lit period comes to about 14 hours and 20 minutes, leaving 9 hours and 40 minutes of darkness. Thus the critical period for this plant was 9 hours 40 minutes. Indoors, if it was given just 10 hours of dark period daily, rather than 12 hours, it would still flower.

Cannabis responds to a lengthening dark period while it is flowering by hastening ripening. Buds ripen faster when they receive an extra hour of darkness after the first three or four weeks of flowering.

Using Critical Time Period Indoors

Outdoor growers who discover the critical time needed to induce flowering can use this information to make more efficient use of their indoor garden. Currently, plants grown under a 12/12 cycle spend half their time in the dark. If the plants have a critical flowering time of, for instance, 10 hours of darkness daily to induce flowering, they can be provided 14 rather than 12 hours of light each day so that they receive almost 17% more energy with which to produce sugars used for more and faster growth.

Two stigmas are attached to each female flower. Both must be pollinated. One becomes the seed and the other the endosperm, food for the embryo.

During the first week of flowering, stigmas begin to appear. If stigmas are unpollinated they remain white for a long time. These plants have been flowering for 24 days.

By day 38 the plants are in full flower and put out layer after layer of stigmas. The bud gets thicker and thicker, and eventually quite hard.

By day 55 the buds start to ripen and the stigmas start turning brown.

All photos by Phil Sullivan / Team Terpene

This Garlic Breath plant has trichomes at varying stages of ripeness. The clear trichome heads are underripe, the milky ones are ripe and the amber ones are overripe. Photo: Kandid Kush

Manipulating Light Outdoors

Perhaps nature didn't get it quite right on cannabis ripening, as far as humans are concerned. If ripening were determined by human needs, the buds would ripen in late spring and be ready to be enjoyed in early summer, the social season. If they ripened at the best time for the farmer, it would be in late summer when the weather is warm and the sun is still shining but it has lost a bit of intensity. Nature has chosen the fall. The harvest can be good, but there's more of a chance of bad weather.

With a bit of effort, the outdoor light cycle can be manipulated to grow and flower the plants at the grower's convenience. To get the most potent and cosmetically beautiful flowers, it is best to harvest during the summer rather than the fall. Buds that ripen in mid or late summer experience more intense light and much more UV spectrum light than fall-ripened buds. The intense light gives the plant energy to grow a bigger bud. The UV light increases its potency. At the same time, stretches of bad weather (cold, rain, snow, and

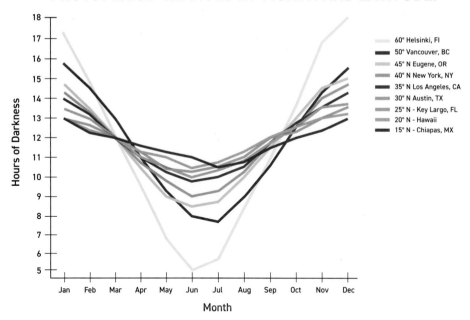

PHOTOPERIOD CHANGES BY MONTH AND LATITUDE.

Legend:
- 60° Helsinki, FI
- 50° Vancouver, BC
- 45° N Eugene, OR
- 40° N New York, NY
- 35° N Los Angeles, CA
- 30° N Austin, TX
- 25° N - Key Largo, FL
- 20° N - Hawaii
- 15° N - Chiapas, MX

Y-axis: Hours of Darkness; X-axis: Month (Jan–Dec)

The further a region is from the equator, the greater the seasonal variations in light period.

wind) are much less likely to occur in summer than in the fall in northern latitudes.

The easiest way is to choose a cultivar that naturally flowers early in the season. For instance, Ed Rosenthal Superbud begins flowering at 37° N around July 16, when there are only 10 hours of darkness.

During the late summer, through winter and early spring, the dark period is long enough to force almost all cultivars to flower. Sativa-dominant hybrids continue to grow even after they have been transitioned to flowering. Indicas can grow from as low as 30 to 100% larger after they are forced to flower.

It is difficult to grow some popular hybrids and indicas outdoors without light extension in many parts of the southern US and regions south toward the equator because the variation in light duration between summer and winter is slight. The dark period is never short enough for the plants to grow vegetatively. Sativa and sativa hybrids produce a better yield in those conditions. Growing these plants at low latitudes requires extending the light period.

The technique is to manipulate flowering so plants continue to grow vegetatively until they reach the desired size before letting them flower. To do this, the dark period is interrupted with light for as little as a few seconds. Think of it as a water spray. All the leaves should be "wet" with light, but once they have been sprayed, they need no more light. The light has reset the phytochrome to the nonflowering mode, and it will require about two hours to return to the flowering position, but the plant will not be in the uninterrupted dark period mode long enough to switch the plants to the flowering mode.

This short interruption of the dark cycle is enough to reset the time count of uninterrupted darkness. By lighting the plants once or twice during the dark period each night, the plants continue to grow vegetatively rather than initiate flowering. When the light interruption stops, the plants immediately start to flower.

As long as there isn't excessive heat, rain, or wind in the forecast, plants can be started any time of the year. The denser they are planted, the less time it takes for them to fill the canopy. Then the lights that interrupt the dark cycle can be turned off. The plants will immediately start to flower. As long as the weather is warm and won't be lower than a night

ACTIVE SPECTRUM OF PHOTOSYNTHESIS

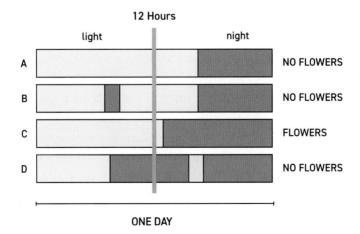

RELATIVE SPECTRAL PHOTON FLUENCE RATE

DAYLIGHT

CANOP

| 400 nm | 500 nm | 600 nm | 700 nm | 800 nm |

WAVELENGTH (Nanometers)

The upper line shows sunlight reaching the top of the canopy. The lower line shows light reaching the under-story. Plants absorb or reflect most of the blue, green, yellow, and red light. Some of it is used for photosynthesis. Far-red light (730 nm) is mostly transmitted or reflected, so there is a much higher ratio of far-red to red light under the canopy than in full sunlight.

FLOWERING CHART

12 Hours

light   night

A	NO FLOWERS
B	NO FLOWERS
C	FLOWERS
D	NO FLOWERS

ONE DAY

A. If the plants receive 18 hours of light, they do not flower. B. If the light cycle is interrupted by a dark period, the plants will not flower. C. When the plants receive 10-12 or more hours of uninterrupted darkness, they flower. D. When the dark period is interrupted, the plants won't flower.

temperature in the 40s F (5°C), the next crop can be planted. Winter harvests are not as large, potent, or attractive as summer crops, but they are worth the effort, especially if the harvest is to be used for concentrates.

In areas that are not quite as warm or as bright, the growth and yield can be increased and the season extended by enhancing natural light with reflective material and electric lights. This is easier to accomplish in small gardens.

To get the best possible harvest, force plants to flower in the late spring to early summer. They will be ready to harvest in mid to late summer. This is the time when the UV and light intensity are strongest, so photosynthesis is occurring at a fast pace, and at the same time the UV light is at its strongest, stressing the plant and increasing its production of THC and terpenes.

Early Harvests & Photoperiod Manipulation

Some zones experience a mild winter, and the light is intense enough and the temperature sufficiently warm to start the garden. In other areas a greenhouse can extend the season by a month or two. The only problem facing the gardener is providing the 16–18 hours of light the plant needs for strong vegetative growth.

Plants started indoors or in a greenhouse with extended light hours in the winter will immediately start to flower when placed outdoors or in a greenhouse using only natural light in the early spring, when there is a long dark period of 10 or more hours of darkness.

Autoflowering plants are excellent choices for early harvest gardens, since they are genetically programmed to ripen in 75 to 90 days and are not affected by light periods.

Late-Summer Crops

A late-summer crop can be generated by moving starter plants, clones, or indoor plants outside late in the season. Many varieties start to flower when they are exposed to 10 to 11 hours of darkness daily.

Plants placed outdoors in midsummer have a chance to grow a bit during the waning days of summer before longer autumn nights force them to flower.

Sativas continue to grow a bit even as they transition to flowering. As flowering progresses, they put all their energy into reproductive development, producing long colas filled with buds. They often require 90 days or more to ripen, so they can only be grown where the growing season extends into the fall.

During the intense days of summer, indoor plants moved outside require conditioning in shade before being placed in bright light. An antitranspirant can be used to help the plants withstand sunburn and adjust to UV light, which is mostly absent indoors under HPS lamps. Plants grown under lights that include UVB spectrum require less adjustment to outdoor light.

Forever Flowering greenhouses have been designed around the specific needs of cannabis growers for over 15 years. Light-deprivation greenhouses are weather resistant and come with automated darkening curtains to control the photoperiod at the touch of a button.

Winter Crops

Plants placed outdoors from late summer through the beginning of spring are triggered to flower by long nights. This technique can be used in subtropical and low-latitude mild-climate zones such as Florida, the Gulf Coast, Hawai'i, Southern California, the Mediterranean zone, parts of South Africa, New Zealand, Australia, Chile, and Argentina, all of which receive sunlight intense enough to support fast growth in winter and rarely drop below 45°F (7°C).

There are many advantages to growing winter crops:

- They require less irrigation than summer crops.
- Non summer crops grow in a better temperature range. Temperatures lower than 85°F (29°C) support rapid growth and dense bud development. Temperatures above 90°F (32°C) stress the plant, decrease growth, and result in looser buds.
- Plants are less likely to be attacked by insects because fewer of them are around, and they are less active in lower temperatures.
- The plants stay much smaller and are more controllable.

Greenhouses

Greenhouses are ideal environments for extending the garden season. Even unheated greenhouses add three weeks of growing time to both the beginning and end of the season. Two weeks of growing time can be gained back using passive heating techniques such as blackened water containers, which absorb sunlight and radiate heat at night. Depending on the zone, heated greenhouses can be used all winter.

Jump-Starting Flowering

Long periods of uninterrupted darkness are nature's trigger to cannabis to begin flowering. This is measured chemically by phytochrome, which is deactivated by red light. The inactive form is referred to as P_r. In the absence of red light, with a peak at 666 nm and effects from about 500–700 nm, P_r drifts into its active form P_{fr} over about two hours. This begins at dusk or when the lights are turned off or during dusk outdoors. This transition period, during which P_{fr} has limited effectiveness, can be dramatically shortened.

P_r is sensitive to far-red light with a peak at 730 nm and is affected in a range of about 700–750 nm. In its presence it changes almost immediately to the active form, P_{fr}. This effect may be useful for shortening the two-hour time it takes plants to switch from the inactive to active form.

Indoors, after the grow lamps are turned off, when the plants are exposed to far-red (730 nm) light, the P_r is turned into P_{fr} much faster and induces flowering within a shorter dark period. Far-red lighting can be provided using LEDs or some fluorescents. Far-red light can also be used to restore the active form of the hormone if the dark is interrupted by light. This may somewhat ameliorate the consequences of interruptions in the dark period.

Outdoors, growers have no control over dawn and dusk, but can force flowering out of season by using far-red lighting to increase the time the plants are under P_{fr}'s flower-inducing influence by 2 hours. Plants receiving 15 hours of light and 9 hours of darkness react as if they were under a lighting regimen of 11 hours of darkness because of the additional 2 hours of active hormone. Most plants initiate flowering under 11 hours of darkness, which is shortened to 9 after exposure to 730 nm far-red light. The plants should be exposed to far-red light each evening at the end of dusk. They need only a few seconds of the light each night.

Unheated greenhouses are often used to grow late-flowering sativas that need some protection from the changing climate. They can also be used to produce a harvest through late planting. By supplementing the weak sunlight of late autumn using lamps during the lit period, the yield can be increased substantially. The amount of light used during the daytime can be adjusted to take into account the sunlight's intensity. For more information on light supplementation, see *Light*.

Late-ripening sativas can be forced to flower using light deprivation. By forcing them in late spring or early summer, they will have enough time to ripen.

Yield is also increased by keeping the plants on a 12-hour schedule by lighting the plants at full intensity throughout the lit period. This can be done outdoors.

UVB Light & Flower Forcing

Cannabis has evolved a very successful survival strategy. It domesticates easily and escapes domestication just as easily. To make a change, there has to be an advantage for at least one species. Humans have always respected cannabis as a fall flowering and ripening crop. However, it turns out that human interests and the plant's natural proclivities have diverged.

John Lydon published his PhD thesis in which he reported on experiments he performed on cannabis that showed the amount of THC that a cannabis plant produces goes up in a direct ratio to the amount of UVB light that the plant receives (Lydon 1985).

The relevance of this information to this discussion is that the angle of the sun to the Earth is most perpendicular on the first day of summer, when UVB light is most intense. As the angle of the Earth and sun becomes more oblique, there is a higher proportion of light from the red spectrum and less blue and UV. By the fall, when sinsemilla normally ripens, not only is the light far less intense, but the amount of UVB being delivered is a small fraction of the amount that is received on the first day of summer.

Cannabis buds that are ripening under the intense sun of early summer grow bigger and denser and are more potent than when they ripen under the waning sun and variable weather of the fall.

UVB Light Chart

The amount of UVB light a plant receives affects THC and terpene production. Plants growing under higher UV levels are more potent.

The amount of UV light that an area receives is determined by the latitude, season, climate, and weather. Light reaches the equator most directly, and that is where it's the most intense. As the latitude increases, light reaches Earth at a more oblique angle, so it becomes less intense.

Throughout the Northern Hemisphere, which includes North America and Europe, UV light is at its lowest levels in December and January. After these months, the levels start rising. The farther from the equator, the longer it takes to peak, the shorter the peak period and weaker the light.

For instance, in San Francisco (37.75°N), UVB reaches its peak with a UVB index between 9 and 11 around May 15. It stays there until around August 15. By September 1 it drops down to 8, and by October down to 6. The UV level at any particular time in any place can now be tracked or monitored using websites and smartphone applications.

When plants ripen during the peak UV period, they will be at their most potent. As the season wears on and the UVB levels decline, the cannabis does not attain the same potency.

DAILY UV INDEX

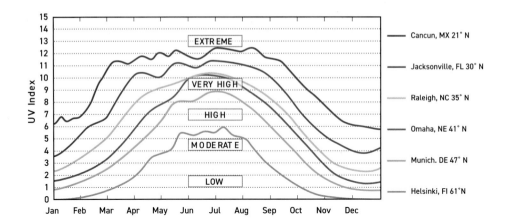

To induce flowering, plants should be placed under 11–12 hours of darkness each day. There are many ways to accomplish this. They range from moving the plants to and from a dark place daily, to covering the garden using an opaque plastic sheet over tunnels, to automated blackout gardens.

To force plants to flower, timing must be punctual and take into account the daily changes in dawn-dusk times to make sure that the plants are getting enough darkness. There are automated systems available that regulate greenhouse curtains.

There are two ways to approach restricting light: darken in the morning or at night. Morning darkening is the preferred method. The shade material is placed over the garden each morning before dawn. The plants need to be shaded counting forward 11–12 hours from dusk. If dusk is at 9:00 p.m. and dawn is 6:00 a.m., curtains should cover the garden before dawn, anytime before 5:30 a.m. They should be removed at 8 a.m. after receiving no light for 11–12 hours.

The other method is to install the curtains in the evening. Count back 12 hours from dawn, which occurred at 6 a.m. in the above example. The curtains are placed over the garden at 6 p.m. Then at 9 p.m., after dusk ends and night begins, the curtains are removed so that any condensed moisture can evaporate into the night air.

To force the plants to flower during the summer, they need to receive the critical dark period each day. Plants are covered with a blackout cloth each day so that they receive 11–12 hours of darkness and are forced into flowering.

In late stages, mold prevention measures should be taken because moisture levels often build up when the plants are covered. Spray the plants with potassium bicarbonate, diluted milk, or other organic fungicides to prevent fungal attacks.

The advantage of placing the curtain over the garden early in the morning rather than before or after dusk is that dew settles after dusk because the temperature drops, increasing relative humidity. Plants stay wet under the tarp. When the tarp is spread in the morning, there is less moisture to deal with. The farther from the plants that the coverings are placed, the less of an effect that condensation has on the garden.

Some of the very best outdoor cannabis is grown using this technique. The reasons are more intense light, more UVB light, and better weather conditions with less chance of cool weather that slows growth and development.

UVB Light Facts

Ultraviolet B (UVB) light is a spectrum of light that is invisible to humans but is visible to insects and many other organisms. On humans it causes suntan and sunburn and is implicated in the formation of eye cataracts. Tanning bulbs emit UVB light.

UVB light affects cannabis potency. The potency of high-quality cannabis increases in direct ratio to the amount of UVB light it receives. This is very significant. In commercial markets, many dispensaries reject much of the fall-harvested outdoor material as inferior. They have found it lacks the potency of indoor crops and is a harsh smoke. However, cannabis grown outdoors that was forced to ripen in the summer was accepted—because it had a high potency and lacked the "aesthetic qualities" of outdoor crops harvested later in the season.

Indoors, under fluorescent and high pressure sodium (HPS) lamps, gardens receive little UVB light. Metal halides (MH) without glass reflectors emit a bit. However, there are ways of supplying the garden with UVB light. Tanning lamps work, that is, lamps that tan people, because of the UVB light they emit. Using tanning lamps increases the THC content of the crop. Reptiles and lizards require the UVB spectrum to stay healthy, so 10% of the output of "reptile fluorescent" lights is UVB. Tanning lamps and UVB-emitting LEDs are available on the internet. UVB supplementation needs to only be a small percentage of the total illumination used in the flowering space. This technology works, but is still in development. Start by using tests in the garden.

Green Light at Night

Plants have evolved for hundreds of millions of years and have never encountered a separation of light spectrums or unusual lighting regimens. When they received light, it came from the sun in a mixture of spectrums from which they could pick and choose. With the advent of gas and then electric lighting, plants encountered unusual regimens and splintered spectrums.

Plants measure day length using the red and far-red light spectrums. While they use other spectrums, they are not sensitive to most of them as far as flowering is concerned.

They use less green light than other spectrums and reflect much of it while absorbing most other spectrums. Plants' insensitivity to green light can be used to a gardener's advantage. Turning a light containing red or blue on in the middle of the dark cycle disturbs the plants' flowering paradigm. HPS, fluorescent, and MH lamps all emit red light. Green fluorescent and LED lights contain no red light and will minimally disturb the flowering plants, allowing growers to enter the garden during the dark period.

This is a schwazzed plant. To sustain healthy growth during the schwazzing process, growers should provide plants with an optimal feeding regiment and nutrients specially formulated to provide macro and micronutrients delivered at exactly the right time during the plant's life cycle.
Courtesy of Joshua Haupt / Three a Light

Extreme Defoliation aka "Schwazzing"

In most conventional cannabis gardens, the cultivator removes leaves to improve air flow and increase light penetration throughout the canopy, which is meant to increase yields. The goal is to remove leaves (especially those that are being shaded or shading other leaves) during the early part of the flower cycle. Deleafing, or defoliation, provides the added benefit of directing carbon allocation in the plant.

Leaves are either carbon sources or carbon sinks depending on how much light they are getting. If a leaf is getting plenty of sunlight and is actively photosynthesizing, it becomes a carbon source. A carbon source provides sugar to other parts of the plant. A carbon sink is a part of the plant that accepts sugar from the carbon sources. Shaded leaves end up being carbon sinks, as they photosynthesize minimally. Removing leaves that are carbon sinks increases the carbon use efficiency by allocating more sugar to the flowers. Optimizing carbon allocation to the flowers increases yield and potency. This is one of the primary reasons why proper deleafing can increase yield in cannabis canopies.

Schwazzing is one method of extreme defoliation. First made popular by Joshua Haupt, author of *Three A Light*, a good schwazze requires intense defoliation during two separate times within the first three weeks of the flower cycle. The first defoliation occurs on day 1. Removing all the fan leaves on the first day of flower seems counterintuitive, but it increases light penetration to the lower bud sites and allows for more air flow through the canopy. On top of that, the plant is now forced to allocate carbon to producing new leaves. Instead of allocating resources to elongating the stem during this stage of growth, the plant must build new leaves, resulting in shorter stems and more compact nodal stacking.

Schwazzing may feel uncomfortable and unnatural to many cultivators, but the science behind it is sound. More light penetration on more bud sites and allocating more resources to those flowers as opposed to stem elongation are the fundamentals behind schwazzing.

After the first schwazze, it is important to temporarily increase the amount of nutrients the plants receive. The big fan leaves, which are removed during the schwazze on day 1, store nutrients. Removing those leaves also removes that nutrient storage pool that the plant can rely on if it needs an added boost of nutrients when actively growing. From days 6 through 10, the nutrient solution concentration should be increased by about 20%, primarily focused on added phosphorus and potassium.

The second schwazze occurs on day 20 of the flowering cycle. It is important not to remove any of the buds, as this is where the flowers develop. Again, the removal of the leaves forces the plant to allocate resources to new leaf production as opposed to elongating the stems. By the time the new leaves have been fully developed, the plant is now in full flower development mode and has bypassed the stage at which stem elongation occurs. Shorter stems mean that more of the buds will develop into each other, creating larger buds.

Extreme defoliation, as opposed to removing lower branches to increase air circulation and light penetration, has the added benefit of not removing potential flower sites. Each bud will develop into a grade A flower if it gets enough light. The increased light penetration provides energy to bud sites lower in the canopy, so that the total volume of high-quality flowers increases, thus increasing yield.

Photo: Zoom Gardens

FINISHING & FLUSHING

Farmers try many methods and techniques for enhancing crop quality and yield because cannabis is such a valuable crop. Fertilizer companies have introduced many products for bud enhancement, described in this chapter. The companies have followed two paths: nature and science.

Finishing Products

All finishing companies keep their formulas proprietary. However, these formulas all work based on one of two theories. Either they bind the nutrients so they are no longer available to the roots (whether they remain or are washed away), or they make the salts more soluble so they flush out of the soil easily. The chart and accompanying ingredient glossary at the end of this chapter lists a range of finishing products readily available in stores and online.

Flushing

Flushing cannabis plants is a controversial subject. Some growers think its usefulness is a myth, while others think it's an essential process that creates the best buds for smoking and vaporizing. There is little science to support one side versus the other, however. Many cannabis connoisseurs suggest that there is no difference between flushed and unflushed bud and the yields are relatively similar. Simultaneously, there are industry professionals who swear by flushing and claim that the difference in the finished product is profound. If flushed flowers are similar in quality and yield to unflushed flowers, then there really is no reason not to flush, as that will save money on fertilizers. Regardless of proven efficacy, this chapter explores how flushing is done and the reasons why growers do or do not do it.

There are many reasons to question the efficacy of flushing:

1. Eliminating or lowering the availability of essential nutrients slows growth at all stages, including the last weeks of flowering.
2. It is difficult to flush large plants that are grown in bags containing 200–300 gallons (760–1,140 l) of planting mix. The plants' roots have a reservoir of nutrients to draw from. Yet these plants are savored by connoisseurs.
3. There are no double-blind studies that have been performed to test the efficacy of flushing.
4. Although certain stresses increase trichome production, it is doubtful that nutrient deficiency is one of them. Trichome and oil production is expensive; it

requires the plant to expend energy. It seems counterintuitive that depriving nutrients would increase cannabinoid and terpene production.

5. Some gardens using perpetual harvest techniques as well as aquaponic grow methods have no provision for flushing but produce fine connoisseur buds. Plants growing in soil in the ground cannot be flushed easily and certainly cannot be used when cannabis is farmed.

6. Large amounts of calcium, one of the mobile nutrients, are required for cell division. To mature, plants must grow new cells. Without a constant supply, maturation slows.

Despite the lack of peer-reviewed studies regarding efficacy, the overwhelming majority of cannabis growers flush. The consensus is that depriving plants of nutrients during the last phases of flowering results in higher-quality bud.

The Basics on Flushing

There are a multitude of flushing methods, but they share a common goal: to remove most of the nutrients available to the roots, thereby encouraging the plant to use the unassimilated salts and nutrients still remaining in the plant.

The result is the plant holds few nutrients in their raw form, instead incorporating them into the plant's tissues or into phytochemicals released by the roots.

In order for roots to absorb nutrients, the nutrients must be dissolved in water. Nutrients that are precipitated, either out of solution or bound in a molecular matrix, are not available to the roots even if they are plentiful.

Flushing with water rinses out the nutrients that are already in the solution. To rinse, use tepid water (about 75°F/24°C) that is adjusted to a pH of about 5.8–6.0, which is the range at which the nutrients are all soluble. With warmer water flushing, more nutrients dissolve and rinse away. The more rinses, the more nutrients that are carried away.

Nitrogen is the most soluble nutrient, and it is the most likely to affect flowering negatively. Even using a rinse that drains only 10% of the added water removes some of the nutrients.

When the pH is out of suggested range (i.e., too high or too low), nutrients fall out of the solution and precipitate. This means that dissolved substances form solids and drop out of solution.

As the flush continues, the ppm of the rinse water drops. This process can be stopped at any time. By leaving some nitrogen in the media, the plant still has some resources for growth, without the abundance that promotes vegetative growth.

Check the ppm of dissolved solids using a meter for both the soil and the water. With larger gardens, it may be more efficient to use just a few plants for trials.

Flushing Techniques

1. Start with a passive flush. This is when the plants use the reserves in the mix. Then perform an active flush close to ripening.
2. Perform a constant flush.

Each time the plants are irrigated, add enough water so 10–20% of it drains. The drain water will be rich in nutrients, so there is little salt buildup in the medium. There are few excess nutrients to flush near ripening.

Some growers encourage vigorous vegetative growth before the plant makes a total switch to flowering. If doing so, leave the plants unflushed, or even supply a small amount of nitrogen during the first two weeks of flowering and let it deplete naturally.

pH

The solubility of the nutrients in the planting mix is pH dependent. The nutrient solution should be adjusted to 5.8–6.0 pH to maximize the solubility of the salts, aka the nutrients, that are dissolved in the solution. It removes more nutrients than water that is not pH-adjusted.

Water Temperature

Salts are more soluble in warmer water. Adjust flush water temperature to 75°F (24°C) if possible. More nutrients will be flushed.

Cannabis Flushing Techniques: Passive, Active & Chemically Enhanced

Cannabis growers use a variety of flushing theories and techniques. There is no one correct technique. Just because it isn't mentioned here doesn't mean it isn't helpful.

Flushing techniques can be divided into three main categories: passive, active, and chemically enhanced.

Passive versus Active Flushing

The difference between passive and active flushing is that at some point in the plant's rush to ripening, either the caretaker or nature makes a decision to help the plant ripen by removing nutrients from the soil. The primary nutrient that is removed in this process is nitrogen, although many other water-soluble nutrients are removed.

Plants growing in mix or soil are flushed using water. Dissolved and soluble salts are drained out. Depending on how thorough the flush, much, most, or nearly all of the soluble nutrients are removed. They are often replaced with a new flowering formula that may contain some macro or micro fertilizers as well as hormones, enzymes, or sugars.

Plants react quickly to this sudden change in the environment by focusing their energy on maturation of flowers rather than continued production of flowers.

Active Flushing

Most modern cannabis plants ripen seven to nine weeks after being forced to flower. Their planting media may include ingredients that gradually release nutrients and are often irrigated using a water-nutrient solution. If the planting medium is composed of the usual ingredients such as peat moss, coir, or compost, its copious carbon-containing molecules bind some of these nutrients and are ready to release them when nutrient levels get low.

Depending on the size of the plant and container, the media type, and the technique being used, this process can take up to three weeks. Irrigate with nutrient-free water so no new nutrients are provided for the last one to three weeks of flowering.

For instance, a nine-week plant won't be fed after the sixth, seventh, or eighth week of flowering.

Enriched organic soils and planting media, especially if they have been used for more than one season, are likely to contain organically locked nutrients that mycorrhizae and other rhizosphere organisms continuously unlock; this provides more nutrients to the roots.

Then, as the residual nutrients are used up, the plant taps into its own reserves. Some of the minerals are mobile— nitrogen (N), phosphorus (P), potassium (K), magnesium (Mg), molybdenum (Mo)—and they translocate to the canopy top, where new growth is happening and where the plant's energy provider, the lights or the sun, is available.

As the leaves lose nitrogen and magnesium, they turn yellow. The loss of P and K results in leaf edge curl and dead spots. After the plant has extracted the valuable nutrients from the leaf, leaving mostly cellulose, it has no further use, and it withers and dies.

These are indications that the flushing is working as intended.

The goal is to time the total loss of nutrients with ripening of the buds so nutrient deprivation does not cause appreciable loss.

Calcium (Ca), sulfur (S), iron (Fe), boron (B), and copper (Cu) are immobile, and their deficiency symptoms, which usually don't occur in late flowering, can be seen in the new growth. Iron (Fe) deficiency, though rare unless the pH around the rhizosphere is abnormally high, often results in bright yellow leaves around the buds. But the same effect could also be caused by N deficiency late in flowering. Lack of zinc, which is rare, causes twisted atypical growth.

As the leaves dry, the buds continue to grow and mature. They use the reserves being drawn from the media, roots, xylem, and leaves.

Flowering formula fertilizers contain little or no nitrogen. Plants growing in soil or planting mixes use the residual nitrogen loosely bound in the media that continues to dissolve. The major nutrient nitrogen, which is mobile, translocates from the lower leaves to the upper canopy. The lower leaves turn bright yellow and then curl and dry. Hydroponic mixes without media reserves require some N during the first half of flowering (usually three to four weeks) and less during the next quarter (10–15 days). The lack of nitrogen toward the end of flowering hastens ripening and maturity. This is one of the cues the plant uses to begin ripening.

Final Flush Recommendations by Medium

Clay Loam: 15–20 days.

Sandy Soil: Flush for a week. It doesn't contain very much organic matter to bind the nutrients, and it rinses readily.

Porous Loam: Flush for 10–15 days. Some nutrients are held tenuously to the matrix and need a bit more flushing than sandy soils.

Heavy Loams and Clays: Flush for 15–20 days. These soils bind nutrients that are hard to rinse away and must be used up by the plant.

Enriched Soils & Mixes: Soils that were enriched using additives such as plant meals and manures may not require any flushing. Soil microorganisms dissolve the nutrients locked in organic compounds and provide them to the roots as needed. Most nutrients that are left are still locked up in organic matter. There is probably very little free nitrogen. However, if bottom leaves are not yellowing, there is too much nutrient left in the soil and the mix should be flushed.

Planting Mixes: Planting mixes differ in their abilities to buffer or hold nutrients, so each should be dealt with in its own manner.

Peat Moss & Coco: Flush one week if bottom leaves are green and three to four days if they are yellow. These media buffer nutrients (nutrients attach to them), but flushing will have a noticeable effect on the crop. The free nutrients are already dissolved and are easily rinsed away.

Hydroponic Systems (nonnutritive media such as rockwool, LECA, and deep water culture): Flush three to four days. As soon as the water-nutrient solution is removed and replaced with pH'd water, the roots have no access to nutrients. The plants react immediately, first showing signs in the lower leaves, which turn yellow. The buds also ripen faster.

Medium-based hydroponic and fertigation systems (drip irrigation, ebb and flow, wick, capillary mat, reservoir, manually irrigated nutrient-water): Flush four to seven days. The roots in these systems are usually anchored in a nonnutritive mix composed mostly of coir or peat moss. Infrequently, clay pebbles or perlite are used. None of these bind tightly to the nutrients, so plants respond immediately to the new nutrient-free environment.

Chemically Enhanced Flushes

The most popular flush is plain water. Salts in the media or in hydroponic units are all water soluble, or they're precipitated, that is, have dropped out of the solution.

Precipitated nutrients cannot be taken up or used by the roots. Other salts are bound to larger organic molecules attached to the planting medium. These are only moderately available to the roots and are made available through mycorrhizae and other organisms in the rhizosphere (the area of the media that surrounds the roots). All other salts are soluble and drain out when flushed.

A few flushes claim they contain chelates that actually draw nutrients from the plants. This may be true but has not been proved yet.

Once plants are flushed, they draw from nutrients within their systems. First, they use the unbound nutrients held in the xylem and the extracellular water channels.

Then the mobile nutrients, nitrogen (N), phosphorus (P), potassium (K), and magnesium (Mg) migrate from the lower parts of the plant to the canopy that is getting light.

A large light-unobstructed plant delivers nutrients to the sunlit sides as well as the top of the plant. Rather than only going up, the nutrients travel out, to the growing tips and maturing flowers.

The immobile nutrients, boron, calcium, copper, iron, manganese, and zinc, remain stationary. Chlorophyll and other mineral-laden organelles in the cells break apart, facilitating the migration of the minerals they contain to the most active areas of the plant. Lacking the macronutrients, these leaves lose their green color created by magnesium, turn yellow, or tan and dry up.

Chart of Finishing Products

Refer to the glossary on the following pages to understand the ingredients listed.

PRODUCT	COMPANY	INGREDIENTS
Big Bud	Advanced Nutrients	L-tryptophan, L-cysteine, L-glutamate and L-glycine, P, K
Big Swell	Aurora Innovations	Yucca, molasses, L-glycine, phosphoric acid, potassium hydroxide
Bloombastic	Atami	P_2O_5, K_2O, chelated Fe
Bloom Blaster	Grotek	KH_2PO_4
Bountea Better Bloom	Bountea	Fish protein, kelp, vegetable and mineral extracts
Bud Burst	Nutrifield	Dried kelp
Bud Factor X	Advanced Nutrients	Chitosan, surfactant
CNS17 (RIPE)	Botanicare	$CaNO_3$, $MgSO_4$, KNO_3, KH_2PO_4, $MnSO_4$, ammonium molybdate
Flawless Finish	Advanced Nutrients	Mg, chelated Mg, sulfur
FloraNectar	General Hydroponics	$MgSO_4$, K_2SO_4, secret ingredient (probably simple sugar)

Ginormous	Humboldt Nutrients	P_2O_5, K_2O, unspecified micronutrients
Honey Chome	Emerald Harvest	$Mg(NO_3)_2$, $KHSO_4$, K_2SO_4, cane sugar, palm sugar, agave nectar
Hydro Bio	Vital Humic	*Lactobacillus plantarum*, *Bacillus subtilis*, *Bacillus licheniformis*, *Bacillus pumilus*, *Bacillus amyloliquefaciens*, *Bacillus megaterium*, *Trichoderma viride*, humic acid, potassium salts, fulvic acid, sea kelp, molasses, evaporated cane juice
Hydroplex	Botanicare	P, K, Mg
Ionic PK Boost	Growth Technology	P, K, nipacide (formaldehyde-based biocide used industrially. This is toxic and should not be used for food products.)
Liquid Karma	Botanicare	Dolomite, K_2CO_3, CO_3, fish meal, seaweed extract, $MgSO_4$, humic acid, B vitamins
Mammoth Microbes	Mammoth	Bacterial culture, alfalfa, water
Massive Bloom	Green Label	N-P-K, amino acids, vitamins B1 and B2, triacontanol, carbohydrates, humic acid, Mg
Nirvana	Advanced Nutrients	Humus, *Laminaria saccharina* (seaweed extract), alfalfa meal, yeast, quilla and yucca extracts, hydrolyzed whey protein, ein, bat guano, azomite
Purple Maxx	Humboldt County's Own	Triacontinol
Terpinator	Rhizoflora, Inc.	K_2SO_4
T-Rex	Cutting Edge Solutions	B1, glutamine, l-cysteine
Vital Flower Powder	Vital Garden Supply	100% soluble organic fish fertilizer
Vitamino	Botanicare	Ammoniacal nitrogen, nitrate nitrogen, vitamin B1
Zyme	Cyco	Amylase

Glossary of Common Finishing Ingredients

Alfalfa Contains triacontanol, a natural plant stimulant.

Algae Extract Kelp extract

Amino Acids Primarily glutamine and cysteine, but includes others. May be absorbed through the root system, increasing stress tolerance, growth, yield, and vitality.

Ammonium Molybdate Molybdenum (Mb) micronutrient

Amylase An enzyme that acts as a catalyst for breaking down starches, turning them into sugars. These sugars provide a source of energy for the plant.

Ascorbic Acids Vitamin C

Azomite A natural mineral complex that stimulates growth.

B Vitamins Use of B vitamins noted in literature or practice.

B1 Vitamin Touted as a stress relief for plants. Proved to have no value.

B2 Vitamin Also known as Riboflavin. There is no direct literature or note of its use in plants, which produce it in abundant quantities. However, it is known to protect some organisms from UV light.

Bat Guano Source of organic N or P.

Bone Meal (Steamed) (N:1.6–2.5, P:21, K:0.2) Moderate release source of P.

$CaCO_3$ Calcium carbonate, source of Ca

Carbohydrates Simple sugars such as glucose or dextrose that plants can uptake.

Carrot (Wild, aka Queen Anne's Lace) Ferments into amino acids that stimulate flower growth.

Charcoal Soil conditioner that stimulates plant growth.

Chelated Many micronutrients are metals that have little availability. When bonded with other elements (chelation), they become much more available.

Chitosan Found in crustacean shells, insect exoskeletons, and fungus cell walls. Chitosan is a plant growth enhancer and bio-pesticide substance that boosts the innate ability of plants to defend themselves against infections.

Citric Acid Vitamin C. When sprayed under stress conditions, improves growth and internal citric acid concentration, and also induces defense mechanisms by increasing the activities of antioxidant enzymes. May play a positive role in stress tolerance.

Cysteine (L) An amino acid high in sulfur. Effective against bacterial infections in plants and may stimulate terpene production.

Dolomite Mined combination of Ca (lime) and Mg.

Extract A preparation containing the active ingredient of a substance in concentrated form.

Fe Iron

$FeSO_4$ Iron sulfate

Fish Meal Made from ground fish by-products and nonfood fish, 60–70% protein. A rich source of amino acids.

Fish Protein Concentrated fish meal

Glutamine (L) (Glutamate) An amino acid involved in plant growth. Supplementation may increase stress resistance and growth.

Guano Seabird or bat poop

Humic Acid A complex of acids that result from the decomposition of plant matter. It contains humic and fulvic acids as well as other molecules. It helps to regulate the bioavailability of nutrients to the roots.

Jasmonic Acid Regulates plant growth and development processes including growth inhibition, senescence, flower development, and leaf abscission.

K Potassium, always used as a compound.

K_2CO_3 Potassium carbonate, a common fertilizer

Kelp The seaweed ascophyllum nodosum

KH_2PO_4 Potassium phosphate, a common fertilizer

$KHSO_4$ Potassium hydrogen sulfate (potassium-bisulfate), a common fertilizer

K_2O Potash, a common fertilizer

KNO_3 Potassium nitrate, a common fertilizer

K_2SO_4 Potassium sulfate, a common fertilizer

Mg Magnesium, an essential element

$MgHPO_4$ Magnesium phosphate

$MgSO_4$ Magnesium sulfate aka epsom salts

Micronutrients Elements used by plants in small quantities. They are: boron (B), zinc (Zn), manganese (Mn), iron (Fe), copper (Cu), molybdenum (Mo), and chlorine (Cl). In total, they constitute less than 1% of the dry weight of most plants.

$MnSO_4$ Manganese sulfate, micronutrient

Molasses Sugar concentrate made from sugarcane.

Mycorrhizae Fungi that grow in association with plant roots in a symbiotic relationship. Ectomycorrhiza form a cell-to-cell relationship with the root hairs. Arbuscular mycorrhizae penetrate the root cells. Both provide nutrients and protection in return for root exudate containing their food, sugars.

N Nitrogen

P Phosphorus, always used as a compound.

Phosphates Phosphorus compounds

Phyto-Acids (Bloom Master, Earth Juice). Undetermined plant products.

PO_4 Phosphate

P_2O_5 Phosphorus pentoxide, commonly used fertilizer

Radish Ferments into amino acids, which are growth stimulators.

Saponins Derived from yucca. Reduce water surface tension and loosen minerals from around roots.

Seaweed Kelp

Sugar Plant food supplement that can be absorbed by roots.

Triacontanol Plant growth stimulator. Large quantities are found in alfalfa.

Tryptophan (L) Boosts flower hormone production.

DO NOT USE

Potassium Sorbate Preservative and fungicide commonly used in foods and cosmetics.

Paraben Widely used in cosmetics as a preservative and bactericide and fungicide. Weak association as an estrogen simulator and with endocrine interruption.

Nipacide Biocide. Kills all living organisms. Made from formaldehyde.

The Vitamin B1 Myth

In 1930, a scientist was growing excised roots in a petri dish. He noticed, or so he thought, that the addition of vitamin B1 (thiamine) stimulated the growth of the roots. After several years of experiments performed under laboratory conditions showing the same stimulating effects, eventually *Better Homes and Gardens* picked up this story and wrote an article for the December 1939 issue on the benefits of vitamin B1 as a root stimulator.

Unfortunately, these results were never reproduced outside laboratory conditions, and likely because an increase in root productivity was due to plant hormones called auxins associated with vitamin B1 in the lab. Auxins are now known to promote root initiation and are widely used as rooting hormones.

Vitamin B1 fell victim to a case of "correlation, not causation." Although the data suggested that vitamin B1 increased productivity in excised roots in petri dishes under laboratory conditions, these results could never be repeated with intact roots in the garden. Scientific studies have since debunked this claim, even as early as 1940 (Hammer 1940). The original author from the 1930 paper said in 1942 that "additions of vitamin B1 to intact growing plants have no significant or useful place in horticultural or agricultural practice."

PART V:

HARVESTING & PROCESSING

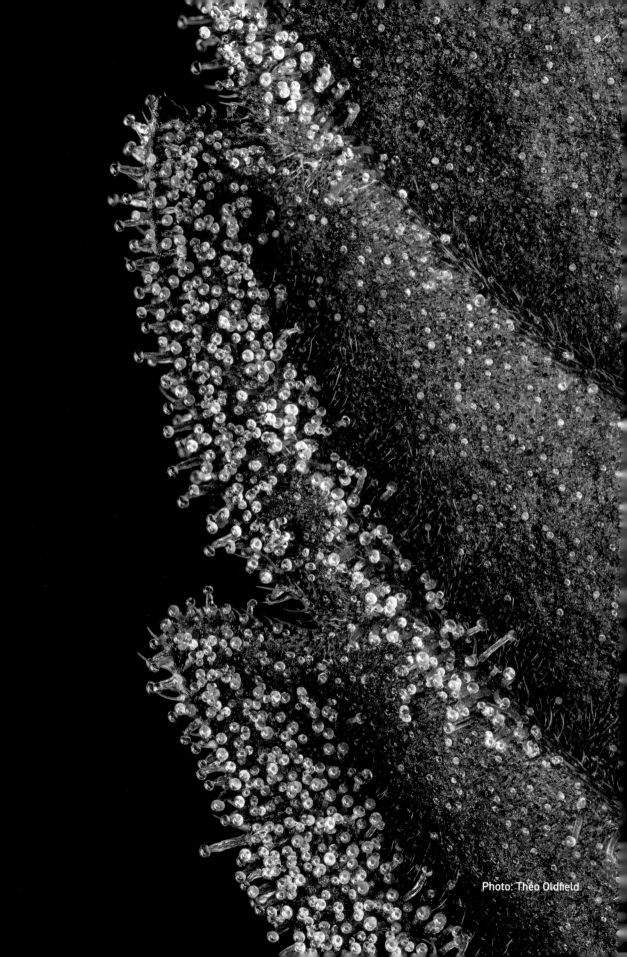

Photo: Theo Oldfield

WHEN & HOW TO HARVEST

Harvesting, drying, curing, and storing are incredibly important processes to growers. Each contributes to the final quality of the flowers and the end-use products processed from them. A good crop followed by poor post-harvest practices is as disastrous as crop failure.

Even a small harvest requires a little bit of labor. Processing a large one adds complexity and requires planning. Determining when to cut the crop, whether to cut whole plants or to judge each bud for its ripeness, when to trim, how and where to dry and cure the buds for use or processing, and how to preserve the aroma and taste by retaining the terpenes and essential oils are important decisions for any harvest.

Growers usually plan their gardens in great detail by setting timetables and cultivation parameters for their plants and bringing the plants to the peak of maturity. However, they often spend a lot less time planning the harvest. Even large commercial operations are sometimes far behind in harvest and post-harvest operations. These final tasks need the most thought; they are the ones most likely to be improperly executed—but they needn't be. With proper preparation the process can flow seamlessly.

For larger operations, try to divide up the tasks so that there are few bottlenecks. The task flow can be divided in many ways. For instance, if a grower has access to an area to store branches or colas but there are insufficient trimming facilities, then bringing in the buds and pulling off fan leaves should be prioritized. The colas can be placed in storage to dry before trimming or under refrigeration to keep them fresh for wet trimming. Then the material can be manicured over a longer period of time.

No matter the situation, plan ahead and prepare for the coming harvest.

The harvest consists of several tasks (not always in this order):
- Cutting the colas (tops) from the plants
- Cutting (bucking) the buds from the branches
- Trimming the buds
- Drying the buds
- Curing and properly storing the buds

Make sure to prepare for each stage. In many cases, even on large farms, not much has changed over the years. Growers tend to get set in their ways; their gardens are easily dated by the techniques they employ. Not all growers realize that new equipment is available to increase efficiency and scale back the manual labor associated with the harvest.

497

As soon as the plant is cut down, instead of focusing on terpene production, growers must focus on terpene retention.

If buds aren't processed correctly, a perfectly good crop can be destroyed. Proper harvesting includes keeping the buds clean and fresh, and preserving flavors and aromas. Cannabis freshness is based on two factors: maintaining enough moisture in the material for it to be pliable without inviting mold, and, just as important, retaining the terpenes found in the trichomes. Terpenes are volatile oils that volatilize at different temperatures, some of them as low as 68°F (20°C). For this reason, at no time during the drying and curing process should the temperature be raised very much above this point.

Before it is consumed, cannabis is judged first by appearance and then by smell. Fresh, aromatic buds are the most likely to be demanded and consumed. It's imperative to plan ahead, know the bottlenecks and schedule accordingly but, most important, as a grower, it is important to know what to do and why.

The Harvesting Process

Picking

Picking is the process of cutting the buds, branches, or whole plant from the root before trimming and/or drying.

Bucking

Bucking is the process of removing the flowers from the stems.

Manicuring

Manicuring is the process of trimming the small leaves that are growing around the buds to sculpt them into shape. This step can be done wet or dry.

Fresh, "wet" vegetation is turgid while it is being clipped, so it is easy to handle. Just as important, the trichomes that hold cannabinoids and terpenes are pliable rather than brittle and are more likely to stay attached to the plant. A downside of trimming wet is that it can require cool storage and a larger trim team or mechanization to keep up with the rate of harvest.

Allowing the crop to dry before trimming eliminates bottlenecks by allowing for a more extended trimming period. Although trichome loss will occur with either method, dry trimming may lead to a higher rate of trichome separation.

Growers sometimes manicure a bit while the plants are still standing. The plants are in a convenient position to remove fan leaves and other vegetation so that there is less damage to the bud. Use this technique only a few days before harvest.

Drying, Curing & Storing

The purpose of drying is to remove enough moisture from the buds to prevent mold developing in storage. Once the plants are initially dried, a second-stage drying process called "curing" is employed to achieve uniform drying while maintaining a slightly spongy texture and a smoother smoke. When properly cured, buds can age nicely for several months. Climate controls and processing techniques are crucial to successful drying, curing, and storing.

Processing

Many plants are not destined to end their journey as simple buds. Growers often will process their harvest into concentrates and extracts, and/or infuse the oil into foods, lotions, and tinctures after harvest.

This Oakland garden harvests, processes, and dries large quantities at once. Photo: Ed Rosenthal

Strategizing for Harvest

Lay out a strategy based on the goals of the garden. (*See Goals*.) If the crop is to be used for its flowers, then the harvesting method may be different from that utilized for extracts and concentrates. As with any blooms, cannabis flowers should be handled gently and with care. Biomass, the entire product of the harvest, is used for extracts or concentrates and can be handled without concern for cosmetic beauty.

There are many strategies to consider. Some require planning during variety selection or before planting, while others can be decided later in the season. Numerous factors play a part in these decisions.

One of the first major decisions a grower faces is how big the garden will be. Whether the plan is for a hobby garden or a large commercial operation, the goals should be realistic.

Assess the resources required in labor and capital and determine whether those resources are available to meet the expenses of production.

With that in mind, consider labor as a factor of time. The main labor factors are setup and harvest. Both of these operations can be carried out over a longer period by a smaller group, or in a shorter time by a larger group.

Personnel and Timing

A smaller group can more easily handle a crop that is harvested over several weeks versus a crop that is harvested all at once.

The biggest factor to consider when choosing a time to harvest the crop is ripening. The efficiency and rate of turnover of each round of flowering also must be considered. It is important to strike a balance between harvesting at peak ripeness and yield versus optimizing the speed and frequency of harvests each year.

Growers must make these choices about how and when to harvest based on their garden and workplace circumstances, ripening time, and desired end use.

Ripening

Ripening times vary by variety, and growers may choose to harvest at different stages of growth in order to obtain the desired effects and use. Before cutting down the plants, the grower must determine when to harvest.

The Ripening Process

Plants and varieties differ in maturation pattern. Some mature all at once, so that the whole plant can be picked. Other varieties mature from the top down or from the outside in. For these varieties, the buds on the outside mature faster than inner buds hidden from the light. Once the outer buds are harvested, the inner branches are exposed to light and quickly ripen. During a staged harvest, it can take up to two weeks of choosing mature buds before the plant is totally picked. Picking the plant a little at a time ensures that every bud is at maximum potency and quality.

A plant's flowering cycle, and its ripening and harvesting time, are variety specific. Each variety is programmed to respond to a critical period of darkness that turns growth from vegetative to flowering. Indoors, this is accomplished when the lights are cut back to 12 hours. Outdoors, the critical dark period usually varies between 9 and 11 hours of darkness. In addition to genetics, flowering time is also affected by light intensity and total light received on a daily basis (DLI), ambient temperature, and nutrients.

The best way to determine the picking time is by watching the development of the trichomes (the stalk-like resin glands that contain the active compounds), which grow on the leaves surrounding the flowers. The flower area becomes covered with these resin glands over time. Tools are available that can measure cannabinoid content in flowers and monitor for its peak when choosing a harvest date. Growers can also use magnification to assess the size, color, and clarity of the trichomes. Combined with lab testing at various points of maturation, visual cues can be used during future harvest rounds to estimate when peak potency has been achieved for each cultivar.

Late-season and long-maturing varieties usually spend about three to five weeks in this period of heavy trichome growth.

As flowers near ripeness, their caps swell with resin and the trichomes become more prominent and stand erect. The viscous, sticky liquid that accumulates contains terpenes and cannabinoids, which are produced on the inside membrane of the trichome cap. As the resin accumulates in the cap, the flower odor becomes more intense.

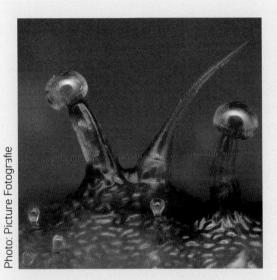

Photo: Picture Fotografie

Types of Trichomes

Bulbous Trichome
Bulbous trichomes have no stalk and are much smaller than the other trichomes. They appear mostly on leaves rather than in the bud area, especially during vegetative growth, and contain cannabinoids.

Crysolith Trichome
These trichomes do not contain cannabinoids. They grow on the bottom of the leaves to deter pests.

Sessile Stalked Capitate Trichome
These trichomes appear during the vegetative growth stage and produce only small amounts of cannabinoids.

Stalked Capitate Glandular Trichomes
These trichomes are the most abundant and contain the desired cannabinoids, terpenoids, and flavonoids that growers seek.

The odor reaches its peak at the same time that the trichomes begin to fluoresce in the light, twinkling like little crystals. In some varieties, the trichomes are so prominent that the whole bud sparkles. Using a magnifying glass, a jeweler's loupe, or a microscope, monitor the buds' progression to the peak of ripeness by watching the resin in the gland tops.

Under magnification, individual glands can be seen turning from clear to cloudy white or amber. This has traditionally been considered the peak harvest time. Cultivators differ in their assessment of the peak harvest period. The controversy is whether the harvest should occur when the trichomes are mostly clear, cloudy, or amber. Plants harvested at each of these stages may produce different effects. Lab testing can be used to determine peak potency and to target harvest dates by desired outcomes.

Ripening cannabis reeks of pungent terpenes, and each day brings increased intensity of odor. Rub the leaves surrounding the bud between clean fingers and inhale. This releases aroma molecules while leaving fingers sticky with resin. Inhale and smell an exotic medley of familiar and unusual odors that may range from sweet to acrid, musky, and skunky.

There are various factors to take into consideration before deciding when it's time to harvest:
- Plants of the same variety flower and ripen at about the same time. Clones from a single plant grown under the same conditions flower and ripen at the same time.
- In most varieties, flowering time is determined by the light regimen, not a plant's age or size.
- When all the buds on small plants get direct sunlight, they tend to ripen at the same time.
- Buds on large plants that are directly lit, whether on the top of the plant or on the sides, mostly ripen at the same time.
- Outdoors, big plants grown with large spaces between them will often get light from three different sides as the sun moves around them. In the Northern Hemisphere, light comes from the east, west, and south; in the Southern Hemisphere, light comes from the east, west, and north. This light pattern is especially prevalent in the autumn, when the sun is at an acute angle and lower on the horizon.
- On large colas, outer buds often ripen, while the inner buds are deprived of direct sunlight.

Harvesting Early or Late

Traditionally many growers have determined when to pick based on the 30/70 rule. They harvest when about 30% of the trichomes have turned amber and the remaining 70% are milky white. This may not be accurate and results are cultivar specific. More research is needed.

Some growers will harvest late, with a goal of buds with a higher cannabinol (CBN) content, which is a product of aged and degraded THC and is used to aid sleep.

Some growers harvest early to produce plants with low-enough THC levels to qualify as "hemp." Cannabis will not continue to ripen after it has been harvested.

Weather

Cannabis flowers in the autumn. At the time when plants could use more light, sun intensity is naturally declining, beginning in the late summer. At the same time, the weather may change from balmy summer to cool autumn, sometimes with wind and rain—weather not conducive to great buds.

A grower may have to make hard decisions and compromises. Consider the following situation: the buds are ten days from early ripeness. The forecast is for cool weather followed by rain and then a long period of sun and warm weather, long enough to ripen the crop. What to do? Cut early and forfeit ripeness, or leave the plants standing and take measures to try to prevent mold attacks? (*See Picking.*)

Gauging Ripeness

Knowing when to pick a ripe bud has historically been more of an art than a science; however, new research is showing that traditional methods may not optimize gauging ripeness. (*See The Science behind Choosing a Harvest Date* later in this chapter.) Growers have their own processes and criteria for determining ripeness, but a savvy grower will watch for several signs. Most follow these steps:

Indoors, most growers induce their plants to flower using twelve hours of uninterrupted darkness. However, plants can be forced to flower at a shorter period of darkness. Outdoors, the first signs of flowering are used as an indicator. The true date of initiation for most varieties is 7–10 days before the plant indicates. The number of hours between dusk and dawn is the number of hours of darkness it takes to force flowering. That is the critical dark period. Hours for daily dusk and dawn vary by region and season and are available online. With an online "sunrise-sunset" calculator, the hours between and including morning and evening "civil twilight" make up the total light period. The hours between and including evening and morning "nautical twilight" make up the total dark period.

During the first weeks of flowering, the stigmas become visible. Stigmas are white or pastel-colored hairs that protrude from the newly forming flower bracts. They're hollow inside and have "brushes" on the outside through which they filter the air containing pollen. When they capture the proper pollen grain, the pollen will form a pollen tube that travels down the hollow stigma to meet the egg (ovule) located in the ovary at the base of the flower bract. If the stigmas are unpollinated, they will retain their vitality for a long time.

By week four, most varieties are in full flower, and they put out layer after layer of stigmas, so the bud gets thicker, denser, and sometimes hardens.

In most varieties the buds start to ripen around week six, and the stigmas start to shrivel and turn brown, orange, or red. The trichomes start to become more prominent; eventually the caps on these glands start filling up.

By week seven or eight, most varieties are about one to two weeks away from peak ripeness. Most of the stigmas have shriveled, and the trichomes are more prominent. The glands continue to fill up with cannabinoids and terpenes and look like mushroom caps. They begin to bulge like balloons. The odor becomes more intense, but the bud is still not ripe. It hasn't yet reached peak intensity.

On ripe buds, the trichomes are totally erect, and the caps on them are prominent. They're bulging with resin, the stigmas are shriveled, and the bracts are swollen, sometimes resembling seed pods.

The Science Behind Choosing a Harvest Date

By Thomas Blank, Kymron DeCesare, Reggie Gaudino, PhD, Caleb King, PhD, and Donald P. Land, PhD

Photo: Professor P of Dynasty Genetics

Cannabis cultivators have traditionally relied on visual and olfactory cues to determine "the readiness" of the inflorescences for harvest. "Cannabis lore" includes looking at the ratio of white to colored/bent stigmas, looking at the color of the trichome head, and checking whether the flower smells ripe (green smelling rather than the expected "bouquet"). Due to the diversity and complexity of cannabis, experience with the plant translates to a better product, whether for breeding or producing quality flowers. The term "results/experience may vary" has never been more appropriate.

There is still a limited understanding of the complex interactions and interplay between the different chemical production systems in cannabis. Thus, these data are a first look at the time-series production of phytochemicals during growth. Understanding this process is further complicated by the considerable variation in cultivation and fertigation practices employed by growers.

The reality is that cannabis is very responsive to its environment, and different growing regimens will produce slightly, or even drastically, different cannabinoid and terpene profiles. In the extreme, the predominant phytochemicals from what is the expected profile for that particular variety can be significantly changed.

The question "When is the best time to harvest?" has been the subject of much debate for a long time. Data presented here may not make that decision much easier. Rather, as with all things cannabis, there is no straightforward answer. "Harvesting for what?" is the only appropriate response. As the data presented here illustrate, what the grower wants, whether it be bud weight or maximum cannabinoid or terpene content, can be the deciding factor of when to harvest.

Here, an effort is made to apply the scientific method, using measurements and analytics in chemistry, biology, and environmental sciences, to identify the most important characteristics of the plant, which can help the experienced cultivator or breeder to determine optimal harvest time.

The information gained can be used to better understand and reproduce those aspects of cultivation that affect the final cannabinoid and terpene content. The data are designed to help better understand the production of cannabinoids and terpenes over the life cycle of the plant and to identify the best time, or time range, to harvest for maximum terpene or cannabinoid content.

Cannabinoids other than THCa and CBDa have become of greater interest in the industry, thanks to literature citing the potential therapeutic utility of these chemical species. Cannabinoids of interest in this study included CBGa, CBGVa, THCa, THCVa, CBDa, CBDVa, and CBCa, as well as other minor cannabinoids.

Cannabinoids were monitored during the growth cycle of several different types of cannabis (Types I, II, III, and IV), including a variety that was augmented in production of propyl (C3) cannabinoids. Both vegetative (leaf) and floral (bud) material, cured with standard USDA guidelines (strictly for determination of cannabinoid content, not with final content or bag appeal as final criteria), were tracked from preflower through harvest. The data presented closely resemble published data elsewhere in the scientific literature (Pertwee 2014; De Meijer 2003, 2005, 2009, 2009).

Terpene profiles are strongly influential in entourage effects and the end users' experience. Cannabis cultivars can be grouped into seven familial clades evolved from a common ancestor and thus share common characteristics based on the most abundant primary terpenes or combinations of the most abundant primary terpenes in the plant oil profile. Plant genes that enable the synthesis of terpenes include highly active terpene synthases responsible for producing the most abundant terpenes in a cultivar.

Clades can involve a single dominant primary terpene or up to three primary terpenes of relatively similar co-abundance. Terpene gene variation in cannabis leads to substantial diversity in cultivar offerings. The potential to breed for specific terpene profiles has sparked new, or perhaps renewed, interest in cannabis terpenes.

Terpene measurements presented here were carried out on flower material that was cured using a procedure that preserves volatile terpene content or "bag appeal." In this study, terpene content was acquired only at weeks five and eight of flowering due to the time and cost of the preparation and testing. The overlap of sampling for both cannabinoids and terpenes at those two time points allows the comparison of terpene content relative to cannabinoid accumulation.

While the data presented here are scientifically robust, some limitations on what can be interpreted must be outlined so that the data can be viewed with the proper perspective. The data represented here are not a comprehensive survey of all varieties but just a representative sampling of several types of varieties currently available: high THC (Type I), mixed ratio (Type II), high CBD (Type III), and high CBG (Type IV). The information presented here can help make it easier to decide what week to harvest after flower initiation, for best terpene and/or cannabinoid content.

Materials and Methods

Cannabis plants producing predominantly THC, CBD, both THC and CBD, or CBG were vegetatively propagated from mother seed stock. All plants, apart from Type II, were grown indoors in one- or two-gallon (7.5 l) plastic pots supplemented with high pressure sodium vapor lighting, filtered water, and macro- and micronutrients.

Type II plants were grown outdoors in Colorado under summer and autumn field conditions with overhead watering and fertigation. All flower samples were obtained from the top third of each plant, with each plant's final sample collected from the most apical flower.

Leaf tissue was obtained within the top third of each plant and from three to four different branches. About one gram of dried leaf and two to five grams of dried flower samples were collected weekly from the same plant. Plant tissues were dried in darkness at 25°C (77°F) with dehumidified air between 30 and 50% relative humidity for 7 to 10 days until a consistent dry weight was obtained. Any residual moisture was neither measured nor subtracted to account for dry weights.

Dried samples were milled to a powder, with stems and seeds mechanically removed. Cannabinoids and terpenoids from 0.5-gram powder aliquots were solvent extracted using ultrasonication. A validated reverse-phase high pressure liquid chromatography (HPLC) method was employed to quantify the amount of CBD, CBDa, Δ^9-THC, Δ^9-THCa, CBC, CBCa, CBG, and CBGa, presented as % weight cannabinoid per mass of herbal material, in the original sample. The sum of acid and neutral cannabinoid percentages do not account for decarboxylation reactions/constants. Terpenoids were quantified using a liquid injection technique on a validated gas chromatography mass spectrometry (GC-MS) method, presented as % weight terpenoid per mass of herbal material.

Results and Discussion

Data were collected for both vegetative (leaf) and floral (bud) material. However, it is important to note that the results show that, in each tissue, the production of cannabinoids and terpenes is not the same, with respect to either the compounds made or the timing in which they are produced.

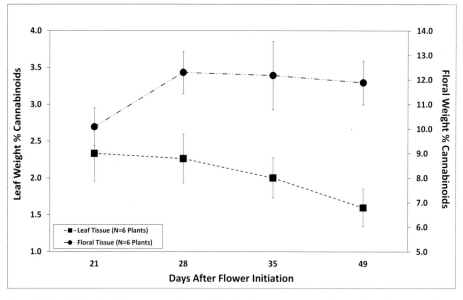

Fig. 1 - Type III leaf and flower total cannabinoids from the same plants throughout female floral development.

All cannabinoid data were taken after flowering was initiated, unless otherwise indicated. Leaf total cannabinoid data is presented in Figure 1. "Total cannabinoid" is defined as the sum of the "major" cannabinoids (THCa, CBDa, CBCa, and CBGa, as well as their less abundant neutral forms).

Figure 1 compares the cannabinoid production in leaf versus floral (bud) tissue. The data here can be misleading, because they do not take into account the change in mass of the leaf tissue between day 21 post initiation and day 49 post initiation. The downward trend could be simply due to the fact that the leaves increase in size while the level of cannabinoid production stays constant (or drops). A steady rise of cannabinoids in floral tissue until weeks five and six is clearly seen in the data presented, not only in Figure 1, but also in Figures 2–4 as well, regardless of whether the variety predominantly makes THC, CBD, or both THC and CBD. No CBCa-dominant plants were ready for testing at the time these data were being collected. Thus the CBCa values presented in Figure 6C are the natural levels found in the varieties used in this study.

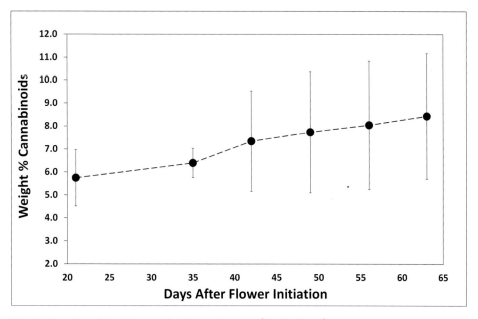

Fig. 2 - Type I total floral cannabinoid development (N = 7 plants)

The Type I cannabis plants described in Figure 2 are atypical of most high-THC-producing varieties. This particular variety produces a significant proportion of minor cannabinoids and matures later. In this particular example, maximum cannabinoid content is more closely tied to maximum flower size (later in the flower cycle means additional accumulation of biomass), and thus the decision process is much simpler.

This sample illustrates the differences between cannabis varieties and further highlights that there is no "one size fits all" solution. Harvest time decisions need to be made differently for the various cultivars and for different growing regimens as they are applied to those cultivars. The variety presented here would be considered a "mid-maturity" variety.

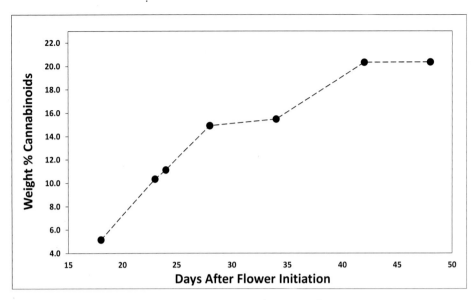

Fig. 3 - Type II total floral cannabinoid development (N = 1 plant)

Type II cannabis plants (mixed ratio, producing both THC and CBD) showed a similar cannabinoid maximum at around six weeks post flower initiation in outdoor trials. A number of environmental factors may have influenced these results, such as an early September snowstorm, which occurred in Colorado at about 28 days post outdoor flower initiation. Total cannabinoid content in Type III plants grown in the same outdoor field plots responded similarly to the environmental perturbation (data not shown).

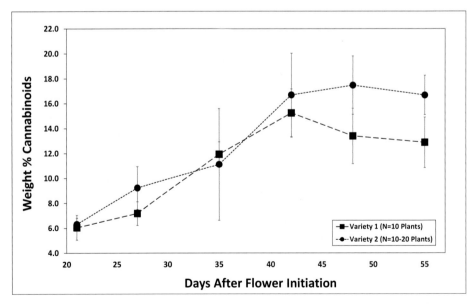

Fig. 4 - Type III total floral cannabinoid development for two genetically distinct varieties.

Two CBD-dominant varieties are presented in Figure 4. Note that one variety peaks at about day 42 (week six) post flower initiation and drops off sharply thereafter, while the other peaks at about day 49 (week seven) post flower initiation before falling off.

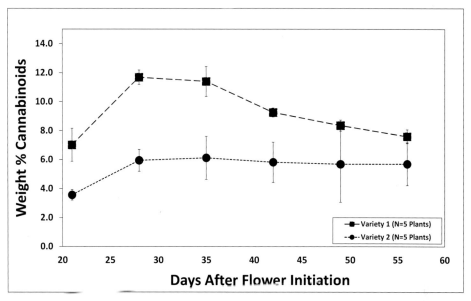

Fig. 5 - Type IV total floral cannabinoid development for two genetically distinct varieties.

Typically, Type IV cannabis plants do not produce significant amounts of "major cannabinoids" (THC or CBD), with the exception of CBC. Thus CBG, the precursor for all major cannabinoid synthesis, accumulates to varying degrees. The data presented here indicate that the peak of CBGa production seems to fall between three and five weeks post flower initiation, which is different from the peak of CBGa production shown in the data for Type III cannabis plants presented in Figure 6D. (See CBG peak in Fig. 6D that seems to be delayed compared with CBG peak in Fig. 5.)

The combined cannabinoid data presented here show that, for THC-dominant, CBD-dominant, and mixed-ratio varieties, there is a general trend for cannabinoid production to reach its peak by about week six after flower initiation (around day 40–42 of flower). For the limited number of CBGa-dominant and CBCa-producing varieties presented here, the data illustrate that the timing of maximum production for CBGa and CBCa may vary.

Terpenes

A key aspect of identifying therapeutic utility of cannabis varieties involves measuring and assessing the plant terpene and terpenoid concentration profile. Terpenes are organic molecules based on 5-carbon "isoprene" units, while terpenoids are terpenes containing oxygen.

Volatile terpenes in cannabis consist of mostly monoterpenes (10-carbon molecules) and the somewhat less volatile sesquiterpenes (15-carbon molecules). For simplicity, the whole group of terpenes and terpenoids is referred to as "terpenes."

Few plants produce the numbers and diversity of terpenes found in cannabis. Over 100

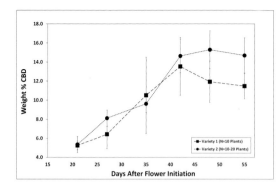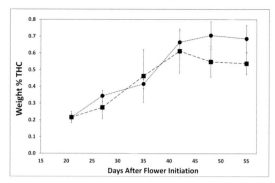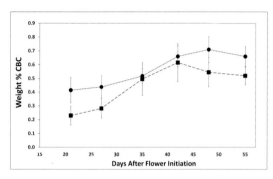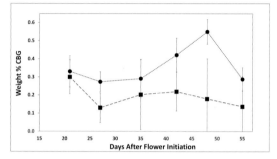

Fig. 6 - Type III individual cannabinoid time series for two genetically distinct varieties.
A. CBD Development (top left) B. THC Development (top right) C. CBC Development (bottom left) D. CBG Development (bottom right): Variety 1 (square), N = 10 Plants; Variety 2 (circle), N = 10–20 Plants]

terpenes have been identified in cannabis, though only a maximum of about 20–25 volatile terpenes are found at significant levels in any cultivar. Each cultivar can have 6–15 volatile terpenes present above trace levels in its profile. Volatility is important in delivery as a vapor. Larger di- and tri-terpenes are not volatile and, hence, cannot be efficiently delivered by vapor.

Here the discussion is focused on the smaller volatile terpenes that have 10 (2 isoprene units) or 15 carbons (3 isoprene units). Terpenes are believed to be the most critical factor in the "entourage effects" of a cultivar, as they largely determine the cultivar-specific effects experienced by the consumer.

Terpenes are the main constituents in essential oils derived from many plants and have been used around the world for centuries to treat many ailments orally, topically, or by aromatherapy (Dagli et al. 2015; Ali et al. 2015).

Terpenes found in cannabis can also be found in the essential oils of many other plants. Over the last few decades, activities of the individual terpene contents of essential oils have been studied and have demonstrated that there is a wide range of therapeutic activity of individual terpenes.

Individual terpenes have been shown in animal and human testing to produce cognitive benefits, sedative effects, and pain relief, and to influence EEG patterns in the human brain (do Vale et al. 2002; Gertsch et al. 2008; Cho et al. 2017; Russo 2011; Sowndharara-

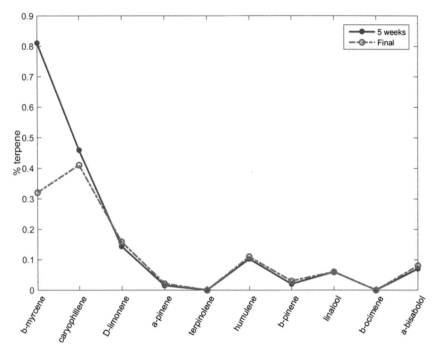

Fig. 7 - Concentrations of the 10 most abundant terpenes at five weeks and final harvest. The β-myrcene value for the final harvest sample shows anomalous results, and the low value is likely the result of poor handling during the preparation process for analysis by GCMS. β-myrcene is a volatile compound that has poorer solubility in certain extraction solvents and thus is sensitive to extraction methodology.

jan 2016; Kei et al. 2016; Teixeira et al. 2017; Lim et al. 2011). Some terpenes introduce a calm focus in the mind, while others can cause the mind to race, and still others act on pain, anxiety, and depression.

Each unique variety contains a terpene profile that acts with cannabinoids to produce an entourage effect (Russo 2011). To a large degree, terpenes are believed to be the compounds primarily responsible for the differences in the effects experienced with different varieties.

Investigation into leaf terpenes showed little correlation to terpenes in flower tissue and are predominantly sesquiterpene in content. Therefore, to focus on the "harvest" aspect, only terpenes during the flowering phase are considered.

Data presented in Figure 7 are from a mixed ratio (~1.2:1 CBD:THC) variety grown in a tent using LED lights. The data were collected at five weeks (mid-flower) and final harvest (around week eight or nine). Note that, as early as week five, terpene production seems to have peaked and remains constant through final harvest.

For comparison, production of several cannabinoids also seems to peak around the five- or six-week mark, regardless of whether they were grown indoors, in a greenhouse, or outdoors. Again, it must be reiterated that, while many varieties follow the timeline of peaking between five or six weeks, Figures 2 and 3 are presented to illustrate that some varieties take much longer to finish and thus would require different harvest considerations.

Conclusions

Trichome Color & Harvest

Some growers use color changes in the trichomes as a way to determine a harvest time. As trichome oil loses monoterpenes to volatilization, or as the ratio of percentage of THCa to percentage of terpenes increases in the oil, THCa can be expected to precipitate as a white solid in the oil, giving a milky appearance.

If THCa crystals are contaminated with some other chemicals, they may turn off-white in color, and then amber, as contaminants rise to higher levels. This color change can be expected because some phytochemicals, including terpenes, have a high susceptibility to oxidation and can turn amber or precipitate out of the trichome oil.

A very small amount of highly colored material can have a large effect on visual appearance. Varieties that do not have abundant oxidizable monoterpenes (e.g., White CBG, White Buffalo, White 99, Super Silver Haze) may not show much of the amber color at peak potency. Thus, color change of trichomes is not a reliable or universally applicable methodology on which to decide when to harvest.

Due to the diversity of cannabis, the likelihood of developing a single methodology to determine peak harvest time is unlikely. The combination of finish times, environmental response, and genetic makeup (responsible for the terpenes and cannabinoids produced) combine to make each variety, or at least groups of similarly classified varieties (based on structure, chemical content, photoperiod, etc.), distinct enough that they may need very specific decisions on why and when to harvest, as well as how to cure.

Curing itself is fraught with several different decision points based on what the final application of the flower will be.

As stated previously, the only valid answer to "When is the right time to harvest?" is "What is the end goal of the harvest?" Cannabinoids and terpenes seem to peak around the same time frame, generally two or more weeks before maximum flower weight. Chemically, the plant is ready for harvest before the flower is fully mature. Thus, as with all things agriculture, perhaps maximum yield is ultimately the real deciding factor.

Primary terpenes are terpenes that can be the most abundant terpene in a cultivar; there are at least six primary terpenes in cannabis.

Primary monoterpenes in cannabis can be present as one of the most abundant terpenes in a cultivar, or they can be present at lower concentrations in a more complementary role.

β-myrcene: the most common terpene in cannabis is an acyclic monoterpene that has mild analgesic, sedative, and muscle-relaxant properties (do Vale et al. 2002). Myrcene also may help carry other terpenes and cannabinoids across the blood-brain barrier. Myrcene smells of mango.

DR-limonene: DR-limonene is the most common monocyclic terpene in cannabis and is a moderate sedative and a muscle relaxant (do Vale et al. 2002). It is known to be an effective antidepressant and anti-anxiety terpene on its own.

α-pinene: α-pinene is a bicyclic monoterpene (two rings) that is a known acetylcholinesterase inhibitor (AChEI). It increases neurotransmitter concentration in the brain by limiting its destruction by enzymes. As an AChEI, alpha-pinene improves memory and cognition, is often associated with "clear headed" effects (Cho et al. 2017), and is known to stimulate the parasympathetic nervous system and to lower blood pressure, producing a calm state. It smells of sweet and mildly pungent pine aroma.

Terpinolene: Terpinolene is a monocyclic terpene found in many trees. Terpinolene has been shown to increase alpha to beta wave power ratios in the brain, leading to a focused calm. Terpinolene is also a mild muscle relaxant and a sedative.

Primary sesquiterpenes are among the most abundant terpenes in cannabis. They are less volatile than monoterpenes and have less influence on flower aromas but are vaporized readily under heating.

β-caryophyllene: β-caryophyllene is the second most common terpene in cannabis and the most common sesquiterpene. A system-wide-acting anti-inflammatory and analgesic compound (Gertsch et al. 2008), it is a bicyclic terpene that is produced in the same synthesis as another sesquiterpene, humulene (aka α-caryophyllene), so they are present together in cannabis.

Farnesenes: This group of linear chain, acyclic sesquiterpenes differ from each other in the placement of double bonds. Farnesenes are less studied than other cannabis terpenes, but they are reported to act as mild sedatives and muscle relaxants. Some isomers also are reported to increase cognitive function with AChEI activity. Farnesenes have a mild aroma of grass and green apples.

Secondary terpenes are present at lower abundance levels than primary terpenes, but they can contribute notably to cultivar effects. Terpenes that are enzyme inhibitors and channel blockers can be potent in small abundances, sometimes making them even more potent overall than the more abundant terpenes in their specific effects.

Secondary monoterpenes can be present at significant levels that may substantially affect the entourage effect. They include β-pinene, linalool, β-ocimene, 3-carene, α-terpinene, eucalyptol, fenchol, α-phellandrene, and eudesmol.

Secondary sesquiterpenes can be present at significant levels that may substantially impact the entourage effect. α-bisabolol, guiaol, trans-nerolidol, trans-bergamotene, and γ-elemene are some secondary sesquiterpenes.

Photo: Doobie Duck

514

PICKING

Harvesting Strategies Outdoors

The harvester has a few choices: cut the whole plant or sections of it; cut individual branches; cut just the ripe buds and leave the rest to ripen; or cut all the buds, separating them into As for "trophy flowers" and Bs for smalls.

Why would a grower consider cutting the whole plant? Perhaps weather conditions are severe enough to require a rapid harvest, or, if the grower is working with a crop that ripens evenly and is ready to harvest at the same time, the grower may choose to cut whole plants in order to harvest the entire crop at once. The choice may be determined by labor availability. A grower can choose a large crew to cut and dry the product all at once, a surge crew to work for a limited period of time, or, depending on financial constraints, a crew to trim when demand for labor is lower.

Another choice is to cut individual branches as they mature. Cutting off the outer branches opens the inner buds to light, hastening their maturity. A grower may harvest individual buds for the same reason: doing so provides the immature buds underneath with more light.

When plants are spaced tightly in rows and bottom-pruned, all the buds grow on the top portion of the plants. They can be cut using a hedge trimmer, leaving the understory to ripen or to be harvested separately for concentrates/extracts.

Other factors may lend themselves to harvesting only the ripest buds. If the weather is predicted to stay fair for a long period, a grower may choose to change the flow of the harvest by slowing the process down and trimming off the best buds as they become perfectly mature.

Buds and branches can be sorted into As and Bs, using the material for different purposes. Shake and imperfect buds are used for concentrates, while high-quality buds are trimmed.

With smaller plants, most of the buds are often ready at the same time. Either the whole plant or the colas can be cut. All material that is removed from the plant should be placed on hygienic tarps, bags, or other containers.

Picking Outdoors

Outdoors, where maximum size or height might not have a limit, huge plants can be harvested over two or three stages by taking the ripened portion of each branch and leaving the unripened portions to finish over the next week or two.

Outdoor growers have little control over temperature, humidity, and wind. Ideal conditions for picking are cool and dry, less than 70°F (21°C), and low humidity. In reality, poor weather may require an early harvest. The best time to harvest is before dawn or early morning, when the plants contain the most terpenes.

Plants grown using a sea-of-green method have a single layer of tops because very little light pierces the canopy. Industrially they can be harvested with a scythe. Monster plants spaced farther apart absorb light over their entire height.

Weather affects ripening time. Cloudy skies and cool temperatures slow growth and ripening. In the Northern Hemisphere, the south-facing sides of the plants ripen first. Plants with low levels of nutrients ripen later. Drier soil or planting medium decreases time to ripening.

Legal considerations may play a role in developing harvesting strategies. In jurisdictions where individual plants are tagged, buds from different plants may not be allowed to be mixed, or they must stay with the plant until some point in the processing.

There are two possible paths, depending on growing conditions and the grower's needs: a slow, elongated period of harvesting, or one big harvest. Most indoor farms use the former, while outdoor operations often use the latter.

Growers who harvest all at once should plan for staff. There is a surge of work that can be accomplished in a burst or over a longer period.

Another strategy eliminates the need for a temporary labor surge. First, all labor is devoted to harvesting. Plants are cut and hung to dry or are placed in a refrigerated space where they remain fresh for processing. Then, they are processed over time.

When only a clone or stabilized seed variety is grown, all the plants ripen within a short window. If labor is limited, using a staged harvest paces the work. These buds are processed as the next group ripens. During the growth cycle, fertigation is easier because the same formula is used for all the plants at the same time. Another way to limit labor surges is to use several varieties that mature at different times so that the harvest takes place over a longer period.

Growers face harvest pressures caused by improperly planning for environmental factors. Sunny, warm, dry weather is ideal for ripening. The sun powers photosynthesis and provides energy for ripening. The warm weather promotes fast growth, and with little moisture there is less chance that powdery mildew or other infections will occur.

Gardens often have those conditions all summer long, but in autumn the plants are in a tug-of-war with nature, ripening just as conditions get more challenging. Light intensity and UV light levels are diminishing, and it may be cloudy, foggy, or rainy—all perilous environmental conditions. Growers must contend with autumn's rapidly changing climate.

Wet Harvest

Harvesting in fog or rain presents special problems because wet vegetation is vulnerable to attack by bacteria and mold. In this situation, prepare the plants or branches by hanging them or placing them on drying racks, leaving more space than usual to promote drying. Quickly remove excess moisture from the leaves by raising the temperature to the mid-70s F (23–24°C) and circulating the air while removing moisture with a dehumidifier. This lowers the risk of infection and decreases drying time. Once the water on the leaf surfaces has dried, resume normal drying techniques.

Preparing for Bad Weather

As the crop ripens, monitor the weather forecasts for at least two weeks before planned picking. Take the forecasts into consideration when selecting harvest dates. Depending on the conditions, growers may choose to harvest, protect the plants with covers or tarps, use drying equipment, and/or spray with protectants. Usually large-scale outdoor growers proceed cautiously They choose not to risk the whole crop to botrytis just to gain a slightly higher cannabinoid potency. Moisture is a problem, as dense, thick buds are more prone to mold than fluffy or thin bud varieties.

If the light-deprivation greenhouse harvest must be picked early and there is sufficient warning, speed up ripening by increasing the dark period to 14 hours daily. This induces the plants to ripen faster at the cost of bud size. Turning off the light a day or two before harvesting also helps a little with ripening and may increase cannabinoid and terpene content. Keep temperatures in the low 70s (around 21°C) and the humidity below 50% in the dark space to prevent mold infections.

Once the grower determines that the buds are ripe, it's time to pick.

Picking: Step-by-Step

1. **Plan:** Estimate the date the buds will first be ready to pick. Schedule time and resources for picking.
2. **Inspect for ripeness:** Regularly examine buds for signs of ripening.
3. **Deleaf:** If convenient, about three weeks before harvest, remove fan leaves that aren't getting light or are blocking buds from direct exposure to light. Remove other fan leaves a week to a few days before harvest.
4. **Prepare:** Ready the tools, equipment, and drying area. Clean and inspect all equipment to make sure it is working. Tune up tools by sharpening, oiling, and charging them. Make sure there are enough tarps and baskets and an area large enough to store the harvest.
5. **Disinfect the processing and drying/curing areas:** Clean all surfaces and tools with hydrogen peroxide, bleach, or other disinfectants.

6. **Cut**: Remove buds when they have reached peak potency. Or cut entire branches of buds the same length for easier processing.

7. **Sort:** Place picked buds or cut branches in trays for transfer to the trimming or drying area. To capture the greatest amount of THC and terpenes, plants should be harvested toward the end of the dark period. If the garden is outdoors, the best time is before sunrise. If the garden is indoors, it is best to leave the lights off during the harvesting process and pick after the plants have gone through a full dark period. Cannabinoids and terpenes accumulate during that time, so an extended period of darkness produces the most cannabinoid content.

Growers have many choices of how to harvest. Here are some different styles.

This 1980s Swiss cannabis farm uses an old-fashioned method of harvest: chopping the whole plant at the base of the stock and hanging it upside down in a large barn, shed, or warehouse. Photo: Ed Rosenthal

Whole Plant

There are several reasons for cutting the whole plant at once:
- The plants are tagged and, due to track and trace compliance, must remain intact until further processing when the tags are removed.
- The buds have matured at the same time. (This often happens on small plants or when the entire plant is fully illuminated. All the buds on sea-of-green plants usually mature at the same time.)
- Weather conditions are threatening.
- The entire plant, or most of it, is to be used for extracts or concentrates, so full cosmetic ripening is not important.
- Space needs to be made for new planting. (If the planting area is scheduled to be

replanted, waiting for some buds to ripen throws off the schedule. It is usually not worth the time delay.)

Pros: The plants are quickly removed from the field or room and away from environmental stresses.

Cons: Not all the buds are perfectly ripe. Some are either overripe or immature and may be best used for concentrates and extracts.

Individual Ripe Branches & Buds

There are several reasons to cut buds and branches (or sections of branches) as they ripen:

- Some branches may be in the shadow of other plants or other obstructions, especially in autumn, when the sun's angle is more oblique. Removing ripe branches often allows light to reach the other less-developed flowering sites.
- Cutting branches may be more labor-efficient than cutting the whole plant.
- A large plant may be too heavy and bulky to cut at the stem, so it has to be taken down in pieces.

The branches are easily bunched for transporting.
Photo: David Downs

Pros: Harvesting individual buds and branches as they ripen gives lower buds hidden inside the canopy the chance to fully mature for another one to two weeks. There is a significant difference in potency and quality between unripe and ripe buds, so the extra time and labor required for multiple harvesting sessions or daily bud inspections are worthwhile. Another advantage is that the most valuable buds are removed first and therefore safeguarded. The inner buds are not nearly as valuable, especially when harvested too early.

Cons: Harvesting individual buds and branches takes more time and labor than cutting whole plants. Some experience is needed to recognize ripeness.

Ripe Portions of Colas

Most colas ripen first at their tips, and the ripeness travels inward. One portion of the cola may be ripe, while the other portion is not. For perfection, the ripe portion can be harvested, and the inner portion will ripen as it receives more light.

Water Deprivation

Experienced growers practice slight water deprivation one to two days before harvest. This creates a stress response so that more cannabinoids and terpenes are produced. The deprivation should not be so severe that it leads to wilting.

Picking Indoors

Adjust the garden temperature down to the low 70s F (21–22°C) and lower than 50% humidity before harvest. The cooler temperature keeps the terpenes from evaporating, and the low humidity minimizes the threat of mold.

Late Picking

Some growers allow extended ripening times for increased density and/or a shift in color. If harvesting is delayed, the risk of trichome caps popping off their stalks increases.

Equipment Used for Picking

- **Schedules:** keep track of the entire process and manage various important factors and tasks.
- **Photographer's loupe or a magnifier:** monitors trichome development and ripeness.
- **Cutting Tools:** described below.
- **Tarps:** place around large plants when cutting them.
- **Shelves or hang lines:** hold whole plants, branches, colas, or buds.
- **Transporting equipment:** moves material from field to processing. This may be a basket or a hand-drawn garden cart, small motorized transport, or a portable conveyor belt.
- **Cold storage:** keeps the buds cool and turgid while awaiting processing or fresh-frozen capabilities.
- **Cleaning supplies:** vacuum cleaners, brooms, dustpans, alcohol and hydrogen peroxide, clean rags, paper towels, soap and water, resin removers such as potassium hydroxide (KOH), or commercial resin solvents.
- **Changing/Sanitation Rooms:** workers should practice proper hygiene, and washing facilities should be available.
- **Gloves:** for all phases of the operation, from plant cutting to manicuring. Canvas, rubber, and/or latex gloves are necessary.
- **Pruning shears, scissors, or power cutters:** sharp and sanitized.
- **Food-grade plastic trays:** hold material for sorting fan leaves, branches, colas, trim, buds, and waste material.
- **Ergonomically correct tables and chairs**
- **Solvent:** such as isopropyl alcohol, olive oil, or commercial resin degreaser to clean resin off scissors and other surfaces.

Find a good pair of gloves

Find comfortable gloves that do not impede work. Thin cotton gardening gloves protect the skin for jobs such as moving branches. When handling larger plants and thick branches, use more protective gloves. Garden gloves are a good choice for handling buds and small branches. Latex gloves are ideal for manicuring. Be sure to choose the right size. They should fit the trimmers' hands snugly; it is difficult to work with loose gloves. After manicuring, trimmers often put latex gloves in the freezer to easily peel the hash that collects on them.

Manual Cutting Tools

Choose tools based on ease of use, efficiency, and comfort. Below is a range of trimmers—small and large, long- and short-handled—as well as a sense of what to look for in a high-quality trimming tool.

The garden section of hardware stores likely has three kinds of hand tools useful for picking cannabis: bypass, anvil, and ratchet tools.

Bypass: A bypass cutting tool works by sliding a straight blade past another blade. The bypass cutter's scissor-like motion works well for cutting live green plants. The firm outer wall of the plant yields easily to this bypass motion. Bypass cutters have a stainless steel curved blade on the bottom of the tool and a straight blade on top. The straight blade passes next to, not on top of, the lower surface, sometimes called the hook. The lower blade's curvature is designed to hold the branch or stem while the cutting blade descends and cuts. Bypass cutters offer a very clean cut because the blade slices all the way through the plant material. Use bypass pruners for branches up to three quarters of an inch (2 cm) thick, bypass loppers for branches up to one inch (2.5 cm) thick, and a handsaw for anything larger.

Anvil: Anvil cutters work by bringing a straight blade down against a wide anvil, often made of rubber or steel. This crushing motion is most effective when working with thick and stiff or dead and dried-out plants. When used on live plants, anvil cutters tend to crush the soft tissue of the plant, stopping the flow of nutrients and prolonging the healing time for the cut surface. An anvil cutter dulls less quickly than a bypass cutter and can't be damaged when twisting the tool in the cut, as can happen with bypass cutters.

Ratchet: Ratchet pruners are used to cut thick branches or stalks. They are either hydraulic or pneumatically driven. One handle is stationary and the other moves. The lower jaw of the pruner hooks around a stalk or branch when the handle is pumped. As the blade sinks into the material, the ratchet gear clicks into place. The user then continues the pumping motion until the cut is complete.

Small pruning saw: When a branch or stem is too large or unwieldy to make a clean cut with a cutter or a lopper tool, a small pruning saw is a good alternative. There are two types of pruning saws: straight and curved blade. As the name indicates, straight-blade pruning saws have straight blades. Though the blades are straight, the handles are often curved, like a pistol grip, making it more comfortable to use. Straight-blade pruning saws are best used for green plant material.

Loppers: The long handles of a lopper allow the reach to be extended with minimal effort, enabling the user to cut anything that can fit between the two blades. Curved blades are best for heavy-duty cutting. The curvature of the blade allows the user to add additional force to the cut, slicing through even the toughest branches and stalks. Using a pruning saw or lopper takes time, so growers working with large plants should consider electric tools to increase efficiency.

Power Trimmers & Clippers

Use of portable electric tools speeds up the process of cutting branches and ripe colas, by a factor of three to eight times the pace of manual work. Electric hand garden trimmers often come with two different blades that facilitate precision work.

They can be used when leafing and are useful when harvesting small plants or buds, or even just the ripe portion of the buds, leaving the unripe portions. Each of the two blades is small, usually a hedge trimmer about 10 inches (25 cm) long and a grass shearer about 3 to 4 inches (7–10 cm) wide. Depending on the bud formation and plant shape, both of these cutters can be used to remove the ripe buds from the plant, leaving the unripe buds or just the branches and the leaves from which the buds stuck out.

Versions of these tools come with pole extensions up to 10 feet (3 m), so tall plants can be trimmed while the worker stands on the ground rather than on a ladder or platform. This is an important issue because workers are more likely to sustain an injury when working while elevated.

Large Hedge Trimmers

Removing branches is easy with a hedge trimmer. Hedge trimmers can also be used to harvest buds or remove just the ripe parts of buds. Hedge trimmers have blades that are 12–24 inches (30–60 cm) long. Smaller trimmers are adequate for most plants and weigh less than models with longer blades, so workers don't tire as quickly. A hedge trimmer with an 18-inch (45 cm) cutting area allows workers to reach tall branches and into bushy plants. Trimmers can be directed very accurately to remove individual buds as well as branches.

If the branches are too thick for the trimmer to handle efficiently, a reciprocating saw or small chain saw can be used. Lightweight models are easy to wield, even for higher branches.

Harvesting time decreases 50% or more when power hand trimmers, hedge trimmers, and power saws are used. Plants growing in a Christmas tree formation can be harvested with five strokes. There are four columns of branches, one on each side. First, a clean tarp is laid down to catch the cut branches. Starting with the top branches on one side of the plant, the branch is cut near the node, where it meets the stem, and the trimmer goes down the length of the plant. All the branches will fall into a neat pile on the tarp. Move to each side consecutively. Then cut the top.

The buds on the branches will be the same size and equal length; only the bare portions of the branches will differ in length. The branches will collect in neat piles because the buds aren't touched while cutting. Bushy plants and plants with multiple branches are also easy to cut using a hedge trimmer. A giant plant that takes up to 15 minutes to cut with hand tools falls to the trimmer in a few minutes. Using power tools results in less contact and thus less damage.

Afterward, either the tarps containing the buds can be rolled up or the buds can be placed in containers. Then they should be quickly moved to a cool area for processing.

Depending on the distance from the field or indoor garden to the next station, a simple garden utility cart, an electric utility vehicle, or motorized transport such as a golf cart may be practical. At this point there are two avenues a grower may choose: trim while the plants are wet or when they are dry. Each has its advantages and disadvantages. (*See Trimming.*)

The inner branches contain no buds and very few leaves. Rather than sorting later, the operator selects only the budded colas for harvest. A tarp is laid around the plant to catch the falling buds. When the cutting is done, the tarp is pulled away from the plant, folded into a bundle, and transported to the processing area.

Since the buds are not touched during the cutting process and are soft and pliant because they are fresh rather than dried, they suffer little damage from exposure to the vibration of power tools.

This photo series started with the low branches already removed. The rest of the plant was cut to the ground in less than 60 seconds. Compared with cutting by hand, there is less damage to the buds. A tarp placed underneath the plant makes it easy to gather the harvest and move it to the processing area—a 5-to-10-minute process completed in less than 2 minutes.

Mini Hedge Trimmers

The efficient way to cut buds from plants with mini hedge trimmers:

- Place a tarp under the plant to catch all the buds or branches that are about to fall. Start with the vegetation closest to the ground and cut the buds along the stem upward. They will fall off the plant in much the same way that hair drops when it is cut. Work up the plant in an orderly manner. If the buds are too tall to reach, use a secure step stool to increase reach. With the right equipment, workers should be able to easily cut the buds from a plant 8–10 feet (2.5–3 m) high.
- Small hedge trimmers are most useful for cutting small branches and individual buds. They work very well on bushy plants. The buds from a garden of sea-of-green plants are easy to harvest using these tools. When the trim has been completed, the plant will still look green but will be bereft of buds or will hold only immature buds left to ripen.

Battery-Operated Shears

Electric clippers do the work, eliminating strained muscles and carpal tunnel syndrome. A hand-held, battery-operated trimmer is useful for removing large leaves and exposing the buds, making more precise trimming easier.

Transportation

Depending on the size of the crop and the distance the buds or branches need to travel to be cleaned, processed, and cured, a variety of transportation methods can be used. The simplest method involves transporting trimmed buds in boxes or hand-drawn carts. Several carts may be connected to make a small train drawn either by humans or by machines. For bigger grows, where the distance from the processing station increases with the quantity of material, efficiency of transport becomes a greater factor, so utility vehicles, trucks, or conveyor belts are used. Cover the produce while it is being transported to avoid dust contamination when transporting harvested cannabis from the field.

Cleaning Outdoor Crops

Sanitation is something to monitor because of stringent quality controls in the commercial market and user sensitivities for home-grown material. Prevent contamination by using tarps to keep plants from touching the ground. Keep dust to a minimum by spraying down dusty gardens before beginning harvesting.

After picking, some outdoor growers clean their crops with hydrogen peroxide. When the plants are growing in a windy environment, the sticky resins trap and hold dust, dirt, mold spores, and bacteria from the air. Both indoors and out, powdery mildew infections can cover a plant. The solution should be about 0.66%. Drugstore H_2O_2 is a 3% solution. A simple equation can be used to calculate how much water is needed to dilute store-bought H_2O_2 to a desired concentration:

$$M_1 \cdot V_1 = M_2 \cdot V_2$$

M = Molarity (or concentration)

V = Volume

The volume of store-bought H_2O_2 at a concentration of 3% needed to get 1-liter (1,000 mL) of 0.66% H_2O_2 is 222 ml; 222 ml of 3% H_2O_2 and 778 ml of water add up to 1,000 ml of 0.66% H_2O_2.

If the hydrogen peroxide used is greater or less than a 3% solution, adjust the water ratio up or down accordingly. Hydrogen peroxide is the preferred sanitary agent if washing outdoor-grown crops is necessary because it leaves no residue.

Dip the freshly cut branches in the solution. Some growers soak branches for up to 30 minutes. Others just do a quick dip. There has been little research on this method of cleaning. The water will turn a muddy color but will not strip the branches of trichomes or chlorophyll, only the dirt. Immediately set the washed material out to dry. Hanging is best. Use wind and fans to quicken the process.

If hydrogen peroxide is unavailable, a similar cleaning technique can be employed by mixing a ¼ cup (60 ml) of lemon juice and a ½ cup (118 ml) of baking soda in 3.5 gallons (13 l) of water.

Some ways to keep dust to a minimum:

- Outdoors, moisten paths and unpaved roads to settle mud and dust. Cover bare soil with old rugs placed upside down.
- Use enclosed trailers for transporting harvested cannabis in dusty areas.
- Inside drying spaces use air cleaners with UVC lights enclosed that capture particles in filters. The UVC lights kill airborne spores and bacteria.
- Filter incoming air. Particulate filters remove the larger particles. Carbon filters clean the circulating air. They keep the smell down inside the room.
- Keep the surfaces "restaurant clean" by regularly wiping down tables, chairs, prep areas, floors and entrance ways with hydrogen peroxide, isopropyl alcohol, or other disinfectants.
- Keep a filtered wet/dry vacuum handy for use in cleaning debris and messes.
- Cover harvested material to prevent it from picking up dust, fungal spores, or bacteria during transport to drying or processing areas.

Hygiene Rules

1. Use best sanitation practices: wash hands, use hygienic gloves, sweep debris, and clean work areas after each project. Everything—tools, cleaning equipment, storage boxes—should have its own space and be labeled with procedure for use, if necessary. Do the same thing for outgoing material. Everything should be sorted and marked.
2. Process the harvest in a different area than the growing space to avoid contamination by workers and their clothing or tools.
3. No pets should be allowed into the growing or processing areas.

Photo: Kandid Kush

TRIMMING

Trimming, sometimes called manicuring, is the preparation of the bud after it has been cut from the plant. How and when buds are trimmed depends on the grower's goals and strategy. The purpose of trimming is to separate the highest-quality part of the plant, the ripe female flower clusters (buds), from the stems and leaves. Manicuring is one of the final steps in the post-harvest process and is a skilled task that requires training and experience.

Trimming should not be confused with pruning, which is the removal of unwanted vegetation from living plants.

Parts to Be Trimmed

The bud is the plant's jewel. It is a cluster of flowers that grow at the nodes along and at the tip of each branch. The flowers squeeze tightly between and on top of one another, forming thick layers until the entire group is a dense floral mass, also called an inflorescence or raceme.

More than one bud grows on each branch. If buds grow large enough, they grow into each other, forming one continuous group called a "cola." Colas are always found on the outer extremity of the branch. The branch may grow at nearly a 90-degree angle to the plant's stem, although branches of some cultivars grow diagonally or curve up.

Trimming starts with the removal of the buds from the branch (bucking). From that point, the order of the trimming process varies greatly, but to create a fully manicured bud:

- The fan leaves are removed.
- The "sugar" leaves and petioles surrounding the buds are removed.
- Any damaged or contaminated material is removed.

What's left is the manicured bud. Fan leaves contain small amounts of cannabinoids, and "sugar" leaves contain a larger amount. Both are usually saved for extracts, concentrates, and infused-products manufacturing.

Trimming Styles & Strategies

There are many ways to trim. Style and method depend on quantity and quality of the crop, goals, and individual preferences. The biggest difference is between wet and dry trimming. This refers to the condition of the harvested flowers, whether the material still contains the moisture it had as a living plant or whether it has been dried prior to trimming. The pro-

Untrimmed (left) versus trimmed (right) flower buds. Photo: Kandid Kush

cess—whether trimming and then drying, or the reverse—requires preparation. The complexity of planning increases with the size of the crop.

Deleafing is the removal of the large fan leaves before harvesting. This opens up the plant canopy so that light can reach the inner buds, enabling them to grow and ripen faster and develop more potency. Later, harvesting and trimming is easier without the bulky leaves.

In the Field: Wet vs. Dry Trimming

Some growers of large outdoor crops use a combination of wet and dry trimming. They must prepare a temporary space, since it's used only once or twice a year, and have the time or people to cut and handle the harvest. Meanwhile, the trimmers are wet-trimming as fast as they can. Harvested plants and branches can be kept fresh by keeping them at the same temperature as a vegetable crisper: 38–40°F (3–4°C) and 60% relative humidity or higher. Sometimes available trim labor is overwhelmed, and harvested buds are hung to dry. This can allow for dry trimming to occur later and over a more extended timeline, when trim labor is more readily available.

Trimming is a routine that requires time and space; whether the garden is run by one person or is a large enterprise, space and labor are set aside specifically for trimming tasks.

Wet Trimming

Wet trimming is a sticky, time-consuming process, but generally produces higher potency finished buds. This is because it generally separates a lower percentage of trichomes from the buds than dry trimming. Wet trimming is popular with growers who are not concerned with processing their harvest quickly or have limited space to dry their crop. Trimmed flowers take up less space in the drying room. The process of trimming wet flowers takes longer, but if there is an entire team of people standing by, growers may not have the luxury of waiting for the entire crop to dry.

Pros:
- A naked bud takes less time to dry than does a bud surrounded by leaves. This is an advantage if space and time are considerations.
- Wet trichomes are more pliant, so fewer snap off.
- Wet hand-trimming produces plentiful "finger hash," hashish that is ready to be smoked soon after it's removed from workers' gloves or hands.
- The crop is manicured soon after it is cut and is ready for testing and packaging once dried and cured.
- Wet-trimmed buds often have a "tidier" appearance than dry-trimmed buds.

Cons:
- A bud surrounded by leaves is more protected during the drying process.
- Wet hand-trimming is slower than dry trimming.
- In surge situations, the size of the crew may need to be temporarily increased to trim the buds before they wilt.

Dry Trimming

Dry trimming is more popular than wet with some producers because it is faster, but dry trichomes are brittle and break off more easily during trimming. Collect them using screens and trays. This powder, called kief, can be smoked, sprinkled over smokable flowers and into joints, pressed into hash, or used for processing into extracts and infused products. (*See Processing.*)

Pros:
- Dry trimming is faster and easier than wet trimming. In addition to using scissors, gloved hands can simply snap off the dried brittle leaves.
- Surge harvesting is processed more easily, because the only tasks essential to the harvest are to cut the buds, colas, or whole plants and provide them the proper environmental conditions to dry. Buds can be trimmed anytime they are dry. There is no immediate need for large crews working around the clock. A small crew can trim for a longer period after the harvest.

Cons:
- Buds allowed to dry on the stems with leaves attached dry more slowly and take up more space than buds manicured wet and dried on screens.
- More trichomes are lost to handling. Once the trichomes are dry and become brittle, they separate from buds more easily.

Trimming Tips

- Separate the processes of deleafing, bucking (removing the buds), sorting, and trimming. This maximizes efficiency. Personnel can be switched between activities as needed.
- Break the colas along their natural structure and reduce them to buds with no stems sticking out. Buds should be no bigger than 3–4 inches (7–10 cm) in length.
- Holding the stem, roll the bud in the hand to best angle it into the blades before cutting.
- Look for mold or mildew. Diseased leaves are a sign of infection. The biggest, densest, and often most beautiful buds are most susceptible to mold.

Setting Up the Hand-Trim Station

- Light each workstation with bright, non-glaring light.
- Install a clean table and adjustable-height chairs that comfortably place trimmers over the table or use a trimming tray that sits on the lap.
- Use comfortable chairs compatible with the job. They should help the operator face forward toward the work.
- Loud noise and interruptions disturb the workflow. The space should be fairly quiet, except for music, talk radio, or recordings that all can agree on. If that's not possible, individuals should use earbuds.
- The space should be kept neat.
- Sweep and vacuum floors and sanitize surfaces frequently.
- Use carbon filters and air cleaners to keep the air dust-free.
- Trimmers should wear clean clothes and practice proper hygiene such as showering and handwashing. Shower space with clean towels should be available. Inform smelly people to clean up.
- Provide appropriate work gloves and hairnets.

How to Hand Trim

- Use gloves at all times. Trimmers should take care not to touch their eyes and face. Cannabis is nontoxic, but sticky trichomes sting the eyes and may cause skin irritation.
- Place a screen under the trimming area to collect trichomes. Trichomes fall off constantly during handling. Capture them using framed stainless steel mesh or silk screen. Prefabricated screens are available online or are easily made with a 100-micron-thick mesh fastened to a frame.
- Disinfect transport bins and tools with hydrogen peroxide, alcohol, bleach, and hypochlorous acid. This helps prevent proliferation of bacteria and viruses.
- Arrange separate bins for top buds, high mid-grade, less desirable buds, extractable

material, and trash. The other material will be used for processing.

- Clip off the smaller buds (also called larf or popcorn). Place them in their own bin.
- Trim off the smaller, multifingered "sugar leaves" surrounding the buds.
- The bud should now appear almost naked, except for some half-cut leaves sticking out from between the flowers. Watch out for buds that are much bigger than the others. They take longer to finish drying and are more susceptible to mold. They can be dried separately or broken down into smaller buds.
- Collect trichomes from the table or trim bin.
- Scrape finger hash from scissors.
- Clean up.

Useful Trimming Tips

Chairs, Tables & Trays

Chairs and tables affect productivity. View the chair and table as a unit. The chair should be adjustable in height as well as position so that the trimmer's back and shoulders are not hunched over and the arms are at a comfortable height, allowing the hands full mobility. Resin or plastic garden chairs do the exact opposite. Both the seat and the back force the body backward rather than toward the work. Office chairs used by typists are good choices. A jeweler's station is an ideal work area. Chairs made for handwork position the trimmer in a more comfortable, forward position. Lap trim trays are very popular because the operator can sit in a comfortable position with arms vertical from the shoulders rather than splayed out over a table. Trays work well but probably are not as efficient as a good chair-table unit.

Keep Blades Clean

With heavy use, trimming shears and scissors become sticky with plant resins. Trimmers use a variety of around-the-house substances to keep blades clear, including commercial products, isopropyl alcohol, vegetable oils, and pH Up. Keep cups near scissors to soak them or dip them to scrub off the excess hash. Seventy percent isopropyl alcohol (IPA) is a better antimicrobial solution than 99% IPA. The higher concentration of water in the 70% IPA helps catalyze the antimicrobial activity of the alcohol. However, 91% and 99% IPA solutions are better for removing resin from trimming scissors.

Trimming tools should be used only for trimming, as opposed to cloning or pruning, in order to prevent the spread of plant-borne infections.

Best Practices

Hiring Workers

Hire and schedule trimmers. Use personal references and interview trimmers about their relevant experience. Always test the trimmer. Inefficient and negligent trimmers can ruin high-grade cannabis flowers and cost far more than they are worth. Slow trimmers slow the pace of production of faster trimmers who often adjust to a slower pace.

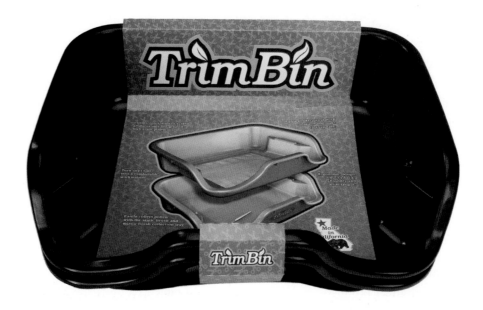

Use a professional work surface: The TrimBin by Harvest-More is sturdy and ergonomically designed to sit atop the worker's lap. It is simple, easy to carry, easy to clean, and promotes organization with various compartments to hold tools. Buds sit atop a stainless steel screen so that trichomes are collected in the plate underneath.

Safety & Comfort

The health and safety of workers is the grower's responsibility. Long-term repetitive work, such as hand trimming, can lead to repetitive stress injuries. It is imperative that trim stations be ergonomic and meet OSHA standards.

Wear gloves, work clothes, appropriate footwear, and goggles when using power equipment. When working near noisy equipment, wear noise filters or headphones that block noise but allow communication with mics and speakers.

Long hair should always be tied back and, along with facial hair, covered with a hat or hair net.

The best lighting sources to use are filtered sunlight coming through windows, skylights, or greenhouses; overhead LEDs or fluorescent lights with a color of about 5,000 kelvin (very similar to sunlight); or table, floor, reading, or workstation lamps that direct light onto the stage where the work is taking place.

Workers should take a break every two hours or less and not skip bathroom breaks or meals. Water and other hydration should be available and close by at all times.

All drinking water should be certified potable water.

Injuries from repetitive stress lead to chronic pain and permanent damage. Anyone who feels significant muscle stress or fatigue should be relieved of duty before they strain their muscles or sustain a more significant injury.

Worker Health

Anyone on the job who develops an allergic reaction to any part of the plant or its dust should not work on the site. An individual's health is worth more than a paycheck.

The most typical allergic reactions that are expressed physically are bumps or rashes, flushing, and a hoarse voice. Much rarer symptoms that need emergency treatment are trouble breathing, feeling lightheaded, or fainting. These symptoms are external manifestations of inflammation and/or anaphylaxis. Internally other body parts, including organs, may also be affected.

Trim Temperature

Trimming should be done at a clean, climate-controlled, comfortable trimming station. Keep the temperature at 65-70°F (18–21°C) to prevent terpene volatilization. Maintain humidity at about 55–60%. Workers might feel chilled—provide sweatshirts of different sizes.

Some growers choose to trim outdoors. Trim when the temperature is cool rather than hot and with little wind so that the buds aren't contaminated with dust. Don't leave plants, buds, or trim in direct sunlight, which rapidly degrades cannabinoids. Use micro-emitters to cool the area, and keep dust down by spraying dry soil.

Varieties of Trimmers & Clippers

Bonsai Pruner, Bud and Leaf Trimmer

Squeezer steel scissors made before 74 CE have been recovered from Pompeii. The metal had to be tempered because they were meant to be pushed in and then returned to the open position. This is a modern version manufactured in 2016. It is just four inches (10 cm) long, with razor-sharp stainless steel blades, spring action, and a delicate handle.

Wiss Clips

The Wiss Clip is a 4.75-inch (12 cm) stainless steel scissor with sharp point blades that are replaceable. It has spring action and a heavy-duty contoured design with industrial PVC plastic handles.

Fiskars

Fiskars have a spring-action, symmetrical, soft-grip handle that works with right- and left-handed users. These are the most popular hand-trimming scissors.

Chicamasa Curved Blade Sap-Resistant Garden Scissors

These scissors are made of the highest-quality stainless steel, with a true curved blade and sap-resistant Florin coating to prevent buildup.

Handheld Machine Trimmers

Electric scissors save hands, wrists, and arms from repetitive stress while maintaining much of the control and the gentleness of hand trimming. About a dozen different types of electrical scissors and clippers are on the market.

Advantages:

- Saves hands
- Doesn't tire
- Prevents repetitive injuries
- Faster

Disadvantages:

- There is a learning curve. Training is required.
- May not be as thorough as a hand trim.
- Machine trimmers require slightly more maintenance than scissors.
- The up-front cost is higher than for manual scissors.

Bucking Machines

Bucking machines automate the process of removing buds from the stock. They can increase productivity by about 50%—some bucking machines can process up to 150 pounds (68 kg) of material per hour. To use a bucking machine, insert the cut end of a branch into the appropriately sized hole. As soon as the branch is inserted, the bucker grabs it and pulls it through the machine, stripping the buds from the stock. Bucking machines have variable speeds to process either wet or dry material. The machine can typically be cleaned with an alcohol spray or a heated pressure washer.

To maintain high-quality flower while bucking wet, two factors need to be managed, temperature and freshness. When it comes to temperature, the cooler the better. Indoor growers may consider turning the lights off and the air conditioning up in the garden the day before harvest. For outdoor growers, avoid harvesting in the middle of the day; try to harvest early in the morning when temperatures are cooler.

When wet bucking, it's very important that the cannabis be as fresh as possible. Cannabis that sits too long between the chop and the bucking machine and has started to wilt can be damaged by the bucking machine. Freshness allows the buds to remain stiff and pop off the stem better as opposed to getting smashed.

The two most important factors for good results while dry bucking is the moisture content of the cannabis and the speed of the machine. The machine should be operated slower, typically the first third of the speed range. When overly dried plants are bucked using a machine, flowers will crumble and fall apart. The big stems and the little stems still need to be pliable so that they can fold, go through the machine, and get stripped.

Munch Machine bucking machines are the industry standard. They are gentle on flowers and come with variable speed control to allow for damage-free bucking on wet or dry cannabis. The superior grip and power allow one Mother Bucker to average 150 pounds (68 kg) per hour when bucking wet, or 37 pounds (~17 kg) per hour when bucking dry. Some users have achieved 250 pounds (113 kg) per hour wet. All equipment is easy to clean and utilizes FDA food-grade materials, coatings, and lubricants to meet current Good Manufacturing Standards.

Mechanize & Automate

Manicuring is a skilled but tedious task. Outdoors it is seasonal, creating bulges in demand for labor for several months. Indoors, full-time, it is monotonous. In a high-powered, automated production system, hand manicuring is expensive and labor intensive. Professional manicurists can trim one to three pounds (0.5–1.5 kg) wet or two to four pounds (1–1.8 kg) dry in an eight-hour workday, depending on cultivar, bud size and shape, and desired trim style. Trim machines can process many times that and are quickly changing the economics of this stage of cannabis processing.

When the first machines were released, cultivators faced the decision of using a machine that simplified processing and saved time and labor at the expense of some cosmetic loss. This is no longer as much of a consideration because newer models are gentler on the buds. Even the gentlest machine trim will result in some trichome loss on the surface of the bud; it's just a matter of how much. Remember, even the best human trimmers also lose surface glands.

Why Machine Trim?

Machine trimming is most efficient for processing commercial and larger-scale gardens. They can be used for all grades of flowers, including top shelf.

Some machines handle top-shelf flowers better than all but the best hand trimmers. Machine trimming has been overly maligned, especially when taking into consideration that the work of human trimmers varies in both quantity and quality. Many trimmers do a lower-quality trim at a far higher cost than a good machine. Even the best human trimmer tires after several hours, let alone several days or weeks on the job. By contrast, a well-maintained machine treats the millionth bud as nicely as the first.

Tight buds are the best candidates for automatic processing machines. The most common type of trimming machines are tumblers, which come in many models. The new models are very gentle and can trim even top-shelf material. The pitch or angle is adjustable, slowing or speeding up the pace at which the buds tumble through the machine. Spending less time in the machine results in a "looser" trim, leaving on more of the tight trim leaf around the bud. Touch-up trimming is sometimes required, but the bud retains more of its trichomes with a loose trim. Automated trimming machines allow for quicker processing in the stage of cannabis production that requires the most labor and attention.

Automating the manicuring of smaller or looser buds is best done using tools that assist the hand trimmer and are mostly operated electrically but are manually controlled. These tools use the operator's skill but eliminate the tediousness of scissors.

The space and time savings of trimming wet with machines adds up quickly. Plants can be cut down with power tools and trimmed faster with machine trimmers than is possible by hand. Trimmers are usually designed to cut either wet or dry buds, although a few can process both. Before choosing, make a basic harvest plan.

The downside of machine trimming dried buds is that the buds are brittle, so trichomes snap off easily when manipulated. Dry trimmers are designed to capture trichomes that break off. Several different designs are available, including tumblers and grill or slider models that don't move the buds around as much. Dry-trim machine advocates say that buds trimmed fully dry both smell and taste better than buds trimmed wet.

State regulations set thresholds on microbiological contamination of cannabis flowers and other products. Wet machine trimming may increase the likelihood of contamination because bacteria counts can build up in wet trimmers that are not cleaned and decontaminated regularly. Contamination spreads easily when the buds come in contact with bacteria. This is much less likely to happen when buds are trimmed dry or when machines are properly sanitized between each harvest batch.

Choosing the Right Machine

Aside from wet versus dry trimming capability, there are other ways to differentiate machines.

- Does the device assist the hand trimmer, or does it do the work?
- Will the buds be cut wet or dry? Grill-style trimmers are used for dry buds. The grill slides back and forth, opening and closing; this movement catches and cuts the leaves from the bud, leaving them trimmed without much agitation. Trim bags are designed for use with dried buds. These are cloth tumblers that are shaken. The tumble gently agitates the leaves, causing them to break away from the buds.
- How many workers does the device need? The tumbler and spinner machines for wet buds do the trimming, and the operators attend to the machine, feeding it and removing finished product. The amount of production from these machines depends on the number of workers operating it.

Return on Investment

Some people see a large price tag on a machine trimmer and are put off. One successful grower wrote: "Don't think in dollars; think in pounds. A $3,000 machine is worth a few pounds of top shelf trimmed buds and does the daily work of a team of hand trimmers. In just the first day of using the trimmer it more than paid for itself as compared to using manual trimmers."

The Plant's Role in Effective Machine Trimming

The plant's shape, density, and moisture levels affect machines' performance. Dense buds sustain less damage than light, airy buds that have lots of peaks and valleys, or undeveloped larf buds.

Slow the machine's speed to trim airy buds. Dense buds with prominent sugar leaves can be trimmed at a faster speed without damage. The size of the load the machine is fed affects the trim. Test to see how large a load the trimmer can handle without overloading and damaging buds.

Machine Trimming Tips

- Remove excessive stems and twigs before wet or dry trimming. Break apart big and asymmetrical buds.
- Hang-dry plants destined for dry machine trimming. If they are dried on trays or screens, they should be turned every other day or they can flatten out, making it difficult for machines to process.
- Not all varieties or all types of bud from a single cultivar are suitable for a single trimming machine. Loose, airy sativas are not as compatible with some models as dense indicas and indica hybrids.

The GreenBroz Model M Lite Dry Trimmer is designed to closely mimic the act of hand trimming while increasing the consistency and efficiency of the harvesting process. The M Lite Dry Trimmer is gentle, quick and capable of processing two to four pounds (0.9 to 1.8 kg) per hour. The patented blade design allows for the gentle rolling of the flower to maintain the natural curves and preserve the trichomes.

Unlike the trimmer assist machines, which increase the speed that the trimmers are able to process buds with tumblers and grates, the processing speed is determined largely by the number of people attending to the machine. Aside from bucking, in which the buds are removed from the stem, up to five people can attend to the machine, so the tumbler or grate is constantly processing. With fewer people, the machine may run empty, lessening its efficiency.

Using Small Dry Trimming Machines

This tumbler trimmer method requires a team of one to five people. With each added person the efficiency increases because the machine is working a greater percentage of the time.

- The branches or colas are cut from the plants and placed in bins.
- The buds are removed from the branches using a bucking machine and fall into another basket.
- The bins are transported to a room cooled to 40–45°F (4–7°C), where they are stored.
- Buds are fed into the tumbler and fall into a waiting basket.
- The basket is taken into the drying room, and the buds are placed on trays or screen racks.

The bladeless technology of Tom's Tumbler works fast while preserving the flowers' structure and trichomes. The PYTHON can dry trim up to 1,200 pounds (544 kg) an hour. The weight of the flowers and their friction against each other are utilized to gently trim, rather than risk slicing up buds or damaging trichomes. Tumblers are available in a range of sizes to meet any grower's needs and are customizable.

Tips

- Wet trim before the flowers begin to wilt and lose their turgidity.
- Dry trim at 10–16% moisture, no more or less. Common moisture meters help ascertain the approximate dampness of buds. Using moisture meters requires a learning curve and should be used consistently for consistent results.
- Optimal feeding speeds vary by variety and environmental conditions. Test speeds and angles for each batch.
- Run the machine flat and slowly increase the angle to adjust the throughput speed. Assess the results and determine the best angle for the specific job. Don't run too steep.

Troubleshooting

Unripe Harvest

If the harvest must be trimmed early in the season, there will be fewer mature, dense buds and a higher proportion of small buds and sugar leaves. If only a small percentage of the buds are grade A and most are loose, not only are they bad candidates for machine trimming because they will get sliced up in the trimmer, but they may not be worth trimming at all. They may be best used for making concentrates.

Lubricants & Anti-sticking Agents

Some trimmers require lubrication of their cutting surfaces and moving parts. Cannabis resin is sticky and easily gums up machines, so some machine-trimmed cannabis will have a tiny amount of residual oil on it. A few trimmers run without oil. Use food-grade oils and minimize their use to avoid contamination.

GREENBROZ

540

AUTOMATION

By Clayton Stewart

It may sound like a daunting task to harvest over 2,200 pounds (~100 kg) from 800 to 900 plants and return the site to clean and sanitized, in less than 24 hours, but with the right type of automation and labor efficiency, savvy commercial growers do this on a daily basis.

Compared with the preceding cultivation stages, the harvesting stage is labor-intensive and often involves many bottlenecks in human processing capabilities. When harvesting hundreds to thousands of plants, even the distance and time spent traveling between the garden and harvesting spaces reduces efficiency.

Automating Climate

For drying and curing rooms, strategically placed probes can provide information on temperature and humidity.

Climate monitoring equipment such as Bluetooth and Wi-Fi-enabled hygrometers are indispensable tools for remote viewing and historical tracking of relative humidity and temperature data in the drying room. These wireless hygrometers, although more expensive than conventional digital ones, offer users the option to view and track environmental criteria without disturbing drying, curing, or storage containers or the need to be in the drying room. With a typical temperature accuracy of ±2°F (~1°C) and relative humidity accuracy of ±3%, these tools are best applied when combined with controls for HVAC, humidification, and dehumidification.

In commercial settings with multiple units working in concert to regulate environmental set points, it is critical to have an understanding of fresh-product, moisture-load expectations, that is, how much water must be removed from the atmosphere to facilitate drying, and to communicate these specifications to HVAC engineers for proper sizing and calibration of the dehumidification and humidification units.

In the process of cooling air, air conditioners remove moisture and provide additional dehumidification. Low humidity can be corrected by pausing dehumidification. The relative humidity rises naturally through the transpiration of water vapor from the plant material.

Propagation

Propagation is a baby cannabis plant's chance at becoming a mature, fruit-bearing female, and typically requires a steady human hand to select a suitable cutting for cloning, or ger-

The Growlink Platform virtually connects all the technology in the cultivation space. Nearly every device and system in the cultivation space is controlled by the grower in ways that are intuitive and easy to use from the Growlink mobile app. Growlink captures valuable crop-level data using custom wireless mesh canopy sensors to drive yields, reduce losses, optimize irrigation, prevent disease, and reduce energy consumption. Growlink unlocks the potential of connected equipment, making climate systems easier to use, irrigation efficient, and sustainable and nutrient delivery precise and effortless. The system comes with 24/7 support, on-site commissioning, and training.

minate a seed, or cultivate tissue in nutrient culture. Micropropagation is a more precise method of stem propagation by which a thumb-nail-size tissue cutting is collected and cultivated in a petri dish. Minimal changes to infrastructure to include laminar flow hoods and HEPA-filtered HVAC can provide a sufficiently clean environment for tissue culture propagation to reap the benefits of reduced chance of microbial infection, reduced labor, and reduced space requirements.

Jack Ford of Agronomix Software, a company that helps plant breeders, crop researchers, and agronomists with yield increases and data management, says of its latest transplant robot: "With simple automation during propagation, a grower could experience a 25% gain in production. Automating the full process could lead to a 50 to 70% gain in efficiency" (*Greenhouse Canada Magazine*, June 14, 2019).

Labor, Time & Space Saving Tools

To eliminate most of the aisles in an indoor garden, growers rely on a rolling pallet bench, also referred to as a Dutch tray table system. While the legs of the table remain in place, the top rolls from side to side. Most of the time the tabletops are next to each other. But there is enough room for an aisle when the top is rolled to one side. To make the next aisle, the next tabletop is moved. Single aisles provide more canopy space and ensure that all light reaches the plants.

Portable conveyor belts are easy to set up and save labor by transporting equipment, plants, tools, and other items from one location to another without the use of labor. For instance, buds or branches can go directly from the harvest room to the processing center without people or vehicles transporting it. It may allow for elimination of walkways.

Picking

Harvesting operations are completely dependent on site conditions, plant spacing, cultivar(s), growth method (with/without trellis), plant size, and total plot area.

To automate equipment for harvesting while avoiding unnecessary downstream processing, the more centralized the buds are toward the top of the plant, the better. This allows for the efficient separation of the colas from the stalks and branches.

Bucking

In an industrial setting, rack drying on perforated baking-style sheets is more time efficient than hang-drying whole plants with their woody stalks and branches still attached.

First, buckers are used to separate the buds from the stalks. This eliminates the first bottleneck of harvesting. Automated buckers come equipped with hoppers that catch and funnel the buds to a desired location. Horizontal and incline step conveyors can take over from that point to direct the buds toward a series of trimming machines. Wherever there is no conveyor, simple transport utilities such as pallet jacks, loadable carts, trolleys, or lightweight electric utility vehicles can move bins of product. "Hand-bombing" and handling buds more than once during the harvest process are known contributors to inefficiencies in the industrial harvest department.

> Pre-bucking, post-bucking, and pre-trimming are excellent times for identifying botrytis or other bud defects. Quality control lines provide a hands-on check so that affected buds can be rejected.

Sorting for Defects

Blueberry grading machines such as The Berry Class by Elifab Solutions use proprietary software to optically recognize defects in blueberries with up to 96% accuracy. This type of technology is adaptable to the cannabis industry and could automatically recognize mold- and fungus-affected buds during the processing of large harvests.

Sanitation

UVC light exposure is another effective way to reduce bioburden and treat surface pathogens such as powdery mildew, which can contribute to a host of other problems. UVC light exposure works by degrading microorganisms' DNA. Aeon CleanLight, a company based out of the Netherlands specializing in UVC disinfection technology, currently offers a ballast system for industrial grow rooms that delivers effective doses of ultraviolet light without harming the plants.

Large-Scale Drying & Curing

During the drying and curing stages, regulation of temperature (heating/air conditioning), relative humidity (humidification/dehumidification), and air circulation is paramount.

Thus, a purpose-built cannabis drying and curing chamber requires all the aforementioned components, as well as Good Manufacturing Practice (GMP) design and compliance, in order to compete with conventional drying and curing spaces in industrial settings.

Systems such as the Cannatrol Dry/Cure Box, Darwin Chamber, and Conviron Walk-In Room offer custom-designed chambers that can effectively reduce drying and curing times by actively managing temperature, airflow, and vapor pressure to encourage the consistent removal of moisture and preserve terpenes. This can allow users to home in on specific repeatable settings, depending on the cultivar. It is important to work with reliable engineer recommendations to determine the installation and calibration of these systems, as their performance will directly depend on the load and frequency of product being introduced.

Another technological application similar to these custom-designed chambers is the radiant energy vacuum dehydration (REV) system, which uses microwave energy and vacuum pressure to heat water and evaporate water molecules while retaining terpene content. Manufacturers claim the process is complete in several hours, with an output of about 26 pounds (12 kg) per hour of ready-to-use dried product.

Kiln Drying

Kiln drying is a technique used in large-scale commercial cultivation of a variety of herbs and agricultural products, such as lumber, tobacco, herbs, and cannabis. Kiln drying is utilized efficiently by hemp-flower growers, who are not interested in preserving terpenes. The primary advantage of kiln drying is the capacity to dry large quantities quickly in an enclosed space with controlled heat and rapidly circulating air, using temperatures up to 95°F (35°C). However, these high drying temperatures result in the loss of terpenes.

Freeze Drying

The Cryo Cure machine uses freeze-drying to rapidly and consistently preserve up to 1,200 pounds (~545 kg) of fresh flowers with no shrinkage, intensified color and flavor, and stabilized THC, terpenes, and trichomes in just a day, making it a great companion for live extract processing.

Processing Pre-Rolls

While a lot of commercial cannabis is destined to be sold in flower form, increasingly more large-scale producers have moved into automated processing of pre-rolled joints. Hand-rolling joints is laborious and time-consuming. Using automation, whole big buds, smalls, and shake is run through bulk grinders and packed into hundreds of cones in a matter of minutes.

Cryo Cure's cannabis- and hemp-curing machines utilize patent pending freeze-drying technology to remove the desired amount of moisture from flower or trim. The results are perfectly preserved flowers with no shrinkage, intensified color and flavor, and stabilized cannabinoids, terpenes, and trichomes. On the right are Cryo Cured cannabis flowers, on the left are traditionally cured. Photo: Bruce Gates Photography

Because Cryo Cure can process large quantities of flower in as little as 24 hours, it eliminates the need for curing and drying spaces. Large quantities of flower go in the tray and come out perfectly cured and and ready to consume hours later. Ed Rosenthal pictured. Photo: Tim Imbriaco

STM Canna's RocketBox Pre-Roll Machine packs 453 joints in 60 seconds or up to tens of thousands of joints per day. The RocketBox produces precise, consistent, and repeatable results using proprietary Smart Density software to measure and achieve weight accuracy. It is durable, built for long-term use, easy to use, and compatible with 84, 98, and 109 mm cones.

The STM Canna Revolution Grinder is designed specifically for cannabis to minimize terpene and cannabinoid loss, and processes 15–30 pounds (6–13.5 kg) of dry flower per hour without whipping or blending the flower into dust. Auto-blade oscillation creates scissor-like cuts that produce consistent, homogeneous grind for pre-rolls and extraction. The Revolution Grinder includes interchangeable fine and coarse particle screens, optimal for pre-rolls and extraction.

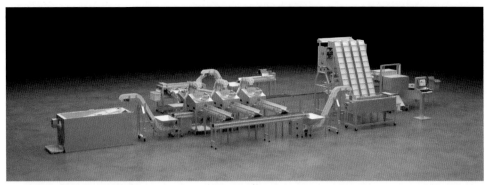

For the first time, commercial cannabis and hemp flower producers fully automate the harvesting process using the GreenBroz end-to-end system. Buds are bucked, sorted, trimmed, and alternately packaged in pre-measured weights, ground, and fed into a joint packing machine and/or directed into the tunnel sifter for kief all through the automation controlled and customized by the grower.

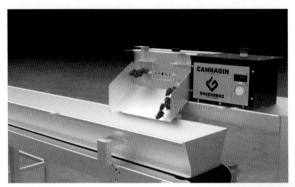

The buds start their journey through the end-to-end system as dried buds on stems. The base of the stems are fed into the CannaGin Destemmer, which bucks the buds from the stem and guides them to the conveyor belt that delivers them to the next step. The CannaGin Destemmer can process multiple stems at once. Each stainless steel shearing door can be adjusted for pressure and speed by the operator for customized precision.

The Rise Conveyor connects machines and processes in this customizable end-to-end system and is compatible with all other GreenBroz automation systems. The buds are moved with precision through continued and metered feeding. The Rise Conveyor holds up to 15 pounds (6.8 kg) and when paired with the sorter can process that quantity in seven minutes.

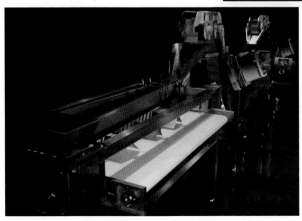

The Rise Conveyor guides the buds to the GreenBroz Precision Sorter, which gently sorts the buds through the gradually farther spaced steel slats. Smalls, mids, and large buds are each guided either into catch containers or the next step in the automated harvest process. Quick, precise sorting means less manual handling. The digital HMI allows the operator to control the speed of the conveyor and the bands' distance on the machine. The digital HMI also provides access to support materials, tech support, and additional machine settings.

Hanging Buds on a DriFlower Rack
Photo: Jordan Goss

DRYING, CURING & STORING

Properly grown, dried, and cured flowers burn smoothly and taste flavorful. The smell and flavor come from the terpenes and flavonoids in the buds. Terpenes also contribute to the cultivar's specific effects. Cannabinoids have no odor.

Using most methods, for quality dried and cured buds, think "low and slow." Drying and curing flowers takes time and patience, but the finished buds are worth the wait.

"Low" refers to temperature. Terpenes evaporate at different temperatures, and some slightly below room temperature. When the air is fragrant with flower odors, the buds are losing their terpenes. Improperly dried and cured buds lose terpenes due to evaporation.

For example, the terpene myrcene—found in mango fruit, hops, bay leaves, eucalyptus, lemongrass, and cannabis—volatizes at just 68°F (20°C). Flowers must be dried at low temperatures for the terpenes to be preserved. Drying at low temperatures and moderate humidity takes longer, hence "low and slow."

Keeping the area clean is imperative when slowly drying buds at low temperatures. No animals are allowed in the area because they shed fur and dander that become airborne and catch on sticky buds.

Workers should wear gloves, hair, and beard nets. Fungal spores are ubiquitous and germinate under favorable conditions: moisture, oxygen, and temperatures between 50 and 70°F (10–21°C), and a mildly acidic surface. Bacteria also prefer moisture, warm temperatures, and a neutral pH.

Buds infected with powdery mildew are considered unfit for consumption. Hydrogen peroxide baths remove powdery mildew. (*See Picking.*) Smoking has not been implicated in any human ailments, but some people may be especially sensitive to inhaling mold.

Buds attacked by bacteria turn brown and crispy. When anaerobic bacteria attack, they emit an acrid ammonia gas and turn buds to mush.

Under cool conditions the plant's cells can stay alive for several days after cutting. It is theorized that during the early part of drying, the plant consumes some of its store of water and carbohydrates. Dried too fast, the buds use fewer starches, resulting in a harsher smoke. Cells on the surface of the plant die first, and the ones farther inside die last. During the first stage of drying, water loss is rapid. At the same time, some of the chlorophyll degrades, creating a smooth smoke. Buds dried slowly and then cured for a few weeks develop the smooth draw of fine herb.

It is hypothesized that a slow drying process, coupled with low to no light conditions, promotes a more thorough breakdown of the plant's primary metabolites such as chlorophyll. These compounds decompose into their congregate parts (sugars, aldehydes, etc.). Then they are available to aerobic bacteria to metabolize during the cure process. The secondary metabolites and compounds resulting from their breakdown add to a harsher smoke, which is why their removal via aerobic bacterial metabolism results in a smoother smoke.

Degraded THC

Heat and light degrade THC into cannabinol (CBN), which has only a fraction of the psychotropic effect and induces sleepiness. When buds, especially large ones, are dried at high temperatures to speed the process, they dry unevenly. By the time the inner portion is dry, some of the THC on the outer portion has turned to CBN.

The Hot Fast Dry

Ocimene Kush by Greenshock Farms
Photo: Mendo Dope

Cultivators are using a wide range of methods, theories, and strategies to dry cannabis. Sometimes these theories are in conflict with one another or accepted science and practice. Further testing and research will determine which methods are best for which cultivators and cultivars and why. A hot and fast dry is one method that seemingly goes against what is known about cannabis, but some growers swear by it.

At Greenshock Farms, plants are hung to dry and then the temperature is raised to 84°F (29°C) and humidity lowered to 30% for two days. Once the plants are bone-dry, the buds are bucked from the branches. This should be done where it is slightly cooler and more humid so that the buds don't lose resin.

Next, the untrimmed buds are put into paper bags for three to four days. Finally, they are stored, sugar leaves on, in freezer bags until it is time to sell them. They say this process speeds up the drying process, allows for a longer storage, and keeps buds greener and fresher. Before they go to market, buds are given a quick water spray to moisten.

They say it is crucial to the process to treat everything delicately so that the flowers are not bruised and the trichomes remain unbroken.

Small-Scale Drying

The drying needs of a small-scale grower are the same as those of a large-scale grower, but climate control is less of a challenge.

Climate-Controlled Drying Chamber

Create a climate-controlled drying chamber in a grow tent, small room, or closet. A small room or a closet is likely to have the right temperature for drying. Add a hygrometer connected to a small dehumidifier, or ventilation in low-humidity situations, and a thermostat regulating a heater or air conditioner.

Drying in a Bag

A brown paper bag is a simple way to keep humidity higher than the humidity in a room and works by slowing evaporation. Recirculate humidity by opening or closing the bag. To keep the humidity lower, place only two or three layers of big buds in the bag and use a hygrometer to measure the moisture level. If the humidity climbs above 55%, open the bag and use a fan to remove moisture-laden air from the space.

Dry on Racks or Screens

The advantage of rack or screen drying is that air flows freely around the buds. Use fans to circulate air and shorten drying time. Rotate buds every two days to prevent flattening.

Not a Drying Space

Don't dry buds in a room with growing plants or in bathrooms because the conditions are incompatible. The result may be mold attacks and loss of potency, color, and quality.

Buds should not be dried in an enclosed container such as a closed box, plastic container, or jar that traps air. As the buds dry, humidity in the container builds up, and water is likely to condense on the sides of the container, increasing the relative humidity. These are ideal conditions for mildews, molds, and bacteria to thrive.

Mold and mildew are likely to attack in closed containers, causing rot (botrytis) and molds. The fungi and aerobic bacteria use up the oxygen. Anaerobic bacteria, which thrive in a nonoxygen environment, flourish. Their telltale sign is the acrid odor of ammonia they emit.

Molds, mildews, and bacteria have a devastating effect on potency and quality. The distinctive odors of the plant diminish and the cannabis smells earthier.

Steps to Drying

1. Clean the space to be used for drying. If it has been used for harvests before, wipe it clean with a hydrogen peroxide, bleach, hypochlorous acid, or other disinfecting solution or just spray the whole space using it. This decreases microorganisms on surfaces. To keep air free from mold spores, hang a UVC sterilizing light.
2. Use an air conditioner and a heater to maintain a temperature of about 60–65°F

(15–18°C) in the drying area. The most volatile terpene, myrcene, evaporates at 68°F (20°C). Set the humidifier or dehumidifier to 50–60% relative humidity. When RH is higher than 60%, the germination and growth of fungi and bacteria on wet material proliferates. Humidity below 50% promotes faster drying, but at that humidity buds have a tendency to dry on the outside while the inside remains moist and produces brittle flowers that result in a harsh smoke. Growers have different climate recipes for temperature and humidity and sometimes adjust temperature throughout the drying process

3. Turn on oscillating circulation fans to keep air moving throughout the space. It is important to keep the air in the drying room flowing over the buds.

4. When drying buds or branches on screens, rotate the buds every other day because gravity flattens them and they won't work well in trimming machines.

5. Monitor the buds during the drying process. This process can last from a few days to three weeks; 5–10 days is optimal. Don't let temperatures get too low or drying will be prolonged. Bud size, crop weight, crop moisture, ambient temperature, and humidity all affect drying time.

Keep the Equipment Clean

It is important to clean equipment in the drying room frequently because fungi and bacteria can colonize air conditioning units, humidifiers, and dehumidifiers. Remove and clean the filter and spray the interior with a 3% hydrogen peroxide or other sanitizing solution. Allow all parts to dry before reassembling.

When Are Flowers Dry Enough?

When the buds first start to dry, they may smell more like hay or freshly mown grass than fragrant flowers. When the plant is cut, it releases stress chemicals called green leaf volatiles (GLVs), which are the same stress-related chemicals lawn grass releases when it is mowed. As the buds dry, they lose color and weight and become more brittle. The green color fades a bit as chlorophyll degrades, making yellow, brown, red, and purple hues more prominent.

Buds are ready for curing when they have reached 10–13% inner moisture. Handheld moisture probes can be used to determine approximate dryness. Because these meters are designed for use with wood and drywall and not cannabis flowers, they require some experience to get accurate readings. Err on the side of caution before container curing or packaging buds for storage.

Without the use of a moisture meter, it can be determined that the first stage of drying is complete when buds feel dry on the outside but retain moisture inside that keeps them pliable. Take an average-size bud and slowly try to fold it in half. If the base of the bud's stem is dry and bends without retracting or snaps, it is ready to cure. Another way of subjectively judging readiness is by lighting up a thinly rolled joint. If it doesn't go out between puffs, then it is ready for curing and storing.

Buds on whole plants take a longer time to dry than on cut branches and drying trays/ screens because there's more vegetation and thus more water to evaporate. Big, thick, dense buds take much longer to dry than smaller buds and are more susceptible to mold and powdery mildew.

Drying Outdoors

Drying outdoors is not ideal; however, it may be necessary in some situations.

The main factors that affect outdoor drying are the same as indoors: temperature and humidity. However, dealing with these factors outdoors is more complicated because humidity and temperature vary over the course of a day. Starting in the morning at sunrise, the day begins to heat, drying any dew that sets during the evening. Heat accumulates until midafternoon, when the temperature drops, increasing relative humidity and the chance that dew will fall. Even in areas with small rises and drops, there may be danger during the hottest part of the day and then again as dew drips onto the plants.

Keep plants away from the sun's heating rays using white reflective material that bounces rather than absorbs the light.

In the shade: Provided that the ambient temperature and humidity stay in a moderate range—50–68°F (10–20°C) and 40–60% RH, plants can be dried outdoors. Buds that experience wider temperature variation lose many more terpenes than those dried in a smaller cooler temperature range. The evening humidity and temperature are critical. Moisture from dew promotes infections. An area exposed to dew is unsuitable for drying unless a dehumidifier is used to eliminate the moisture. Another possibility is to maintain temperature at 68°F (20°C) using a heater; electric heaters are best because they do not emit moisture or particulates, decreasing RH. When the temperature rises with no increase in the water content of the air, humidity decreases.

In a covered area with no sidewalls: An outdoor area that is covered and has no sidewalls is suitable for drying, provided the temperature and humidity stay within range. White roofs reflect light, so they stay cool. Fans are needed to exchange air and to prevent dew from forming on the leaves.

Quick Drying

There are several methods to dry cannabis quickly for testing, but none will yield high-quality, well-dried buds. However, fast-dried buds are an indication of what to expect once the rest of the harvest is dried. Fast-dried buds retain their minty chlorophyll taste and have a harsh smoke.

- Place the buds in the microwave for 30 seconds or longer so that some of the moisture is removed, and then lower the power to 2 and dry the buds until dry enough to test. Microwaves kill seeds, so they should be removed before microwaving.

- Food dehydrators fast-dry buds, but many of the terpenes evaporate in the elevated temperature. They never get very hot, so the THC remains but many of the flavors dissipate. This method also kills seeds.
- A small bud is placed on top of a warm appliance such as a computer or refrigerator.
- Cannabis should be dried in an oven on the lowest setting. Even so, the heat will evaporate many of the terpenes before the buds are dried. Set the temperature at 100°F (38°C) if possible. This may kill seeds.

Rehydrating Overdried Buds

There are plenty of myths and old-fashioned methods for rehydrating overdried buds. One calls for placing fresh tortillas or fruit in a sealed container with the buds so they can absorb the moisture from them. This is unsanitary.

Either put the buds in a climate-controlled room with humidity increased to about 70% or use a tea kettle to add steam to a Rubbermaid container full of buds and close the lid tightly. Leave the steam in the container for a couple of hours. Check the buds to determine if they are remoistened enough or if they are too moist and need to be dried again.

Using a paper towel that is slightly moistened can add moisture into the environment that the flowers are stored in. Be sure not to allow the buds to come in contact with the paper towel. Place the wet towel in an open container inside a cure tote to increase the humidity and add some moisture back to the bud.

Although hydration packs are primarily used for maintaining appropriate water content in dried flowers that will be stored for longer periods of time, they can also be used to rehydrate overdried buds. Returning moisture to overdried buds with a moisture packet will not improve a cure. However, moisture packs can be used to rehydrate buds that will soon be consumed.

These methods cannot salvage buds that have lost their terpenes due to overdrying.

Curing

The vast majority of water is removed during the first phase of drying. This usually happens within 5 to 10 days. The second phase, removing more water while more evenly distributing the remaining moisture and retaining the terpenes, is known as curing. It is analogous to the tobacco curing process, in that it uses a precise climate and time to bring out the aromas of the plant.

Curing is essential to the taste and experience of the finished buds. Like aged wines, well-cured buds are smooth and flavorful. Uncured buds still "work" but are not nearly as enjoyable or desirable. Some buds sold commercially are not cured, just dried.

Curing does not make buds more potent than they already are.

Keys to Curing:

1. Start with mostly dried buds or colas. Buds should feel dry to the touch yet remain slightly spongy when squeezed. The stems at the base of each bud should break or snap when bent, while the bud's inner stem should remain lightly pliable.

2. Place initially dried buds into an enclosed container or bag, filling it about three quarters of the way and leaving space for air at the top. Some cultivators use glass jars or plastic or stainless steel bins, and others use paper bags.

3. Leave curing buds in closed containers to allow capillary action to wick the inner moisture from their cores. This will cause the inner buds to dry slightly and the outer surface area to remoisten slightly while evaporating some of the moisture into the air of the curing container or bag.

4. This evaporation increases the relative humidity of the air in the container, which must be "burped" periodically. Steps to burping the curing container:
   - Open the container.
   - Smell the off-gassing air to ensure that the buds retain their sweet and/or skunky aroma. If there is even a slight musty odor, pour the buds out and allow them to air dry for another 24 hours before restarting the curing process.
   - Feel the buds. They should begin to feel more evenly moist but still dry to the touch and lightly spongy. If they feel overly moist or soggy, pour them out and allow them to air dry for 12-24 hours before restarting the curing process.
   - Gently rotate the buds, so that the buds at the top of the curing container are mixed with the buds from the bottom of the container. Rough handling damages resin glands.
   - Close the container.

5. Sweating or condensation indicates high humidity, not only on the container's interior, but also on the buds. Invariably, with even mild sweating, aerobic bacteria become active and can change the aroma and taste.

6. Burping should occur more frequently in early curing and less frequently in late curing. It is recommended to burp at least:
   - Once per day during the first week of curing.
   - Two to three times per week during the second week of curing.
   - Once per week for week three and beyond.

7. The room containing these curing containers or bags should be climate-controlled, with consistent temperature and relative humidity, so that when burped, the moist air escapes the curing container and is replaced by cooler, drier air.
   - Temperature: 60–65°F (15–18°C)
   - Humidity: 50–60%
   - Create continuous circulation using oscillating and/or ceiling fans on low.
   - Keep it dark. Bright light, especially ultraviolet light, degrades cannabinoids and terpenes. Curing buds should sit in low light to total darkness.

8. Curing time: One week to two months, before placing into storage.

9. By the end of the cure, all hay-like odors should be gone and terpenes should be prominent. A bud's pigments are expressed more without chlorophyll's green dominance. When pinched, a nug should be dry to the touch from the surface to the stem but should bounce back from squeezing, much like a sponge. When bent, the bud should snap in the middle.

Think Outside the Jar

Cannabis cured in sealed containers runs the risk of mold or infection. The water condenses on the inside, and bacterial and fungal spores thrive in the contained high-humidity environment. Fungal spores and bacteria are ubiquitous and germinate under favorable conditions: moist environment, oxygen, temperatures between 50 and 70°F (10–21°C), and a mildly acidic surface.

Usually the first to attack are aerobic molds and fungi. They destroy terpenes and chlorophyll, changing the odor to woody or earthy and the color from green to brown. When all the oxygen is used up, anaerobic bacteria start to grow. The acrid smell of ammonia is a telltale sign that the bacteria are at work. They leave the buds mushy and, when they dry, crumbly.

Open-Air Curing Spaces

Although most cultivators have traditionally cured in closed containers, curing can also occur in an open, climate-controlled space. The conditions should be similar to the drying room, but with slightly elevated humidity to slow down this second-stage drying process and reap the benefits of curing buds outlined above. Open curing rooms should maintain the following conditions so that the buds equalize their moisture content, lose water at a slow, stable pace, and retain their potency:

- Temperature: 60–65°F (15–18°C)
- Humidity: 60–65%
- Continuous air circulation using oscillating and/or ceiling fans on low
- Bright light, especially ultraviolet light, degrades cannabinoids and terpenes. Curing buds should sit in low light to total darkness.
- Buds or colas hung on lines, placed loosely on trays, or in a thin layer in open bags

Pros of Room Curing

Delicacy: Handle the material as minimally as possible. Each bud movement breaks off trichomes and decreases value. By curing in a room, the buds remain undisturbed.

Less Labor and Time: Batch-curing a large, room-size crop requires much less time in monitoring and burping than curing in containers.

Drying Straight into Storage

Some growers don't cure their buds. They leave the crop in place in a controlled drying room until it's time to bag for storage. The only time the buds are touched is during trimming or packaging.

The supply chain can act as a curing agent. A proper dry and cure can take two to three weeks. Buds stay in the supply line for many days to weeks before they reach the end user. They continue to cure during that time.

The Cannatrol™ Cool Cure Box with patented Vaportrol® Technology, gives the small grower precision control over the drying and curing processes. Dial in the optimal conditions, and close the door. Water is removed gently, so that the trichomes will not be damaged and potency and flavor are retained. The fully programmable system dries and cures up to 2.2 pounds (1 kg) of wet buds per cycle and can store up to 4 pounds (1.8 kg) of finished flower in ideal conditions.

Fast Curing

Sometimes there isn't enough time to cure, and that's okay. Plenty of people can't tell the difference. There is no such thing as "fast curing": that's an oxymoron. By its nature, curing is a slow process that takes time.

Using Moisture Packs

Hydration packs are primarily used for maintaining appropriate water content in dried flowers that will be cured and/or stored in sealed containers. They can be used to ensure that moisture levels inside storage containers do not exceed or fall short of optimal levels for curing and storage.

Moisture Meters

Buds are ready for storage when they have reached 8–11% inner moisture. Handheld moisture probes can be used to determine approximate dryness. Because these meters are designed for use with wood and drywall and not cannabis flowers, they require some experience to get accurate readings. Err on the side of caution before packaging buds for storage.

Storing

Cannabis quality and potency change over time.

In the living plant, the precursors of THC and CBD are found in their non-psychotropic acid forms, THCa and CBDa. Only when they lose a portion of their molecules do they become active as THC and CBD. This occurs naturally over time and is accelerated in the presence of heat and light, especially ultraviolet light.

Once buds are dried and cured, quality for use is at its peak. Over time THC gradually degrades and is far less psychotropic.

Research conducted at the University of Mississippi on low-quality cannabis stored for four years at room temperature (68–72°F/20–22°C) found that the percentage loss of THC was proportional to time in storage, with the greatest loss in the first year. As the THC level declined, the concentration of CBN increased (Ross and Elsohly 1999).

YEARS IN STORAGE	TOTAL THC LOSS	ANNUAL NET THC LOSS
1	16.6%	–
2	26.8%	10.2%
3	34.5%	7.7%
4	41.4%	6.9%

This research is consistent with the experiences of cannabis users. Cannabis loses potency over time as the psychotropic THC converts to CBN or other cannabinoids, which induces sleep. Storing buds in the freezer or refrigerator slows deterioration. Freezing keeps buds fresh and preserves them the longest. However, even in a deep freeze, THC deteriorates at a rate of nearly 4% a year. In deep freeze (below 0°F/-18°C), deterioration slows further. At refrigerator temperatures, THC deteriorates at the rate of about 5.4% a year.

Terpene molecules vary in size, and the smallest ones evaporate at lower temperatures, starting in the high 60s Fahrenheit (18–20°C). Buds kept at room temperature in an open container will experience some loss of terpenes. Storing buds in a refrigerator or freezer keeps terpenes in a liquid state, rather than gassing off. A freezer is best for long-term storage; a refrigerator is good for protecting terpenes in the short term.

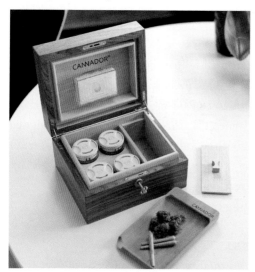

Cannador® manufactures storage products that separate cultivars and keep them at the appropriate relative humidity in order to maintain the flower's natural terpenes and mitigate evaporative loss. They are lockable and come in different sizes that can range in capacity from one to six ounces.

There are several problems with storing cannabis in a freezer, especially when supercooled to 0°F (-18°C).

Even under higher temperatures in the freezer, glandular trichomes become very brittle and are easily and inadvertently shaken off buds. For that reason, once placed in the freezer, the container should be handled very gently, and when removed, the buds should be given time to warm up so that they become more pliable.

The moisture in the air in the container freezes and can form ice crystals, especially during long storage. This may also occur when buds have not been dried sufficiently.

In several experiments, properly dried cannabis in a plastic container developed no ice crystals when placed in a freezer for several months. The trichomes remained intact. If moisture is a problem, vacuum sealing mostly eliminates it, although the process may result in crushed buds. Another solution is to purge the air with moisture-free gas such as carbon dioxide or nitrogen. These can be injected into the container as the ambient air exits through another hole. Then both holes are sealed.

When freezing cannabis in glass containers, choose shoulder-less containers, as shouldered containers are more likely to develop cracks. Metal, wood, and some plastic containers are better candidates for freezing.

One way to store frozen cannabis is in small containers. Just enough for a week's use is stored in each container. The rest of the stored material is not disturbed when a single container is removed, so the glands are not at risk.

Heat and light, especially UV light, evaporate terpenes and erode quality. Only an opaque container will completely protect the terpenes and therefore the quality of the buds stored inside. An opaque container with a white exterior reflects heat, keeping the contents cool.

Chlorophyll Degradation during Drying & Curing
By Clayton Stewart

Abstract

The cannabis plant contains over 500 identified compounds, 140 terpenes (potentially more), at least 144 cannabinoids, 34 noncannabinoid phenols, 32 carbohydrates, 33 fatty acids, 23 flavonoids, 11 phytosterols, 7 alcohols, and 1 vitamin (mb-labs 2020). Chlorophyll degradation is considered a necessary component to the post-harvest treatment of high-quality smokable cannabis. How and when chlorophyll degradation is taking place is not a well-understood concept in the nascent cannabis industry.

Introduction

Chlorophyll is the most abundant pigment on Earth and a critical molecule for life because of its role in transferring electron energy via light absorption in photosynthesis, yet the "basic knowledge about the chlorophyll degradation machinery and its regulation is uncertain" (Ghandchi, Caetano-Anolles, Clough, and Ort 2016).

Chlorophyll is broken down into the pheophorbide-a oxygenase (PAO) pathway, which aims to detoxify and dispose of the phototoxic pigments that operate during leaf senescence and fruit ripening (Hörtensteiner and Kräutler 2011).

During chlorophyll catabolism, enzymes such as chlorophyllase and oxygenase are responsible for severing chlorophyll's long hydrocarbon tail and the opening of its chlorin ring. Degradation of chlorophylls into pheophytin and pheophorbide are shown to have anti-oxidative properties. They ultimately break down into colorless metabolites sent to the cell vacuole for disposal (Hörtensteiner and Kräutler 2011).

The primary pigment of photosynthesis is chlorophyll-a. Chlorophyll-a absorbs light from the orange-red and violet-blue spectrum and transfers harvested sunlight energy to the reaction center and electron transport chain powering further metabolic reactions.

Chlorophyll-b is an accessory pigment: its primary role is to expand the absorption spectrum of usable light. Chlorophyll-c, similar to chlorophyll-a and b, helps the organism gather light and passes excited electrons to the photosynthetic reaction center (Dougherty et al. 1970).

Pheophytin is the product of degraded chlorophyll (Singh and Pandey 2020).

Methodology

One ounce (28g) of commercially grown Fruit Cake was acquired in fresh state about 48 hours after being severed from the plant stalk. The sample had already begun the drying phase at this point, and so 7 grams were immediately weighed and separated as "fresh sample." The fresh sample was sealed in a clean, mason jar at ~19°C (66°F) and transported to the laboratory the next day for analysis.

Of the remaining 21 grams, 7 grams were selected as "dry sample" and another 7 grams selected as "cure sample." The remaining 7 grams were dried in a refrigerator freezer in an unrelated experiment.

The dry sample was dried inside a loosely sealed cardboard box in a low-humidity environment so as to mimic desiccation and dry the sample to the lowest relative humidity (%) possible. The temperature was maintained at ~20°C (68°F). The sample was left to continue drying in this environment for 14 days while curing of the cured sample took place.

The cured sample was dried in the same manner as the dry sample but was removed from the drying environment when the stems of the buds exhibited snapping when bent (about three days into the dry cycle). Those buds were then moved into a clean, sealed mason jar and "burped" two times per day while the aroma gradually transformed from "green smelling" to sweet and pungent aromas holding an internal relative humidity of about 51%. Buds were kept in the curing environment at a temperature of about 19°C (66°F) for 14 days. Note that a "standard cure" is recommended for 30 days.

Results

Fresh:
MC% = ?, Chlorophyll (a) = 717, (b) = 343, (c) = 632, Phaeophytin = 597
Dried:
MC% = 11.5, Chlorophyll (a) = 795, (b) = 222, (c) = 127, Phaeophytin = 247
Cured:
MC% = 8.9, Chlorophyll (a) = 828, (b) = 227, (c) = 131, Phaeophytin = 251

Trends:

1. increasing amounts of chlorophyll-a from control to dried to cured.
2. slightly higher amount of "chlorophyll-b" in fresh. Similar amounts are in dried and cured.
3. 5x higher chlorophyll-c in fresh. Similar amounts are in dried and cured.
4. 3x higher degraded chlorophyll (phaeophytin) in fresh. Similar amounts are in dried and cured.

*Potential sources of error include:

1. no moisture value for fresh sample
2. moisture values for "dried" and "cured" seem reversed
3. short duration of cure (two weeks)
4. increasing amounts of "chlorophyll a" through testing

Conclusion

Data show that degradation of chlorophyll is taking place but not as expected. Higher levels of phaeophytin in the fresh sample may suggest more rapid chlorophyll degradation began early in the drying process, but with rising values for chlorophyll-a and unknown moisture content of the fresh sample, this relationship is uncertain.

This study is preliminary. While there is more work to be done, the results were shocking enough to present the data early.

Storing Materials

Cannabis can be properly stored in different materials, each with pros and cons that make them more or less suitable depending on function.

Glass

Glass makes great, inert, hard, nonbiodegradable storage containers. Different types of glass are used to store food. The color of the glass determines the type of light and heat that can penetrate the barrier. The downside is that most glass jars are clear, and light degrades trichomes, which doesn't matter if buds are stored in the dark. For storing buds exposed to light, an opaque glass is best.

Stainless Steel

Stainless steel tubs with plastic seals and flip-top locking mechanisms are popular because they're strong and can be stacked. The metal does not interact with the buds and is impervious to outside air. Stainless steel containers are an excellent choice for storage.

True Liberty® Bags and Liners are industrial strength and intended to be used as a protective device to maintain sterility and prevent cross-contamination. True Liberty® nylon bags and liners can be used in applications as low as -100°F (-73°C) up to about 400°F (204°C). True Liberty Can Liners are 100% food-grade nylon, double bottom sealed, sterile, smell-proof, and durable. The Can Liner is 48 by 30 inches (1.2 by 0.7 m) and designed to line a 30 gallon (113 l) drum or 20 (76 l) gallon trash can.

True Liberty® Bags, sometimes called "Turkey bags" or "oven bags," have long been used as an industrial strength and smell-proof way to protect and store cannabis. The Bin Liner size was specifically developed based on industry demand and is 100% food-grade nylon, side-sealed, sterile, smell-proof, and durable. The standard Bin Liner is 48 by 30 inches (1.2 by 0.7 m) and designed to line a 25–37 gallon (95–140 l) tote bin. The Bin Liner XL provides more bag height at 48 x 36 inches.

Plastic

Cannabis is slightly acidic and lipophilic, so it degrades some plastics. Plastics are stickier than glass or stainless steel. Turkey bags are popular because they contain almost all odors and are inexpensive. However, they are easily pierced by stems and offer no protection from shaking and movement, which leads to more damage and separation of sugar leaves and trichomes. Five-gallon (19 l) buckets sealed with airtight lids protect buds from getting crushed and can be stacked.

Moisture Control Packs

Moisture control packs made for cannabis storage attempt to maintain a preset moisture level by absorbing or releasing moisture. Using one of these packs maintains a set humidity of about 55–62% ensuring the proper level of moisture is retained without causing mold. They are also available at higher humidities to remoisten overdried buds.

Vacuum Sealing

Vacuum packaging is popular because it decreases the amount of oxygen present in a storage container. Oxygen is corrosive and degrades the buds' color. Decreased presence of oxygen also discourages the growth of spoilage bacteria. However, anaerobic bacteria thrive in low and no-oxygen, damp environments. Never seal and store wet or damp buds except when freezing for fresh frozen storage.

Gas-Based Storage

Gas-flushed, sealed Mylar bags are excellent packaging for long-term storage. The process injects the bag with nitrogen, purging the oxygen, and seals it. Unlike oxygen, nitrogen is inert and doesn't burn. Purging packages of oxygen extends the life of the buds and prevents growth of mold and discoloration, similar to vacuum sealing. Some automated packaging technologies offer nitrogen bagging using tamper-proof packaging.

Storing Fresh-Frozen

Harvested biomass can be processed directly into concentrates or freezer-stored fresh to be processed later. This saves energy and labor. With fresh-frozen storage, extracting the material can be postponed to a more convenient time.

Fresh frozen buds can be used for making "live" concentrates. For hash making, first, the frozen buds are added to ice water. Then agitation from a paint mixer or other tool makes the glandular trichomes brittle; they break off and are collected in a series of filters that catch different-size glands. When collected, the glands can be sold/consumed as hash or used as an intermediate for making "live rosin."

Light hydrocarbon extractors commonly use butane and propane as solvents to turn fresh frozen cannabis into "live resin." The result is a high-quality dabbable concentrate with very high terpene content.

Evaluating Cannabis Quality

By Max Montrose

This material was originally published in *Interpening: The Art and Science of the Cannabis Sommelier* (Trichome Institute, 2019) and is reprinted with permission from the author.

Interpening is the science of evaluating cannabis flower to determine quality, variety type designation, and psychotropic effects, through physical and aromatic inspection. An interpener can be thought of as a cannabis sommelier. Interpening is important for industry professionals and consumers because speciation, cultivar names, and lab testing do not provide the consumer with much information about the quality or the effects of cannabis today. Interpening teaches people how to evaluate cannabis with a deductive process that encompasses both technical sciences and sensory observations that enable people to identify the quality and effect types of cannabis varieties.

Summary of Visual Evaluation

When visually evaluating flower with the naked eye, hold it about one foot (30 cm) away from the face in a properly lit environment. While evaluating the flower, note if there are any faulty characteristics such as discolorations, odd-looking structures, excess trim, or white spots. After this initial inspection, look closer with a magnifying glass, jeweler's loupe, or scope, to determine the ripeness, health, and density of the trichomes. During this close-up evaluation, search for flaws ranging from insects to mold, and other flaws discussed in the following sections.

Photo: Max Montrose

Visual Evaluation Checklist

Faulty Flower Structure

The first thing to look for when evaluating quality is the integrity of the flower structure. When qualifying the structure of flower, simply decide if it came from a healthy plant or not. Quality is determined by the natural shape, color, trichome density, ripeness, and attractiveness of the flower. If the plant was grown properly, the flowers will be robust, beautiful in color, and alluring. Yet, if the plant was grown poorly, flower can look dull, unattractive, and weathered.

Photo: Kale Worden

Anthers

Anthers are male stamens that contain pollen and are often referred to as "hermies" or "bananas." If an anther that looks like a banana-shaped sack is visible, evaluate the flower more carefully to see if seeds are present, as seeds are harsh to inhale and take away from a pleasant cannabis experience, making the flower quality unacceptable.

564

Premature Flower

Premature flower is tricky because the flower may have already formed with trichomes and stigmas, and smells good when fresh, but ultimately lacks potency due to the early harvest. If the stigmas of the flower are pale orange, yellow, or white, it's an indication of a premature flower. Use a loupe for a closer evaluation of the trichomes.

Poor-Quality Trichomes

When evaluating trichome quality, use a jeweler's loupe or scope to confirm if the majority of the trichomes are clear (premature), milky (mature), or amber (overripe). Sometimes all three of these ripeness levels can be found within the same inflorescence. Non-glandular trichomes and broken heads will still make flower look amazing from a distance, but a jeweler's loupe is necessary to reveal these flaws and determine quality.

Poor Trim

All leaves should be completely removed from the flower during the trimming process. Look for untrimmed sugar leaves and their stems (aka "crow's feet").

Visible Mold

The primary indicator of botrytis is color and off-putting odor. If a flower looks healthy but smells suspicious or off-putting, break it open vertically, exposing the stem, and examine the interior. If there are any indications of a reddish-brown or light-gray fuzzy mold in between the bracts and around the stem, it's most likely botrytis. Off colors close to the base of the flower such as gray, red, tan, or brown indicate that the botrytis is very light and may be difficult to smell. Heavy botrytis has a very specific odor that is semisweet and acrid simultaneously and can easily upset the stomach upon smelling it. When this fungus comes in contact with the plant's trichomes, it can turn them brown, dissolve them, and destroy them.

Powdery mildew (PM) is much easier to spot on a living plant, as that is when it thrives. If PM spots are visible on a cured flower, it means the PM is much worse than is seen because the majority of the mold's structure has dehydrated and shrunk. PM does not produce any odor and is not systemic, unlike botrytis.

Photo: Max Montrose

Jar Rot

Jar rot is the same fast-growing, light-gray mold found on strawberries that are left in the refrigerator for too long. If jar rot is fresh, it will smell slightly damp, and a gray fuzzy mold will be present. If the flower has jar rot and then dries out, mold residue can be seen faintly but will not have an odor. This material is unsuitable for smoking or ingesting.

Discoloration

A bright lime-green color can indicate a possible nutrient overdose depending on the variety. It is rare to find flowers that have been dyed purple or blue, but those chemical dyes do exist, and some growers use them; be suspicious of flowers with unnatural, wild-looking colors and investigate further before consuming. Cannabis with dyes are harsh to inhale and taste like burning plastic. However, deep purple colors do naturally occur. This natural purple color is beautiful, harmless, and easy to distinguish from unnatural dyes.

Insects

Insects injure flowers, leaves, branches, and roots by eating or sucking them, leaving residual by-products such as carcasses, fecal matter, eggs, webs, and exoskeletons. Some insects that infest flowers are too small to be seen by the naked eye, which is why a microscope or jeweler's loupe is needed to detect them. Freckles on leaves can be spotted from a distance and are the result of insects eating the underside of the leaf. Always look for small, discolored spots on the leaves and trim because if a plant has them, it most likely contains a whole spider mite or thrip life cycle, which should not be consumed.

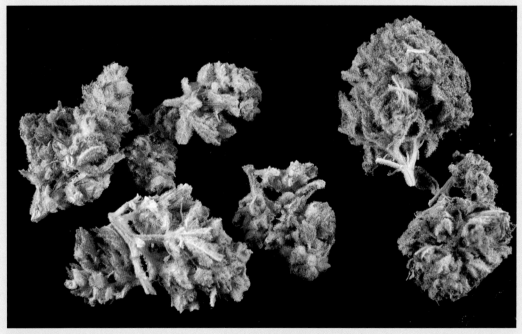

Old vs. fresh buds. Photo: Max Montrose

Burning

If a plant has a multicolored burn toward the top of the inflorescence, it is most likely "light burn" from growing too close to the lights. If the trim coming out of the flower is brown or scorched, that is usually a sign of "nutrient lock," which burns the internal tissues of the plant from excess or improperly added nutrients. Consuming flowers with nutrient lock can cause coughing and discomfort.

Old Cannabis

Old flower is very easy to identify because it looks dull, tarnished, and tan. Flower that is just beginning to age generally starts deteriorating in color from the base of the flower stem and moves up toward the top. The major factors to look for when determining if the flower is old are its vibrancy, color spread, and scent. The natural green-to-purple colors from the chlorophyll and flavonoids within the bracts will diminish to tan tones, and the orange-to-red stigmas will start to look rusty and brown.

Trichome Institute provides a variety of high-level cannabis courses and certification including the cannabis sommelier, Interpening. Interpening is the art and science of evaluating cannabis flower to determine quality, variety type, and psychotropic effects, through physical and aromatic inspection. Check out Trichome Institute to learn more about its courses, books, tools, and more.

Fresh rosin being pressed.   Photo: Dabsel Adams

PROCESSING

The journey for many buds ends with curing, storing, and smoking, but more and more, buds and trim are used to create concentrates and extracts that are consumed as is or are used to produce infused products like edibles, tinctures, topicals, and more.

There are many methods that are safe for home growers and also scale easily for commercial producers, but also many methods that are unsafe to perform outside of controlled, licensed, and professional operations.

Home cultivators have many options: solventless hashes, rosins, full-extract cannabis oil (FECO), kief, and infused tinctures, foods, drinks, and topicals can all be safely made at home. They are also popular on dispensary shelves. At the same time, technologies continue to improve for both home and commercial cultivators.

Glandular Trichomes

The cannabis plant produces three basic types of resin-rich glands that grow to different sizes expressed in microns or micrometers, which is a metric measurement equal to one millionth of a meter. Trichomes range from as small as 15 microns to as large as 500 microns, allowing them to easily be separated by using mesh screens of corresponding sizes.

The bulbous glands are the smallest, ranging from 10 to 15 microns. These tiniest glands perch atop equally tiny one-cell stalks that cover the leaves of vegetative plants. The capitate-sessile glands are the middle size, ranging from 25 to 100 microns, and are more numerous than the bulbous glands. "Capitate" means globular, and that's what they look like—spherical globs of resin that lie on the leaf and flower surfaces. The third type, capitate-stalked glands, are most visible on the buds of mature, flowering plants, as these rich resin balls are the largest at 100–500 microns in diameter. They sit high on three to four cell stalks that can reach 500 microns.

The maturity of the plant, its variety, and environmental conditions all affect gland size. For instance, many Moroccan varieties may have glands that are under 80 microns. Many equatorial varieties also have small glands. "Hash Plant" varieties often have glands that are 120 microns or larger. Most hybrid varieties are in the midrange, between 80 and 110 microns.

For a sense of these sizes, 500 microns equals about 0.02 inches (0.5 mm): a human hair is about 70 microns or a bit more in width; the finest beach sand is 100 microns; playground sand is roughly 250 microns; and the eye of a needle is more than 1,200 microns.

To measure the size of the glands with precision, use a microscope and a slide with a micron scale etched on it. Some microscopes come equipped with a scale called a reticule built into one of the eyepieces to measure microns. Count the number of hash marks of the gland's width and multiply by the conversion factor for the magnification power.

The Processing Hierarchy

This list prioritizes salvageable material according to its cannabinoid content and value from the processing of cannabis.

1. Grade A (Top Shelf) Flower: These large and medium buds are the highest-quality portion of the harvest and are found on the "top shelf" of a cannabis dispensary. Cannabinoid content can be upward of ~30% THC or 20% CBD.

2. Smalls: These flowers are smaller than typical Grade A flowers; however, smalls can be just as dense and potent.

3. Popcorn/Larf/B Buds: These flowers are usually found on lower parts of the plant that did not receive as much light as the top Grade A buds. The flowers are loose and airy. They still have cannabinoid content but typically not as much as Grade A or smalls. THC content typically ranges from 10–20%.

4. Shake: Sometimes called a "bag shake," the term refers to leaves and small flowers that have shaken down to the bottom of a bag of stored cannabis flowers. This is a combination of sugar leaf and smaller buds. THC content typically ranges from 8–15%.

5. Trim: The trim is the portion of the harvest that is collected after the Grade A and smalls are manicured. These are primarily derived from the leaves right around the buds that are trimmed away. THC content typically ranges from 8–15%.

6. Fan Leaves: These leaves tend to have very little THC content; however, the fan leaves closest to the female flowers will have trichomes on them as well. THC content can vary quite a bit but is typically around 5%.

7. Vegetative Leaf: These leaves are similar to the mature fan leaves; however, they are positioned far away from the female flowers, so they do not have any significant trichome development. These leaves have insignificant amounts of cannabinoid content.

Kief
Skill Level: beginner

Kief is the building block of many other by-products such as other forms of hash or edibles. Kief, also known as "dry sift," is composed of the unpressed glands separated from dried mature flowers and leaves using a screen. It is very popular because it is simple and cost-effective.

Kief is the easiest cannabis by-product to make. Tiny resin-filled glands cover the buds and leaves. These tiny stalked glands, known as trichomes, are the only part of the plant that contain significant amounts of cannabinoids, such as THC and CBD, as well as the pungent terpenes that give each cultivar its distinctive aroma, taste, and medical and psychoactive qualities. Making kief consists of collecting those trichomes. There are a number of techniques for separating them from the plant material and sorting.

Kief can be smoked just as it is collected by simply adding it to a pipe. It is often pressed to make hash. It can also be used to produce tinctures or other infused products.

Because kief is so easy to collect from dried cannabis, it is one of the oldest cannabis preparations and is known in many corners of the world. Alternatively spelled as kif, kief, kef, or kiff, the word appears in many languages.

The origin of the word is the Arabic "kayf," which means well-being or pleasure. The term was historically used in Morocco and elsewhere to mean a mixture of cannabis and tobacco, not unlike modern-day spliffs or blunts, though it was typically smoked using hookahs. This combination probably started in the mid-17th century, after Sir Walter Raleigh introduced tobacco to England and Europe. In Amsterdam and other parts of Europe, kief is sometimes called pollen or polm. Although kief is not cannabis pollen, many of the screens and devices used to separate kief from other plant material are called pollen screens or pollen sifters.

Preparing Leaf for Screening

Very little preparation is needed to sieve plant material for kief. In fact, kief making is so quick that small quantities can be done while the trash is being sorted or prepared for another process. It can also be done in large batches.

The best kief comes from dry but not crisp flowers, trim, and leaves. Very dry material is brittle and crumbles into smaller pieces or dust that passes through the screen. Kief made from such material contains more vegetative matter. Compacted material or "brick" cannabis does not work as well for making kief as loose material does because the gland caps are broken, spilling their contents, which congeal to the leaves.

On the other hand, in the mountains of the Hindu Kush region, hash makers wait for cold, dry weather to sift plant material. The connection between the glands and the dry leaves becomes brittle, so they break away easily when they are frozen.

Another advantage of using cold material is that the thick oils of the resin do not clog the screen; however, the cold also promotes crumbling so that finely ground plant material sifts through.

Traditional resin screening in Balkh, Afghanistan. Photo: Lucas Strazzeri

Excellent kief can be made in temperate conditions. To make kief of the finest caliber, cool temperatures, lower than 60°F (15°C), are best. Low to moderate humidity is okay, and the presence of a little humidity is even welcome if the material is particularly dry.

In countries close to the 30th parallel north, such as Nepal, Afghanistan, and Lebanon, small amounts of kief have traditionally been made using a silk scarf stretched tightly over a bowl. Dried cannabis, frequently cured for as long as six months, is rubbed on the taut silk cloth. The cloth's fine weave allows the small glands to pass through to the bowl, leaving the vegetative material on top. Silk scarves are still used in parts of the world, but stainless steel mesh screens (often called "silk screens") are more durable and come in a variety of dimensions and mesh sizes. Nylon screens are also used, but they become stale, and microplastics chip off the mesh.

The simplest way kief is made is by gently rubbing the plant material over a fine screen. The size of the openings in the screen determines which size glands and how much residual plant material drops through the screen. The vigor used in rubbing the material has a profound effect on the quality of the final product.

Different grades of kief are produced by varying the amount of time the material is sifted, the screen's gauge, and the pressure used. Sifting the same material a few times yields more kief, but each sift results in a higher proportion of plant matter mixed with the glands. Kief color ranges from golden white for the purest kief to various shades of green. The greener it is, the more plant material it contains.

Kief or pollen-sifting boxes are good tools for making small amounts; they can be as simple as wooden stash boxes with a screen above a pullout drawer that catches the glands that fall off in normal handling. Other boxes are made specifically to capture different grades of kief, separating the glands from the vegetation by shaking it.

Overvigorous shaking or rubbing may be counterproductive because too much vegetation is collected, lowering the quality. However, kief that will be used for cooking or topicals may benefit from the added plant material, because the goal might be to recover as many cannabinoids as possible.

Some larger sifters are automated, much like a front-loading washing machine, so all that is required is to add the material, flip a switch, and let the sifter do the work.

Compact DIY solutions are inexpensive and easy to make from screens used for printing T-shirts and posters. All that is needed is the proper screen, a frame to stretch it on, and a smooth hard surface such as glass or metal to collect the kief.

Printing screens made of nylon, polyester, or metal are available at art supply stores or online. A stainless mesh screen lasts forever and is easily cleaned. The mesh sizes are typically described in terms of the number of threads per inch, so a higher number is a finer screen. Meshes range from around 40 to 400, with 110 and 156 being the most common for printing T-shirts. Screen mesh can be purchased pre stretched in aluminum or wood frames or as rolls or sheets.

Glands & Screens: A Guide

Inches	LPI	Microns	Millimeters
0.0021	270	53	0.053
0.0024	230	63	0.063
0.0029	200	74	0.074
0.0035	170	88	0.088
0.0041	140	105	0.105
0.0049	120	125	0.125
0.0059	100	149	0.149
0.0070	80	177	0.177

Matching screen size to gland size is important for maximizing kief yield. Most glands are between 75 to 125 microns or micrometers in diameter and vary based on the cultivar, the maturity of the plant, and other factors. Mesh screens are usually sized by a "mesh" measurement that indicates how many strands of wire or nylon it has per inch (2.5 cm). Detailed mesh-to-micron conversion charts can be found online, but this chart shows common mesh sizes and the micron size of the openings between strands. (LPI stands for lines per inch.)

Kief sifting works best with screens between 100 and 130 microns. Plants with larger trichomes need a screen of 150 microns to capture the glands. Screens in the range of 100–150 lines per inch usually work well, but not all mesh sizes are created equal. The size of the openings varies based on the diameter of the strands. Screens made of nylon, polyester, or stainless steel have different strand diameters at any particular mesh size, and finer mesh screens use strands of smaller diameters. Stainless steel screens are the most durable and don't shed. Plastic and nylon screens should be replaced periodically because they shed strands as they age and wear.

The GreenBroz Alchemist 420 ensures the most value is extracted from the harvest. The Alchemist 420 has a capacity of eight cubic feet (0.22 m³) and can fit as much as 10 pounds (4.5 kg) of trim at a time while producing a high-quality yield of 15–25% by weight. For each 10 pounds (4.5 kg) of trim, as much as 1.5 to 2.5 pounds (0.6–1.1 kg) of kief are produced. It can be used as a stand-alone or integrated into the GreenBroz automated harvesting end-to-end system.

Dry Ice Kief: The Manual Method

Perhaps the cheapest, simplest way to concentrate cannabinoids is also one of the newest. Since 2009, hash makers have been turning to dry ice (frozen carbon dioxide) to yield an impressive amount of kief. Dry ice sieving is one of the fastest methods to produce kief, is very inexpensive to set up, and results in very little mess or cleanup. Dry ice kief is very smooth and contains a lot of terpenes because it's made cold.

Equipment:
- Cannabis (1 ounce, dry trim or fresh frozen)
- Bubble Bags (durable 160- and 220-micron water bubble bags)
- 5-gallon bucket
- Clean, sanitary surface area, at least four feet (1.2 meters) long
- Collection tool (such as a plastic scraper)
- (1.3 kg) dry ice, broken up into small pieces*

Dry ice is so cold that it will "burn" human skin. Never touch dry ice with bare hands; use proper protective gloves (such as an oven mitt or thick, waterproof insulating gloves).

Manual dry ice sieving uses the -106°F (-76°C) temperature of dry ice to freeze the waxy stalks of the trichomes, making them brittle enough to snap off when agitated. The snapped glands then fall through the 160- or 220-micron bag onto a surface and are collected.

First, designate a sanitary indoor space and a table with a smooth, clean surface. Place trim or ground bud in the bucket. Add dry ice. Tightly affix the 160-micron bubble bag over the top of the bucket using large rubber bands so that when the bucket is turned upside down, the dry ice and trim fall onto the screen.

Dry-ice kief is a fast and easy method of extracting high-quality kief. (Left) Flowers and dry ice are placed in a drum and covered with a screen. Kief is shaken out of the drum onto the table where it just needs to be scraped up. (Right) Kief made with the dry ice method. Photos: Lizzy Fritz

Pick up the bucket and gently shake to help distribute the cold. After a minute, turn the bucket upside down and hold it over the table. The dry ice and trim fall to the bottom of the bag firmly attached to the top of the bucket.

Lightly shake the dry ice and trim mix up and down, moving longitudinally along the surface of the table so that the falling kief creates a trail several feet long.

As the bucket is shaken, the kief dust rains down from the bag onto the table, amid little puffs of evaporating carbon dioxide. Keep shaking for 30 seconds to sieve the trichomes through the filter. The first glands are a pale golden-yellow. As the process continues, the trail of glands gets greener because more vegetative material is in the mix. The first material to fall, the golden glands, is the highest quality.

A scraper is used to collect the kief, which can be stored in a glass jar.

Repeat the process using the 220-micron bag and collect the kief. One ounce of dried sugar leaf trim can yield up to four grams of kief at 160 microns, and six lower-grade grams of kief at 220 microns.

Hash & Hashish

Isolating the resin glands that contain the flavors and effects of cannabis from the largely inert plant material is far from a new idea. The old methods of concentration are used to create hashish, often called hash. The practice began millennia ago, probably in Asia near the Hindu Kush region, but there is a rich historical tradition of cannabis extraction across Asia, the Middle East, and North Africa, home to historical hash capitals including India, Nepal, Afghanistan, Pakistan, Lebanon, and Morocco.

Perhaps the oldest way of making hash is hand-rubbing fresh plants, collecting the resin that accumulates on fingers and palms, then rolling it into balls or coils. This is called charas. The resulting product is prized globally, and the legends of its unique potency still attract travelers to the northern Himalayas, where it's made on a large scale.

The yields from charas are low. It requires much more material and far more labor than other methods. The process can produce extremely high-quality hash, but because the resin is collected fresh from the plant and is still very sticky, it is pressed by working it with palms and fingers into a ball or patty until it dries a bit.

Another classic method of hash production involves suspending dried cannabis plants over tarps and collecting the glands that fall naturally and pressing them into hashish.

New techniques can all trace their lineage directly to hash makers of antiquity, because the core physical principles are unchanging: manually removing the resin glands using cold and physical agitation, then concentrating the resin using heat, pressure, and time.

This is traditional Afghani pressed hashish and a pressing stamp. Photo: Lucas Strazzeri

Traditional hash smoking in Mazar-i-Sharif, Afghanistan. Photo: Lucas Strazzeri

Hashish
Skill Level: beginner to intermediate

Pressing unrefined hash into balls, cakes, or slabs creates hashish; all steps of the process are consumable, but making hashish is a two-step process. First, the glands are collected; second, the collected material is compressed into bricks or balls.

Pressing hash involves a combination of force and mild heat to condense the glands into a solid mass. The shape and size of hash varies depending on the pressing method. When hand pressed, hash is often ball-shaped. Flat-pressed hash may look like thin shale rock, with hardened shelf-like layers that chip along the creases. Mechanically pressed hash is usually a neat cake, like a bar of soap.

Hashish ranges in color and pliability.

The cultivar used, manufacturing method, temperature, and the purity of the kief influence its color, which ranges from light yellow-tan to charcoal black, and its texture, which ranges from pliable taffy to hard and brittle. It oxidizes and darkens from exposure to light, oxygen, and heat. Regardless of its texture, high-quality hash should soften when plied with the simple warmth of human hands.

In the region of traditional hash making, kief is typically aged, sometimes for a year or more, before it's pressed. Most modern hash makers do not wait that long.

> TIP: Unpressed kief oxidizes in warm temperatures, while hash is more resilient to warmth as long as it's pressed when it's totally dry. When pressed wet, it molds. Kief can be stored in a cool, dark place. Hash stored frozen suffers little from aging.

Preparing Resin by Hand

Hand rubbing plants to collect hash has been used for thousands of years in Asia. It is still used in some parts of the world. However, the effort required to produce a substantial yield is greater than the other methods. It can be messy and labor intensive, and it contains contaminants from plant debris and hands as well as a substantial amount of water, making it likely to spoil if it isn't used fresh or dried.

The amount of material collected through hand rubbing is dependent on timing and technique. It is best to collect for hash when the plants' stigmas have started to turn amber as they reach full maturity, but before the leafy material has become brown or dry. The more dead or dry the plant material, the more plant debris will be mixed into the hash. Removing dead or dried material before collection increases the quality of the hash.

Collection should not be done when the plants are wet because this increases water content. In the cool of the morning, after any dew has evaporated, is the best time for rubbing. It's dry but cool, before the terpenes start to evaporate.

The most popular technique is to cup both hands around the part of a cola closest to the stem and then draw the hands up to the top of the bud with firm but not tight pressure. Experienced collectors often coat their hands very lightly with vegetable oil to improve yield because the resins stick to the oil.

Removing the collected resin from hands can be an involved task. One way to solve this problem is by using non-powdered latex, vinyl, or plastic gloves. When the collector is finished rubbing the plants, the gloves are placed in the freezer. The hash peels off easily. This procedure does not work well with bare hands.

For the most part, Westerners' attitude toward hand rubbing is that it is best used when the goal is a small amount of quality hash before or during harvest and manicuring.

Hash Pressing by Hand

Hand pressing is a method for transforming kief into hashish a few grams at a time. Pressing by hand is convenient, since it requires no additional equipment, but it takes considerable energy and the results are better with a practiced technique. Those unaccustomed to hand pressing may find it difficult to make the material bind together. The considerable work it takes to get well-pressed hash can easily result in sore hands.

This method works best using freshly sieved medium to high-quality kief. If the kief contains a significant amount of vegetative material, it's harder to mold into hash and may not stick together properly. To hand press, a small mound of fresh kief that will fit comfortably in the hand is measured out, usually a few grams. This material is pushed together as the hands press against each other. After a few minutes it begins to cohere into a solid piece. Then it is rubbed between the palms, or between palm and thumb. After 10 minutes or more of manipulating the material, it begins to change density.

Dry, aged kief lacks some of its original stickiness and takes longer to stick together. If it was stored properly, it should cooperate, though it may require more kneading. When a piece of hashish has not been pressed properly, it crumbles easily at room temperature.

If the kief is particularly stubborn and won't stick together to form a mass, mild heat may help.

The material can be wrapped in food-grade cellophane, ensuring that it is completely sealed and all the air is squeezed out. This package is wrapped in several layers of thoroughly wetted cloth or paper towels. Turning frequently, it is warmed in a skillet that is set on the lowest heat. It doesn't need to be heated as long as other methods because the only point of heating is to get the material to stick together so it can be kneaded into a solid piece.

Another heating method is to press the package for a few seconds on each side using an iron set on a very low heat setting.

The concept of using a hot-water bottle is similar to pressing by hand. However, more heat is applied to thoroughly melt each trichome head's waxy cuticle.

A pile of resin on cellophane or parchment paper is then folded in half. Next, a glass bottle is filled with boiling hot water and allowed to cool for five minutes. Then, the bottle is placed on the paper-covered resin and allowed to sit for 30 seconds.

The darkening stain of the warming resin can be seen through the bottle. If the color is changing quickly, the resin will press very quickly. If the resin barely begins to change after 30 seconds, the resin will have to be "worked" considerably more. Using a series of passes, roll the bottle over the resin using minimal pressure. Allow the heat to melt the material without forcing. Flip the paper over and repeat the process.

The resin should no longer be a mound but flatter and more like a patty. When the paper is opened, the resin should be sticky and have a nice sheen. The resin is folded in half and then pressed again. This process is repeated one more time before the warm resin is held in the palm of the hand.

The ball is rolled between the two palms as if it were a ball of clay to create a modern-day "temple ball." It is rolled with firm pressure to compress the resin and push out any air. Resin that has lumps, lines, or wrinkles needs to be worked more thoroughly.

Ice Water Hash
Skill Level: intermediate

Ice water hash making uses a process of collecting glandular trichomes from the trim, leaf, and buds using agitation in an ice water bath. The process

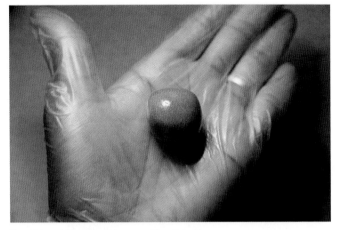

Traditional Nepalese pressed hash ball.
Photo: The Dank Duchess

works because cannabinoids are not water soluble, so once collected, they are easily separated from the ice water and ice.

Ice water hash comes out as loose, granular resin. It can be smoked as is or pressed into traditional hashish or rosin using a press. High-quality, loose hash is easily pressed into hashish using nothing more than the palm of one hand and some light, brisk friction, applied using the thumb of the other hand. Modern rosin presses automate this process using two heated plates pressed together with high pressure. Loose or pressed, many people are still enthralled by the unique, entourage effect of this potent natural product.

Producing solventless hashes is safe because the process doesn't involve the use of any flammable/explosive chemicals or dangerous gases/machinery.

All that is needed is water, ice, and agitation to separate resin glands from plant material. Water and plant material are placed in a bucket that has been lined with filtration bags, similar in composition to the screens used for making dry sift kief. Like those screens, the bags filter the glands by micron size, which indicates quality. A micron is one-millionth of a meter, or 0.001 millimeters. The material is stirred to knock the trichomes free, and while the plant material floats in the top bag, the glands (which are heavier) sink and are collected in the lower bags.

Ready-made systems use multiple bags that sort the glands by size: unlike kief making, the material is separated in one step rather than through repeated sieving. Usually the material is processed once, but some commercial hash makers process it a second time to further isolate more glandular trichomes.

The Original Bubble Bags are professional quality, heavy-duty bags for extracting bubble hash and are rated to last an average of 200 washes. Bubble Bags feature German top-quality precision heat-pressed monofilament polyester screen, exact within 1 micron, and 800-thread count nylon sidewalls. The 8-bag kit is the most popular kit and provides every micron needed to capture the best-quality product possible.

As with all extraction methods, cold temperature is a key element of water hash production. First, freezing the biomass to be extracted is recommended. The ice keeps the water and material very cold during the separation process so that the glands remain brittle and snap off with agitation. After the material is agitated in ice water, it's allowed to settle. The top bag collects the plant material. Next, the lower bags are separated, and the different-size glands are removed from each one. After the ice water hash is dried, it's ready to smoke.

Ice water hash varies in color and can be many shades of white, brown, red, and even purple. When extracted from the finest-grade material, the potency of water hash can test as high as many solvent hash products, with up to 80% cannabinoid content. Content between 40 and 60% is more typical.

A Note on Yields

Processing 227 grams of high-quality material usually yields between 18 grams (5% yield) to 35 grams (15% yield) of hash. Yields increase with the quality of the starting material and optimization of the process.

There are considerations other than cannabinoid yield; the entourage full-spectrum effects and natural flavor profile of water hash are unique because the process preserves the terpenes in the glands. For this reason, some people prefer high-quality water hash to solvent-extracted products.

Water Hash Tips

All gland-bearing plant material (leaf, trim, buds, shake, or any combination of the four) can be used to make water hash. Dried or frozen material can also be used.

It is important to keep the material and the environment very cold when making water hash. Low-temperature water, near freezing, makes trichomes brittle enough to snap off. A cool room keeps terpenes from evaporating.

Humidity is also a factor. Avoid humid storage conditions to prevent deterioration from bacteria or molds. One method is to store wet or dried cannabis in the freezer. When using material that has not been stored in this way, place it in the freezer prior to processing.

It's crucial to treat the cannabis delicately to preserve the glands and keep them on the vegetation prior to processing. Take the utmost care when bucking buds from twigs and stems. Don't pulverize the material from excessive trimming or grinding. Coarsely chopped cannabis is most convenient. Remove twigs, stems, and twist ties, because they can tear the hash-making bags.

Thoroughly dry collected and scraped ice water hash. Water hash that is stored before it is dried will mold, ruining it.

Water and mash left over at the end of the process contain nutrients present in the plant material. The water is great for watering plants, and the mash can be used as mulch or added to compost.

Ice water hash can be made in small or large quantities, and turnkey extracting systems can be purchased to simplify the process. Personal and industrial-size systems are available. It is also possible to make water hash using home-gathered equipment, but with inexpensive kits available, the savings are often negligible. Premade systems offer increased precision and efficiency for the ice water hash process, and due to its increasing popularity, concentration technologies and methods are constantly evolving.

Ready-Made Bags

For water hash, the ready-made bag systems are an excellent choice.

Bubble Bags are the design of Fresh Headies in Canada. Bubbleman, the head hash master of Fresh Headies, has traveled extensively, spreading the good word of water hash for decades. He can also be found moderating online forums on this topic. Bubble Bags are available in 1-gallon (~4 l), 5-gallon (~19 l), and 20-gallon (75 l) sizes. All filtration systems are available in sets of four or eight bags and as singles.

There are several other brands of bags. The eight-bag system separates hash into finer categories. The size difference between just-ripe glandular trichomes and overly mature or premature ones allows them to be separated into grades.

Using Bubble Bags

First, the coarse filter bag is secured in a bucket and the water and ice cubes are added. For instance, a 5 gallon (19 l) bucket uses about 5 pounds (2.25 kg) of ice. A 30 gallon (113.5 liter) container requires about 30 pounds (13.6 kg). Then, plant material is added. The cannabis is agitated using a kitchen mixer or a drill with a paint-mixing attachment. The material is stirred to knock the trichomes free, and as the plant material floats in the top bag, the glands (which are heavier) sink and are separated into the ice water. After the material settles, the starter bag is pulled out and squeezed. The bulk of the plant material now held in this bag is set aside. This material can be processed again, but the resulting product will be lower grade, though still suitable for infused products.

Line a second, empty bucket with the additional filter bags. The finest bag goes in first, so it will be on the bottom. The green water from the initial process is poured into the bucket, lined with the filtering bags. Pull the bags out one by one and collect the material in the bottom of each one. Allow the end product to dry. Toss the water out or use it for watering plants.

Homemade Bags

Bags can be constructed using silk screens of the appropriate mesh size. Standard silk-screen material is available in several size increments between the desired 100–150 strands per inch. The screen must be attached to a tightly woven, water-resistant material (nylon works well) so that the silk screen forms the bottom of the bag.

A separate bag made for coarse filtering (200 to 250-micron-size gaps) is used to separate the bulk of the vegetation from the glands in the first phase. This bag should line the bucket. It does not get layered with the other bags, so it should be as large as the bucket allows. The screen is lifted out of the container removing with it the vegetative material, leaving green water that also contains the trichomes behind.

Multiple bags can be made with different screening levels in the 50 to 150-micron range for separating the water hash by quality. The finest screen produces the purest hash. The bags should be designed to fit inside one another, with the finest mesh bag being the largest, and the coarsest mesh bag being the smallest

Fresh-frozen material works best. If it was not stored in the freezer, it is ideally placed inside until it's frozen. Fresh material can also be used.

A standard blender, two-beater mixer, drill with a paint-mixing attachment, or commercial kitchen mixer can be used. Let it run for 15–20 minutes to fully agitate the cannabis biomass.

The bags are pulled out one by one. The glands are found inside the finer screens. The material is scraped from the screens and dried thoroughly.

Methods for Drying Water Hash

There's a delicate balance in drying: trying to remove moisture from the hash without vaporizing the terpenes. Drying should be done in a room with a temperature lower than 68°F (20°C), the evaporation temperature of the lightest terpenes such as myrcene. Humidity is also a factor, with 30–45% humidity being optimal, but it can vary by cultivar.

Drying is accomplished in a number of ways, including the chop, sieve, microplane, and freeze-drying methods.

- **Chop Method:** The chop method is accomplished by chopping damp resin into small pieces so that it can be spread over a wide surface area to dry.

Resin is chopped swiftly in a cold room, using a small knife to create rows of damp material. Then rows are shaped perpendicular to the first row. On a swatch of parchment paper, the chopped resin is spread over the surface, taking care to keep the clumps as separate as possible. The chop method is the least effective method for thoroughly drying the resin because clumps tend to trap moisture.

- **Sieve Method:** Using the sieve method results in very small clumps of resin that do dry thoroughly.

    Two strainers and three spoons are placed in the freezer. After the wash, resin dries on the 25 micron screen. The screen is wrapped around the resin and wrapped again within a clean paper towel. Place in the refrigerator for two hours. To utilize the sieve method, the material has to be cold and devoid of excess moisture.

    After two hours one of the frozen strainers and spoons are taken out of the freezer and the resin out of the refrigerator. The partially dried resin is placed in one of the strainers above parchment paper. Using a circular motion, the cold spoon is lightly run over the mass of resin. A fine rain of resin falls onto the parchment paper or a clean box.

    The parchment is covered in a light dusting of resin powder, taking care not to pile resin on top of itself. When the resin begins either sticking to the strainer or the spoon, a fresh, frozen instrument is exchanged for the warmer one. When resin warms, it sticks together, making sieving nearly impossible, so work quickly.

    Allow resin to dry between 3 and 14 days, depending on the cultivar and the conditions of the room. When ice water hash is dry, it looks and sounds like sugar crystals when poured.

- **Zesting:** The zesting method is a favorite among many hash makers because it consistently allows the resin to dry thoroughly.

    Three lemon zesters and the resin rests on a drying screen in the freezer. It's important that the puck be frozen. The next day, in a cold room, remove a zester and a puck. Using quick movements, grate the resin over a large sheet of parchment paper.

    Allow resin to dry between 3 and 14 days, depending on the cultivar and the conditions of the room. When the resin is dry, it looks and sounds like sugar crystals when poured.

    The main drawback of this method is that the trichome heads are sliced open, thereby allowing terpenes to escape. Also, ripped heads are less stable, leading to shortened shelf life.

- **Freeze-Drying Method:** Freeze-drying is an excellent option for getting resin to its absolute driest. The basic idea behind freeze-drying is to have water frozen inside resin pucks sublimate to vapor, completely bypassing the liquid stage. Over the course of about 24 hours, frozen resin becomes like dry sand.

Whichever process is used, the key is to achieve complete drying. Under magnification, the final product will look like sandy heaps of trichome heads. Store in a cool, dark, and dry place, and don't press until the material is completely dry.

Machine Pressing

Making hash is very easy using a mechanical press. In the past, bookbinding presses, called nipping presses, and hand-pumped hydraulic presses were used.

For small amounts, a pollen press can be used in conjunction with a handheld kief-collecting grinder. Kief is added to this small metal tube. The tension pin is placed in, and the pollen press is screwed shut. The next day, the kief is pressed into a neat hash block. Many companies have similar presses now, including one made of stainless steel with a low torque T-handle.

Today the best way to make hash is to use a rosin press, which is made for the purpose. It provides controlled and even pressure.

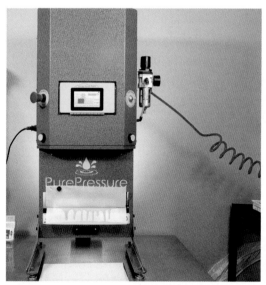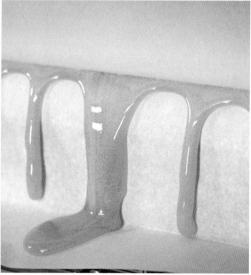

The PurePressure Automated Longs Peak rosin press utilizes an 8-ton pneumatic cylinder as opposed to higher tonnage hydraulic cylinders to achieve smoother actuation and precision force control. It also features an intuitive touch-screen interface and automated pressure control system so that users can fully take advantage of the extremely accurate aluminum-heated plates while pressing any type of rosin imaginable (accurate to within 1°F). The Longs Peak is the go-to press for high-output solventless processors and is built in the USA in Denver, Colorado.

The PurePressure Bruteless™ ice water hash-washing vessels are made for the modern bubble hash producer and feature full food-contact-grade sanitary welded stainless steel. The systems are available in multiple sizes to meet the needs of home washers and large-scale commercial processors. These vessels utilize a custom porous stainless steel false bottom that enables detached trichomes to gently settle at the bottom and away from the agitation for better preservation, as well as numerous strategically placed ports to attach drain valves, skim valves, sight glasses, and temperature gauges. They also come with a one-inch (2.5 cm) thick neoprene insulation sleeve, which enables processors to use half as much ice as is typically needed in a non-insulated vessel.

Rosin

Skill Level: beginner to intermediate

Rosin is the simplest, least expensive way to extract concentrate from raw buds or hash for more effective dabbing. Instead of a chemical process, rosin technologies rely on heat and pressure to squeeze trichomes from the source material. It is a very fast process: a batch of rosin can be produced in moments and consumed immediately. Another advantage of rosin production is that it poses minimal risk of physical injury.

The physical science of rosin is simple: applying heat melts the terpenes and cannabinoids into a pliable resin. Then it is squeezed using a press. Some lipids and waxes melt at the same temperatures. Thus the finished product is generally not as refined as the results of some other methods.

There are a number of tools that can be used to make rosin. The choice depends mostly on the quantity being pressed. On the hobby level, household items can be used. For commercial production, industrial processors use pneumatic or hydraulic presses.

No matter the size of the project, the start-up costs of this method are very low compared with chemical extraction, where just the cost of the safety equipment and laboratory modifications exceeds the cost of even an elaborate large-scale rosin operation. However, running a solvent extraction setup yields a higher extraction efficiency than rosin systems.

The Flat Iron Technique

The easiest way to understand rosin is to make a small batch. It's simple and can be done using a flat iron (for hair) or a clothing iron that has precise temperature settings or a digital display dial. It should be set between 280 and 330°F (138–165°C).

The bud is placed inside the tea bag or filter (if applicable) and folded inside parchment paper. Bags and filters reduce the risk of contaminating the rosin while removing plant material.

When the iron is at the appropriate temperature and the bud is secured in its envelope, the envelope is pressed with the iron, concentrating the pressure on the buds in the middle. If clamps are being used, they are tightened for three to eight seconds. The process is complete when the sizzle sound of resin escaping and interacting with the heat is heard.

The iron is released, the envelope opened, and the buds removed. The envelope is then placed on a cool surface for a few minutes before the rosin is collected.

Oaksterdam University's Commercial Extraction and Manufacturing Certification Course demystifies the complex process of extracting the essence of the plant that cannabis is prized for—the cannabinoids, terpenes, and flavonoids. From the safety and compliance requirements to the science and business of extraction and manufacturing consumer goods, this cutting-edge course explores the market trends that are driving the evolution of the sector.

Gutenberg's Dank Pressing Co.'s rosin press bags filter rosin from the plant material inside the bag, producing a pure, clean finished rosin. The bags are made from 100% food grade premium quality dye-free nylon. The double stitch sewing makes these bags durable and strong enough to withstand tons of pressure while also producing maximum clean-filtered yields.

Rosin Processing

There are three types of material that can be pressed into rosin: buds, hash, and kief. To produce the best-quality rosin, the best material is pressed. Size doesn't matter but quality does, so small buds and some residue from trimming can be pressed into rosin.

Freshly cured, resin-rich material results in the best rosin. Conversely, older, drier material results in lower yields of a darker, less flavorful rosin.

When rosin is pressed from hash, it's the second time the material is being concentrated, resulting in a higher concentration of cannabinoids. Creating a stunning product requires exceptional starting material: fresh, with a high ratio of oil to plant matter.

Rosin pressed from ice water hash collected from different-grade filters results in rosins with distinctly different effects. The size of the glands seems to affect their chemical content.

Kief, especially secondary grades resulting from processing for a long duration, contains a high percentage of plant material but can still be pressed into rosin.

The more plant matter removed from the trichome heads, the higher the potency and the cleaner and smoother the resulting rosin.

Industrial Rosin Presses

There are practical limits on how much rosin production can be scaled, but industrial presses are available. They apply low heat and high pressure, resulting in a uniform product.

A big factor in choosing a press is the amount of pressure it produces. Most commercially available rosin-specific presses have been designed to press only hash. Higher pressure is required to process flowers.

Collecting Rosin

Gathering up rosin after pressing is often more challenging than the press itself. Depending on the starting material, moisture, temperature, and timing, a wide range of consistencies can result. It can be a stable, easy-to-gather material or a sticky sap. Hash rosin is more stable (less sticky and gooey) than flower rosin, which is often difficult to gather.

Rosin is viscous and sticky at room temperature, so it is processed in a cold area to keep it more solid. Gloves and hairnets prevent contamination and getting rosin stuck on skin. After the rosin is pressed, it is chilled in the refrigerator, where it becomes more solid and easier to handle.

Curing & Storage

Once the hashish is pressed, it can be kept for months or possibly years with little deterioration to its potency and flavor, with proper storage. A frost-free freezer is the best place for storing hash.

Light, heat, moisture, and oxygen work together to oxidize the outside of the hash, destroying its potency.

The inside is not exposed to higher levels of light and oxygen and remains potent. Forming a large ball is a good way to protect most of the hash from oxidation and to prevent the evaporation of terpenes.

Metal, glass, or silicone containers are preferred for storage. Plastics and rubber are not recommended because the terpenes—responsible for the flavor and aroma of the hash—are somewhat volatile compounds that interact chemically with plastic or rubber, degrading both the hash and the container. However, this happens slowly under freezing conditions.

Always store rosin in sealed containers in the refrigerator or freezer. This preserves the terpenes and prevents oxidation.

Rosin shows its consistency instantly. Depending on temperature, the rosin will either stabilize, budder up, or turn to crumble. If the rosin is becoming budder directly out of the press, it's a sign that the entire batch is going to turn to crumble. If it's not buddering up in the press, there's about a 50% chance of it staying shatter.

Edibles, Tinctures & Topicals

There are several easy methods for home extraction of cannabis for cooking and making tinctures and topicals. All these processes can be done at home in a kitchen or scaled for industrial production.

Edibles

The modern history of cannabis edibles dates back centuries before prohibition. In 19th-century Paris, the Club de Hashischins met for the express purpose of eating hashish. Authors and poets whose works are now considered classics were members.

In the 1920s, Alice B. Toklas published her infamous brownie recipe that popularized brownies as the cannabis food of choice in modern times. More recently, "medicated" foods have become a common therapeutic alternative for medical cannabis use.

Eating cannabis provides a different experience than inhaling it. It isn't an immediate rush. Instead, the sensation begins gradually, about half an hour to an hour after ingestion. The length of the lag time depends mostly on stomach contents. When cannabis is eaten on a full stomach, the high takes longer to come on and is not as intense. On an empty stomach, the inverse is true. The high comes in "waves," reaching a peak an hour or two hours after the first effects are felt. Then it tapers over the next hour. Altogether, the high usually lasts three to four hours.

Taking the right dose is more important when ingesting than inhaling. The onset of the high is rapid when inhaled; it is easy to self-titrate to find the proper level of high or medication. It is harder to adjust the dose because the effects take longer to occur after eating. New users should err on the side of too little rather than too much. More can always be eaten. Although eating too much can be an unpleasant experience, it is not dangerous.

The secret to creating tasty and effective cannabis food lies in transforming cannabis into a cooking ingredient. Using cannabis preparations and a little ingenuity, any tried-and-true favorite or cookbook recipe can be converted into cannabis treats.

Cannabinoids are not water-soluble. To create a satisfactory cannabis consumable, plant material must be combined with an ingredient that can dissolve it. Ingredients with this capacity are alcohol, oil, butter, or fat and lecithin-containing milk products.

Mild heat also plays a role in cannabis cooking. For THCa and CBDa to convert to their active forms, they must lose their carbonate molecule, COOH, which evaporates under low heat.

Decarboxylation Explained

Some THC and CBD in resin is present in the form of THCa and CBDa. These forms have a carboxyl group (COOH) attached. To decarboxylate is to remove the carboxyl group, which simply means breaking the bond between the COOH group and the rest of the cannabinoid molecule. This is usually accomplished through mild heat such as smoking, vaping, or cooking. When the carboxyl group is removed from the cannabinoid acid, the COOH volatizes in conjunction with the water vapor (H_2O) and carbon dioxide (CO_2), and the cannabinoid is left behind. Converting THCa through decarboxylation improves the available THC content, sometimes called "potentiating" the THC.

When heating cannabis, the temperature should be kept below 100°F (38°C) so that fewer terpenes evaporate. THC has a boiling temperature of 392°F (200°C). Once it reaches or passes this temperature, it begins evaporating into the air. To activate the THC without evaporating it, pay attention to the cooking temperature used.

In recipes such as the ever-famous brownies, the oven temperature is often set at 400°F (205°C). This is okay. The batter never reaches this temperature. Baking temperatures indicate oven temperature settings, not the temperature of the food.

The real danger of cannabinoid depletion comes with stovetop cooking. Sautéing or frying temperatures reach 400°F (205°C), and at this temperature the cannabinoids boil off. Closely monitor stovetop cooking to avoid cooking away cannabinoids. The best way to use cannabis in a sauté is to add it when the dish is almost done. Treat the cannabis as an herb like basil: use it last and only allow it to be under the heat briefly. This way the active ingredient doesn't heat up and evaporate.

Making edibles is not difficult once the cannabis is infused with base ingredients. Trichomes are fat-soluble, so most recipes are infused with fat or oil. With infused butter or oil on hand, it can be easily incorporated into any recipe. To avoid using a fatty ingredient, sprinkle kief or ground trim in with the flour or dry ingredients of a recipe.

How to Make Butter: Aunt Sandy Style

"Aunt Sandy" Moriarty's cannabis butter became a local favorite in the San Francisco Bay Area as the first dispensaries were opening. Sandy taught cooking classes at Oaksterdam University, and her edibles were available in Oaksterdam-affiliated dispensaries. Her notorious lemon bars were delicious and potent, and almost completely lacked the grassy flavor typically associated with old-school edibles, which can be attributed to this method of extracting cannabis into butter. This recipe yields two cups (500 ml) of butter and can be adjusted for potency by adding more or less cannabis.

Equipment:
- Scale
- 5-quart stock pot (no lid)
- Strainer or colander and catch pot
- Potato masher or stiff spoon
- Cheesecloth
- Kitchen gloves (plastic or non-powdered latex)
- Ice cream scoop or big spoon
- Food storage bags or containers

Ingredients:
- Cannabis leaf trim: varies from one-eighth of an ounce (3.5 g) to four ounces (~113 g) depending on personal preferences and tolerance
- One pound (453 g) butter of choice
- Water

Weigh desired amount of plant material on scale. Add the butter and cannabis and fill the stock pot with water. Bring the mixture to a boil and then reduce heat and let simmer uncovered for three to four hours. The mixture will cook down and concentrate, and a lot of the water will evaporate. The idea is to cook as much of the liquid off as possible without burning the plant material.

Turn off the stove and remove from heat. Use a second pot and a strainer to strain the plant material from the water and butter mixture. Place the plant-material-filled strainer over the pot and allow the liquids to drain into it. Use a potato masher or a stiff spoon to apply pressure to the plant material to release the remaining water-butter mixture.

Allow the mixture to cool further and then strain through a cheesecloth. Use heat-resistant gloves in order to strain the remaining liquid out of the cloth. Place the remaining water-butter mixture in the refrigerator overnight. The butter will congeal and separate from the remaining water mix. The following day use a scoop or spoon to remove the solid butter from the top of the pot. Let the butter dry, or pat with a paper towel to remove left-over moisture. Store the butter in appropriate food storage containers and/or food storage bags. The butter can be melted briefly if needed to accommodate storage.

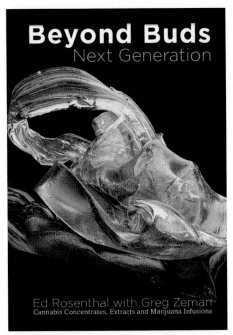

To learn more about professional and home extractions of cannabis, check out *Beyond Buds, Next Generation: Marijuana Concentrates and Cannabis Infusions*, by Ed Rosenthal, with Greg Zeman.

Shelf life is roughly three months in the refrigerator and six months in the freezer. Butter can be added to any recipe that calls for it or melted on top of foods after they are cooked.

Dosing is tricky; it is important to start low and go slow. Keep track of how much cannabis was infused and start by eating a fraction of a serving (i.e., a quarter of a cookie) and waiting a full three to four hours to gauge the effects. From here, appropriate dosing can be customized.

Other Infusions

Using either raw flowers, kief, or extracting into fat, it is easy to process cannabis into a wide-variety of products including infused foods, tinctures, and lotions, salves, and other topical ointments. Methods covered in this chapter are the basis of making all of these byproducts. However, while this book covers the very basics in home-safe extraction, *Beyond Buds: Next Generation* by Ed Rosenthal with Greg Zeman covers industrial and solvent-based extraction, topical processes and cooking in far greater detail.

Photo: Zoom Gardens

APPENDIX A: CLONING

Plant cells have a property called totipotency; any plant cell can dedifferentiate and redifferentiate into any other type of tissue. In other words, an epidermal cell can turn into a root cell, and that is exactly what happens when a cultivator takes a cutting to clone a plant. This is an example of asexual or vegetative reproduction. Since the cutting has the same genetics as the "mother" plant from which it was taken, it will have the same characteristics.

Using clones has several advantages over using seeds.
- Clones are faster and easier to start than germinating seeds.
- Seeds require sexing. Clones are the same sex as the plant from which they are cut.
- Plants grown from seeds of the same variety can vary in quality. Clones are uniform.
- Clones have been selected for high quality.

A potential disadvantage of using clones rather than seeds is that they may not grow as vigorously, especially outdoors. Unlike seeds, clones do not have a taproot.

Plant roots need oxygen. That's why the cutting's planting medium is selected for its ability to provide oxygen to the root zone. When cuttings receive abundant amounts of oxygen in the water or planting medium, they form a larger root mass, capable of taking up more water and nutrients, resulting in faster growth and healthier plants.

Cuttings are best made while the plant is still in its vegetative growth stage. However, they can be taken even as the plant is being harvested. Cuttings generally root within one to two weeks when they are given a clean, humid, moist, and warm environment.

Cuttings do not have any roots, so they have a limited ability to absorb water. Keep the humidity between 75 and 85%, so they aren't placed under stress.

Cuttings root fastest when they are kept at about 75–80°F (24–7°C). It is important that both the air and the rooting area are kept warm. At lower temperatures the clones root slower.

At first, use a moderate amount of light, between 100–200 $\mu mol \cdot m^{-2} \cdot s^{-1}$. (*See Light.*) A 4-foot (122 cm) long rack holds four 10 x 20 inch (25 x 50 cm) trays. High-output T5 fluorescents can provide enough light until the cuttings start to root; however, this is old technology, and fluorescents in older fixtures can be replaced with LED arrays. With new dedicated LED fixtures, there is the added benefit of light intensity control. After cuttings have rooted, they require twice the light, which can be supplied by adjusting the LED's brightness.

Cuttings can be rooted in coir, vermiculite, perlite, peat moss, Excel plugs, rockwool, soil, commercially available rooting plugs, and other porous rooting materials.

Most professional cloners prefer rockwool, which promotes very fast rooting. Most cloning machines use aeroponics or water sprays. Other cloning machines hold the cuttings in place while the stems soak in aerated water, which adds the benefit of a highly oxygenated environment ideal for new root production.

Rooting hormones are compounds used to promote root initiation. These hormones mimic the activity of the plant's natural auxins. Auxins will promote the dedifferentiation and then redifferentiation of plant cells into root tissue.

Cloning: Step-by-Step

Equipment

- Scissors: use sharp, sanitized, and comfortable scissors. Spring-loaded scissors are easy on the muscles because they do not have to be pulled back to open position.
- Clean, well-lit work area.
- Small jars or glasses filled with water to hold the cuttings before they are prepared for planting.
- Alcohol, hydrogen peroxide, bleach, hypochlorous acid, or another disinfectant in a spray bottle and cloth or paper towels for sterilization.
- Root dip solution. Most rooting hormones contain naphthalene acetic acid (NAA), indole-3 acetic acid (IAA), indole-butyric acid (IBA), or a combination of these three root stimulators. Many brands are available.
- Containers with sterile medium, or cubes that are ready for clones. If using rockwool that has not been prewashed of lime, soak it in water pH adjusted to 5.5 for 24 hours. This removes the lime.
- Lighted shelf.
- Trays, humidity domes, heat mats, and thermostat.

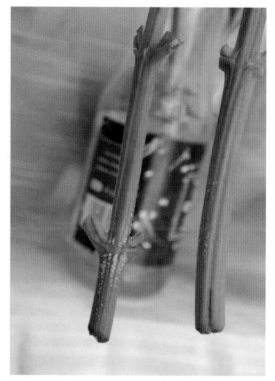

These plant tops were placed in water five days earlier and are now showing budding roots. Water was changed daily. Photo: Ed Rosenthal

These clones were started in Excel cubes and have been transferred to LECA clay pellets. They will be transferred to a larger hydroponics system soon. Photo: Ed Rosenthal

Directions

- Wipe down the work space and scissors with hydrogen peroxide, bleach, hypochlorous acid, or another disinfectant to sterilize.
- Wash hands and put on a pair of sanitary gloves.
- From the mother plant, take cuttings about 4–6 inches (10–15 cm) in length, and place the cut ends in a glass of water to prevent dehydration. See the additional trimming instructions following this section in order to choose where to cut the clone.
- Trim the cuttings. Place them in a second glass of water until they are ready to be placed.
- Line the clones up by the leaf canopy and then cut the stems so that the clones are the same length.

The misters (red) constantly spray very fine oxygenated water at the cuttings. Photo: Ed Rosenthal

- Wipe the scissors with sterilizer and then cut the stems an eighth of an inch (3 mm) from the end.
- Dip the cuttings in the rooting solution to about half an inch (13 mm).
- Place the clones at least 1 inch (25 mm) deep in the medium.
- Irrigate using water adjusted to a pH of 5.8–6. They need no enhancers or nutrients for the first few days.
- Various rooting enhancers are available. They contain plant hormones and nutrients and are added to the water solution.
- Compost tea or mycorrhizae-beneficial bacteria mixes can also be added once roots have begun to grow into the medium. The mycorrhizae develop symbiotic relationships with the roots.
- Spray the top of the medium with hydrogen peroxide as an antiseptic.

Trimming the Clone

The strongest clones are cut from the new growth at the ends of the branches. These cuttings are four to six inches (10–16 cm) long. A cut is made with a sterile blade at a 45° angle in order to create more surface area on the stem to pull water into the cutting. Remove the large leaves and vegetative growth except for three medium-size leaves surrounding the growing tip. At the end of the trimming, only one to two inches (2.5 to 5 cm) of leaf should remain at the top of each cutting. The rest of the stem is bare. Care should be taken that at least one removed node, where a leaf's petiole was attached, is near the base of the stem, ensuring that it will be inserted into the rooting medium. Cuttings with nodes in the medium root faster than those with nodeless stems. Roots emerge from the node site faster than along the stem's internode. Trim back the laminae, or blades of the leaf, to reduce the amount of leaf material. This will help the plant retain water as it eliminates stomata, pores in the leaf where water vapor is released. Leave at least 1 to 2 inches (2.5–5 cm) of leaf surface. Try to get all the cuttings to be about the same length. The uniformity will mean that longer cuts don't shade neighbors and thus slow the rooting process.

Clone preparation techniques vary. Larger or smaller clones can be taken. Both have advantages. Larger clones require less time in the vegetative stage. Smaller clones allow the grower to produce more cuttings from a mother plant and to produce more of them in a small space.

If large numbers of cuttings are being taken, a system using multiple stem cuttings from one branch can be used. Cuttings can be made from many of the internodes along the branch, which have vegetative growth. These cuttings are at least four inches (10 cm) long and have some leaf material and a node to plant.

If a technique works well for the grower, and the grower is satisfied with the results, then it is the right way.

Rooting in Water

Cannabis cuttings can be rooted in room temperature water. Using tap water is fine but change the water every day to make sure it has enough oxygen. Shake the water before using it to oxygenate it. Several commercial units use oxygenated water as a rooting medium.

Another technique uses a piece of Styrofoam board with holes punched to hold the clones. The board floats in a tray with water heated and aerated using an air pump and a bubbler. When the cuttings begin to root, they are moved to a solid planting medium. Aerating and heating the water to 72°F (22°C) speeds up the rooting process.

Aeroponic Rooting

Most cloning machines use aeroponics for rooting. The plant canopy is held above the reservoir while the stems hang down in a chamber or are held in a mesh cup. Misters emit fine sprays that bathe the stem in highly oxygenated water. Clone machines promote very fast rooting because they provide an excellent balance of water, oxygen, and root zone temperature.

Aeroponic and water culture cuttings do not require as high humidity as those rooted into planting mediums. They can be kept at 50–60% humidity. Aeroponic and water culture systems get the cuttings past the most difficult phase, the first few days after being cut. Transfer them to other mediums as soon as roots appear.

One popular commercial cloning kit consists of a tray that holds peat pellets in a min-

Cuttings in a commercial water cloner produce vigorous roots quickly as long as water oxygen levels are maintained. Photo: Ed Rosenthal

iature greenhouse. The cuttings are placed one to a peat pellet. Fairly small-to-large-size cuttings can be placed in these pellets. Peat pellets are especially convenient for rooting plants that will be placed in indoor or outdoor soil mixes.

Maintaining Temperature & Humidity

In gardens where only a few clones or a few trays of clones are being propagated, high humidity and temperature can be maintained using horticultural heat mats, or a heated propagation tray with a high dome. Heating clones helps promote plant respiration. Plants not only absorb water and nutrients through their roots but also respire, and the rate of respiration is directly related to the plant's temperature.

Maintaining high temperature and humidity in a small room or even a closet-size space takes some effort. The lighting helps raise temperature, and humidifiers keep the humidity high. CO_2 generators burn propane or natural gas. They also produce heat and humidity. Use a thermostat to regulate the generator. Even with the added moisture, the room is likely to have humidity of less than 80%. Use a humidifier regulated by a humidistat. Five-micron misters are an efficient alternative. Once installed, they require little maintenance and are inexpensive to operate.

Silver
Back

S.

APPENDIX B: TISSUE CULTURE
by Bill Graham

When a clone is cut and planted, roots grow along the vascular tissues, on the ribs that run up and down the stem. Small bunches of cells were laid down during development just in case the limb found itself fallen over in the dirt or any other circumstance that would put the stem in contact with moist soil that it may have to root into.

These root cell clusters are called primordia and are stimulated to grow by rooting hormones known as auxins, which are produced in growing tips of the shoots and diffuse down the stem by gravity. Another group of hormones called cytokinins are produced in the root tips. These cytokinins move up the roots and shoots, in contrast to the auxins, which travel down the plant. When the stem is cut, the source of cytokinins is cut off and the auxins begin to accumulate around the cut end and lower vascular tissues. The ratio of auxin to cytokinin rises until a threshold is reached, which stimulates the root primordia and dedifferentiated stem tissue to multiply and differentiate into root tissue. These are the bumps that will quickly emerge as stringy and feathery roots in an environment of satisfactory conditions of moisture and oxygen at a rate determined by the temperature.

Growers take advantage of this natural rescue system to root clones with energy provided by the carbohydrates stored in the wood and sugar-storing tissues like leaves and green stems. But how small can the cuttings be and still have enough energy to develop the root primordia? Every grower who experiments sees that the smaller the cutting, the longer it takes to root and that cuttings will not grow below a specific size, depending on cultivar, cutting size, and the amount of stored energy in the cutting. Feeding sugar directly to the plant tissues to provide more energy for the small cuttings makes up the difference and is the basis of plant tissue culture.

Tissue culture, also known as micropropagation or microcloning, is growing small parts of plants in a liquid or agar-solidified nutrient media, typically using exogenous sugar as the tissues' energy source.

Plant tissue culture gained popularity with specialty plant growers as early as the 1980s because of the availability of prepared kits and lab-quality supplies. Commercial greenhouses use TC techniques to clone their plants by the thousands, and even millions. Most crops not grown from seeds, including houseplants, pineapples, fruit trees, and agave plants, begin life in small glass and plastic jars and are "harvested" to grow into full-size plants.

Cannabis growers today are making tissue culture clones at home in closets, bathtubs, and other small gardening spaces. They begin by surface-sterilizing small limb tips and node meristems and placing them on media of nutrients, vitamins, hormones, and sugar, often hardened using agar from kelp or gellan gum from dried bacteria slime.

The small half-inch (1.25 cm) and taller plants are often grown in glass or plastic jars and test tubes to increase their numbers and make new plants while providing a safety backup, revealing systemic or other diseases, and allowing growers to grow and clone the clean ones.

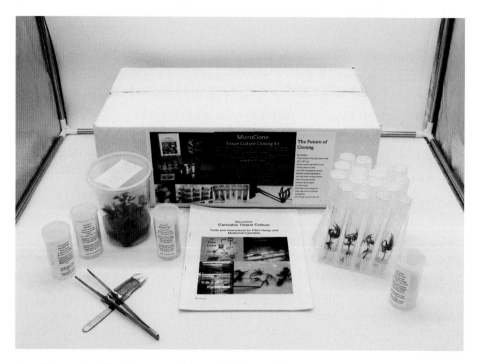

Microclone Propagation Services created the original cannabis tissue culture techniques in California's early medical market and today are the cannabis industry's number one choice for tissue culture tools for both large and small growers. Setup and use is simple and inexpensive and allows growers to store and transport genetics safely as well as constantly renew their garden with a steady supply of healthy disease-free clones. Equipment is quick and easy to upgrade.

Most of what it takes to grow in tissue culture is knowledge that growers already have. Growers will recognize the media, for tissue culture is made with the same nutrients as hydroponics, plus sugar for energy. Vitally, the media are sterilized to prevent anything but the plant from growing in the sweet, sugary solution. It is cloning, but cleaner, using smaller plants and containers.

The most basic method of tissue culture is called Tissueponic. Two-inch (5 cm) tips of thin inner limbs are surface sterilized and put into tissue culture media containing rooting hormone for only three weeks before moving into sterile rockwool or rooter plugs and acclimating back to new little plants. The broader technique of micropropagation adds the extra steps of growing small rootless plants in culture containers, where they branch and grow to a few inches (3 to 5 cm) tall. Every month or so they are removed from their culture jars and put into several distinct pieces, some into tissue culture rooting and the smaller bits into a fresh multiplication medium to grow and make new plants all over again.

Typical Five-Stage Micropropagation

Stage 0: Care and Preparation of the donor plant prior to taking mini-cutting.

Stage 1: Introduction: Small cuttings put into vessels of low- or no-hormone media.

Stage 2: Multiplication: Media of branching hormone encourages short nodes and branching and prevents roots.

Stage 3: In-Culture Rooting: Media of rooting hormones encourages rooting and stretching.

Stage 4: Rooting Out of Culture: Pre-rooted plants are removed from culture into plugs.

Micropropagation Stage 1 starts when small node and tip cuttings are put into culture, usually wide test tubes first, so that any plants that may still harbor fungus or bacteria from the cleaning will only spoil the single plant, and the neighboring tubes are protected. The healthy plants acclimate to culture over a few weeks and are moved into larger vessels containing a medium made with hormones called cytokinins, which encourage branching and tight nodes where they grow to a few inches tall and sprout branches. This is tissue culture's **Stage 2** or multiplying stage. Tissue culture cloning jars produce five to eight new plants every four to six weeks. When plants reach three quarters of an inch (2 cm) or larger, they are removed for rooting, and the less-developed material is moved onto fresh Stage 2 media to repeat the cycle.

Stage 3 rooting of the clones is initiated in tissue culture using auxins, the same hormones that growers use to start roots on cuttings. The clones are smaller, and more than 200 can be produced in a square foot under only a few watts of light. When tissue culture plants are removed from culture into the environment outside the tubes, they are **Stage 4**, the last stage, and very tender, so a controlled environment is especially important.

Moderate light levels, temperatures, and high humidity are needed to prevent transpiration and drying of the thin surface tissues and from the new leaves' stomata. Plants are given humid, circulated air for a few days until they develop a protective waxy coating, or cuticle, and enough roots develop to supply the shoots with enough water to avoid wilting. Rooting takes a few weeks until they are ready to transplant.

Personal Gardens

The basic tissue culture grow space has a protected surface for cutting and handling plants, lighted and unlighted shelves for active and prepared tubes, respectively, and a HEPA air filter to capture airborne particles. Growers also need a place to prepare sterile media using a pressure cooker. A microwave is used for preheating media and sterilizing rockwool for rooting when the plants leave culture.

Commercial Tissue Culture

Larger operations use the same basic principles as the single rack used by the home grower. A laminar airflow hood is a covered bench that gently moves HEPA-filtered air from the back of the work surface into the face of the user sitting across from it. Filtered air is blown into a space behind the one micron or lower filter and moves across the worktop a few inches a second and at the exact same speed at the corners as in the center, allowing the technician to work longer without the risk of microbial contaminants landing on the plant or cutting plate.

Larger systems use bigger and faster autoclaves to produce sterile media.

Labs use a lot of tubes and jars, so a commercial restaurant dishwasher saves a lot of time and labor.

In commercial labs, rooting the clones from culture is scaled, creating large environments with controlled heat and humidity. One successful tissue culture producer roots into 132 plug 10 x 20 inch (15 x 50 cm) propagation trays, placed on lighted racks. Warm water circulates through radiant pipes placed along the walls of an insulated room. A large humidifier with a circulating fan keeps air moving across the new foliage without removing too much moisture.

Tissue culture, also known as micropropagation or microcloning, is growing small parts of plants in a liquid or agar-solidified nutrient media, typically using exogenous sugar as the tissues' energy source.

Photo: Christian Petke

Advantages of Tissue Culture

Tissue culture is being used by cannabis growers because it offers advantages in cost, ease of entry, and space savings. Tissue culture ensures growers the plants they are cloning are disease-free and healthy. Diseases are revealed during the ex-plant's growth while in the tubes, on plants, and media and as halos around the cut end of the plants where they grow into the clear gel. Contaminated plants are removed, and visual inspection and selective removal eliminates over 99% of contaminated stock. The clean plants go on to produce all the new stock.

In 2019, viruses and viroids as well as other systemic diseases such as the Hop Latent Viroid were discovered in many popular cultivars. Tissue culture plays an important role in testing and maintaining virus- and viroid-free tissue. Small pieces of isolated tissue from culture are tested against DNA tests that look for specific sequences unique to viruses, viroids, and other pathogens such as powdery mildew and fusarium. Those that show no such contamination are saved to produce future stock.

Two of the main advantages of tissue culture are the ease and space savings when storing genetics. The self-contained tubes provide a month's feeding at a time. The plants take care of themselves and are separated from environmental hazards. Tissue culture is a safety backup for valuable cultivars; the plants can go without light for a few days, feeding on their sugar nutrients. The small amount of light ordinarily provided helps growth and maintains the healthy green chlorophyll and light pigments.

Another method of storing genetics using tissue culture is artificial seeds. These are not ordinary seeds and must be carefully stored in a special solution and planted back into tissue culture in order to develop in larger adult plants. They are made by encapsulating small, single nodes containing a growing point in a few milliliters of nutrient solution coated with agar. They look like fish roe with the tiny plants inside. The artificial seeds then may be refrigerated to slow their growth or carefully frozen in liquid nitrogen.

Although further advances are expected, at this writing the process of making and restoring artificial seeds from cannabis today takes more risk and effort than the easier method of maintaining cultures every four to six weeks or so.

"Genetic drift" is the term given to clones that do not behave or exhibit the potency, vigor, or flavor that they used to before years of cloning; however, this is likely not the function of a change in genetics. The hypothesis is that the transcription of DNA in cloned plants grown in ideal conditions indoors for generations is made more efficient by blocking stress genes that have not been needed. The chemical nature of the blocking is called methylation, and it prevents transcription by RNA, blocking the expression of genes for extra cannabinoid production, for instance. The genes themselves do not change, but whether or not the genes are transcribed does change.

The study of methylated DNA and how it affects gene expression is called epigenetics. The first strategy should be to raise and clone some plants outdoors every summer in sunshine-rich UV, or simulate the hot days, cool nights, wind, and other outdoor environmental factors that stimulate the DNA to activate those stress genes again. When plants are tissue-cultured, a similar demethylation appears to occur. Some plants retrieved from tissue culture seem to be restored to their original but lost characteristics after several cycles of tissue culture.

Tissue culture has expanded and eased genetic transfers, since it is so convenient to ship tubed clones. It also creates opportunities to improve cannabis crops genetically. For instance, tissue culture has the potential to induce polyploidy, a naturally occurring mutation that increases the number of chromosomes in every cell, resulting in larger and more vigorous plants.

Chromosome doubling can be induced in tissue culture by adding chemicals such as colchicine or Sulfluran to the media. Although colchicine is the most cited, the chemical Sulfluran is less toxic and can be purchased in farm supply and hardware stores, where it is sold as a weed killer. The chemicals disrupt mitosis, the cell division process. Instead of dividing into two new cells after the chromosomes duplicate, the division pauses, and the cell begins growing again but with twice as much DNA as it should have, and thus grows larger and stronger.

APPENDIX C: PRODUCING SEEDS

by Humboldt Seeds

Seasoned growers and breeders know all too well the horrible feeling of loving and losing a particular cannabis varietal. Cultural changes, disease, legal challenges, and a host of other factors have led to the loss of many special and much-loved cultivars. Seed production is a great way for backyard gardeners to preserve and stabilize their favorite varietals and save them for future seasons and future generations.

The process is the same whether setting up a breeding project with seeds found in a bag of herb or creating a new varietal with seeds ordered online. Start by germinating as many seeds as possible.

Segregating males from females is key. Select a choice male with the desired characteristics and be sure to keep him separated from the female garden. He can be used to pollinate a lower branch of each female plant during the second to fourth week of flowering, depending on specific varietals.

Use a paper bag with pollen inside and a rubber band to keep the bag closed after it is slipped over the lower branch to prevent the pollination of the entire crop. A couple of small male flowers full of pollen go a long way. Outdoors, pollinate on a dry windless day. Indoors, shut off the fans. This will make the whole process much easier and help limit the possibility of an unwanted incident.

Spray the area with water to neutralize any remaining pollen grains as the paper sack is being removed. Attach a piece of tape to the pollinated branch, noting the male and female used. Once flowers are mature, select a choice female.

Gather the seeds from the special plant(s). The seeds tend to take a couple of weeks longer to mature than the harvest time for flowers. During this time the seeds will change color from light tan to green to dark brown, and when finished will appear dry and hard.

Two good ways to check seed maturity is to press on one with a fingernail or crack one between the teeth. When the seeds are ready, they will not dent easily with either of these tests. (See *Selecting Seeds* in *Getting Started*.) It is okay to harvest all but the pollinated branches, allowing the seeds to finish.

With the first generation of seeds, as many plants as (are legally) possible are grown. Each is carefully labeled, and notes and photos are taken of the preferred parents from the last generation and this new crop of offspring.

In plant breeding "like begets like." One method is to select the male based on growth habits and terpene profile, which can be obtained by rubbing a stem. Male plants can be tested for cannabinoid content at cannabis testing labs. Choosing the right male(s) is more

Pinch & Pull is the only fully self-contained male pollen pouch delivery system. It is great for breeders large and small, and all Pinch & Pull bags are 97% biodegradable, breathable, and fully contained; everything inside is fertilized while no pollen escapes to surrounding buds. Not only does it deliver pollen in a controlled fashion; it helps track seed parentage, giving breeders the ability to seed just the buds they choose without turning whole plants or crops to seed. Pollen is completely contained within an externally loaded pouch and dissipates inside the inner pouch over four to five days.

important than the female because the male will be a "stud" pollinating many females.

Keep this "like" male alive and separated. Pollinate the selected female and repeat season after season until the population all resembles the original choice female. At this point, the seeds are a homozygous population, meaning the line is stable. Depending on the genetic background of the original seed stock, this can take three to seven breeding cycles. Generally, hybrids require more backcrossing than purebreds. It's important to adhere to the original selection, as deviating from this delays achieving the goal of stable seeds. (*See Basic Breeding.*)

Breeding from Clone

Seeds can be bred from clones, but it is important to be familiar with the variety. Does it have issues if stressed? What are its optimal growing conditions? Is this clone really worth the time spent to develop a stable seed line?

Clonal male plants are rare but can sometimes be produced. Even so, it's usually easier to start from seed in selecting a male pollen donor. When choosing this male, it's best to select from a similar seed variety based on the most desired characteristics, structure, color, aroma, and so on. Grow out as many regular seeds as legally possible, selecting the male that most resembles the chosen clone. Remember "like begets like" in plant breeding.

Keep the male separated and only pollinate a small clone off a lower branch of a larger clone plant. Collect the seeds from this clone and then grow out as many as possible, ultimately selecting a male that most resembles the clone mother.

Next, cross this "son" back into the clone mother, creating a "backcross 1" (BX1). Once this has been done, select a choice male from this population, and backcross him into his now "grandmother clone." This creates BX2. The population will begin to appear very similar, with 75% resembling the original clone. Continue this process and repeat two more times to result in a 93% homozygous population to the original clone.

Generation % When Backcrossing

Generation	%
BX1	50
BX2	75
BX3	87.5
BX4	93.75
BX5	96.875
BX6	98.4375

At this point seeds may begin to display signs of inbreeding depression, such as stunted growth and increased intersex expression in the flowers (i.e., hermaphrodites). If this process is carried out with two different parallel populations and those are crossed, the result will be homozygous seeds, which are like the similar parents but with hybrid vigor. This is considered a pure cultivar. If two different varieties that have been backcrossed are bred together, they will produce F1 hybrid plants with uniform characteristics. This is the holy grail of plant breeding, a true F1 hybrid.

For large-scale growers, seed production can be a way to develop new and novel varieties to differentiate themselves in the market. Breeding and seed propagation can also be a way to pollinate an entire crop intended for flower. Pollination separation is vital. Use of sterile technique with all equipment and persons visiting the pollination area is important, especially if there are other flowering plants in the facility. Cull all donor males immediately after pollination has occurred. (*See Basic Breeding.*)

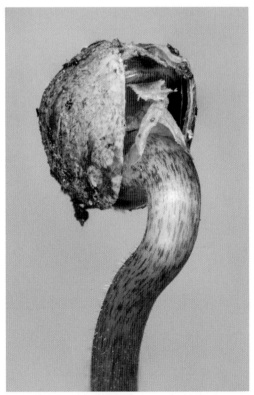

The stem of a new seedling emerging from the shell. Photo: CannaGraphics, Courtesy of Humboldt Seed Company

607

Photo: Ed Rosenthal

APPENDIX D: REGENERATION

Regeneration, colloquially called "re-vegging," is the process of reverting plants that have ended flowering back to vegetative growth. This is done for two purposes:

1. Saving genetics: If clones have not been taken before flowering initiation, reverting the plant to vegetative growth preserves the genetics.
2. It is often faster, easier, more convenient, and less labor intensive than cloning or starting with seeds.

Regenerated plants pruned of just their buds have complete infrastructures, so they can be fairly sizable without taking a lot of time in vegetative growth.

When a plant is pruned, new leaves and branches usually begin to grow within a few weeks. Growers can do the same thing with their plants. The regeneration process begins at harvest. There is no seed sowing or repotting involved. When harvesting, take the buds but leave at least a few branches with some leaf material and buds on them. The more that is left, the larger the plant will be when it starts growing again. The rest of the plant can be harvested as usual.

It is important that vegetative material is left on the branches because the plant won't regenerate without it.

Growers who wish to grow single-stem plants should harvest most branches, leaving only a few bud sites on the stem. The plants' energy will focus on this remaining growth site.

Once the plants are harvested, the lights should be left on continuously until the plants show signs of regeneration. The plants switch to the vegetative cycle and start to grow again in about 10 days. First, a vegetative branch will sprout from an old bud. Then the plants can be kept in the vegetative regimen of 18–24 hours of light daily to serve as clone mothers, or they can be forced to flower when they reach the desired size.

During this period, the new vegetative growth may look different from what would be expected. The leaves will be round and twisted; however, this is normal and can be expected. Those leaves will eventually be removed as the new vegetative growth returns to normal production.

Regenerated plants tend to sprout many branches, which results in a bushy plant with many small buds. To grow larger buds, prune the plants so that there are fewer branches. The plant will put its energy into the remaining branches, resulting in fewer but bigger buds.

Most people practice regeneration only once or twice and then start again with new plants, although a few growers harvest and regenerate repeatedly.

One popular method of using regeneration is by harvesting indoor plants and then placing harvested plants outdoors in the spring or summer. The plant regenerates and produces an autumn harvest. In warmer climates plants can be placed outdoors for a winter or spring harvest and then regenerated for autumn harvest. If plants are forced to flower in spring or early summer using light deprivation, they can be pruned for regeneration, and they will flower again in the autumn.

A fungus gnat is getting stuck with sticky trichomes.   Photo: Picture Fotografie

APPENDIX E: PEST & DISEASE
Revised by Saul Alba

Pests and diseases are a fact of life in agriculture. Between the 1950s and the 1990s the go-to solution for pest and disease management was almost exclusively eradication with pesticides. In 1942 Rodale started the magazine *Organic Farming and Gardening* to promote chemical-free practices. Then in 1959, Vernon Stern introduced the concept of integrated pest management (IPM) in the landmark paper "The Integration of Chemical and Biological Control of the Spotted Alfalfa Aphid: The Integrated Control Concept." His ideas are still the basis of modern agricultural pest management, whether conventional or organic.

What is now commonly known as the organic agriculture movement arose from the desire to protect the consumer, the farm worker, and the environment. Farmers began to embrace the use of "soft" pesticides as well as other practices that reduced the reliance on pesticide applications to their crops. To a great extent this started as a search for alternatives to banned or regulated chemicals.

Using IPM for cannabis crops is especially important. As more states legalize cannabis, the idea that a product that is primarily consumed through inhalation should be clean of toxic residues guides much of the legislation. Presently, the use of all cannabis crop protection materials is tightly regulated. Many of the pesticides and fungicides that informal market cannabis growers use have been outlawed for legal cannabis production. This has resulted in an increased interest in true integrated pest management.

IPM is an approach to pest management in which the grower relies on several control strategies. As many strategies as can work together are employed, hence the term "integrated." The different approaches can be broken down into four principles of IPM: resistance, exclusion, disruption of the pest life cycle, and eradication. These are not mutually exclusive principles, and strategies often fit into more than one category.

The Four Principles of IPM

1. Resistance
When the grower selects a cultivar that is particularly resistant to a pest or disease, there is a greater chance of protecting the crop. Some cultivars are more resistant than others to fungal attack. Some terpene profiles are more attractive and others more repellent to certain arthropod pests. Flower architecture affects the crop too. Large, tight buds are less resistant to bud rot. When the grower chooses cultivars that are less susceptible to infestation and/or infection, pest and disease management is easier and cheaper.

2. Exclusion

There are many techniques used to prevent plant pests from interfering with the plants no matter where they are being grown.

Outdoors:

- Place netting over plants to keep out many small insects, including moths that lay eggs.
- Use high netting around the garden to prevent infiltration by some wind-borne pests.
- Create an exclusionary zone around the planting space consisting of an unplanted area or planted with pest repellent plants such as sages and mints.
- Put up high fences to protect against herbivores and prowlers.

Greenhouses:

- Screen and filter all incoming air.
- Use exclusionary spaces.
- Dust control around greenhouses prevents the entry of airborne mites, other small invertebrates, and pathogens.
- Change from street clothes to greenhouse work clothes, including shoes.
- Use hair and beard nets.

Indoors:

- Create exclusionary space around building.
- Change from street clothes to work clothes.
- Use hair and beard nets.
- Screen any air being exchanged.

3. Treating and Quarantining New Plants

Quarantine all plants entering the space in a separate area. They should be kept in quarantine for about 15 days. Any infection should be apparent during that time. Plant quarantine can prevent years of suffering from pests and diseases. Thoroughly inspect all plants when they enter quarantine and throughout the period. That should be the last thing done that day.

Sanitation practices can be thought of as exclusion. Built-in air curtains blow pests or spores off anyone who enters the space. Provide clean apparel for workers to change into. Wet sanitation mats, disposable gloves, beard and hair nets, and hand sanitizers help keep disease out of the garden.

How to Quarantine:

1. **Isolate the new plants in a sanitized quarantine space**

    "Social distancing" is important for plants when they are suspected of being carriers of pest and disease. An infected or infested plant cannot spread disease to other plants if they are properly isolated.

2. **Inspect new clones closely**

   Look for the presence of pests, their eggs, or pest damage on the plants. Use a magnifying lens or jeweler's loupe to identify the small pests.

3. **Mechanically remove pests and treat with IPM**

   Either spray or dip plants in a solution to treat against potential pests. Spraying with or dipping in an insecticidal soap solution and herbal pesticide is very effective in killing soft-bodied arthropods like spider mites, aphids, thrips, and so forth. A root dip with an entomopathogenic fungal spore solution such as Beauveria bassiana will inoculate the growing medium to mitigate root pests like root aphids but not mites. Entomopathogenic fungi infect insects and arachnids and parasitize them. The pests eventually die from the infection, and the fungus will release more spores from the pest's carcass.

4. **Install sticky traps in the quarantine area**

   Both yellow and blue sticky traps will show pest presence. The yellow traps show the presence of winged insects, such as winged aphids, whiteflies, and fungus gnats. Blue sticky traps attract the leaf miners and thrips.

5. **Sanitize the quarantine area**

   Fungal spores, zoospores, bacteria, and so on should be neutralized so that disease does not spread. Hydrogen peroxide (H_2O_2), isopropyl alcohol, bleach, hypochlorous acid, and other disinfectant products like Zerotol or OxiPhos work well as antimicrobial sprays.

6. **Sanitize tools, shoes, clothes, hands**

   Spores are all around: in the air, on tabletops, and on the ground. It is important to also sanitize anything that goes from the quarantine area into any area where plants are already growing. Spores can spread from clothing or hands if non-quarantined plants are handled in unsanitary conditions.

7. **Install air cleaners, including a negative ion generator and UVC light air cleaners**

8. **Isolate new plants for as long as needed**

   Typically, the new cuttings will stay in quarantine for a few days; however, if a robust and active IPM program throughout the vegetative and flowering stages is followed, the quarantine time can be abbreviated.

4. Disruption of Life Cycle

This is somewhat of a catch-all principle because it borrows strategies from the others. However, it is important to understand that all pests and diseases have a life cycle and disrupting particular stages can help control them. The life cycle stages are categorized as (1) birth or germination, (2) feeding or infection, (3) reproduction or proliferation, and (4) dissemination. Growers should become intimately familiar with the different life stages of the pest and consider ways that they can be interfered with. Approaching IPM strategy from this angle often reveals options that had not been considered.

Birth or germination is when the pest or disease starts operating. In the case of invertebrates it can be hatching or live birth, and with diseases it's germination of spores or other propagules. Numerous strategies can be used to disrupt birth or germination.

It's important to consider how much environmental conditions affect the life cycle stages of pests and diseases. Many fungal disease spores germinate only when exposed to particular temperatures and humidity levels. In fact, the best management strategy for the most common fungal pathogens found on cannabis is climate control. Other methods are minor tools.

Feeding or infection can be considered the first real attack by the pest or disease on the plant. After a pest is hatched or a spore germinates, penetrating the plant tissue is the life stage that follows. How can the grower disrupt feeding or germination? Azadirachtin is a neem tree extract that is known to repel insect feeding and also to reduce their appetite. Numerous herbal extracts have similar properties. Some spores need wounds in plant tissue in order to infect the plant, so minimizing wounding or treating wounds can be effective. Some plant biostimulants can elicit a resistance response that cause thickening of cell walls, thereby making feeding and infection more difficult.

ARBICO Organics Pest Traps work as a visual attractant for a wide range of crawling and flying insect pests drawn in by the bright color. Once they are trapped, the gridded surface makes it easy to identify and count how many have landed and been captured on the trap. Adult pests are caught there and the reproductive cycle is interrupted.

Eradication

Once the grower has taken into consideration all the previous principles of IPM and developed a strategy, then it is time to think about eradication of the pest or disease. Too often growers devote excessive resources to spray materials, spray equipment, and labor, forgetting that the integrated approach can help their applications perform better. This overreliance on sprays is why the concept of IPM took hold. In fact, most farmers who practice sustainable agriculture look at sprays as a last resort for controlling a problem.

One reason for rethinking the spray-first approach is that biological control, while a very effective eradication strategy, is difficult to integrate with spray programs. Monocropping disrupts natural ecology, giving an advantage to plant pests and diseases. The statement "Nature abhors a vacuum," attributed to Aristotle, is an appropriate explanation.

Crops are artificial ecosystems that don't contain the checks and balances of a true ecosystem. It's conducive to the growth of plants, but also to herbivorous organisms that feed on the crop. The farmer has created a vacuum where these herbivores' natural enemies aren't present.

Most pests can reproduce rapidly and fill the vacuum, resulting in a population explosion. Even if natural enemies arrive, the pest and natural enemy populations are so out of balance that the predator cannot keep up with its prey's reproductive rate.

Biological control rebalances the prey-predator relationship by increasing the population of the herbivore's natural controls. This is done by introducing commercially reared natural enemies indoors and creating habitats that attract natural enemies from the wild in outdoor gardens.

The true goal of IPM is an effort to reduce or eliminate the need for chemical applications to control pests. Sprays and drenches can be thought of as the last-ditch effort of pest management. Sprays are sometimes likely to be used in some circumstances, but an integrated approach seeks to reduce their use and impact on the farm ecosystem and the plants themselves. In some jurisdictions no sprays of any kind are permitted. Farmers in these areas must rely on other sources of protection.

Monitoring

The foundation of modern IPM is monitoring to answer the following questions:
- What is out there?
- Where is it?
- How much of it is there?
- What stage of development is it in?

Decision-making about control options is handicapped until these questions are answered. The larger the pest infestation, the harder it is to control. It is easier to deal with a small population or infection than a large one. Monitoring helps the farmer find sparks or smoldering embers and extinguishes them before they become raging wildfires. It also helps the grower rein in pest management costs by identifying pest or infection "hot spots" so that more resources can be allocated to those areas.

Pests and infections can be identified by their signs and symptoms.

Signs are the pests themselves or something they leave on the plant that can be used to identify them. Eggs, mycelia, excrement, shed exoskeletons, and webbing are all evidence pests leave behind.

Symptoms are the effects observed on a plant that are caused by an infection or pest attack. Common symptoms can be feeding damage, yellowing, leaf deformation and wilt, weird growth, rot, stem damage, unhealthy color, and lack of vitality. It is of utmost importance that the grower is intimately familiar with both signs and symptoms of the infections and pests that can injure the crop.

A very useful technique for monitoring pests is "beat sheet" scouting, which involves using a white sheet and beating on the foliage to knock pests off the plant and onto the sheet, where they can be seen. Pheromone lures are available for some pests. Indicator plants that preferentially attract pests can be used as an early detection tool.

Prevention

Pests are among the most annoying and difficult problems facing gardeners. The best way to deal with them is to prevent them from entering. No matter the growing method, pests will infect the garden if they are given a chance. Here are some ways of preventing them from getting in.

Pets: Pests enter using pets as transportation. Don't let pets in the garden. Their fur and dander can also accumulate on sticky buds.

Clothing: Clothing worn outdoors can carry in pests. Even a single pest can be a vector for a fast-growing colony. After going outside, wash and dress in freshly laundered clothes.

Plant Quarantine: Before letting a plant enter a pest-free garden, place it in quarantine and use a pesticide/fungicide spray or dip just to be sure.

Planting Mix: Make sure the planting mix is composed of inert or pasteurized ingredients. Planting mix that is not inert or pasteurized may contain pests and diseases.

Pest Highways & Airways: Make sure all air coming into the garden space is filtered. Repair any cracks, holes, or other open spaces.

The Common Pests of Cannabis

The following section provides information to help the grower recognize and control pests that commonly affect cannabis. A description of each pest is provided to identify both signs and symptoms, and some effective control options are reviewed.

Invertebrate Pests

Ants herding aphids. Photo: Alexander Wild

Aphids

Aphids are small oblong or pear-shaped soft-bodied insects about one to three millimeters long. There are thousands of species that vary in color from green to yellow, black, or brown. Depending on the species and the stage of life the aphid is in, it may have wings and a wax or "wool" made from their secretions.

A common trait of aphids that distinguishes them from all other insects is the pair of tailpipe-like cornicles that extend from the tail end of their abdomens.

Aphids colonize the stems and undersides of plant leaves. Some species, such as the black bean aphid, are quite noticeable because their color stands out from the plant. Others, such as the green peach aphid or the cannabis aphid, are often colored spring green and blend in with young leaves. The most problematic aphid pest of cannabis by far is the cannabis aphid, which evolved on cannabis and is highly specialized to feed and reproduce exclusively on this plant. Another problematic aphid is the subterranean rice root aphid, which evolved feeding on grass roots but has been able to host on roots of several broadleaf plants, cannabis included.

Aphids are true bugs. They puncture stems, branches, and leaves and suck sap from them using a straw-like mouth, called a stylet. To obtain enough nutrients, aphids must suck a lot of dilute sap, refine it, and excrete the excess concentrated sugar solution, referred to as "honeydew." It attracts food for ants that herd the suckers, protecting them from predators. Honeydew is a growth medium for sooty mold fungus, which causes necrosis of plant tissue and interferes with photosynthesis.

Heavy aphid infestations cause leaf curl, wilt, and stunted and delayed growth. Aphids are vectors for hundreds of diseases and can quickly cause an epidemic. They transfer viruses, bacteria, and fungi from plant to plant.

During warm weather, each generation takes only a few days to complete a life cycle, and each aphid can produce numerous offspring, depending on the species. This high reproduction rate makes aphids seem to appear overnight. Indoors, with no predators to keep them in check, they can overrun a garden very quickly.

The Cannabis Aphid

It's believed that the cannabis aphid evolved along with the cannabis plant. No other plant host is known. This makes it a formidable pest of cannabis, as the plant meets all its predator's nutritional needs, allowing it to reproduce incredibly fast.

The cannabis aphid has a similar appearance to other green aphids, so the grower must pay attention to its distinguishing behaviors and features. It colonizes the underside of leaves but also infests branches. A branch infestation resembles a freeway traffic jam. Other aphids that feed on cannabis tend not to feed on branch tissues.

It is usually almost white during early nymph stages and light green at older stages and adulthood, but it has a broad color range, including brown. Some populations have three green stripes running lengthwise along the dorsal surface of the abdomen. These stripes are more prominent in the darker-colored forms. The winged form is generally a greenish yellow with a dark spot on its back. The main distinguishing features can only be seen under high magnification. They are two horn-like projections between the antennae. The hairs associated with these projections and the antennae have a bulbous tip.

The Rice Root Aphid

The rice root aphid is a pest of cereal crops and some broadleaf crops such as celery and cannabis. Like most aphids, it has a broad range of colorations. Most are green with an orange tail end. Many are completely orange, but their tail ends tend to be a darker orange. These aphids usually feed on cannabis roots but do occasionally infest and feed on leaves.

Monitoring

- Signs: check for colonies, which tend to be most prevalent along the upwind edge of the garden, close to outside sources of aphids; check leaf undersides, where many species hang out. Root aphid colonies are easily identifiable feeding in clusters on roots.
- Signs: look for winged forms.
- Signs: look for shed exoskeletons. The shed exoskeletons are white and for foliar aphids can be seen on leaves under the infestation. Root aphids are found near colonies.
- Signs: look for honeydew. Often exoskeletons stick to the honeydew.
- Signs: look for sooty mold.
- Signs: look for ant presence.
- Symptom: leaf curling.

Resistant Varieties

The industry is still too young for aphid-resistant varieties to be recognized. There are anecdotal observations that some varieties are more susceptible to infestations.

Exclusionary Practices

- Use filtration and screening. Generations of some species are airborne for part of their life cycle, so a fine filter in the air intake prevents aphid entry.
- Hang air curtains at entries to the garden.
- Weed along the perimeter of the garden.
- Use quarantine procedures for new plants.
- Use of repellents such as herbal insecticides, garlic oils, or other herbal extracts.

Disruption of Life Cycle

- Use molting disruptors such as azadirachtin.

Eradication

- Biological controls: aphid parasitoid wasps (*A. colemani, A. ervi*) are extremely effective. They lay eggs in the developing aphid and emerge "Alien" style. Other good options: the aphid predatory midge (*A. aphidimyza*), generalist insect predators (lacewing larva, *Orius insidiosus*), lady bird beetles, sprays (foliar aphids) and drenches (root aphids) of entomopathogenic fungi (*B. bassiana, I. fumosorosea*).
- Sprays: herbal/botanical oils (rosemary, thyme, garlic, peppermint, neem, capsaicin, cinnamon oil, cloves, coriander oil, garlic), insecticidal soaps, pyrethrum.

Spider mites leave behind telltale webbing on the colas.
Photo: Ed Rosenthal

Spider Mites

Spider mites are very common and are among the most serious pests in the cannabis garden.

Spider mites are barely visible to the naked eye, since they are only 0.02 inch (0.4 mm) long. They are arachnids (relatives of spiders), and like other arachnids they have four pairs of legs and no antennae. Their color range includes red, brown, black, yellow, and green, depending on their diet, species, and the time of year. Spider mites are so tiny that most of these details are visible only with magnification.

Spider mites live on the plants, mostly on the underside of the leaves, but are also found around the buds. They can be found moving from leaf to leaf and plant to plant using their silvery webbing as highways.

Spider mites are sap-feeders, like many other garden pests. They are a major threat due to their high rate of reproduction. Spider mites pierce the surface of leaves and then suck plant juices from them. These punctures appear on the leaves as tiny yellow spots. As the population grows, the mites produce webbing that they use as a pedestrian bridge between branches or plants.

Spider mites multiply quickly. They are most active in warmer climates than cold ones.

Reproduction Rate & Life Cycle

Newly hatched mites have a 3:1 ratio of females to males, and each female lays up to 200 eggs. This life cycle can repeat as often as every eight days in warm, dry conditions such as an indoor garden. This means that a spider mite population can explode with shocking speed, and this rapid reproduction is what makes them so troublesome.

Monitoring

- Signs: colonies
- Signs: eggs
- Signs: shed exoskeletons
- Signs: webbing
- Symptoms: stippling (puncture) damage

Exclusionary Practices

- Control dust along the perimeter of the garden.
- Use fine filtration of air inlets.

- Use air curtains.
- Weed along the perimeter of the garden.
- Quarantine new plants. Almost all spider mite infestations enter the garden on an infested plant.

Disruption of Life Cycle
- Control relative humidity. Spider mites thrive in dry climates. High humidity slows spider mite development and reproduction. This can be used in vegetative and early flowering stages to slightly slow population increase.

Eradication
- Biological controls: predatory mites (*P. persimilis, N. californicus, A. andersonii, N. fallacis, G. occidentalis*), the spider mite predatory midge *Feltiella acarisuga*, the spider mite ladybird beetle predator *Stethorus punctillum*, generalist insect predators (lacewing larva, *Orius insidiosus*).
- Sprays: herbal/botanical oils (cinnamon, clove, lemon grass, rosemary, thyme, garlic, peppermint), insecticidal soaps, miticidal sulfur sprays.

ARBICO Organics Leafhopper Assassin Bugs (*Zelus renardii*) are excellent general predators in gardens and greenhouses because they remain predatory in all life stages. Their rapid feeding habits and tendency to kill for the sake of killing make them ideal for continued control of various pest insect populations including leafhoppers, aphids, mealybugs, thrips, small caterpillars, and more. Assassin Bugs also have the ability to feed on larger prey than many of their beneficial insect counterparts. Their wide range of food sources and high reproduction rate allow Assassin Bugs to maintain and even grow their population without high pest numbers. They are active in a wide range of temperatures and have a two-month lifespan, providing continuous control.

Release fast-feeding *Phytoseiulus persimilis* at first sign of spider mite infestation. *P. persimilis* are red relative to the pest mites they feed on and are best used to combat active mite populations. *P. persimilis* will leave the area in search of alternative food sources if pest levels drop too low. *P. persimilis* consume egg, nymph, and adult stages of pest mites.

Hemp Russet Mites (HRM)

Hemp russet mites are very small in comparison with other cannabis pests, and an individual is nearly impossible to see without magnification. As a size comparison, the length of their bodies is roughly the diameter of a spider mite egg. The body shape of HRM is very different from most other mites in that it is elongated and almost worm-like, with their legs near the head at the thick end of the body. They resemble tiny carrots.

Their only known host is cannabis; hence, HRM can be a devastating pest to the crop that can completely destroy flowers. It is an insidious pest in that often the symptoms of an infestation are only visible after the population is enormous. These sap-feeding mites cause a leaf deformation typically called "canoeing" because the leaves curl downward and resemble a canoe. This symptom is not always indicative of HRM feeding. Another symptom of HRM infestation is a "rust" discoloration of branches and young flowers. Finding this symptom usually takes a trained eye.

The primary strategy for control is exclusion of infested plants. Most russet mite infestations were inherited by less-than-dedicated growers who did not quarantine and scout plants that were brought in from other gardens. The mites are also suspected of using wind currents to get from one plant to another.

Once in a garden they are nearly impossible to eradicate. The go-to strategy is the use of elemental sulfur sprays, but these are risky to consumers and also when used shortly after applying oil sprays because it dramatically increases the risk of phytotoxicity.

Herbal sprays such as Ed Rosenthal's Zero Tolerance control the mites when used regularly.

All mite sprays should be applied using a fogger so that they coat the undersides of the leaves, where the mites hang out.

There are anecdotal reports that commercially available natural enemies can control an HRM infestation. One promising exception would be the Western Predatory Mite, *Ga-*

Ed Rosenthal's Zero Tolerance Pesticide has been formulated from food-grade cinnamon, clove, rosemary, and thyme oils to create a powerful tool to kill and repel plant pests and pathogens. It has been designed for repeated use.

lendromus occidentalis, which controls russet mites of other crops. One thing that the grower needs to consider before attempting to use predatory mites for HRM control is that they will likely feed on their preferred prey if it is present and ignore HRM.

Monitoring
- Signs: colonies.
- Symptoms: leaf deformation ("canoeing").
- Symptoms: stem discoloration ("rust-like").
- Symptoms: flower discoloration ("rust-like").

Resistant Varieties
- The industry is still too young for HRM-resistant varieties to be recognized; however, there have been observations of preferences for plants with certain terpene profiles.

Exclusionary Practices
- Use air curtains.
- Weed out "volunteer" hemp plants along the perimeter of the grow.
- Employ quarantine procedures for new plants.
- Enforce worker hygiene protocols.

Eradication
- Potential for biological control of early infestations by *Galendromus, Amblyseius,* and *Neoseiulus* predatory mites (*G. occidentalis N. californicus, A. andersonii, N. fallacis*).
- Sprays: elemental sulfur sprays and clone dips, insecticidal soaps, and paraffinic oils.

Broad Mites

Broad mites are a microscopic mite pest of cannabis. Unlike hemp russet mites, broad mites are pests of many other crops too. The body shape of broad mites is similar to that of other mites, but there is a sizable gap between its two front legs, which tend to point forward, and its two hind legs, which tend to be oriented to the back. Unlike hemp russet mites, they are very mobile.

One other sign of broad mite infestation is the presence of their eggs on leaf surfaces. These eggs are tiny, oblong, and translucent, and have what appear to be a dimpled surface. They are very distinct, and scouts should know what to look for.

Symptoms of broad mite infestation can be similar to those of hemp russet mites. Leaf deformation from feeding tends to be more "blister-like," and there is often what appears to be more of a sheen to the leaves. Leaves often lose their sheen and tend to curl up, so "canoes" or downward-curling leaves are more likely to indicate russet mites.

As with hemp russet mites, the primary strategy for control is exclusion of infested plants and worker hygiene. Since they are very mobile, they can be introduced on clothing and have even been reported to hitchhike on whiteflies.

Herbal oil and sulfur sprays can also be used for broad mite control. Two commercially available predatory mites, *Galendromus*, *Amblyseius* and *Neoseiulus* mites successfully control them in a number of crops.

Monitoring
- Signs: mobile adults.
- Signs: distinct eggs.
- Symptoms: leaf deformation ("blistering").
- Symptoms: leaf deformation (upward curl of the leaf edge).

Exclusionary Practices
- Use air curtains.
- Employ quarantine procedures for new plants.
- Enforce worker hygiene protocols.

Eradication
- For biological control of early infestations use *Galendromus, Amblyseius,* and *Neoseiulus* predatory mites (*G. occidentalis N. californicus, A. andersonii, N. fallacis*).
- Sprays: herbal oils, elemental sulfur sprays, and insecticidal soaps.

Photo: Ed Rosenthal

Caterpillars
In spring and summer, caterpillars are common outdoors, but rare indoors.

Caterpillars are the larval stage of butterflies and moths. They have soft, segmented bodies with a head, thorax, and abdomen. The thorax contains three pairs of jointed legs that have hooks and the abdomen up to five pairs of stumpy, "false" legs. Caterpillars are often the same color as leaves, so they are hard to spot. There are a range of caterpillars that commonly infest cannabis.

Corn Earworm
Adults are gray to brown with a wingspan of about 35 mm (1.3 inches). Coloration of the larvae varies from green to brown, and they have a dark stripe that runs the length of their backs as well as along both sides. There is typically a lighter coloration of the underbelly. Eggs can be laid singly or in clusters.

Cutworms
The adults are gray to dark brown moths with wingspans of 1.25–1.75 inches (3–4.5 cm). The caterpillars grow to 1–1.5 inches (2.5 to 3.75 cm) long. Colors include brown, green,

gray, and black. Eggs vary widely by species but are usually laid on the stems or the upper sides of leaves in clusters. The caterpillars hide in the soil and leaf litter and feed on the aboveground parts of the plant at night.

Cabbage Worms

The most common cabbage worm is the Imported Cabbage Worm. The adult moths are off-white with one or two black spots on each wing. They have a wingspan of about 1.5–2 inches (3.75–5 cm). The caterpillars are green and may grow up to 1.5 inches (3.75 cm) long. Eggs are ridged and dome-shaped and usually laid singly on the undersides of leaves.

Corn Borers

The adults are yellow or tan-colored nocturnal moths with wingspans of about an inch (2.5 cm). The caterpillars are about one inch long, light brown in color with a brown head, and spots on each segment. Eggs are white to pale yellow in color, laid in clusters of 20 to 30 on the undersides of leaves.

Caterpillars eat both leaves and the soft stems. Others bore into the stem and eat the pith, the stem's soft inner tissue. Cutworms feed at night and spend the day in shallow burrows near the plants. Corn borers attack mature plants: they need a stem large enough to hold their bodies. After the eggs are laid on the leaves, they hatch and the young larvae eat the leaves around the eggs for two weeks to a month, leaving close clusters of tiny holes. To catch borers early, look for these small holes. Later in the season look for small holes in the plant stalks, possibly covered with thin silky webbing. After borers have been at work for a while, they sometimes cause the stalk to develop "fusiform galls," or bulges in the plants' stalks that widen in the middle and taper at both ends. The borers may leave visible trails on the stalks leading to the galls.

The branches and leaves above the caterpillar's feeding damage wilt, since they receive no water or nutrients. If it is a main stem, the whole plant dies. If it is a side stem, only that branch succumbs. In addition to the direct damage they cause, caterpillars leave behind damaged tissues that are vulnerable to infection as well as feces that can serve as inoculation points for numerous microbes.

Caterpillars are voracious eating machines and can savage plants very quickly. They chew continuously to support their high growth rate. They can destroy a tray of seedlings overnight.

Leaf-eaters leave large holes as calling cards in the leaves they dine on. Corn earworms, cabbage worms, and other caterpillars also infest buds. A bud that turns brown and wilts "for no reason" may house a caterpillar consuming it from within.

Cutworms are perhaps the most obvious of all caterpillars: plants damaged by cutworms are literally chewed through at the soil line, causing the plant to topple. Seedlings and young plants are completely consumed.

Moths can produce many generations per year in warm climates. Each female lays several hundred eggs. The adults mate in spring to early summer, and the caterpillars emerge in the early summer to fall. The caterpillars feed until they are ready to enter the pupal stage. They then spin cocoons or dig burrows and continue their development until they emerge as adult moths. The generation that emerges in late summer and fall often overwinter as caterpillars, emerging in early spring to begin feeding again. This is especially common with cutworm species.

Caterpillars reproduce slowly compared with many pests, but they have large appetites, and each one can cause a lot of damage.

Monitoring
- Signs: adults fly around lights at night or are caught on pheromone traps.
- Signs: eggs.
- Signs: larva (caterpillars).
- Signs: leaves that are rolled with silk (some species).
- Signs: pupae.
- Signs: silky webbing.
- Signs: feces.
- Symptoms: chewing damage.
- Symptoms: "Fusiform galls" from corn borer feeding.
- Symptoms: dried-up buds.

Exclusionary Practices
- Use light traps outside the garden.
- Screen air inlets.
- Use pheromone mating disruption of some species.
- Use row covers to prevent egg laying.
- Weed alternate hosts.
- Protect young plants by growing vegetatively indoors.
- Use insect trapping glue applied as cutworm barriers on the stems of seedlings and young plants.

Eradication
- Biological control: BT Trichogramma wasps, spined soldier bugs, generalist insect predators (lacewing larva, *Orius insidiosus*), parasitic nematodes (*S. feltiae*) for subterranean caterpillars, *Bacillus thuringiensis kurstaki* (Btk) sprays, praying mantis.
- Sprays: herbal/botanical oils (rosemary, thyme, garlic, peppermint, neem), herbal teas (cinnamon), insecticidal soaps, insect neurotoxins (pyrethrins, spinosads), commercially available polyhedral occlusion bodies of numerous caterpillar viruses.
- Hand removal of the larva.

Thrips
Thrips are not commonly considered major pests of cannabis. However, in some indoor and greenhouse conditions they can be serious pests.

Thrips are tiny, no more than 0.06 inch (1.5 mm) long, but can still be seen by the naked eye. Adults have wings but do not fly well; they jump when startled. The head and body range from yellow to dark brown. The larvae are about half the size of adults, lighter in color, and wingless.

Thrips attack the leaves and are seen on both surfaces.

Thrips use a saw-like structure to pierce and scrape the leaf surfaces until sap begins to flow. They then suck up the juices and leave a surface of patchy white or silvery scrapings often called "rasping" damage. The leaf surface looks scarred or scabby. If the infestation is heavy and goes unchecked, the leaves lose much of their chlorophyll and turn white. Thrips leave behind greenish black specks of feces on and under leaves. The scar tissue shows up in silver patches. Thrips damage can resemble that of spider mites or leaf miners at first.

Damaged leaves can't be healed, and their ability to absorb light is compromised. If the thrips are not controlled, the plants die. Thrips also carry pathogens that they transfer through feeding, although it is yet to be confirmed that any of these pathogens can infect the cannabis plant.

Outdoors, thrips hibernate over the winter in soil and plant debris. Thrips become active when the temperature climbs above 60°F (16°C). The warm, stable temperatures of indoor gardens allow them to be active year-round. Thrips are a more serious problem indoors because of this and also because a natural soil-dwelling fungus that infect thrips pupae may not be present in indoor grows.

Reproduction Rate & Life Cycle
Females lay eggs (anywhere from 40 to 300 depending on species) in plant crevices or insert them into the leaves and stems. The larvae of Western Flower Thrips feed until they enter what is known as a pre-pupal stage, when they fall to the ground, burrow, spend two developmental stages in the soil or leaf litter, and then emerge as reproductive adults.

Depending on the species and temperature (optimum is 77–82°F/26–28°C), the larval thrips hatch, pupate, and mature into egg-laying adults in 7 to 30 days.

Monitoring
- Signs: identify adults and larvae either on the plant by using the "beat scouting" technique or on blue or yellow sticky cards.
- Signs: green to black feces near feeding damage.
- Symptoms: "rasping" feeding damage.
-

Exclusionary Practices
- Barrier placed between soil and plant canopy.
- Use air curtains.
- Thrips screening.
- Weed along the perimeter of the grow.
- Employ quarantine procedures for new plants.

- Western Flower Thrips pupae live in the soil after they drop from the plant. By placing a barrier around the top of the container, the pupae can't get to the soil and die. As with fungus gnat larvae, a layer of diatomaceous earth on top of the soil also helps destroy the thrips pre-pupae.

Disruption of Life Cycle
- Molting disruptors such as azadirachtin.

Eradication
- Biological control of early infestations by *Amblyseius* predatory mites (*A. swirskii*, *A. cucumeris*), generalist insect predators (lacewing larva, *Orius insidiosus*), entomopathogenic fungi (*B. bassiana*, *I. fumosorosea*), parasitic nematodes (*S. feltiae*), soil predatory rove beetle (*D. coriaria* formerly *Atheta*), soil predatory mite (*S. scimitus* formerly *Hypoaspis*).
- Sprays: herbal/botanical oils (rosemary, thyme, garlic peppermint, neem), herbal teas (capsaicin, cinnamon oil, cloves, coriander oil, garlic), insecticidal soaps, insect neurotoxins (pyrethrins, spinosads).
- Trapping with yellow or blue sticky tape, trap crops such as marigolds.
- Crop vacuuming.

ARBICO Organics offers six species of beneficial nematodes to choose the best options for the indoor garden, greenhouse, row crop, or container. Beneficial nematodes mainly parasitize insect pests that have soil-dwelling larvae or pupae; however, they have been known to parasitize above ground stages of certain pests as well. Their wide range of prey makes them exceptional for general pest control in chemical-free growing environments.

Fungus Gnats

Fungus gnats are common indoors. They are found outdoors occasionally in moist warm areas.

Fungus gnats are a tenth to a twelfth of an inch (3-4 mm), dark grayish black, and have a slender build with delicate long legs and long wings. The larvae are clear to creamy-white with a shiny black head and can be up to a quarter inch (6 mm) long.

Adults fly close to the soil level and through the lower region of the plant canopy. Fungus gnat larvae live at the root level, usually from one to three inches (2.5 to 7.5 cm) below the soil line. In shallow containers the larvae may be found wriggling in the drain tray after watering. Outdoors, adults and larvae live in moist, shady areas.

Fungus gnat larvae weaken the plant by eating roots, root hairs, and organic matter growing in planting mix, rockwool, soil, and other planting mediums. They can also be vectors for disease. Adult gnats do not eat. They live only to reproduce. However, when they develop into large-enough swarms, they can stick to trichomes on flowers.

Adult females lay eggs at the surface of moist soil, near the plant stem. The larvae hatch out in 4 to 10 days, depending on temperature, and feed off algae, fungus, and plant matter (including plant roots), and then pupate in the soil and emerge as adults. The total time from egg to reproductive adult is about four weeks, and females lay several hundred eggs in small batches over their lifetime. Indoors, they breed continuously throughout the year and reproduce very rapidly.

Monitoring
- Signs: adults flying or crawling under the canopy or trapped in yellow sticky cards.
- Signs: larva in the soil or feeding on potato halves. Potato halves can be placed on the soil surface cut-side down and checked periodically. The larva will be found feeding on the potato.

Exclusionary Practices
- Use air curtains.
- Use screening.
- Employ quarantine procedures for new plants.

Disruption of Life Cycle
- Barrier placed between soil and plant canopy. Paper, cloth, or another barrier placed over the soil prevents larvae from completing their life cycle, part of which is spent in the soil.
- Control irrigation so that there is no overwatering. Algae attracts adults that grow in areas of standing water and pot surfaces.
- A layer of diatomaceous earth can prevent the fungus gnat adult from laying eggs in the soil. If algae develops on the surface of the diatomaceous earth, then its effectiveness diminishes.

Eradication

- Biological control with parasitic nematodes (*S. feltiae*), soil predatory rove beetle (*D. coriaria* formerly *Atheta*), soil predatory mite (*S. scimitus* formerly *Hypoaspis*), *Bacillus thuringiensis israelensis* (Bti) drenches.
- A drench with hydrogen peroxide / peracetic acid solutions can kill fungus gnat larvae.
- Sprays: herbal/botanical oils (cinnamon, rosemary, thyme, garlic, peppermint, neem), insecticidal soaps, insect neurotoxins (pyrethrins).
- Trapping: putting yellow sticky tape under the canopy lowers population levels.

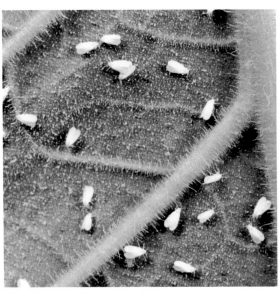

Photo: Nature's Control

Whiteflies

Whiteflies are common pests indoors and outdoors. Whiteflies resemble tiny moths but are neither moths nor true flies. They are relatives of aphids and scales. They are 0.04 inch (1 mm) long, and their soft bodies are covered in a powdery wax, which gives them protection.

Whiteflies infest the undersides of leaves. If the plant is disturbed, they take flight and are seen fluttering around the plant.

They are true bugs, using a modified mouth shaped like a straw to puncture plants and suck sap. They are vectors for viruses. Like aphids, whiteflies exude sticky honeydew, and this can contribute to mold problems on the plants. Leaves appear spotty, droop, and lose vigor.

Whiteflies quickly build up a large population and suck the life out of the plants, but they are not difficult to get rid of. Plants are easily checked for whiteflies by shaking them. If they are present, they'll fly off and then settle right back onto the leaves.

Reproduction Rate & Life Cycle

Females each lay about 100 tiny eggs on the underside of leaves. Eggs hatch in about 7 to 10 days, and the larvae drain sap from leaves. Larvae mature in two to four weeks, and the adults live for four to six weeks after that. Like all arthropods, their reproductive rate is temperature dependent: most whitefly species do best in a temperature range of 80 to 90°F (27–33°C).

Monitoring

- Signs: adults flying or feeding under leaves or trapped in yellow sticky cards. The glue from yellow sticky cards removes their waxy covering so they appear clear.

- Signs: waxy exudates left on the leaves where there was a colony.
- Signs: eggs laid in a circular pattern.
- Signs: nymphs that look like miniature trilobites, usually with red eyes.
- Signs: pupae that look like hockey pucks. Some species have long hair protruding from them.
- Signs: translucent, empty pupal cases.
- Signs: honeydew.
- Signs: sooty mold.
- Signs: ant presence.

Exclusionary Practices
- Use air curtains.
- Screen.
- Weed areas around the garden.

Disruption of Life Cycle
- Molting disruptors such as azadirachtin.

Eradication
- Biological control with parasitoid wasps (*E. formosa*, *E. eretmocerus*), *Amblyseius swirskii* (the predatory mite), the Mullein Bug Dicyphus hesperus, generalist insect predators (lacewing larva, *Orius insidiosus*), entomopathogenic fungi (*B. bassiana*, *I. fumosorosea*).
- Sprays: herbal/botanical oils (cinnamon, rosemary, thyme, garlic, peppermint, neem), limonene-oil-based repellents, insecticidal soaps, insect neurotoxins (pyrethrins).
- Trapping with yellow sticky tape under the canopy.
- Crop vacuuming.

Slugs & Snails

Snails and slugs occasionally attack greenhouse and outdoor gardens, especially young plants with leaves close to the ground. They are rare indoors.

Slugs range in color from pale gray to tan and grow to as long as two inches (5 cm) long. Their bodies are soft and fleshy, and glisten with a clear slime that the slugs secrete to retain moisture and help their movement. Two small "horns" atop the slug's head are actually the slug's "eyes," which sense light (slugs have no sense of sight).

Snails are slugs with shells. They are built almost identically to slugs, except for a coiled shell of calcium carbonate that protects most of a snail's body. Snails can withdraw completely into their shells when threatened. Shells of common garden snails can reach up to an inch and a half (3.75 cm) in diameter, and are gray, brown, and black.

Snails and slugs are found on the leaves and edges of leaves and flowers when it is moist, usually after dusk. When it is dry or light, they hide in dark moist areas such as piles of fallen leaves, crevices, and moist shady areas.

Snails and slugs eat leaves. Holes in leaves and/or clipped edges of leaves and flowers, accompanied by a silvery, slimy trail, indicate snail or slug damage. A single snail can savage many small plants in one night.

These pests thrive in moist, dark environments. They hide in mulch, short and stubby plants, under boards, and in soil. They avoid sunlight, so they are seldom seen during the day, but come out to feast at night.

There is one particular kind of snail that should be left alone. Decollate snails sometimes attack plants, but their main food is other snails and slugs. The fastest way to tell a "good" snail from a plant-eating pest is the shape of the shell: common garden snails usually have round shells that coil in a simple spiral. Most species of decollate snails have cone-shaped shells. If these are the only snails found in the garden, then go ahead and get rid of them, because they eat plants if there is no other food in their habitat. But if there are other snails present as well, then the decollate snail is a friend.

Reproduction Rate & Life Cycle
Slugs and snails are hermaphroditic, so every individual lays eggs in clutches of 30 to 120 eggs, one to two inches (2.5 to 5 cm) in moist soil. When conditions are suitable (not too dry or too cold), slugs and snails can lay eggs as often as once a month, so their numbers can increase rapidly during damp spring and fall weather.

Monitoring
- Signs: adults and eggs that are laid in the soil.
- Signs: dried slime trails.
- Signs: feces.
- Symptoms: feeding damage.

Exclusionary Practices
- Screen.

- Eliminate areas of excessively humid soil.
- Use copper-based barriers (copper salts, copper tapes).

Eradication
- Biological control with decollate snails, arthropod predators (rove beetles, carabid beetles), all manner of vertebrates (amphibians, reptiles, birds, and mammals).
- Iron granular slug baits.
- Trapping with beer traps.
- Hand picking.

Ants

Ants are abundant both indoors and outdoors. Most of the species that affect cannabis do so because they protect honeydew-producing pests such as aphids and other sap-sucking bugs.

Ants can be found in the soil or planting medium, where they nest. They climb the stalk and graze their herds of aphids and other sap feeders on the leaves. They nest in underground colonies, occasionally causing damage to the roots.

Ants are attracted to plants that already have colonies of aphids or any other sap-feeding bugs. They tend to these pests and protect them from predators, often moving them to new grazing areas. It is important to control ants not so much for the damage they might cause to the plant directly but because they make control of other pests more difficult.

Ants are social creatures, living in colonies centered around queens and supported by workers. Some species have only one queen per colony, while others may have several. The ant life cycle begins with an egg laid by a queen, progresses through a larval and pupal stage, and then adulthood. In many species only the oldest adults work outside the colony. Ninety percent of the ants work in the nest. Colonies reproduce when a newly hatched queen selects several males and either walks or flies to a new location.

Ants regulate their reproductive rates depending on conditions in the colony and the outside environment. They do this partly by regulating the length of the pupal stage and partly by varying how many larvae or pupae are transformed into queens. With suitable weather, ample food, and water, the reproductive rate increases. To protect the plant, the colony must be eliminated.

Monitoring
- Signs: adults crawl on floors and walls, on the plants, on the soil and pots and near colonies of sap-sucking insects.

Exclusionary Practices

- Place ant poison baits along the perimeter of the garden.
- Place ant traps along the perimeter of the garden.
- Use perimeter insecticidal sprays or powders such as ground cinnamon or cloves.
- Destroy ant colonies adjacent to the garden.
- Use water moats. Ants don't swim, so moats prevent them from crawling from floor or table to the container. A simple moat can be made using a wide tray and a support such as a thick piece of Styrofoam or a block of wood. Place the plant container on top of the support. Fill the tray with water or place the table legs in a moat.
- Spread diatomaceous earth along the garden perimeter.
- Use sticky substances painted on or wrapped around plant stalks and stems, pots, and tables, which can interfere with their harvesting behavior.

Eradication

- Sprays: herbal/botanical oils (rosemary, thyme, garlic, peppermint, neem), insecticidal soaps, insect neurotoxins (pyrethrins, spinosads).
- Bait stations placed within the garden. Poisonous bait stations are a fast and efficient way to control ant infestations. Boric acid is an organic material that when mixed with a sugary bait will be taken back to the colony and fed to others. If ingested regularly it will kill the colony.

Vertebrate Pests

Vertebrate pests tend to be problematic in the outdoor grow environment, although they can also wreak havoc inside the greenhouse. The best way to manage them is through exclusionary practices.

Burrowing Mammals: Gophers & Moles

Gophers and moles are subterranean mammals. Gophers are more of a problem for farmers because they feed on plant roots and kill them, while moles are predators of invertebrates and don't feed on plant material. Both can cause damage to roots if they dig near plants. These tunnels can be extensive, and injuries to workers who step into them are another potential problem. Both can also damage irrigation lines.

Gophers are medium-size rodents ranging from about 5 to nearly 14 inches (13–36 cm) long (not including tail). Their fur is very fine and ranges in color from nearly black to pale brown. The forepaws have strong claws. The head is small and flattened, with small ears and eyes and very prominent incisor teeth.

Gophers feed on plants in three ways; (1) they feed on roots that they encounter when digging their tunnels, (2) they may venture short distances (only a body length or so) from their tunnels to eat vegetation on the surface, and (3) they pull vegetation into their tunnels from below. Gophers may also attract predators that feed on them, and these may cause considerable damage when digging for their food.

Moles are also burrowing mammals about five to seven inches (13–17 cm) long, weighing three to four ounces (85–115 g). They have soft dark fur, very small eyes, pointed snouts, and strong digging claws on their front feet. Moles seldom appear on the surface, but the gardener usually notices their burrows instead.

Moles build tunnel complexes in rich soil. They eat insects and earthworms, and therefore favor moist soils with a lot of soil-dwelling insect life.

When gophers are suspected, the first task is to make sure that they aren't moles instead.

First, check their diggings: a molehill tends to be a rough cone with a hole or an earthen "plug" near the center. A gopher mound is more fan-shaped, with the hole or plug near one edge. Next, look for damage. Moles generally cause very little damage. Gophers may chew the plants' roots, causing them to wilt and making it possible to pull them up with just a slight tug. If plants are chewed off completely at the soil line, or completely gone roots and all, then chances are good that there is a gopher problem.

Reproduction Rate & Life Cycle

Gophers mate once a year, in the spring, and produce a litter of up to five young in late spring to early summer. They live for up to 12 years.

Moles generally have one litter of two to five pups per year, in mid to late spring. Except for the spring breeding period, they tend to be solitary and highly territorial. They fight other moles even to the death if one invades another's tunnel system.

Monitoring

- Signs: tunnels and piles of earth from their digging.
- Signs: gophers occasionally exit their tunnels
- Symptoms: wilted plants, roots show chewing damage or have been completely eaten.

Exclusionary Practices

- Install gopher screens under the soil before planting.
- Use traps. Gopher and mole traps can be very different, since they are designed to take advantage of their different burrowing and feeding habits.
- Use perimeter repellents. Gophers and moles are repelled by several different substances. Castor oil is a commonly used organic repellent, but synthetic repellents are also available. Odor repellents such as predator urine can also work.

Eradication

- Biological control: owl boxes are often erected near grows to attract females to nest.

Owls hunt at night when gophers may find it safer to emerge from their burrows.

- Fumigants: toxic substances such as poison gases, carbon monoxide (engine exhaust fumes), and carbon dioxide, either as a gas or as dry ice, can be pumped into their tunnels to kill entire colonies. Commercial fumigants are generally paper or cardboard cartridges filled with charcoal and potassium nitrate. They're ignited and dropped into the tunnel openings, and the gasses they produce as they burn kill the gophers. Watch for wisps of smoke rising from the ground, as these may mark other exits from the gopher's tunnel. Sealing the exits with packed earth or heavy rocks is critical to keeping the toxic gases inside the burrow and also to prevent escapes while the fumigation is performed.

- Poison baits: there are commercially available organic and conventional toxic baits for burrowing pests of agriculture. Some of these are very fast acting; others require multiple feedings. What must always be considered are any nontarget effects on predators of gophers and moles. If predators feed on a poisoned pest, the toxins that killed it are ingested by them (dogs, cats, owls, raptors) and may in turn poison them.

Deer

Deer populations vary widely, both geographically and by habitat. Deer favor light forest and grasslands near forested areas, as they dislike getting more than a few hundred yards from cover. Gardens in suburban areas built near suitable forestland may have problems with grazing deer. Garden plots set up in wild or rural areas are very likely to be visited by deer if the habitat supports them.

Deer are grazers with graceful bodies, thin legs, and long necks. They vary greatly in size depending on species, age, and sex, but usually range between four and six feet (1.2 and 1.8 m) long and weigh 80 to 220 pounds (35 to 100 kg). Usually the heavier species are found in the north and the smaller lighter ones in the south. The males carry antlers beginning in late summer and usually shed them in very late winter or spring.

Deer emerge from forest cover at night to browse on plants, but flee quickly when approached. They have excellent senses, so most of the time the gardener knows them only by their tracks and the damage they leave. Some deer have become accustomed to humans and don't flee on sight.

Deer prefer fresh leaves, fruit, and other rich plant matter. In the cannabis garden they tear up and eat entire small plants, strip plants of leaves, and trample them. Cannabis evolved cannabinoids in part as protection against herbivores. Most mammals find the leaves and flowers unpleasant. Deer are among the few exceptions. This means that in areas that have large deer populations, they may be attracted to the garden simply because it's a food supply that most other herbivores leave alone. Even so, they prefer young, tender plants. As cannabis matures and cannabinoid levels increase, they become less palatable to deer.

Deer lack upper incisor teeth. They do not bite plants the way a rabbit or similar animal might. Instead the deer takes hold of leaves with its lips and lower teeth and then tears them off. This makes for ragged browse damage, very different from the neatly clipped leaves left by rodents. Look also for deer tracks and droppings near the garden.

Reproduction Rate & Life Cycle

Deer follow a normal mammalian life cycle. Adults mate in the late autumn through mid-winter, and the female gives birth to one or occasionally two fawns in late spring to early summer. Deer usually mature in 1 to 2 years and live for 10–20 years if not killed by predators or disease.

Monitoring

- Signs: adults and young.
- Signs: tracks.
- Signs: feces.
- Symptoms: leaf feeding damage that appears ragged. Younger plants are eaten entirely.

Exclusionary Practices

- Use fencing. Fencing must be tall enough so that the deer can't jump over it. A deer can jump any fence under eight feet (2.5 m) high if it can get close enough. Fencing can be electrified to make it more effective. A variant called a "Minnesota fence" actually uses an attractive bait such as peanut butter to get the deer to lick the fence or a foil tag attached to the fence. The deer get a mild shock and avoid the fence completely after that.
- Use perimeter repellents. Deer find the odors of garlic, capsaicin, and rotten eggs offensive, and several brands of commercial repellents containing these ingredients are available. Anything that carries a human's scent such as barbershop clippings, worn clothing, or human urine also works. Urine or scat from dogs or other predators is another option. Predator urine is available commercially. Scat is sometimes available from a local zoo or pet store. Scented bar soap can be used suspended in a net bag near the plants. If it is unknown whether a repellent is safe for use on food plants, surround the cannabis plants with other plants that will not be ingested. Replace the repellent according to the manufacturer's instructions or every few days for the other scent repellents listed above.
- Use sounds and lights. Anything that startles or frightens deer is effective. Buy several home motion detectors at a hardware store and set them up in a perimeter around the grow site. Depending on the resources at the site, motion detectors can be rigged to trigger high-pressure water sprinklers (these are sold as "scarecrow sprinklers"),

bright lights, battery-powered radios, or ultrasonic noise when a deer approaches. Remember to set up lights to point away from the plants, and if discretion is important, then shield the lights or lower the radio volume so the deer can detect them but nearby watchers cannot.

Eradication
- Use traps.
- Hunt them (follow local regulations).

Rodents: Rats & Mice

Rats and mice are not common pests in cannabis gardens, but sometimes they kill plants by gnawing or digging. They are an environment-specific problem, as they view cannabis as a target of opportunity.

Rats and mice are common wherever humans live, although they are not always visible. Some rats live in the wild, feasting on insects, nuts, fruits, and nature's detritus. They lair in burrows, walls, piles of trash, dense brush, attics, or wherever they can build a secure nest.

Cannabis is not a primary food source for rats, but they like to chew the woody stalks of plants. This cuts the plants down. These rodents' teeth grow constantly, and gnawing behavior is instinctive.

Rodents can also be indirect pests of cannabis. Many growers use slow-release sachets of predatory mites as a biological control strategy for several different pests such as spider mites, thrips, and whiteflies. These sachets are essentially tiny breeding colonies of predatory mites that are hung in the canopy where their prey live. As the members of the breeding colony reach maturity, they emerge from the sachets and begin hunting in the crop for their pest prey. The sachets contain a wheat bran carrier that is attractive to rodents. If the rodent population in and around the garden is sizable, they can destroy all the sachets within a few nights. If the grower wishes to use slow-release sachets as part of a biological control program, it is essential that rodents be controlled.

Rodents are a problem for the garden when the garden is close to something that they like to eat. Gardens near cornfields, orchards, food warehouses, areas with nuts or berries growing wild, and other similar places are at risk. Food at campsites draws rats and mice close to the garden, so secure all food and destroy or remove all food scraps.

Rodents are prolific breeders. They breed year round if they have sufficient food and a warm place to keep their young. They produce numerous litters a year, but they adjust their population automatically to the local food supply.

Monitoring

- Signs: rodent runways. When rodents leave their nests, they prefer to move close to walls following scent paths left during previous excursions. These pathways are known as runways and can often be identified visually by the gray or brown marks on the walls adjacent to the runway that oil from their fur has left behind.
- Signs: feces. These are prominent along runways and entrances into walls. Products that dye rodent feces with a fluorescent compound after they are digested can be used to find feces.
- Signs: holes in slow-release sachets.
- Symptoms: chewing damage on stalks.

Exclusionary Practices

- Repair cracks in the walls of grow rooms or greenhouses. The repair material should be made of something that rodents can't chew through such as steel plate or steel wool.
- Use traps. There are numerous different kinds of traps. Lethal traps are usually set and kill the individual that triggered it. Live-catch traps can capture an individual rodent or they can be multi-catch, which do not have to be reset. Runways are the most strategic location to place traps.
- Use perimeter repellents. Castor oil is a commonly used organic repellent, but synthetic repellents are also available. Odor repellents such as predator urine can also work.

Eradication

- Biological control: owl boxes, cat sentries.
- Poison baits: there are commercially available organic and conventional toxic baits for rodent pests of agriculture. An organic poison is cholecalciferol, a Vitamin D3 that requires multiple feedings. As with other poisons, the grower needs to be careful to not poison their non-target predators. Predators feeding on rodents killed by cholecalciferol are much less likely to be poisoned.

The Common Diseases of Cannabis

Disease can strike cannabis plants at any stage. The diseases that affect cannabis fall into three broad categories: fungal, viral, and bacterial. The spores that cause plant diseases are ubiquitous. Viral and viroid particles live either in the plant or inside an insect that vectors them. A garden's susceptibility to disease is often traceable to environmental imbalances in temperature, moisture, light conditions, airflow, and pH, among others.

Fungus grows when it finds the right levels of moisture, temperature (the range varies by species), acidic conditions, and a reliable source of nutrition.

Viruses or viroids live in plant tissues, and in cannabis are transmitted mechanically.

Bacteria are much more likely to invade when the environment has been compromised, in conditions such as oxygen deprivation, which make their attack more successful.

Once disease hits, it is important to act quickly. However, prevention is the best solution.

Botrytis infected plants Photo: Ed Rosenthal

Gray Mold & Brown Mold (Botrytis)

Gray mold, *Botrytis cinerea*, is found almost everywhere and can cause disease on most plants, including cannabis. It causes damping off, stem canker, and bud rot. It is one of the most common fungal diseases that attack cannabis.

The fungus can germinate only on wet plant tissue when the temperature is between 55 and 70°F (13–21°C). This often happens in dry weather as dew accumulates on the leaves. Once it starts growing, it can tolerate a wide range of humidity and temperatures, but high humidity and cool temperatures help it thrive. Lowering the humidity often stops it from continuing to grow.

Gray mold, like most other fungi, enters and easily infects any part of a plant that is either wounded, damaged from pests and pruning, or beginning to die. Thus, it is very important to sanitize pruning equipment between cuts.

Cuts and lesions are a normal part of plant life, so all plants are subject to attack when conditions are favorable to the mold. Unhealthy or shaded areas of plants or crevices in buds are ideal conditions for mold. Spores travel mostly via wind and rain and even in tap water, but they can be brought into gardens on clothing and pets.

Shaded areas of the plant that do not get a lot of light are usually infected first. Then the disease spreads quickly through growth and spores.

Gray mold does the greatest amount of damage during flowering. It attacks the flowering tops, leaves, and stalks. Seedlings and seeds can also be infected and killed.

The mold starts out whitish like powdery mildew, but then darkens to a smoky gray or brown. It has a fuzzy appearance, and light to dark brown rot forms in the damaged tissue.

Leaves and buds turn yellow. In higher humidity, the gray mold leaves a brown slimy substance on the leaves and turns the bud to rot, especially when the tissue is dense late in flowering.

Stems with unhealed breaks can be infected with B. cinerea, causing stem cankers, which then affect the rest of the plant by depriving it of nutrients and water.

Monitoring

- Signs: spore-trap sampling of the air and surface swabs. There are numerous methods to identify and quantify the spore load in an air space or on surfaces, which have been developed for other industries. Some of these use spore identification by microscopy; others require the captured spores to be cultured on a nutrient media for identification; and others use PCR technology.
- Signs: transmission-light microscopes can be used to identify botrytis. The structure to look for is a branched reproductive mycelia with oval spores in clusters on the tips of the branches. They are reminiscent of grape bunches.
- Symptoms: gray or brown fuzz inside buds that eventually advances to the outside, turning green buds gray or brown.
- Infected area turns brown and dries up. It may be soft if wet or brittle if it has dried.
- Stem canker or stem rot.

Resistant Varieties

- Although this pathogen can be devastating to crop yield, several resistant cultivars are available. Varieties that produce smaller flowers are likely to be more resistant than those that produce large, compact flowers that create a micro-environment conducive to fungal germination, proliferation, and sporulation. Cultivars that have a much more open branch architecture may allow for better airflow and humidity control. It's quite possible that cultivars which prefer tropical environments will be less susceptible to this pathogen.

Exclusionary Practices

- Use HEPA filtration of air inlets.
- Decontamination of the grow environment air and incoming air can be accomplished using peroxides, ultraviolet light, chlorine dioxide, ozone gas, ionizers, and antimicrobial fogging. Hospitals, food processors, and laboratory clean rooms use different technologies and materials to reduce pathogen loads in the air.
- Create work procedures that forbid going from infected to uninfected rooms, and general worker hygiene to prevent movement of spores from infected areas to clean areas.
- Sanitize hands and tools.
- Fungicidal clone dips.
- Remove plant debris post-harvest and around the vicinity of the garden to exclude aerial spores from disseminating to clean plants. Botrytis can form a protective structure called a sclerotium, which allows it to survive in debris and soil.
- Rogue infected tissue: carefully remove infected flowers to prevent spore dissemination.

Disruption of Life Cycle

- Climate control is especially important as harvest approaches. The best strategy to control botrytis is to keep the temperature and humidity outside the range that allows for spore germination, mycelial proliferation, and sporulation. This includes the macroclimate of the garden and the microclimate in the canopy and inside the flower. The temperature should be raised to a minimum of 75°F (24°C) day and night if possible. Outdoors, heaters can be used to keep small gardens warm.

- Control air movement: air currents can disseminate spores to plants in areas of the garden that haven't been infected or to younger plants.
- Use bio stimulants: numerous substances are known to elicit defensive responses that cause plants to thicken their cell walls. This thickening of the cell walls can make it much more difficult for a spore that has germinated to penetrate the flower tissue and infect it.

Eradication

- Preventative biological control with numerous competitive microorganisms (*B. subtilis, B. amyloliquefaciens, S. lydicus, U. oudemansii*).
- Use fungicidal sprays: some materials that can help control the spread of spores are herbal sprays containing cinnamon or clove oil. These kill the organisms and dry the infected areas in place.
- Use a 10% milk solution (32 ounces per gallon) to prevent mold. It can be used after rain or during humid weather.
- Use a 1% potassium bicarbonate ($KHCO_3$) solution (1.25 ounces per gallon). Sodium bicarbonate (baking soda, $NaHCO_3$) can also be used, although it delivers sodium, which presents problems if it builds up.

Chlorine Dioxide for Pest & Disease Control

Chlorine dioxide (ClO_2) is a yellowish-green gas that has antimicrobial properties and shows great potential as a disinfectant in cannabis cultivation, drying, curing, and trim rooms. It is less corrosive than other gaseous disinfectants such as ozone; however, it has been shown to neutralize fungal spores for crops other than cannabis (Lee et al. 2020). This paper shows that ClO_2 is very effective in killing Aspergillus spores for storing fresh coffee beans. Plant pathogens such as powdery mildew (PM) are also susceptible to ClO_2 (Sharma et al. 2017).

Many cultivars are especially susceptible to PM infection, and one of the most effective preventative measures against infecting a crop (applying sulfur to the canopy) should not be used once the flowers appear on the stems. Sulfur application will impart an unpleasant aroma and flavor on cannabis flowers. The application of sulfur does not kill PM spores; however, it creates an environment that makes it difficult for the spores to germinate.

Using a slow-release ClO_2 product, such as ProKure D, in combination with sulfur can be the one-two punch that prevents PM from rearing its ugly head. A slow-release ClO_2 product sanitizes the air and the plant tissue, so that the PM spores are neutralized. Once the flowers develop in the canopy, stopping the application of sulfur and switching to hanging ClO_2 packets above the canopy at a regular interval will prevent PM without leaving a residual aroma or flavor on the cannabis flower. ClO_2 is gaseous and breaks down into chloride ions and oxygen. Chloride is naturally found in plants and does not impart any flavor.

This product is OMRI listed and registered with the EPA as a fungicide, disinfectant, algaecide, virucide, and deodorizer, so it goes beyond just eliminating PM from the canopy.

Powdery mildew. Photo: Ed Rosenthal

Powdery Mildew

Powdery mildew is a fungal disease that affects a wide range of plant species. Each species of powdery mildew has a very limited host range, but all are characterized by an easily recognizable white or gray powdery growth on the upper surfaces of leaves. The strains that attack hops also attack cannabis.

Mildew spores can be found everywhere. Powdery mildew is a common problem for both indoor and outdoor growers whenever the temperature and humidity fall into its favored range.

Mildew spores are ubiquitous and endemic. In areas where grapes, strawberries, cannabis, or hops are being grown, wind and air ventilation are the main vectors. Another major factor is contaminated cuttings. Clothing, pets, and wild animals can also deliver spores to the garden.

Spores can remain dormant until triggered by environmental factors, which include a suitable host, adequate humidity, moderate temperatures, low light intensity, and acidity.

Powdery mildew is most likely to attack young leaves, up to two or three weeks old. The infection spreads over the plant and spreads to other plants in the garden. It affects buds, stems, stalks, and leaves.

The first signs of an infection are raised bumps on the upper leaf surfaces. Plant leaves look like they've been dusted with flour or confectioners' sugar. At first, it might appear on just a small portion of the leaf in an irregular circle pattern. It quickly spreads, and soon the entire leaf is covered as if it had been powdered.

Infected plants prematurely yellow, brown, and eventually die. If untreated, black specks can arise in the white powdery mildew. Buds have a stale, moist smell and are coated with white powdery-looking mycelia. Powdery mildew hinders photosynthesis, crippling yields.

Infected buds and leaves are not acceptable for smoking.

As with other aboveground pathogenic fungi that affect cannabis, climate control is the key. Many of the strategies for identification and control of botrytis apply to powdery mildew as well. One major difference is that powdery mildew is much easier to control with sprays than botrytis since it primarily infects leaves. However, it can move into flowers if left unchecked.

Monitoring
- Signs: spore-trap sampling of the air and surface swabs. Numerous methods to identify and quantify the spore load in an air space or on surfaces have been developed for other industries. Some of these use spore identification by microscopy, others require the captured spores to be cultured on a nutrient media for identification, and others use polymerase chain reaction (PCR) technology.
- Signs: transmission-light microscopes can be used to identify powdery mildew. The structure to look for is a reproductive mycelium terminating in a chain of oval spores. They are reminiscent of a pearl necklace.
- Symptoms: white, powdery mycelia that emerge from the leaf upper surfaces.

Resistant Varieties
- Powdery mildew is a common problem in cannabis production, and there may be varieties that are less susceptible to it. As with botrytis, strains that have a much more open branch architecture might allow for better airflow and humidity control.

Exclusionary Practices
- Use HEPA filtration of air inlets.
- Decontaminate the grow environment air and incoming air by using UVC light, chlorine dioxide, ozone gas, ionizers, antimicrobial fogging, clean uniform changes, and restricting worker movement.
- Sanitize hands and tools.
- Fungicidal clone dips.
- Removal of plant debris.

Disruption of Life Cycle
- Climate control: this is especially important as harvest approaches. The best strategy to control powdery mildew is to keep the temperature and humidity outside the range that allows for spore germination, mycelial proliferation, and sporulation. This includes the macroclimate of the garden and the microclimate in the canopy. Do not let the temperature dip below 75°F (24°C) day or night.
- Control air movement: air currents can disseminate spores to plants in areas of the garden that haven't been infected or to younger plants. Use UVC lights to clean airstreams of living organisms
- Biostimulants: numerous substances are known to elicit defensive responses that

cause plants to thicken their cell walls. This thickening of the cell walls can make it much more difficult for a spore that has germinated to penetrate the flower tissue and infect it.

Eradication

- Use preventative biological control with numerous competitive microorganisms (*B. subtilis, B. amyloliquefaciens, B. pumilus, S. lydicus*).
- Use fungicidal sprays: elemental sulfur, potassium bicarbonate, organic acids such as sorbic, citric, peracetic, and acetic, hydrogen peroxide, fungicidal soap, herbal/botanical oils, copper soaps and salts, and skim milk.

Is Powdery Mildew Systemic, and Does It Matter?

It is easy to see the means of powdery mildew transmission. The white powdery-looking growth on top of leaves is the reproductive organs of the fungus. The spores' transmission can be by airborne invasion, by touch from plant to plant or plant to animal to plant and splashing water. It dies in streams and standing water.

This doesn't answer the question of whether powdery mildew is systemic. Asked another way, does it invade the plant's vascular system? A systemic disease may be asymptomatic at times. However, given the right conditions (such as temperature, humidity, and food source), it quickly invades and digests cells in the leaf, then produces reproductive organs.

Plants that have expressed signs of powdery mildew must be monitored for symptoms. When cloning, it seems as though plants that have expressed powdery mildew but are asymptomatic can still transmit the disease. These might be indications of systemic disease. However, the general consensus in the scientific community is that it doesn't travel through the plant's vascular system but along the leaf epidermis, eventually covering the plant completely, though it might remain asymptomatic until the right conditions occur, and then the pathogen has an explosive eruption that can turn the plant white.

The fungus can infect the entire plant, so it doesn't matter whether it happens through internal or external action. Once the plant is infected, the fungus may be controlled but not eliminated.

The Threat of Viral Cannabis Diseases

Cannabis cryptic virus (CanCV) was recently identified in several European industrial hemp cultivars, and infected plants exhibit symptoms that may previously have been confused with tobacco viruses. Alfalfa mosaic virus (AMV), cucumber mosaic virus (CMV), and Arabis mosaic virus (ArMV) all originate in other plants and have also been identified in European industrial hemp cultivars.

Hop latent viroid infected plant. Photo: Dark Heart Nursery

Recently, lettuce chlorosis virus (LCV) was found in Israeli glasshouse medicinal cannabis crops, and beet curly top virus (BCTV) was reported from plants grown outdoors in Colorado. All could pose economically significant problems in the future.

Out of the 900 plant viruses that have been described, only a limited number have been studied for cannabis, and so far just two cannabis-specific viruses have been identified: the hemp streak virus (HSV) and the hemp mosaic virus (HMV), whose spread is facilitated by viral vectors including aphids, thrips, and whiteflies.

Hop Latent Viroid (HpLVd)

The Hop Latent Viroid (HpLVd) is a recently identified pathogen of cannabis that has the potential to become a pest of serious economic importance. Hops is a relative of cannabis, as both plants belong to the Cannabaceae family. It is unknown how it was transmitted from hops to cannabis.

It is important to understand that this is not a plant virus. Viruses are composed of nucleic acids (like DNA and RNA) and have a protein coat. Viroids do not have a protein coat and are composed entirely of nucleic acids. These nucleic acid chains are also very short, making viroids the smallest known pathogens to infect plants. Similarly to viruses, viroid particles enter a cell and hijack the cell's gene replication machinery in order to replicate themselves. It is still not known how this process causes the symptoms associated with infection.

Ironically, HpLVd is of major concern in cannabis, although it is mostly asymptomatic in hops. As of publication, the California Department of Food and Agriculture (CFDA) has given HpLVd a temporary disease rating of "Z" in hops, meaning that it "may be expected to score low as a pest of agriculture or the environment and/or that are of common occurrence and generally distributed in California."

The temporary Z rating means that not enough research is available to conclude that it is a pathogen of significance in California hops. It is expected that this will be changed to a rating of "C," meaning that it is "used for pests that score medium to low as a pest of agriculture or the environment and that are of general distribution."

In a recent CDFA publication, an HpLVd disease rating of C was also given to the viroid in hemp production.

Hops production in California is very small in comparison with cannabis. Research and time will determine what economic impact this pathogen will have on cannabis production.

Transmission of viroids is thought to be primarily mechanical, meaning that it is transmitted when the particles from an infected plant are moved through a wound or an opening in an uninfected plant. This vectoring can occur through pest feeding or through contaminated tools. Aphids are known to readily transmit viroids in other plant species. Scissors used for pruning or taking clones can also move it through a garden. Contaminated hands can also move the viroid.

Tracking and tracing of the viroid is critical. What makes this pathogen so insidious is that it is frequently asymptomatic in plants, and even those that will show symptoms sometimes may not until a few weeks into flowering. It is believed that an asymptomatic plant may develop symptoms as a result of some stressor. Once a plant has tested positive, it is essential that all progeny either be tested and found clean or destroyed. This is a very difficult task and can become very expensive. The viroid was only recently identified, and many states have had a legal cannabis industry for years, so one can assume that it is everywhere now. As new states legalize cannabis, it may be necessary to introduce legislation on mandatory testing and certification.

Monitoring
- Signs: genetic testing reveals the presence of the viral RNA. Genetic testing is absolutely essential to monitoring for this viroid because it is a latent viroid, meaning that many plants are asymptomatic. These asymptomatic plants can still serve as a source for infection.
- Symptoms: reduced trichome production or diminished size of the gland heads.
- Symptoms: reduced flower yield.
- Symptoms: stunting.
- Symptoms: fragile stalks and stems.

Exclusionary Practices
- Test all incoming plant material for presence of the virus and keep the new plants quarantined until negative results are confirmed.

- Maintain populations of clean tested plants as the sole source for propagation material.
- Hand and tool sanitation is the most important control strategy available to the grower. Proper protocols and training of all workers who come in contact with plants is essential.
- Worker hygiene.

Disruption of Life Cycle
- There are no known strategies for interfering with the viroid's life cycle.

Eradication
- Destroy plants that have tested positive or show symptoms.
- Micro-propagation of apical meristem tissue is one way to remove the viroid.

Hop Latent Viroid Screening Protocol

It is ineffective to screen for infection by looking for short, stunted plants early in vegetative growth because clones can be cut at different sizes and from different parts of the mother. Lateral stem growth is the best screening method outside of getting plant tissues tested at a lab.

Starting at the second week of vegetative growth, as the lateral branches start to develop, each plant is examined to determine abnormal lateral growth. Each cultivar will have different lateral stem angles, so the abnormal lateral growth will differ from cultivar to cultivar if there is a symptomatic infection. Qualitative assessment is usually sufficient to screen most of the plants. If a lateral branch looks abnormally more horizontal than average, lightly push down on it. If it easily separates from the main branch, it's likely infected with HpLVd. Repeat screening as plants are transitioning from vegetative growth to flowering; however, at this stage the infected plants should also show signs of stunting.

Process:
- At week 2 of vegetative growth, screen each plant for abnormally horizontal lateral branching.
- Lightly press down on the lateral branch. If it easily separates from the main branch, it is likely infected with HpLVd.
- Separate/quarantine plants that are assumed to be infected.
- Do NOT cut on these plants without sanitizing the cutting tool.
- Isopropyl alcohol does not sanitize the tools quickly enough.
- Bleach (at full strength or 10% dilution) or Virkon are the only cleaning agents that work quickly enough.
- Follow the instructions from a qualified testing lab and send plant tissue to be tested. If results come back as positive, the quarantined plants must be removed and destroyed.

GLOSSARY

Aeroponics is a technique of growing in which the roots hang in the air of an enclosed chamber. A continuous spray of fine mist irrigates the roots with droplets that cover them with a thin film of highly oxygenated water.

Alkalinity is the ability of the water to buffer acids.

Anti-transpirants are compounds applied foliarly that reduce transpiration, or plant sweating, and preserve and protect plants from drying out too quickly. Anti-transpirants can also be used to protect leaves from salt burn and fungal diseases.

Apical Meristem is the growing tip of the stem. Cells in the apical meristem are capable of dividing indefinitely, and their main function is the production of new growth. There are two apical meristems on the plant, the shoot apical meristem (SAM) and the root apical meristem (RAM).

Autoflower is a plant that flowers without environmental cues such as light period or heat.

Auxins are hormones that regulate or modify the growth of plants, including form or shape as well as root formation and bud growth.

Ballast is an attachment that converts electrical current to the appropriate current needed to power the light.

Bracts are the outer leaves that envelope the ovule (seed pod). Bracts are often misidentified as calyxes.

Calyxes are the smaller green sepals that hold the petals at the base of the flower.

Cannabichromene (CBC) is the third most prevalent phytocannabinoid after THC and CBD. CBC is used as an analgesic and anti-inflammatory. It is nonpsychotropic, or nonintoxicating.

Cannabidiol (CBD) is a cannabinoid found in cannabis. CBD is not intoxicating. It relieves convulsion, inflammation, anxiety, and nausea, as well as inhibits cancer cell growth. It does not dock on the brain's CB1 receptor, but only on the CB2 receptors located in areas outside the brain.

Cannabigerol (CBG) is referred to as the "mother cannabinoid," as it is the precursor to THCa, CBDa, and CBCa. CBG has medicinal properties and is nonintoxicating.

Cannabimimetic is a name used for non-cannabinoid molecules that are known to act on the human endocannabinoid system (e.g., compounds found in frankincense, liverwort, and echinacea; McPartland et al. 2014).

Cannabinoids are biologically active chemical compounds that bind with receptors in the endocannabinoid system. There are four main types of cannabinoids: endogenous, phyto, pharmaceutical, and synthetic. There are hundreds of identified cannabinoids, the most well known being the phytocannabinoids THC and CBD.

Capillary Mats are about a quarter inch (60 mm) thick. They are made from soft polyester covered with opaque polyethylene perforated with small holes. They have great wicking ability and are used in subirrigation systems.

Chemotype refers to the chemical profile of a cannabis cultivar, including cannabinoids, terpenes, and flavonoids.

Chlorophyll is the green pigment in plants that photosynthesizes by absorbing light.

Chloroplast is a semi-autonomous organelle that holds the chlorophyll. It contains some of its own genetic material and has some ability to direct the synthesis of its own proteins.

Chlorosis is a reduction in or loss of the normal green coloration caused by a lack of chlorophyll.

Consemilla refers to a mature marijuana bud with seeds. From the Spanish "con" for "with," and "semilla" for "seed," meaning "with seed."

Cotyledons are the pair of embryonic leaves that appear at germination.

Cytokinins are plant hormones that work with auxin to promote cell division (general growth) and lateral growth.

Dopamine is an essential brain chemical that regulates movement and emotion. A lack of dopamine in the brain contributes to Parkinson's disease.

Efficacy measures the output of light in μmols of photons.

Efficiency is the amount of light emitted per unit of energy.

Endocannabinoids are endogenous cannabinoid, or endocannabinoid, a naturally occurring cannabinoid produced within the body.

Fan leaves are large leaves that collect sunlight. The leaf symbol is commonly associated with cannabis.

Fertigation is the application of fertilizers to planting mix using an irrigation system.

Foot-candle (fc) is a unit used to define the amount of illumination the inside surface of a 1 foot (30 cm) radius sphere would be receiving if there were a uniform point source of one candela in the exact center of the sphere.

Friable refers to the consistency of the soil; friable soil forms a clod when squeezed into a fist but easily crumbles when it is poked.

Ganja is the term for marijuana in Jamaica and is the same as in India. Indian immigrants brought the tradition with them.

Genotype is the genetic makeup of cannabis varieties.

Gibberellins are plant hormones that stimulate the growth and stretching of leaves and shoots. Unlike auxins, they tend to affect the whole plant.

Hemp is the common name for plants of the entire genus cannabis, although the term commonly refers to cannabis strains cultivated for industrial (nondrug) use. Hemp is cultivated for oil and fiber.

Hermaphrodites are plants that have both male and female flowers. This may be caused genetically, by stress, or by using hormones and chemicals.

Hydrocarbons are compounds that contain carbon and hydrogen.

Hydroponics is a method of growing plants supplying dissolved nutrients through the irrigation water, rather than the growing medium. Plants are either held anchored by their roots in an inert (chemically inactive) medium or held using a collar that supports the stem.

Incandescent lights are common screw-in lamps powered by an electrically heated filament.

Kali is the traditional Jamaican term for the best weed and is named for the Indian killer goddess.

Lumen is a unit for measuring light.

Lux is a metric measure of light.

Macronutrients are the nutrients that are used in large quantities by the plant. They are nitrogen (N), phosphorus (P), and potassium (K).

Micronutrients are the nutrients that are used in smaller quantities by the plant. They are calcium (Ca), sulfur (S), magnesium (Mg), iron (Fe), copper (Cu), manganese (Mn), zinc (Zn), and boron (B).

Myrcene is the most prevalent terpene found in most varieties of marijuana. It smells clove-like, earthy, green-vegetative, citrus, fruity with tropical mango or minty nuances. It is a potent analgesic, anti-inflammatory and antibiotic.

Necrosis is dead patches of tissue on a leaf.

Node is the spot where the leaf joins the stem.

Organelles are specialized bodies within the cell that have a specialized function. In most cases, the organelle is separated from the rest of the cell by selectively permeable membranes and maintains its own DNA.

Overwinter describes techniques used to live through the winter season. Insects overwinter as adults, pupae, or eggs.

Petiole is the stalk or support that attaches the blade of a leaf to the stem.

Phenotype refers to physical traits like plant height, yield, leaf size, terpene profile, cannabinoid ratios, flavonoid content, time to harvest, and so forth.

Photosynthesis is the chemical reaction, powered by energy from light, by which the plant uses light energy to combine water and CO_2 to make sugars and release oxygen.

Photosynthetic Photon Flux (PPF) is the total number of photons ($\mu mol \cdot s^{-1}$) produced by the lighting source.

Photosynthetic Photon Flux Density (PPFD) is a measurement that most accurately describes light received by plants, since it weighs all photons of light in the PAR spectrum equally, unlike lux.

Photosynthetically Active Radiation (PAR) refers to light in the range of 400–700 nanometers.

Phytochrome is a photoreversible pigment that controls flowering. It exists in two forms: red and far-red sensitive.

Pistil is the ovule-bearing organ of a flower.

Porosity refers to the texture of soil and the space between solid particles that can hold water and air.

Psychoactive refers to substances that cross the blood-brain barrier and are active in the brain.

Psychotropic refers to substances that create mind-altering, intoxicating, or psychedelic "highs."

Rhizosphere is the area of soil immediately surrounding the plant roots, which contains many organisms living in a community.

Ruderalis is a variety of cannabis that is not dependent on the light cycle or other environmental cues to flower.

Serotonin is a neurotransmitter involved in sleep, depression, memory, and other neurological processes.

Short-Day Plants flower based on a critical dark period.

Sinsemilla is Spanish for "without seeds," this refers to a seedless cannabis female flower.

Stigmas are the pollen catchers. Cannabis pistils consist of two stigmas and an ovule (prospective seed).

Stomata are the pores on the underside of the leaves that collect carbon dioxide in the air and transpire water and oxygen.

Stretching is the elongation of the stem caused by a combination of heat and inadequate light.

Supercropping is a technique of training top branches to grow horizontally so that the primary bud is exposed to more light.

Terpenes are the essential oils of plants that create the odors we smell. Plants produce terpenes for three reasons: to attract pollinators, to attract predators of herbivores, and to repel or kill herbivores. Cannabis is wind-pollinated, so it doesn't need to attract pollinators, and outdoors it is resilient to insect predation.

Δ⁹ tetrahydrocannabinol (THC) is the main psychoactive substance found in cannabis.

Transpiration is the loss of water vapor from a plant to the outside atmosphere. It takes place mainly through the stomata of the leaves. Although its function is disputed, it may reduce leaf temperature, but what is definitely known is that water vapors are emitted through the leaves and water is lost.

Trichomes are glands growing off the leaves and buds that contain THC.

BIBLIOGRAPHY

Marijuana Grower's Handbook (2010)

Ashman, M. R., and G. Puri. *Essential Soil Science*. Oxford, UK: Blackwell Science, 2002. Print.

Baker, Jerry. *Terrific Garden Tonics!* Wixom, MI: American Master Products, 2004. Print.

Bickford, Elwood D., and Stuart Dunn. *Lighting for Plant Growth*. Kent, OH: Kent State University Press, 1972. Print.

Carr, Anna. *Color Handbook of Garden Insects*. Emmaus, PA: Rodale, 1979. Print.

Catton, Chris, and James Gray. *The Incredible Heap: A Guide to Compost Gardening*. New York: St. Martin's, 1983. Print.

Clarke, Robert Connell. *Hashish!* Los Angeles: Red Eye, 1998. Print.

Elsohly, Mahmoud. *Marijuana and the Cannabinoids*. Totowa, NJ: Humana, 2007. Print.

Enoch, Herbert Z. , and Bruce A. Kimball. *Carbon Dioxide Enrichment of Greenhouse Crops: Physiology, Yield, and Economics*. Vol. 2. Boca Raton, FL: CRC, 1986. Print.

Fisher, Paul, and Erik Runkle. *Lighting Up Profits: Understanding Greenhouse Lighting*. Willoughby, OH: Meister Media, 2004. Print.

Foster, Rick, and Brian R. Flood. *Vegetable Insect Management*. Willoughby, OH: Meister Media, 2005. Print.

Freeman, Worth. *Biology of Plants*. 6th ed. New York: W. H. Freeman, 1999. Print.

Gillman, Jeff. *The Truth about Garden Remedies*. Portland, OR / London: Timber, 2008. Print.

Green, Joey. *Joey Green's Gardening Magic*. Emmaus, PA: Rodale, 2003. Print.

Grotenhermen, Franjo, and Ethan Russo. *Cannabis and Cannabinoids*. Binghamton, NY: Haworth Integrative Healing Press 2002. Print.

Heinz, Kevin M., Roy G. Van Driesche, and Michael P. Parrella. *Bio Control in Protected Culture*. Batavia, IL: Ball, 2004. Print.

Hicklenton, Peter R. *CO_2 Enrichment in the Greenhouse*. Vol. 2. Portland, OR: Timber, 1988. Print.

Hill, Lewis. *Cold-Climate Gardening: How To Extend Your Growing Season by at Least Thirty Days*. Pownal, VT: Storey Communications, 1987. Print.

Ingham, Elaine. *The Compost Tea Brewing Manual*. 5th ed. Corvallis, OR: Soil Foodweb, 2002. Print.

Ingham, Elaine, and Carole Ann Rollins. *Adding Biology for Soil and Hydroponic System*s. Corvallis, OR: Sustainable Studies Institute and Nature Technologies, 2006. Print.

Iversen, Leslie L. *The Science of Marijuana*. New York: Oxford University Press, 2000. Print.

Joiner, Jasper N. *Foliage Plant Production*. Edgewood Cliffs, NJ: Prentice-Hall, 1981. Print.

Kaiser, Diane. *A Book of Weather Clues*. Washington, DC: Starhill, 1986. Print.

Kohnke, Helmut, and D. P. Franzmeier. *Soil Science Simplified*. 4th ed. Prospect Heights, IL: Waveland, 1995. Print.

Levitan, Lois. *Improve Your Gardening with Backyard Research*. Emmaus, PA: Rodale, 1980. Print.

Lewis, Wayne, and Jeff Lowenfels. *Teaming with Microbes: A Gardener's Guide to the Soil Food Web*. Portland, OR / London: Timber, 2006. Print.

Lydon, John. *The Effects of Ultraviolet-B Radiation on the Growth, Physiology, and Cannabinoid Production in Cannabis Sativa L.* Ann Arbor, MI: University Microfilms, 1985. Print.

Mainly, Marseene. *How to Supercharge Your Garden.* 2nd ed. Richmond, BC, Canada: Mainly Productions, 1996. Print.

McCaskill, J. A. *Plant Nutrient Facts for Hydroponic Container Growing.* Hemet, CA: Jim McCaskill Independent, 1979. Print.

McDonald, Maurice S. *Photobiology of Higher Plants.* West Sussex, UK: John Wiley & Sons, 2003. Print.

McPartland, J. M., R. C. Clarke, and D. P. Watson. *Hemp Diseases and Pests: Management and Biological Control.* New York: CABI, 2000. Print.

Molyneux, C. J. *A Practical Guide to NFT.* Ormskirk, Lancashire, UK: Nutriculture, 1988. Print.

Morgan, Lynette. *Fresh Culinary Herb Production.* Tokomaru, New Zealand: Suntec (NZ), 2005. Print.

Olkowski, William, Sheila Daar, and Helga Olkowski. *The Gardener's Guide to Common-Sense Pest Control.* 2nd ed. Newton, CT: Taunton, 1995. Print.

Olkowski, William, Sheila Daar, and Helga Olkowski. *Common-Sense Pest Control.* Newton, CT: Taunton, 1991. Print.

One Thousand and One Gardening Secrets. FC & A Publishing, 2004. Print.

Page, Jessica, and Paul Horne. *Integrated Pest Management for Crops and Pastures.* Collingwood, Australia: Landlinks, 2008. Print.

Parnes, Robert. *Fertile Soil: A Grower's Guide to Organic and Inorganic Fertilizers.* Davis, CA: agAccess, 1990. Print.

Pfeiffer, Ehrenfried. *Weeds and What They Tell.* Wyoming, RI: Bio-Dynamic Literature, 1981. Print.

Reed, David W. *Water, Media, and Nutrition for Greenhouse Crops.* Batavia, IL: Ball, 1996. Print.

Resh, Howard M. *Hydroponic Food Production: A Definitive Guidebook for the Advanced Home Gardener and the Commercial Hydroponic Grower.* 4th ed. Santa Barbara, CA: Woodbridge, 1991. Print.

Resh, Howard M. *Hobby Hydroponics.* Boca Raton,

FL / London / New York: CRC / Taylor & Francis Group, 2003. Print.

Resh, Howard M. *Hydroponics: Questions and Answers for Successful Growing.* Mahwah, NJ: Newconcept, 1998. Print.

Roberto, Keith. *How-to Hydroponics.* 4th ed. Farmingdale, NY: Futuregarden, 2004. Print.

Romer, Joe. *Hydroponic Crop Production.* Kenthurst, Australia: Kangaroo, 1993. Print.

Steel, Damascus. *CO_2 Secrets.* Deluxe ed. 1992. Print.

Stout, Ruth. *How to Have a Green Thumb without an Aching Back.* New York: Simon & Schuster, 1987. Print.

Stout, Ruth, and Richard Clemence. *The Ruth Stout No-Work Garden Book.* Emmaus, PA: Rodale, 1971. Print.

Styer, Roger C., and David Koranski. *Plug and Transplant Production: A Grower's Guide.* Batavia, IL: Ball, 1997. Print.

Van Patten, George F. *Gardening: The Rockwool Book.* Portland, OR: Van Patten, 1991. Print.

Walls, Ian G. *The Complete Book of the Greenhouse.* 4th ed. London: Ward Lock, 1988. Print.

Wright, Paul. *Totally Organic Hydroponics.* Organiponics, 2004. Print.

Yepson, Roger. *1,001 Old-Time Garden Tips.* 2nd ed. Emmaus, PA: Rodale, 2003. Print.

Magazines

Greenhouse Product Management
Grow Magazine
High Times
HortIdeas
Integrated Pest Management
Maximum Yield
Organic Gardening
Pacific Horticulture
Science News
Scientific American
Skunk Magazine

Understanding the Effects of Cannabis

Alshaarawy, Omayma, and James C. Anthony. "Are Cannabis Users Less Likely to Gain Weight? Results from a National Three-Year Prospective Study." International Journal of Epidemiology, March 16, 2019. https://academic.oup.com/ije/article/48/5/1695/5382155.

Blasco-Benito, Sandra, Marta Seijo-Vila, Miriam Caro-Villalobos, Isabel Tundidor, Clara Andradas, Elena Garcia-Taboada, Jeff Wade, et al. "Appraising the 'Entourage Effect': Antitumor Action of a Pure Cannabinoid versus a Botanical Drug Preparation in Preclinical Models of Breast Cancer." Biochemical Pharmacology, June 27, 2018. https://pubmed.ncbi.nlm.nih.gov/29940172/.

Clarke, Robert Connell, and Mark Merlin. Cannabis Evolution and Ethnobotany. Berkeley: University of California Press, 2016.

de Meijer, E. "The Chemical Phenotypes (Chemotypes) of Cannabis." In Handbook of Cannabis, edited by R. Pertwee, 89-110. Oxford: Oxford University Press, 2016.

Devane, W. A., L. Hanus, A. Breuer, R. G. Pertwee, L. A. Stevenson, G. Griffin, D. Gibson, A. Mandelbaum, A. Etinger, and R. Mechoulam. "Isolation and Structure of a Brain Constituent That Binds to the Cannabinoid Receptor." Science, December 18, 1992. https://pubmed.ncbi.nlm.nih.gov/1470919/.

Crippa, José A., Antonio W. Zuardi, Alline C. Campos, and Francisco S. Guimarães. "Translational Investigation of the Therapeutic Potential of Cannabidiol (CBD): Toward a New Age." Frontiers in Immunology, September 21, 2018. https://pubmed.ncbi.nlm.nih.gov/30298064/.

Devane, W. A., F. A. Dysarz III, L. S. Melvin, and A. C. Howlett. "Determination and Characterization of a Cannabinoid Receptor in Rat Brain." Molecular Pharmacology, November 1988. https://pubmed.ncbi.nlm.nih.gov/2848184/.

Gallily, Ruth, Zhannah Yekhtin, and Lumir Hanus. "Overcoming the Bell-Shaped Dose-Response of Cannabidiol by Using Cannabis Extract Enriched in Cannabidiol." Pharmacology & Pharmacy, January 2015. https://www.researchgate.net/publication/273352080_Overcoming_the_Bell-Shaped_Dose-Response_of_Cannabidiol_by_Using_Cannabis_Extract_Enriched_in_Cannabidiol.

Gerdeman, Gregory. "Endocannabinoids at the Synapse: Retrograde Signaling and Presynaptic Plasticity in the Brain." ResearchGate, January 2008. https://www.researchgate.net/publication/227031210_Endocannabinoids_at_the_Synapse_Retrograde_Signaling_and_Presynaptic_Plasticity_in_the_Brain.

Gertsch, Jürg, Marco Leonti, Stefan Raduner, Ildiko Racz, Jian-Zhong Chen, Xiang-Qun Xie, Karl-Heinz Altmann, Meliha Karsak, and Andreas Zimmer. "Beta-Caryophyllene Is a Dietary Cannabinoid." PNAS, July 1, 2008. https://www.pnas.org/content/105/26/9099.

Herkenham, M., A. B. Lynn, M. D. Little, M. R. Johnson, L. S. Melvin, B. R. de Costa, and K. C. Rice. "Cannabinoid Receptor Localization in Brain." Proceedings of the National Academy of Sciences of the United States of America, March 1990. https://pubmed.ncbi.nlm.nih.gov/2308954/.

Jansen, C., L. M. N. Shimoda, J. K. Kawakami, L. Ang, A. J. Bacani, J. D. Baker, C. Badowski et al. "Myrcene and Terpene Regulation of TRPV1." Channels (Austin, TX), December 2019. https://www.ncbi.nlm.nih.gov/pmc/articles/PMC6768052/.

Kaneko, Yosuke, and Arpad Szallasi. "Transient Receptor Potential (TRP) Channels: A Clinical Perspective." British Journal of Pharmacology, May 2014. https://pubmed.ncbi.nlm.nih.gov/24102319/.

Katona, István, and Tamás F. Freund. "Endocannabinoid Signaling as a Synaptic Circuit Breaker in Neurological Disease." Nature Medicine 14, no. 9 (September 2008): 923–30. https://doi.org/http://njms2.njms.rutgers.edu/vija/documents/FreundKatona2008.pdf.

Lewis, Mark A., Ethan B. Russo, and Kevin M. Smith. "Pharmacological Foundations of Cannabis Chemovars." Planta Medica, March 2018. https://pubmed.ncbi.nlm.nih.gov/29161743/.

Maccarrone, Mauro, Itai Bab, Tamás Bíró, Guy A. Cabral, Sudhansu K. Dey, Vincenzo Di Marzo, Justin C. Konje et al. "Endocannabinoid Signaling at the Periphery: Fifty Years after THC." Trends in

Pharmacological Sciences, May 2015. https://pubmed. ncbi.nlm.nih.gov/25796370/.

McPartland, John M., Geoffrey W. Guy, and Vincenzo Di Marzo. "Care and Feeding of the Endocannabinoid System: A Systematic Review of Potential Clinical Interventions That Upregulate the Endocannabinoid System." *PLoS One*, March 12, 2014. https://www.ncbi.nlm.nih.gov/pmc/articles/ PMC3951193/.

McPartland, J. M., and G. W. Guy. "The Evolution of Cannabis and Coevolution with the Cannabinoid Receptor—a Hypothesis." *In The Medicinal Use of Cannabis and Cannabinoids*, edited by G. W. Guy, B. A. Whittle, and P. J. Robson, 71–101. London: Pharmaceutical Press, 2004.

Mechoulam, Raphael, and Shimon Ben-Shabat. "From Gan-Zi-Gun-Nu to Anandamide and 2-Arachidonoylglycerol: The Ongoing Story of Cannabis." *Natural Product Reports*, January 1, 1999. https:// pubs.rsc.org/en/content/articlelanding/1999/np/ a7039/3e#!divAbstract.

Morena, Maria, Sachin Patel, Jaideep S. Bains, and Matthew N. Hill. "Neurobiological Interactions between Stress and the Endocannabinoid System." *Neuropsychopharmacology: Official Publication of the American College of Neuropsychopharmacology*, January 2016. https://www.ncbi.nlm.nih.gov/pmc/articles/ PMC4677118/.

Muller, Chanté, Paula Morales, and Patricia H. Reggio. "Cannabinoid Ligands Targeting TRP Channels." Frontiers in *Molecular Neuroscience*, January 15, 2019. https://www.ncbi.nlm.nih.gov/pmc/articles/ PMC6340993/.

Munro, Sean, Kerrie L. Thomas, and Muna Abu-Shaar. "Molecular Characterization of a Peripheral Receptor for Cannabinoids." *Nature News*, September 2, 1993. https://www.nature.com/articles/365061a0.

O'Sullivan, Saoirse Elizabeth. "An Update on PPAR Activation by Cannabinoids." *British Journal of Pharmacology*, June 2016. https://www.ncbi.nlm.nih.gov/ pmc/articles/PMC4882496/.

Pellerin, Cheryl. *Healing with Cannabis: The Evolution of the Endocannabinoid System and How*

Cannabinoids Help Relieve PTSD, Pain, MS, Anxiety, and More. New York: Skyhorse, 2020.

Pertwee, R., and M. Grazia Cascio. "Known Pharmacological Actions of Delta-9-tetrahydrocannabinol and of Four Other Chemical Constituents of Cannabis That Activate Cannabinoid Receptors." In *Handbook of Cannabis*, edited by R. Pertwee, 115–36. Oxford: Oxford University Press.

Rees, Amy, Georgina F. Dodd, and Jeremy P. E. Spencer. "The Effects of Flavonoids on Cardiovascular Health: A Review of Human Intervention Trials and Implications for Cerebrovascular Function." *Nutrients*, December 1, 2018. https://pubmed.ncbi. nlm.nih.gov/30513729/.

Russo, Ethan B., Andrea Burnett, Brian Hall, and Keith K. Parker. "Agonistic Properties of Cannabidiol at 5-HT1a Receptors." *Neurochemical Research*, August 2005. https://pubmed.ncbi.nlm.nih. gov/16258853/.

Russo, Ethan Budd, and Jahan Marcu. "Cannabis Pharmacology: The Usual Suspects and a Few Promising Leads." *Advances in Pharmacology*, June 2017. https://www.researchgate.net/publication/317354478_Cannabis_Pharmacology_The_ Usual_Suspects_and_a_Few_Promising_Leads.

Russo, Ethan B. "History of Cannabis and Its Preparations in Saga, Science, and Sobriquet." Chemistry and Biodiversity, August 21, 2007. https://onlinelibrary.wiley.com/doi/abs/10.1002/cbdv.200790144.

Russo, Ethan B. "Taming THC: Potential Cannabis Synergy and Phytocannabinoid-Terpenoid Entourage Effects." *British Journal of Pharmacology*, August 2011. https://www.ncbi.nlm.nih.gov/pmc/articles/ PMC3165946/.

Sulak, Dustin, Bonni Goldstein, and Russell Saneto. "The Current Status of Artisanal Cannabis for the Treatment of Epilepsy in the United States." *Epilepsy & Behavior*, February 2017. https://pubmed.ncbi. nlm.nih.gov/28254350/.

Terpenes

Almeida, Jackson Roberto Guedes da Silva, Grasielly Rocha Souza, Juliane Cabral Silva, Sarah Raquel Gomes de Lima Saraiva, Raimundo Gonçalves de Oliveira Júnior, Jullyana de Souza Siqueira Quintans,

Rosana de Souza Siqueira Barreto, Leonardo Rigoldi Bonjardim, Sócrates Cabral de Holanda Cavalcanti, and Lucindo José Quintans Junior. "Borneol, a Bicyclic Monoterpene Alcohol, Reduces Nociceptive Behavior and Inflammatory Response in Mice." *Scientific World Journal*, April 18, 2013. https://www.hindawi.com/journals/tswj/2013/808460/.

Arruda, D., F. D'Alexandri, A. Katzin, and S. Uliana. "Antileishmanial Activity of the Terpene Nerolidol." Antimicrobial Agents and Chemotherapy, May 1, 2005. Retrieved February 8, 2021, from https://aac.asm.org/content/49/5/1679.

"Author Index to Volume 5." *Anti-Inflammatory & Anti-Allergy Agents in Medicinal Chemistry (Formerly Current Medicinal Chemistry—Anti-Inflammatory and Anti-Allergy Agents)* 6, no. 1 (2007): 1–2. https://doi.org/10.2174/187152307779939750.

Bahi, Amine, Shamma Al Mansouri, Elyazia Al Memari, Mouza Al Ameri, Syed M. Nurulain, and Shreesh Ojha. "β-Caryophyllene, a CB2 Receptor Agonist Produces Multiple Behavioral Changes Relevant to Anxiety and Depression in Mice." *Physiology & Behavior*, June 13, 2014. https://www.sciencedirect.com/science/article/abs/pii/S0031938414003400.

Breitmaier, Eberhard. *Terpenes: Flavors, Fragrances, Pharmaca, Pheromones.* Weinheim: WILEY-VCH, 2008.

Capaldo, C., N. Beeman, R. Hilgarth, P. Nava, N. Louis, E. Naschberger, . . . A. Nusrat. IFN-γ and TNF-A-Induced GBP-1 Inhibits Epithelial Cell Proliferation through Suppression of β-catenin/TCF Signaling." Mucosal Immunology, November 2012. Retrieved February 8, 2021, from https://www.ncbi.nlm.nih.gov/pmc/articles/PMC3481006/.

Cavaleiro, C., E. Pinto, M. Gonçalves, and L. Salgueiro. "Antifungal Activity of Juniperus Essential Oils against Dermatophyte, Aspergillus and Candida Strains." Journal of Applied Microbiology, January 1, 1970. Retrieved February 8, 2021, from https://agris.fao.org/agris-search/search.do?recordID=US201500153336.

Chan, Weng-Keong, Loh Teng-Hern Tan, Kok-Gan Chan, Learn-Han Lee, and Bey-Hing Goh. "Nerolidol: A Sesquiterpene Alcohol with Multi-Faceted Pharmacological and Biological Activities." *Molecules* (Basel, Switzerland), April 28, 2016. https://www.ncbi.nlm.nih.gov/pmc/articles/PMC6272852/.

Choudhary, M. I., I. Batool, M. Atif, S. Hussain, and A. Rahman. "Microbial Transformation of (-)-guaiol and Antibacterial Activity of Its Transformed Products." Journal of Natural Products, May 2007. Retrieved February 8, 2021, from https://pubmed.ncbi.nlm.nih.gov/17385913/.

d'Alessio, Patrizia A., Massoud Mirshahi, Jean-François Bisson, and Marie C. Béné. "Skin Repair Properties of d-Limonene and Perillyl Alcohol in Murine Models." *Anti-Inflammatory & Anti-Allergy Agents in Medicinal Chemistry* 13 (2014): 29–35.

De Lucca, A. J., A. Pauli, H. Schilcher, T. Sien, D. Bhatnagar, and T. J. Walsh. "Fungicidal and Bactericidal properties of Bisabolol and Dragosantol." Journal of Essential Oil Research, December 9, 2011. Retrieved February 8, 2021, from https://www.tandfonline.com/doi/abs/10.1080/10412905.2011.9700457.

Ehrnhöfer-Ressler, Miriam M., Kristina Fricke, Marc Pignitter, Joel M. Walker, Michael Rychlik, and Veronicka Somoza. "Identification of 1,8-Cineole, Borneol, Camphor, and Thujone as Anti-Inflammatory Compounds in a Salvia Officinalis L. Infusion Using Human Gingival Fibroblasts." *Journal of Agricultural and Food Chemistry*, April 10, 2013. https://pubmed.ncbi.nlm.nih.gov/23488631/.

Fernandes, E. S., G. F. Passos, R. Medeiros, F. M. Da Cunha, J. Ferreira, M. M. Campos, . . . J. B. Calixto. "Anti-inflammatory Effects of Compounds Alpha-humulene and (-)-trans-caryophyllene Isolated from the Essential Oil of Cordia Verbenacea." European Journal of Pharmacology, August 27, 2007. Retrieved February 8, 2021, from https://pubmed.ncbi.nlm.nih.gov/17559833/.

Grassman, J., S. Hipprli, R. Spitzenberger, and E. Elstner. "Chemical Composition and Antibacterial Activity of Essential Oil of Heracleum Rechinger Manden from Iran." Natural Product Research, June 12, 2005. Retrieved February 8, 2021, from https://pubmed.ncbi.nlm.nih.gov/20552523/.

G. Agullo, L. Gamet-Payrastre, K. C. Park, G. S. Bae, I. Seckiner, O. Bayrak, A. Pichette, S. Bourgou,

G. M. Brodeur, R. Vrolix, K. Brusselmans, C. Brannock, J. L. Cadet et al. "Antioxidative, Anticancer, and Genotoxic Properties of α-Pinene on N2a Neuroblastoma Cells." *Biologia*, January 1, 1997. https://www.researchgate.net/publication/258831837_Antioxidative_anticancer_and_genotoxic_properties_of_a-pinene_on_N2a_neuroblastoma_cells/fulltext/563e00dd08ae45b5d28c3607/Antioxidative-anticancer-and-genotoxic-properties-of-a-pinene-on-N2a-neuroblastoma-cells.pdf.

Huang, Xia-Ling, Xiao-Jun Li, Qui-Fang Qin, Yu-Sang Li, Wei Kevin Zhang, and He-Bin Tang. "Anti-Inflammatory and Antinociceptive Effects of Active Ingredients in the Essential Oils from Gynura Procumbens, a Traditional Medicine and a New and Popular Food Material." *Journal of Ethnopharmacology*, July 15, 2019. https://pubmed.ncbi.nlm.nih.gov/31034956/.

Hur, Jinyoung, Sok Cheon Pak, Byung-Soo Koo, and Songhee Jeon. "Borneol Alleviates Oxidative Stress via Upregulation of Nrf2 and Bcl-2 in SH-SY5Y Cells." Pharmaceutical Biology, December 26, 2011. https://www.tandfonline.com/doi/abs/10.3109/13880209.2012.700718.

Jeong, Jong-Geun, Young Sup Kim, Yong Ki Min, and Seong Hwan Kim. "Low Concentration of 3-Carene Stimulates the Differentiation of Mouse Osteoblastic MC3T3-E1 Subclone 4 Cells." Phytotherapy Research, August 8, 2007. https://onlinelibrary.wiley.com/doi/abs/10.1002/ptr.2247.

Khan, A., K. Vaibhav, H. Javed, R. Tabassum, M. E. Ahmed, M. M. Khan, . . . F. Islam, F. "1,8-Cineole (Eucalyptol) Mitigates Inflammation in Amyloid Beta Toxicated pc12 cells: Relevance to Alzheimer's Disease." Neurochemical Research, February 2014. Retrieved February 8, 2021, from https://pubmed.ncbi.nlm.nih.gov/24379109/.

Klauke, A.-L., I. Racz, B. Pradier, A. Markert, A. M. Zimmer, J. Gertsch, and A. Zimmer. "The Cannabinoid CB2 Receptor-Selective Phytocannabinoid Beta-Caryophyllene Exerts Analgesic Effects in Mouse Models of Inflammatory and Neuropathic Pain." *European Neuropsychopharmacology*, October 22, 2013. https://www.sciencedirect.com/science/article/pii/S0924977X13003027.

Legault, J., W. Dahl, A. Pichette, and J. Madelmont.

"Antitumor Activity of Balsam Fir Oil: Production of Reactive Oxygen Species Induced by Alpha-Humulene as Possible Mechanism of Action. Planta Medica, May 2003. Retrieved February 8, 2021, from https://pubmed.ncbi.nlm.nih.gov/12802719/.

Lee, S., J. Han, G. Lee, M. Park, I. Choi, K. Na, and E. Jeung. "Antifungal Effect of Eugenol and Nerolidol against Microsporum Gypseum in a Guinea Pig Model." Biological and Pharmaceutical Bulletin, January 2007. Retrieved February 8, 2021, from https://pubmed.ncbi.nlm.nih.gov/17202684/.

Li, Yan-Hong, Xiao-Ping Sun, Yin-Qing Zhang, and Ning-Sheng Wang. "The Antithrombotic Effect of Borneol Related to Its Anticoagulant Property." *American Journal of Chinese Medicine*, 2008. https://pubmed.ncbi.nlm.nih.gov/18711769/.

Maurya, A. K., M. Singh, V. Dubey, S. Srivastava, S. Luqman, and D. U. Bawankule. "A-(-)-Bisabolol Reduces Pro-inflammatory Cytokine Production and Ameliorates Skin Inflammation." Current Pharmaceutical Biotechnology, 2014. Retrieved February 8, 2021, from https://pubmed.ncbi.nlm.nih.gov/24894548/.

Miller, Jessica A., Patricia A. Thompson, Iman A. Hakim, H. H. Sherry Chow, and Cynthia A. Thomson. "D-Limonene: A Bioactive Food Component from Citrus and Evidence for a Potential Role in Breast Cancer Prevention and Treatment." *Oncology Reviews*, July 15, 2015. https://arizona.pure.elsevier.com/en/publications/d-limonene-a-bioactive-food-component-from-citrus-and-evidence-fo.

Miller, Jessica A., Julie E. Lang, Michele Ley, Ray Nagle, Chiu-Hsieh Hsu, Patricia A. Thompson, Catherine Cordova, Amy Waer, and H. H. Sherry Chow. "Human Breast Tissue Disposition and Bioactivity of Limonene in Women with Early-Stage Breast Cancer." *Cancer Prevention Research*, June 1, 2013. https://cancerpreventionresearch.aacrjournals.org/content/6/6/577.abstract.

Nokhodchi, A., K. Sharabiani, M. Rashidi, and T. Ghafourian. "The Effect of Terpene Concentrations on the Skin Penetration of Diclofenac Sodium." International Journal of Pharmaceutics, April 20, 2007. Retrieved February 8, 2021, from https://pubmed.ncbi.nlm.nih.gov/17174049/.

Okumura, N., H. Yoshida, Y. Nishimura, Y. Kitagishi, S. Matsuda. "Terpinolene, a Component of Herbal Sage, Downregulates AKT1 Expression in K562 Cells." Oncology Letters, February 2012. Retrieved February 8, 2021, from https://www.ncbi.nlm.nih.gov/pmc/articles/PMC3362481/.

Park, Tae-Ju, Yong-Soo Park, Tae-Gyun Lee, Hyun-jung Ha, and Kyong-Tai Kim. "Inhibition of Acetylcholine-Mediated Effects by Borneol." *Biochemical Pharmacology*, January 1, 2003. https://pubmed.ncbi.nlm.nih.gov/12473382/.

Patella, Jessica. "Effects of Rosemary Essential Oil on Mood and Memory." Natural Health Research Institute, July 29, 2013. Retrieved February 8, 2021, from https://www.naturalhealthresearch.org/rosemary-essential-oil/.

Peana, A., P. D'Aquila, F. Panin, G. Serra, P. Pippia, and M. L. Moretti. "Anti-inflammatory Activity of Linalool and Linalyl Acetate Constituents of Essential Oils." Phytomedicine, December 9, 2002. Retrieved February 8, 2021, from https://pubmed.ncbi.nlm.nih.gov/12587692/.

Pichette, A., P. Larouche, M. Lebrun, and J. Legault. "Composition and Antibacterial Activity of Abies Balsamea Essential Oil." May 20, 2006. Retrieved February 8, 2021, from https://pubmed.ncbi.nlm.nih.gov/16619365/.

Rohr, Annette C., Cornelius K. Wilkins, Per A. Clausen, Maria Hammer, Gunnar D. Nielson, Peder Wolkoff, and John D. Spengler. "Upper Airway and Pulmonary Effects of Oxidation Products of (+)-Alpha-Pinene, d-Limonene, and Isoprene in BALB/c Mice." *Inhalation Toxicology*, July 2002. https://pubmed.ncbi.nlm.nih.gov/12122569/.

Russo, Ethan B. "Taming THC: Potential Cannabis Synergy and Phytocannabinoid-Terpenoid Entourage Effects." *British Journal of Pharmacology*, August 2011. https://www.ncbi.nlm.nih.gov/pmc/articles/PMC3165946/.

Russo, Ethan B., and Jahan Marcu. "Nerolidol." Cannabinoid Pharmacology, 2017. https://www.sciencedirect.com/topics/pharmacology-toxicology-and-pharmaceutical-science/nerolidol.

Su, Jianyu, Haoqiang Lai, Jianping Chen, Lin Li,

Yum-Shing Wong, Tianfeng Chen, and Xiaoling Li. "Natural Borneol, a Monoterpenoid Compound, Potentiates Selenocystine-Induced Apoptosis in Human Hepatocellular Carcinoma Cells by Enhancement of Cellular Uptake and Activation of ROS-Mediated DNA Damage." *PLoS One*, May 20, 2013. https://pubmed.ncbi.nlm.nih.gov/23700426/.

Wang, Shu, Dan Zhang, Jinsheng Hu, Qi Jia, Wei Xu, Deyuan Su, Hualing Song et al. "A Clinical and Mechanistic Study of Topical Borneol-Induced Analgesia." *EMBO Molecular Medicine*, June 2017. https://pubmed.ncbi.nlm.nih.gov/28396565/.

Wu, Hai-Yin, Ying Tang, Li-Yan Gao, Wei-Xiang Sun, Yao Hua, Shi-Bao Yang, Zheng-Ping Zhang et al. "The Synergetic Effect of Edaravone and Borneol in the Rat Model of Ischemic Stroke." *European Journal of Pharmacology*, June 27, 2014. https://www.sciencedirect.com/science/article/abs/pii/S0014299914004865.

Yang, Zhiwei, Nan Wu, Yuangang Zu, and Yujie Fu. "Comparative Anti-Infectious Bronchitis Virus (IBV) Activity of (-)-Pinene: Effect on Nucleocapsid (N) Protein." *Molecules* (Basel, Switzerland), January 25, 2011. https://www.ncbi.nlm.nih.gov/pmc/articles/PMC6259611/.

Basic Breeding

Campbell, L. G., J. Dufresne, and S. A. Sabatinos. "Cannabinoid Inheritance Relies on Complex Genetic Architecture." *Cannabis and Cannabinoid Research* 5, no. 1 (February 27, 2020):105–16. doi: 10.1089/can.2018.0015.

Stubbornly Seedless Cannabis

Mansouri, H., and M. Bagheri. "Induction of Polyploidy and Its Effect on Cannabis Sativa L." In Cannabis sativa L.: Botany and Biotechnology, edited by Suman Chandra, Hemant Lata, and Mahmoud A. ElSohly (Springer, January 1, 1970). Retrieved February 8, 2021, from https://link.springer.com/chapter/10.1007/978-3-319-54564-6_17.

Parsons, J. L., S. L. Martin, T. James, G. Golenia, E. A. Boudko, and S. R. Hepworth. "Polyploidization for the Genetic Improvement of Cannabis sativa." Frontiers in Plant Science, April 2019. Retrieved February 8, 2021, from https://www.researchgate.net/publication/332765433_Polyploidization_for_

the_Genetic_Improvement_of_Cannabis_sativa.

Photosynthesis

Chandra, S., H. Lata, I. A. Khan, and M. A. Elsohly. "Photosynthetic Response of Cannabis Sativa L. to Variations in Photosynthetic Photon Flux Densities, Temperature, and CO_2 Conditions. Physiology and *Molecular Biology of Plants* 14, no. 4 (2008): 299–306. doi:10.1007/s12298-008-0027-x.

Light

Albright, L. D., and A. J. Chiu. "Controlling Greenhouse Light to a Consistent Daily Light Integral." Transactions of the ASAE 43, no. 2 (2000): 421–31.

Baskin, J. M., and C. C. Baskin. "Promotion of Germination of Stellaria Media Seeds by Light from a Green Safe Lamp." *New Phytologist* 82 (1978): 381–83.

Borthwick, H. A., and H. M. Cathey. (1962). "Role of Phytochrome in Control of Flowering of Chrysanthemum." *Botanical Gazette* 123, no. 3 (1962): 155-62. http://www.jstor.com/stable/2472998

Both, A. J., B. Bugbee, C. Kubota, R. G. Lopez, C. Mitchell, E. S. Runkle, and C. Wallace. "Proposed Product Label for Electric Lamps Used in the Plant Sciences." *HortTechnology*, 27, no. 4: 544–49. https://doi.org/10.21273/HORTTECH03648-16.

Boyle, G. 2004. *Renewable Energy: Power for a Sustainable Future.* 2nd ed. Oxford: Oxford University Press.

Butler, W. L., S. B. Hendricks, H. W. Siegelman. "Action Spectrum of Phytochrome in Vitro." *Photochemistry and Photobiology* 3 (1964): 521–28.

Cashmore, A. R., J. A. Jarillo, Y. J. Wu, and D. Liu. "Cryptochromes: Blue Light Receptors for Plants and Animals." *Science* 284, no. 5415 (1999): 760–65. https://doi.org/10.1126/science.284.5415.760.

Cathey, H. M., and H. A. Borthwick. "Photoreversibility of Floral Initiation in Chrysanthemum." *Botanical Gazette* 119, no. 2 (1957): 71–76. http://www.jstor.org/stable/2473021.

Cathey, H. M., and L. E. Campbell. 1980. "Light and Lighting for Horticultural Plants." *Horticulture Review* 2.

Davis, P. A., and C. Burns. "Photobiology in Protected Horticulture." *Food and Energy Security* 38. https://doi.org/10.1002/fes3.97.

Faust, J. E., and J. Logan. (2018). Daily Light Integral: A Research Review and High-Resolution Maps of the United States. *HortScience* 53, no. 9 (2018): 1250–57. https://doi.org/10.21273/HORTS-CI13144-18 (https://endowment.org/dlimaps/).

Folta, K. M., and S. D. Carvalho. "Photoreceptors and Control of Horticultural Plant Traits." *HortScience* 50, no. 9 (2015): 1274–80.

Franklin, K. A. "Shade Avoidance." *New Phytologist* 179, no. 4 (2008): 930–44. https://doi.org/10.1111/j.1469-8137.2008.02507.x.

Gupta, S. D., ed. *Light Emitting Diodes for Agriculture.* Springer, 2017.

Haitz, R., and J. Y. Tsao. "Solid-State Lighting: "The Case" Ten Years After and Future Prospects. *Physica Status Solidi (A) Applications and Materials Science* 208, no. 1 (2011): 17–29. https://doi.org/10.1002/pssa.201026349.

Hernández, R., and C. Kubota. "Physiological Responses of Cucumber Seedlings under Different Blue and Red Photon Flux Ratios Using LEDs." *Environmental and Experimental Botany* 121 (2016a): 66–74. https://doi.org/10.1016/j.envexpbot.2015.04.001.

Hernández, R., T. Eguchi, M. Deveci, and C. Kubota. "Tomato Seedling Physiological Responses under Different Percentages of Blue and Red Photon Flux Ratios Using LEDs and Cool White Fluorescent Lamps. *Scientia Horticulturae* 213 (2016b): 270–80. https://doi.org/10.1016/j.scienta.2016.11.005.

Hogewoning, S. W., G. Trouwborst, H. Maljaars, H. Poorter, W. van Ieperen, and J. Harbinson. "Blue Light Dose-Responses of Leaf Photosynthesis, Morphology, and Chemical Composition of Cucumis sativus Grown under Different Combinations of Red and Blue Light." *Journal of Experimental Botany* 61, no. 11 (2010): 3107–17. https://doi.org/10.1093/jxb/erq132.

Hogewoning, S. W., E. Wientjes, P. Douwstra, G. Trouwborst, W. van Ieperen, R. Croce, and J. Harbinson. "Photosynthetic Quantum Yield Dynamics: From Photosystems to Leaves." *Plant Cell* 24, no. 5 (2012): 1921–35. https://doi.org/10.1105/tpc.112.097972.

Holley, J., B. Poel, M. Yelton, S. Hulick, and P. Shaw. "Use a High Yield Photoperiod to Increase Lettuce Production by 40 Percent." *Greenhouse Production News*, 2018. https://gpnmag.com/news/use-a-high-yield-photoperiod-to-increase-lettuce-production-by-40-percent/.

Jenkins, G. I. "The UV-B Photoreceptor UVR8: From Structure to Physiology." *Plant Cell* 26, no. 1 (2014): 21–37. https://doi.org/10.1105/tpc.113.119446.

Koontz, H. V., and R. P. Prince. "Effect of Sixteen and Twenty-Four Hours Daily Radiation (Light) on Lettuce Growth. *HortScience* 21 (1986): 123–24.

Kopsell, D. A., C. E. Sams, and R. C. Morrow. "Blue Wavelengths from LED Lighting Increase Nutritionally Important Metabolites in Specialty Crops." *HortScience* 50, no. 9 (2015): 1285–88. https://doi.org/10.21273/hortsci.50.9.1285.
Korczynski, P. C., J. Logan, and J. E. Faust. "Mapping Monthly Distribution of Daily Light Integrals across the Contiguous United States." *HortTechnology* 12, no. 1 (2002): 12–16.

Kusuma, P., M. Pattison, and B. Bugbee. 2020. "From Physics to Fixtures to Food: Current and Potential LED Efficacy." *Nature-Horticulture Research* 7 (2020): 56. https://doi.org/10.1038/s41438-020-0283-7.

Kusuma, P., and B. Bugbee. "Far-Red Fraction: An Improved Metric for Characterizing Phytochrome Effects on Morphology." *Journal of the American Society for Horticultural Science* 146, no. 1 (2020): 3-13. https://doi.org/10.21273/JASHS05002-20.

Lund, J. B., T. J. Blom, and J. M. Aaslyng. "End-of-Day Lighting with Different Red/Far-Red Ratios Using Light-Emitting Diodes Affects Plant Growth of Chrysanthemum x morifolium Ramat. 'Coral Charm.'" *HortScience* 42, no. 7 (2007): 1609–11.

Massa, G. D., H.-H. Kim, R. M. Wheeler, and C. A. Mitchell. *HortScience* 43, no. 7 (2008): 1951–56. http://hortsci.ashspublications.org/content/43/7/1951.full.

Mccoshum, S., and J. Z. Kiss. "Green Light Affects Blue-Light-Based Phototropism in Hypocotyls of Arabidopsis thaliana Author." *Journal of the Torrey Botanical Society* 138, no. 4 (2011): 409–17.

McCree, K. J. "The Action Spectrum, Absorptance, and Quantum Yield of Photosynthesis in Crop Plants." *Agricultural Meteorology* 9, no. C (1971): 191–216. https://doi.org/10.1016/0002-1571(71)90022-7.

McCree, K. J. "Significance of Enhancement for Calculations Based on the Action Spectrum for Photosynthesis." *Plant Physiology* 49, no. 5 (1972): 704–6. https://doi.org/10.1104/pp.49.5.704.

Morrow, R. C. "LED Lighting in Horticulture." *HortScience* 43, no. 7 (2008): 1947–50. https://doi.org/10.21273/hortsci.43.7.1947.

Nelson, J. A., and B. Bugbee. "Economic Analysis of Greenhouse Lighting: Light Emitting Diodes vs. High Intensity Discharge Fixtures." *PLoS ONE* 9, no. 6 (2014). https://doi.org/10.1371/journal.pone.0099010.

Ouzounis, T., E. Rosenqvist, and C. O. Ottosen. "Spectral Effects of Artificial Light on Plant Physiology and Secondary Metabolism: A Review." *HortScience* 50, no. 8 (2015): 1128–35. https://doi.org/10.21273/hortsci.50.8.1128.

Park, Y. G., and B. R. Jeong. "Night Interruption Light Quality Changes Morphogenesis, Flowering, and Gene Expression in Dendranthema grandiflorum." *Horticulture Environment and Biotechnology* 60, no. 2 (2019): 167–73. https://doi.org/10.1007/s13580-018-0114-z.

Pintó-Marijuan, Marta, and Sergi Munné-Bosch. "Photo-Oxidative Stress Markers as a Measure of Abiotic Stress-Induced Leaf Senescence: Advantages and Limitations." Journal of Experimental Botany 65, no. 14 (2014): 3845–57. https://academic.oup.com/jxb/article/65/14/3845/2877459.

Pocock, T. "Light-Emitting Diodes and the Modulation of Specialty Crops: Light Sensing and Signaling Networks in Plants." *HortScience* 50, no. 9 (2015): 1281–84.

Sager, J. C. "Spectral Effects on the Growth of Lettuce under Controlled Environment Conditions." *Acta Horticulturae* 148 (1984): 889-96.

Shinomura, T., A. Nagatani, H. Hanzawa, M. Kubota, M. Watanabe, and M. Furuya. "Action Spectra for Phytochrome A- and B-Specific Photoinduction of Seed Germination in Arabidopsis thaliana." *Proceedings of the National Academy of Sciences of the United States of America* 93, no. 15 (1996): 8129-33. http://www.jstor.com/stable/40175.

Smith, H. L., L. Mcausland, and E. H. Murchie. "Don't Ignore the Green Light: Exploring Diverse Roles in Plant Processes." *Journal of Experimental Botany* 68, no. 9 (2017): 2099–110. https://doi.org/10.1093/jxb/erx098.

Steigerwald, D., J. Bhat, D. Collins, R. Fletcher, M. Holcomb, M. Ludowise, P. Martin, and S. Rudaz. "Illumination with Solid State Lighting Technology." *IEEE Journal on Selected Topics in Quantum Electronics* 8 (2002): 310–20.

Stutte, G. W. "Light-Emitting Diodes for Manipulating the Phytochrome Apparatus." *HortScience* 44, no. 2 (2009): 231–34. https://doi.org/10.21273/hortsci.44.2.231.

Terashima, I., T. Fujita, T. Inoue, W. S. Chow, and R. Oguchi. "Green Light Drives Leaf Photosynthesis More Efficiently Than Red Light in Strong White Light: Revisiting the Enigmatic Question of Why Leaves Are Green." *Plant and Cell Physiology* 50, no. 4 (2009): 684–97. https://doi.org/10.1093/pcp/pcp034.

Wallace, C., and A. J. Both. "Evaluating Operating Characteristics of Light Sources for Horticultural Applications." *Acta Horticulturae* 1134 (2016): 435–43. https://doi.org/10.17660/ActaHortic.2016.1134.55.

Wang, Y., and K. M. Folta. "Contributions of Green Light to Plant Growth and Development." *American Journal of Botany* 100, no. 1 (2013): 70–78. https://doi.org/10.3732/ajb.1200354.

Zhang, T., and K. M. Folta. "Green Light Signaling and Adaptive Response." *Plant Signaling and Behavior* 7, no. 1 (2012). https://doi.org/10.4161/psb.7.1.18635

Zhen, S., M. Haidekker, and M. W. van Iersel. "Far-Red Light Enhances Photochemical Efficiency in a Wavelength-Dependent Manner." *Physiologia Plantarum* 167, no. 1 (2019): 21–33. https://doi.org/10.1111/ppl.12834.

Zhen, S., and B. Bugbee. "Far-Red Photons Have Equivalent Efficiency to Traditional Photosynthetic Photons: Implications for Redefining Photosynthetically Active Radiation." *Plant, Cell & Environment* 43 (2020): 1259–72. https://doi.org/10.1111/pce.13730.

Zhen, S., and B. Bugbee. "Substituting Far-Red for Traditionally Defined Photosynthetic Photons Results in Equal Canopy Quantum Yield for CO_2 Fixation and Increased Photon Capture during Long-Term Studies: Implications for Re-defining PAR." *Frontiers in Plant Science* (2020). https://doi.org/10.3389/fpls.2020.581156.

Zhen, S., and B. Bugbee. "Far-Red Photons Have Equivalent Efficiency to Traditional Photosynthetic Photons: Implications for Re-defining Photosynthetically Active Radiation." *Plant, Cell & Environment* (2020). https://doi.org/10.1111/pce.13730.

Zhen, S., and M. W. van Iersel. "Far-Red Light Is Needed for Efficient Photochemistry and Photosynthesis." *Journal of Plant Physiology* 209 (2017) 115–22. https://doi.org/10.1016/j.jplph.2016.12.004.

Carbon Dioxide

Goorahoo, D., S, F. C., G. Carstensen, and S. Ashkan. *Crop Growth Enhancement with CO_2 Injection into the Crop Canopy with Drip Irrigation.* Fresno, CA: CSU Fresno Center for Irrigation Technology and the Agricultural Gas Company, 2003.

Water

Argo, W., and P. R. Fisher. *Understanding pH Management.* Meister Media, 2008.

Argo, W., and P. R. Fisher. "Understanding Plant Nutrition: Irrigation Water Alkalinity and pH." Greenhouse Grower, June 12, 2008. https://www.greenhousegrower.com/production/fertilization/understanding-plant-nutrition-irrigation-water-alkalinity-ph/.

Hong, C., G. W. Moorman, W. Wohanka, and

C. Buttner. 2017. "Biology, Detection, and Management of Plant Pathogens in Irrigation Water." APS Publications, 2017. https://doi.org/10.1094/9780890544914.

Lee, Eric, and Lorence R. Oki. "Slow Sand Filters Effectively Reduce Phytophthora after a Pathogen Switch from Fusarium and a Simulated Pump Failure." *Water Research*, 2013. https://pubmed.ncbi.nlm.nih.gov/23866129/.

Lévesque, Serge et al. "Inactivation of Rhizoctonia Solani in Fertigation Water Using Regenerative in situ Electrochemical Hypochlorination." *Scientific Reports* 9, no. 1 14237. (October 2019). doi:10.1038/s41598-019-50600-7.

McGehee, C. S., P. Apicella, R. Raudales, G. Berkowitz, Y. Ma, S. Durocher, and J. Lubell. "First Report of Root Rot and Wilt Caused by *Pythium myriotylum* on Hemp (Cannabis sativa) in the United States." 2019. https://doi.org/10.1094/PDIS-11-18-2028-PDN.
Marcelis, L. F. M., and E. Heuvenlink, eds. *Achieving Sustainable Greenhouse Cultivation*. Burleigh Dodds Science, 2019. doi:10.19103/AS.2019.0052.

Park, E. J., E. Alexander, G. A. Taylor, R. Costa, and D. H. Kang. "The Decontaminative Effects of Acidic Electrolyzed Water for *Escherichia coli* O157:H7, *Salmonella typhimurium*, and *Listeria monocytogenes* on Green Onions and Tomatoes with Differing Organic Demands. *Food Microbiology* 26, no. 4 (2009): 386-90.

Raudales, R. E., J. L. Parke, C. L. Guy, and P. R. Fisher. "Control of Waterborne Microbes in Irrigation: A Review." *Agricultural Water Management* 143 (2014): 9–28.

Sonneveld, C., and W. Voogt. *Plant Nutrition of Greenhouse Crops*. Springer, 2009.

Siddiqui, Mohammed. *Postharvest Disinfection of Fruits and Vegetables*. Elsevier, 2018.

Oxygen
Jacobs, K., J. MacDonald, A. Berry, and L. Costello. "The Effect of Low Oxygen Stress on *phytophthora cinnamomi* Infection and Disease of Cork Oak Roots." US Forest Service, January 1, 1997. Retrieved February 12, 2021, from https://www.fs.usda.gov/treesearch/pubs/28218.

Nutrients & Fertilizers
Cockson, P., H. Landis, T. Smith, K. Hicks, and B. Whipker. "Characterization of Nutrient Disorders of *Cannabis sativa*." Applied Sciences 9, no. 20 (2019): 4432. Retrieved February 8, 2021, from https://www.mdpi.com/2076-3417/9/20/4432/htm.

Veazie, Patrick, and Paul Cockson. "Nutrient Monitoring in Cannabis Cultivation: A Step-By-Step Guide." *Cannabis Business Times*, August 2, 2020. https://www.cannabisbusinesstimes.com/article/nutrient-monitoring-for-cannabis-step-by-step-guide/.

Epstein, E., and A. J. Bloom. Mineral Nutrition of Plants: *Principles and Perspectives*. Sunderland, MA: Sinauer Associates, 1994.

Mattson, N. S., and C. J. Currey. "Advances in Nutrient Management in Greenhouse Cultivation. In *Achieving Sustainable Greenhouse Cultivation*, L. F. M. Marcelis and E. Heuvelink. Cambridge, UK: Burleigh Dodds Science, 2019.

Soil
Alori, Elizabeth T., Bernard R. Glick, and Olubukola O. Babalola. "Microbial Phosphorus Solubilization and Its Potential for Use in Sustainable Agriculture." Frontiers in Microbiology, May 15, 2017. https://www.frontiersin.org/articles/10.3389/fmicb.2017.00971/full.
Glick, Bernard R. "Modulation of Plant Ethylene Levels by the Bacterial Enzyme ACC Deaminase." *FEMS Microbiology Letters* 251, no. 1 (2005): 1–7. https://doi.org/10.1016/j.femsle.2005.07.030

Gaskin, J. W., P. Hartel, E. Little, and G. Harris. "Soil Inoculants." University of Georgia College of Agricultural and Environmental Sciences Cooperative Extension, August 2013. https://secure.caes.uga.edu/extension/publications/files/pdf/C%20990_2.PDF.

Souza, R. de, A. Ambrosini, and L. M. P. Passaglia. "Plant Growth-Promoting Bacteria as Inoculants in Agricultural Soils." *Genetics and Molecular Biology* 38, no. 4 (2015): 401-19. doi:10.1590/S1415-475738420150053.

The California Appellation of Origin Garden
Actimage, R. "Demarcation of Production Areas and Protection of Soils." Retrieved February 8, 2021,

from https://www.inao.gouv.fr/eng/The-National-Institute-of-origin-and-quality-Institut-national-de-l-origine-et-de-la-qualite-INAO/Missions/Demarcation-of-production-areas-and-protection-of-soils.

Actimage, R. "Ouvrages sur les signes de qualité ou d'origine." Retrieved February 8, 2021, from https://www.inao.gouv.fr/Institut-national-de-l-origine-et-de-la-qualite/Ouvrages-sur-les-signes-de-qualite-ou-d-origine.

Beans, C. "How Does a Crop's Environment Shape a Food's Smell and Taste?" Science News, September 18, 2020. Retrieved February 8, 2021, from https://www.sciencenews.org/article/terroir-food-crops-environment-smell-taste.
California Legislative Information. California Senate Bill No. 185 CHAPTER 841 An act to amend Sections 26001 and 26063 of the Business and Professions Code, relating to cannabis. October 12, 2019. Retrieved February 8, 2021, from https://leginfo.legislature.ca.gov/faces/billTextClient.xhtml?bill_id=201920200SB185.

Sustainability
Oxford College of Procurement and Supply. "How Sustainable Is Sustainability?" November 12, 2019. Retrieved February 8, 2021, from https://www.oxfordcollegeofprocurementandsupply.com/how-sustainable-is-sustainability/#:~:text=The%20current%20definition%20of%20sustainability,term%20depletion%20of%20natural%20resources%E2%80%9C.

Pleasant, B. "Five Ways to Build Soil in Winter." GrowVeg, October 22, 2015. Retrieved February 09, 2021, from https://www.growveg.com/guides/5-ways-to-build-soil-in-winter/.

Getting Started
Nelson, P. V., C. Song, and J. Huang. "What Really Causes Stretch?" Greenhouse Product News, January 11, 2002. Retrieved March 12, 2021, from https://gpnmag.com/article/what-really-causes-stretch/.

Finishing & Flushing
Kontaxis, D. G., and D. Cox. "Effect of Vitamin B1 on Vegetable Transplants." California Agriculture, September 1984. Retrieved February 8, 2021, from http://calag.ucanr.edu/download_pdf.cfm?article=ca.v038n09p15.

Hammer C. "Effects of Vitamin B1 upon the Development of Some Flowering Plants." *Botanical Gazette*, 102, no. 1 (1940). https://doi.org/10.1086/334942.

Re, G., R. Barbero, A. Miolo, and V. Di Marzo. "Palmitoylethanolamide, Endocannabinoids, and Related Cannabimimetic Compounds in Protection against Tissue Inflammation and Pain: Potential Use in Companion Animals." Vet Journal, January 2007. Retrieved February 8, 2021, from https://pubmed.ncbi.nlm.nih.gov/16324856/.

Schalau, J. "Vitamin B-1 and Root Stimulators." Backyard Gardener, March 26, 2008. Retrieved February 8, 2021, from https://cals.arizona.edu/yavapai/anr/hort/byg/archive/vitaminb1androotstimulators.html.

When & How to Harvest: The Science behind Choosing a Harvest Date
Babar, Ali, Naser Ali Al-Wabel, Saiba Shams, Aftab Ahamad, Shah Alam Khan, and Firoz Anwar. "Essential Oils Used in Aromatherapy: A Systemic Review." *Asian Pacific Journal of Tropical Biomedicine* 5, no. 8 (2015): 601-11. https://doi.org/10.1016/j.apjtb.2015.05.007.

Cho, K. S., Y. Lim, K. Lee, J. Lee, J. H. Lee, and I.-S. Lee. "Terpenes from Forests and Human Health." *Toxicological Research* 33, no. 2 (2017): 97–106. http://doi.org/10.5487/TR.2017.33.2.097.

Dagli, N., R. Dagli, R. S. Mahmoud, K. Baroudi "Essential Oils, Their Therapeutic Properties, and Implication in Dentistry: A Review." *Journal of International Society of Preventive and Community Dentistry* 5, no. 5 (2015): 335-40. doi:10.4103/2231-0762.165933.

De Meijer, et al. "The Inheritance of Chemical Phenotype in Cannabis sativa L. (II): Cannabigerol Predominant Plants." 2005.

De Meijer, et al. "The Inheritance of Chemical Phenotype in Cannabis sativa L. (III): Variation in Cannabichromene Proportion." 2009a.
De Meijer, et al. "The Inheritance of Chemical Phenotype in Cannabis sativa L. (IV): Cannabinoid Free Plants. 2009b.

do Vale, T. G., E. C. Furtado, J. G. Santos Jr., G. S.

Viana. "Central Effects of Citral, Myrcene and Limonene, Constituents of Essential Oil Chemotypes from Lippia alba (Mill.) n.e. Brown." *Phytomedicine* 9, no. 8 (2002): 709–14. doi:10.1078/09447110232 1621304.

Gertsch, Jürg, Marco Leonti, Stefan Raduner, Ildiko Racz, Jian-Zhong Chen, Xiang-Qun Xie, Karl-Heinz Altmann, Meliha Karsak, and Andreas Zimmer. *Proc Natl Acad Sci U S A.* 105, no. 26 (2008): 9099–104.

Kei, H., C. Song, and Y. Miyazaki. *Journal of Wood Science* 62 (2016): 568.

Lima, D. F., M. S. Brandão, J. B. Moura, J. M. Leitão, F. A. Carvalho, L. M. Miúra, J. R. Leite, D. P. Sousa, and F. R. Almeida. *Journal of Pharmacy and Pharmacology* 64, no. 2 (2012): 283–92. doi: 10.1111/j.2042-7158.2011.01401.x.

Russo, E. B. "Taming THC: Potential Cannabis Synergy and Phytocannabinoid-Terpenoid Entourage Effects." *British Journal of Pharmacology* 163, no. 7 (2011): 1344–64.

Sowndhararajan, K, and S. Kim. "Influence of Fragrances on Human Psychophysiological Activity: With Special Reference to Human Electroencephalographic Response." *Scientia Pharmaceutica* 84, no. 4 (2016): 724-51. doi:10.3390/scipharm84040724. Teixeria, Gisele Facanha Diogenes, Antonio Eufrasio Viera-Nieto, Flavio Noguerada Costa, Angelo Roncalli Alvese Silva, and Adriana Rolim Campos. Biomedicine & Pharmacotherapy 91 (July 2017): 9 46–50.

Drying, Curing & Storing

Dougherty, R. C., H. H. Strain, W. A. Svec, R. A. Uphaus, and J. J. Katz. "Structure, Properties, and Distribution of Chlorophyll c." Journal of the American Chemical Society, May 1, 1970. Retrieved February 8, 2021, from https://pubs.acs.org/doi/pdf/10.1021/ja00712a037.

Ghandchi, F., G. Caetano-Anolles, S. Clough, and D. Ort. "Investigating the Control of Chlorophyll Degradation by Genomic Correlation Mining." PLos One, September 12, 2016. Retrieved February 09, 2021, from https://journals.plos.org/plosone/article?id=10.1371%2Fjournal.pone.0162327#:~:-text=The%20key%20controlling%20enzyme%20

involved,in%20the%20reaction%20%5B3%5D
Higdon, Jane. "Chlorophyll and Chlorophyllin." Linus Pauling Institute, January 1, 2021. https://lpi.oregonstate.edu/mic/dietary-factors/phytochemicals/chlorophyll-chlorophyllin.

Hörtensteiner, S., and B. Kräutler. "Chlorophyll Breakdown in Higher Plants." BBA: Biogenetics 1807, no. 8 (2010): 977–88. Retrieved February 9, 2021, from https://www.sciencedirect.com/science/article/pii/S0005272810007942.

Martin, L. "What Are the Roles of Chlorophyll A & B?" Sciencing, July 24, 2019. Retrieved February 9, 2021, from https://sciencing.com/what-are-the-roles-of-chlorophyll-a-b-12526386.html.

Ross, S. A., and M. A. Elsohly. "UNODC - Bulletin on Narcotics - 1997 Issue 1 - 008." United Nations: Office on Drugs and Crime, December 1, 1999. https://www.unodc.org/unodc/en/data-and-analysis/bulletin/bulletin_1997-01-01_1_page008.html.

Seely, G. R. "Chlorin." ScienceDirect Topics, 1966. https://www.sciencedirect.com/topics/biochemistry-genetics-and-molecular-biology/chlorin.

Singh, A. K., and A. K. Pandey. "Chlorophyll." ScienceDirect Topics, 2020. Retrieved February 9, 2021, from https://www.sciencedirect.com/topics/chemistry/chlorophyll.

Steep Hill. "Terpenes." Steep Hill, n.d. Retrieved February 9, 2021, from https://www.steephill.com/science/terpenes.

Appendix E: Pest & Disease

Lee, H., J. H. Ryu, H. Kim. "Antimicrobial Activity of Gaseous Chlorine Dioxide against Aspergillus flavus on Green Coffee Beans." *Food Microbiology* 86(April 2020). doi: 10.1016/j.fm.2019.103308.

Sharma, Ajay & Sawant, Indu & Saha, Sujoy & Kadam, Pratiksha & Somkuwar, Ramhari. (2017). Aqueous chlorine dioxide for the management of PM vis-a-vis maintaining quality of grapes and raisins. *Journal of Eco-Friendly Agriculture.* 12. 59-64.

GARDEN CONSULTANTS

Saul Alba
IPM Specialist
(805) 325-9389

Justin Arriola
Arriola.J@intelligentengineeringsolutions.com

Joey Ereñeta
Horticulture Department Chair,
Oaksterdam University
Let It Grow Consulting
joey@letitgrowconsulting.com

Bill Faulconer
bill@roomtogrowav.com

Mike Finley
Cultivo, Inc.
mikefinely@cultivoinc.com
(831) 332-6582

Dr. Robb Flannery
info@drrobbfarms.com

Bill Graham
microclone100@gmail.com
(650) 346-8009

Jake Holley
jakemarkholley@gmail.com
(303) 502-7677

Jeff Jones
Product Development and Field Testing
at Oaksterdam University and
Quick Trading
Jeff@oaksterdamuniversity.com

Autumn Karcey
CEO, Cultivo, Inc,
(530) 379-8588
autumn@cultivoinc.com

Ed Rosenthal
https://www.edrosenthal.com/contact

Clayton Stewart
clayton.dl.stewart@gmail.com
(604) 619-2416
cscannabissolutions.com

Surna, Inc.
(303) 993-5271
info@surna.com
Surna.com

Photo: Stinkbud

GARDEN RESOURCES

800+ CANNABIS PROJECTS | SINCE 2006

COMPREHENSIVE CANNABIS ENVIRONMENT SOLUTIONS

An efficient and precise environment is critical to maintaining a healthy, consistent crop and a successful business. Don't hope for the best when it comes to your HVAC/D design and equipment; choose Surna's experienced team to provide a climate solution specific to your facility's unique needs and budget.

CLIMATE (HVAC/D) SYSTEMS

Environmental systems and equipment designed for energy efficiency and plant health.

MEP ENGINEERING

Cannabis-focused MEP engineering & design with fully stamped construction documents.

CONTROL SYSTEMS

Intelligent data mangement with schedules, trends, and system alarms at your fingertips.

MAINTENANCE SERVICES

Proactivley address problems with your HVAC/D system before they impact your bottom line.

+1 (303) 993 5271 | WWW.SURNA.COM

24/7 DATA

-⋏- pulse

CULTIVATION
MONITORING & ALERTING

PROTECTING GARDENS OF ALL SIZES IN OVER 40 COUNTRIES

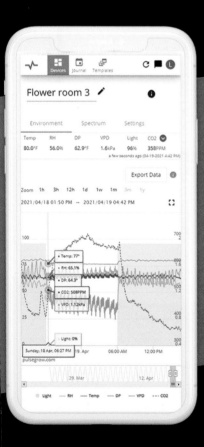

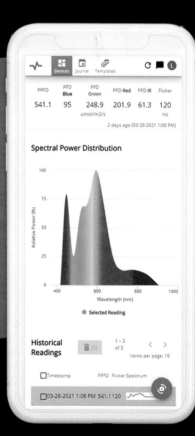

CO₂

DEW POINT

HUMIDITY

LIGHT SPECTRUM

PAR/PPFD

TEMPERATURE

VPD

LEARN MORE & CONNECT

 1-888-537-8573 @PULSEGROW

monitor | control | analyze | predict

Precision Climate   Precision Fertigation   Fanatical support

We build tightly integrated hardware and software backed by fanatical support
to power the future of farming.

growlink.com / 1-800-432-0160

SEED STRAIN:
Witchy Wonder

20 20
3RD PLACE
HIGHLIFE CUP
WINNER

Earth Witch Seeds

Worlds 1st Vegan Plant-Based Cannabis Seed Company

OFFICIALEARTHWITCHSEEDS.COM

@officialearthwitchseeds | FOR INQUIRES: ewsofficialtyson@galaxyhit.com

– Founded in Amsterdam 2018 –

grow your own escape

PREMIUM CANNABIS SEEDS

SHOP "MAUI WOWIE" AND 500+ STRAINS

BEAVER SEEDS

JAY
KITCHEN

CO-FOUNDER
UPTOWN
GROWLAB

AUTHOR:
THE KITCHEN

NEWEST PROJECT:
2021 CANNABIS ANNUAL

YOUTUBE STATS:

2,500+ VIDEOS
10 MILLION VIEWS
100,000 VIEWS PER MONTH

2021
CANNABIS ANNUAL

A YEAR IN REVIEW AND GUIDE TO ALL THINGS CANNABIS

www.uptowngrowlab.live

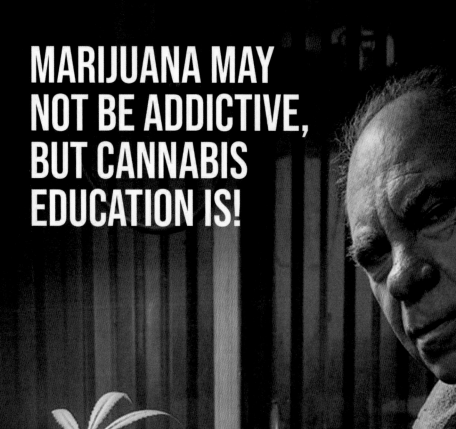

Know More. Grow More.

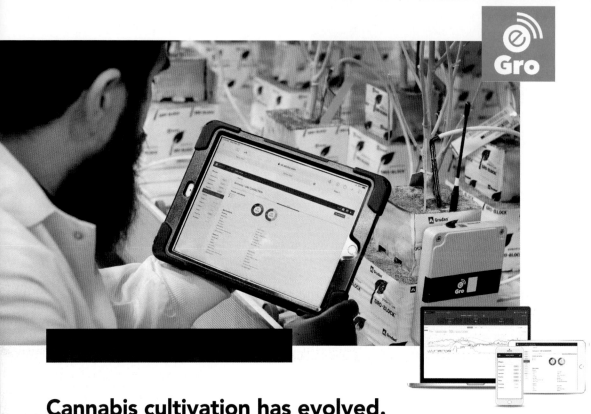

Cannabis cultivation has evolved.

Before, growers based their growing strategies on intuition and experience. Today, Master Growers use data and technology to control production, quality and profitability. e-Gro from Grodan is the revolutionary online platform that integrates GroSens Rootzone and Climate sensors for deep insights of the entire facility with 24/7, real time, remote access to data:

- Optimize crop steering, strain specific strategies and maximize yields
- Compare irrigation and climate strategies in different rooms and zones
- Track individual batches, including mother plants, from cloning through to harvest for consistent end product quality
- Receive real-time notifications when readings go outside of your set parameters
- Ensure SOPs are followed across the team
- Leverage Grodan's 50+ years of crop steering expertise and the power of Data Scientists from world renowned universities

Are you ready to master your cannabis production with data driven cultivation? Check out e-Gro today at www.grodan101.com/e-Gro

Growing in Grodan is as easy as

1 Saturate

Saturate Grodan Starter Plugs and Cubes in a nutrient solution of roughly 1.5 EC and 5.5 pH with a course spray or submerged in the solution for up to 1 minute. Let drain.

pH 5.5 – 6.5

2 Take Cuttings

Choose equal length and diameter cuttings from new growth, no more than 14 days old, near top of plant. Apply rooting solution to cut only, preventing it from getting on the stem.

Insert stem ½ inches into the conditioned Grodan starter plug.

- Place Starter Cubes in a propagation dome or humidity tent.

Monitor the wet weight. Once the wet weight reaches about half, apply an irrigation with a nutrient solution of 1.5 EC and 5.5 pH. Drain excess to prevent mould, algae and disease.

3 Transplant

When starters are well rooted with strong white roots emerging from the plug, transplant the cutting to a larger Grodan Gro-Block.

Saturate Grodan Gro-Blocks with a nutrient solution of 1.5 to 2.0 EC and 5.5 to 6.0 pH by watering wand / boom with several slow passes on a flood table, or submerge in the nutrient solution until they sink.

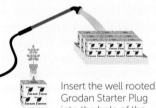

Insert the well rooted Grodan Starter Plug into the hole of the conditioned Grodan Gro-Block.

Measure the weight of the block at saturation and throughout the growing cycle. When the water content of the blocks is 55% to 65% apply the first irrigation.

4 Irrigation: Golden Rule is Transpiration Before Irrigation

Apply at least one irrigation within 1 hour after lights on

Second irrigation close to mid-day

Achieve 10 - 30% runoff of the daily irrigation for proper re-saturation and nutrient replacement

Adjust irrigation throughout the life cycle for strain, environment and root zone conditions.

- In Veg use smaller volumes of nutrient solutions (3%) at a higher frequency for vigorous leaf, stem and structural tissue growth.

- In Flower use larger volumes of water (6%) at lower frequency to steer growth generatively.

Do NOT over saturate the Grodan Gro-Blocks to prevent algae, slow plant growth and disease pressure.

Do NOT allow the Grodan Gro-Blocks to dry back below 50% of wet weight to prevent slow growth, slow root development and inconsistencies between plants. Drying back beyond 50% of wet weight will make it harder to re-saturate the media and create dry spots in the blocks.

For more information on Grodan products and using them for optimal crop quality and yield, check out www.grodan101.com

Part of the ROCKWOOL Group

RAGING
kale

DRAGON
alpha

RAGING
kush

Being able to control the type (quality) of light your plants are getting during the different phases of growth is mandatory if you are trying to influence the morphology of the plant. With Scynce LED's "full power spectrum tuning" you have complete control over the spectrum delivered without the loss of power (intensity) and no need to swap out bulbs or fixtures, ever!

🌐 scynceled.com | 📷 @scynceled

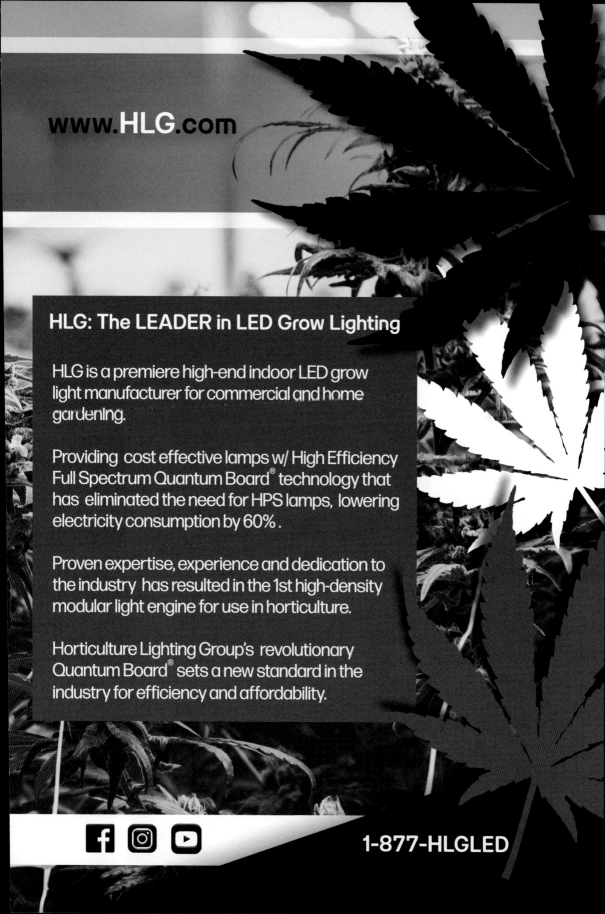

HERE'S WHAT YOU'LL FIND INSIDE:

BASE NUTRIENTS:
pH Perfect Sensi Grow Parts A + B
pH Perfect Sensi Bloom Parts A + B

BUD TASTE & TERPENE ENHANCEMENT:
Bud Candy

BIGGER BUDS:
Big Bud
Overdrive

ROOT MASS EXPANDERS:
Voodoo Juice

BUD POTENCY & STALK STRENGTHENER:
B-52

SENSI GROW: A&B Feed your plants the exact nutrients they need for robust vegetation and prime them for a flourishing harvest.

SENSI BLOOM: A&B This two-part base nutrient system provides comprehensive nutrition for a bountiful bloom phase.

BUD CANDY: Promote explosive bursts of sugar-coated buds when you feed your plants Bud Candy, the industry's leading horticultural carbohydrates formula.

BIG BUD: This legendary bloom booster provides customized ratios of phosphorus and potassium to unlock bigger yields.

OVERDRIVE®: Overdrive® is a late-season bloom booster engineered to reinvigorate flower late in the game for swelling buds packed with potency.

VOODOO JUICE: Bigger roots mean bigger fruits. Hand-selected microbes promote a robust root system, which is crucial for getting dense, resin-coated colas.

B-52: B-52 contains vitamin B1 and other ingredients that allow the plant to focus its energy on developing sturdy stalks and bigger buds.

AWARD-WINNING NUTRIENTS

Add even more value to your harvest by using the same tools the pros rely on to ahcieve their best yields. Each kit includes a trichome magnifier, measuring cup, feed chart, and two 10ML pipettes, making it easier than ever to grow your own garden.

Visit Your Local Authorized Retailer to Start Today
100% Money Back Grower Guarantee

TOOLS FOR THE
MODERN GARDENER
SUITELEAF.COM

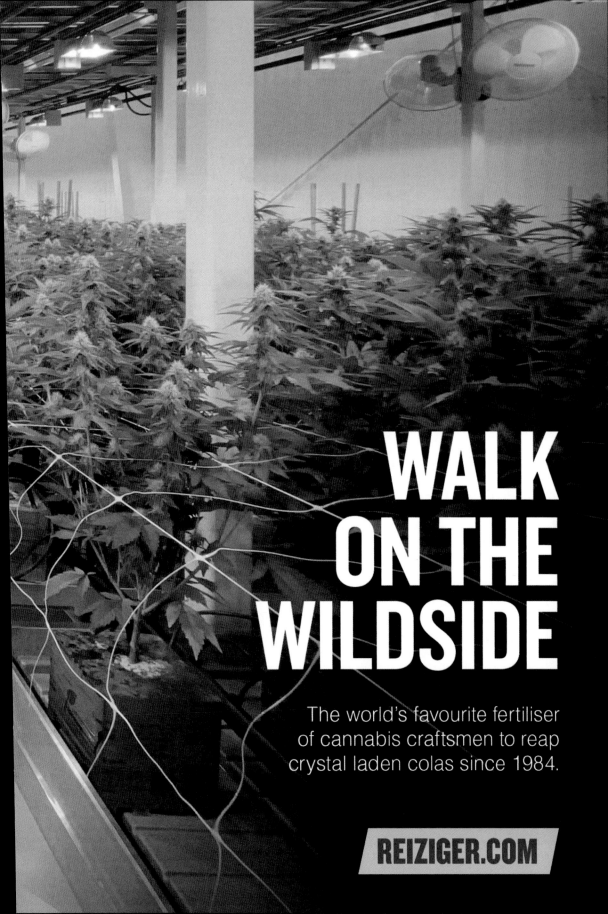

WALK ON THE WILDSIDE

The world's favourite fertiliser of cannabis craftsmen to reap crystal laden colas since 1984.

REIZIGER.COM

Control Powdery Mildew & Pro-TeKt® Your Harvest!

Studies have shown that consistent application of soluble silicon to your plants increases their natural defenses against fungi and insects and can reduce powdery mildew infections by 80%.

Dyna-Gro is complete, easy to use and, cost-effective. Our highly concentrated nutrient formulas are the only one-part nutrient solutions on the market that contain all 16 macro and micronutrients required for optimum plant health.

For more than 38 years, Dyna-Gro has been a top supplier of nutrients for the cannabis community. We were the first company in the U.S. to bring a soluble silicon product to the horticulture market. Use with Foliage-Pro in veg, and BLOOM and Mag-Pro during flower. It's all you need to grow great weed!

www.dyna-gro.com   800-DYNA-GRO

Find Dyna-Gro products online and at your local hydro store!

PREMIUM ORGANICS

TRIPLE CERTIFIED FERTILIZERS

www.vitalgardensupply.com

Guard Your Grow
PLAN • PREPARE • CONTROL

IPM Solutions to Protect Your Bottom Line

Natural Pesticides & Botanicals

Planning & Record Keeping

Trap & Monitor

IPM

Biological Controls

Mechanical Controls

Cultural Controls

Beneficial Nematodes

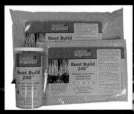

Root Build 240

Predatory Insects & Mites

Pest Insect Traps

Your Source For Year-Round Growing Solutions

Guaranteed Live Delivery
Experienced IPM Specialists

Call Today!
1-800-827-2847
www.arbico-organics.com

Serving Growers Since 1979.

SASQUATCH™
SOIL CO.

Legend has it, plants love it.°

OUR MISSION

We want to make gardening easier, healthier and more plentiful for everyone. Whether you have a horticulture degree or just a desire to grow a garden, Sasquatch Soil gives plants beneficial nutrients and gives you legendary results.

1.5 | Cubic Feet | Premium Garden Soil

A Beastly Blend of organic input materials, Compost, Forest fiber material, Forest humus, perlite, volcanic rock, composted rice hulls, organic worm castings, organic limestone, organic gypsum, kelp meal, trace minerals, organic humic acid, organic fish meal, organic mushroom compost, organic mycorrhizae

REGISTERED
cdfa
ORGANIC INPUT MATERIAL

Fueled by legend, backed by science, Sasquatch Soil Co. specializes in creating unique blends of soil that naturally replicate the nutrient rich forest.

By the Bag, Bulk or Tote

530.433.5733

f /sasquatchsoilco

@sasquatchsoil.co

. . . .

sasquatchsoil.co

NATURAL & ORGANIC
Momo's Mix

Bio Harmonic Tonic

Involving life and living organisms   **A component frequency of an oscillation or wave**   **A medicine that invigorates and strengthens**

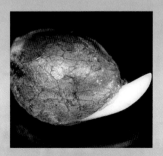

PROFESSOR P
Dynasty Genetics, Oregon
"I've witnessed tremendous results germinating seeds with Bio Harmonic Tonic. Over the course of several tests it has increased germination % on older seeds as well as faster growth from the beginning."

MOSCA NEGRA
Mosca Seeds, Colorado
"Recently, we began adding Bio Harmonic Tonic, soaking our rooting plugs in the solution and continued adding it during every watering. We were excited to see the accelerated root growth and development- Amazing!"

LUCAS DOWLING
Medical Marijuana Grower, Oregon
"I was astounded with the results and terpene/flavor profiles of everything in the garden! By far my best harvest yet, particularly with regards to cannabinoid and terpene profile."

Email Us: James@HappyTreeMicrobes.com
Instagram: @BioHarmonicTonic

Bio Harmonic Tonic can be used indoor, outdoor, greenhouse, soil, coco, hydroponics and in conjunction with your favorite nutrients. Bio Harmonic Tonic will run through any standard irrigation or drip system.

HappyTreeMicrobes.com

Increase Root Development

Increase Plant Growth & Yield

Increase Plant Available Phosphorus

Bio harmonically active microbial mix with Amazon Botanicals and Gemstone Harmonics Robust expression of plant growth and bloom

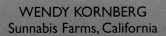

Robust Expression in Growth

WENDY KORNBERG
Sunnabis Farms, California

"With Bio Harmonic Tonic, the plants are able to uptake and mobilize nutrients much better than the control group."

Savory Expression in Bloom

MATT MILLEMAN
Bold Coast Farms, Maine

"BHT provides my seedlings with strong roots and a hearty immunity that allows them to thrive throughout their flower period."

HappyTreeMicrobes.com

'GROW LIKE YOU MEAN IT'

Bio Harmonic Tonic establishes robust life interactions in the root zone, these bio reactions supercycle nutrient uptake, accelerating plant growth, yield and flower.

Increases Roots

Increases Growth

Increases Flower

"Bio Harmonic Tonic, the proof is in the pot!"
Patrick "Soil" King
2019 Emerald Cup MVP

"Bio Harmonic Tonic, Easy to use! Gets results!"
Jeff Lowenfels
Teaming with Microbes

TrimBin ™

High walls keep your work contained and make cleanup easy.

150 micron stainless screen produces only fine-grained, high-grade pollen.

Ergonomic design reduces back, shoulder and wrist fatigue.

Easily collect pollen with the static brush and mirror-finish collection tray.

Increases productivity by alleviating user fatigue and discomfort.

Turn any chair into a comfortable workstation!

Made in California.

HarvestMore ®

harvest-more.com

ALL-PURPOSE
BAGS AND LINERS

- 100% Food-Grade Nylon
- BPA Free, FDA Approved
- Save Time and Money on Cleanup
- Resistant to Punctures & Tears
- Approved for Irradiation
- Vacuum Sealable

- Protect Your Harvest
- Preserve Flavor & Freshness
- Prevent Cross-Contamination
- Temperatures from -100°F to 400°F
- Stabilize Moisture Level
- Maximize Shelf Life

Available in 10, 25, 100 & Bulk packs			
Name	**Dimensions**	**Volume**	**Tips**
2 Gallon Bag	12" x 20"	2 Gallons	Holds 1lb, vacuum sealed
3 Gallon Bag	18" x 20"	3 Gallons	Holds 1 lb, bag tied
4 Gallon Bag	18" x 24"	4 Gallons	Lines 5 gallon bucket
8 Gallon Bag	24" x 40"	8 Gallons	Holds 5 lbs, bag tied
Bin Liner	48" x 30"	27 - 37 Gallons	Lines 27-37 gallon tote bins
Bin Liner XL	48" x 36"	27 - 37 Gallons	More bag material for closure
Can Liner	30" x 48"	20 - 30 Gallons	Lines 20 gallon trash can or 30 gallon drum
Drum Liner	36" x 48"	55 Gallons	Lines 55 gallon drum
Additional Products Available			
Multi-Pack (16 bags)	Varies	Varies	2 x 2 Gallon Bags, 2 x 3 Gallon Bags, 2 x 4 Gallon Bags, & 10 x 3 Quart Bags
3 Quart Bag (100 bags)	8" x 16"	3 Quarts	Holds 1/4 lb, bag tied
Canister XL (100 liners)	18" x 36"	13 Gallons	Lines XL canister
Rolling Bench Table Liner	80" x 500"	1 roll	Lines growing trays or rolling benches
Pallet Container Liner	55" x 44" x 90"	1 roll / 30 liners	Lines standard pallet size container
Bottomless Bags & Dispensers	12" x 100' 18" x 100' 24" x 100' 24" x 500'	---	Various widths and lengths; Cut and seal to preferred size; Dispensers are mountable

REDUCE – REUSE - RECYCLE

MADE IN THE USA

INDUSTRIAL STRENGTH
HARVEST SOLUTIONS

OPTIMIZE EFFICIENCY
FROM START TO FINISH

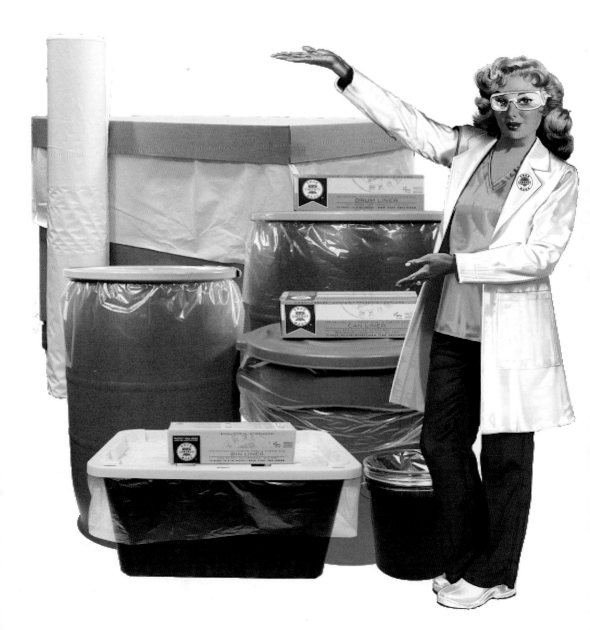

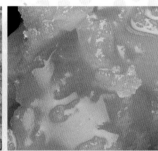

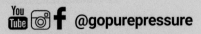

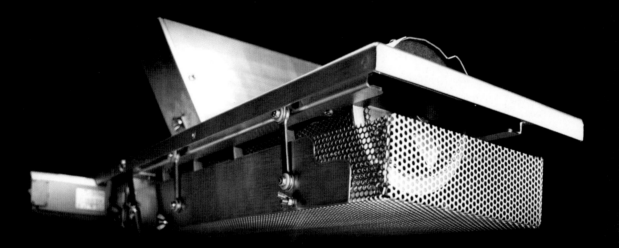

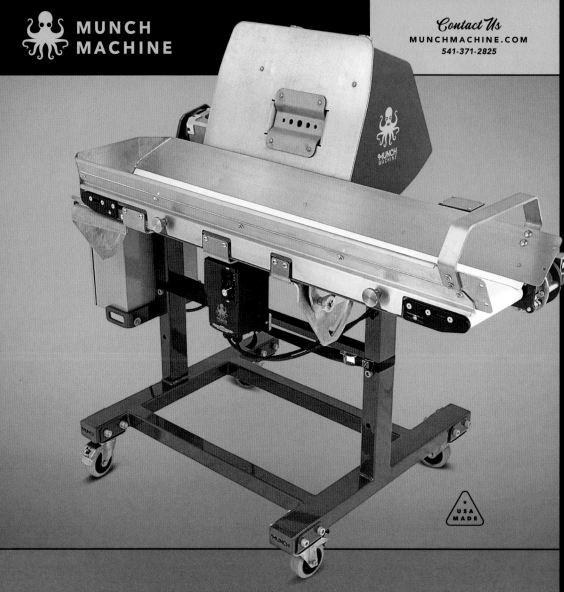

ACHIEVE THE PERFECT GROW

Integrated Environmental Controls for your Grow Space

Bluetooth-enabled UIS Controls at Your Fingertips

CONTROLLER 69
Pairs with the AC INFINITY App

CLOUDLINE Series
Inline Fans

CLOUDRAY Series
Clip-on Fans

IONGRID Series
LED Grow Lights

AC INFINITY

Products subject to change.

Integrate various grow equipment and easily automate them all from one central smart controller. Monitor climate data and program triggers, timers, schedules, alert notifications, and other advanced controls to attain the perfect environment for your plants.

@acinfinityinc

www.acinfinity.com

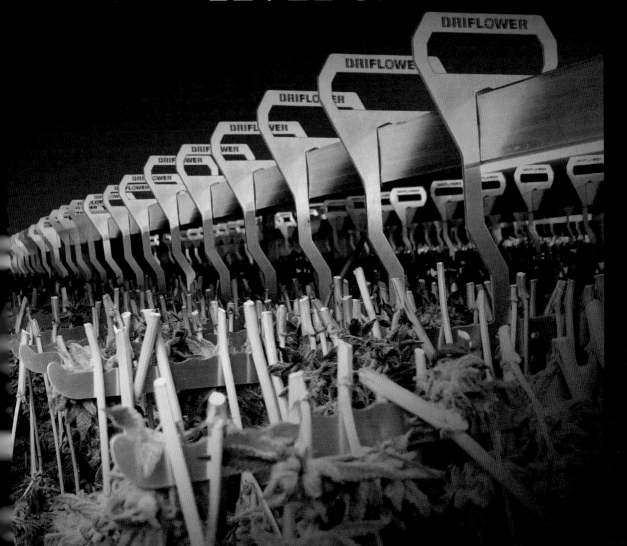

CRYO CURE™

SKILLFULLY DRIED CANNABIS IN 14 HOURS

Actual Cryo Cured Flower

Incredible Looking Flower With No Degradation

No Finished Flower Shrinkage | Live Resin Flower
Faster Curing Time | Higher THC Testing
Preserves Terpenes & Trichomes

@CRYOCURECANNABIS

CRYOCURE.COM

INDEX

for fungus gnats, 629

for hemp russet mites, 621–622, *621*

herbal/botanical oils, 618, 620, 623, 625, 627, 629, 630, 633

insect neurotoxins, 625, 627, 629, 630, 633

for spider mites, 620

for thrips, 627

for whiteflies, 630

See also pest management

stadium garden structures, 332

staffing, 359, 500, 515, 516, 528, 529, 531, 535, 541

See also safety issues

Star Anise, *49*

stems, *431*, *607*

apical meristems, 102–103, 435, 647, 648

auxins and, 101, 458

bending and crimping, 457, 459

botanical description, 38

branching and, 104

clone trimming, 595–596

cultivar selection, 434, 605

diploid and triploid, *97*

disease pathogens of, 182, 434, 565, 639, 640, 647

expansion and growth, 102, 147, 434

flowers and, 466

gibberellins, 96, 649

harvesting and, 523

hypoxic roots and, 270

internodes development, 129

leaves from, 456

micropropagation and, 542

nodes and, 102

phosphorous and, 215

plant growth and, 103

plant tissue culture and, 599

SAM/RAM and, 103

sativa vs. indica, 60

sessile trichomes and, 467

silicon and, 224–225

single-bud plants and, 457, 609

SOG system and, 282

taproot and, 426, 428

See also stretching

Stewart, Clayton, 541–547, 559–561

Sticky Flower Farm (Oklahoma), 377–381, *378*

stigmas

cannabis breeding and, 90, 91

cannabis flowering process and, 464–465, 466, 467

definition of, 40–41, *40*, *472*, 651

harvest timing and, 503, 504

nutrient deficiencies and, 222

quality evaluation and, 565, 567

resin collecting and, 577

wind pollination and, 106, 465

stomata, *110*

blue light and, 124

CO_2 and, 109, 111, 153, 154, *159*, 161

definition of, 109, 651

oxygen and, 109, 153, 191

photosynthesis and, 109, 111, 191

stomatal conductance, 111

transpiration and, 109, 111, 197

water deficits and, 446–447

stone wool. *See* rockwool

storage, 435, 497, 557–559, *558*, 561–563, *562*, 588

strains. *See* cannabis cultivars

stretching

definition of, 651

defoliation and, 483

hormones and, 96, 601

light and, 69, 145, 146, 227, 433, *433*, 434

phosphorus and, 198, 434

red light and, 123–124, 461

sativa vs. indica, 60

temperature and, 227, *433*, 434

See also gibberellins

substrates. *See* inorganic/inert substrates for hydroponics

Sulfluran, 603

sulfur (S), 220, *220*

amending alkaline soils, 278, 279

on fertilizer labels, 200

flushing and, 488

gypsum and, 278–279

as immobile nutrient, 488

as micronutrient, 650

as plant growth essential, 176

powdery mildew and, 641, 644

soil tests and, 274

water management and, 178

water pH and, 172

Sunboldt Grown Farms (Shively, California), *396*, 397–398, *398*

sunlight

acclimation to, 441, 445

advantages of, 129–130

appellation of origin (AO) programs and, 392

cultivar selection and, 67, 69

flowering and, 121, 473–476

germination and, 432–433

in greenhouses, 130–132, 237

hydroponics and, 314, 327

Korean Natural Farming methods and, 411

measurement of, 117, 118, 130

photoperiod and, 105, 121, 473–476

plant size and, 69

seedling vulnerabilities and, 434–435

supplementation of, 130, 133, 441, 442

terpenes and, 44

UV light and, 441, 444, 445

vegetative growth and, 441–442

supercropping, 458–459, 651

sustainability, 311, 411, 416–422

T

taproot, 426, 428

Teaming with Microbes (Lowenfels and Lewis), *295*

tea tree, *51*

temperature, 231–232

air conditioning (AC), 238–242, 342, 344–345, 347, 349, 421, 425, 541

as cannabis growth limiting factor, 112

carbon dioxide and, 162

cloning and, 593, 597

disease management and, 227–228, 229, 641, 643

for drying and curing, 543–544, 549

early plant growth and, 439

for hydroponics, 185

pest management and, 626

potting mixes and, 190

roots and, 185, 245–246

stretching and, 227, *433*, 434

for trimming, 531, 533

for vertical gardens, 383

water and oxygen, 185, 186, *190*, 246

terpenes, 42–53

aromatic essential oils and, 42–43

cannabis types of, 45–53, 71, 512, 513

chemical components of, 42, 43

definition of, 651

drying and curing, 498, 549, 598

entourage effect and, 25, 29, 31, 43

fragrance and, 25

harvest timing and, 505

hash and, 580

human brain effects of, 43

humulene and, 36–37, 50–51

interactions and, 53

lab-created extracts, 43–44

as plant benefits, 470

resistance to pests and, 470, 611

in tree-sized cannabis plants, 400

in trichomes, 25, 44, 467–468

volatility of, 44, 45, 247

Terpineol, 51

terpinolene, 51, 513

terroir, 389, 390, 419

THC (Δ^9 tetrahydrocannabinol), *23*

definition of, 22, 651